GRAMMAR
FOR THE WELL-TRAINED MIND

KEY TO PURPLE WORKBOOK
- REVISED EDITION -

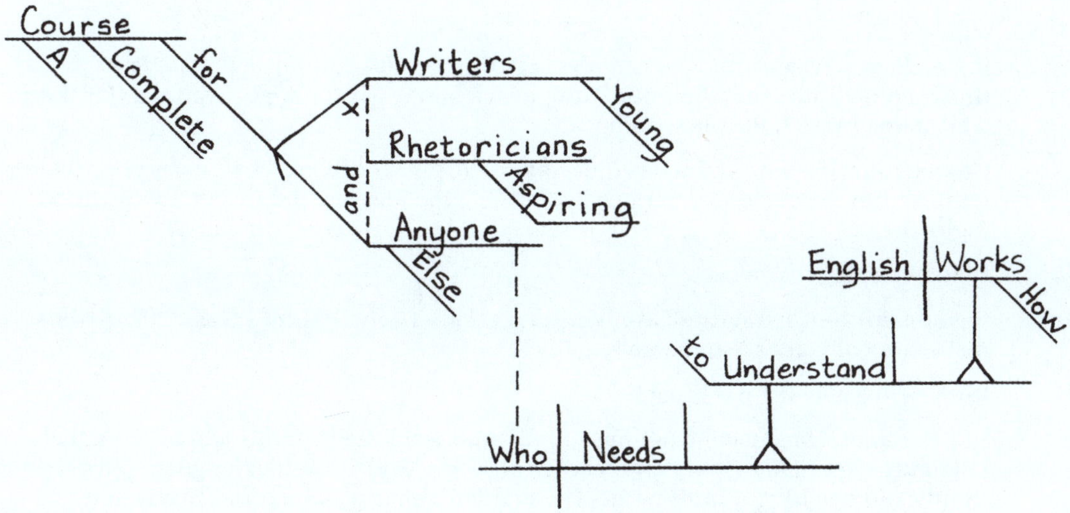

By Susan Wise Bauer
and Audrey Anderson,
Diagrams by Patty Rebne

Layout and Design by Shannon Zadrozny

WELL-TRAINED MIND PRESS

Names:	Bauer, Susan Wise, author. | Anderson, Audrey, 1986- author. | Rebne, Patty, illustrator. | Zadrozny, Shannon, designer. | Bauer, Susan Wise. Grammar for the well-trained mind. Purple workbook.
Title:	Grammar for the well-trained mind. Key to Purple workbook / by Susan Wise Bauer, with Audrey Anderson ; diagrams by Patty Rebne ; layout and design by Shannon Zadrozny.
Other titles:	Key to Purple workbook
Description:	Revised edition. | [Charles City, Virginia] : Well-Trained Mind Press, [2024] | For instructors of grades 5 and above.
Identifiers:	ISBN: 978-1-944481-61-2 (paperback)
Subjects:	LCSH: English language--Grammar--Study and teaching (Middle school) | English language-- Grammar--Study and teaching (Secondary) | English language--Rhetoric--Study and teaching (Middle school) | English language--Rhetoric--Study and teaching (Secondary) | BISAC: JUVENILE NONFICTION / Language Arts / Grammar. | JUVENILE NONFICTION / Language Arts / General. | JUVENILE NONFICTION / Study Aids / General.
Classification:	LCC: LB1631 .B3953 2024 | DDC: 428.00712--dc23

Table of Contents

WEEK 1

Introduction to Nouns and Adjectives

— LESSON 1 —

Introduction to Nouns
Concrete and Abstract Nouns

Exercise 1A: Abstract and Concrete Nouns

Decide whether the underlined nouns are abstract or concrete. Above each noun, write *A* for abstract or *C* for concrete. If you have difficulty, ask yourself: Can this noun be touched, seen, or experienced with another one of the senses? If so, it is a concrete noun. If not, it is abstract.

All that glitters is not gold [C]. (English and Spanish)

Forget injuries; never forget kindness [A]. (Chinese)

Study the past [A] if you would define the future [A]. (Chinese)

We learn little from victory [A], much from defeat [A]. (Japanese)

The shrimp [C] that falls asleep gets carried away by the current [C]. (Spanish)

He who conquers his anger [A] has conquered an enemy. (German)

The oldest trees [C] often bear the sweetest fruit [C]. (German)

Pride [A] is no substitute for a dinner [C]. (Ethiopian)

A leaky house [C] can fool the sun [C], but it can't fool the rain [C]. (Haitian)

Exercise 1B: Abstract Nouns

Each row contains two abstract nouns and one concrete noun. Find the concrete noun and cross it out.

hunger	thirst	~~bread~~
delight	~~frosting~~	pleasure
confusion	victory	~~torch~~
shock	fear	~~monster~~
~~guard~~	sadness	tranquility
self-control	boredom	~~mob~~

— LESSON 2 —

Introduction to Adjectives
Descriptive Adjectives, Abstract Nouns
Formation of Abstract Nouns from Descriptive Adjectives

Exercise 2A: Descriptive Adjectives, Concrete Nouns, and Abstract Nouns

Decide whether the underlined words are concrete nouns, abstract nouns, or descriptive adjectives. Above each, write *DA* for descriptive adjective, *CN* for concrete noun, or *AN* for abstract noun.

DA CN AN
The cowardly lion wished for courage.

DA CN AN
The shy tinman wished for love.

DA CN AN
The silly scarecrow wished for intelligence.

DA DA CN AN
The lost little girl wished for the power to go home.

DA DA CN CN DA CN
The Yellow Brick Road led through a field of crimson poppies.

> **Note to Instructor:** You may need to explain that *brick* can be a noun when it refers to a concrete object ("a brick") but that in this sentence, *brick* acts as an adjective because it describes what kind of road the Yellow Brick Road is. If the student is already familiar with compound proper nouns, he or she may identify *Yellow Brick Road* as one noun. This is also an acceptable answer.

CN AN CN
The travelers were overcome with sleepiness when they smelled the flowers.

Exercise 2B: Turning Descriptive Adjectives into Abstract Nouns

Change each descriptive adjective to an abstract noun by adding the suffix *-ness*. Write the abstract noun in the blank beside the descriptive adjective. Remember this rule: **When you add the suffix *-ness* to a word ending in *-y*, the *y* changes to *i*.** (For example, *grumpy* becomes *grumpiness.*)

sad	sadness
truthful	truthfulness
effective	effectiveness
ugly	ugliness
silly	silliness
sluggish	sluggishness
eager	eagerness
bulky	bulkiness

Exercise 2C: Color Names

Underline all the color words in the following paragraph. Then write *A* for adjective or *N* for noun above each underlined color word. If you are not sure, ask yourself, "[Color name] *what*?" If you can answer that question, you have found a noun that the color describes. That means the color is an adjective.

Rachel held her sister Dana's hand as they walked up the turquoise [A] path into the yellow [A] candy store. Candy of every imaginable flavor covered the walls. Dana immediately headed to the magenta [A] jellybeans. Rachel laughed; Dana's favorite color was magenta [N], and she always wanted magenta [A] clothes and notebooks for school. Rachel raced over to the bright red [A] strawberries covered in white [A] chocolate. Right next to the strawberries were green [A] bonbons. She usually liked green [N], but this trip was not about color. It was about taste!

— LESSON 3 —

Common and Proper Nouns
Capitalization and Punctuation of Proper Nouns

Exercise 3A: Capitalizing Proper Nouns

Write a proper noun for each of the following common nouns. Don't forget to capitalize all of the important words of the proper noun. Underline the names of the book and movie you choose, to show that those names should be in italics if they were typed.

Answers will vary.

Exercise 3B: Proper Names and Titles

On your own paper, rewrite the following sentences properly. Capitalize and punctuate all names and titles correctly. If you are using a word processing program, italicize where needed; if you are writing by hand, underline in order to show italics.

I just finished reading *The Secret Garden*.

My uncle subscribes to the magazine *Time*.

My favorite campfire song is "Bingo."

The sinking of the *Titanic* was a terrible disaster.

Lewis Carroll's poem "Jabberwocky" has many made-up words.

Exercise 3C: Proofreading for Proper Nouns

In the following sentences from *The Story of the World, Volume 3,* by Susan Wise Bauer, indicate which proper nouns should be capitalized by underlining the first letter of the noun three times. This is the proper proofreader mark for *capitalize.* The first word in the first sentence is done for you.

But not very many europeans traveled to russia, and those who settled in russia lived apart from the russians, in special colonies for foreigners.

peter's only port city, archangel, was so far north that it was frozen solid for half the year.

The sea of azov led right into the black sea, which led to the mediterranean. azov belonged to the ottoman turks.

The turks waved their turbans in surrender. azov had fallen!

— LESSON 4 —

Proper Adjectives
Compound Adjectives (Adjective-Noun Combinations)

Exercise 4A: Forming Proper Adjectives from Proper Nouns

Form adjectives from the following proper nouns. (Some will change form and others will not.) Write each adjective into the correct blank below. If you are not familiar with the proper nouns, you may look them up online on Encyclopaedia Britannica, Wikipedia, or some other source (this will help you complete the sentences as well). This exercise might challenge your general knowledge! (But you can always ask your instructor for help.)

Great Wall	Ireland	January	Victoria
Italy	Los Angeles	Shinkansen	Canada
Goth	Friday	Double Ninth Festival	Christmas

Traditionally, Double Ninth Festival cakes are made by layering lard, rice flour paste, and a bean paste diluted with white sugar, but each area of China has its own variation on the recipe.

Note to Instructor: The student may answer "Double Ninth Festival cakes." Technically this is not incorrect, but point out that "Double Ninth" is the more common adjective form of the proper noun.

The January festival known as Plough Monday marked the return to work after Twelfth Night.

Gothic cathedrals were built by medieval journeymen—guilds of craftsmen who were expert woodcarvers, blacksmiths, stonemasons, plasterers, ironworkers, and glaziers.

During the Victorian period in England, many farmers left their land to live in cities and work in factories.

By Los Angelean standards, Hollywood Hills and Culver City are just a stone's throw from each other.

The diagonal section of the Huangyaguan section of the Ming Wall is called Heartbreak Hill by many runners in the Great Wall Marathon.

My favorite Christmas cookies are gingerbread men and spritz.

The Shinkansen train carries over 143 million passengers from Tokyo to Shin-Osaka every year, sometimes at speeds as high as 200 miles per hour.

I found the recipe for *gelato di fragola* in my Italian cookbook.

On Bloody Sunday (21 November 1920), fourteen British military operatives and fourteen Irish civilians were killed in Dublin.

Er Shun, a giant panda on loan to the Canadian zoo in Toronto, gave birth to twin cubs in October of 2015; each one was the size of a stick of butter.

It was such a difficult week that we were all more than ready for the Friday holiday and the long weekend.

Exercise 4B: Capitalization of Proper Adjectives

In the following sentences, correct each lowercase letter that should be capitalized by using the proofreader's mark (three underlines beneath each). Circle each proper adjective. Finally, write an *S* (for "same") above the proper adjectives that have not changed form from the proper noun.

the portuguese explorers were the first european travelers to reach the australian region, but spanish navigators were not far behind.

thomas abercrombie was a legendary national geographic photographer who worked in the arabian desert, the antarctic continent, the entire middle eastern region, and the south pole. he photographed jacques cousteau, the first indian white tiger brought to the north american continent, and the islamic pilgrimage to mecca.

the october farmers' market was a panorama of colorful leaves, halloween costumes, pumpkins, and heirloom squash. the blue hubbard and golden hubbard varieties were my favorite.

Note to Instructor: While some sources do not capitalize the proper adjectives *Blue Hubbard* and *Golden Hubbard*, these squashes are specific proprietary varieties and so should be capitalized.

the laws of the elizabethan age allowed french and dutch protestants to have their own london churches, although english citizens were not supposed to enter them. diplomats from catholic countries were allowed to celebrate mass, but only in their own homes, and english subjects were banned from those services as well.

Exercise 4C: Hyphenating Attributive Compound Adjectives

Hyphens prevent misunderstanding! Explain to your instructor the differences between each pair of phrases. The first is done for you. If you're confused, ask your instructor for help.

Note to Instructor: These are intended to be fun, not frustrating. Use the suggestions below to help the student, and give the answers if the student is stumped.

a small-town boy
a small town boy

a small-town boy is a boy from a small town
a small town boy is a town boy of diminished size: a small boy who is also a town boy

(both a small boy and a town boy)

a violent-crime conference
a violent crime conference

a violent-crime conference is a conference about violent crime
a violent crime conference is a crime conference that turns ugly

(both a violent conference and a crime conference)

a high-chair cover
a high chair cover

a high-chair cover is a cover for a baby's seat
a high chair cover is a chair cover that's too far off the ground

(both a high cover and a chair cover)

a cross-country runner
a cross country runner

a cross-country runner is a runner who goes across country
a cross country runner is a rural runner in a bad mood

(both a country runner and a cross runner)

an ill-fated actress
an ill fated actress

an ill-fated actress is an actress who's doomed to suffer very bad luck
an ill fated actress is an actress facing a particular fate with an upset stomach

(both an ill actress and a fated actress)

WEEK 2

Introduction to Personal Pronouns and Verbs

— LESSON 5 —

Noun Gender

Introduction to Personal Pronouns

Exercise 5A: Introduction to Noun Gender

How well do you know your animals? Fill in the blanks with the correct name (and don't worry too much if you don't know the answers . . . this is mostly for fun).

Animal	Male	Female	Baby	Group of Animals
cattle	bull	cow	calf	drove of cattle
chicken	rooster	hen	chick	brood of chickens
deer	buck	doe	fawn	herd of deer
owl	owl	owl	chick	parliament of owls
horse	stallion	mare	foal	herd of horses
rabbit	buck	doe	bunny	nest of rabbits
mouse	buck	doe	pup OR pinkie	mischief of mice
swan	cob	pen	cygnet	flock OR wedge of swans

Exercise 5B: Nouns and Pronouns

Write the correct pronoun above the underlined word(s). The first is done for you.

They

Astronomers predicted that the comet would crash into Jupiter on or about July 25, 1994.

—Theo Koupelis, *In Quest of the Universe*

This particular slab of black basalt was different from anything that had ever been discovered. [It] The slab carried three inscriptions.

—Hendrik van Loon, *The Story of Mankind*

[We] Jenny and I read a book about inventors.

Benjamin Franklin not only invented objects such as the lightning rod, but [he] Benjamin Franklin also invented the expression "pay it forward" to teach people to repay kindness by being kind to others.

Wilbur and Orville Wright had always loved construction. [They] Wilbur and Orville Wright began as bicycle mechanics and eventually constructed the first successful airplane!

The wheel is one of the most important inventions of all time. [It] The wheel was probably invented for chariots in ancient Mesopotamia, which is now part of Iraq.

"Why," said Effie, "I know what it is. It is a dragon like the one St. George killed." And [she] Effie was right.

—E. Nesbit, *The Book of Dragons*

Exercise 5C: Substituting Pronouns

Does the passage below sound awkward? It should, because it's not what the Brothers Grimm actually wrote. Choose the nouns that can be replaced by pronouns, cross them (and any accompanying words, such as *the*) out, and write the appropriate pronouns above them.

Note to Instructor: Answers that replace other nouns by pronouns are acceptable as long as the pronouns are the correct gender and the passage reads well. It is not necessary for the student to replace every noun below, as long as the sentences no longer sound awkward.

Then Dullhead fell to at once to hew down the tree, and when [it] ~~the tree~~ fell [he] ~~Dullhead~~ found amongst the roots a goose, whose feathers were all of pure gold. [He] ~~Dullhead~~ lifted [her] ~~the goose~~ out, carried the [her] ~~goose off~~, and took [her] ~~the goose~~ to an inn where [he] ~~Dullhead~~ meant to spend the night.

Now the landlord of the inn had a beautiful daughter, and when [she] ~~the daughter~~ saw the goose, the daughter[1] was filled with curiosity as to what this wonderful bird could be and [she] ~~the daughter~~ longed for one of the golden feathers.

Note to Instructor: This noun is not replaced by *she* because the pronoun could be construed to refer to the goose, the nearest previous feminine noun.

Exercise 5D: Pronouns and Antecedents

Circle the personal pronouns in the following sentences, and draw an arrow from each pronoun to its antecedent. If the noun and pronoun are masculine, write *M* in the margin. If they are feminine, write *F*; if neuter, write *N*. Some sentences have two personal pronouns. The first is done for you.

Although Helen Keller was blind and deaf, she became a famous author and speaker. F

The man selected a cake covered with violet icing and bit into it. It appeared to be filled with jam. N

Sylvia was not much comforted. She moved along to the middle of the seat and huddled there. F

—Joan Aiken, *The Wolves of Willoughby Chase*

Andreas Vesalius showed immense curiosity about the functioning of living things. He often caught and dissected small animals and insects. M

—Kendall Haven, *100 Greatest Science Discoveries of All Time*

The Wart copied Archimedes in zooming up toward the branch which they had chosen. M

—T. H. White, *The Once and Future King*

Mother Teresa was born in Albania; she worked for 45 years caring for the poor people of India. F

Mahatma Gandhi led peaceful protests against the persecution of poor people and women in India. He disobeyed unfair laws but quietly suffered the punishment. M

Even though he spent 27 years in prison, Nelson Mandela, a follower of Gandhi, helped to bring democracy for all races to South Africa. M

Being the scientist that he was, Carver decided that he would take the peanut apart. M

—Robert C. Haven, *Seven African-American Scientists*

"Why," said Effie, "I know what it is. It is a dragon like the one St. George killed." And she was right. F, N

—E. Nesbit, *The Book of Dragons*

— LESSON 6 —

Review Definitions
Introduction to Verbs
Action Verbs, State-of-Being Verbs
Parts of Speech

Exercise 6A: Identifying Verbs

Mark each underlined verb *A* for action verb or *B* for state-of-being verb. Condensed slightly from W.S.B. Mathews, *A Popular History of the Art of Music.*

We here enter [A] upon one of the most interesting and important chapters in the history of music.

The art of polyphony originated [A] at the same period as the pointed arch and the great cathedrals of Europe. In music, polyphony represents [A] the same bounding movement of mind, filled with high ideals. In the same country arose [A] the Gothic arch, the beauties of Notre Dame in Paris, and the involved and massive polyphony of music.

Polyphonic is [B] a term which relates [A] itself to two others. They are [B] Monodic and Homophonic. The musical art of the ancients was [B] an art in which a single melodic formula doubled [A] in a lower or higher octave, but where no harmony was [B]; variety came [A] through rhythm alone. Monodic art was [B] an art of melody only. Our modern art of homophony is [B] like that, in having but a single melody at each moment of the piece; but it differs [A] from the ancient in the addition of a harmonic support for the melody tones. This harmonic accompaniment rules [A] everything in modern music. It is [B] within the power of the composer to support [A] the melody tone with the chord which would most readily suggest [A] itself, within the limitations of the key. Instances of this use of harmonic accompaniment are [B] numerous in Wagner's works, and form [A] the most obvious peculiarity of his style.

Halfway between these two types of musical art stands [A] polyphony, which means [A] etymologically "many sounds," but which in musical technique is [B] "multiplicity of melodies." In a true polyphony, every tone of the leading voice possesses [A] melodic character, but all the tones are [B] themselves elements of other, independently moving melodies. The essence of polyphony is [B] canonic imitation. The simplest form of this is [A] the "round," in which one voice leads [A] off with a phrase, and immediately a second voice begins [A] with the same melody at the same pitch, and follows [A] after. At the proper interval a third voice enters [A]. Thus, when there is [B] only one voice, we have [A] monody; when the second voice enters [A] we have [A] combined sounds of two elements; and when the third enters [A] we have [A] chords of three tones.

A round goes (A) on in an endless sequence until the performers stop (A) arbitrarily. There is (B) no innate reason why it might not continue (A) indefinitely!

Exercise 6B: Action Verbs and State-of-Being Verbs

Provide an appropriate action and state-of-being verb for each of the following nouns. The first is done for you.

Note to Instructor: The student's answers should be exactly the same as those listed in the state-of-being column. The verbs in the action column are samples; answers may vary.

	State-of-Being	Action
The rabbit	was (or is)	hopped
Dinosaurs	are/were	fought
The sun	is/was	shines
Trains	are/were	speed
I	am/was	sing
The student	is/was	reads
Molecules	are/were	move
The wind	is/was	blows
Wolves	are/were	howl
You	are/were	study

Exercise 6C: Strong Action Verbs

Good writers use descriptive and vivid verbs. First underline the action verbs in the following sentences. Then rewrite a different, vivid verb in the space provided. The first is done for you. You may use a thesaurus if necessary.

Note to Instructor: Sample action verbs are provided, but answers may vary.

Ellen spoke to her friend after their fight.	apologized
Edgar moved away from the angry tiger.	scurried, scrambled, hurtled
The starving man ate his dinner.	gobbled, devoured, inhaled
The delicate lamp broke on the floor.	shattered, splintered
The frightened little girl asked for her mother.	begged, sobbed
After the snowstorm, Carrie came down the hill in her sled.	barrelled, hurtled
Alexander the Great beat his enemies.	vanquished
The Blackfoot moved across the land.	crept

— LESSON 7 —

Helping Verbs

Exercise 7A: Action and Helping Verbs

Underline the action verbs in both columns of sentences once. The sentences in the second column each contain at least one helping verb. Underline these helping verbs twice. The first is done for you.

These sentences are adapted from *A Complete Geography* by Ralph Tarr and Frank McMurry.

COLUMN 1	COLUMN 2
Waves form in the ocean.	Waves are formed by winds which blow over the water.
Waves endanger small ships.	Waves are constantly endangering small ships.
Waves damage the coast.	The constant beating of the waves is slowly eating the coast away.
Tides rise and fall.	Tides are caused by the moon and the sun.
The sun pulls on the earth.	The ocean is drawn slightly out of shape when the sun's pull affects it.
Spring tides rise high.	The high tides at full and new moon are called spring tides.

Exercise 7B: Helping Verbs

Fill in each blank in the story with a helping verb. Sometimes, more than one helping verb might be appropriate. This excerpt is adapted from *King Arthur: Tales of the Round Table,* by Andrew Lang.

Long, long ago, after Uther Pendragon died, there was no king in Britain, and every knight hoped for the crown himself. Laws were broken on every side, and the corn grown by the poor was trodden underfoot, and there was no king to bring evildoers to justice.

When things were at their worst, Merlin the magician appeared and rode fast to the place where the Archbishop of Canterbury lived. They took counsel together, and agreed that all the lords and gentlemen of Britain would/should ride to London and meet on Christmas Day in the Great Church. So this was done.

On Christmas morning, as they left the church, they saw in the churchyard a large stone, and on it a bar of steel, and in the steel a naked sword __was__ held, and about it __was__ written in letters of gold, "Whoever pulls out this sword is by right of birth King of England."

The knights __were__ anxious to be King, and they tugged at the sword with all their might; but it never stirred. The Archbishop watched them in silence. When they __had__ exhausted themselves from pulling, he spoke: "The man is not here who __can/will/shall/should/may/might/must/could__ lift out that sword, nor __do__ I know where to find him. But this is my counsel—that two knights __are/be__ chosen, good and true men, to keep guard over the sword."

This was done. But the gentlemen-at-arms cried out that every man had a right to try to win the sword, and they decided that, on New Year's Day, a tournament __would/should/might/must__ be held and any knight who wished __could/would/might__ enter the lists.

Among them was a brave knight called Sir Ector, who brought with him Sir Kay, his son, and Arthur, Kay's foster-brother. Now Kay __had__ unbuckled his sword the evening before, and in his haste to be at the tournament __had__ forgotten to put it on again, and he begged Arthur to ride back and fetch it for him. But when Arthur reached the house the door __was__ locked, for the women __had__ gone out to see the tournament, and though Arthur tried his best to get in, he could not. Then he rode away in great anger, and said to himself, "Kay __will/shall/must/can__ not be without a sword this day. I __shall/will/should/must/can/could__ take that sword in the churchyard and give it to him." He galloped fast till he reached the gate of the churchyard. Here he jumped down and tied his horse tightly to a tree; then, running up to the stone, he seized the handle of the sword, and drew it easily out.

— LESSON 8 —

Personal Pronouns

First, Second, and Third Person

Capitalizing the Pronoun *I*

Exercise 8A: Capitalization and Punctuation Practice

Correct the following sentences. Mark through any incorrect small letters and write the correct capitals above them. Insert quotation marks if needed. Use underlining to indicate any italics.

Note to Instructor: Inserted caps are bolded. This exercise assumes that students know to capitalize the first word in a sentence (if not, remind them).

On the night of **M**ay 6, 1915, as his ship approached the coast of **I**reland, Captain **W**illiam **T**homas **T**urner left the bridge and made his way to the first-class lounge, where passengers were taking part in a concert and talent show, a customary feature of **C**unard crossings.

> **Note to Instructor:** The title *Captain* is capitalized because it has become part of the full proper name of the *Lusitania's* captain: Captain William Thomas Turner. The word *captain* occurring on its own would not be capitalized.

On the morning of the ship's departure from **N**ew **Y**ork, a notice had appeared on the shipping pages of **N**ew York's newspapers. **P**laced by the **G**erman embassy in **W**ashington, it reminded readers of the existence of the war zone and cautioned that "vessels flying the flag of **G**reat **B**ritain, or of any of her allies, are liable to destruction" and that travelers sailing on such ships "do so at their own risk." **T**hough the warning did not name a particular vessel, it was widely interpreted as being aimed at **T**urner's ship, the **L**usitania, and indeed in at least one prominent newspaper, the **N**ew **Y**ork **W**orld, it was positioned adjacent to **C**unard's own advertisement for the ship.

Rev. **H**enry **W**ood **S**impson, of **R**ossland, **B**ritish **C**olumbia, put himself in **G**od's hands, and from time to time repeated one of his favorite phrases, "**H**oly **G**host, our souls inspire." **H**e said later he knew he would survive.

His life jacket held him in a position of comfort, "and **I** was lying on my back smiling up at the blue sky and the white clouds, and **I** had not swallowed much sea water either."

But, strangely, there was also singing. **F**irst "**T**ipperary," then "**R**ule, **B**rittania!" **N**ext came "**A**bide **W**ith **M**e."

> **Note to Instructor:** If the student asks, the quotation mark goes outside the punctuation mark after each song, but since this rule has not been covered, count any placement as correct.

Wilson believed that if he went then to **C**ongress to ask for a declaration of war, he would likely get it.

—Erik Larson, *Dead Wake*

The supposedly snobbish **F**rench leave all personal pronouns in the unassuming lowercase, and **G**ermans respectfully capitalize the formal form of "you" and even, occasionally, the informal form of "you," but would never capitalize "**I**."

The growing "**I**" became prevalent in the 13th and 14th centuries, with a **G**eoffrey **C**haucer manuscript of **T**he **C**anterbury **T**ales among the first evidence of this grammatical shift.

—Caroline Winter, "Me, Myself and I," in *The Times Magazine* 8/3/2008

Exercise 8B: Person, Number, and Gender

Label each personal pronoun in the following selection with its person (*1*, *2*, or *3*) and number (*S* or *PL*). For third-person singular pronouns only, indicate gender (*M*, *F*, or *N*). The first two are done for you.

I [1S] was standing with Mr. and Mrs. Elbert Hubbard when the torpedo struck the ship. It [3SN] was a heavy, rather muffled sound; a second explosion quickly followed, but I [1S] do not think it [3SN] was a second torpedo, for the sound was quite different. I[1S] turned to the Hubbards and suggested, "You[2PL] should go down to get life jackets." They[3PL] had ample time to go there and get back to the deck, but both seemed unable to act.

I[1S] went straight down to find a life belt, took a small leather case containing business papers, and went back up on deck to the spot where I[1S] had left the Hubbards. They[3PL] had gone; I[1S] never saw the Hubbards again.

A woman passenger nearby called out to Captain Turner, "Captain, what should we do?" He[3SM] answered, "Ma'am, stay right where you[2S] are. The ship is strong and she[3SF] will be all right." So she[3SF] and I[1S] turned and walked quietly aft and tried to reassure the passengers we[1PL] met. There was no panic, but there was infinite confusion.

—Slightly condensed from Charles E. Lauriat, *The Lusitania's Last Voyage* (1931)

WEEK 3

Introduction to the Sentence

— LESSON 9 —

The Sentence
Parts of Speech and Parts of Sentences
Subjects and Predicates

Exercise 9A: Parts of Speech vs. Parts of the Sentence

Label each underlined word with the correct part of speech AND the correct part of the sentence.

part of speech — noun, verb

The cat licks its paws.

part of the sentence — subject, predicate

part of speech — pronoun, verb

I actually prefer dogs.

part of the sentence — subject, predicate

part of speech — noun, verb

The dog runs down the road.

part of the sentence — subject, predicate

part of speech — pronoun, verb

He runs down the road.

part of the sentence — subject, predicate

Exercise 9B: Parts of Speech: Nouns, Adjectives, Pronouns, and Verbs

Label each underlined word with the correct part of speech. Use *N* for noun, *A* for adjective, *P* for pronoun, and *V* for verb.

One day (N), while I (P) was playing with my new (A) doll (N), Miss Sullivan (N) put (V) my big (A) rag (A) doll into my lap also, spelled (V) "d-o-l-l" and tried (V) to make me understand that "d-o-l-l" applied to both.

Earlier in the day we [P] had had a tussle over the words [N] "m-u-g" and "w-a-t-e-r." Miss Sullivan had tried to impress it upon me that "m-u-g" is *mug* [N] and that "w-a-t-e-r" is *water* [N], but I persisted [V] in confounding the two. In despair she [P] had dropped the subject [N] for the time [N], only to renew it [P] at the first [A] opportunity [N]. I became [V] impatient at her repeated [A] attempts and, seizing the new doll, I dashed [V] it [P] upon the floor [N].

—From Helen Keller, *The Story of My Life*

Exercise 9C: Parts of the Sentence: Subjects and Predicates

In each of the following sentences, underline the subject once and the predicate twice. Find the subject by asking, "Who or what is this sentence about?" Find the predicate by asking, "Subject what?" The first is done for you.

George ate the banana. *Who or what is this sentence about?* George. *George what?* George ate.

Owls are birds of prey.

Owls see in both the day and night.

Vultures eat carrion.

Hawks hunt live prey.

Ospreys catch fish.

Kites prefer insects.

Falcons steal the nests of other birds.

— LESSON 10 —

Subjects and Predicates

Diagramming Subjects and Predicates

Sentence Capitalization and Punctuation

Sentence Fragments

Exercise 10A: Sentences and Fragments

If the group of words expresses a complete thought, write *S* for sentence in the blank. If not, write *F* for fragment.

birds can land on the ground	S
small birds flapping their wings	F
or landing on the water	F
large birds can only hover for a short time	S

hummingbirds can beat their wings 52 times per second — S

because their feet act like skids — F

some birds are flightless — S

Exercise 10B: Proofreading for Capitalization and Punctuation

Add the correct capitalization and punctuation to the following sentences. In this exercise you will use proofreader's marks. Indicate letters which should be capitalized by underlining each letter three times. Indicate ending punctuation by using the proofreader's mark for inserting a period: ⊙. Indicate words which should be italicized by underlining them and writing *ITAL* after the sentence. If a word has to be both italicized AND capitalized, underline it once first, and then add triple underlining *beneath the* first underline. The first two are done for you.

once there was a very curious monkey named george ⊙

we booked a cruise on a ship called sea dreams ⊙ ITAL

the titanic had a sister ship called the olympic ⊙ ITAL

the titanic had a gym, a swimming pool, and a hospital with an operating room ⊙ ITAL

the millionaire john jacob astor and his wife were on board ⊙

the titanic hit an iceberg on april 14 ⊙

when the ship began to sink, women and children were loaded into the lifeboats first ⊙

the survivors in the lifeboats heard the band playing until the end ⊙

the carpathia brought the survivors to new york ⊙ ITAL

Exercise 10C: Diagramming Subjects and Predicates

Find the subjects and predicates in the following sentences. Diagram each subject and predicate on your own paper. You should capitalize on the diagram any words which are capitalized in the sentence, but do not put punctuation marks on the diagram. If a proper name is the subject, all parts of the proper name go onto the subject line of the diagram. The first one is done for you.

Note to Instructor: If the student has difficulty finding the subjects and predicates, remind her to ask "Who or what is this sentence about?" to find the subject. Once the subject is located, the student should ask, "[Subject] what?"

Example: Many hurricanes form in the southwest North Pacific.
Who or what is this sentence about? Hurricanes.
Hurricanes what? Hurricanes form.

Joseph Duckworth earned an Air Medal.

Joseph Duckworth | earned

Many hurricanes form in the southwest North Pacific.

hurricanes | form

Few hurricanes arise on the equator.

Sometimes, hurricanes develop over land.

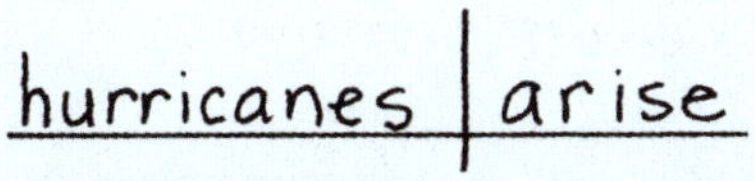

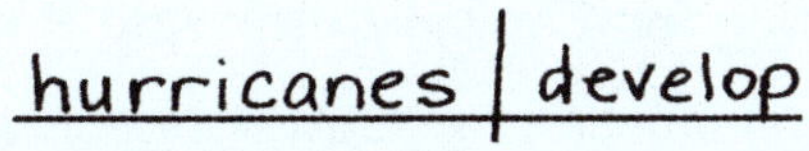

Satellites photograph hurricanes.

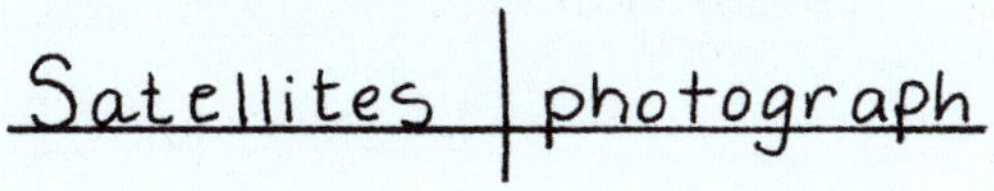

Radar tracks hurricanes.

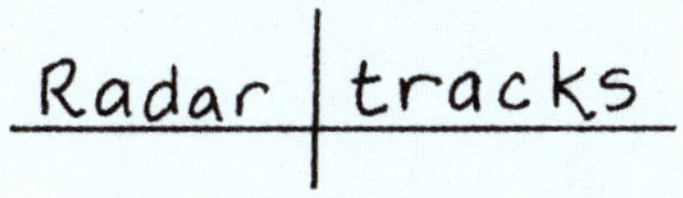

Meteorologists issue hurricane warnings.

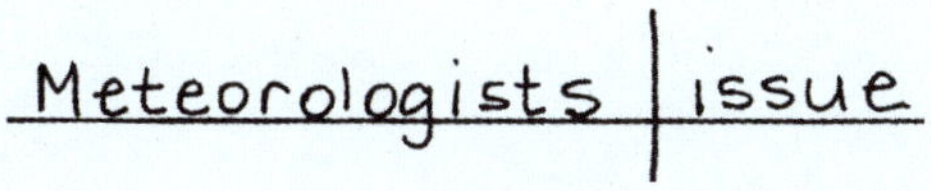

Red flags with black centers are warnings of approaching hurricanes.

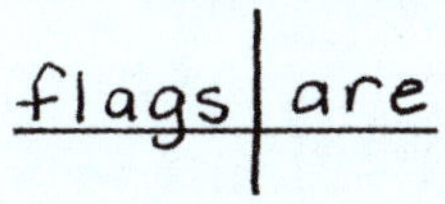

— LESSON 11 —

Types of Sentences

Exercise 11A: Types of Sentences: Statements, Exclamations, Commands, and Questions

Identify the following sentences as *S* for statement, *E* for exclamation, *C* for command, or *Q* for question. Add the appropriate punctuation to the end of each sentence.

	Sentence Type
Aunt Karen is teaching me how to make strawberry pie.	S
Do we make the piecrust or the filling first?	Q
Don't touch that stove! *or* .	C
Roll the dough until it is very thin.	C
I stirred the filling, and Aunt Karen poured it into the pan.	S
How long do we bake the pie?	Q
This pie is delicious! *or* .	E
Eat this. *or* !	C
Do you mind if we sit down?	Q
I am getting tired.	S

Exercise 11B: Proofreading for Capitalization and Punctuation

Proofread the following sentences. If a small letter should be capitalized, draw three lines underneath it. Add any missing punctuation.

what a beautiful morning!

please come with me on a bike ride. or !

my bicycle tires are flat.

will you help me with the air pump?

did you pack the water bottles and snacks?

don't forget to put on sunscreen. or !

let's go. or !

Exercise 11C: Diagramming Subjects and Predicates

On your own paper, diagram the subjects and predicates of the following sentences. Remember that the understood subject of a command is *you,* and that the predicate may come before the subject in a question.

Learn quietly.

(you) | Learn

Are you hungry?

you | Are

Sometimes, students work hard.

students | work

Other times, students stare out of windows.

students | stare

The book is open.

book | is

Close the book.

(you) | Close

Did you?

you | Did

You did a good job today.

You | did

— LESSON 12 —

Subjects and Predicates
Helping Verbs
Simple and Complete Subjects and Predicates

Exercise 12A: Complete Subjects and Complete Predicates

Match the complete subjects and complete predicates by drawing lines between them.

Note to Instructor: The completed sentences are listed below, but accept any reasonable answers.

The hard storm	huddled close together under a low-branching tree.
The chickens	became cool and clear.
The horses	appeared, first one, then six, then twenty.
Out in the meadow, the sheep	ran for the open door of the hen-house.
The wind	were already in their comfortable stalls with hay.
The loud thunder	flew across the sky.
The clouds, too,	swayed the branches.
At last the air	came in the night when the farmers were asleep.
Next, the stars	made the lambs jump.

Exercise 12B: Simple and Complete Subjects and Predicates

In the following sentences (adapted from Connie Willis's wonderful novel *Bellwether*), underline the simple subject once and the simple predicate twice. Then, draw a vertical line between the complete subject and the complete predicate. The first is done for you.

The little ewe | kicked out with four hooves in four different directions, flailing madly.

A deceptively scrawny ewe | had mashed me against the fence.

The flock | meekly followed the bellwether.

The sheep | were suddenly on the move again.

Out in the hall, they | wandered aimlessly around.

In the stats lab, a sheep | was munching thoughtfully on a disk.

A fat ewe | was already through the door.

Exercise 12C: Diagramming Simple Subjects and Simple Predicates

On your own paper, diagram the simple subjects and simple predicates from Exercise 12B.

The little ewe kicked out with four hooves in four different directions, flailing madly.

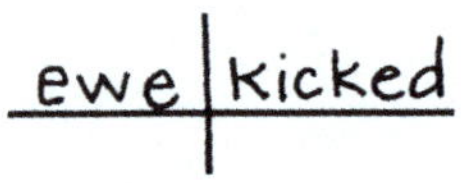

A deceptively scrawny ewe had mashed me against the fence.

The flock meekly followed thc bellwether.

The sheep were suddenly on the move again.

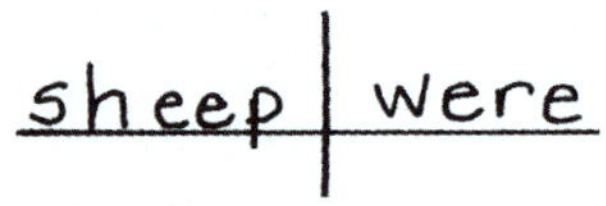

Out in the hall, they wandered aimlessly around.

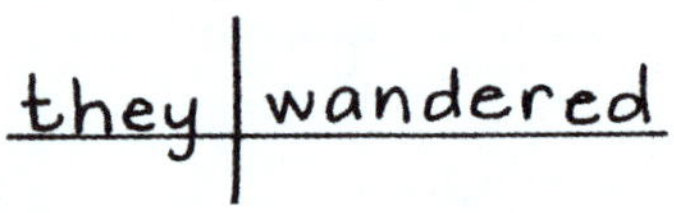

In the stats lab, a sheep was munching thoughtfully on a disk.

A fat ewe was already through the door.

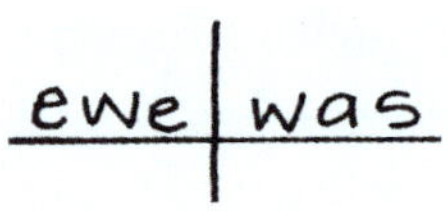

— REVIEW 1 —

Weeks 1-3

Topics
Concrete/Abstract Nouns
Descriptive Adjectives
Common/Proper Nouns
Capitalization of Proper Nouns and First Words in Sentences
Noun Gender
Pronouns and Antecedents
Action Verbs/State-of-Being Verbs
Helping Verbs
Subjects and Predicates
Complete Sentences
Types of Sentences

Review 1A: Types of Nouns

Fill in the blanks with the correct description of each noun. The first is done for you.

	Concrete / Abstract	Common / Proper	Gender (M, F, N)
teacher	C	C	N
Alki Beach	C	P	N
Miss Luzia	C	P	F
jellyfish	C	C	N
terror	A	C	N
Camp Greenside	C	P	N
determination	A	C	N
daughter-in-law	C	C	F
gentleman	C	C	M
vastness	A	C	N
President Jefferson	C	P	M

Review 1B: Types of Verbs

Underline the complete verbs in the following sentences. Identify helping verbs as *HV*. Identify the main verb as *AV* for action verb or *BV* for state-of-being verb. The first is done for you.

Erosion, rain, and winds have (HV) created (AV) the Grand Canyon over many years.

A massive flood could (HV) have (HV) contributed (AV) to the formation of the Grand Canyon.

Even experienced geologists are (HV) puzzled (AV) by this phenomenon.

AV
Many rock layers compose the cavernous walls.

HV AV
The Grand Canyon is considered one of the seven natural wonders of the world.

BV
The Great Barrier Reef and Mount Everest are other natural wonders.

HV BV
My grandparents and I might be at the Grand Canyon next September.

HV BV
The Grand Canyon will be my first wonder of the world.

HV AV
Maybe next I will travel to Australia for the Great Barrier Reef.

HV HV AV
By the time I am 50 I will have seen all seven wonders of the world!

Review 1C: Subjects and Predicates

Draw one line under the simple subject and two lines under the simple predicate in the following sentences. Remember that the predicate may be a verb phrase with more than one verb in it.

Hot air balloons were constructed long before the invention of airplanes.

French scientists invented hot air balloons in the late 1700s.

They originally were very dangerous.

These first contraptions utilized a cloth balloon and a live fire.

Later modifications improved the safety of hot air balloons.

Soon, even tourists could ride in hot air balloons.

However balloonists also attempted more impressive feats.

Many have died in their attempts to break new ballooning records.

Three bold adventurers in the 1970s flew in a balloon across the Atlantic Ocean.

Review 1D: Parts of Speech

Identify the underlined words by writing the following abbreviations above them: *N* for noun, *P* for pronoun, *A* for adjective, *AV* for action verb, *HV* for helping verb, or *BV* for state-of-being verb.

The following excerpt is from the novel *Out of My Mind* by Sharon Draper (Atheneum, 2010), pp. 3-4.

N AV P AV P A A A
When people look at me, I guess they see a girl with short, dark, curly hair strapped into a
N BV A N HV AV
pink wheelchair. By the way, there is nothing cute about a pink wheelchair. Pink doesn't change
N
a thing.

They'd see (AV) a girl with dark brown (A) eyes that are full of curiosity (N). But one of them (P) is (BV) slightly out of whack.

Her head (N) wobbles (AV) a little.

Sometimes she (P) drools (AV).

She's really tiny for a girl who is (BV) age ten and three quarters.

… After folks (N)… finished (AV) making a list of my problems (N), they (P) might (HV) take (AV) time to notice that I have a fairly nice (A) smile (N) and deep dimples—I think (AV) my dimples are (BV) cool.

I wear (AV) tiny gold (A) earrings (N).

Sometimes people (N) never even ask my name, like it's not important or something. It (P) is (BV).

My name (N) is Melody (N).

Review 1E: Capitalization and Punctuation

Use proofreading marks to indicate correct capitalization and punctuation in the following sentences. Be careful: Some of these may have more than one sentence, so ending punctuation will need to be inserted to split sentences correctly!

Small letter that should be capitalized: ≡ beneath the letter.

Italics: single underline | insert period: ⊙ | insert exclamation point: ↑
insert question mark: ^? | insert quotation marks: “ | insert comma: ^,

the first day of winter was tuesday, december 21 ⊙

mr. collins, my history teacher, taught us about osiris, an ancient egyptian god ⊙

francisca sat outside café gutenberg and read gulliver's travels ⊙

does thanksgiving always fall on a thursday ⊙

in canada, thanksgiving is celebrated on the second monday in october ⊙

the trans-siberian railway, the longest railway in the world, runs from moscow to vladivostok ⊙

the opera california youth choir, a korean american choir, performed mozart's requiem in los angeles ⊙

did geraldine bring a copy of today's washington post ^?

do we need to finish the call of the wild by friday for ms. hannigan's class ^?

Review 1F: Types of Sentences

Identify the following sentences as *S* for statement, *C* for command, *E* for exclamation, or *Q* for question. If the sentence is incomplete, write *F* for fragment instead.

The following sentences were adapted from Pam Muñoz Ryan's *The Dreamer* (Scholastic, 2010), a fictional story about the poet Pablo Neruda (pp. 16-19).

	Sentence Type
The next day, Mamadre was far more watchful, and Neftalí could not escape from his bed.	S
"Tell me all that you can see."	C
"I see rain."	S
"Tell me about the stray dog."	C
"What color is it?"	Q
"I cannot say."	S
"Maybe brown."	F
"Tell me about the boot that is missing."	C
"It has no shoestrings."	S
"I will rescue it and add it to my collections."	S
"You do not know where it has been."	S
"Or who has worn it."	F
To what mystical land does an unfinished staircase lead?	Q

WEEK 4

Verb Tenses

— LESSON 13 —

Nouns, Pronouns, and Verbs

Sentences

Simple Present, Simple Past, and Simple Future Tenses

Exercise 13A: Simple Tenses

	Simple Past	Simple Present	Simple Future
I	grabbed	grab	will grab
You	behaved	behave	will behave
She	jogged	jogs	will jog
We	enjoyed	enjoy	will enjoy
They	guessed	guess	will guess

Exercise 13B: Using Consistent Tense

When you write, you should use consistent tense—if you begin a sentence in one tense, you should continue to use that same tense for any other verbs in the same sentence. The following sentences use two verb tenses. Cross out the second verb and rewrite it so that the tense of the second verb matches the tense of the first one.

The first sentence is done for you.

Annie leaped up and ~~hugs~~ hugged her mother.

Alison walked to the ticket booth and ~~picks~~ picked up tickets for her first football game.

Her brother accompanied her to the game and ~~will explain~~ explained the rules.

The game will continue for a long time, and the players ~~work~~ will work hard.

The running back steals the ball and ~~scored~~ scores a touchdown!

Alison and her brother jump in the air and ~~will cheer~~ cheer for the team.

It will be a fun trip home because her brother ~~stops~~ will stop for ice cream to celebrate.

Exercise 13C: Forming the Simple Past Tense

Using the rules for forming the simple past, put each one of the following verbs in parentheses into the simple past. Write the simple past form in the blank. Be sure to spell the past forms of regular verbs correctly, and to use the correct forms of irregular verbs.

These sentences are taken from *The Emerald City of Oz*, by L. Frank Baum.

The Nome King was in an angry mood, and at such times he was very disagreeable. Every one kept away from him, even his Chief Steward Kaliko.

Therefore the King __stormed__ and __raved__ all by himself, walking up and down in his jewel-studded cavern and getting angrier all the time. Then he __remembered__ that it was no fun being angry unless he had some one to frighten and make miserable, and he __rushed__ to his big gong and __made__ it clatter as loud as he could.

In came the Chief Steward, trying not to show the Nome King how frightened he was.

"Send the Chief Counselor here!" __shouted__ the angry monarch.

Kaliko ran out as fast as his spindle legs could carry his fat, round body, and soon the Chief Counselor __entered__ the cavern. The King __scowled__ and __said__ to him:

"I'm in great trouble over the loss of my Magic Belt. Every little while I want to do something magical, and find I can't because the Belt is gone. That makes me angry, and when I'm angry I can't have a good time. Now, what do you advise?"

"Some people," said the Chief Counselor, "enjoy getting angry."

"But not all the time," __declared__ the King. "To be angry once in a while is really good fun, because it makes others so miserable. But to be angry morning, noon and night, as I am, grows monotonous and prevents my gaining any other pleasure in life. Now what do you advise?"

"Why, if you are angry because you want to do magical things and can't, and if you don't want to get angry at all, my advice is not to want to do magical things."

Hearing this, the King __glared__ at his Counselor with a furious expression and __tugged__ at his own long white whiskers until he __pulled__ them so hard that he __yelled__ with pain.

"You are a fool!" he __exclaimed__.

"I share that honor with your Majesty," said the Chief Counselor.

The King __roared__ with rage and __stamped__ his foot.

"Ho, there, my guards!" he __cried__. "Ho" is a royal way of saying, "Come here." So, when the guards had hoed, the King said to them, "Take this Chief Counselor and throw him away."

Then the guards took the Chief Counselor, and bound him with chains to prevent his struggling, and __locked__ him away. And the King __paced__ up and down his cavern more angry than before.

— LESSON 14 —

Simple Present, Simple Past, and Simple Future Tenses
Progressive Present, Progressive Past, and Progressive Future Tenses

Exercise 14A: Forming the Simple Past and Simple Future Tenses

Form the simple past and simple future of the following regular verbs.

Past	Present	Future
added	add	will add
shared	share	will share
patted	pat	will pat
cried	cry	will cry
obeyed	obey	will obey
danced	dance	will dance
groaned	groan	will groan
jogged	jog	will jog
kissed	kiss	will kiss

Exercise 14B: Progressive Tenses

Circle the ending of each verb. Underline the helping verbs.

was chewing
will be dancing
am decorating
will be exercising
am floating
was gathering
will be copying

Exercise 14C: Forming the Past, Present, and Progressive Future Tenses

Complete the following chart. Be sure to use the spelling rules above.

Note to Instructor: This exercise drills progressive verbs and also prepares the student for the introduction of person in next week's lessons. If the student asks why the helping verbs change, you may either say, "You'll find out next week" or turn to Lesson 18 and do it out of order. (The first method is recommended; person has not yet been covered in order to allow the student to concentrate on the tenses being introduced.)

	Progressive Past	Progressive Present	Progressive Future
I run	I was running	I am running	I will be running
I chew	I was chewing	I am chewing	I will be chewing
I grab	I was grabbing	I am grabbing	I will be grabbing
I charge	I was charging	I am charging	I will be charging
You call	You were calling	You are calling	You will be calling
You fix	You were fixing	You are fixing	You will be fixing
You destroy	You were destroying	You are destroying	You will be destroying
You command	You were commanding	You are commanding	You will be commanding
We dare	We were daring	We are daring	We will be daring
We educate	We were educating	We are educating	We will be educating
We jog	We were jogging	We are jogging	We will be jogging
We laugh	We were laughing	We are laughing	We will be laughing

Exercise 14D: Simple and Progressive Tenses

Fill in the blanks with the correct form of the verb in parentheses.

The scientist Antoni van Leeuwenhoek _was experimenting_ when he _tested_ the water of the inland lake Berkelse Mere.

When he _looked_ through his lens, he _discovered_ that microscopic creatures _were swimming_ in the water.

The French surgeon Ambroise Pare _was cauterizing_ wounds when he ran out of boiling oil.

He _used_ salve instead, but he _remarked_ to another doctor, "In the morning, the wounds _will be festering_."

In the morning, the wounds he _treated_ with salve _were healing_ better than the wounds that were treated with cauterization.

Johannes Kepler _was studying_ the orbit of Mars.

Finally, Kepler _decided_ that the orbit must be elliptical.

— LESSON 15 —

Simple Present, Simple Past, and Simple Future Tenses
Progressive Present, Progressive Past, and Progressive Future Tenses
Perfect Present, Perfect Past, and Perfect Future Tenses

Exercise 15A: Perfect Tenses

Fill in the blanks with the missing forms.

Simple Past	Perfect Past	Perfect Present	Perfect Future
I jogged	I had jogged	I have jogged	I will have jogged
I planted	I had planted	I have planted	I will have planted
I refused	I had refused	I have refused	I will have refused
I shrugged	I had shrugged	I have shrugged	I will have shrugged
We cheered	We had cheered	We have cheered	We will have cheered
We sighed	We had sighed	We have sighed	We will have sighed
We managed	We had managed	We have managed	We will have managed
We listened	We had listened	We have listened	We will have listened
He missed	He had missed	He has missed	He will have missed
He knitted	He had knitted	He has knitted	He will have knitted
He juggled	He had juggled	He has juggled	He will have juggled
He hammered	He had hammered	He has hammered	He will have hammered

Exercise 15B: Identifying Perfect Tenses

Identify the underlined verbs as perfect past, perfect present, or perfect future. The first one is done for you.

perfect present
I have decided to set up a saltwater fish tank in my room today.

perfect past
I had read a book about marine biology before deciding to set up my tank.

perfect present
I have put coral and damselfish in my tank, and I am buying a clown fish tomorrow morning.

perfect present
I have tried to regulate the salt and light levels in the tank, so that the corals and fish can live in an environment similar to the ocean.

perfect past
Last night I was looking for my clown fish because I had failed to see him all day.

perfect past
I had become afraid for my clown fish, but he was hiding in the coral!

perfect future
In fifteen years I will have finished studying marine science, and I will be working at a dolphin center.

Exercise 15C: Perfect, Progressive, and Simple Tenses

Each underlined verb has been labeled as past, present, or future. Add the label *perfect, progressive,* or *simple* to each one. The first has been done for you.

progressive PRESENT ... perfect PRESENT
Roopa is living with her parents and two little sisters in Chennai, India. She has lived there all her life.

progressive PAST ... simple PAST
Roopa was eating her lunch of curry and bread while she looked out the window.

progressive PAST ... simple PAST
Women were hurrying through the streets. They wore colorful saris with jasmine flowers in their hair.

perfect PAST ... simple PAST ... progressive FUTURE
Monsoon season had started already. Soon, thought Roopa, the rains will be flooding the streets.

simple PRESENT ... simple FUTURE
When the monsoon rages, the palm trees will bend close to the ground under the pressure of the wind and rain.

perfect PAST ... simple PAST ... progressive PAST
Roopa had finished her food by now. She picked up her cup of chai tea, happy that she was sitting inside, safe and dry.

— LESSON 16 —

Simple Present, Simple Past, and Simple Future Tenses
Progressive Present, Progressive Past, and Progressive Future Tenses
Perfect Present, Perfect Past, and Perfect Future Tenses
Irregular Verbs

Exercise 16A: Irregular Verb Forms: Simple Present, Simple Past, and Simple Future

Fill in the chart with the missing verb forms.

Note to Instructor: We have not yet covered number and person of verbs, which affect some irregular forms. If the student uses an incorrect form, simply tell her the correct form. Have her cross out the incorrect answer and write the correct answer in its place.

	Simple Past	Simple Present	Simple Future
I	ate	eat	will eat

	Simple Past	Simple Present	Simple Future
You	felt	feel	will feel
She	wrote	writes	will write
We	were	are	will be
They	got	get	will get
I	had	have	will have
You	went	go	will go
He	kept	keeps	will keep
We	made	make	will make
They	thought	think	will think
I	ran	run	will run
You	sang	sing	will sing
It	spoke	speaks	will speak
We	knew	know	will know
They	swam	swim	will swim
I	wrote	write	will write
You	threw	throw	will throw
We	became	become	will become
They	taught	teach	will teach

Exercise 16B: Irregular Verbs, Progressive and Perfect Tenses

Fill in the remaining blanks. The first is done for you.

Note to Instructor: This is only the first practice run with irregular verbs, designed to increase the student's familiarity: give all necessary help. Since we have not yet covered person and number, the student should follow the pattern established in the first line of the chart.

Simple Present	Progressive Past	Progressive Present	Progressive Future	Perfect Past	Perfect Present	Perfect Future
give	was giving	am giving	will be giving	had given	have given	will have given
feel	was feeling	am feeling	will be feeling	had felt	have felt	will have felt

Simple Present	Progressive Past	Progressive Present	Progressive Future	Perfect Past	Perfect Present	Perfect Future
write	was writing	am writing	will be writing	had written	have written	will have written
grow	was growing	am growing	will be growing	had grown	have grown	will have grown
keep	was keeping	am keeping	will be keeping	had kept	have kept	will have kept
make	was making	am making	will be making	had made	have made	will have made
think	was thinking	am thinking	will be thinking	had thought	have thought	will have thought
run	was running	am running	will be running	had run	have run	will have run
sing	was singing	am singing	will be singing	had sung	have sung	will have sung
speak	was speaking	am speaking	will be speaking	had spoken	have spoken	will have spoken
know	was knowing	am knowing	will be knowing	had known	have known	will have known
swim	was swimming	am swimming	will be swimming	had swum	have swum	will have swum
write	was writing	am writing	will be writing	had written	have written	will have written
throw	was throwing	am throwing	will be throwing	had thrown	have thrown	will have thrown
become	was becoming	am becoming	will be becoming	had become	have become	will have become
teach	was teaching	am teaching	will be teaching	had taught	have taught	will have taught
is	was being	am being	will be being	had been	have been	will have been

WEEK 5

More About Verbs

— LESSON 17 —

Simple, Progressive, and Perfect Tenses
Subjects and Predicates
Parts of Speech and Parts of Sentences
Verb Phrases

Exercise 17A: Simple, Progressive, and Perfect Tenses

All of the bolded verbs are in the past tense. Label each bolded verb as *S* for simple or *PERF* for perfect.

Now in these subterranean caverns **lived** [S] a strange race of beings, called by some gnomes, by some kobolds, by some goblins. There **was** [S] a legend current in the country that at one time they **lived** [S] above ground, and were very like other people. But for some reason or other, concerning which there were different legendary theories, the king **had laid** [PERF] what they thought too severe taxes upon them, or **had required** [PERF] observances of them they did not like, or **had begun** [PERF] to treat them with more severity, in some way or other, and impose stricter laws; and the consequence was that they **had** all **disappeared** [PERF] from the face of the country. According to the legend, however, instead of going to some other country, they **had** all **taken** [PERF] refuge in the subterranean caverns, whence they never **came** [S] out but at night, and then seldom **showed** [S] themselves in any numbers, and never to many people at once. It was only in the least frequented and most difficult parts of the mountains that they were said to gather even at night in the open air. Those who **had caught** [PERF] sight of any of them **said** [S] that they **had** greatly **altered** [PERF] in the course of generations; and no wonder, seeing they **lived** [S] away from the sun, in cold and wet and dark places.

—From *The Princess and the Goblin*, by George MacDonald

Exercise 17B: Identifying and Diagramming Subjects and Predicates, Identifying Verb Tenses

Underline the subject once and the predicate twice in each sentence. Be sure to include both the main verb and any helping verbs when you underline the predicate. Identify the tense of each verb or verb phrase (*simple past, present,* or *future*; *progressive past, present,* or *future*; *perfect past, present,* or *future*) on the line. Then, diagram each subject and predicate on your own paper.

These sentences are taken from *The Light Princess and Other Fairy Stories*, by George MacDonald.

Her atrocious aunt had deprived the child of all her gravity. perfect past

aunt | had deprived

One day an awkward accident happened. simple past

accident | happened

The princess had come out upon the lawn. perfect past

princess | had come

She had almost reached her father. perfect past

She | had reached

He was holding out his arms. progressive past

He | was holding

A puff of wind blew her aside. simple past

puff | blew

We have fallen in! perfect present

We | have fallen

He was swimming with the princess. progressive past

He | was swimming

I have quite forgotten the date. perfect present

I | have forgotten

By that time, they will have learned their lesson. perfect future

they | will have learned

She found her gravity! simple past

she | found

Down the narrow path they went. simple past

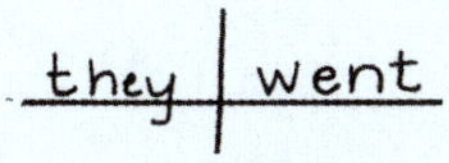

They reached the bottom in safety. simple past

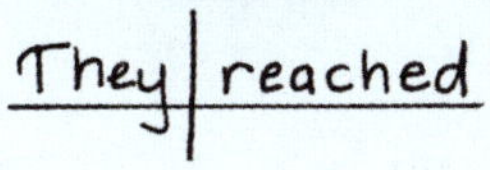

— LESSON 18 —

Verb Phrases

Person of the Verb

Conjugations

Exercise 18A: Third-Person Singular Verbs

In the simple present conjugation, the third-person singular verb changes by adding an *-s*. Read the following rules and examples for adding *-s* to verbs in order to form the third-person singular. Then, fill in the blanks with the third-person singular forms of each verb.

The first of each is done for you.

Usually, add *-s* to form the third-person singular verb.

First-Person Verb	Third-Person Singular Verb	
I shatter	it	shatters
I skip	she	skips
I hike	he	hikes

Add *-es* to verbs ending in *-s, -sh, -ch, -x*, or *-z*.

First-Person Verb	Third-Person Singular Verb	
we brush	he	brushes
we hiss	it	hisses
we catch	she	catches

If a verb ends in *-y* after a consonant, change the *y* to *i* and add *-es*.

First-Person Verb	Third-Person Singular Verb	
I carry	it	carries
I study	she	studies
I tally	he	tallies

If a verb ends in *-y* after a vowel, just add *-s*.

First-Person Verb	Third-Person Singular Verb	
we stray	she	strays
we buy	he	buys
we play	it	plays

If a verb ends in *-o* after a consonant, form the plural by adding *-es*.

First-Person Verb	Third-Person Singular Verb	
I go	she	goes
I do	it	does
I echo	he	echoes

Exercise 18B: Simple Present Tenses

Choose the correct form of the simple present verb in parentheses, based on the person. Cross out the incorrect form.

Hana Suzuki is fourteen. Every morning, she (~~eat~~/eats) rice and soup.

She is Japanese, and she (~~live~~/lives) in Canada with her family.

She has twin brothers. They (gobble/~~gobbles~~) their food and always (finish/~~finishes~~) before she does.

"You (chew/~~chews~~) too fast," her mother (~~say~~/says).

"But the food (~~taste~~/tastes) better if you (eat/~~eats~~) it quickly," they always (argue/~~argues~~).

"I (think/~~thinks~~) that you (enjoy/~~enjoys~~) the food more if you (slow/~~slows~~) down."

But they never (hear/~~hears~~).

They always (run/~~runs~~) out of the house too soon!

Exercise 18C: Perfect Present Tenses

Write the correct form of the perfect present verb in the blank. These sentences are drawn from Charles Dickens's novel *Oliver Twist.*

"I am very hungry and tired," replied Oliver, the tears standing in his eyes as he spoke. "I have walked a long way—I have been walking these seven days."

"Speak the truth; and if I find you have committed no crime, you will never be friendless while I live."

"He has gone, sir," replied Mrs. Bedwin.

"I consider, sir, that you have obtained possession of that book under very suspicious and disreputable circumstances."

"There, my dear," said Fagin, "that's a pleasant life, isn't it? They have gone out for the day."

"We have considered your proposition, and we don't approve of it."

— LESSON 19 —

Person of the Verb

Conjugations

State-of-Being Verbs

Exercise 19A: Forming Progressive Present Tenses

Fill in the blanks with the correct helping verbs.

Regular Verb, Progressive Present

	Singular	Plural
First person	I am conjugating	we are conjugating
Second person	you are conjugating	you are conjugating
Third person	he, she, it is conjugating	they are conjugating

Exercise 19B: Forming Progressive Past and Future Tenses

Fill in the blanks with the correct helping verbs.

Regular Verb, Progressive Present

	Singular	Plural
First person	I am conjugating	we are conjugating
Second person	you are conjugating	you are conjugating
Third person	he, she, it is conjugating	they are conjugating

Regular Verb, Progressive Past

	Singular	Plural
First person	I was conjugating	we are conjugating
Second person	you were conjugating	you are conjugating
Third person	he, she, it was conjugating	they were conjugating

Regular Verb, Progressive Future

	Singular	Plural
First person	I will be conjugating	we will be conjugating
Second person	you will be conjugating	you will be conjugating
Third person	he, she, it will be conjugating	they will be conjugating

— LESSON 20 —

Irregular State-of-Being Verbs

Helping Verbs

Exercise 20A: Simple Tenses of the Verb *Have*

Try to fill in the missing blanks in the chart below, using your own sense of what sounds correct as well as the hints you may have picked up from the conjugations already covered. Be sure to use pencil so that any incorrect answers can be erased and corrected!

Simple Present

	Singular	Plural
First person	I have	we have
Second person	you have	you have
Third person	he, she, it has	they have

Simple Past

	Singular	Plural
First person	I had	we had
Second person	you had	you had
Third person	he, she, it had	they had

Simple Future

	Singular	Plural
First person	I will have	we will have
Second person	you will have	you will have
Third person	he, she, it will have	they will have

Exercise 20B: Simple Tenses of the Verb *Do*

Try to fill in the missing blanks in the chart below, using your own sense of what sounds correct as well as the hints you may have picked up from the conjugations already covered. Be sure to use pencil so that any incorrect answers can be erased and corrected!

Simple Present

	Singular	Plural
First person	I do	we do
Second person	you do	you do
Third person	he, she, it does	they do

Simple Past

	Singular	Plural
First person	I did	we did
Second person	you did	you did
Third person	he, she, it did	they did

Simple Future

	Singular	Plural
First person	I will do	we will do
Second person	you will do	you will do
Third person	he, she, it will do	they will do

WEEK 6

Nouns and Verbs in Sentences

— LESSON 21 —

Person of the Verb
Conjugations
Noun-Verb/Subject-Predicate Agreement

Exercise 21A: Person and Number of Pronouns

Identify the person and number of the underlined pronouns. Cross out the incorrect verb in parentheses. The first one is done for you.

These sentences are taken from *The Once and Future King*, by T.H. White.

	Person	Singular/Plural
They (do/~~does~~) love to fly.	third	plural
He (was/~~were~~) seeing one ray beyond the spectrum.	third	singular
We (~~has~~/had) better fly.	first	plural
You (~~is~~/are) beginning to drop out of the air.	second	singular
It (is/~~are~~) confusing to keep up with you.	third	singular
I (was/~~were~~) a fish.	first	singular
You (~~has~~/have) to glide in at stalling speed all the way.	second	singular
They (prefer/~~prefers~~) to do their hunting then.	third	plural

Exercise 21B: Identifying Subjects and Predicates

Draw two lines underneath each simple predicate and one line underneath each simple subject in the following sentences. If a phrase comes between the subject and the predicate, put parentheses around it to show that it does not affect the subject-predicate agreement.

Leafcutter ants live in the southern United States and South America.

These creatures, (strong and resourceful,) create gardens and complex societies.

The tiny leafcutter ant carries almost ten times its own body weight.

The ants (within the kingdom) consist of a queen ant, soldier ants, and worker ants.

The queen (of the colony) lays eggs.

The soldiers, (bigger than the workers,) protect the colony.

The workers cut leaves for their gardens.

Exercise 21C: Subject-Verb Agreement

Cross out the incorrect verb in parentheses so that subject and predicate agree in number and person. Be careful of any confusing phrases between the subject and predicate.

Caitlin (~~go~~/goes) to the beach to surf every weekend.

The waves, glittering under the sun, (crash/~~crashes~~) against the shore.

She (~~use~~/uses) her small surfboard because the waves are huge.

The other surfers in the ocean (smile/~~smiles~~) at her.

Boards of all shapes and colors (float/~~floats~~) on the water.

"I (~~has~~/have) all day to surf!" she (~~think~~/thinks) happily.

— LESSON 22 —

Formation of Plural Nouns
Collective Nouns

Exercise 22A: Collective Nouns

Write the collective noun for each description. Then fill in an appropriate singular verb for each sentence. (Use the simple present tense!) The first is done for you.

Note to Instructor: Accept any verb that makes sense, as long as it is singular, simple present, third-person.

Description		Collective Noun	Verb	
mother, father, sister, brother	The	family	eats	together.
nine baseball players	The	team	wins, plays, OR loses	the game.
many students learning together	The	class	takes	the test.
people playing different musical instruments	The	band OR orchestra	plays, rehearses OR likes	the piece.
52 playing cards	The	deck	is	incomplete.
many mountains	This	range	is	high and icy.
a group of stars that forms a picture	This	constellation	shines or twinkles	brightly.

Exercise 22B: Plural Noun Forms

Read each rule and the example out loud. Then rewrite the singular nouns as plural nouns in the spaces provided.

Note to Instructor: Make sure that the student reads the rule out loud!

Usually, add *-s* to a noun to form the plural.

Singular Noun	Plural Noun
desk	desks
willow	willows
spot	spots
tree	trees

Add *-es* to nouns ending in *-s*, *-sh*, *-ch*, *-x*, or *-z*.

Singular Noun	Plural Noun
mess	messes
splash	splashes
ditch	ditches
fox	foxes
buzz	buzzes

If a noun ends in *-y* after a consonant, change the *y* to *i* and add *-es*.

Singular Noun	Plural Noun
family	families
salary	salaries
baby	babies
hobby	hobbies

If a noun ends in *-y* after a vowel, just add *-s*.

Singular Noun	Plural Noun
toy	toys
donkey	donkeys
valley	valleys
guy	guys

Some words that end in *-f or -fe* form their plurals differently. You must change the *f* or *fe* to *v* and add *-es*.

Singular Noun	Plural Noun
leaf	leaves
shelf	shelves
wife	wives
thief	thieves

Words that end in *-ff* form their plurals by simply adding *-s*.

Singular Noun	Plural Noun
sheriff	sheriffs
cliff	cliffs
tariff	tariffs

Some words that end in a single *-f* can form their plurals either way.

Singular Noun	Plural Noun
scarf	scarfs/scarves
hoof	hoofs/hooves

If a noun ends in *-o* after a vowel, just add *-s*.

Singular Noun	Plural Noun
patio	patios
radio	radios
rodeo	rodeos
zoo	zoos

If a noun ends in *-o* after a consonant, form the plural by adding *-es*.

Singular Noun	Plural Noun
potato	potatoes
hero	heroes
volcano	volcanoes
echo	echoes

To form the plural of foreign words ending in *-o*, just add *-s*.

Singular Noun	Plural Noun
piano	pianos
burrito	burritos
kimono	kimonos
solo	solos
soprano	sopranos

Irregular plurals don't follow any of these rules!

Singular Noun	Irregular Plural Noun
child	children
foot	feet
tooth	teeth
man	men
woman	women
mouse	mice
goose	geese
deer	deer
fish	fish

Exercise 22C: Plural Nouns

Complete the following excerpt by filling in the plural form of each noun in parentheses. There is *one* collective noun (singular in form) in the passage. Find and circle it.

The following is slightly condensed from the introduction to *The Pirate's Who's Who*, by Philip Gosse (1924).

Surely (pirate) pirates are as much entitled to a biographical dictionary of their own as are (clergyman) clergymen, (race-horse) race-horses, or (artist) artists. Have not the medical (man) men their Directory, the (lawyer) lawyers their List, the (peer) peers their Peerage? There are (book) books which record the (particular) particulars of (musician) musicians, (dog) dogs, and even white (mouse) mice. Above all, there is that astounding and entertaining volume, *Who's Who*, found in every club smoking-room, and which grows more bulky year by year, stuffed with information about the (life) lives, the (hobby) hobbies, and the (marriage) marriages of all the most distinguished (person) persons OR people in every profession. But there has been until now no work that gives immediate and trustworthy information about the lives, and—so sadly important—the (death) deaths of our pirates.

Delving in the *Dictionary of National Biography*, it has been a sad disappointment to the writer to find so little space devoted to the careers of these picturesque if, I must admit, often unseemly persons. There are, of course, to be found a few pirates with household (name) names such as Kidd, Teach, and Avery. But I compare with indignation the meagre show of pirates in that monumental work with the rich profusion of (divine) divines! Even during the years when piracy was at its height, the pirates are utterly swamped by the (theologian) theologians. Can it be that these two (profession) professions flourished most vigorously side by side, and that when one began to languish, the other also began to fade?

My original intention was that only pirates should be included. To admit (privateer) privateers, (corsair) corsairs, and other (sea-rover) sea-rovers would have meant the addition of a vast number of names, and would have made the work unwieldy. But the difficulty has been to define the exact meaning of a pirate. A pirate was not a pirate from the cradle to the gallows. He usually began his life at sea as an honest mariner. He perhaps mutinied with other of the ship's crew, killed or otherwise disposed of the captain, seized the ship, and sailed off.

Often it happened that, after a long naval war, (ship) ships were laid up and (navy) navies reduced, thus flooding the countryside with begging and starving (seaman) seamen. These were driven to go to sea if they could find a berth, often half-starved and brutally treated, and always underpaid, and so easily yielded to the temptation of joining some vessel bound vaguely for the "South Sea," where no (question) questions were asked and no (wage) wages paid, but every hand on board had a share in the adventure.

— LESSON 23 —

Plural Nouns
Descriptive Adjectives
Possessive Adjectives
Contractions

Exercise 23A: Introduction to Possessive Adjectives

Read the following nouns. Choose a person that you know to possess each of the items. Write that person's name, an apostrophe, and an *s* to form a possessive adjective.

Note to Instructor: Even if the person's name ends in *-s*, the student should still add *'s* to form the possessive: "Marcus's football."

Example: Aunt Catherine — Aunt Catherine's coffee mug

[Name]'s pickup truck

[Name]'s anteater

[Name]'s knitting needles

[Name]'s bus ticket to Seattle, Washington

[Name]'s cat food

Exercise 23B: Singular and Plural Possessive Adjective Forms

Fill in the chart with the correct forms. The first row is done for you. Both regular and irregular nouns are included.

Noun	Singular Possessive	Plural	Plural Possessive
plant	plant's	plants	plants'
child	child's	children	children's
family	family's	families	families'
pirate	pirate's	pirates	pirates'
match	match's	matches	matches'
class	class's	classes	classes'
sheep	sheep's	sheep	sheep's
tortilla	tortilla's	tortillas	tortillas'
galley	galley's	galleys	galleys'
video	video's	videos	videos'
ox	ox's	oxen	oxen's

Exercise 23C: Common Contractions

Drop the letters in grey print and write the contraction on the blank. The first is done for you.

Full Form	Common Contraction	Full Form	Common Contraction
I am	I'm	let us	let's
he is	he's	is not	isn't

we are	we're	were not	weren't
you have	you've	do not	don't
she has	she's	can not	can't
they had	they'd	you are	you're
he will	he'll	it is	it's
you would	you'd	they are	they're

— LESSON 24 —

Possessive Adjectives
Contractions
Compound Nouns

Exercise 24A: Using Possessive Adjectives Correctly

Cross out the incorrect word in parentheses.

My sunglasses are lost. Could I borrow (yours / ~~your's~~)?
When (~~your~~ / you're) finished reading, could you lend me (your / ~~you're~~) magazine?
(~~Its~~ / It's) swelteringly hot today!
The car won't start. (Its / ~~It's~~) battery must be dead.
(His / ~~he's~~) rollerblades are too tight.
Did you remember (your / ~~you're~~) backpack? I think (~~its~~ / it's) still on the chair.
(They're / ~~Their~~) so absentminded. (They're / ~~Their~~) always losing (~~they're~~ / their) belongings.
Whose pencil is that? (~~Its~~ / It's) not a red pencil; (~~its~~ / it's) blue, and (its / ~~it's~~) eraser is chewed.
(Their / ~~They're~~) restaurant is known for (its / ~~it's~~) fabulous desserts.
(It's / ~~Its~~) not fair that (she's / ~~hers~~) always using (your / ~~you're~~) pencils instead of (~~she's~~ / hers).

Exercise 24B: Compound Nouns

Underline each simple subject once and each simple predicate (verb) twice. Circle each compound noun.

The post office will close early today.

Sunrise comes very late in the wintertime.

My mother-in-law forgot her checkbook.

I was running for the bus stop with all my dry cleaning in my arms.

The commander-in-chief arrived with great pomp and circumstance.

I really need a truckful of manure for my garden.

I had a horrendous headache last night.

"You Brush Your Teeth" is a song about toothbrushes.

Exercise 24C: Plurals of Compound Nouns

Write the plural of each singular compound noun in parentheses in the blanks to complete the sentences.

Note to Instructor: The rules governing each compound noun are provided for your reference. Discuss with the student as needed.

Both of our (brother-in-law) brothers-in-law are (chef de cuisine) chefs de cuisine at Ethiopian restaurants in Washington, D.C.

If a compound noun is made up of one noun along with another word or words, pluralize the noun (*brothers*). If the compound noun includes more than one noun, choose the most important to pluralize (*chefs*, not *cuisine*).

All three (sergeant major) sergeants major have testified at multiple (court-martial) courts-martial.

If a compound noun is made up of one noun along with another word or words, pluralize the noun (*sergeants*, *courts*). *Major* and *martial* are both adjectives.

The four (secretary of state) secretaries of state had a top-secret meeting.

If the compound noun includes more than one noun, choose the most important to pluralize (*secretaries*, not *states*).

I like to put three (teaspoonful) teaspoonfuls of curry spice into my chicken curry.

If a compound noun ends in *-ful*, pluralize by putting an *-s* at the end of the entire word.

Those annoying (good-for-nothing) good-for-nothings have stolen all of the (bagful) bagfuls of canned goods I was collecting for the food bank.

If a compound noun is made up of one noun along with another word or words, pluralize the noun (*nothings*; *nothing* is a noun, *good* is an adjective, *for* is a preposition).

If a compound noun ends in *-ful*, pluralize by putting an *s* at the end of the entire word (*bagfuls*).

My mother keeps two (tape measure) tape measures in each of her (toolbox) toolboxes.

If the compound noun includes more than one noun, choose the most important to pluralize (*measures* not *tape*, *boxes* not *tool*, since both name the essence of the noun).

The (Knight Templar) Knights Templar were almost wiped out in France in 1307.

If a compound noun is made up of one noun along with another word or words, pluralize the noun (*Knights* is a noun, *Templar* is an adjective).

Matija Bećković and Charles Simić are both past (poet laureate) poets laureate of Serbia.

If a compound noun is made up of one noun along with another word or words, pluralize the noun (*poets* is a noun, *laureate* is an adjective).

— REVIEW 2 —

Weeks 4-6

Topics
Simple, Progressive, and Perfect Tenses
Conjugations
Irregular Verbs
Subject/Verb Agreement
Possessives
Compound Nouns
Contractions

Review 2A: Verb Tenses

Write the tense of each underlined verb phrase above it: *simple past, present,* or *future*; *progressive past, present,* or *future*; or *perfect past, present,* or *future*. The first is done for you. Watch out for words that interrupt verb phrases but are not helping verbs (such as *not*).

progressive present
I am reading *The Word Snoop*.

perfect present / perfect future
By the time I have finished this book, I will have learned everything there is to know about the English language!

progressive future
The next section that I will be reading is about silent letters.

perfect present / simple future
After I have completed the section on silent letters, I will study the history of punctuation.

The following sentences are taken from *The Word Snoop*, by Ursula Dubosarsky (New York: Dial Books, 2009).

simple present
It is time to talk about silent letters.

simple present
They are the ones that creep sneakily into words at the beginning, middle, or end when you
progressive present
are not expecting them.

progressive present
What are you doing there, silent letters!

simple past
You frightened me!

simple present / simple present
English is not the only language with silent letters, but it has more than most.

progressive present / perfect present
This can be really hard when you are learning to spell, as you have probably realized already.

simple past
Then other people thought it would be good if English looked more like Latin, so a *b*, for example,

perfect past
was dumped back into the word *doubt*, even though it had been taken out because no one pronounced it that way anymore.

perfect present
And have you ever wondered about words like *psalm* and *rhubarb*?

simple past
They came from ancient Greek words.

perfect present
Quite a few of today's silent letters have not always been so quiet.

progressive past
Imagine yourself back when you were learning the alphabet for the very first time.

simple future — progressive present
You will have to crack the special code if you want to know what I am saying.

Review 2B: Verb Formations

Fill in the charts with the correct conjugations of the missing verbs. Identify the person of each group of verbs.

PERSON: Third

	Past	Present	Future
SIMPLE	she wiggled	she wiggles	she will wiggle
PROGRESSIVE	she is wiggling	she is wiggling	she will be wiggling
PERFECT	she had wiggled	she has wiggled	she will have wiggled

PERSON: First

	Past	Present	Future
SIMPLE	I shuffled	I shuffle	I will shuffle
PROGRESSIVE	I was shuffling	I am shuffling	I will be shuffling
PERFECT	I had shuffled	I have shuffled	I will have shuffled

PERSON: Second

	Past	Present	Future
SIMPLE	you itched	you itch	you will itch
PROGRESSIVE	you were itching	you are itching	you will be itching
PERFECT	you had itched	you have itched	you will have itched

PERSON: Third

	Past	Present	Future
SIMPLE	they sneezed	they sneeze	they will sneeze
PROGRESSIVE	they were sneezing	they are sneezing	they will be sneezing
PERFECT	they had sneezed	they have sneezed	they will have sneezed

Review 2C: Person and Subject/Verb Agreement

Circle the correct verb in parentheses.

The following sentences are taken from *The 2,548 Best Things Anybody Ever Said*, by Robert Byrne (New York: Simon & Schuster, 1990)

It (is / are) a good thing for an uneducated man to read books of quotations.
—Winston Churchill

I (hates / hate) quotations.
—Ralph Waldo Emerson

We (doesn't / don't) know a millionth of one percent about anything.
—Thomas Alva Edison

He (writes / write) so well he (makes / make) me feel like putting my quill back in my goose.
—Fred Allen

I (considers / consider) exercise vulgar. It (makes / make) people smell.
—Alec Yuill Thornton

If you (isn't / aren't) fired with enthusiasm, you'll be fired with enthusiasm.
—Vince Lombardi

Children (is / are) guilty of unpardonable rudeness when they (spits / spit) in the face of a companion; neither are they excusable who spit from windows or on walls or furniture.
—St. John Baptist de La Salle

Seriousness (is / are) the only refuge of the shallow.
—Oscar Wilde

Of all the animals, the boy (is / are) the most unmanageable.
—Plato

Plato (is / are) a bore.
—Friedrich Nietzsche

In expressing love we (belongs / belong) among the most undeveloped countries.
—Saul Bellow

Only young people (worries / worry) about getting old.
—George Burns

The two biggest sellers in any bookstore (is / are) the cookbooks and the diet books. The cookbooks (tells / tell) you how to prepare the food and the diet books (tells / tell) you how not to eat any of it.

—Andy Rooney

Review 2D: Possessives and Compound Nouns

Circle the TEN possessive words in the following excerpt. Include possessive words formed from both nouns and pronouns.

Find and underline the SIX compound nouns. Write the plurals of those compound nouns on the blanks at the end of the excerpt.

The following excerpt is taken from *Mary Poppins*, by P.L. Travers (New York: Harcourt Books, 1997).

Jane, with (her) head tied up in Mary (Poppins's) bandanna handkerchief, was in bed with earache. . . .

So Michael sat all the afternoon on the window-seat telling her the things that occurred in the Lane. And sometimes (his) accounts were very dull and sometimes very exciting.

"There's Admiral Boom!" he said once. "He has come out of (his) gate and is hurrying down the Lane. Here he comes. (His) nose is redder than ever and he's wearing a top-hat. Now he is passing Next Door—"

"Is he saying, 'Blast (my) gizzard!'?" enquired Jane.

"I can't hear. I expect so. There's (Miss Lark's) second housemaid in (Miss Lark's) garden. And Robertson Ay is in (our) garden, sweeping up the leaves and looking at her over the fence. He is sitting down now, having a rest."

. . . "Mary Poppins," said Jane, "there's a cow in the Lane, Michael says."

"Yes, and it's walking very slowly, putting (its) head over every gate and looking round as though it had lost something."

handkerchieves	earaches	afternoons
window-seats	top-hats	housemaids

Review 2E: Plurals and Possessives

Write the correct plural, possessive, and plural possessive forms for the following nouns.

Noun	Possessive	Plural	Plural Possessive
ghost	ghost's	ghosts	ghosts'
ox	ox's	oxen	oxen's
trolley	trolley's	trolleys	trolleys'
thrush	thrush's	thrushes	thrushes'
Johnson	Johnson's	Johnsons	Johnsons'
rodeo	rodeo's	rodeos	rodeos'
city	city's	cities	cities'
person	person's	persons/people	persons'/people's

Review 2F: Contractions

Finish the following excerpt about Helen Keller by forming contractions from the words in parentheses.

The excerpt is from *Miss Spitfire: Reaching Helen Keller*, by Sarah Miller (Boston, Mass.: Atheneum Press, 2007).

How do I dare hope to teach this child—Helen—when I've (I have) never taught a child who can see and hear? I've (I have) only just graduated from the Perkins Institution for the Blind myself. Worse, it's (it is) not simply that Helen can't (cannot) hear words or see signs . . . The very notion that words exist, that objects have names, has never even occurred to her . . . At least I know that task isn't (is not) impossible; Perkins's famous Dr. Howe taught my own cottage mate Laura Bridgeman to communicate half a century ago, and she's (she is) both deaf and blind.

Even so, I'm (I am) afraid . . .

More than that, I'm (I am) afraid Helen's family expects too much from me. If they've (they have) read the newspaper articles about Laura, they're (they are) prepared for a miracle. They don't (do not) know Laura's "miraculous" education was hardly perfect . . .

If the Kellers are hoping for another Laura Bridgeman, I don't (do not) know how I—an untrained Irish orphan—can please them. I can't (cannot) tell them there may never be another Laura Bridgeman . . .

There's (There is) not a relative alive who'd (who would) have me, and I wouldn't (would not) know where to find them now anyhow. I'd (I would) die of shame if I had to go back to Perkins a failure.

WEEK 7

Compounds and Conjunctions

— LESSON 25 —

Contractions
Compound Nouns
Diagramming Compound Nouns
Compound Adjectives
Diagramming Adjectives
Articles

Exercise 25A: Contractions Review

Write the two words that form each contraction on the blanks to the right. Some contractions have more than one correct answer. The first is done for you.

Contraction	Helping Verb	Other Word
we're	are	we
I've	have	I
mightn't	might	not
doesn't	does	not
mustn't	must	not
that's	is OR was	that
you'd	had OR would	you
it's	is	it
you're	are	you

Exercise 25B: Diagramming Adjectives and Compound Nouns

On your own paper, diagram every word of the following sentences.

Unfortunate mix-ups happen.

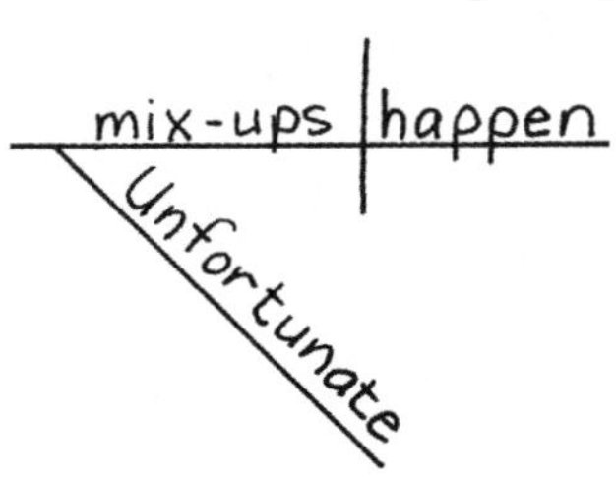

Your desk lamp illuminates.

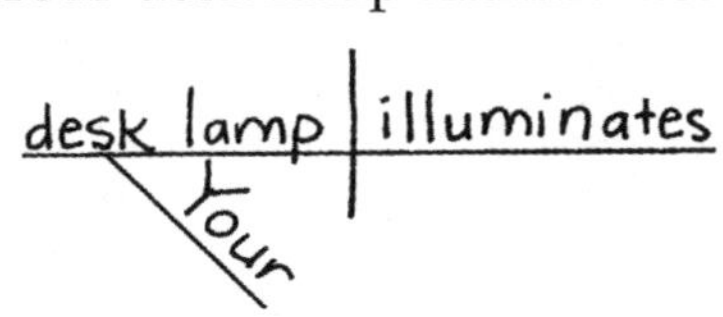

Early trout fishing succeeds.

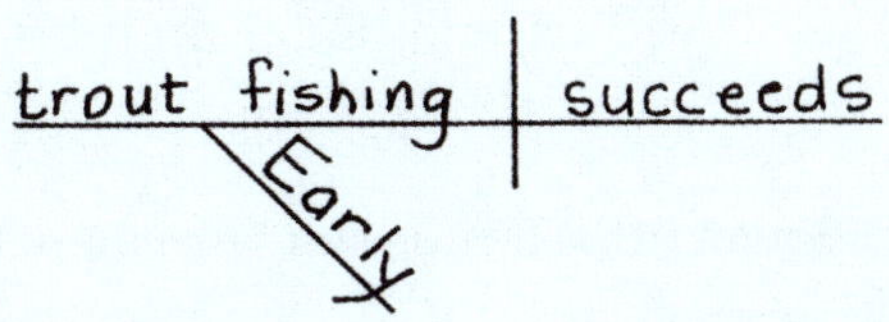

Star Wars entertains.

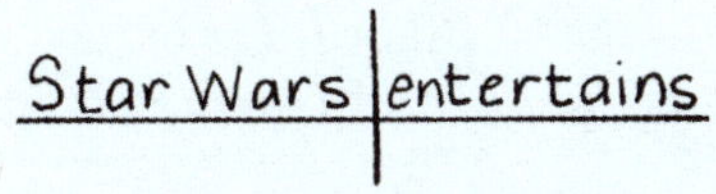

Exercise 25C: Compound Nouns

Draw a line to match each word in Column A with the correct word in Column B to form a single-word compound noun. Then rewrite the new compound noun on the space provided.

Column A	Column B	New Compound Noun
farm	fly	farmhouse
pot	sill	potpie
butter	post	butterfly
court	house	court-martial
lamp	pie	lamppost
window	martial	windowsill

Note to Instructor: Tell the student that the only way to know for sure whether a compound noun should be hyphenated is to consult a dictionary! Many compound nouns can be written either with or without a hyphen.

Linguists often consider a hyphen to be an "intermediate step" in the formation of a compound noun. When English speakers first begin to join nouns together, the hyphen is used, but as a compound noun becomes more common, the hyphen is dropped. You will notice that older texts often hyphenate words which modern texts write as a single noun.

Exercise 25D: Compound Adjectives

Correctly place hyphens in the following phrases.

sixty-one students

a thirty-minute presentation

bluish-green water

a first-class ticket

twenty-four black-and-white copies

two-thirds majority

man-eating grizzly bear

Exercise 25E: Diagramming Adjectives, Compound Nouns, and Compound Adjectives

On your own paper, diagram every word in the following sentences. These are adapted from Jules Verne's *Twenty Thousand Leagues Under the Sea.*

An iron-plated monster had risen.

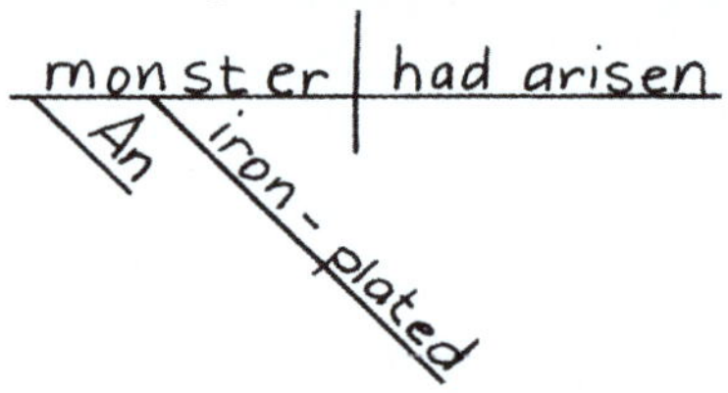

The hideous, powerful sea-monster thrashed.

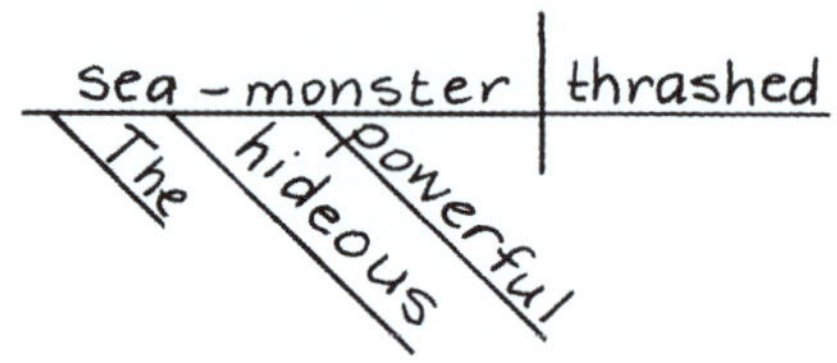

The magnificent chestnut-brown sea otter hissed.

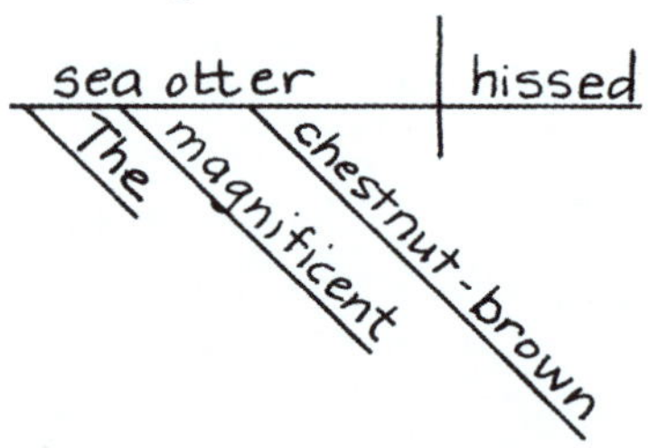

A colossal, billowing storm-cloud threatened.

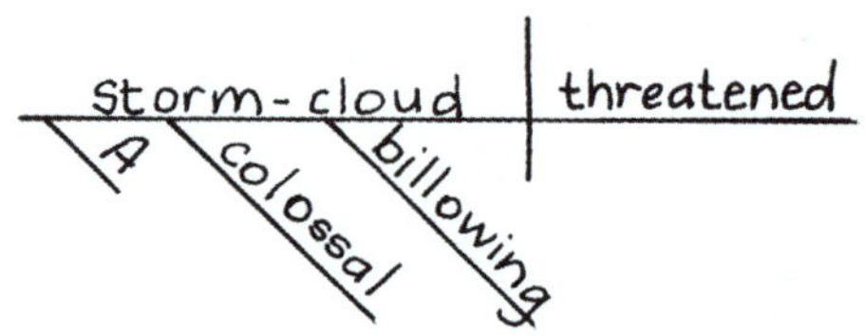

The monster's formidable death-rattle shook.

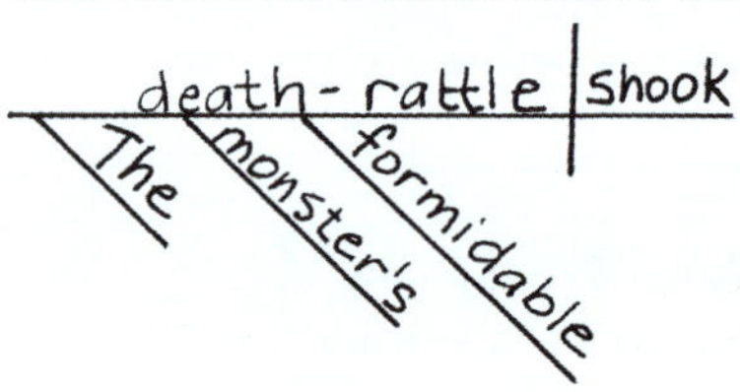

— LESSON 26 —

Compound Subjects
The Conjunction *And*
Compound Predicates
Compound Subject-Predicate Agreement

Exercise 26A: Identifying Subjects, Predicates, and Conjunctions

Underline the subject(s) once and the predicate(s) twice in each sentence. Circle the conjunctions that join them. The first one is done for you.

These sentences are adapted from *Discoverer of the Unseen World: A Biography of Antoni van Leeuwenhoek*, by Alma Payne Ralston.

Here he scooped up a generous sample of the marshy water and put it into a container.

The following night he assembled his simple equipment and prepared to observe the Berkelse Mere water by the light of a single candle.

He put the container in the office-laboratory where he did all of his work and study and waited until the following night.

Particles, green streaks, and little animalcules filled the slide.

The motion of most of these animalcules in the water was so swift and so various.

The streaks were arranged after the manner of copper or tin worms and moved rapidly as he watched.

Exercise 26B: Diagramming Compound Subjects and Predicates

Underline the subject(s) once and the predicate(s) twice in the following sentences. Circle any conjunctions.

When you are finished, diagram the subjects (and any articles modifying the subjects), predicates, and conjunctions (ONLY) of each sentence on your own paper.

The last three sentences in the exercise are taken from L. Frank Baum's *Tik-Tok of Oz*.

Marcos and Carolina are making cookies with their mother.

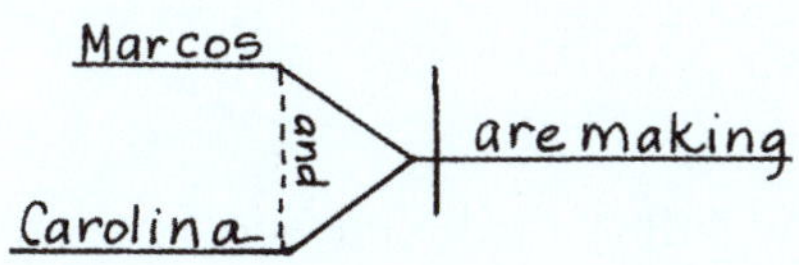

Marcos and Carolina cut and design the cookies.

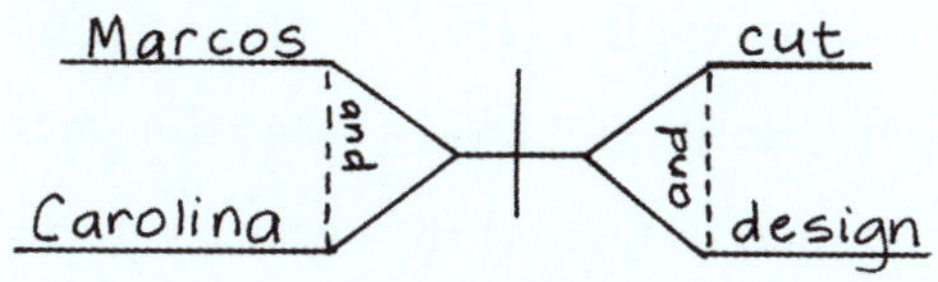

Marcos adds and stirs the ingredients.

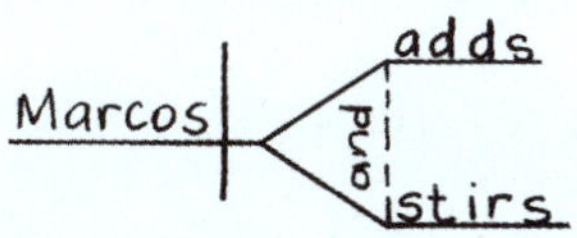

The Rainbow's Daughter and the Rose Princess approached them.

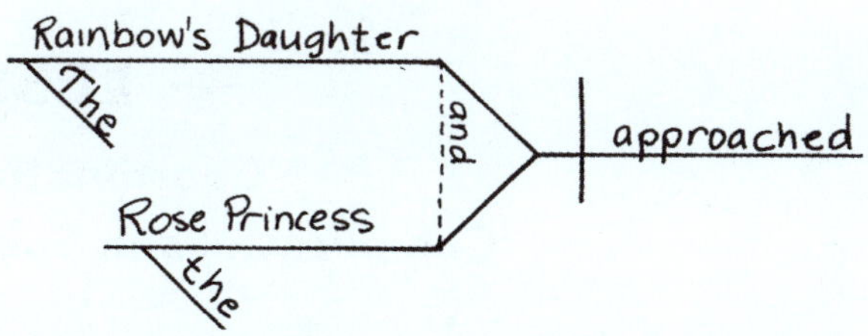

The Shaggy Man grasped the bundle of copper and dumped it upon the ground.

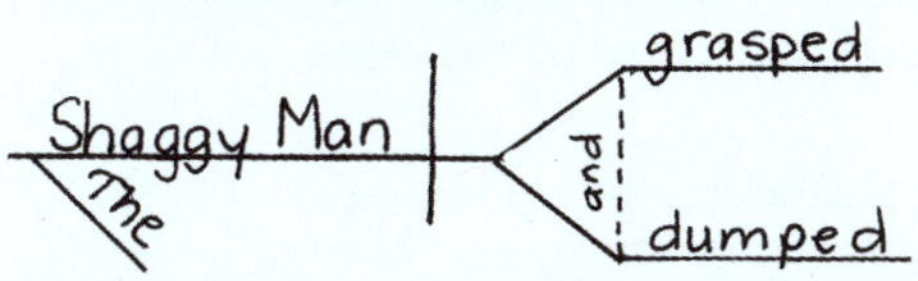

They had raised him and had balanced him upon his feet.

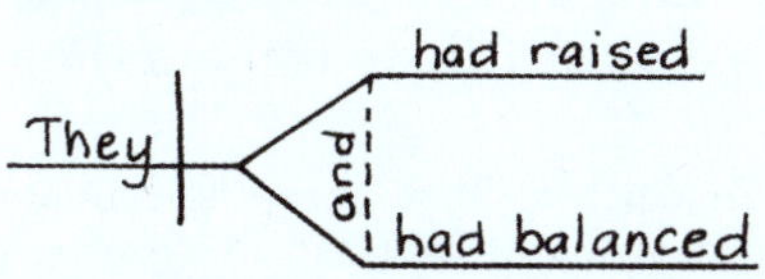

Exercise 26C: Forming Compound Subjects and Verbs

Combine each of these sets of simple sentences into one sentence with a compound subject and/or a compound predicate joined by *and*. Rewrite the new sentences on your own paper.

The architect plans buildings.

The architect designs buildings.

The architect plans and designs buildings.

The audiologist helps children who cannot hear well.

The speech pathologist helps children who cannot hear well.

The audiologist and the speech pathologist help children who cannot hear well.

The electrician installs wires.
The electrician repairs wires.
The electrician installs and repairs wires.

The software designer conceptualizes new websites.
The graphic designer conceptualizes new websites.
The software designer creates new websites.
The graphic designer creates new websites.
The software designer and the graphic designer conceptualize and create new websites.

Exercise 26D: Subject-Verb Agreement with Compound Subjects

Choose the correct verb in parentheses to agree with the subject by crossing out the incorrect verb.

The pilot, copilot, and flight attendants (manage/~~manages~~) the aircraft.

The pilot and the copilot (fly/~~flies~~) the plane.

The flight attendants (assist/~~assists~~) the passengers.

The airplane mechanic and the security guard (ensure/~~ensures~~) the safety of the passengers.

The air traffic controller (~~communicate~~/communicates) with and (~~guide~~/guides) the airplanes.

— LESSON 27 —

Coordinating Conjunctions
Complications in Subject-Predicate Agreement

Exercise 27A: Using Conjunctions

Fill the blanks in the sentences below with the appropriate conjunctions. You must use each conjunction at least once. (There is more than one possible answer for many of the blanks.)

Note to Instructor: Other acceptable answers are in brackets. Make sure that the student has used each conjunction at least one time.

The copper man lost his balance and tumbled to the ground in a heap.
— L. Frank Baum, *Tik-Tok of Oz*

There was always the danger of English or [and] Spanish ships appearing on the green waters of the Gulf.
— Thomas B. Costain, *The Mississippi Bubble*

Pare and his fellow surgeons treated gunshot wounds by cauterizing them with boiling oil of elder.
— John Simmons, *Doctors and Discoveries*

The sun was setting outside, and [for, so] the light that came through the windows was red and gold, but [yet] it did not reach all the way into the corners of the room.

The princess was a sweet little creature, but at the time my story begins was about eight years old, I think, and she got older very fast.
— George MacDonald, *The Princess and the Goblin*

The goblins were now, not ordinarily ugly, but either absolutely hideous, or ludicrously grotesque in face and form.
— George MacDonald, *The Princess and the Goblin*

There are two or three old towers in the field, forlorn, with wall and [or] towers suggesting a splendor that has now departed.

Riches cannot save us from pain, nor can they be taken with us into another world.

During the summer, the lake lost this clearness and became whitish in color.

I could not sleep, for I was troubled in mind.

The copper man was silent, so [and] Betsy wound him up with the key beneath his left arm.
— L. Frank Baum, *Tik-Tok of Oz*

The song of the icy sea is not loud, yet [but] it can be heard to a great distance.

No bather would have a chance if he once got within the grasp of such a monster, nor could a canoe resist the strength of its pull.
— John Timbs, *Eccentricities of the Animal Creation*

Exercise 27B: Subject-Predicate Agreement: Troublesome Subjects

Choose the correct verb in parentheses to agree with the subject noun or pronoun in number. Cross out the incorrect verb.

After breakfast, half of the bananas (are/~~is~~) left, but two-thirds of the bread (~~have~~/has) already been eaten.

The patients (~~was~~/were) still alive.

I (am/~~is~~) moved by an exceedingly powerful desire for knowledge of the heavens.

The choir and the orchestra (listen/~~listens~~) carefully to the conductor.

The trombone players or the saxophonist (is/~~are~~) behind the beat.

My family always (~~eat~~/eats) a lot in the morning.

The cars on the bridge (zoom/~~zooms~~) quickly by.

The celebrity couple (~~was~~/were) filing for divorce.

The raccoon or the squirrels (~~has~~/have) been eating from the birdfeeder.

Nearly three-fourths of the sky (was/~~were~~) covered in fog.

An animal in the bushes (~~growl~~/growls) menacingly.

Fifteen hundred dollars (~~was~~/were) handed out to eleven hundred lottery winners.

Three weeks (is/~~are~~) not enough time to finish my paper!

Two-thirds of his shirt (was/~~were~~) eaten by the tiger.

The band (~~begin~~/begins) to play.

Fifty miles (lie / lies) between the ultramarathoner and the finish line. [either could be argued!]

The hockey team (~~was~~/ were) arguing amongst themselves.

He and the rest of his shirt (~~has~~/ have) escaped.

Exercise 27C: Fill in the Verb

Provide the correct third-person number (singular or plural) of a verb (any verb!) that makes sense.

Note to Instructor: Accept any reasonable answer as long as it is in the correct person and number.

The truthfulness of these men and women ___was, is, etc.___ indeed exemplary. **(3rd singular)**

A profusion of sweet treats ___leads, can lead, etc.___ to extra pounds around the holidays. **(3rd singular)**

Socrates and Plato ___were, are, etc___ the best-known philosophers of ancient Greece. **(3rd plural)**

The discomfort and unhappiness ___were, are, etc.___ very great in that place. **(3rd plural)**

The ship, with all the sailors aboard, ___sank, was sunk, foundered, etc.___. **(3rd singular)**

Sides A, B, and C ___make up, form, constitute, etc.___ a triangle. **(3rd plural)**

My father, my brother, or my sister ___is going, will go, went, etc.___ with me to the movies. **(3rd singular)**

The nation ___is, has become, was, etc.___ very powerful. **(3rd singular)**

The council ___were, are, etc.___ divided in their opinions. **(3rd plural)**

— LESSON 28 —

Further Complications in Subject-Predicate Agreement

Exercise 28A: Subject-Verb Agreement: More Troublesome Subjects

Choose the correct verb in parentheses and cross out the incorrect verb.

The New York Times (~~arrive~~/ arrives) every day at 5:00 a.m.

My mother's eyeglasses (are / ~~is~~) missing, but she reads the paper anyway.

Our friend and neighbor (is / ~~are~~) going away for a long vacation.

"Politics (~~are~~/ is) an interesting subject," she mumbles.

The reviewers as well as the editor (believe / ~~believes~~) that the book is worth reading.

The suspect's whereabouts (is / ~~are~~) unknown at this time.

Luckily, there (are / ~~is~~) muffins baking in the oven.

Each of the cherries (is / ~~are~~) perfectly ripe.

Forty percent of the staff (~~is~~/ are) discontent with the working conditions.

Haunted house phenomena (~~is~~/are) more common than you might think.

There before him (was/~~were~~) a veritable swimming pool.

Here (was/~~were~~) a chance for him.

Kinetics (is/~~are~~) my favorite class in school.

Every one of the soldiers (is/~~are~~) afraid of the coming invasion.

Almost no data (~~was~~/were) gathered from the last set of experiments.

Mumps (was/~~were~~) a common childhood disease before immunizations became common.

Genetics (~~determine~~/determines) the color of your eyes.

You or he (~~are~~/is) the right person for the job.

Forty percent of my time (is/~~are~~) spent on homework.

The appendices (~~was~~/were) found at the end of the paper.

The chef and owner (~~has~~/have) come out to say hello to the diners.

Exercise 28B: Correct Verb Tense and Number

Complete each of these sentences from the *Norwegian Fairy Book* by writing the correct number and tense of the verb indicated.

There lives in Kvam a marksman by the name of Per Gynt. [simple present of *live*]

There are more forests on the Fjäll, and all sorts of beasts dwell in them. [simple present of *am*]

With the exception of three dairy-maids, all the herd-folk are leaving [progressive present of *leave*]

The three beautiful princesses in the castle were longing for rescue. [progressive past of *long*]

Forty-two trolls are marching towards the peasants. [progressive present of *march*]

Dogs or a crying child is disturbing the service. [progressive present of *disturb*]

Fifty shillings is the cost of a fine sword. [simple present of *am*]

A pair of gold shears was hanging by the fireplace. [progressive past of *hang*]

A pattern of black and blue spots covers his whole body. [simple present of *cover*]

The master and commander orders the ship to set sail. [simple present of *order*]

A chest of bright silver coins lies beneath the roots. [simple present of *lie*]

Once upon a time there were seven sons of a king. [simple past of *am*]

Once upon a time there was a king with seven sons. [simple past of *am*]

WEEK 8

Introduction to Objects

— LESSON 29 —

Action Verbs

Direct Objects

Exercise 29A: Direct Objects

In the following sentences, underline the subjects once and the predicates twice. Circle each direct object.

Note to Instructor: Provide all necessary help.

Simon visited his great-aunt in Quebec.

He spends time with her every summer.

His aunt cooked crepes for him for lunch.

At home, he made crepes for his friends and added chocolate, bananas, and cream.

The little princess could see the sky only during the day.

They had got a king and a government.

They heartily cherished the ancestral grudge.

Nature recycles dead leaves.

The dead leaf material protects the soil.

Juliana recycles too.

She built a bin for compost.

She added dried leaves, food scraps, and grass clippings.

Many bugs and worms lived in her compost bin.

The compost nourished her garden.

The herbs and flowers grew and produced leaves and blooms.

Exercise 29B: Diagramming Direct Objects

On your own paper, diagram the subjects, verbs, direct objects, and any necessary conjunctions in the sentences from Exercise 29A.

Simon visited his great-aunt in Quebec.

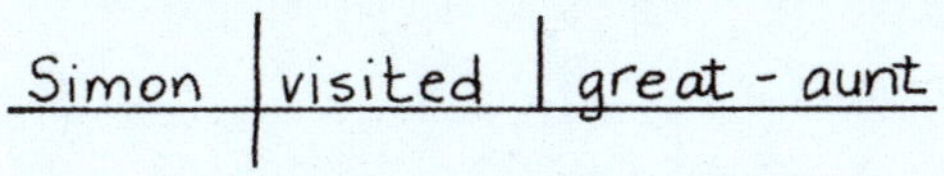

His aunt cooked crepes for him for lunch.

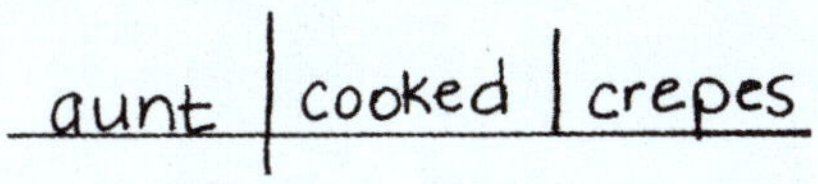

The little princess could see the sky only during the day.

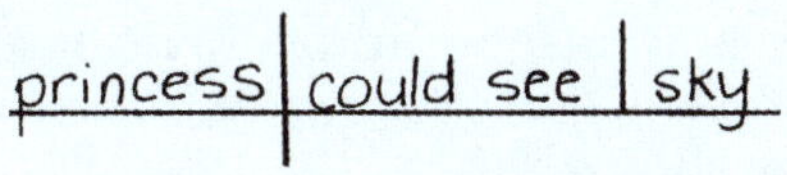

They heartily cherished the ancestral grudge.

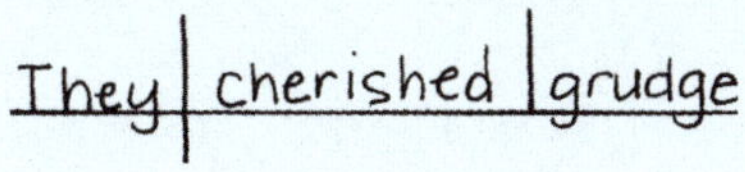

The dead leaf material protects the soil.

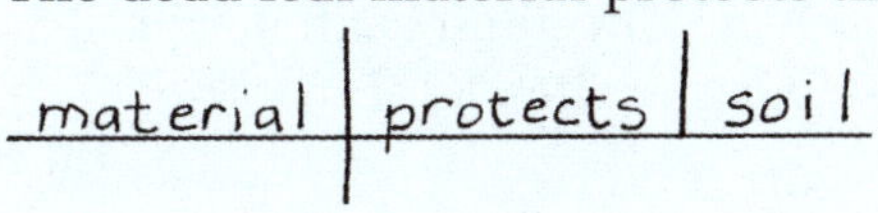

She built a bin for compost.

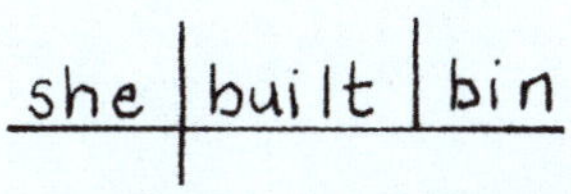

Many bugs and worms lived in her compost bin.

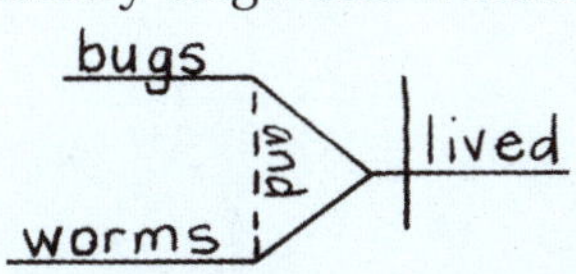

He spends time with her every summer.

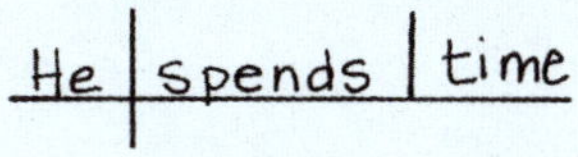

At home, he made crepes for his friends and added chocolate, bananas, and cream.

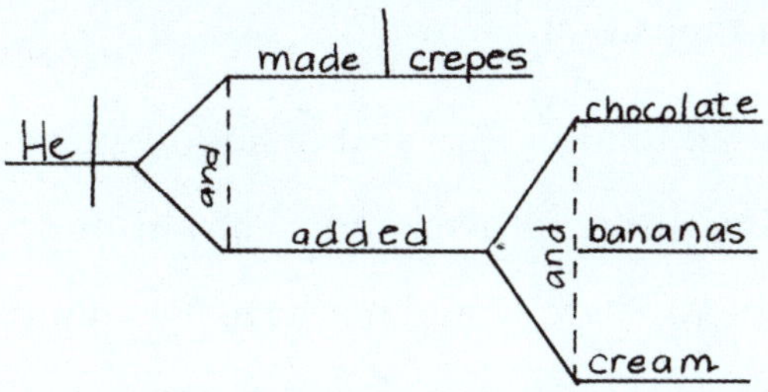

They had got a king and a government.

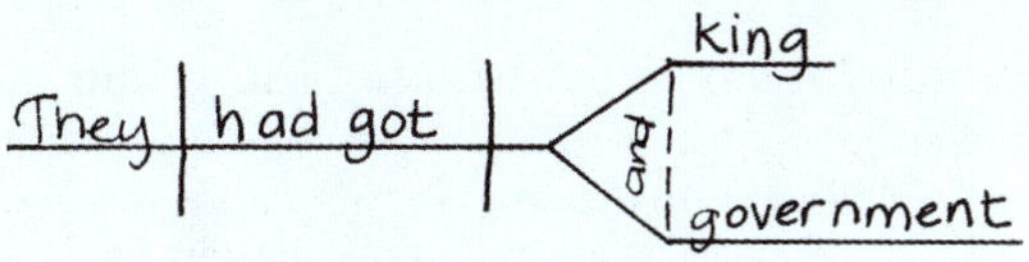

Nature recycles dead leaves.

Juliana recycles too.

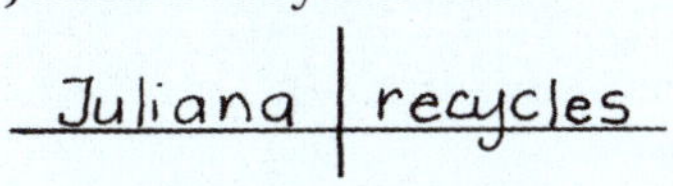

She added dried leaves, food scraps, and grass clippings.

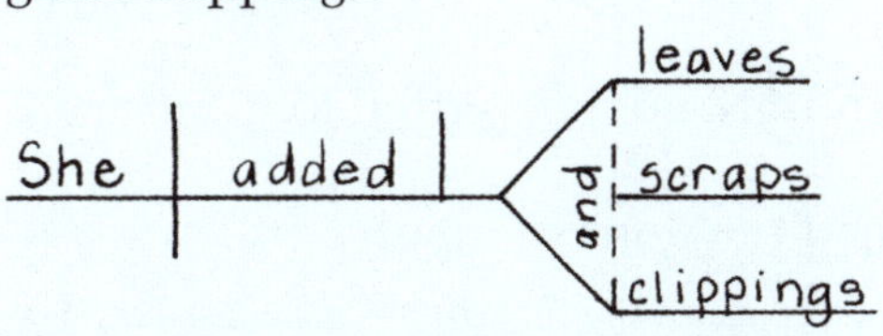

The compost nourished her garden.

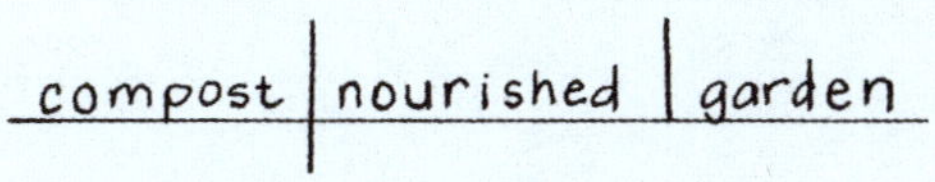

The herbs and flowers grew and produced leaves and blooms.

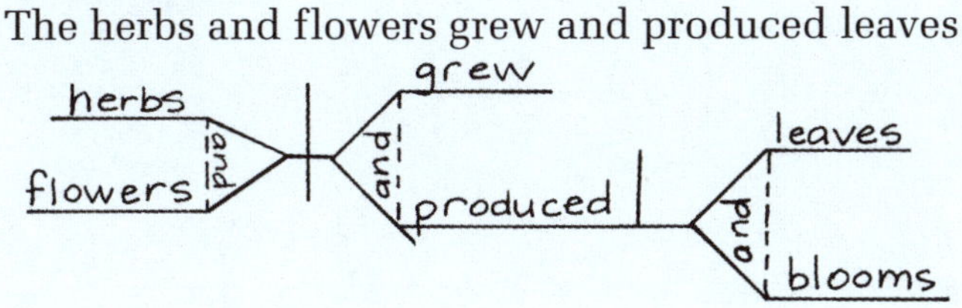

— LESSON 30 —

Direct Objects
Prepositions

Exercise 30A: Identifying Prepositions

In the following sentences from George MacDonald's *The Princess and the Goblin,* find and circle each preposition.

These mountains were full (of) hollow places; huge caverns, and winding ways, some (with) water running (through) them, and some shining (with) all colours (of) the rainbow when a light was taken (into) them. There would not have been much known (about) them, had there not been mines there, great deep pits, (with) long galleries and passages running (from) them, which had been dug to get (at) the ore (of) which the mountains were full. (In) the course (of) digging, the miners came (upon) many (of) these natural caverns. A few (of) them had openings (onto) the side (of) a mountain, or (into) a ravine.

> **Note to Instructor:** In the phrase *which had been dug to get, to* is part of the infinitive, not a preposition. However, since this has not yet been studied, you may accept *to* if the student circles it.

Exercise 30B: Word Relationships

The following sentences all contain action verbs. Underline each subject once and each action verb twice. If the sentence has an action verb followed by a direct object, write *DO* above the direct object.

If the sentence contains a preposition, circle the preposition and draw a line to connect the two words that the preposition shows a relationship between. The first is done for you.

The train (in) the depot puffed loudly.

He opened the door (DO) suddenly.

My father is hanging pictures (DO) today.

The brook (under) the bridge flows sluggishly.

I opened the door (DO) (of) the car immediately.

The car (in) the distance slowed.

She suddenly slowed the car (DO).

The twelve white cabins (beside) the blackened lot sit deserted.

Dark draperies hung upon the walls.

The tunnel through the mountain flooded.

The dog was hiding under the porch.

The clockmaker wound the clock every morning.

Exercise 30C: Diagramming Direct Objects

On your own paper, diagram the subjects, predicates, and direct objects only from the sentences above. If a sentence does not have a direct object, do not diagram it.

He opened the door suddenly.

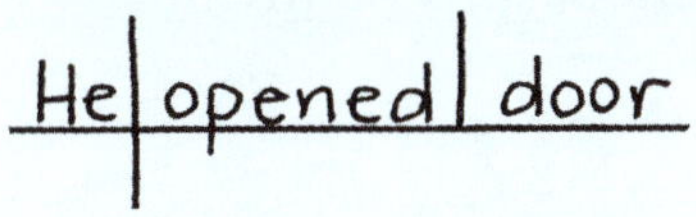

My father is hanging pictures today.

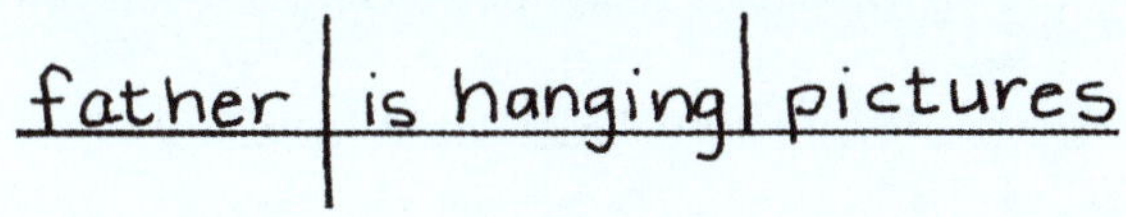

I opened the door of the car immediately.

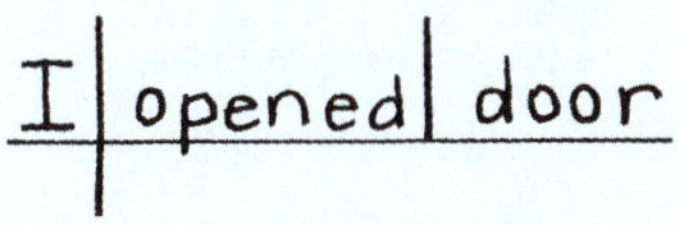

She suddenly slowed the car.

The clockmaker wound the clock every morning.

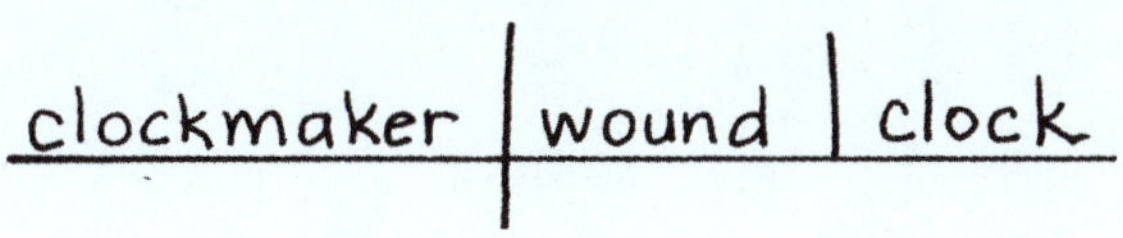

— LESSON 31 —

Definitions Review
Prepositional Phrases
Object of the Preposition

Exercise 31A: Objects of Prepositional Phrases

Fill in the blanks with a noun as the object of the preposition to complete the prepositional phrases.

Note to Instructor: Answers will vary. Suggested answers are given below.

Georgie hid his string beans underneath his _____________. [bread]

Everett always wanted to travel across _____________. [America]

Above the _____________ soared the eagle. [trees]

Samantha has the best hide-and-seek spot, between the __________ and __________. [barn, road]

Wally cried when he fell down the _____________. [slide]

Ronald does not venture into the woods after _____________. [dusk]

Exercise 31B: Identifying Prepositional Phrases

Can you find all ten of the prepositional phrases in the following excerpt from Arthur Conan Doyle's *The Hound of the Baskervilles*? Underline the complete prepositional phrases. Circle the prepositions. Label each object of the preposition with OP. (A *gig* is a small horse-drawn carriage.)

I can well remember driving to his house in the evening some three weeks before the fatal event. He chanced to be at his hall door. I had descended from my gig and was standing before him, when I saw his eyes fix themselves over my shoulder and stare past me with an expression of the most dreadful horror.

Exercise 31C: Remembering Prepositions

Can you remember all 46 prepositions without looking back at your list? On your own paper, write them down in alphabetical order. The first letter of each preposition and the number of prepositions that begin with that letter are found below, as a memory aid.

A	B	D	E	F	I	L
aboard	before	down	except	for	in	like
about	behind	during		from	inside	
above	below				into	
across	beneath					
after	beside					
against	between					
along	beyond					
among	by					
around						
at						

N	O	P	S	T	U	W
near	of	past	since	through	under	with
	off			throughout	underneath	within
	on			to	until	without
	over			toward	up	
					upon	

— LESSON 32 —

Subjects, Predicates, and Direct Objects
Prepositions
Object of the Preposition
Prepositional Phrases

Exercise 32A: Identifying Prepositional Phrases and Parts of Sentences

In the following sentences, adapted from *Japanese Fairy Tales*, by Yei Theodora Ozaki, circle each prepositional phrase. Once you have identified the prepositional phrases, underline subjects once and predicates twice, and label direct objects with *DO*.

The kind-hearted, hard-working old man and the cross-patch wife lived in Japan with the old man's tame sparrow.

DO

The old woman spoiled the happiness of her home by her scolding tongue.

DO DO

After a hard day's work, the old man opened the cage of the sparrow, talked to her, gave treats, and played with her.

DO

The old woman hated the sparrow and quarrelled with her husband about the little bird.

DO DO

She drove the sparrow into exile with spite and spread the laundry in the sun.

In the evening, the old man came into the house with anticipation and was disappointed.

DO

The old man shed painful tears after dark.

He rose before dawn and searched for the sparrow over the hills, through the woods, in bamboo forests.

Lady Sparrow was with her family.

DO

She thanked him with many polite bows for all the kindnesses of the past years.

Exercise 32B: Diagramming

On your own paper, diagram all of the uncircled parts of the sentences from Exercise 32A.

The kind-hearted, hard-working old man and the cross-patch wife lived.

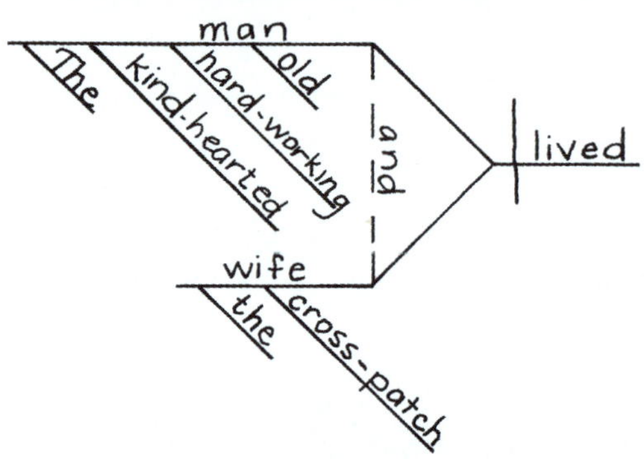

The old woman spoiled the happiness.

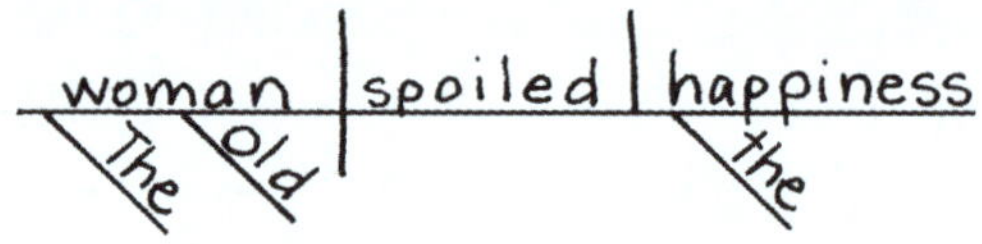

The old man opened the cage, talked, gave treats, and played.

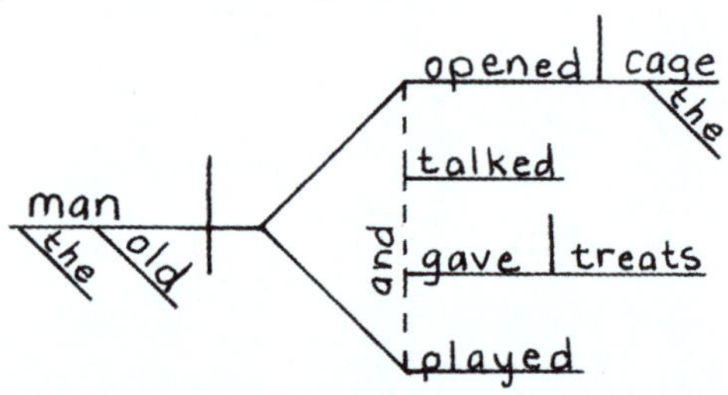

The old woman hated the sparrow and quarrelled.

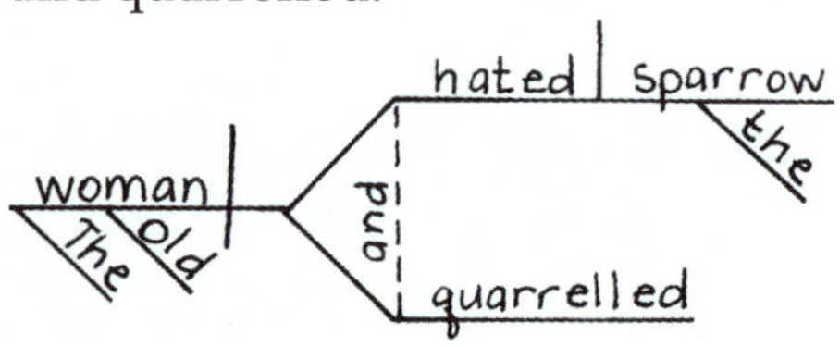

She drove the sparrow and spread the laundry.

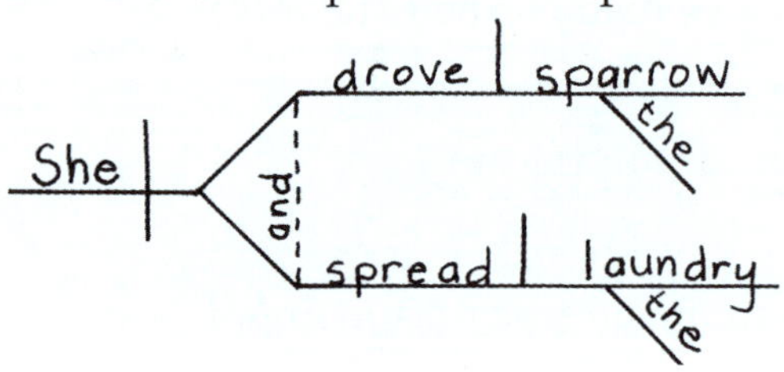

The old man came and was disappointed.

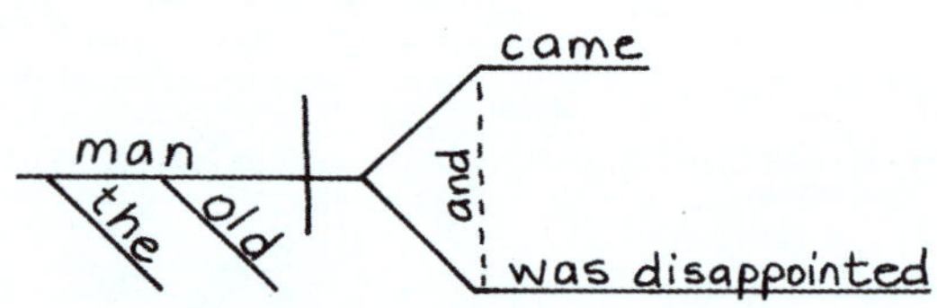

The old man shed painful tears.

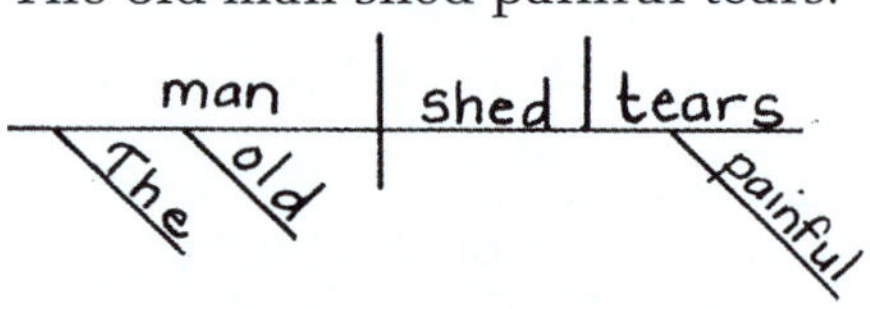

He rose and searched.

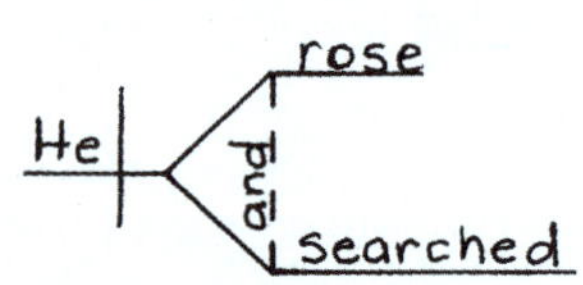

Lady Sparrow was.

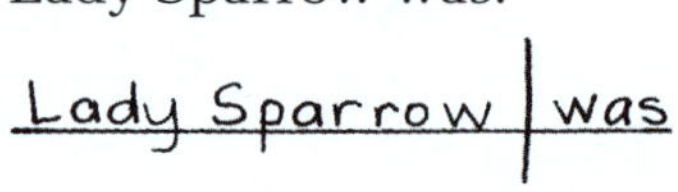

She thanked him.

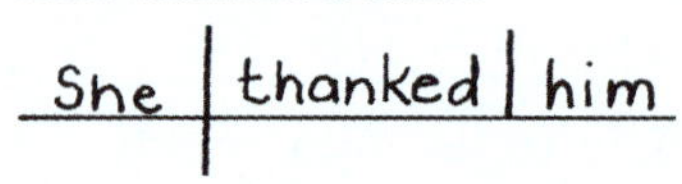

WEEK 9

Adverbs

— LESSON 33 —

Adverbs That Tell How

Exercise 33A: Identifying Adverbs That Tell How

Underline the adverbs telling *how* in the following sentences, and draw arrows to the verbs that they modify. Some sentences contain more than one adverb.

Elizabeth I angrily charged Essex, on his allegiance, not to leave Ireland without her permission.

The Taj Mahal stands magnificently in the city of Agra, India.

The grand structure extravagantly honors Queen Mumtaz Mahal, wife of Emperor Shah Jahan.

After the death of the queen, Emperor Shah Jahan mourned despondently and inconsolably for two years.

The Emperor painstakingly constructed the Taj Mahal over a period of 22 years.

Within the marble walls of the Taj Mahal, the Emperor could properly honor his beloved wife.

Fittingly, this architectural masterpiece has been called one of the Seven Wonders of the World.

As he said once laughingly, it is the best opportunity to tell him all of the things he should hear.

Immediately he pulls his feet from his sandals.

She sang sweetly and played handsomely on the lute.

Exercise 33B: Forming Adverbs from Adjectives

Turn the following adjectives into adverbs.

Adjective	Adverb	Adjective	Adverb
odd	oddly	handy	handily
angry	angrily	beautiful	beautifully
fond	fondly	clever	cleverly
hesitant	hesitantly	shrewd	shrewdly
gaudy	gaudily		

Exercise 33C: Diagramming Adverbs

On your own paper, diagram the following sentences.

They rested peacefully.

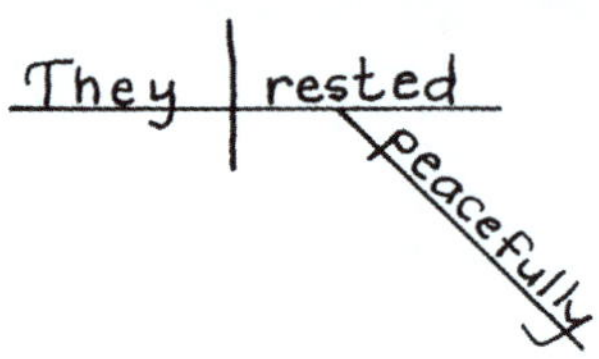

Suddenly he stopped.

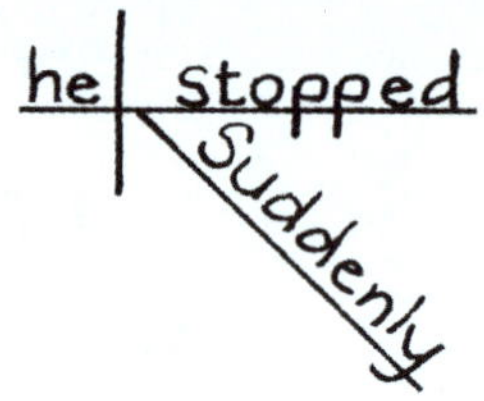

Rosa played hockey aggressively.

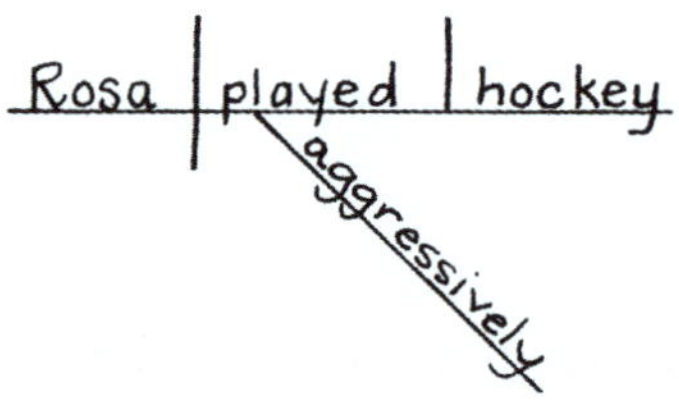

James kindly fixed sweet lemonade.

Did they work diligently?

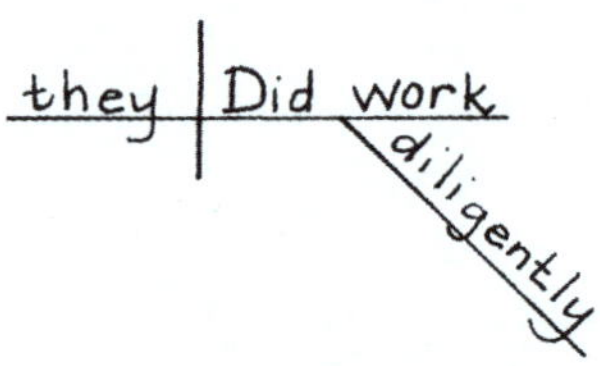

The new tadpoles were wiggling furiously.

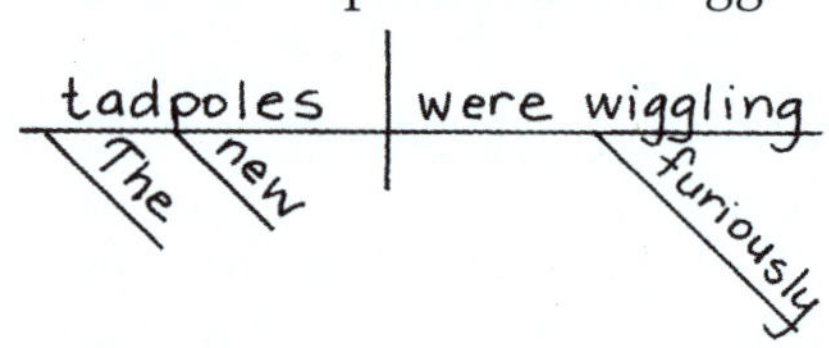

— LESSON 34 —

Adverbs That Tell When, Where, and How Often

Exercise 34A: Telling When

Angeline dropped her recipe cards for French toast. Help her to get organized by numbering the following sentences from 1 to 5, so that she can make breakfast.

4 Later, fry the soaked bread on both sides in a hot skillet.

2 Second, beat three eggs with a bit of milk, sugar, and cinnamon.

5 Finally, enjoy with fresh maple syrup and cream.

1 First, slice a loaf of French bread into thick slices.

3 Next, place the bread in the egg mixture and soak for ten minutes.

Exercise 34B: Distinguishing Among Different Types of Adverbs

Put each of the following adverbs in the correct category according to the question it answers.

tomorrow	occasionally	there	now
carefully	inside	above	first
comfortably	always	rarely	fast

When	Where	How	How Often
tomorrow	there	comfortably	occasionally
now	inside	fast	always
first	above	carefully	rarely

Exercise 34C: Identifying Adverbs of Different Types

Underline the 13 adverbs in the following sentences that tell *when*, *where*, or *how often*.

Estefan has never missed a soccer practice.

The team practices daily outside.

First, the team runs laps.

There they go!

Later they practice drills.

Soccer is usually called *futebol* or *football* in Brazil.

Brazil's national team has repeatedly won the World Cup.

Those who saw him for the first time were often charmed by the eager cordiality of his address.

She had worn some of the dresses once or twice.

It was always strong and confident and it was never dull.

Exercise 34D: Diagramming Different Types of Adverbs

On your own paper, diagram the following sentences.

Tomorrow I am camping there.

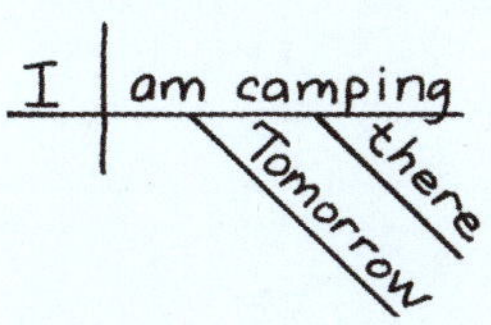

Where are you sleeping?

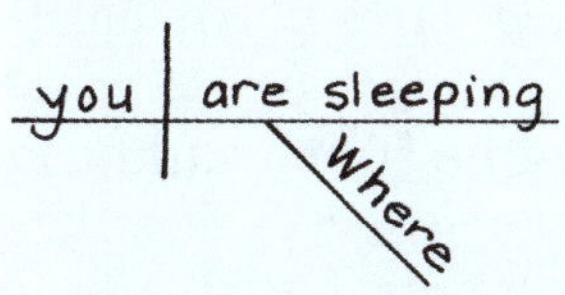

When did you eat dinner?

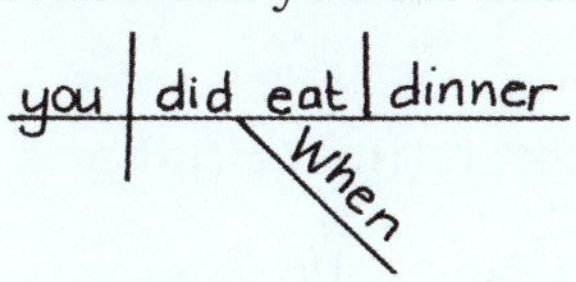

I will never forget you.

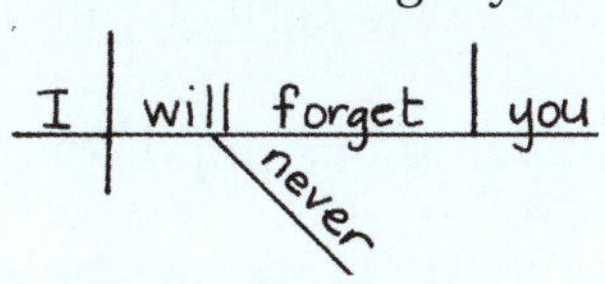

Leo rang his bell twice and tapped his foot impatiently.

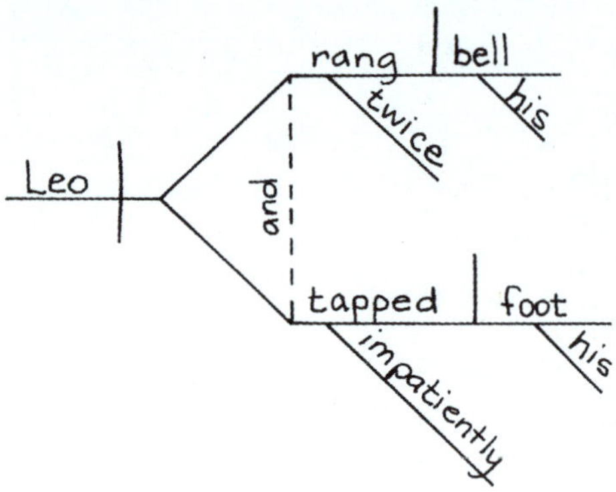

— LESSON 35 —

Adverbs That Tell To What Extent

Exercise 35A: Identifying the Words Modified by Adverbs

Draw an arrow from each underlined adverb to the word it modifies.

Mom told us rather unexpectedly about the plans to move to a new house.

Jordan and I were not especially excited about the idea.

We had worked very hard to make friends in this neighborhood.

The new town would be much larger and less familiar.

We rode with Dad to see our brand new house.

Dozens of enormously grand trees very gently shaded the porch.

A beautifully designed tree house had already been built in the back yard.

Mom and Dad had tried particularly hard to find a place that we would like.

Maybe the kids across the street could come right now to see our tree house!

His face may have been ugly, but all admit that it was remarkably expressive.

His attitude at the piano was perfectly quiet and amazingly dignified.

"Unnaturally patient," says one pupil, "he would have a passage repeated a dozen times till it was to his mind"; "infinitely strict in the smallest detail," says another, "until the right rendering was obtained."

(The following sentences are from Stacy Schiff's *Cleopatra: A Life.*)

She was incomparably richer than anyone else in the Mediterranean.

Cleopatra descended from a long line of murderers and faithfully upheld the family tradition but was, for her time and place, remarkably well-behaved.

Exercise 35B: Diagramming Different Types of Adverbs

On your own paper, diagram every word of the following sentences.

Very talented Lily can jump extremely high.

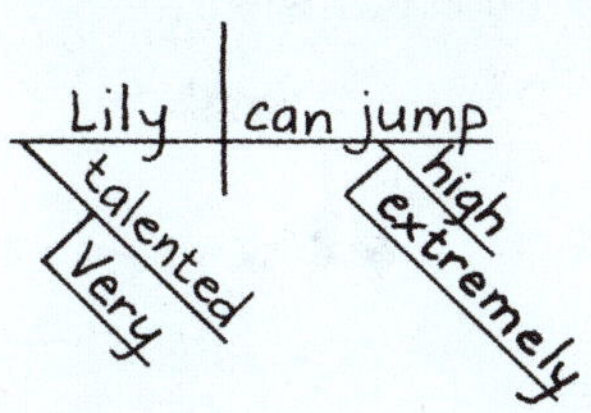

Traffic stopped quite suddenly.

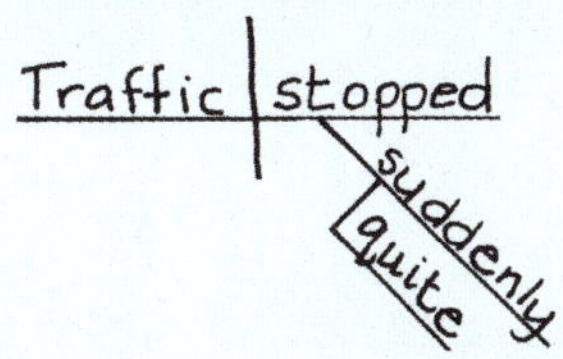

Drive much more carefully!

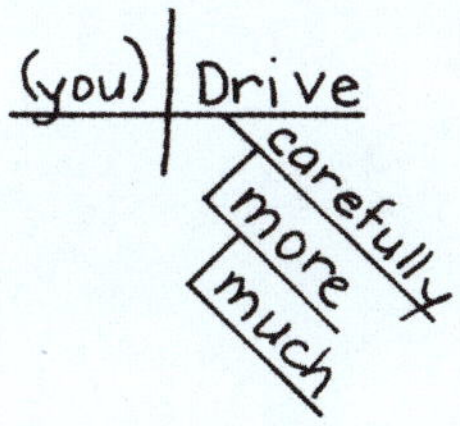

Luke gave very strict orders extraordinarily sharply.

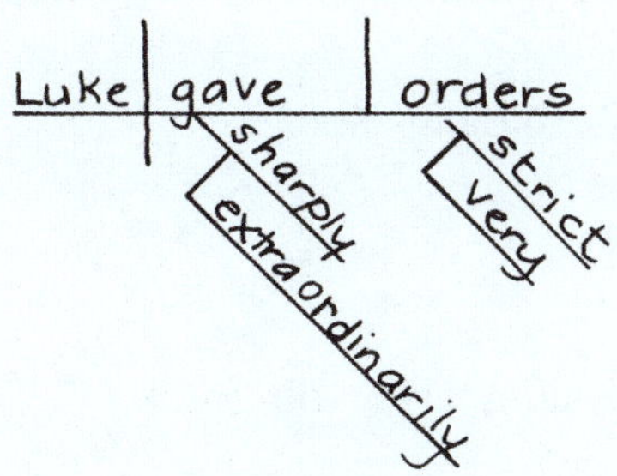

Aunt Lou fixes especially fine meals.

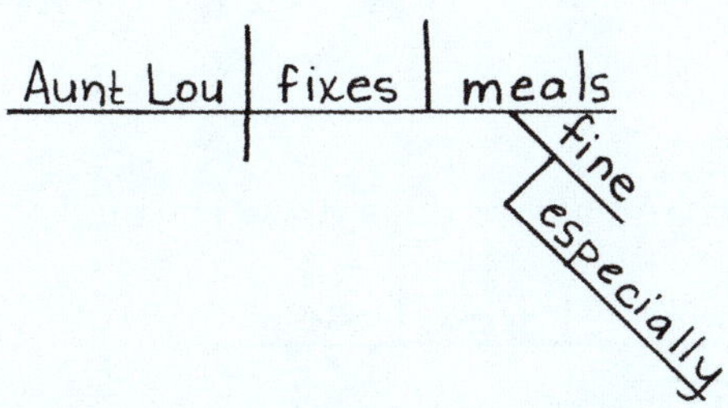

Your excessively rude cousin pinched me particularly hard.

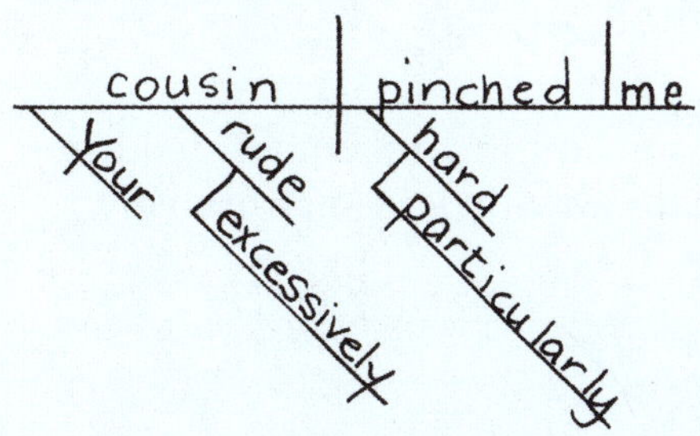

— LESSON 36 —

Adjectives and Adverbs
The Adverb *Not*
Diagramming Contractions
Diagramming Compound Adjectives and Compound Adverbs

Exercise 36A: Practice in Diagramming

On your own paper, diagram every word of the following sentences. These are adapted from Jack London's *The Call of the Wild.*

Buck didn't read the newspapers or journals.

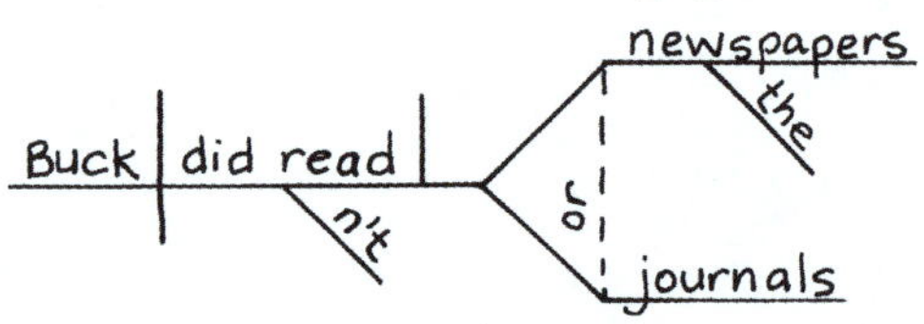

The prospectors wanted strong and heavy dogs.

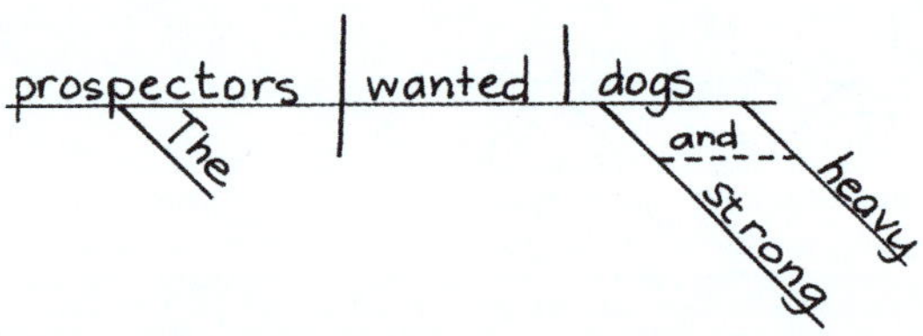

They crassly and dishonestly stole Buck.

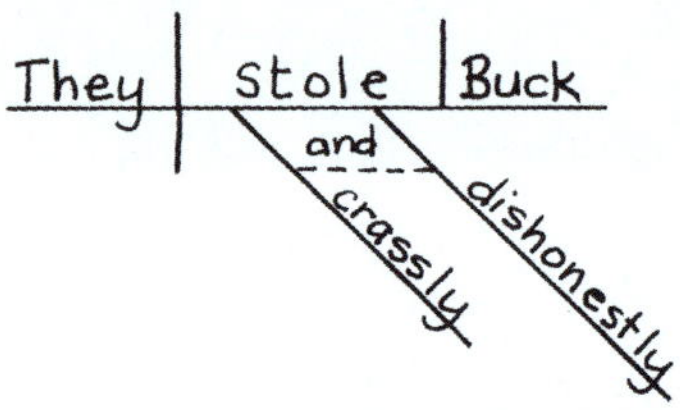

A great fear seized him and contracted his muscles spasmodically and instinctively.

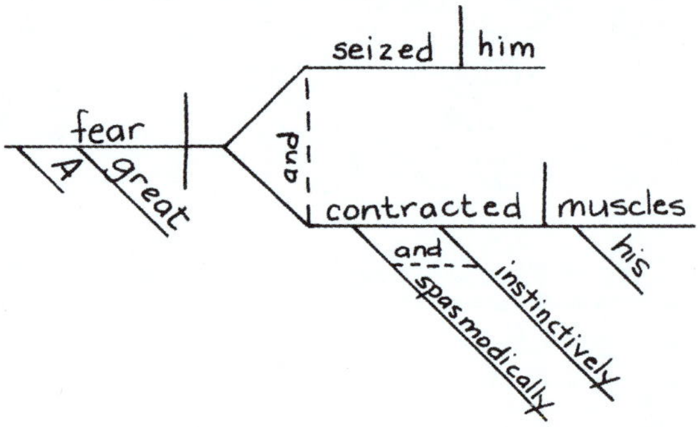

Men had found a yellow metal and were rushing out.

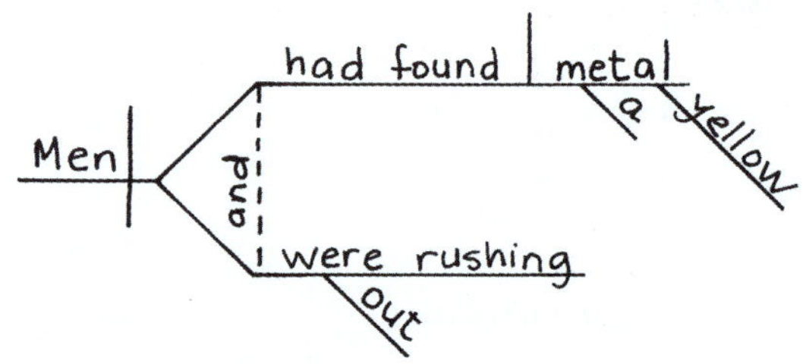

They didn't always buy dogs.

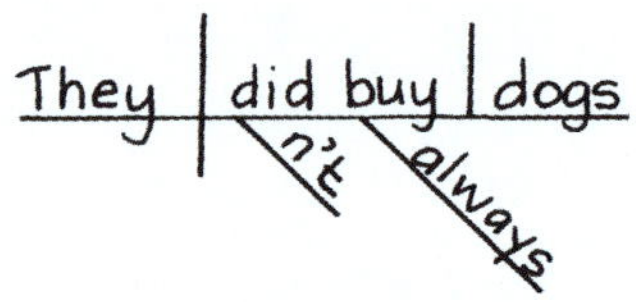

Buck now faced a great and difficult problem.

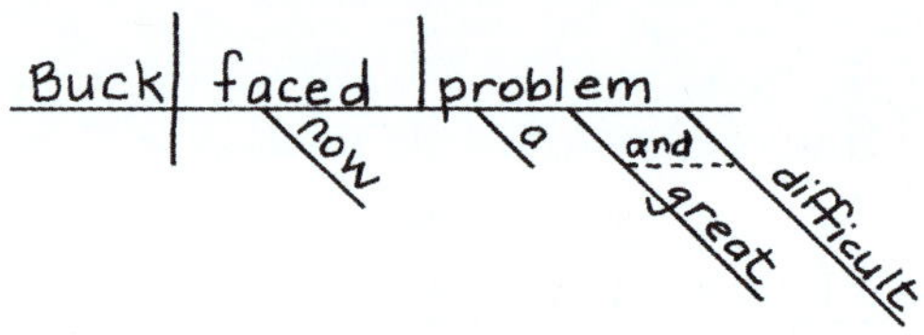

Twelve alert and active dogs drew the sled.

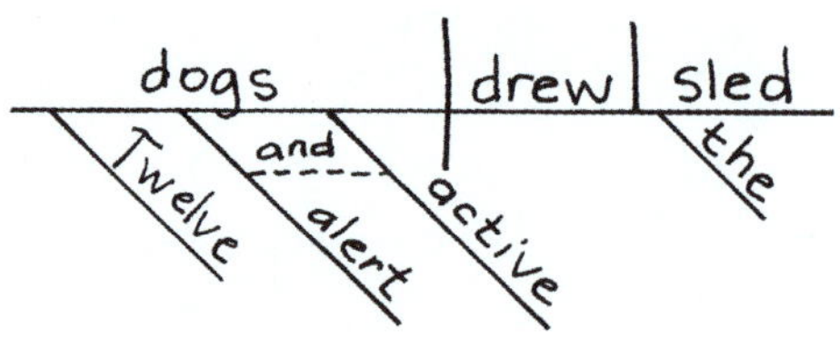

He was struggling and delayed the start.

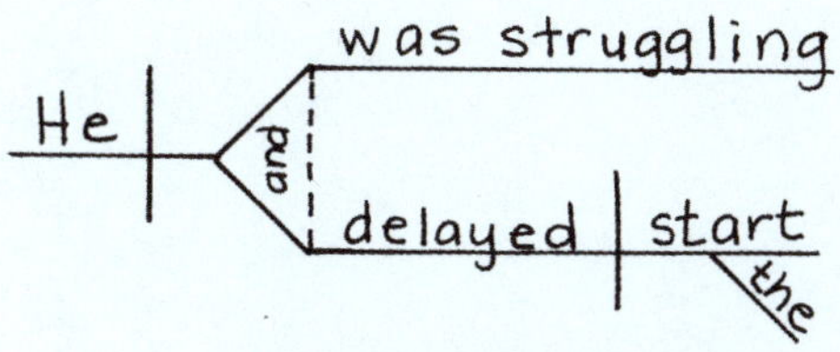

He was not always running forward.

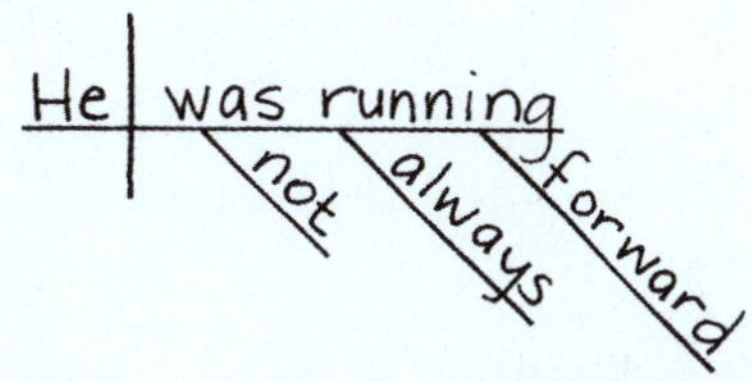

Note to Instructor: *Always* is ambiguous. I have placed it beneath the verb, on the assumption that the sentence means *He was not always running*, but the student could also choose to place it beneath the adverb *forward*, on the assumption that Buck was always running, but was sometimes running sideways or backwards rather than forward. In that case, *not* would also modify *forward*, rather than *was running*. Remember that English grammar does not always act scientifically!

— REVIEW 3 —

Weeks 7-9

Topics
Parts of Speech
Compound Parts of Sentences
Prepositions
Prepositional Phrases
Objects of Prepositions
Subjects and Predicates
Subject-Verb Agreement
Verbs and Direct Objects

Review 3A: Parts of Speech

Identify the underlined words as *N* for noun, *ADJ* for adjective, *ADV* for adverb, *PREP* for preposition, or *CONJ* for conjunction. The first sentence is done for you.

The following excerpt is taken from *A Wrinkle in Time*, by Madeleine L'Engle (New York: Yearling, 1973), pp. 3-8.

ADJ CONJ ADJ
It was a dark and stormy night.

PREP N N ADJ PREP PREP
In her attic bedroom Margaret Murry, wrapped in an old patchwork quilt, sat on the foot of
ADJ PREP
her bed and watched the trees tossing in the frenzied lashing of the wind. Behind the trees clouds
ADV PREP PREP
scudded frantically across the sky. Every few moments the moon ripped through them, creating
ADJ N PREP
wraith-like shadows that raced along the ground.

The house shook.

Wrapped in her quilt, Meg shook.

ADV ADV
She wasn't usually afraid of weather. –It's not just the weather, she thought. –It's the weather
PREP N ADJ N
on top of everything else. On top of me. On top of Meg Murry doing everything wrong. . . .

"Why didn't you come up to the attic?" Meg asked her brother, speaking as though he were at
ADJ ADV
least her own age. "I've been scared stiff."

ADV ADV
"Too windy up in that attic of yours," the little boy said. "I knew you'd be down. I put some
PREP
milk on the stove for you." . . .

N PREP ADV ADV
How did Charles Wallace always know about her? How could he always tell? He never
CONJ CONJ CONJ
knew—or seemed to care—what Dennys or Sandy were thinking. It was his mother's mind, and
PREP ADJ N
Meg's, that he probed with frightening accuracy.

Review 3B: Recognizing Prepositions

Circle the 46 prepositions in the following bank of words. Try to complete the exercise without looking back at your list of prepositions.

beside or under to nowhere except was with
like near and since that for fly
also around bring us upon aboard sail of
anyone beyond into through though throughout across
below inside what among here past about
from being during thing above off mine
beneath after but at against until should
between by wrong along this toward before
fry underneath up down right left over within without
out front behind side in so on board

Review 3C: Subjects and Predicates

In these sentences from poems by Edward Lear, draw one line under the subject and two lines under the predicate. Watch out for compound subjects and predicates!

The owl and the pussycat went to sea in a beautiful pea-green boat.

They took some honey, and plenty of money, wrapped up in a five-pound note.

The owl looked up to the stars above and sang to a small guitar.

Hand in hand, on the edge of the sand, they danced by the light of the moon.

Two Owls and a Hen, four Larks and a Wren, have all built their nests in my beard!

The Cups and the Saucers danced madly about.

The Plates and the Dishes looked out of the casement.

The Soup-ladle peeped through a heap of Veal Patties and squeaked with a ladle-like scream of surprise.

The Tea-kettle hissed and grew black in the face.

They galloped away to a beautiful shore.

In silence they rode and made no observation.

Review 3D: Complicated Subject-Verb Agreement

Cross out the incorrect verb form in parentheses.

Yann or Marilou (is / ~~are~~) the best candidate for class president.

The class (votes / ~~vote~~) at 10:00 on Thursday.

The class (~~was~~ / were) whispering amongst themselves about the upcoming election.

"Five dollars (is / ~~are~~) too much to pay for school lunch," Yann claims.

Yann and his running mates (~~plans~~/ plan) to lower the price of the daily lunch.
But Marilou (has /~~have~~) decided to get a new basketball hoop for the playground.
The principal or the teachers (~~is~~/ are) counting the votes.
Aesop's Fables (does /~~do~~) not seem terribly interesting as the class waits to hear the election results.
The envelope with the results (rests /~~rest~~) temptingly on the table.
The teacher's glasses (~~slides~~/ slide) down her nose when she announces the winner.
Two-thirds of the students (~~has~~/ have) voted for Marilou.
The news (spreads /~~spread~~) quickly throughout the class.
After school there (is /~~are~~) a grand party.
Yann and Marilou graciously (~~shakes~~/ shake) hands.

Review 3E: Objects and Prepositions

In the following paragraph from Charles Dickens's novel *A Tale of Two Cities,* identify the underlined words as *DO* for direct object or *OP* for object of a preposition. For each direct object, find and underline twice the action verb that affects it. For each object of the preposition, find and circle the preposition to which it belongs.

There is one compound object of a preposition, and one compound adjective. When you find them, write *compound OP* and *compound adj* in the margin next to them. Draw arrows from each compound form to the appropriate label in the margin.

The coach lumbered on again, with heavier wreaths of mist closing round it as it began the descent. The guard soon replaced his blunderbuss in his arm-chest, and, having looked to the rest of its contents, and having looked to the supplementary pistols that he wore in his belt, looked to a smaller chest beneath his seat, in which there were a few smith's tools, a couple of torches, and a tinder-box. For he was furnished with that completeness that if the coach-lamps had been blown and stormed out, which did occasionally happen, he had only to shut himself up inside, keep the flint and steel sparks well off the straw, and get a light with tolerable safety and ease (if he were lucky) in five minutes.

WEEK 10

Completing the Sentence

— LESSON 37 —

Direct Objects

Indirect Objects

Exercise 37A: Identifying Direct Objects

Underline the action verbs and circle the direct objects in these sentences, adapted from *The Mississippi Bubble*, by Thomas B. Costain. Remember that you can always eliminate prepositional phrases first if that makes the task easier.

French guns could sweep the horizon.

The lookout could keep a sharp eye on the beach.

Any settlement would need a strong fort.

The outer wall had bastions.

This made a snug little harbor.

The defenders could meet the attacks.

Exercise 37B: Identifying Direct Objects, Indirect Objects, and Objects of Prepositions

Underline every object in the following sentences. Label each one: *DO* for direct object, *IO* for indirect object, or *OP* for object of the preposition.

At Christmas (OP), Benjamin makes his aunt (IO) an ornament (DO).

Sarah's mother cooks the family (IO) a huge dinner (DO) in October (OP) for Canadian Thanksgiving (OP).

For each (OP) of the eight days (OP) of Hanukkah (OP), Maddie's parents give her (IO) and her brother (IO) a present (DO).

On Australia Day (OP), Ramon bakes his sister (IO) meat pie (DO).

Mr. Takahashi always brings his nieces (IO) and nephews (IO) souvenirs (DO) from different Japanese cities (OP).

Hong's grandfather gives him (IO) money (DO) for Chinese New Year (OP).

Exercise 37C: Diagramming Direct Objects and Indirect Objects

On your own paper, diagram the following sentences.

Isabella made us cocoa.

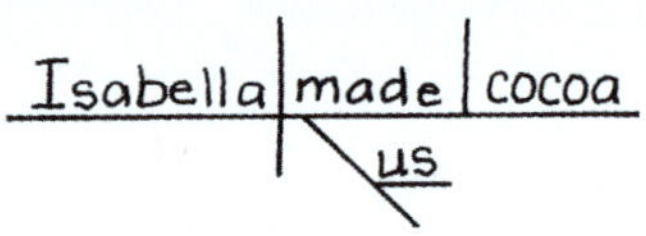

Aunt Debbie taught me Polish.

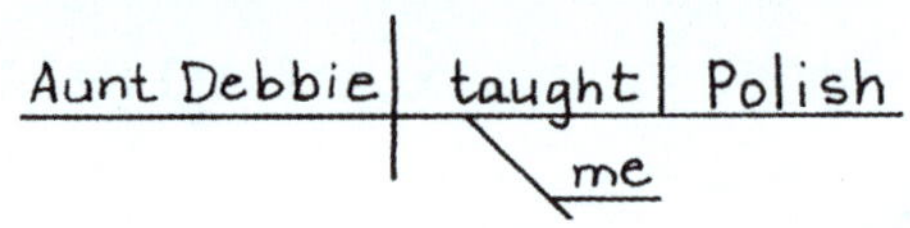

Sean bought us brunch.

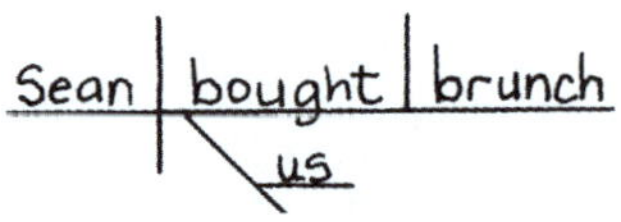

Uncle Walter mailed Joey the cookies.

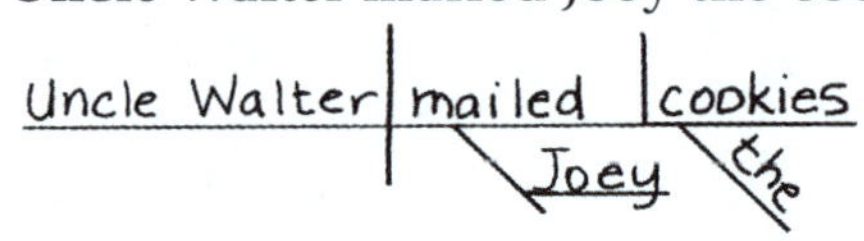

I knitted Grandma the mittens.

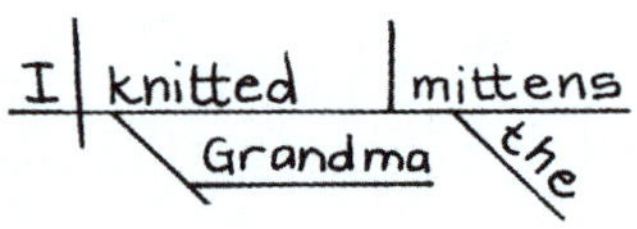

She gave me and my brother hugs and kisses.

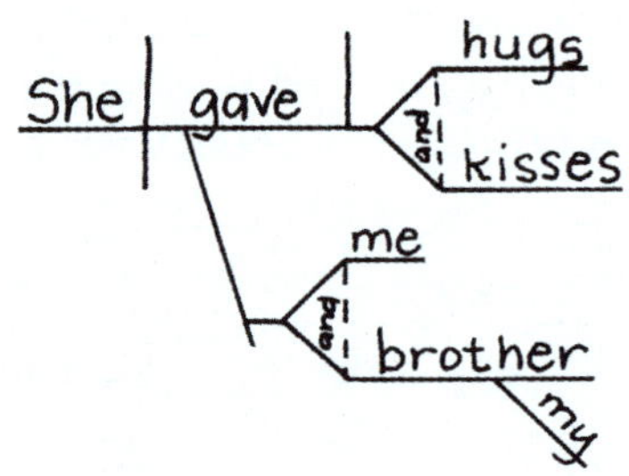

Can you give me help?

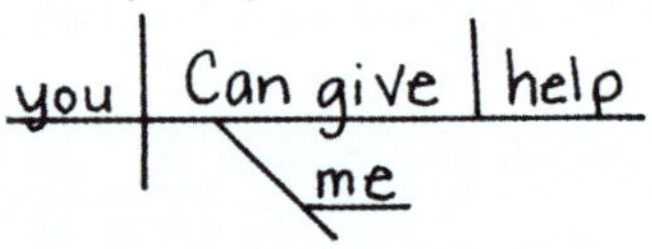

— LESSON 38 —

State-of-Being Verbs
Linking Verbs
Predicate Adjectives

Exercise 38A: Action Verbs and Linking Verbs

In the following sentences, adapted from *A Christmas Carol*, by Charles Dickens, underline the subjects once and the predicates twice. If the verb is a linking verb, write *LV* over it, circle the predicate adjective, and label it *PA*. If the verb is an action verb, write *AV* over it, circle the direct object, and label it *DO*. The first is done for you.

Hint #1: Predicate adjectives and direct objects will never be found in prepositional phrases. Remember—eliminating prepositional phrases can help you find the other parts of the sentence more easily.

Hint #2: Don't forget that *not* is an adverb—never part of the verb.

LV PA
The knocker on the door was very large.

AV DO
Scrooge had seen the knocker night and morning, during his whole residence.

Scrooge saw Marley's face.

It was not angry and ferocious.

The eyes were wide open and perfectly motionless.

He turned the key and shut the door.

Scrooge was not fearful of echoes.

Darkness is cheap.

Scrooge liked it.

Quite satisfied, he closed his door and locked it.

The fire was low and dim.

Someone was dragging a heavy chain.

He heard the noise much louder on the floors below.

Exercise 38B: Diagramming Direct Objects and Predicate Adjectives

On your own paper, diagram *only* the words you labeled (simple subjects, simple predicates, predicate adjectives, direct objects, and indirect objects), along with any conjunctions used to connect compounds, from the sentences in Exercise 38A.

The knocker on the door was very large.

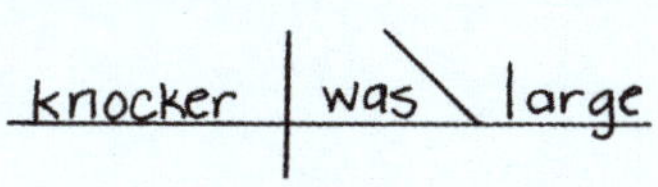

Scrooge had seen the knocker, night and morning, during his whole residence.

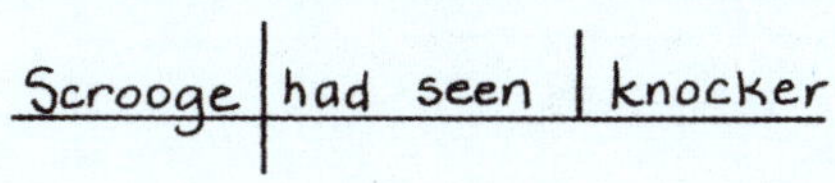

Scrooge saw Marley's face.

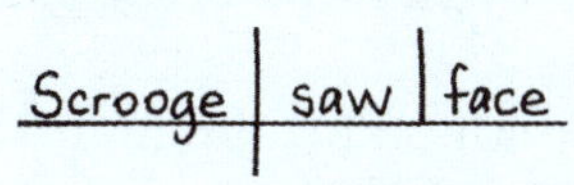

It was not angry and ferocious.

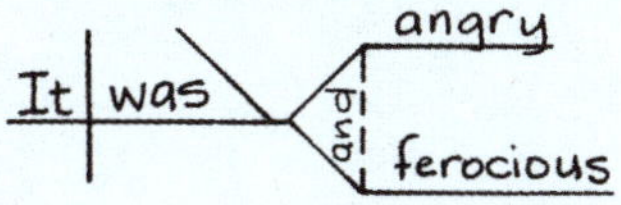

The eyes were wide open and perfectly motionless.

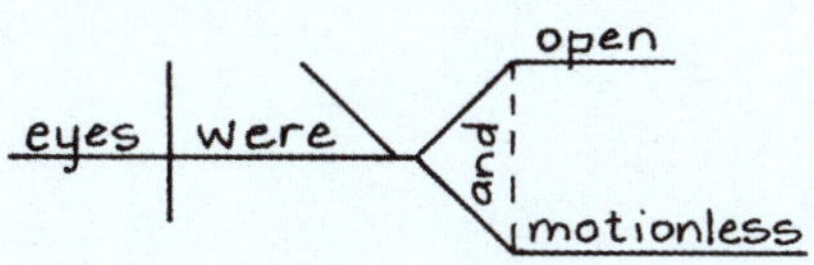

He turned the key and shut the door.

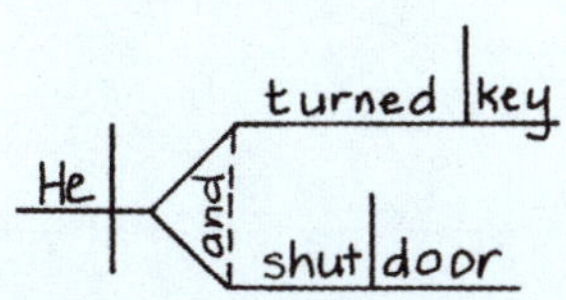

Scrooge was not fearful of echoes.

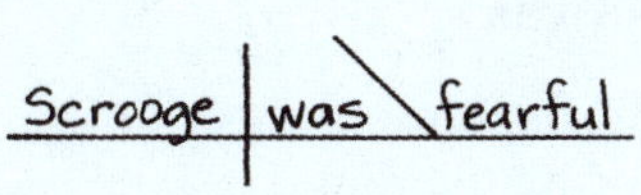

Darkness is cheap.

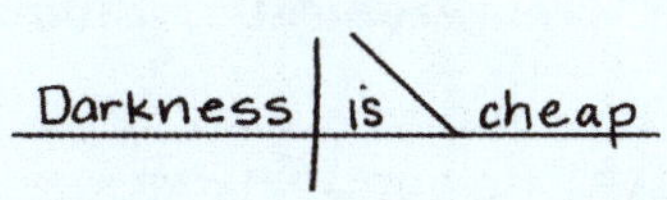

Scrooge liked it.

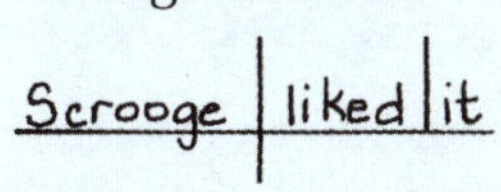

Quite satisfied, he closed his door and locked it.

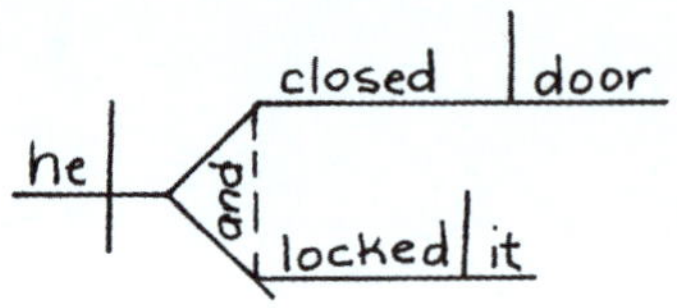

The fire was low and dim.

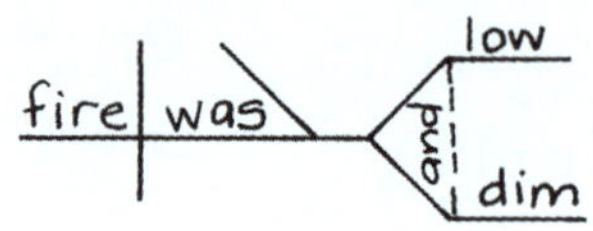

Someone was dragging a heavy chain.

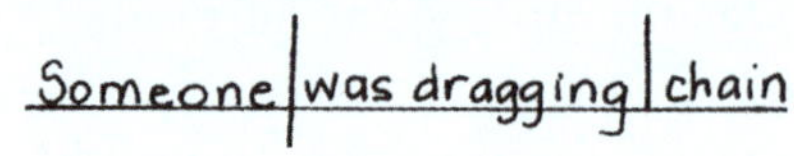

He heard the noise much louder on the floors below.

— LESSON 39 —

Linking Verbs
Predicate Adjectives
Predicate Nominatives

Exercise 39A: Finding Predicate Nominatives and Adjectives

Underline the linking verbs in the following sentences, and circle the predicate nominatives or adjectives. Draw a line from each predicate nominative or adjective to the subject that it describes. There may be more than one of each.

Ethiopia is a country in eastern Africa.

Amharic is the national language of Ethiopia.

Ethiopian foods can be extremely spicy.

Common Ethiopian dishes are veggies, meat, and sourdough flatbread.

Everyone is happy there.

His face was round.

His name is Mr. Mo.

A growing lad is always hungry.

Exercise 39B: Distinguishing Between Predicate Nominatives and Adjectives

Underline the predicate nominatives and predicate adjectives in the following sentences. Identify them by writing *PN* above the predicate nominatives and *PA* above the predicate adjectives.

The Western landscape is mountainous.

That large shadow was a mountain (PN).

A good education is a great advantage (PN).

Matthew's education was advantageous (PA) in his career search.

The selling point of the car was its color (PN).

In the setting sun, the sky was bright (PA) and colorful (PA).

The saxophone music was soulful (PA) and beautiful (PA).

The appeal of the music was its soul (PN) and beauty (PN).

European fortifications were crude (PA).

One is saline (PA), bitter (PA), and stinking (PA).

The walls were dirty (PA).

It was entirely separate (PA).

It was cold, bleak, biting weather (PN).

Exercise 39C: Diagramming

On your own paper, diagram every word of the following sentences.

Rainforests are magnificent.

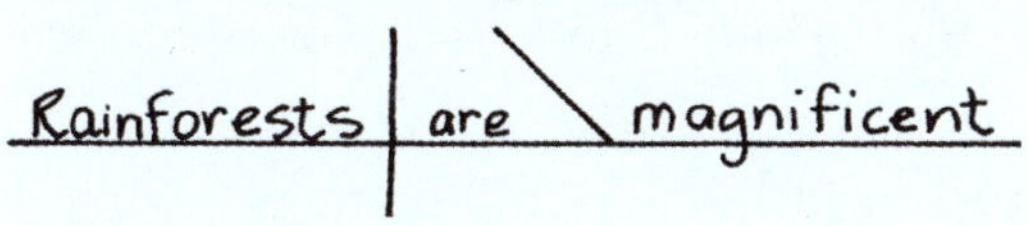

Bats are flying mammals.

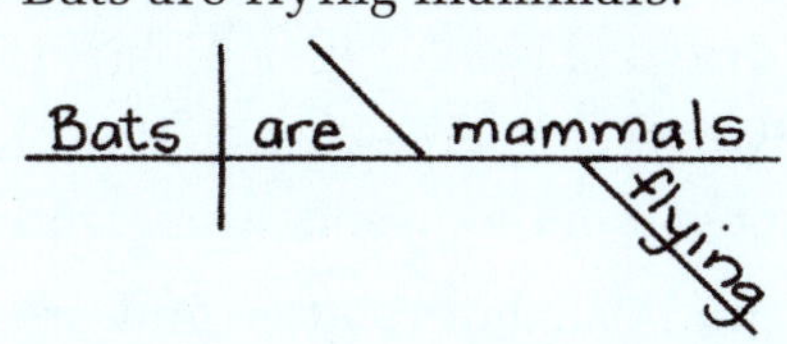

Most bats are insectivores.

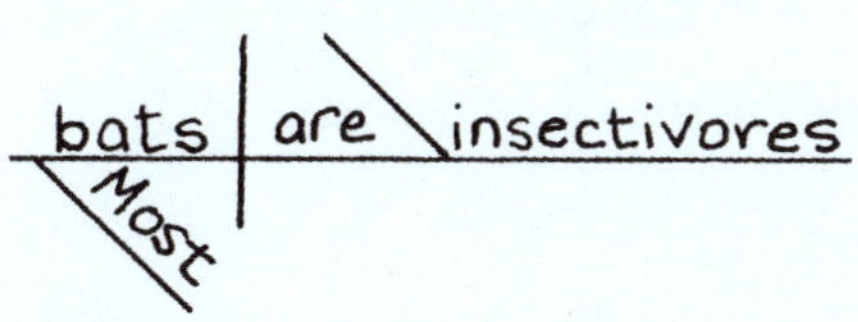

Bat caves can be dark and creepy.

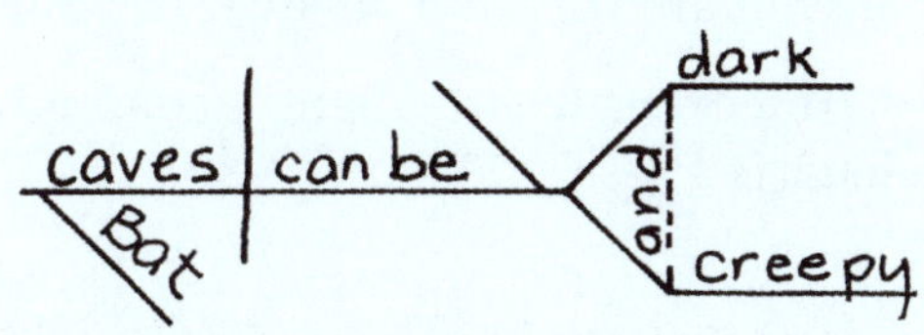

Be careful!

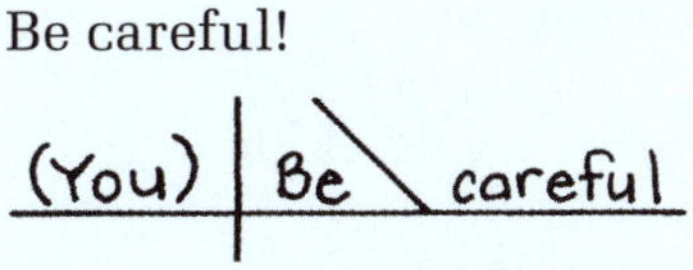

Dark clouds gathered.

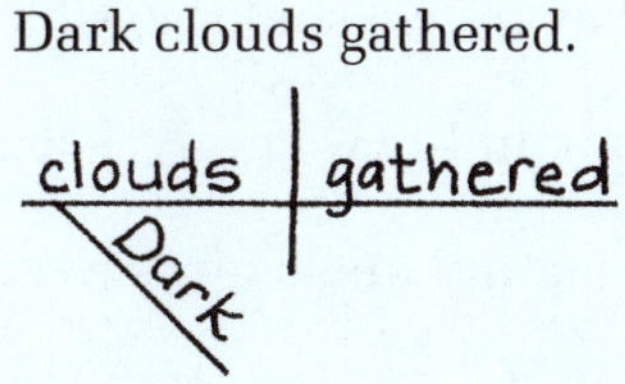

Loud thunder frightened little Timmy.

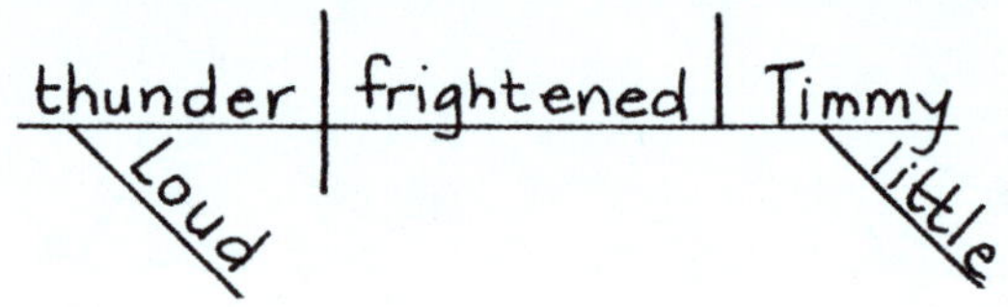

Are you afraid?

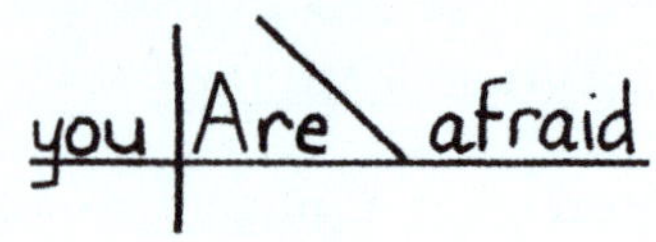

Heavy rains nourished thirsty plants.

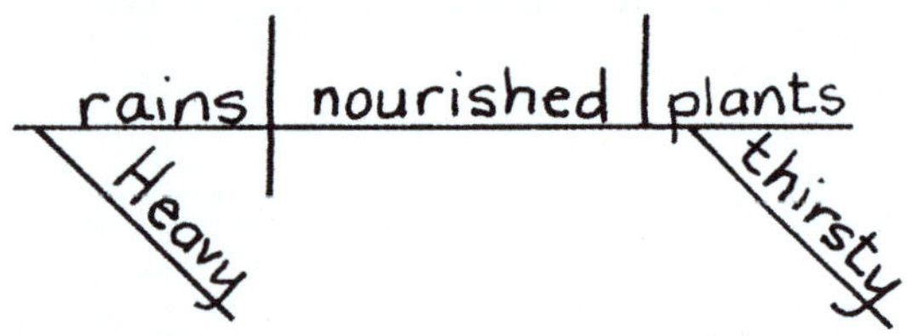

— LESSON 40 —

Predicate Adjectives and Predicate Nominatives
Pronouns as Predicate Nominatives
Object Complements

Exercise 40A: Reviewing Objects and Predicate Adjectives and Nominatives

Identify the underlined words as *DO* for direct object, *IO* for indirect object, *OP* for object of a preposition, *PN* for predicate nominative, or *PA* for predicate adjective.

- For each direct object (or direct object/indirect object combination), find and underline twice the action verb that affects it.
- For each object of the preposition, find and circle the preposition to which it belongs.
- For each predicate nominative and predicate adjective, find and draw a box around the linking verb that it follows.
- When you are finished, answer the questions at the end of the selection.

The following excerpts are slightly adapted from *A Thousand Never Evers*, by Shana Burg (New York: Delacorte Press, 2008), pp. 1-5.

Note to Instructor: This is intended to be a challenging exercise. Give all necessary help.

Now get this: a boy in Jackson [is] so rich [PA] that when he finished high school, his daddy bought him [IO] a brand-new car [DO]. At least that's what I heard. In my family, we don't have that kind (of) money [OP], but my uncle gives a whole dollar [DO] (to) any Pickett [OP] who graduates Acorn Elementary School. It['s] tradition [PN].

So here I am, soaring (through) the sky [OP] (on) my swing [OP] that hangs (from) the oak tree [OP], when

DO DO
Uncle Bump calls out the door of his shed, "Go on. Get your brother. He'll take you." He
DO OP
stretches a dollar bill (between) both hands and I jump right off. . . .

I nod so my brother will think I know what he's talking about. But I wonder why he
DO IO DO
can't answer my questions plain and simple. If he's so smart, why doesn't he tell me this: Why
DO OP
do they call it the movement? How can he swipe (under) his nose and stop crying? And why did
IO DO
Medgar Evers's mama give him such a silly name?

1. Find the compound adjective in this passage. Write it in the blank below and cross out the incorrect choice.
   brand-new is in the attributive/~~predicative~~ position.

2. Find the object complement in this passage. Write it in the blank below and cross out the incorrect choices.
   movement is an ~~adjective~~/noun that ~~describes~~/renames the direct object.

Exercise 40B: Parts of the Sentence

Label the following in each sentence: *S* (subject), *LV* (linking verb), *AV* (action verb), *DO* (direct object), *OC-A* (object complement-adjective), *OC-N* (object complement-noun), *IO* (indirect object), or *PN* (predicate nominative).

S AV DO OC-A
The king considered Anne beautiful.

S AV DO
The king considered Anne politely.

S AV IO DO
The king offered Anne Boleyn a crown.

S AV DO OC-N
The king crowned Anne Boleyn queen.

S AV DO OC-A
She found the situation perplexing.

S AV DO OC-A
The old woman kept the cottage neat.

S AV DO
The old woman kept the cottage carefully.

S AV DO OC-A
The sound struck the merrymakers dumb.

S AV DO OC-N
The teacher appointed you monitor.

S LV PN
The monitor was you.

S AV DO OC-A
The dim light rendered large objects barely visible.

Exercise 40C: Diagramming

Diagram the sentences from Exercise 40B on your own paper.

The king considered Anne beautiful.

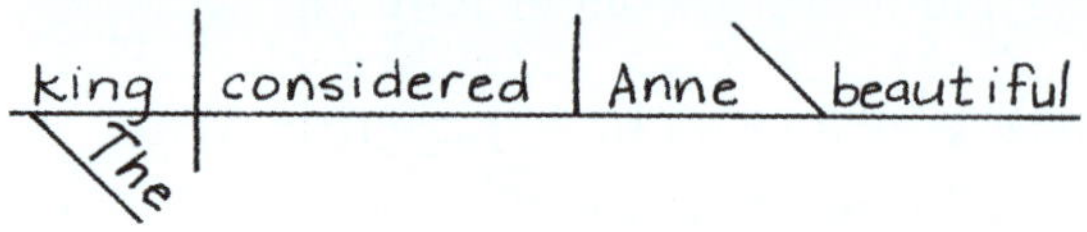

The king considered Anne politely.

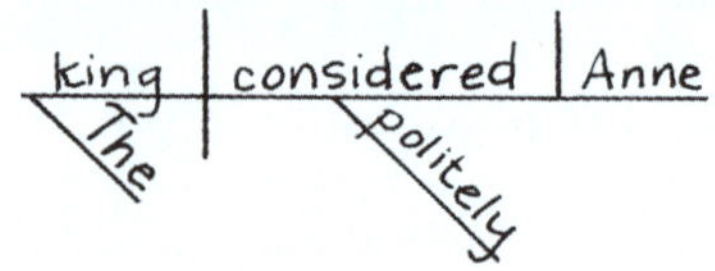

The king offered Anne Boleyn a crown.

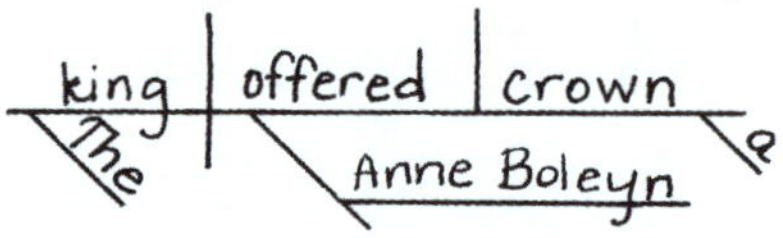

The king crowned Anne Boleyn queen.

She found the situation perplexing.

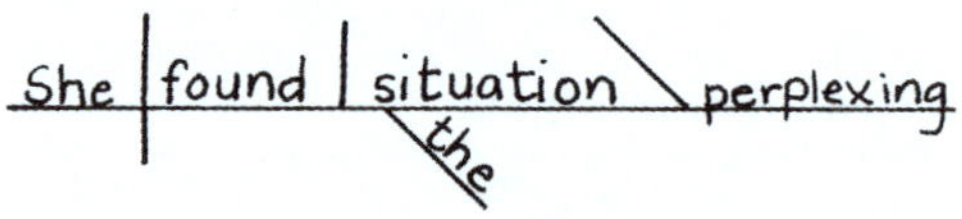

The old woman kept the cottage neat.

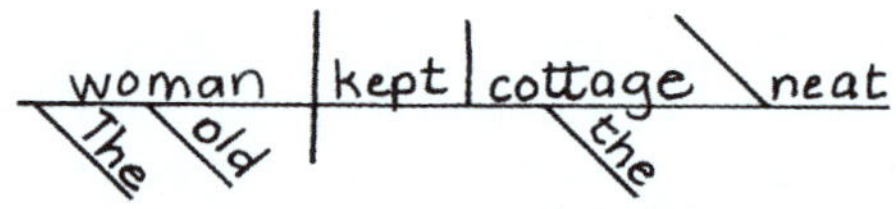

The old woman kept the cottage carefully.

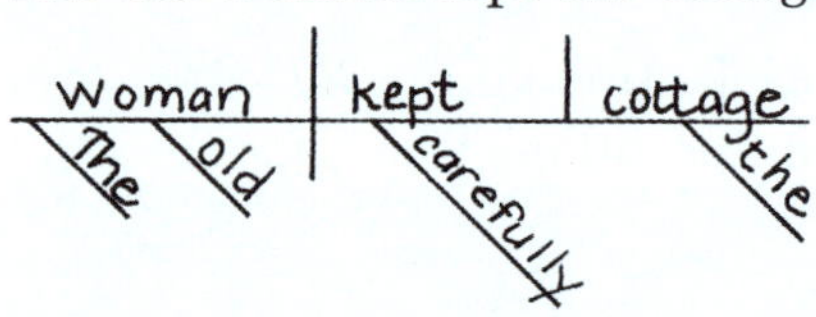

The sound struck the merrymakers dumb.

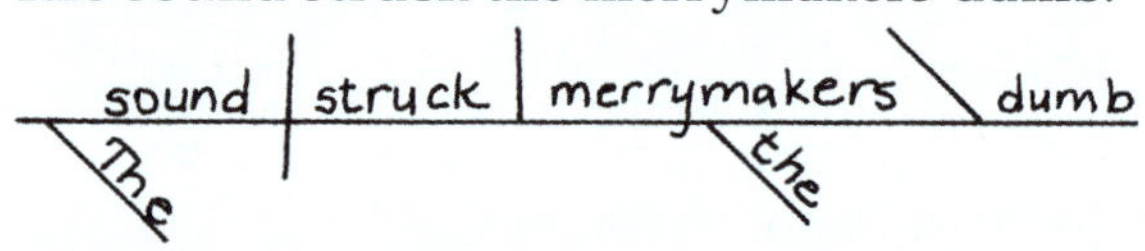

The teacher appointed you monitor.

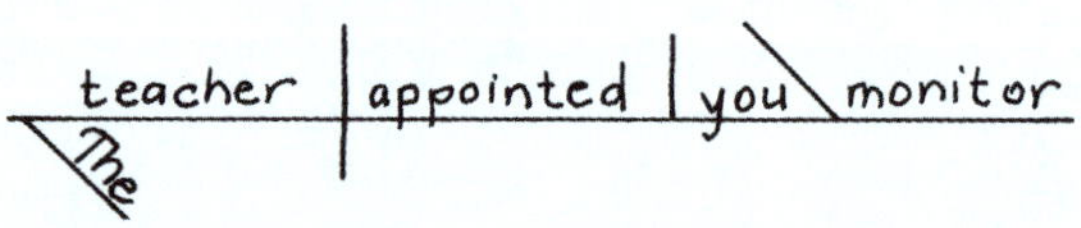

The monitor was you.

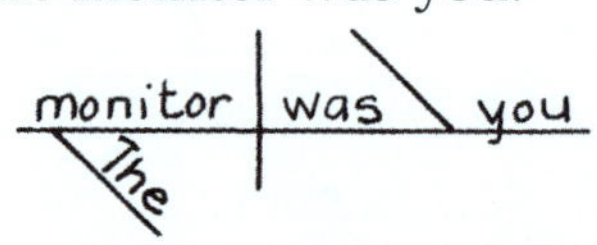

The dim light rendered large objects barely visible.

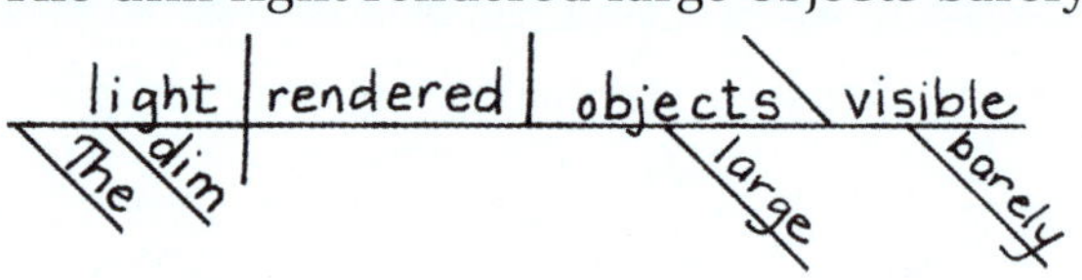

WEEK 11

More About Prepositions

— LESSON 41 —

Prepositions and Prepositional Phrases
Adjective Phrases

Exercise 41A: Identifying Adjective Phrases

Underline the adjective phrases in the following sentences. Draw an arrow from each phrase to the word it modifies. The first is done for you.

Queen Victoria was a great ruler of England.

She started some of our most popular fashions.

Many brides before Queen Victoria wore black wedding dresses.

White was a color for funerals.

But Queen Victoria wanted to wear a wedding dress with beautiful white lace.

Queen Victoria in her spotless white gown stunned the nation.

Women today still follow this trend of hers.

The following sentences are from Ian Ridpath's T*he Illustrated Encyclopedia of Astronomy and Space.*

The total number of comets is enormous.

The study of their physical structure and behavior . . . is now an increasingly important field of research.

The Sun's heat melts the nucleus, releasing huge volumes of gas.

Exercise 41B: Diagramming Adjective Phrases/Review

Diagram the following sentences on your own paper. Follow this procedure, and ask yourself the suggested questions if necessary.

1) Find the subject and predicate and diagram them first.
   What is the verb?
   Who or what [verb]?

2) Ask yourself: Is the verb an action verb? If so, look for a direct object.
   Who or what receives the action of the verb?
   If there is a direct object, check for an indirect object.
   To whom or for whom is the action done?

Remember that there may be no direct object or no indirect object—but you can't have an indirect object without a direct object. If there is an indirect object, it will always come between the verb and the direct object.

3) Ask yourself: Is the verb a state-of-being verb? If so, look for a predicate nominative or predicate adjective.
   Is there a word after the verb that renames or describes the subject?

4) Find all prepositional phrases. Ask yourself: Whom or what do they describe?

5) Place all other adjectives and adverbs on the diagram. If you have trouble, ask for help.

Brides in India wear red.

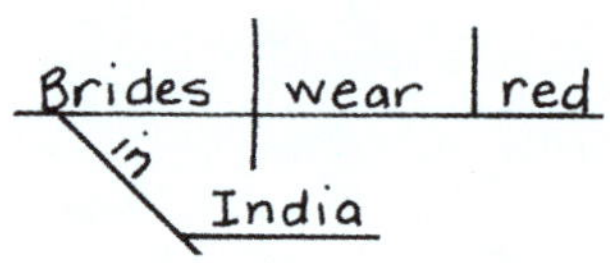

Many of our traditions have unusual origins.

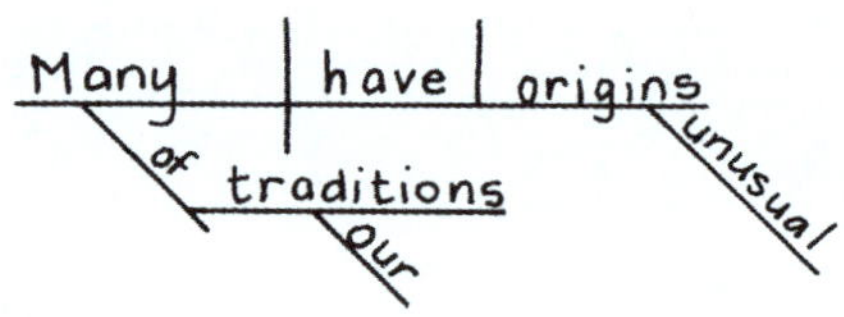

History can tell us stories about ourselves.

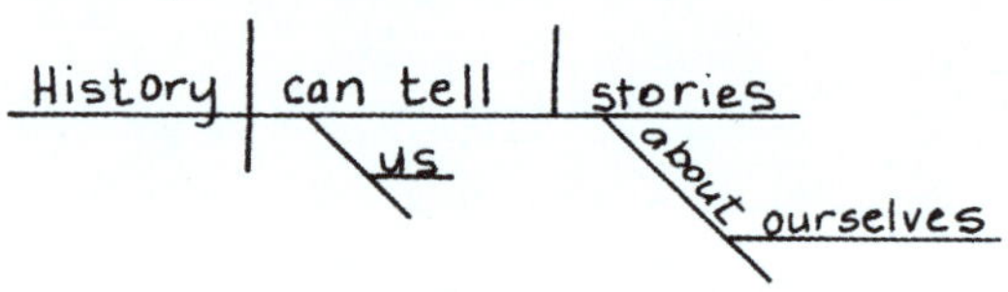

Queen Victoria was a great ruler of England.

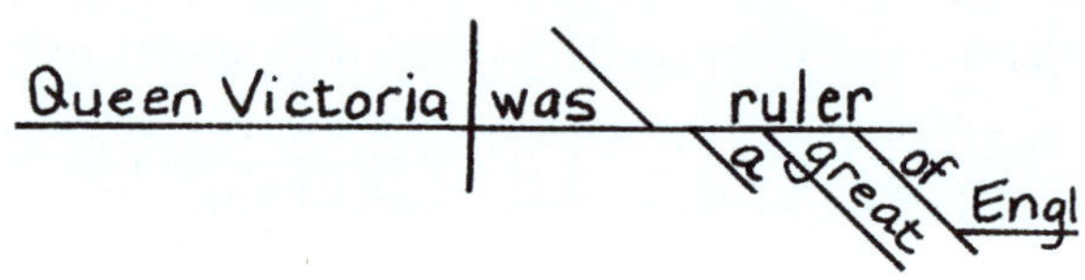

Many brides before Queen Victoria wore black wedding dresses.

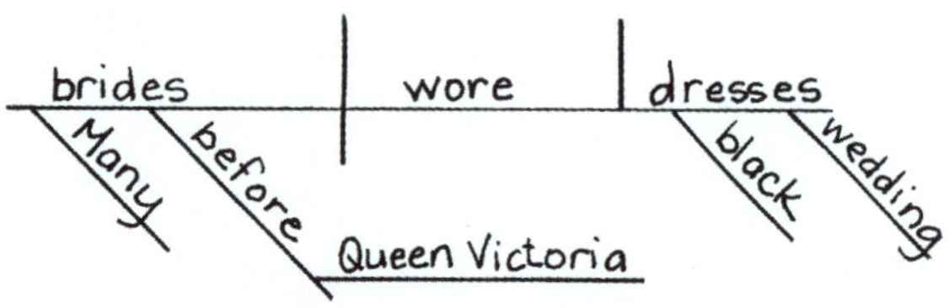

White was a color for funerals.

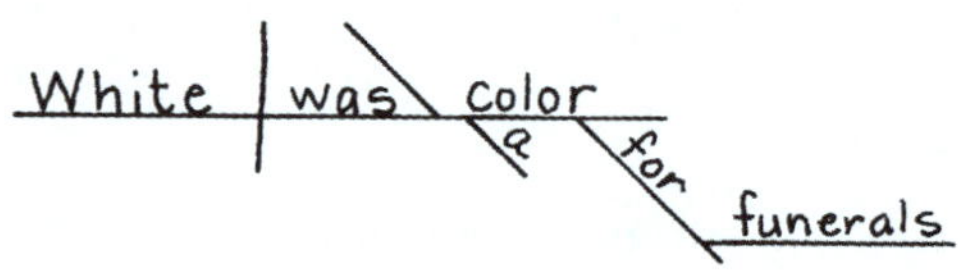

Queen Victoria, in her spotless white gown, stunned the nation.

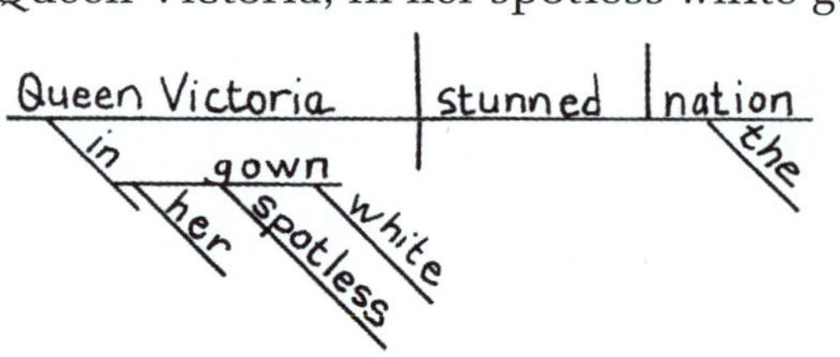

— LESSON 42 —

Adjective Phrases
Adverb Phrases

Exercise 42A: Identifying Adverb Phrases

Underline the adverb phrases in the following sentences and circle the preposition that begins each phrase. Draw an arrow from the phrase to the word it modifies. The first is done for you.

Ozzie's family traveled to California for a volcano tour.

In northern California they toured Mount Shasta.

Through some volcanic craters, you can see bubbling lava.

Active volcanoes have erupted during recent history.

Extinct volcanoes have not erupted in millennia.

Gas builds up in the volcano with increasing pressure.

Volcanic eruptions are caused by this buildup.

With incredible force, the volcano can shoot dangerous gas and ash into the air.

At this stage, the storm goes into decline.

Some species are born larger and immediately drop to the bottom.

The octopus lays her eggs in capsules and attaches them to a rock with a string-like substance.

She defends the nest against intruders.

Exercise 42B: Diagramming Adverb Phrases

On your own paper. diagram the following five sentences from *The Adventures of Tom Sawyer*, by Mark Twain.

Tom eagerly drew his sore toe from the sheet and held it up for inspection.

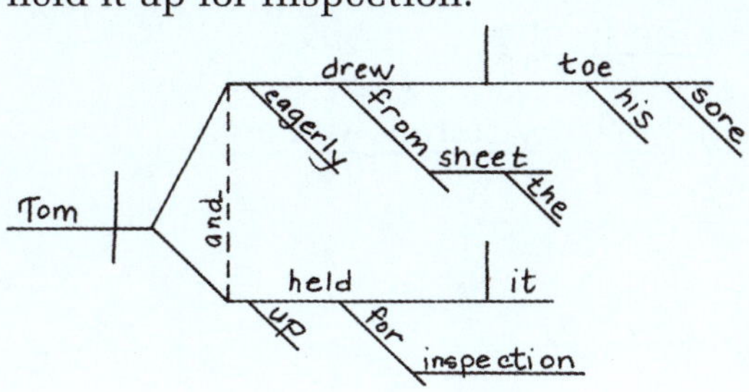

Tom was panting with his exertion by this time.

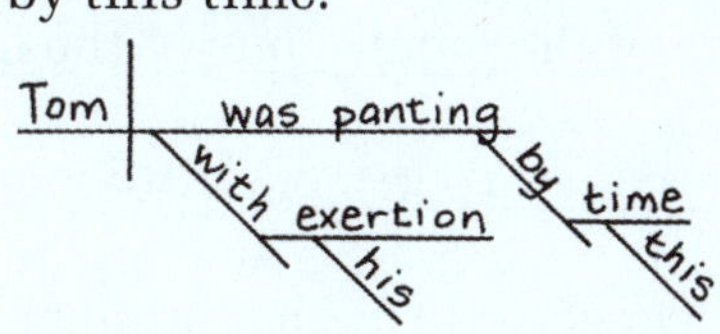

Sid yawned, stretched, and then brought himself up on his elbow with a snort and stared at Tom.

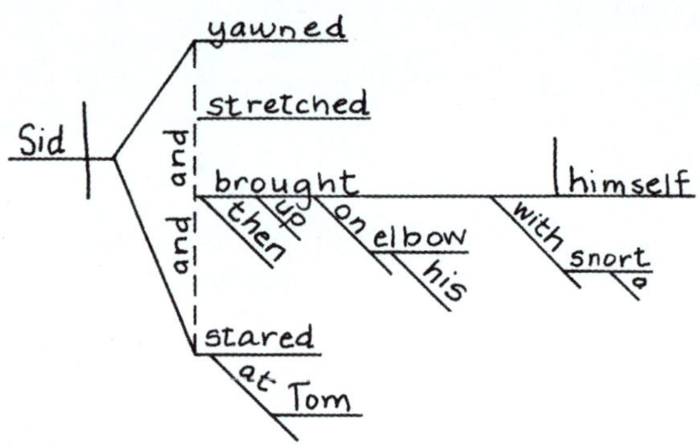

Tom was suffering in reality now.

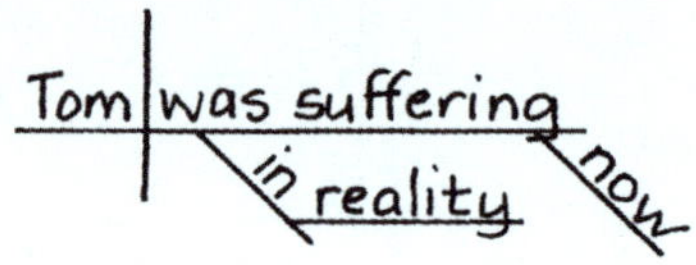

The pain vanished from the toe.

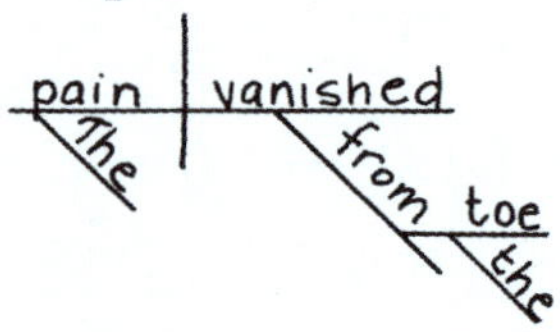

— LESSON 43 —

Definitions Review
Adjective and Adverb Phrases
Misplaced Modifiers

Exercise 43A: Distinguishing Between Adjective and Adverb Phrases

Underline all of the prepositional phrases in the following sentences. Write *ADJ* above the adjective phrases and *ADV* above the adverb phrases.

ADV ADJ
On her birthday, Etta received a powerful telescope with a tripod.

ADV ADJ ADJ
With her new telescope, she could see four of the moons of Jupiter.

ADV
She tracked their movement over several weeks.

ADV ADJ
At the beginning of the month, they were spaced almost equally distant.

ADV ADJ ADJ ADV
By the middle of the month, one of the moons was hidden behind Jupiter.

ADV ADJ ADV
After her telescope experiment, Etta viewed the stars of the night sky with renewed awe.

ADV ADJ
A thunderstorm goes through a number of stages.

ADV ADV
Rain drops may remain in a liquid form for some time.

The octopus climbed out of the tank (ADV), slithered to the corner (ADV) of the table (ADJ), felt with its tentacles (ADV) for a table leg (ADV) that it could not see, slid down the table leg (ADV), dragged itself across the deck (ADV) and dropped to the safety (ADV) of the sea (ADJ) below.

From Derek K. Hitchins, *Systems Engineering: A 21st Century Systems Methodology*

Even the largest octopus can squeeze through a narrow opening (ADV) in the top (ADJ) of an aquarium (ADJ). Once it escapes, an octopus can live a long time on land (ADV).

From Katie Kubesh, Kimm Bellotto, and Niki Mcneil, *Predators of the Deep*

Exercise 43B: Correcting Misplaced Modifiers

Circle the misplaced adjective and adverb phrases in the following sentences. Draw an arrow to the place where the phrase should be. The first is done for you.

The lady bought two peaches (with large, dangly earrings.)

(Inside the doughnut,) Derek licked the cream filling.

I fondly remembered the chicken my grandmother fried (in my mind.)

The doctor (inside the patient's joint) felt the hard lump.

Alistair gave a rosemary plant to his mother (in a hand-painted pot.)

(With three legs,) Welles built a kitchen stool.

Erin (of chocolate and peanut butter) baked cookies.

The man squirted honey into his tea (with long hair and ripped shoes.)

(Under the bed,) Gertrude found the missing earring.

The boy picked up the lizard (with checkered pants.)

My uncle told us how he used to scrub dirty dogs (at the table.)

— LESSON 44 —

Adjective and Adverb Phrases

Prepositional Phrases Acting as Other Parts of Speech

Exercise 44A: Prepositional Phrases Acting as Other Parts of Speech

In each sentence below, circle any prepositional phrases. Underline the subject of the sentence once and the predicate twice. Then, label the prepositional phrase as *ADJ* (adjective phrase), *ADV* (adverb phrase), *S* (subject), *PA* (predicate adjective), *PN* (predicate nominative), or *OP* (object of the preposition).

The waiters are (in elaborate green uniforms) PA.

The house (on the secluded lane) ADJ is (on fire) PA.

(In the south) S was her lost home.

Molting makes a snake moody and depressed.

Note to Instructor: This is a compound object complement.

The best time (for us) ADJ is (after dinner) PA.

We drove (through the large gateway) ADV, (up a slight hill) ADV (to the door) ADV (of the great white house) ADJ.

(Before breakfast) S is too early!

(Beyond the fence) S is the park.

My favorite ride is (in a private jet) PN.

A growl rumbled (from (beneath the roof) OP) ADV.

Exercise 44B: Diagramming

On your own paper, diagram the sentences from 44A.

The waiters are in elaborate green uniforms.

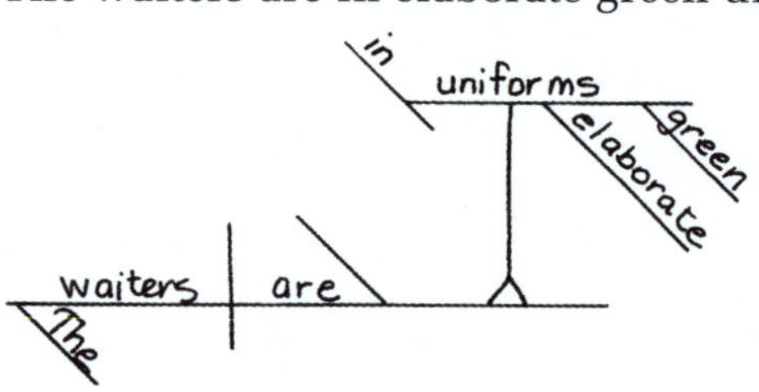

The house on the secluded lane is on fire.

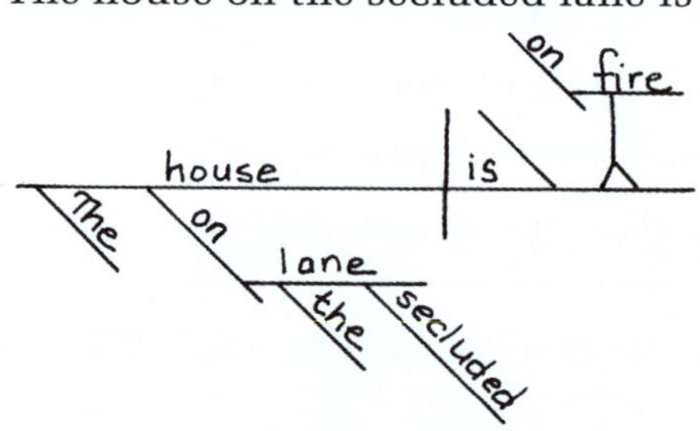

In the south was her lost home.

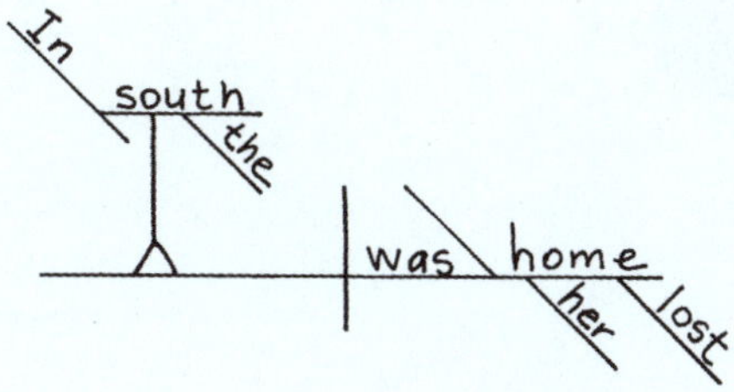

Molting makes a snake moody and depressed.

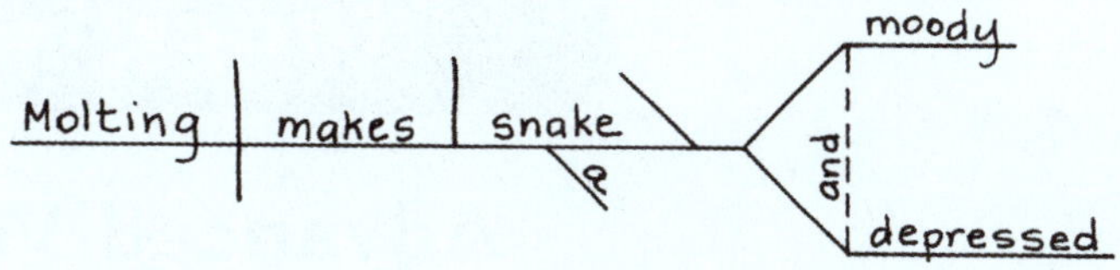

The best time for us is after dinner.

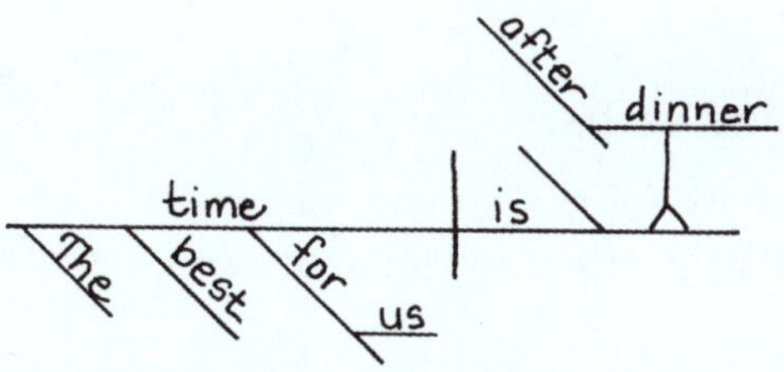

We drove through the large gateway, up a slight hill, to the door of the great white house.

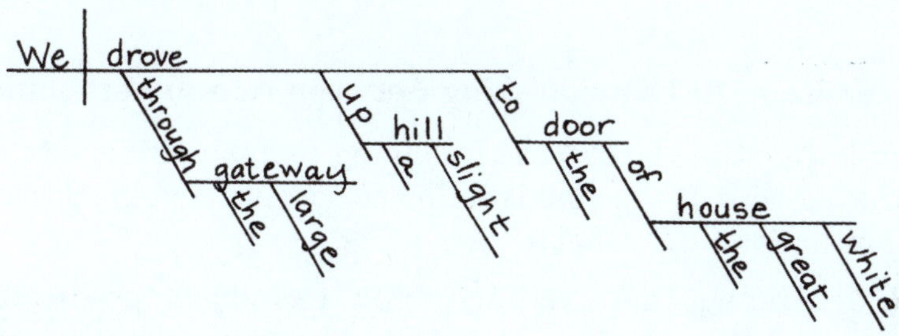

Before breakfast is too early!

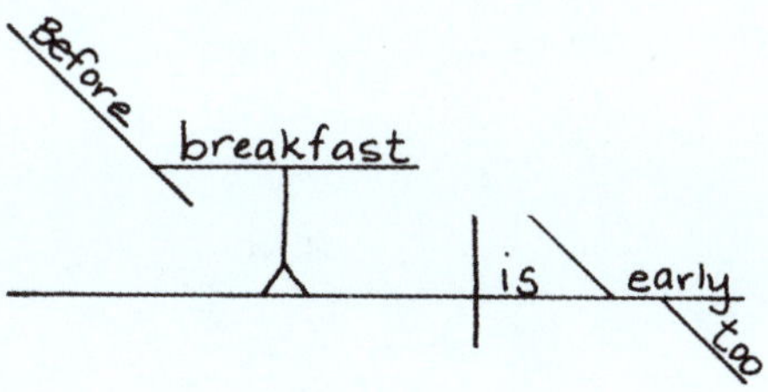

Beyond the fence is the park.

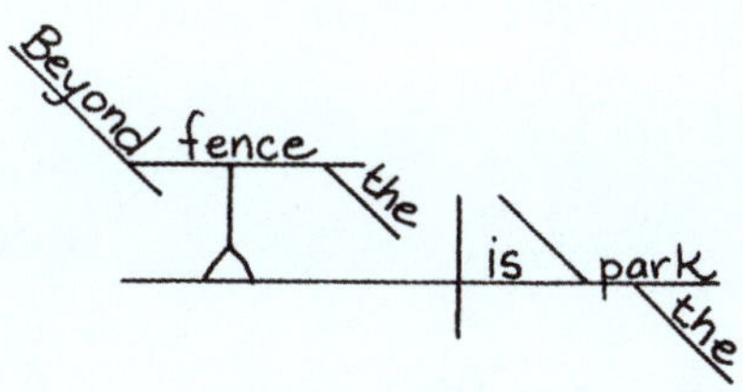

My favorite ride is in a private jet.

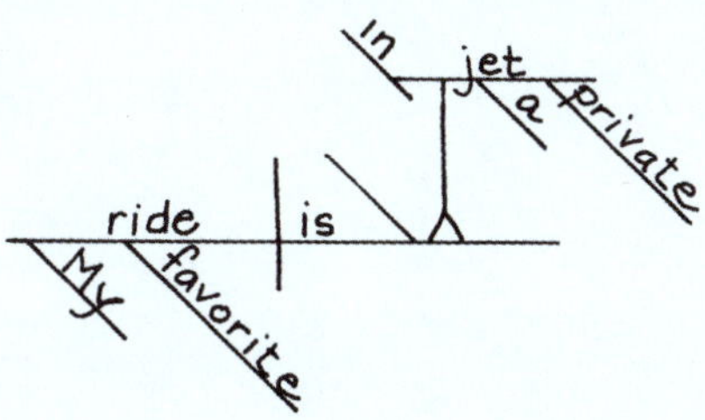

A growl rumbled from beneath the roof.

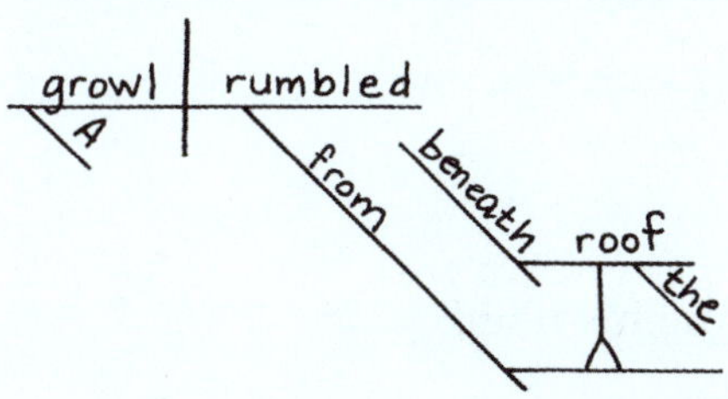

WEEK 12

Advanced Verbs

— LESSON 45 —

Linking Verbs

Linking/Action Verbs

Exercise 45A: Distinguishing Between Action Verbs and Linking Verbs

Underline the verbs in the following sentences. Identify them as *AV* for action verb or *LV* for linking verb. If the verb is followed by a direct object (*DO*), predicate adjective (*PA*), or predicate nominative (*PN*), label it.

Remember that a verb with *no* direct object, predicate adjective, or predicate nominative will most likely be an action verb. Also remember that direct objects, predicate adjectives, and predicate nominatives are never found in prepositional phrases.

AV DO
Maggie smelled the week-old milk.

LV PA
The milk smelled strange.

AV DO
She threw the milk away.

AV
Casey remained in the cellar during the tornado.

LV PA
He stayed calm in the stressful situation.

LV PA
The storm seemed endless.

LV PA
Casey was nervous.

AV DO
His little sister was holding his hand.

LV PA PA
Soon the sky became clear and still.

LV PN
The sapling became an oak.

AV
Trees grow on either side of the road.

LV PA
It looks untidy.

LV PA
Castles of various sorts were common.

AV DO
Peking reflected the dominance of the imperial household.

Exercise 45B: Distinguishing Among Different Kinds of Nouns

Underline all of the nouns in the following sentences. Identify them as *S* for subject, *IO* for indirect object, *DO* for direct object, or *PN* for predicate nominative.

S DO
Susana planted a garden.

S DO DO DO
Susana grew tomatoes, basil, and peppers.

S IO DO DO
Susana gave her little plants water and care.

S PN
Soon the seeds were tiny little green shoots.

S
The veggies became ready to harvest.

S DO IO DO
Susana picked the vegetables and made her sister a delicious salad.

S PN
Now Susana is a chef!

Exercise 45C: Diagramming Action Verbs and Linking Verbs

On your own paper, diagram the following sentences.

They seem anxious.

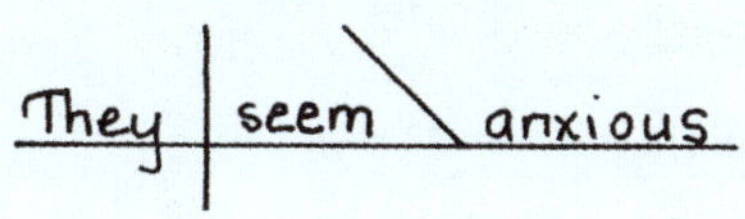

Daniel fixed Mom dinner.

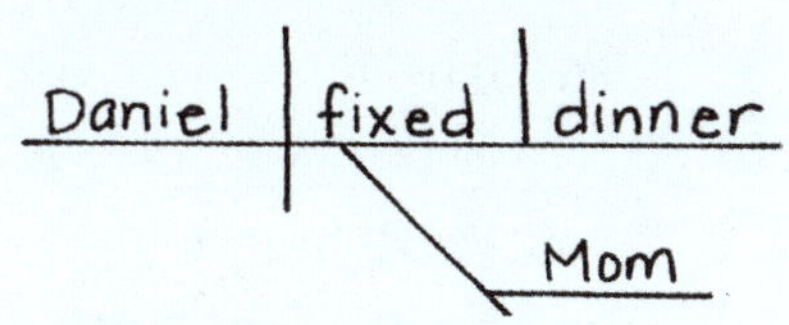

Toads are amphibians.

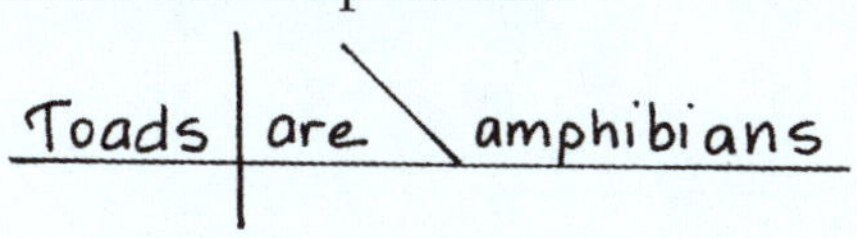

Toads are hopping.

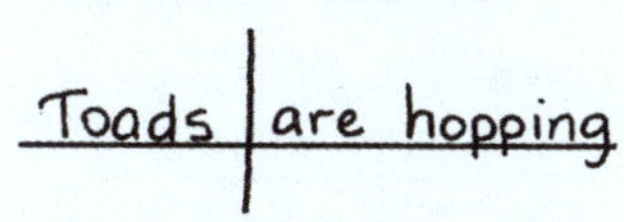

He tasted couscous.

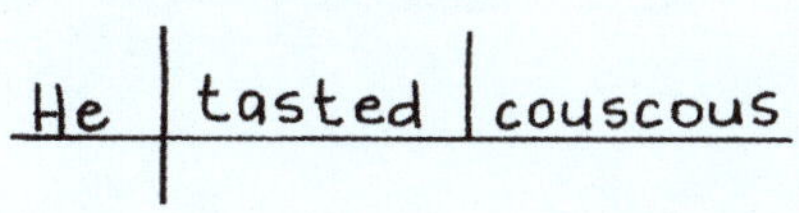

This tastes delectable.

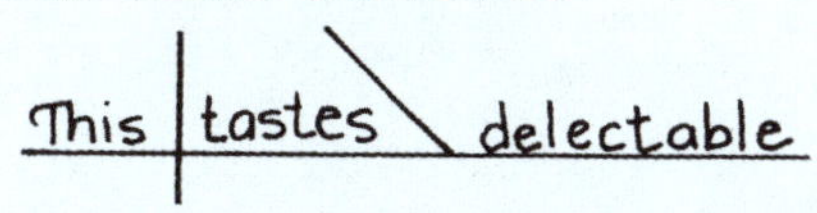

— LESSON 46 —

Conjugations
Irregular Verbs
Principal Parts of Verbs

Exercise 46A: Forming Simple, Perfect, and Progressive Tenses

Fill in the missing blanks in the chart below.

Simple Present

	Singular	Plural
First person	I breathe	we breathe
Second person	you breathe	you breathe
Third person	he, she, it breathes	they breathe

Simple Past

	Singular	Plural
First person	I breathed	we breathed
Second person	you breathed	you breathed
Third person	he, she, it breathed	they breathed

Simple Future

	Singular	Plural
First person	I will breathe	we will breathe
Second person	you will breathe	you will breathe
Third person	he, she, it will breathe	they will breathe

Perfect Present

	Singular	Plural
First person	I have breathed	we have breathed
Second person	you have breathed	you have breathed
Third person	he, she, it has breathed	they have breathed

Perfect Past

	Singular	Plural
First person	I had breathed	we had breathed
Second person	you had breathed	you had breathed
Third person	he, she, it had breathed	they had breathed

Perfect Future

	Singular	Plural
First person	I will have breathed	we will have breathed
Second person	you will have breathed	you will have breathed
Third person	he, she, it will have breathed	they will have breathed

Progressive Present

	Singular	Plural
First person	I am breathing	we are breathing
Second person	you are breathing	you are breathing
Third person	he, she, it is breathing	they are breathing

Progressive Past

	Singular	Plural
First person	I was breathing	we were breathing
Second person	you were breathing	you were breathing
Third person	he, she, it was breathing	they were breathing

Progressive Future

	Singular	Plural
First person	I will be breathing	we will be breathing
Second person	you will be breathing	you will be breathing
Third person	he, she, it will be breathing	they will be breathing

Exercise 46B: Latin Roots

The following English words were created from Latin words. Draw lines matching the English word with the Latin root word. You do not need to know Latin to do well on this exercise!

English word	Latin root	Meaning
ambulance	A. *frango*	("to break")
audible	B. *claudo*	("to close")
exclude	C. *audio*	("to hear")
dictate	D. *habito*	("to live")
edible	E. *fugio*	("to flee")
fragile	F. *ambulo*	("to walk")
refugee	G. *edo*	("to eat")
habitat	H. *dico*	("to speak")

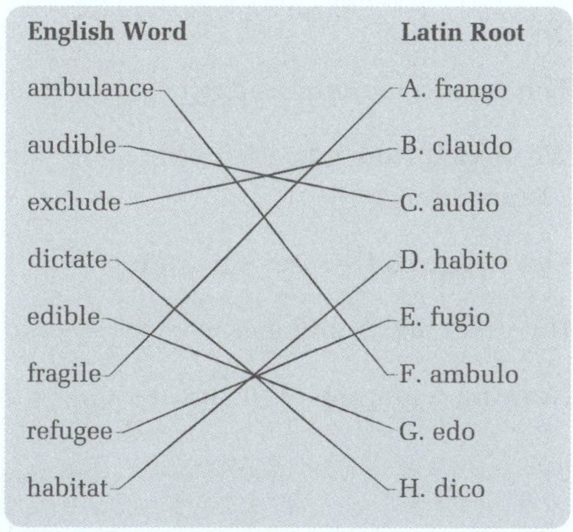

Exercise 46C: Principal Parts of Verbs

Fill in the chart with the missing forms.

	First Principal Part Present	Second Principal Part Past	Third Principal Part Past Participle
I	climb	climbed	climbed
I	flop	flopped	flopped
I	sniffle	sniffled	sniffled
I	juggle	juggled	juggled
I	announce	announced	announced
I	wink	winked	winked
I	plan	planned	planned
I	wave	waved	waved
I	roast	roasted	roasted
I	lift	lifted	lifted

Exercise 46D: Distinguishing Between First and Second Principal Parts

Identify the underlined verb as 1 for first principal part or 2 for second principal part.

These sentences are taken from *The Greely Arctic Expedition: As Fully Narrated by Lieut. Greely, U.S.A., And Other Survivors.*

The crystal mountains dash (1) against each other backward and forward.

We passed (2) from a heated cabin at 30° above zero to 47° below zero in the open air without inconvenience.

The sea-gulls fly (1) away screaming.

Her great masts and massive ribs of solid timber cracked (2).

Nothing remained (2) of the great ship.

— LESSON 47 —

Linking Verbs
Principal Parts
Irregular Verbs

No exercises this lesson.

— LESSON 48 —

Linking Verbs
Principal Parts
Irregular Verbs

Exercise 48A: Principal Parts

Fill in the blanks in the following chart of verbs.

Present	Past	Past Participle
meet	met	met
wind	wound	wound
am	was	been
read	read	read
fit	fit	fit
begin	began	begun
come	came	come
run	ran	run
drink	drank	drunk
shrink	shrank	shrunk
ring	rang	rung
sing	sang	sung
swim	swam	swum
learn	learned	learned
know	knew	known
wear	wore	worn
do	did	done
go	went	gone
lie	lay	lain
see	saw	seen
catch	caught	caught
hide	hid	hidden
speak	spoke	spoken
steal	stole	stolen
take	took	taken
write	wrote	written
walk	walked	walked
ride	rode	ridden
hear	heard	heard
make	made	made
send	sent	sent

Present	Past	Past Participle
hurt	hurt	hurt
lead	led	led
listen	listened	listened
shut	shut	shut
lend	lent	lent
lay	laid	laid
tell	told	told
lose	lost	lost
dig	dug	dug
choose	chose	chosen
become	became	become

Exercise 48B: Forming Correct Past Participles

Write the correct third principal part (past participle) in each blank. The first principal part is provided for you in parentheses. The first is done for you.

I have __made__ (make) a chocolate cake for my grandmother.

My grandmother has __come__ (come) from Oregon to visit!

She has __brought__ (bring) hot cocoa with her to share.

I had already __read__ (read) the book about the history of chocolate that she had __given__ (give) me during our last visit.

The book was __written__ (write) by a historian and culinary anthropologist.

By the time we finished talking about the book, my grandmother and I had __drunk__ (drink) three cups of cocoa.

We decided that we had __been__ (be) very studious historians.

Exercise 48C: Forming Correct Past Tenses

Write the correct second principal part (past) in each blank. The first principal part is provided for you in parentheses. The first is done for you.

I __told__ (tell) my grandmother what I had learned about the history of chocolate.

Chocolate __came__ (come) from a bean called *cacao*.

An unknown person in Latin America __was__ (am) the first to make chocolate.

They __drank__ (drink) chocolate as a spicy beverage.

Spanish conquistadors __brought__ (bring) the *cacao* beans back to Spain.

They __put__ (put) sugar in the chocolate and __made__ (make) desserts from it.

As she __ate__ (eat) a big bite of chocolate cake, my grandmother __said__ (say) that she __was__ (am) grateful to the first person who ever made chocolate.

Exercise 48D: Proofreading for Irregular Verb Usage

Find and correct the SIX errors in irregular verb usage in the following excerpts from the Norwegian folktale "Why the Sea is Salt." Cross out the incorrect forms and write the correct ones above.

But Christmas is a time when even selfish people give gifts. So he ~~gived~~ gave his brother a fine ham, but ~~telled~~ told him never to let him see his face again.

The merchant ~~knowed~~ knew how to start the mill, but he did not know how to stop it; no matter which way he turned it, it ~~goed~~ went on grinding and grinding. The heap of salt ~~growed~~ grew higher and higher, until at last the ship went down, making a great whirlpool where it ~~sinked~~ sank.

Exercise 48E: Diagramming

On your own paper, diagram the following four sentences.

Who made you the judge of your brother?

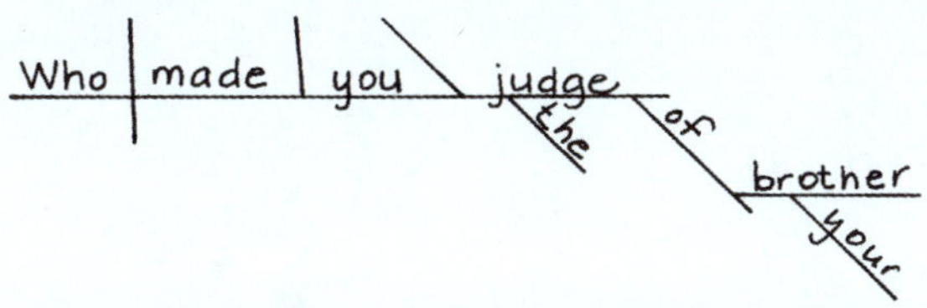

The gratin of potato and cheese smelled absolutely delightful.

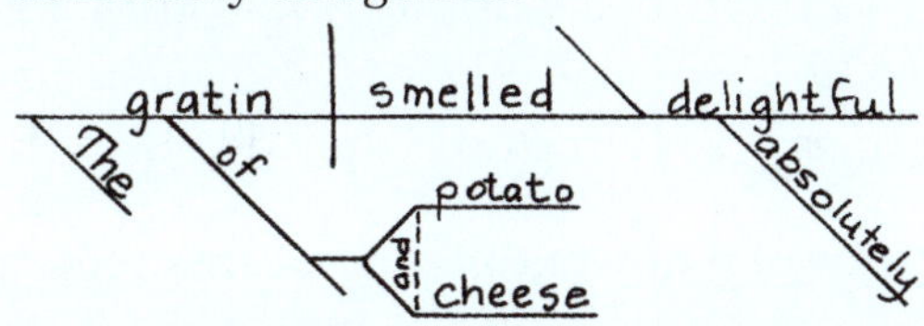

In the morning is the best time for exercise.

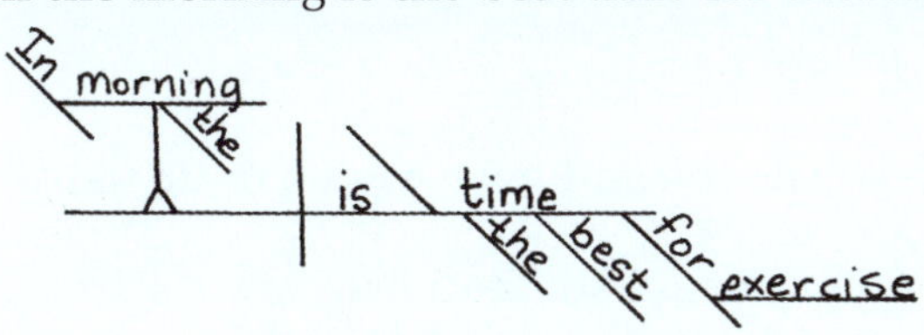

Queen Abigail smelled the bouquet of roses and lilies without enthusiasm.

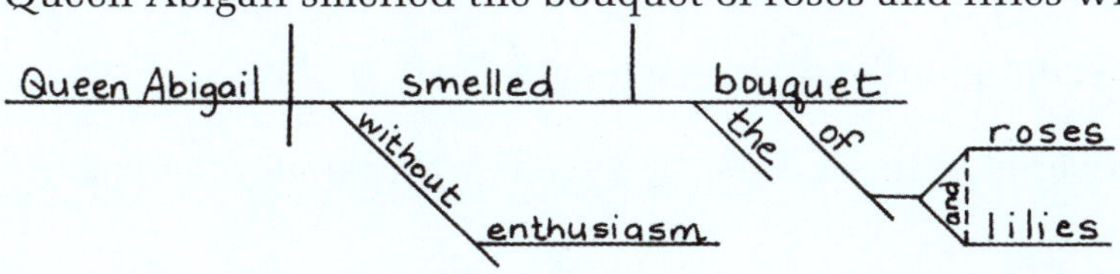

— REVIEW 4 —

Weeks 10-12

Topics
Direct and Indirect Objects
Linking Verbs
Predicate Adjectives
Predicate Nominatives
Articles
Adjective Phrases
Adverb Phrases
Action vs. Linking Verbs
Irregular Verbs
Principal Parts (Present, Past, Past Participle)

Review 4A: Action vs. Linking Verbs

Identify the underlined verbs as *A* for action or *L* for linking.

Over half of earth's living creatures dwell [A] in the depths of the sea.

The identities of many of these creatures remain [L] unknown.

Deep-sea creatures are [L] perhaps the most bizarre animals on earth.

Many deep-sea animals may seem [L] nightmarish but in reality are harmless.

The fish have developed [A] over time in the dark, cold depths of the sea and have grown [L] quite ugly.

Because of the shortage of light and food, the fish have grown [A] unusual adaptations.

Because their eyes are [L] large, and their skin is [L] devoid of pigment, these creatures appear [L] alien-like.

The grisly fangtooth fish may look [L] fearsome, but it only grows [A] to a length of six inches.

We can only imagine [A] what strange, undiscovered animals must live even farther under the waters!

Review 4B: Predicate Adjectives and Predicate Nominatives

Underline the linking verb in each of the following sentences. If the sentence concludes with a predicate nominative or predicate adjective, circle each and write *PA* for predicate adjective or *PN* for predicate nominative above it.

Grandpa Harold is my mother's father [PN].

He is my only grandparent [PN].

Grandpa Harold's hair has grown gray [PA] and thin [PA].

His back has become somewhat bent (PA)

But his laugh is still clear (PA) and joyous (PA)

Sometimes he seems younger (PA) than my serious cousin Leslie.

She is a teenager (PN) but she seems much more mature (PA)

Her perfume smells spicy (PA) and floral (PA)

Review 4C: Adjective and Adverb Phrases

In the following excerpt from Russell Freedman's *Give Me Liberty! The Story of the Declaration of Independence,* identify each underlined prepositional phrase as *ADJ* for adjective phrase or *ADV* for adverb phrase.

William Gray, a master rope maker, knew there was going to be trouble in Boston (ADV) that night. He wanted no part of it (ADJ). As dusk fell, he closed the shutters of his house and shop (ADJ). After supper, he sent his apprentice, fourteen-year-old Peter Slater, upstairs and locked the boy in his room (ADV).

Peter waited until the house was quiet. Then he knotted his bedding together, hung it out the window (ADV), and slid to freedom (ADV). He wasn't a rope maker's apprentice for nothing.

He hurried along dark cobbled streets (ADV) to a secret meeting place (ADV), a blacksmith's shop where a crowd of men and boys seemed to be getting ready for a costume party. They were smearing their faces with coal dust and red paint (ADV) and wrapping old blankets around their shoulders (ADV), disguising themselves as Mohawk Indians (ADV). . . .

Note to Instructor: *As Mohawk Indians* modifies the verb form *disguising* and answers the question *how*, which makes it an adverb phrase.

Review 4D: Forming Principal Parts

Complete the following excerpt (from *Animals on the Edge: Science Races to Save Species Threatened with Extinction*, by Sandra Pobst) by writing the correct principal part (PP) of the verb (first, second, or third) in parentheses.

Some people wonder (*wonder*, 1st PP) why we should make (*make*, 1st PP) the effort to save animals that are in danger of becoming extinct. After all, species have been (*be*, 3rd PP) going extinct throughout history as natural conditions changed (*change*, 2nd PP).

The changes occurring today, however, are (*be*, 1st PP) primarily the result of human activity. As the world's population has grown (*grow*, 3rd PP), forests have been cut (*cut*, 3rd PP) down, prairies plowed (*plow*, 3rd PP) under for farms, cities have expanded (*expand*, 3rd PP), and factories and cars have spewed (*spew*, 3rd PP) pollution into the air and water. Illegal killing of animals has also increased (*increase*, 3rd PP) as some cultures highly value (*value*, 1st PP) products made from protected animals.

Review 4E: Irregular Verbs

Find and correct the SIX errors in irregular verb usage in the following excerpt from *Island of the Blue Dolphins*, by Scott O'Dell. Cross out each incorrect form and write the correct form above it.

I ~~finded~~ found nothing in the canoes under the cliff. Then, remembering the chest the Aleuts had ~~brung~~ brought to shore, I ~~setted~~ set out for Coral Cove. I had ~~saw~~ seen that chest on the beach during the battle but did not remember that the hunters had ~~took~~ taken it with them when they ~~flood~~ fled.

Review 4F: Misplaced Modifiers

Circle the misplaced adjective and adverb phrases in the following sentences. Draw an arrow to the place where each phrase should be.

The girl caught a lake trout (with two blond braids).

The canoe rocked precariously in the waves (with two seats).

(From the plate) the dog gobbled the cake that had fallen.

The snake wriggled through the grass (with the red stripes).

Marta accidentally bumped a man carrying books (with her elbow).

Uncle Bruce told us stories about his trip to the Caribbean (in the dining room).

I heard that the mayor is coming to our school (from Hillary's brother).

(In the campfire) the boy with the ripped jeans toasted his marshmallow.

Review 4G: Diagramming

On your own paper, diagram the following sentences.

Before the invention of money, people bartered for goods.

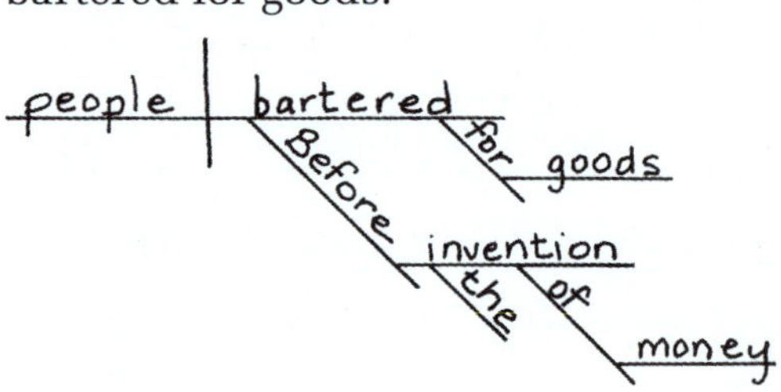

Luke trades Matt a chicken for a basket of apples.

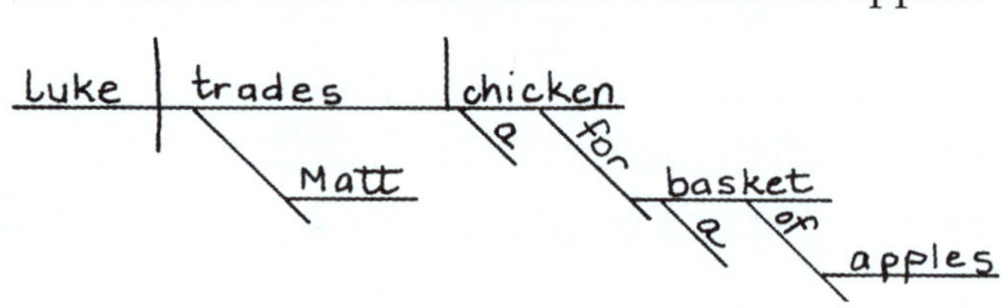

Barter can be complex and problematic.

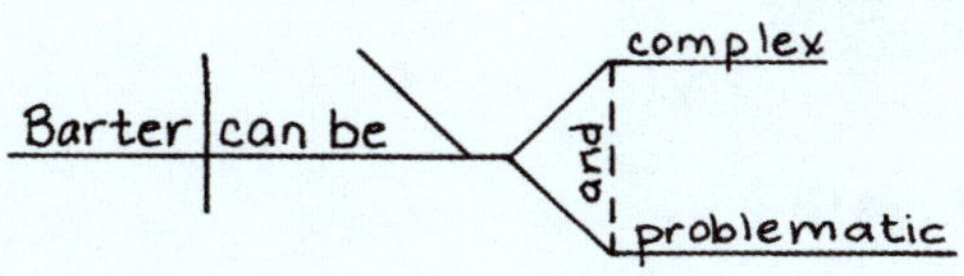

Money was invented for simplification.

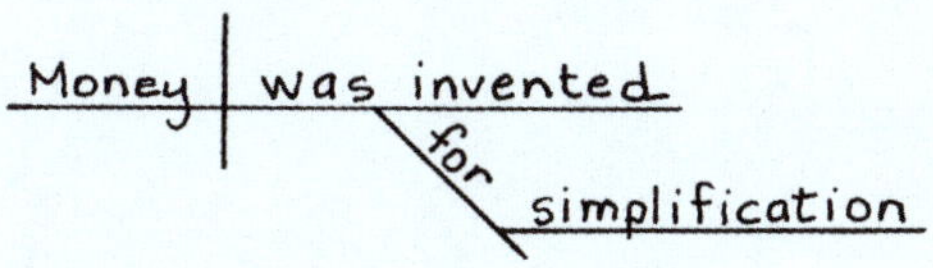

Today we give stores paper money.

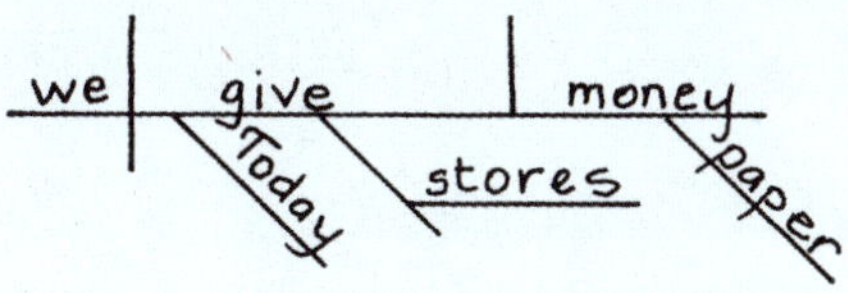

Cowry shells became money in ancient Chinese society.

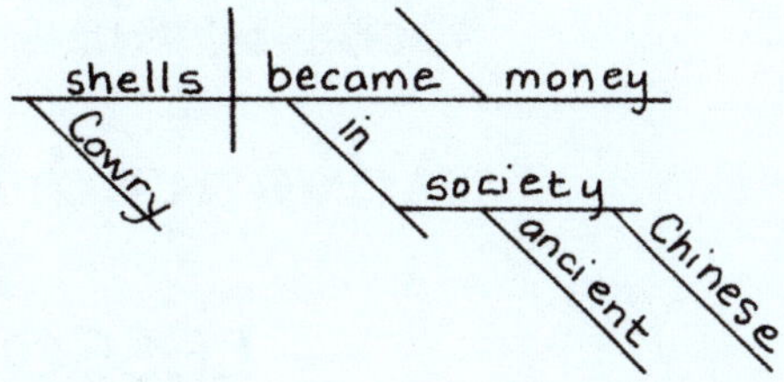

Over the years, silver and gold became standards of currency.

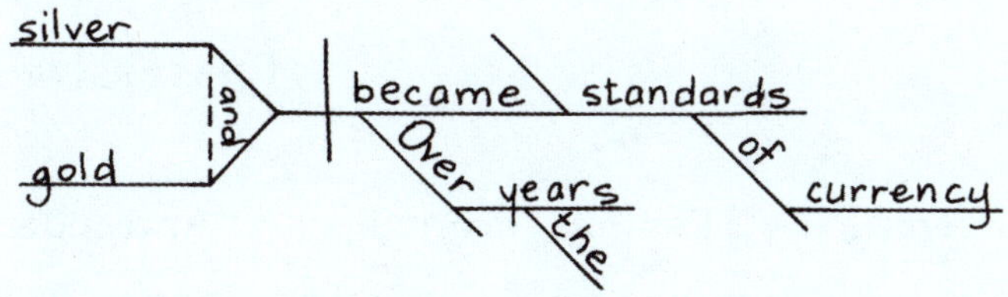

Will all money be electronic in the future?

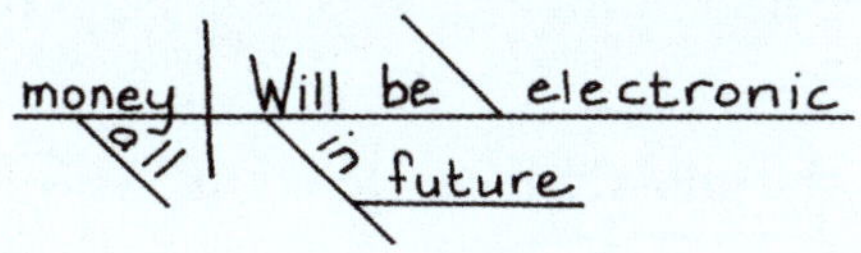

WEEK 13

Advanced Pronouns

— LESSON 49 —

Personal Pronouns
Antecedents
Possessive Pronouns

Exercise 49A: Personal Pronouns and Antecedents

Circle the personal pronouns in the following sentences, adapted from *A Christmas Carol*, by Charles Dickens. Draw an arrow from each pronoun to the antecedent. In the margin, write the gender (*F*, *M*, or *N*) and number (*S* or *PL*) of each pronoun.

Scrooge gazed at the ghostly face. He could see it clearly. M, S and N, S

Though the eyes were wide open, they were perfectly motionless. N, PL

Darkness is cheap, and Scrooge liked it. N, S

Scrooge was not a man to be frightened by echoes. He fastened the door. M, S

Exercise 49B: Identifying Possessive Pronouns

Underline the possessive pronouns in the following sentences from *The Travels of Marco Polo*. Each possessive pronoun is acting as an adjective. Draw an arrow from the pronoun to the noun it modifies. There may be more than one pronoun in each sentence.

On its summit is erected an ornamental pavilion, which is likewise entirely green.

Here, on the southern side of the new city, is the site of his vast palace.

In the rear of the body of the palace are large buildings containing several apartments, where is deposited the private property of the monarch, or his treasure in gold and silver bullion, precious stones, and pearls, and also his vessels of gold and silver plate.

Exercise 49C: Using Possessive Pronouns

Write the correct possessive pronoun above the underlined noun(s).

his
Theodore Roosevelt loved bull terrier dogs. After biting many people, Theodore Roosevelt's pet dog was sent away from the White House.

His / Her
Theodore Roosevelt's daughter Alice received a present from the Empress of China. The Empress's gift was a small Pekingese dog.

her
The first animal launched into orbit in space was a Russian female dog, Laika. Laika, a stray from the streets of Russia, had already proven Laika's ability to withstand harsh conditions.

our
My family and I named my family's and my first pet dog Laika after the famous astronaut dog.

their
Animals depend on animals' owners.

their
The Wesley sisters take turns looking after the Wesley sisters' pet dog.

her
It's Stephanie's turn today.

hers / mine
This puppy is Penny's, but that puppy is my puppy.

Its
There is a problem with this dog collar. The collar's buckle is broken.

Exercise 49D: Diagramming Pronouns

On your own paper, diagram every word in the following sentences.

The *North Star* made her way into a small inlet in the ice.

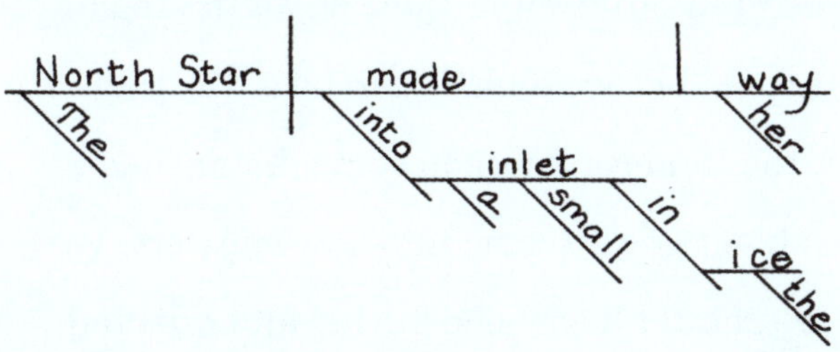

Note to Instructor: *Into a small inlet* is a prepositional phrase acting as an adverb because it answers the question *where*. Because it is an adverb, it is diagrammed beneath the verb.

In the ice is a prepositional phrase describing which inlet, so it acts as an adjective.

She was caught by the ice, and was completely destroyed.

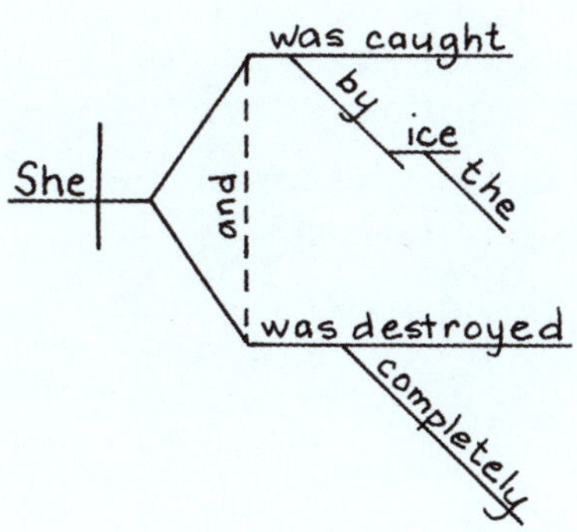

Note to Instructor: *By the ice* is a prepositional phrase acting as an adverb because it answers the question of how the ship was caught, so it is diagrammed beneath the verb.

Her great masts and her massive ribs of solid timber cracked and broke.

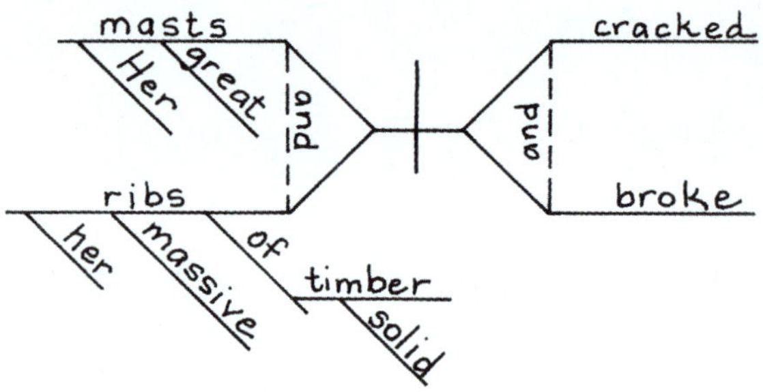

Note to Instructor: *Of solid timber* is a prepositional phrase acting as an adjective. It answers the question "What kind of ribs?"

— LESSON 50 —

Pronoun Case

Exercise 50A: Subject and Object Pronouns

Underline all the personal pronouns in the following paragraph. Identify them as *S* for subject, *O* for object, or *P* for possessive.

This description of a pyroclastic flow was written by the Roman lawyer Pliny the Younger after he lived through the eruption of Mount Vesuvius in the year 79. This translation by Betty Radice comes from *The Letters of the Younger Pliny* (Penguin Books, 1963), Book VI.

Ashes were already falling, not as yet very thickly. I[S] looked round: a dense black cloud was coming up behind us[O], spreading over the earth like a flood . . . We[S] had scarcely sat down to rest when darkness fell, not the dark of a moonless or cloudy night, but as if the lamp had been put out in a closed room. You[S] could hear the shrieks of women, the wailing of infants, and the shouting of men; some were calling their[P] parents, others their[P] children or their[P] wives, trying to recognize them[O] by their[P] voices . . . A gleam of light returned, but we[S] took this to be a warning of the approaching flames rather than daylight. However, the flames remained some distance off; then darkness came on once more and ashes began to fall again, this time in heavy showers. We[S] rose from time to time and shook them[O] off, otherwise we[S] should have been buried and crushed beneath their[P] weight.

Exercise 50B: Using Personal Pronouns Correctly

Choose the correct word(s) in parentheses and cross out the incorrect choice(s). Be sure to choose the grammatically correct choice for writing and not the choice that sounds the best.

My brother and sister and (~~me~~/I) decided to clean the yard for our father's birthday.

My mother helped (us/~~we~~) to find the tools.

Daniela and (~~him~~/he) raked, and I trimmed the bushes.

Mom lent (Diego and me/~~Diego and I~~) a hand when we bagged the leaves.

At the end of the day, (~~us~~/we) were very tired but very pleased.

Dad gave Daniela, Diego, and (me/~~I~~) a huge compliment.

He said that the best gifts of all were (~~us~~/we).

Exercise 50C: Diagramming Personal Pronouns

On your own paper, diagram the following sentences. Personal pronouns are diagrammed exactly like the nouns or adjectives they replace.

They offered us advice.

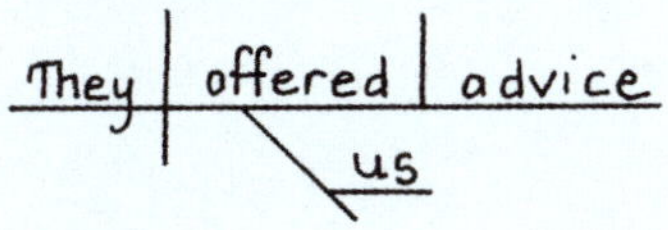

It is I.

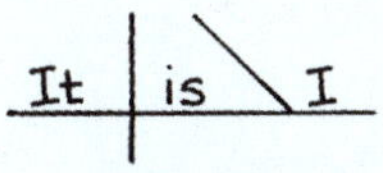

I understand you.

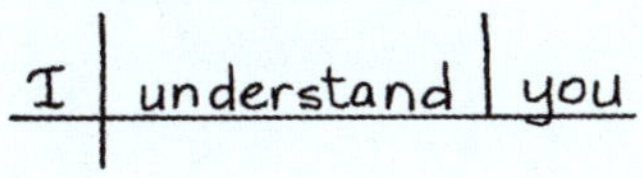

We beat them!

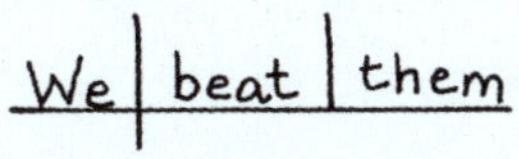

He fixed me lunch.

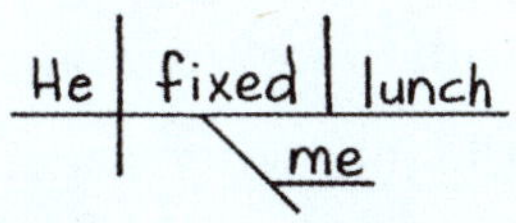

Their companions were we.

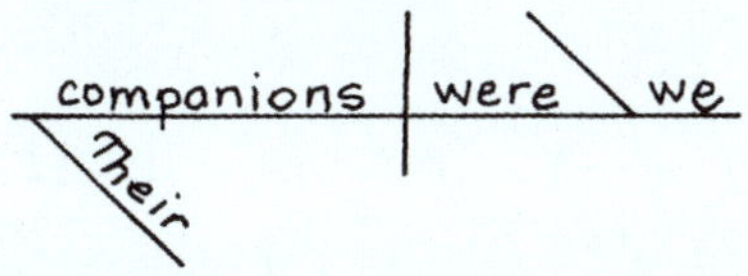

— LESSON 51 —

Indefinite Pronouns

Exercise 51A: Identifying Indefinite Pronouns

Underline all of the indefinite pronouns in the following sentences. Each sentence may contain more than one pronoun.

Sitting-room, bedroom, lumber-room. All as they should be. Nobody under the table, nobody under the sofa; a small fire in the grate; spoon and basin ready; and the little saucepan of gruel (Scrooge had a cold in his head) upon the hob. Nobody under the bed; nobody in the closet; nobody in his dressing-gown, which was hanging up in a suspicious attitude against the wall.

—From Charles Dickens, *A Christmas Carol*

The summer heat has withered everything except the mesquite, the *palo verde*, the grease wood, and the various cacti.

—From John Charles Van Dyke, *The Desert: Further Studies in Natural Appearances*

Nothing besides gilding and painting presents itself to the eye.

—From Marco Polo and John Masefield, *The Travels of Marco Polo the Venetian*

Exercise 51B: Subject-Verb Agreement: Indefinite Pronouns

Choose the correct verb in parentheses. Cross out the incorrect verb.

Both of the Travis twins (~~is~~/are) throwing a birthday party.

Everyone (has/~~have~~) been invited!

All of the decorations (~~was~~/were) purchased and hung.

A few of the guests (~~has~~/have) arrived already, but some (~~is~~/are) going to be late.

Most of the cupcakes (~~has~~/have) been made.

But some of the icing (is/~~are~~) missing!

(Does/~~Do~~) anyone know where the icing is?

One of the Travis twins (was/~~were~~) holding up Tiger, the cat.

All of his furry face (was/~~were~~) covered in icing.

Exercise 51C: Diagramming Indefinite Pronouns

On your own paper, diagram the following sentences, drawn from *Oliver Twist*, by Charles Dickens.

Nobody knows him.

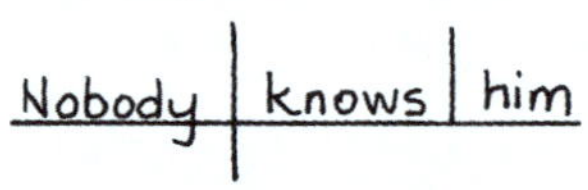

Neither of them are employed.

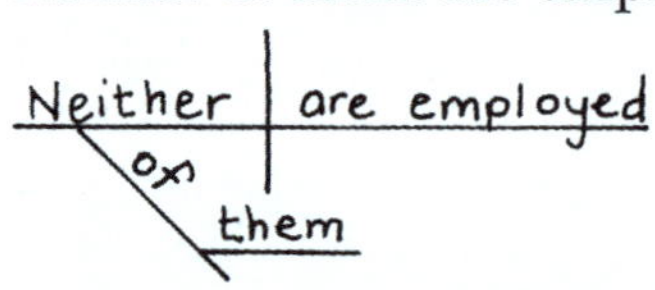

Few people were stirring.

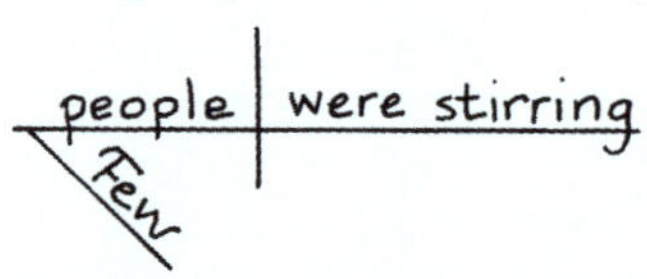

They were both daughters.

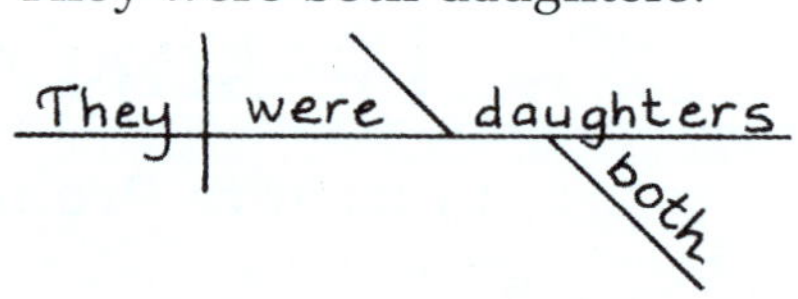

Both of them were wrapped in shabby outer garments.

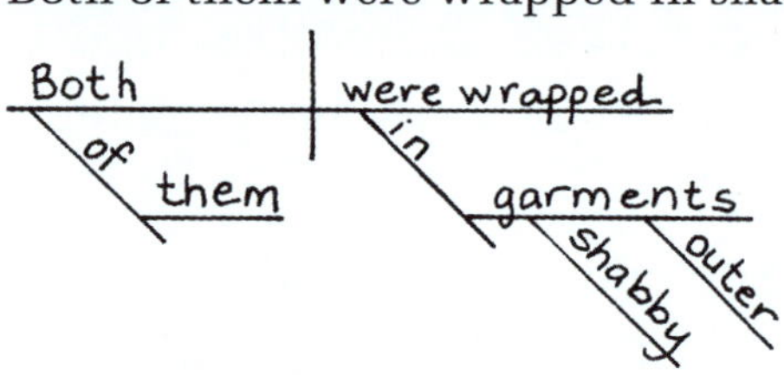

— LESSON 52 —

Personal Pronouns
Indefinite Pronouns

Exercise 52A: Subject and Object Pronouns

In the following sentences from E. Nesbit's *The Railway Children*, cross out the incorrect pronoun.

And (he/~~him~~) did not like the feeling which thinking this gave (~~he~~/him).

That night at tea (he/~~him~~) asked Mother if (she/~~her~~) had a green leather note-book with silver corners.

(She/~~Her~~) had not; but when (she/~~her~~) heard what (he/~~him~~) wanted it for (she/~~her~~) gave (~~he~~/him) a little black one.

"It has a few pages torn out," said (she/~~her~~), "but it will hold quite a lot of numbers."

After all, it was (she/~~her~~) who had thought of packing up the odds and ends of things to eat.

"Is (he/~~him~~) all killed?" asked Phyllis.

"All (we/~~us~~) can do, you and (I/~~me~~) and Daddy, is to be brave, and patient."

"Phil and (I/~~me~~) are going away."

"(I/~~Me~~) don't know how to thank you for making it possible for (~~I~~/me)."

"Father and (I/~~me~~) used to go on the river at Marlow before (we/~~us~~) were married."

"Besides parting from Father, (he/~~him~~) and (I/~~me~~) have had a great sorrow—oh, terrible—worse than anything you can think of."

"If you take his feet and Phil and (I/~~me~~) take his head, (we/~~us~~) could carry him."

"(I/~~Me~~) know that you love mother and Peter and Phil and (~~I~~/me)."

"Phil and (I/~~me~~) can wash (~~they~~/them)," said Bobbie, "if you'll iron (~~they~~/them), Mother."

(She/~~Her~~) and her mother and that awful sheet of newspaper were alone in the room together.

Exercise 52B: Possessive and Indefinite Pronouns

In these sentences from E. Nesbit's *The Enchanted Castle,* cross out the incorrect word in each set of parentheses.

"I ought to," she said, "if anybody (does/~~do~~)."

The sun was blazing in at the window; the eight-sided room was very hot, and everyone (was/~~were~~) getting cross.

Everyone (was/~~were~~) very hungry, and more bread and butter had to be fetched.

Something enormously long and darkly grey came crawling towards him, slowly, heavily. The moon came out just in time to show (its/~~their~~) shape.

No one (was/~~were~~) to be seen.

And the nearer they came to the Temple of Flora, in the golden hush of the afternoon, the more certain each (was/~~were~~) that they could not possibly have done otherwise.

Both the others (~~was~~/were) used to Gerald's way of telling a story while he acted it.

Everyone grew calmer and more contented with (his/~~their~~) lot.

Part of the shelf near it held, not bright jewels, but rings and brooches and chains, as well as queer things that she did not know the names of, and all (~~was~~/were) of dull metal and odd shapes.

Then everyone sat or lay down on (his/~~their~~) couch and the feast began.

All (was/~~were~~) still as the sweet morning itself.

There (~~was~~/were) a few bunches of flowers among the vegetables, and the children hesitated, balanced in choice.

But none of the houses (~~turns~~/turn) into enchanted castles.

A few words (~~was~~/were) exchanged.

None of the children (~~was~~/were) at all sure what the utmost rigour of the law might be.

Some (~~was~~/were) dipping (~~his~~/their) white feet among the gold and silver fish, and sending ripples across the faces of the seven moons.

Some (~~was~~/were) pelting each other with roses so sweet that the girls could smell them even across the pool.

Others (~~was~~/were) holding hands and dancing in a ring, and two (~~was~~/were) sitting on the steps playing cat's-cradle which is a very ancient game indeed with a thread of white marble.

Some of us (~~is~~/are) very hungry.

Exercise 52C: Writing Sentences from Diagrams

Use the diagrams below to reconstruct these sentences from E. Nesbit's *Five Children and It*. Write the original sentence on the blank below each diagram. Pay careful attention to each part of speech! Punctuate each sentence properly.

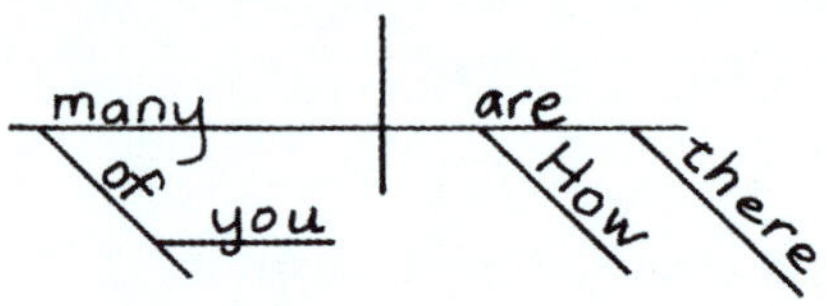

How many of you are there?

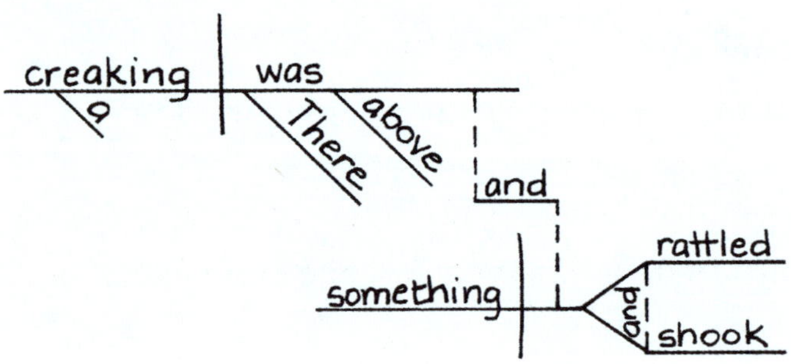

There was a creaking above, and something rattled and shook.

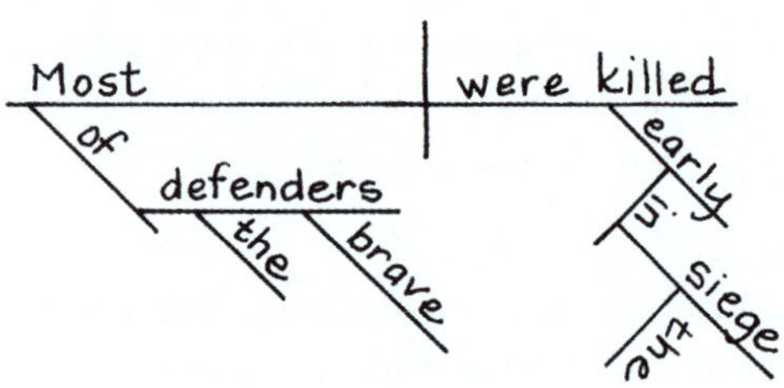

Most of the brave defenders were killed early in the siege.

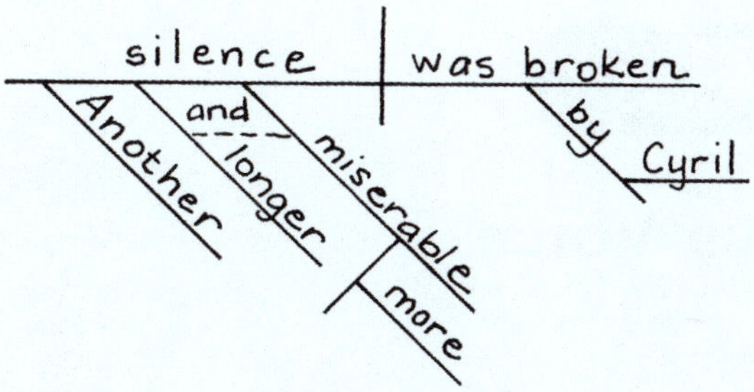

Another silence, longer and more miserable, was broken by Cyril.

> **Note to Instructor:** *Another longer and more miserable silence was broken by Cyril* is also correct.

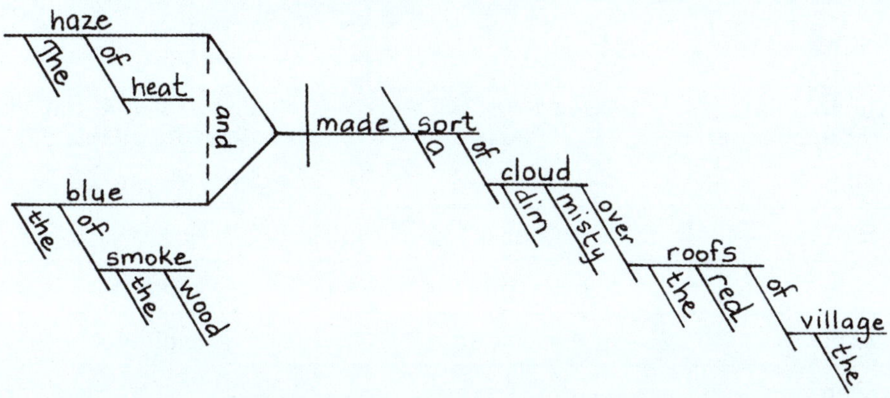

The haze of heat and the blue of the wood smoke made a sort of dim misty cloud over the red roofs of the village.

WEEK 14

Active and Passive Voice

— LESSON 53 —

Principal Parts

Troublesome Verbs

Exercise 53A: Principal Parts of Verbs

Fill in the chart with the missing forms.

	First Principal Part Present	Second Principal Part Past	Third Principal Part Past Participle
I	clap	clapped	clapped
I	quit	quit	quit
I	hide	hid	hidden
I	avoid	avoided	avoided
I	keep	kept	kept
I	say	said	said
I	see	saw	seen
I	break	broke	broken

Exercise 53B: Using Correct Verbs

Choose the correct verb in parentheses. Cross out the incorrect verb

Katrin loves to (~~lay~~/ lie) in her bed on cold mornings in Iceland.

But today Katrin (rose / ~~raised~~) early from bed, because her *amma,* or grandmother, is turning 80 years old today.

Amma (~~rose~~/ raised) six children, including Katrin's father.

Katrin's father (~~lay~~/ laid) the marinated salmon on the grill.

Katrin's parents had (~~let~~/ left) her alone for the afternoon and (let / ~~left~~) her go horseback riding.

After she returned, she and her mother (set / ~~sat~~) the table.

Her mother had (laid / ~~lain~~) the embroidered cloth napkins next to the plates.

After eating dinner, they all (~~set~~/ sat) at the table for hours and talked and laughed.

Very late that night, Katrin (lay / ~~laid~~) down to sleep.

Exercise 53C: Correct Forms of Troublesome Verbs

Fill in the blanks with the correct form of the indicated verb.

I __lie__ some time in a situation which no language can describe. (*lie*)
—Karl Friedrich Hieronymous, *The Adventures of Baron Munchausen*

She then gathers more pollen, __lays__ another egg, and builds another partition. (*lay*)
—Anna Botsford Comstock, *Handbook of Nature Study*

She always __leaves__ a space for a vestibule near the door. (*leave*)
—Anna Botsford Comstock, *Handbook of Nature Study*

After listening for some time, I __raised__ my head and looked around. (*raise*)
—Karl Friedrich Hieronymous, *The Adventures of Baron Munchausen*

This means that if you __sat (OR sit)__ in one in Hawaii you might be boiled like a lobster. (*sit*)
—Bill Bryson, *A Short History of Nearly Everything*

Exercise 53D: Proofreading for Correct Verb Usage

Find and correct *six* errors in verb usage by crossing out the incorrect verbs and writing the correct forms above them.

Last year, my brother and I ~~rose~~ raised a crop of peanuts. Our parents ~~let~~ left a quarter of the garden free for us to plant the peanuts. As soon as the sun had ~~rose~~ risen, we ran to the garden to plant our peanuts. We planted unroasted peanuts that we had bought from the grocery store. Soon they sprouted, producing little green shoots that ~~raised~~ rose out of the ground. We were patient and waited a long time, but we never saw any peanuts. The leaves began to turn yellow, so we decided to pull up the plants. My brother pulled up the first plant and ~~lay~~ laid it on the ground. The dirt fell off the roots, and we saw the peanuts ~~laying~~ lying there on the grass. They had been growing underground the whole time.

— LESSON 54 —

Verb Tense

Active and Passive Voice

Exercise 54A: Reviewing Tenses

Write the tense of each underlined verb above it. These two excerpts are from the Sherlock Holmes story "The Adventure of the Speckled Band," written by Arthur Conan Doyle. The first is done for you.

"It seems that a young lady has arrived (perfect present) in a considerable state of excitement, who insists (simple present) upon seeing me. She is waiting (progressive present) now in the sitting-room. Now, when young ladies wander (simple present) about the metropolis at this hour of the morning and knock sleepy people up out of their beds, I presume (simple present) that it is something very pressing which they have (simple present) to communicate."

He had ceased (perfect past) to strike, and was gazing (progressive past) up at the ventilator, when suddenly there broke (simple past) from the silence of the night the most horrible cry to which I have ever listened (perfect present).

Exercise 54B: Distinguishing Between Active and Passive Voice

Identify the following sentences as *A* for active or *P* for passive. If you're not sure, ask yourself: Is the subject *doing* the verb, or is the verb *happening to* the subject?

The Battle of Marathon was fought thousands of years ago between Athens and Persia. P
Many interesting legends have been told about the battle. P
The Athens army was outnumbered. P
The Athens army asked Sparta for help. A
A messenger boy named Pheidippides was sent to Sparta to request aid. P
The Persians were defeated! P
Pheidippides had been delivering messages for days! A
Nonetheless, the messenger boy carried news of victory 26 miles back to Athens. A
Today, the famous 26.2-mile race is called a marathon. P

The following sentences are taken from *The Adventures of Baron Munchausen*, by Karl Friedrich Hieronymous.

We sailed from Amsterdam with dispatches from their High Mightinesses the States of Holland. A
The natives of the island were half-starved by his oppressive and infamous impositions. P
In about six weeks we arrived at Ceylon. A
We were received with great marks of friendship and true politeness. P
The skin of the crocodile was stuffed in the usual manner. P
The lion's skin was properly preserved. P
We measured the crocodile. A

Exercise 54C: Forming the Active and Passive Voice

Fill in the chart below, rewriting each sentence so that it appears in both the active and the passive voice. Be sure to keep the tense the same. The first is done for you.

Active	Passive
The Greeks created the Olympic Games.	The Olympic Games were created by the Greeks.
A cook named Coroebus won the first Olympic race.	The first Olympic race was won by a cook named Coroebus.
France was hosting the first modern Olympics.	The first modern Olympics was being hosted by France.

Active	Passive
The Olympics bring together many countries.	Many countries are brought together by the Olympics.
A famous athlete will light the Olympic torch.	The Olympic torch will be lit by a famous athlete.
Olympic champions have inspired many people.	Many people have been inspired by Olympic champions.

— LESSON 55 —

Parts of the Sentence
Active and Passive Voice

Note to Instructor: You should adapt the following review to the student's level of knowledge. If the student is clear on the concepts learned so far, and is able to diagram the sentences correctly, you do not need to follow every line of dialogue for every sentence. However, the student should be able not only to diagram the sentences, but to name the parts of the sentence and explain their use (for example, in the first sentence, if you ask the student, "What kind of phrase is *to the ground* and what does it do?" the student should be able to answer, "A prepositional phrase acting as an adverb").

These sentences are adapted from Jonathan Swift's classic adventure novel *Gulliver's Travels.*

Sentence #1

Instructor: Read me the first sentence from your workbook.

Student: My arms and legs were strongly fastened to the ground.

Instructor: What is the predicate?

Note to Instructor: In the dialogues that follow, prompt the student whenever necessary.

Student: Were fastened.

Instructor: Who or what were fastened?

Student: My arms and legs.

Instructor: *Arms and legs* is the compound subject. Diagram the compound subject and the predicate. Does the subject perform the action? (Are the *arms and legs* fastening something?)

Student: No.

Instructor: *Arms and legs* receives the action of the verb. Is *were fastened* an active or passive verb?

Student: Passive.

Instructor: Repeat after me: In a sentence with a passive verb, the subject receives the action.

Student: In a sentence with a passive verb, the subject receives the action.

Instructor: What kind of pronoun is *my*?

Student: Possessive pronoun.

Instructor: What are possessive pronouns also known as?

Student: Possessive adjectives.

Instructor: *My* modifies the noun *arms.* Place it on your diagram. What part of speech is *strongly*?

Student: An adverb.

Instructor: What questions do adverbs answer?

Student: How, when, where, how often, to what extent.

Instructor: Which of these questions does the adverb *strongly* answer?

Student: How.

Instructor: Adverbs modify verbs, adjectives, and other adverbs. What part of speech does *strongly* modify?

Student: The verb.

Instructor: Diagram it beneath the verb. What part of speech is *to*?

Student: A preposition.

Instructor: What does a preposition do?

Student: A preposition shows the relationship of a noun or pronoun to another word in the sentence.

Instructor: This preposition shows the relationship between Gulliver's arms and legs and the ground. *To the ground* is a prepositional phrase. It answers the question *where.* What part of speech answers the questions *how, when, where, how often, to what extent*?

Student: An adverb.

Instructor: *To the ground* is a prepositional phrase acting as an adverb. Diagram it beneath the verb.

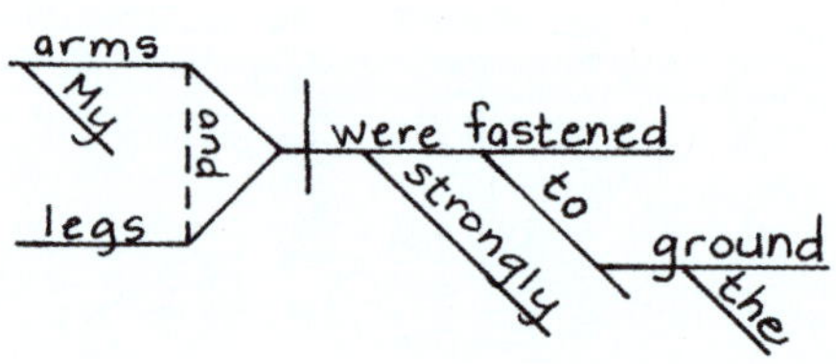

Sentence #2

Instructor: Read the second sentence out loud.

Student: I felt something alive on my left leg.

Instructor: What are the subject and predicate of the sentence?

Student: I felt.

Instructor: I felt what?

Student: Something.

Instructor: *Something* receives the action of the verb *felt.* What part of the sentence is *something*?

Student: Direct object.

Instructor: When a sentence has a direct object, you can be pretty sure that the subject is performing the action! Repeat after me: In a sentence with an active verb, the subject performs the action.

Student: In a sentence with an active verb, the subject performs the action.

Instructor: Diagram the subject, predicate, and direct object on your own paper. *Something* is the direct object. What part of speech is *something*? What kind of word is it? (Hint: You learned about this word in Lesson 51.)

Student: Indefinite pronoun.

Instructor: What are indefinite pronouns?

Student: Indefinite pronouns are pronouns without antecedents.

Instructor: You can see why Gulliver would use an indefinite pronoun—he doesn't know *what* is on his left leg! Whatever it is, it's alive. *Alive* follows the direct object *something* and describes it. What kind of word describes a noun or pronoun?

Student: An adjective.

Instructor: What do we call a word that follows the direct object and describes or renames it?

Student: Object complement.

Instructor: Diagram *alive* as an object complement. What is the prepositional phrase in this sentence?

Student: On my left leg.

Instructor: What is the object of the preposition *on*?

Student: Leg.

Instructor: It isn't always easy to know what word a prepositional phrase modifies. Ask yourself: Does this phrase answer one of the *adverb* questions (*how, when, where, how often, to what extent*)? Or does it answer one of the *adjective* questions? Repeat those after me: *What kind, which one, how many, whose.*

Student: What kind, which one, how many, whose.

Instructor: Where did Gulliver feel the *something alive?*

Student: On his left leg.

Instructor: This is a prepositional phrase acting as an adverb, because it answers the question *where.* What parts of speech do adverbs modify?

Student: Verbs, adjectives, other adverbs.

Instructor: Diagram *on my left leg* beneath the verb.

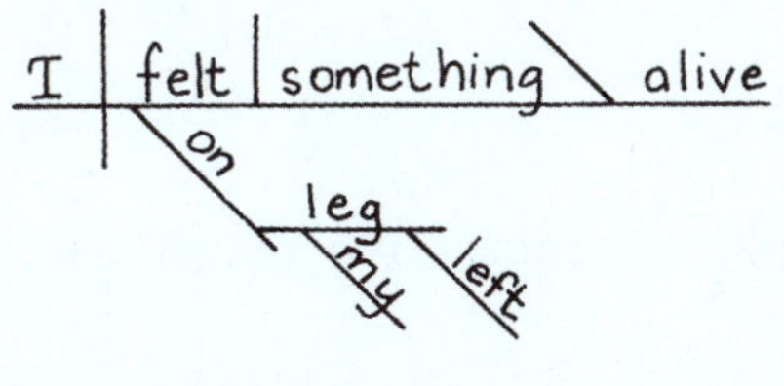

Sentence #3

Instructor: Read me the third sentence.

Student: I saw a tiny human creature with a bow and arrow.

Instructor: What are the subject and verb of this sentence?

Student: I saw.

Instructor: Is this an active or passive verb?

Student: Active.

Instructor: The subject *I* is *doing* the seeing, so the verb is active. What does the subject see?

Student: A tiny human creature.

Instructor: What is the one word that acts as the direct object?

Student: Creature.

Instructor: Diagram the subject, predicate, and direct object. There are three adjectives that modify *creature*. What are they?

Student: A, tiny, human.

Instructor: *A* is a particular kind of adjective called an *article*. What are the three articles?

Student: A, an, the.

Instructor: What is the prepositional phrase that finishes out the sentence?

Student: With a bow and arrow.

Instructor: There is one preposition in this phrase, but there are two of something else. What are there two of?

Student: Objects of the preposition.

Instructor: Does the phrase *with a bow and arrow* answer an adjective question, or an adverb question?

> **Note to Instructor:** If necessary, remind the student of the adverb and adjective questions. This phrase answers the question *which tiny human?* (The tiny human with a bow and arrow.)

Student: Adjective.

Instructor: Diagram the adjective phrase beneath the noun it describes.

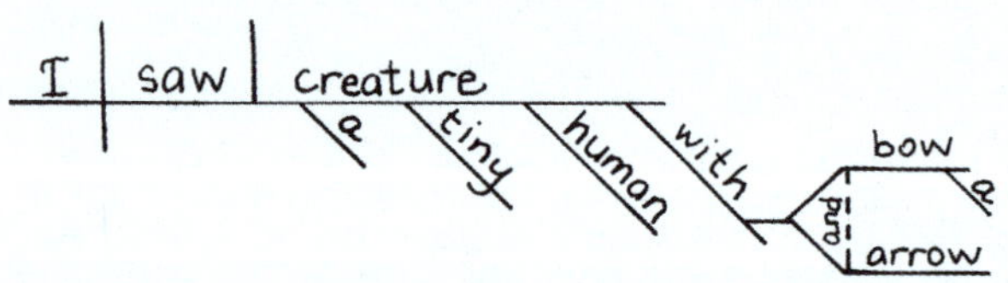

Sentence #4

Instructor: Read me the fourth sentence.

Student: They ran back in a fright.

Instructor: What are the subject and predicate?

Student: They ran.

Instructor: What tense is the verb? Remember to tell me perfect, simple, or progressive as well as past, present, or future.

Student: Simple past.

Instructor: Diagram the subject and predicate now. Where did they run?

Student: Back.

Instructor: What part of speech answers the question *where*?

Student: Adverb.

Instructor: *Back* is an adverb. Diagram it beneath the verb *ran*. *How* did they run?

Student: In a fright.

Instructor: What part of speech answers the question *how*?

Student: Adverb.

Instructor: The prepositional phrase *in a fright* functions as an adverb. Diagram it beneath the verb *ran* as well.

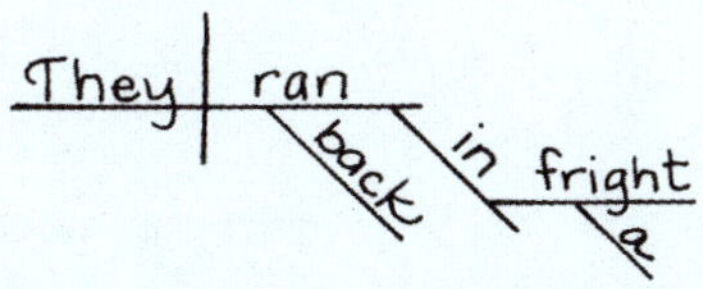

Sentence #5

Instructor: Read me the fifth sentence.

Student: Some of them were hurt by the fall.

Instructor: What is the subject?

Student: Some.

> **Note to Instructor:** If necessary, remind the student that a subject can never be inside a prepositional phrase.

Instructor: What kind of pronoun is *some*?

> **Note to Instructor:** If necessary, ask, "Does *some* have an antecedent?"

Student: Indefinite.

Instructor: To find out whether *some* is singular or plural, look at the prepositional phrase that follows the pronoun. What is that prepositional phrase?

Student: Of them.

Instructor: Does *of them* tell you that *some* is one tiny human creature, or more than one tiny human creature?

Student: More than one.

Instructor: In this sentence, the subject is plural and takes a plural verb. What is the plural verb?

Student: Were hurt.

Instructor: Is the subject hurting, or being hurt?

Student: Being hurt.

Instructor: The subject isn't performing the action of hurting; the subject is receiving the action. Is the verb active or passive?

Student: Passive.

Instructor: Diagram the subject, the prepositional phrase that describes it, and the verb. What prepositional phrase remains in the sentence?

Student: By the fall.

Instructor: What question does this prepositional phrase answer?

> **Note to Instructor:** If necessary, go through the adjective and adverb questions one at a time. Does *by the fall* answer the questions *what kind, which one, how many, whose*? Or does it answer the *questions how, when, where, how often, to what extent*? The answer is *how*. How were they hurt? By the fall.

Student: How.

Instructor: Is the phrase acting as an adverb or adjective?

Student: Adverb.

Instructor: Diagram it beneath the verb.

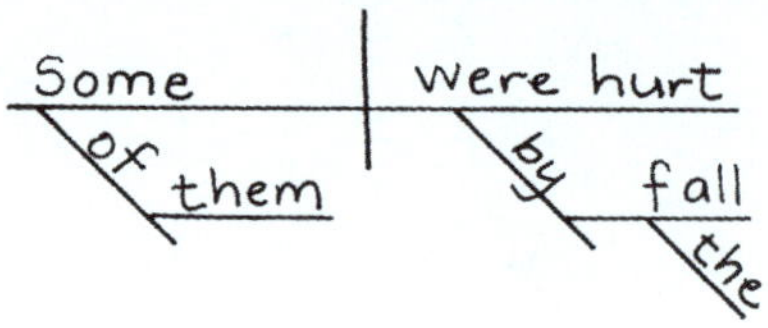

— LESSON 56 —

Active and Passive Voice
Transitive and Intransitive Verbs

Exercise 56A: Transitive and Intransitive Verbs

Underline each verb in the following sentences. Write *T* above each transitive verb and *IT* above each intransitive verb. Circle the direct object of each transitive verb.

Most of these sentences are adapted from *Mexico: An Encyclopedia of Contemporary Culture and History* (ABC-CLIO, 2004).

He was sleeping in the Iberia hotel.

The advent of modernism laid the groundwork for a distinctly Mexican poetry.

Diego Rivera complained about the stifling training at the National Academy of San Carlos.

Samuel Ruiz sent priests and other volunteers to support peasant activism.

The solution to Mexico's problems lay in political reform at the national level.

Comedy-fantasies like Carlos Vela's *Cinco de chocolate y uno de fresa* entertained audiences.

Mexico broke diplomatic relations with the Axis but did not declare war until May 1942.

The city was sitting atop dry lake beds in a valley.

Francisco Villa broke publicly with the First Chief of the Constitutionalist Army.

The government looked to the oil industry as a major source of revenue.

The road to power ran through the federal bureaucracy.

Many years of bloody fighting lay ahead.

Especially popular with students and the middle class, he ran a strong campaign.

Rebel groups even ate in company cafeterias.

Changes in immigration laws in 1990 raised Mexico's annual quota.

The Maya laid siege to Merida in 1848.

The best Golden Age films entertained and instructed.

Exercise 56B: Active and Passive Verbs

In the blanks below, rewrite each sentence with an active verb so that the verb is passive. Rewrite each sentence with a passive verb so that the verb is active.

These sentences are adapted from *Mexico: A Primary Source Cultural Guide*, by Alan Cobb (Rosen Publishing Group, 2004).

Quetzalcoatl brought a small tree to the Toltecs.
A small tree was brought by Quetzalcoatl to the Toltecs.

The tree grew flowers and then brown pods.
Flowers and then brown pods were grown by the tree.

Quetzalcoatl picked the pods and dried them.
The pods were picked and dried by Quetzalcoatl.

The women were taught to roast and grind the pods by Quetzalcoatl.
Quetzalcoatl taught the women to roast and grind the pods.

He instructed the Toltecs to mix the pods with hot water and hot peppers.
The Toltecs were instructed by him to mix the pods with hot water and hot peppers.

First honey, and then milk and sugar, was added by the Toltecs to this bitter drink.
The Toltecs added first honey, and then milk and sugar, to this bitter drink.

The gods gave them their sacred chocolate drink.
Their sacred chocolate drink was given to them by the gods.

Exercise 56C: Diagramming

On your own paper, diagram every word in the following sentences.

She took her coat down and locked the door of the cottage behind her and walked down the dim road towards the curve.

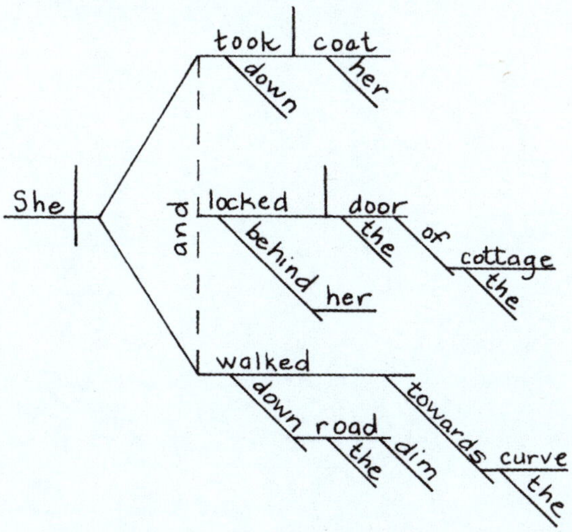

Napoleon was alarmed by the news of the loss of the battle and the retreat of the army beyond the Seine.

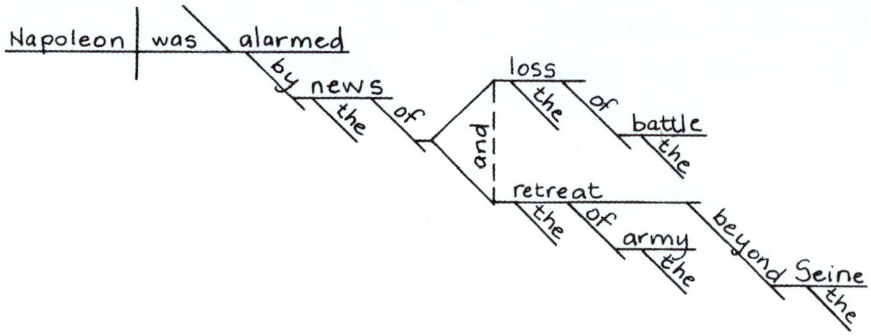

You can buy a "Goat for Peace" for your aunt's birthday.

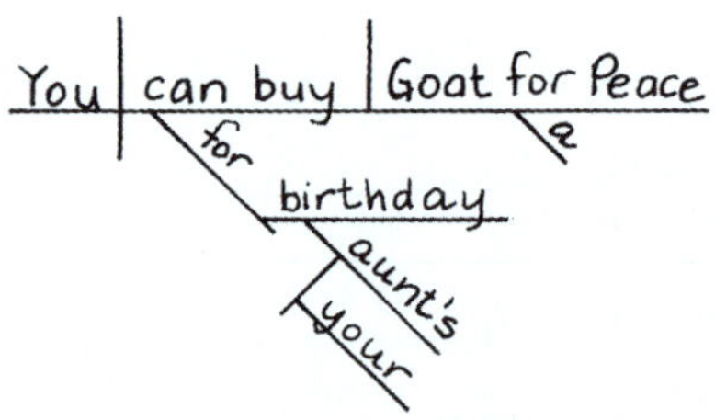

A goat is a milk and fertilizer factory and can provide self-sufficiency.

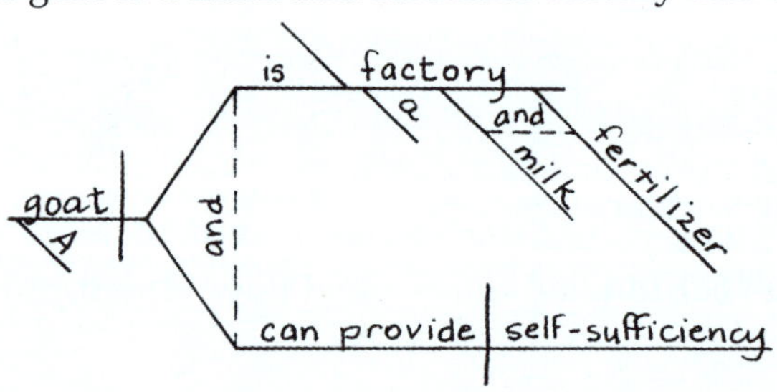

WEEK 15

Specialized Pronouns

— LESSON 57 —

Parts of Speech
Parts of the Sentence
Intensive and Reflexive Pronouns

Exercise 57A: Identifying Intensive and Reflexive Pronouns

Underline the intensive and reflexive pronouns in the following sentences. Above each pronoun, write *I* for intensive or *R* for reflexive. If the pronoun is reflexive, also mark it as *DO* (direct object), *IO* (indirect object), or *OP* (object of the preposition). The first is done for you.

Esther treated herself (R DO) to a giant brownie sundae.

Control yourselves (R DO)!

The mayor himself (I) presented the award.

We ourselves (I) cleaned the entire house.

I bought myself (R IO) a new board game.

I myself (I) bought the new board game.

The following sentences are adapted from *Galileo: Astronomer and Physicist*, by Paul Hightower.

Some professors came to see Galileo make a fool of himself (R OP).

The book itself (I) was a brilliant and important work.

He constructed himself (R IO) a working model of the new telescope.

Galileo wrote to Kepler, "I count myself (R DO) happy in the search for truth."

The stars themselves (I) did not move.

Exercise 57B: Using Intensive and Reflexive Pronouns Correctly

Each of the following sentences contains errors in the usage of intensive and reflexive pronouns. Cross out the incorrect word and write the correction above it.

himself
Felix cut ~~hisself~~ when he tripped over the root.

ourselves
We asked ~~ourself~~ what we should do.

me
Stuart gave him and ~~myself~~ excellent advice.

themselves
The Guzman brothers ~~theirselves~~ made the rhubarb pie.

he
Chelsea and ~~himself~~ ate the entire dessert!

her
We ourselves picked up Emory and ~~herself~~ from the train station.

Exercise 57C: Diagramming Intensive and Reflexive Pronouns

On your own paper, diagram every word in the following sentences.

He occupied himself with a collection of old books.

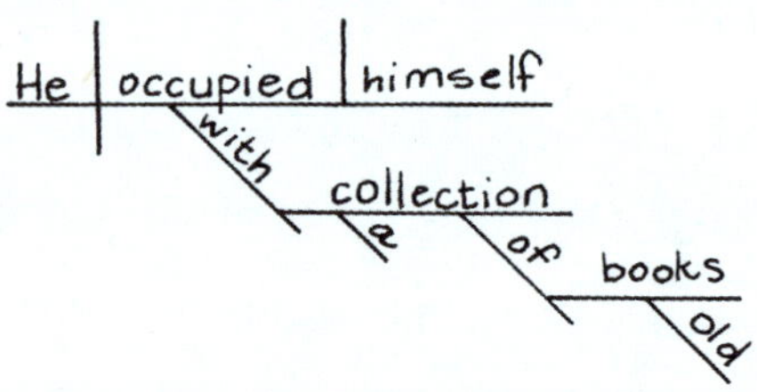

The three inner satellites are themselves eclipsed by the shadow of Jupiter.

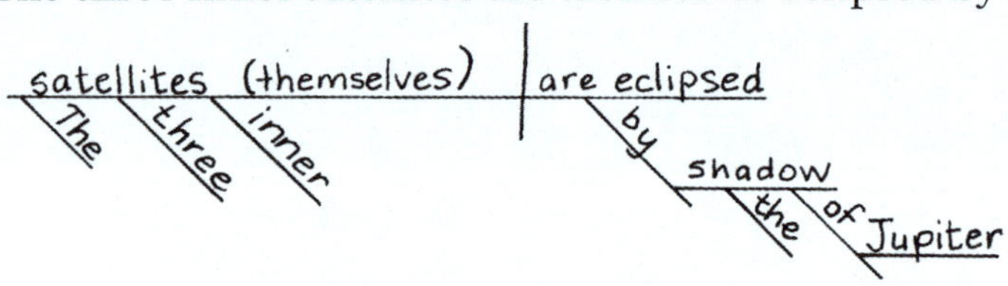

A new problem now presented itself to the scientist.

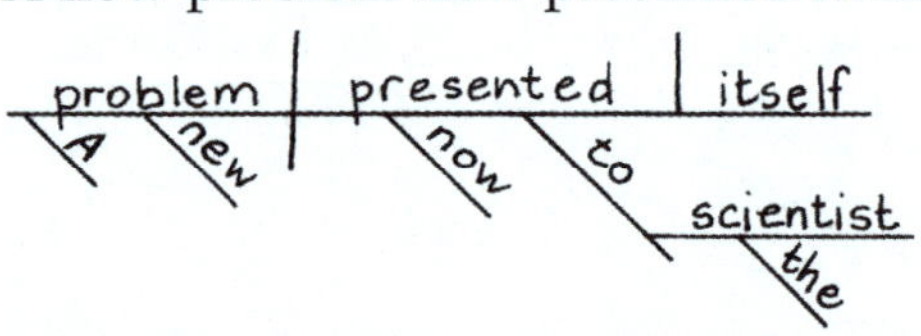

The power of the earth draws the moon to itself.

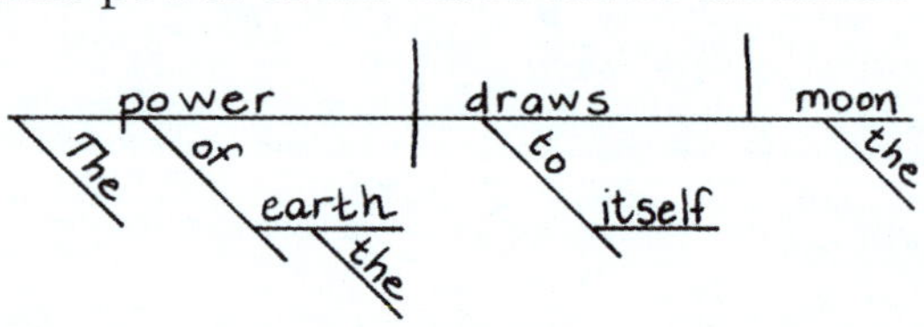

— LESSON 58 —

Demonstrative Pronouns
Demonstrative Adjectives

Exercise 58A: Demonstrative Pronouns and Demonstrative Adjectives

In the sentences below, label every occurrence of *this, that, these* and *those* as either *DP* (for demonstrative pronoun) or *DA* (for demonstrative adjective). Draw an arrow from each demonstrative adjective to the noun it modifies. Label each demonstrative pronoun as *S* (subject), *DO* (direct object), *IO* (indirect object) or *OP* (object of the preposition).

These sentences are slightly adapted from *The Civil Rights Movement*, by Elizabeth Sirimarco (Marshall Cavendish, 2005).

DA
The driver asked us to stand up and let him have those seats.

DP S
Medgar Evers was effective, and that made him a target of hate.

DA
This leaking old wreck of a shanty must be nearly half a century old.

DA DA
"This time, on this issue," said Johnson, "there must be no hesitation and no compromise with our purpose."

DP S
That finally brought a reaction from a police officer.

DA
"I quit being white, and free, and an American citizen when I climbed aboard that Jim Crow coach," wrote Sprigle.

DP OP
All of this is on account of us wanting to register.

DA
These strong feelings gave rise to the Black Power movement.

DP S
She was apparently calm, but those of us who knew her were aware of the great perturbation beneath her serene exterior.

DP DO
The leaders passed these on to the followers.

DP S
Yes, this is the United States, I thought to myself.

DA
We will achieve these goals because most Americans are law-abiding citizens.

DA
It was during those days that the sonnet "If We Must Die" exploded out of me.

And he said, "Well, if you don't stand up, I'm going to call the police and have you arrested."

DP DO
I said, "You may do that."

DP OP
Segregation was legal as long as blacks were provided with facilities "equal" to those of whites.

Exercise 58B: Demonstrative Pronouns

In the blank beneath each sentence, write a possible description of the thing or person that the underlined demonstrative pronoun stands for. Make sure to choose the correct number. (And use your imagination.)

Note to Instructor: Any answers of the correct number are acceptable.

That is completely disgusting.
[Answer should be singular, e.g., The rat sunning himself in the middle of my kitchen floor]

Those are my very favorites.
[Answer should be plural, e.g., The jam-filled doughnuts sprinkled with sugar]

This really hurts.
[Answer should be singular, e.g., Pulling out nose hairs]

These smell horrible.
[Answer should be plural, e.g., The fourteen rotten eggs in the nest]

Exercise 58C: Diagramming

On your own paper, diagram every word in the following three sentences.

There must be no hesitation and no compromise with our purpose.

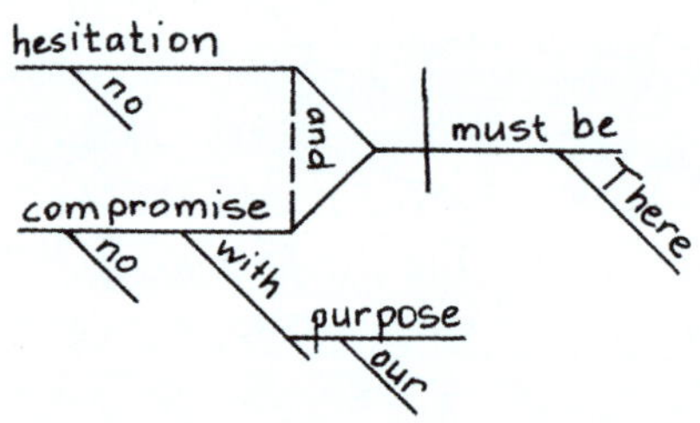

During those days, the sonnet itself exploded out of me.

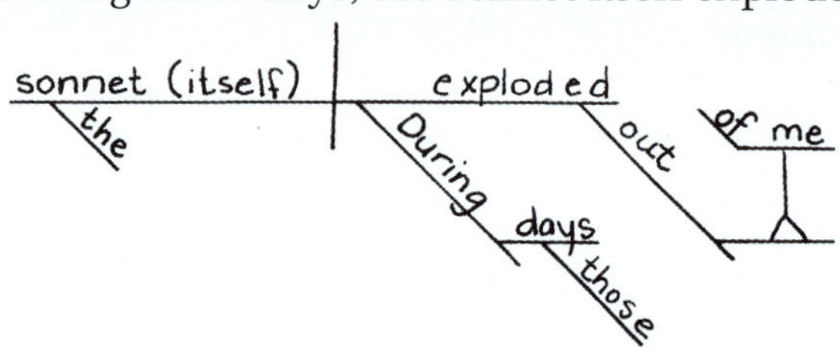

All of this is on account of us.

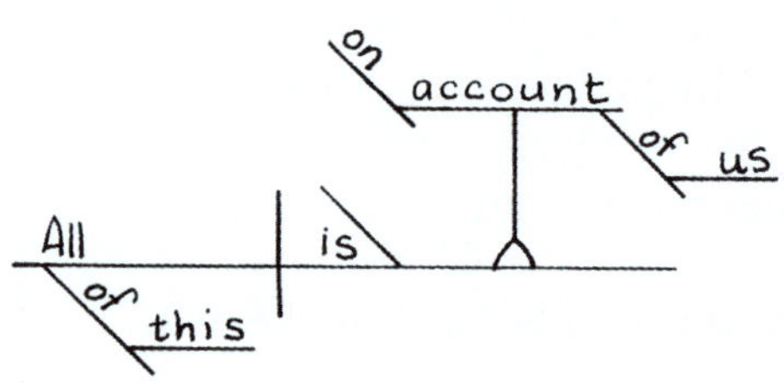

— LESSON 59 —

Demonstrative Pronouns
Demonstrative Adjectives
Interrogative Pronouns
Interrogative Adjectives

Exercise 59A: Identifying Demonstrative and Interrogative Pronouns

Underline all of the demonstrative and interrogative pronouns in the sentences. There may be more than one in each sentence.

This was lucky; he was about to begin to groan, as a "starter," as he called it, when it occurred to him . . . his aunt would pull it out, and that would hurt.

"Look here, Joe Harper, whose is that tick?"

This restored her and she said: "Tom, what a turn you did give me. Now you shut up . . . and climb out of this." ___

Who comes here into Sherwood Forest without my pass?

"Which of us does he mean?" gasped Huckleberry.

"What's the row there? Who's banging? What do you want?"

— Mark Twain, *The Adventures of Tom Sawyer*

This meant . . . some ships fought in the battle for a much longer time than others.

— Roy Adkins, Nelson's *Trafalgar: The Battle That Changed the World*

On entering the huts they found two large parrots (*guacamayos*) entirely different from those seen until then by the Spaniards.

— R.A. Van Middledyk, *The History of Puerto Rico: From the Spanish Discovery to the American Occupation*

Exercise 59B: Using Interrogative and Demonstrative Pronouns Correctly

Choose the correct word in parentheses. Cross out the incorrect word.

(~~Whose~~/ Who's) going to the concert in the park tonight?

(Who / ~~What~~) is the lead singer for the band tonight?

(Who / ~~Whom~~) is that lovely girl in the yellow dress?

(This / ~~These~~) is Marcela's favorite music.

(Whose / ~~Who's~~) are these purple dancing shoes?

(These/~~Those~~) are my dance shoes right here, so (~~those~~/those) must be Keith's shoes over there.
(~~Who~~/Whom) did she ask to dance?
(Who's/~~Whose~~) dancing with Marcela now?
(~~Who~~/Whom) did you invite to dinner?
(This/~~These~~) has been a lovely evening.
(Who/~~Whom~~) is organizing the event next week?
With (~~who~~/whom) will you get a ride home?

Exercise 59C: Diagramming Interrogative and Demonstrative Pronouns

On your own paper, diagram the following sentences.

Whose are these lovely mittens?

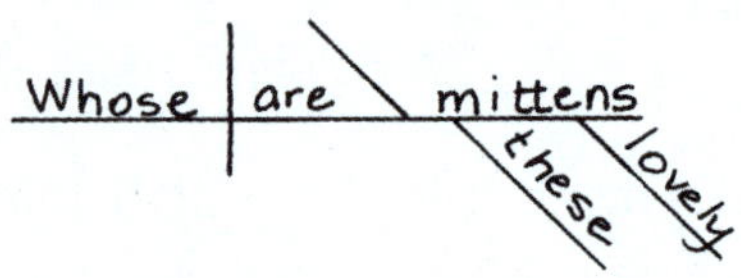

He did what?

They talked lazily of this and that.

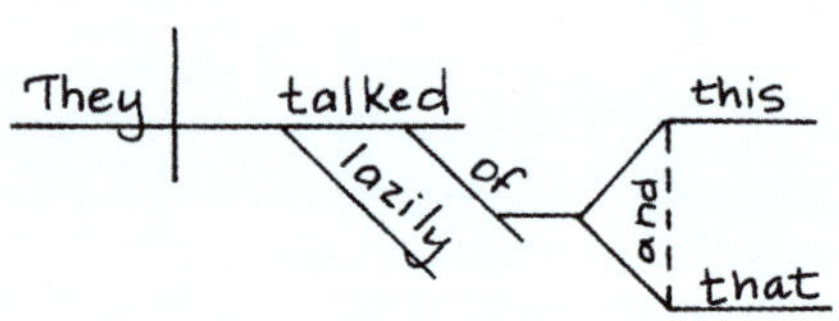

Who brought this?

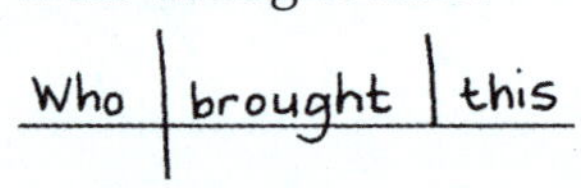

For whom was the letter intended?

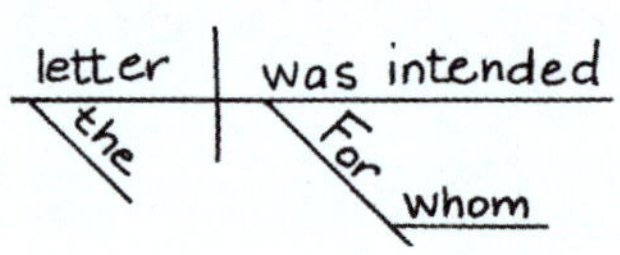

Which is the best road to San Diego?

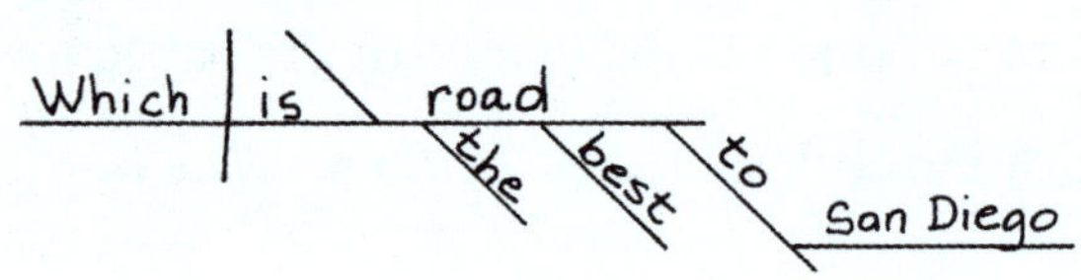

You must try this cheesecake and those truffles!

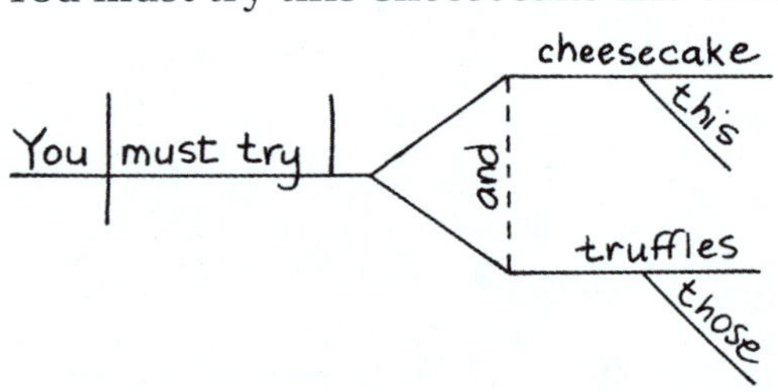

— LESSON 60 —

Pronoun Review

Sentences Beginning with Adverbs

Exercise 60A: Singular/Plural Indefinite Pronouns

Cross out the incorrect verb in each sentence.

All of the family (~~were~~/was) at the ball.

[The family is acting as a single unit.]

None of us (are/~~is~~) able to help our nature.

[There is more than one person who cannot help.]

Some of the gentlemen (were/~~was~~) gone to the stables.

[More than one gentleman went to the stable.]

(~~Are~~/Is) any of the pie left?

[There is only one pie.]

Most of the books (were/~~was~~) locked up behind glass doors.

[There is more than one book.]

Exercise 60B: Interrogatives and Demonstratives

In each of the following sentences, underline the interrogatives and demonstratives. If they are acting as adjectives, draw a line from each to the noun it modifies. If they are acting as other parts of the sentence, label them (*S* for subject, *DO* for direct object, *IO* for indirect object, or *OP* for object of the preposition).

These sentences are taken from a 19th-century fairy tale called "The Peasant and His Son."

Oho, my friend, <u>what</u> (S) is the meaning of <u>this</u> (OP)?

<u>These</u> (S) are most elaborate preparations.

I was in one of <u>those</u> three eggs. [those → eggs]

<u>Who</u> (S) took away your father's cow?

You will find <u>that</u> (DO) out in the evening, perhaps.

And you will expose yourself to <u>this</u> danger? [this → danger]

<u>This</u> (S) is a very strange proceeding!

<u>Whose</u> daughter is she? [Whose → daughter]

His feelings were wounded by <u>these</u> words.

Exercise 60C: Diagramming Practice

On your own paper, diagram every word of the following sentences, adapted from Charlotte Bronte's *Jane Eyre.*

The cold winter wind had brought with it somber clouds and a chilly rain.

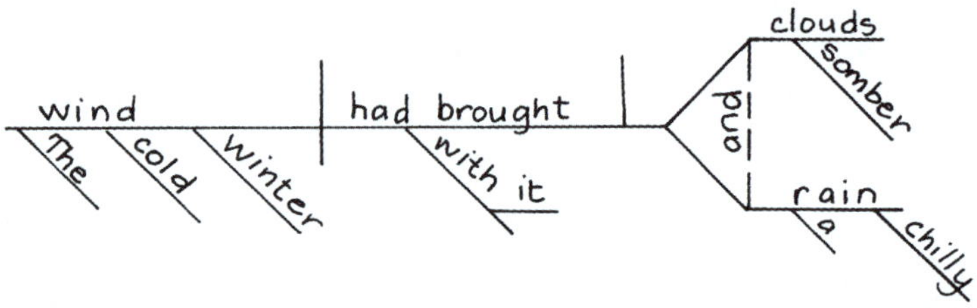

Where are my powers for this dread undertaking?

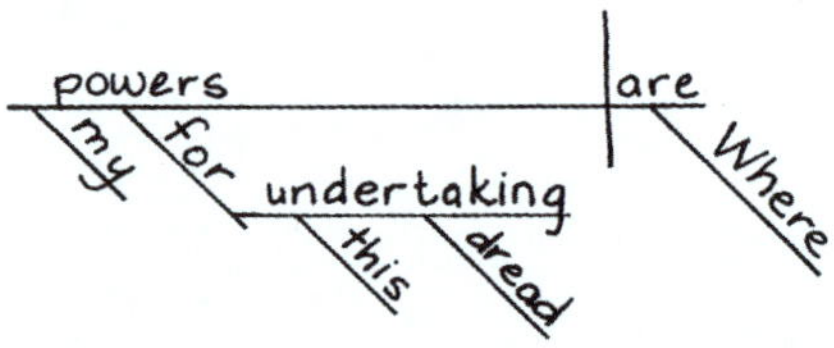

Dreadful to me was the return from the walk with nipped fingers and toes.

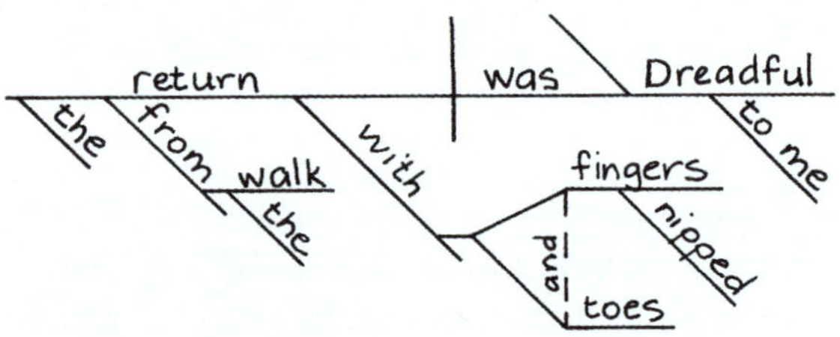

Note to Instructor: You may need to explain that *dreadful* cannot be the subject of the sentence because it is an adjective. *Return,* the noun, is the subject, and *dreadful* is the predicate adjective. This is called "inverted order." *To me* is a prepositional phrase acting as an adverb and modifying the adjective *dreadful.* It answers the question *how. From the walk* and *with nipped fingers and toes* both answer the question *which return.* (The return from the walk and the return with nipped fingers and toes!)

There were the two wings of the building, the garden, and the hilly horizon.

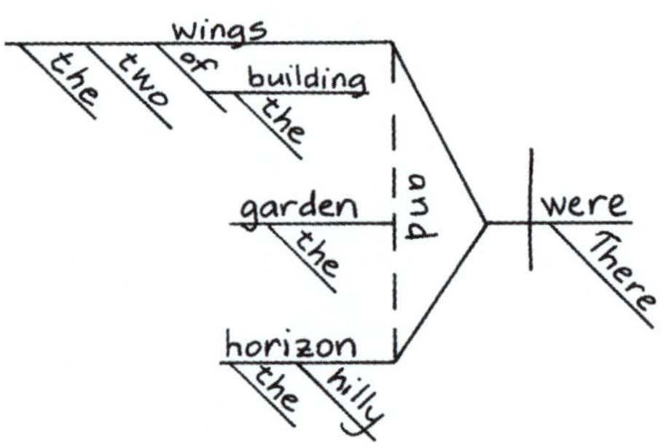

— REVIEW 5 —

Weeks 13-15

Topics
Pronouns and Antecedents
Possessive Pronouns
Subject and Object Pronouns
Indefinite Pronouns (and Subject-Verb Agreement)
Troublesome Verbs
Active and Passive Voice
Conjugating Passive Voice
Intensive and Reflexive Pronouns
Demonstrative and Interrogative Pronouns

Review 5A: Types of Pronouns

Put each pronoun in the word bank into the correct category of pronoun.

this themselves mine me some which whom
those few itself our they us anyone
its ourselves whose she I that him

Personal Subject	she	they	I
Personal Object	me	us	him
Personal Possessive	mine	our	its
Indefinite	some	anyone	few
Demonstrative	this	those	that
Interrogative	whom	which	whose
Intensive/Reflexive	themselves	itself	ourselves

Review 5B: Using Correct Pronouns

Cross out the incorrect pronoun in parentheses.

(~~Whose~~/Who's) coming with Nettie and (~~I~~/me) to the market?
(Whose/~~Who's~~) car will we use to get (there/~~their~~)?
The first person to arrive was (he/~~him~~).
Gena, Kayleigh, and (she/~~her~~) are arguing about (~~whose~~/who's) the best at grammar.
(There/~~their~~) was a fire near (~~there~~/their) house, and (~~their~~/they're) worried for (their/~~they're~~) neighbors.

(Who / ~~Whom~~) is the boy that hurt (himself/ ~~hisself~~) this morning?

Christie and (I/ ~~myself~~) would prefer to build the fort by (~~ourself~~/ ourselves).

(~~Who~~/ Whom) are (they / ~~them~~) speaking with?

The last two people on the train were Buford and (she / ~~her~~).

Candace and (he / ~~him~~) are sitting next to (~~who~~/ whom)?

Review 5C: Pronouns and Antecedents

Circle the NINE personal pronouns (subject, object, and possessive) in the following excerpt from *Tuck Everlasting*, by Natalie Babbitt. Draw arrows to each pronoun's antecedent.

One pronoun does not have a written antecedent. Can you guess why?

One day at that time, not so very long ago, three things happened and at first there appeared to be no connection between (them).

At dawn, Mae Tuck set out on (her) horse for the wood at the edge of the village of Treegap. (She) was going there, as (she) did once every ten years, to meet (her) two sons, Miles and Jesse.

At noontime, Winnie Foster, whose family owned the Treegap wood, lost (her) patience at last and decided to think about running away.

And at sunset a stranger appeared at the Fosters' gate. (He) was looking for someone, but (he) didn't say who.

No connection, (you) would agree. But things can come together in strange ways.

Pronoun without a written antecedent: you (because *you* are the antecedent, and the author doesn't know who you are!)

Review 5D: Agreement with Indefinite Pronouns

Choose the correct word in parentheses to agree with the indefinite pronouns. Cross out the incorrect word.

(~~Is~~/ Are) all of these books required reading for the summertime?

Some of these shirts (~~is~~/ are) still wrinkled.

Has anyone left (her / ~~their~~) necklace here on the chair?

No one here (knows / ~~know~~) how to soft-boil an egg.

Both (~~was~~/ were) late to the meeting because of the power outage.

(Has / ~~Have~~) all of the milk been drunk?

(Is / ~~Are~~) someone picking up some more milk on (his / ~~their~~) way home?

Most of the audience (was / ~~were~~) clapping enthusiastically.

Many (~~is~~/ are) called, but few (~~is~~/ are) chosen. —Matthew 22:14

Review 5E: Distinguishing Between Active and Passive Voice

Identify each sentence as *A* for active voice or *P* for passive voice. The verbs are underlined for you.

These sentences were adapted from *Walking the Appalachian Trail*, by Larry Luxenberg (Stackpole Books, 1994), an account of hiking the Appalachian Trail ("A.T."), a 2,147-mile-long trail along the eastern coast of the United States.

Each year as many as two thousand people start out to hike the whole A.T. A

Hikers are well advised to camp at or near the first four shelters along the trail. P

Ranger training includes frequent night patrols. A

Hikers can also be assured that what these Rangers go through in their seventeen-day stint in these mountains is infinitely more difficult than the thru-hikers' transit. P

Jeff is renowned on the A.T. for examining hikers' packs. P

Tourists can still pan for gold in the area. A

The name Dahlonega is said to be the Cherokee name for "precious yellow or gold." P

Springer Mountain is revered among hikers for its prominent role on the A.T. P

Because of the high winds, Robie jumped two miles upwind of Springer. A

His canopy was caught in two trees. P

Review 5F: Troublesome Verbs

Circle the correct verb form in parentheses. Cross out the incorrect form.

These sentences were taken from *The Dollmaker*, by Harriette Arnow (Simon & Schuster, 1983), the story of a mother raising her family in rural Appalachia.

She waited, calling to him with her eyes, but he never (raised/~~rose~~) his head.

She had (~~laid~~/lain) there in her bed and heard it and felt alone in the hearing.

Black coal smoke (~~raised~~/rose) from the post-office chimney.

Last night's thin snow still (lay/~~laid~~) in the cup-like hollows of the leaves.

Enoch, the nine-year-old, (sat/~~set~~) stiff and straight on the chair like a boy.

Gertie hesitated. She seldom (let/~~left~~) Cassie go visiting alone.

She pressed Cassie's face close against her coat, (~~lay~~/laid) her hands on her scarf-wrapped ears, all the while conscious of the watching, listening children.

Mrs. Hull took the lamp from the mail shelf and (~~sat~~/set) it on the meat counter.

He went into the main room to put on the clean overalls she had (~~lay~~/laid) out on the rocking chair.

Gertie watched a little saucer fall from a corner of the flimsy crumpling box and (~~lay~~/lie), a bright spot of red in the snow.

WEEK 16

Imposters

— LESSON 61 —

Progressive Tenses
Principal Parts
Past Participles as Adjectives
Present Participles as Adjectives

Exercise 61A: Identifying Past Participles Used as Adjectives

Underline the past participles used as adjectives in the following sentences, taken from Jim Kjelgaard's classic novel *Big Red*. Draw a line from each past participle to the word modified.

Not long, just long enough to get a ripped foot or a slashed side before Danny could send home the shot that would kill the bear.

But all he saw was the plainly imprinted tale of how the red dog had come upon the bear.

He found the bear's trail in the scuffed leaves there.

But his tongue was a dry, twisted thing that clung to the roof of his mouth.

By a broken bramble, a bit of loosened shale, or an occasional paw print between the boulders, he worked out the direction that Old Majesty had taken.

Exercise 61B: Identifying Present Participles Used as Adjectives

Underline the present participles used as adjectives in the following sentences. Draw a line to the word modified.

The first four sentences are from *Big Red*; the last three are from Alma Payne Ralston's *Discoverer of the Unseen World.*

He had turned for the first time to face the pursuing dog.

Old Majesty had left his retreat by the beech tree, and with whipping front paws had tried to pin the red dog to the earth.

Old Majesty had climbed straight up the long, sloping nose of a hump-backed ridge and had run along its top.

He would come . . . with snapping jaws and slashing paws.

In reality the instrument was "a simple magnifying glass."

In the coming months, Galileo worked to create telescopes that were more and more powerful.

The telescope that Galileo created is known today as a refracting telescope.

Exercise 61C: Diagramming Participles Used as Adjectives

On your own paper, diagram the following sentences.

Whistling teakettles sound homey.

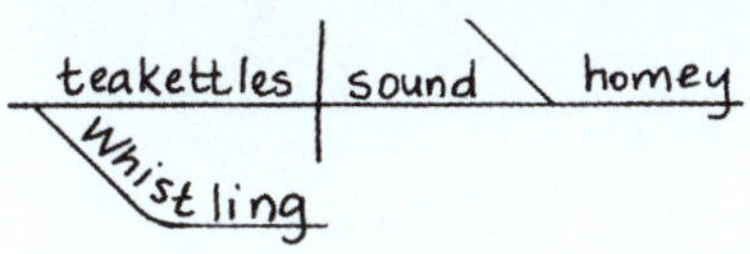

Boiling water steeps aromatic tea.

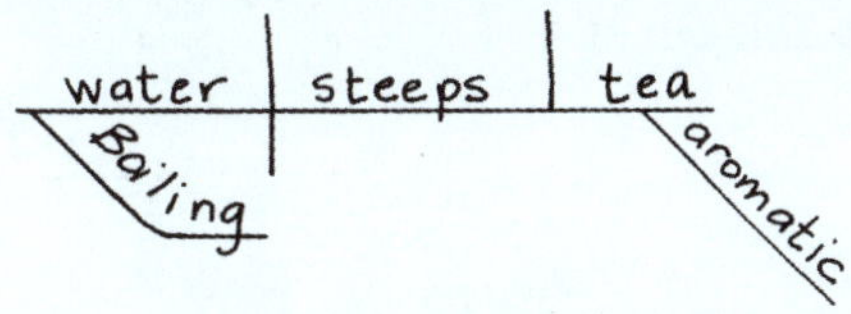

Chipped teacups leak.

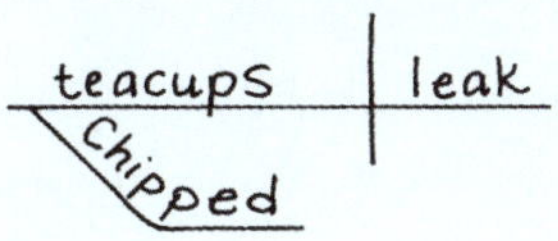

Steaming mugs warm frozen fingers.

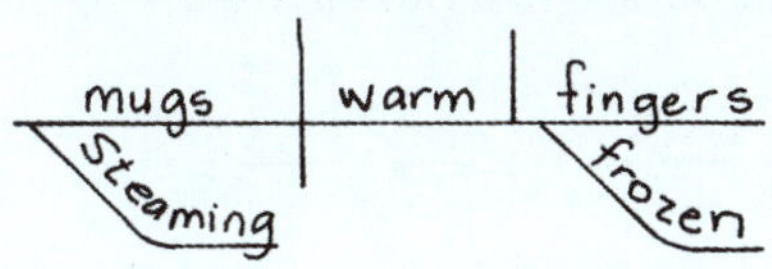

— LESSON 62 —

Parts of Speech and Parts of Sentences
Present Participles as Nouns (Gerunds)

Exercise 62A: Identifying Gerunds

In the following sentences, adapted from H. A. Guerber's *Myths of the Norsemen from the Eddas and Sagas*, underline each subject once and each predicate twice. Write *DO* above any direct objects, *IO* above any indirect objects, and OP above any objects of prepositions. Circle each gerund.

OP DO DO OP
The waving of Hrim's mane sent dew and frost to the earth.

DO OP
The Northmen feared the winter chilling of the earth.

DO OP
Dwarves spent their time in mining.

DO OP
Heimdall's trumpet announced the coming of the frost-giants.

IO DO
Odin offered the starving his own oxen.

Exercise 62B: Diagramming Gerunds

On your own paper, diagram every word in the following sentences.

Galloping exhausted the little mare.

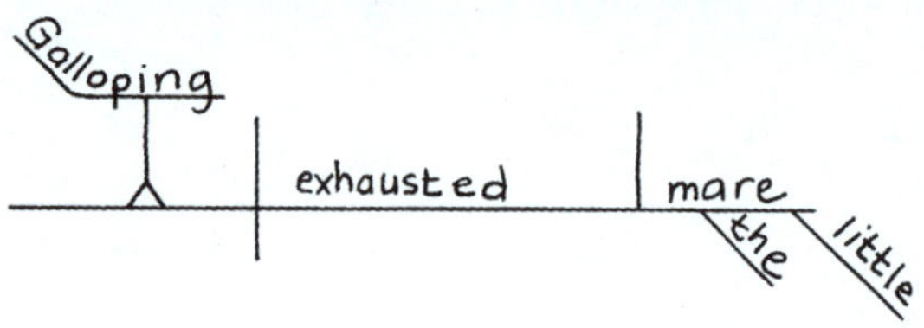

The Giant was tired of working.

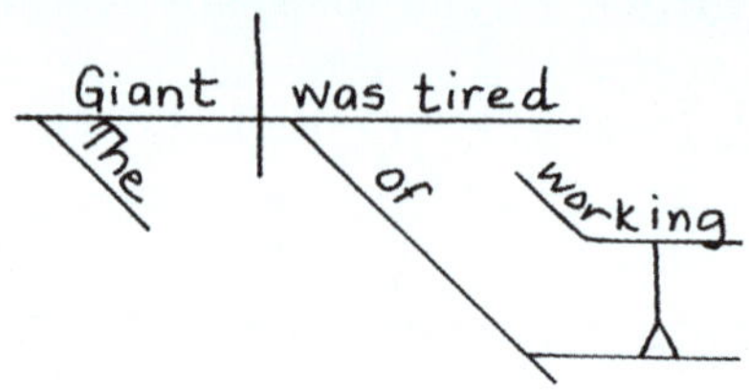

The great eagle's wings were flapping.

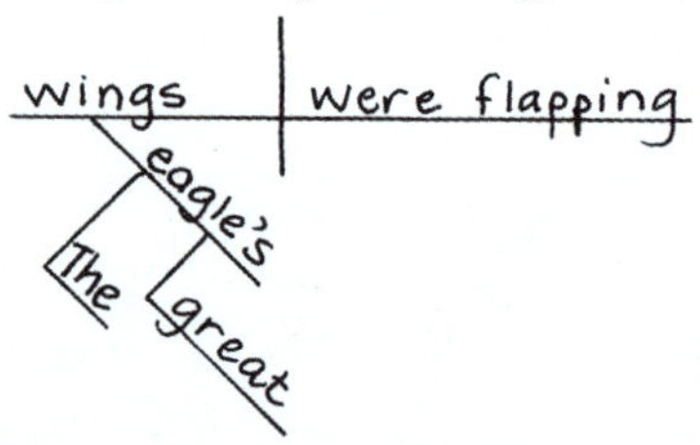

Loki heard flapping.

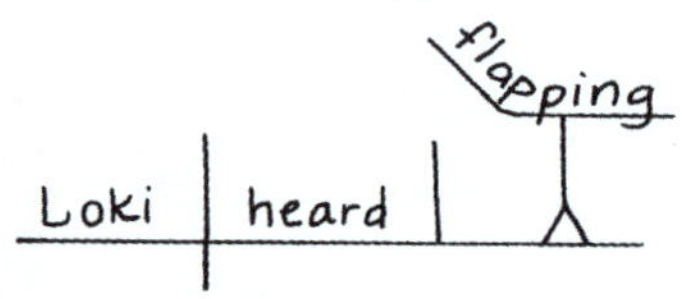

The cunning Ice Dwellers were planning an invasion.

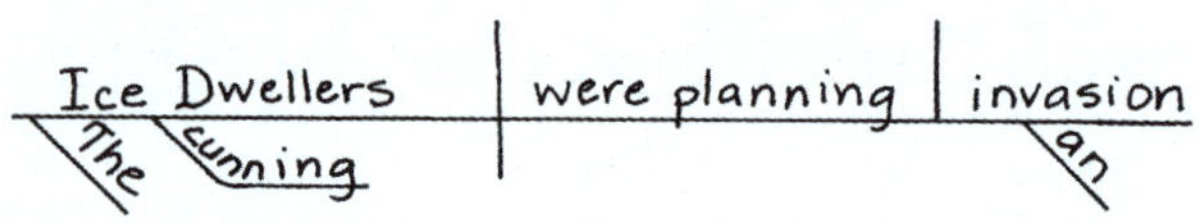

— LESSON 63 —

Gerunds
Present and Past Participles as Adjectives
Infinitives
Infinitives as Nouns

Exercise 63A: Identifying Gerunds and Infinitives

Underline the gerunds and infinitives in the following quotes. Identify the imposters as *G* for gerund or *I* for infinitive. Then, identify each gerund or infinitive as a subject (*S*), predicate nominative (*PN*), direct object (*DO*), or object of a preposition (*OP*).

I S (To give); I PN (to receive)
To give your best is to receive the best. —Raymond Holliwell

G S (Loving)
Loving is never a waste of time. —Astrid Alauda

I DO (to die); I DO (to conquer)
The old soldier did not fear to die; he hoped to conquer. —Alexandre Dumas

I S (To imagine); I S (To know)
To imagine is everything. To know is nothing at all. —Anatole France

It is not how much we do, but how much love we put in the doing [G OP]. It is not how much we give, but how much love we put in the giving [G OP]. –Mother Teresa

To judge [I S] another is to lose [I PN] an opportunity. –Unknown

I have never developed indigestion from eating [G OP] my words. —Winston Churchill

To be [I S] or not to be [I S] . . . is the question. —Shakespeare, *Hamlet*

I love eating [G DO], I love drinking [G DO], I love painting [G DO]. —Wang Meng

How many legs does a dog have if you call a tail a leg? Four. Calling [G S] a tail a leg doesn't make it a leg. —Abraham Lincoln

On all sides were heard rejoicing [G S] and congratulation. —Julius Caesar

Tracking [G S] over the boulders was painfully slow work. —Jim Kjelgaard, *Big Red*

There was one chance in fifty of killing [G OP] that huge bear with a single shot. —Jim Kjelgaard, *Big Red*

Exercise 63B: Diagramming Gerunds and Infinitives

On your own paper, diagram the following sentences.

To give is to receive.

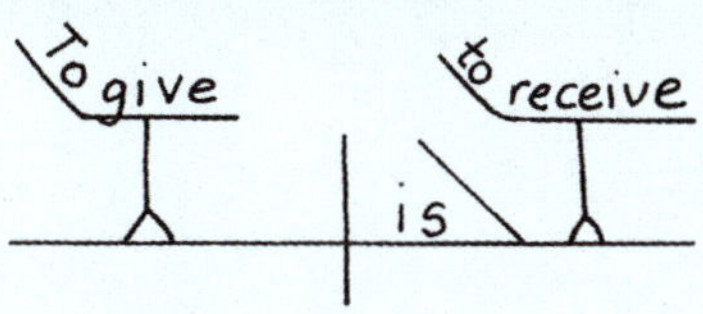

Loving is never a waste of time.

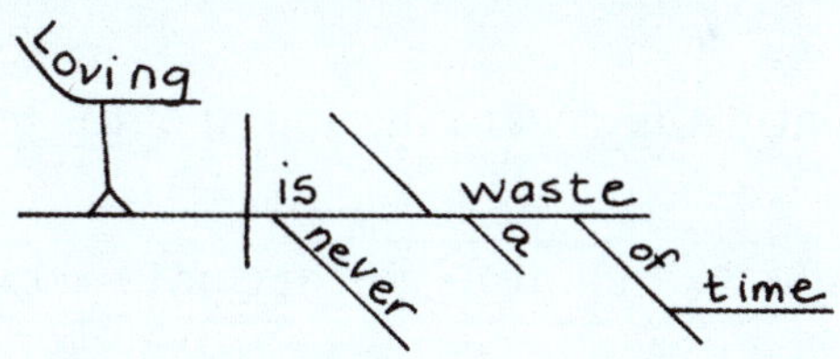

The old soldier did not fear to die.

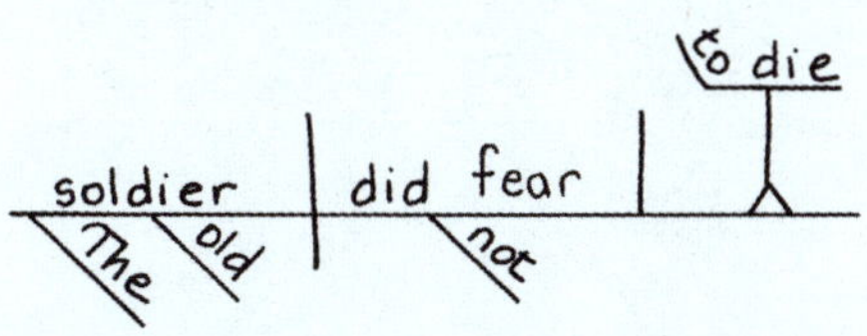

I love eating.

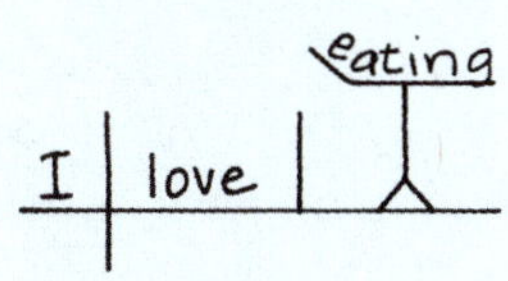

On all sides were heard rejoicing and congratulations.

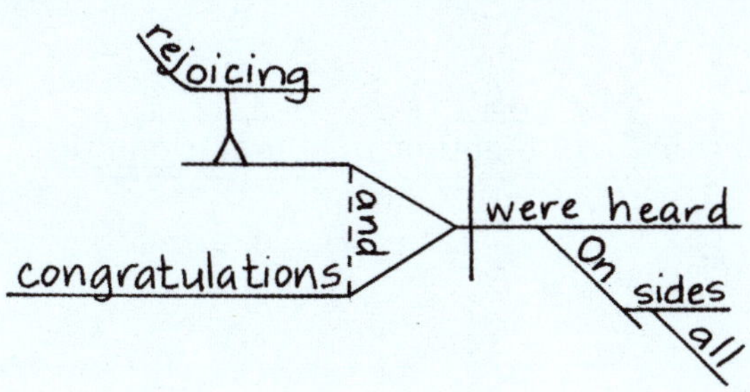

Tracking was painfully slow work.

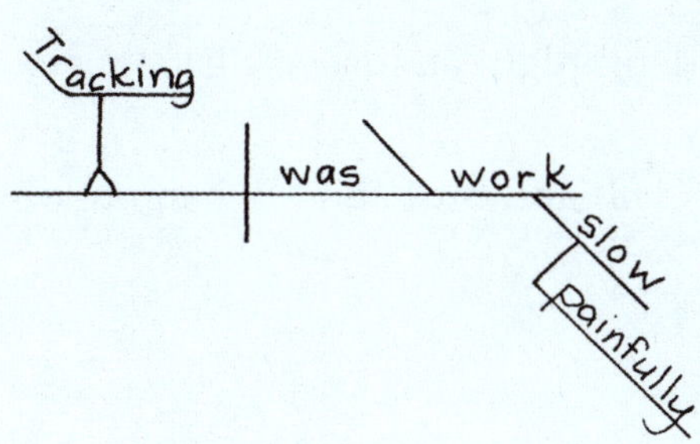

— LESSON 64 —

Gerunds
Present and Past Participles
Infinitives
Gerund, Participle, and Infinitive Phrases

Exercise 64A: Identifying Phrases That Serve as Parts of the Sentence

In the following sentences, begin by underlining each prepositional phrase.

Then, circle each group of words that contains a gerund, infinitive, present participle, or past participle. Each one serves as a part of the sentence. (Those circled phrases might include some of your prepositional phrases!) Label each circled phrase. Your options are as follows: *ADJ* (adjective), *ADV* (adverb), *S* (subject), *IO* (indirect object), *DO* (direct object), *OC* (object complement), *OP* (object of the preposition), *PN* (predicate nominative), or *PA* (predicate adjective).

These sentences are taken from *The Story of the Champions of the Round Table*, by Howard Pyle.

ADJ [modifies *terror*] ... ADJ [modifies *flame*]

With terror (growing greater in his heart,) he saw the flame of fire (consuming the town and the castle.)

ADV [modifies *sat*]

Meanwhile, Queen Helen and Folio sat together (waiting for him to return).

Note to Instructor: It is also acceptable for the student to put one circle around *waiting for him* and the other around *to return. Waiting* modifies *sat together* and *to return* modifies *him.*

ADJ [modifies *hooves*]

Presently, they heard the sound of his horse's hooves (coming down that rocky path.)

PA (or PN) [modifies *I*]

I was (to wait for arms and armor to aid me).

Note to Instructor: The student may circle the entire phrase as indicated, or may use two circles to separate out each infinitive phrase instead. If separate phrases are used, *to aid me* modifies *arms and armor.*

ADV [modifies *made*]

Thus Queen Helen found him, and (finding him) made no outcry of any kind.

PA

Were they not (broken of heart?)

ADJ [modifies *knight*]

(The fallen) knight embraced Sir Lancelot about the knees.

ADJ [modifies *permission*]

Sir Percival and Sir Lamorak had obtained permission (to ride forth together in companionship.)

Exercise 64B: Diagramming

On your own paper, diagram all of the sentences from Exercise 64A.

> **Note to Instructor:** Provide all necessary help. The student may need assistance deciding where modifying phrases go; remind her to use the adverb questions (*where, when, how, how often, to what extent*) and adjective questions (*which one, what kind, how many, whose*) about each phrase. You may also need to remind the student that verb forms acting as adjectives are simply diagrammed on a bent line beneath the word modified, while verb forms acting as nouns are diagrammed on a bent line placed on a tree in the correct diagram space.

With terror growing greater in his heart, he saw the flame of fire consuming the town and the castle.

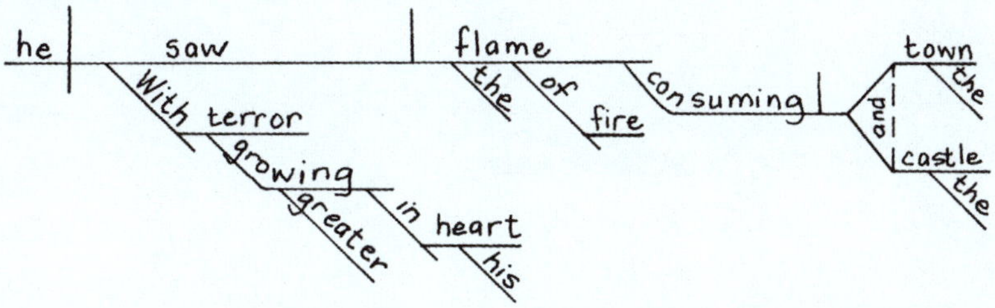

Meanwhile, Queen Helen and Folio sat together waiting for him to return.

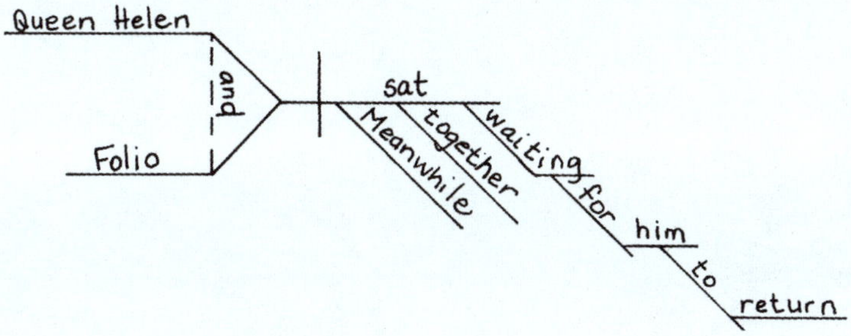

Presently, they heard the sound of his horse's hooves coming down that rocky path.

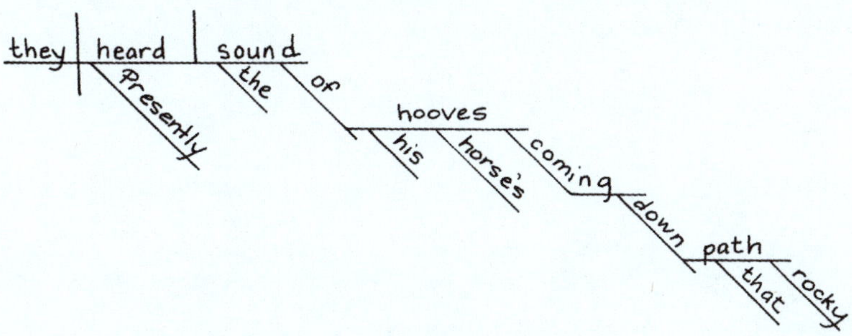

I was to wait for arms and armor to aid me.

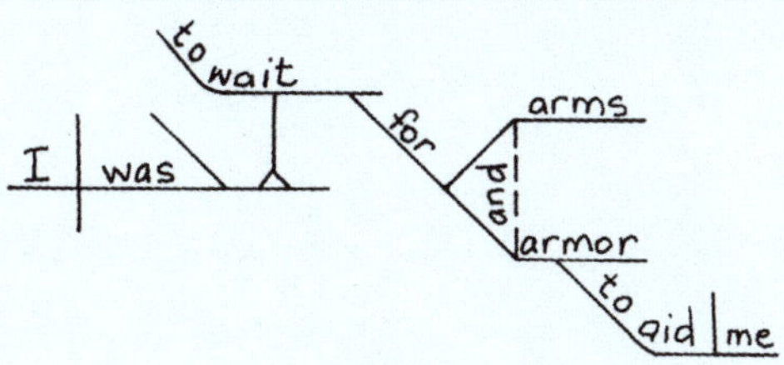

Thus Queen Helen found him, and finding him made no outcry of any kind.

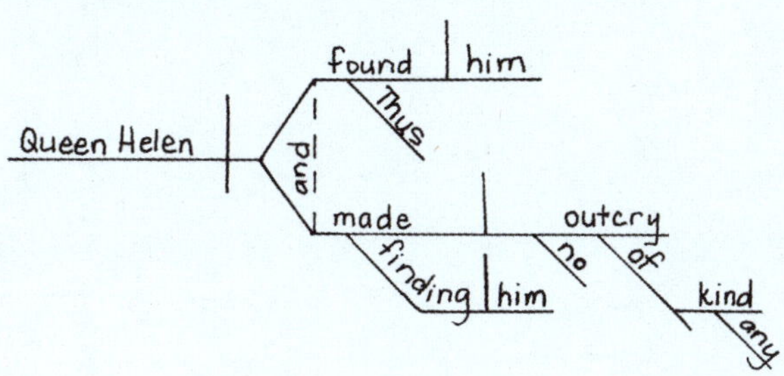

Were they not broken of heart?

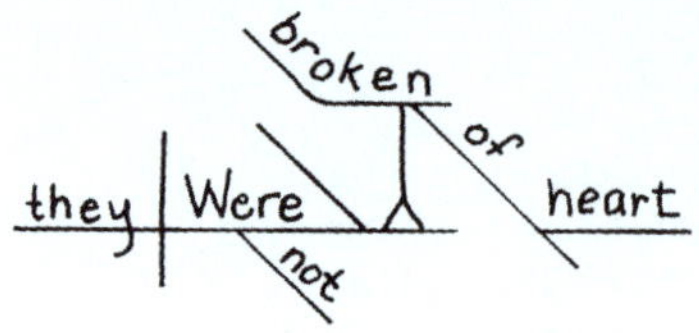

The fallen knight embraced Sir Lancelot about the knees.

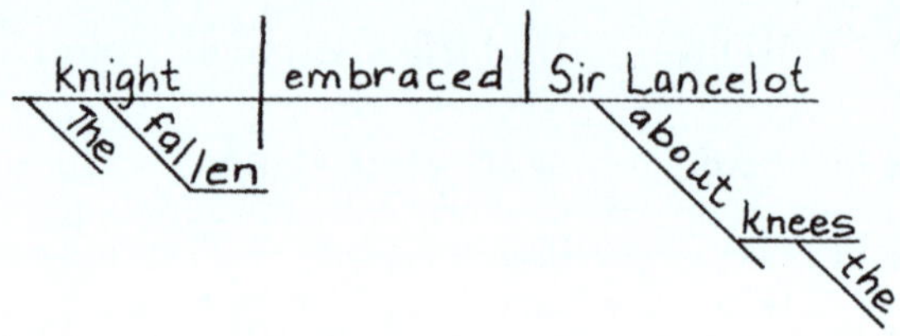

Sir Percival and Sir Lamorak had obtained permission to ride forth together in companionship.

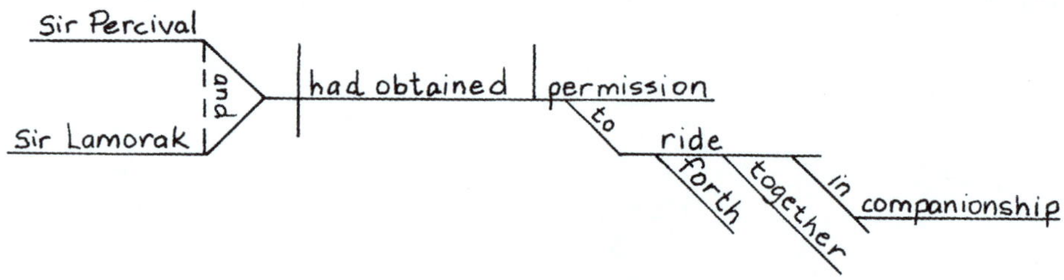

WEEK 17

Comparatives and Superlatives
Subordinating Conjunctions

— LESSON 65 —

Adjectives
Comparative and Superlative Adjectives

Exercise 65A: Identifying Positive, Comparative, and Superlative Adjectives

Identify the underlined adjective forms as *P* for positive, *C* for comparative, or *S* for superlative.

The first two sentences are from Matthew Pilkington's *A General Dictionary of Painters*; the third sentence is from Alison Weir's *The Six Wives of Henry VIII*; the last two sentences are from Albert Frederick Pollard's *Henry VIII*.

Jan Brueghel the Younger (C) would also become a painter.

One of their finest (S) joint performances was the picture of Adam and Eve in Paradise.

He was nearly forty-five now, growing bald (P), and running to fat . . . more egotistical (C), more sanctimonious (C), and more sure (C) of his own divinity, while still seeing himself as a paragon of courtly and athletic (P) knighthood.

His suspicion was aroused on the slightest (S) pretext.

He was beginning to look grey and old (P), and was growing daily more corpulent (C) and unwieldy.

Exercise 65B: Forming Comparative and Superlative Adjectives

Fill in the blank with the correct form of the adjective in parentheses. All of these comparisons will end in *-er* or *-est*.

Note to Instructor: If the student chooses the wrong form, remind him that the comparative compares *two* things, while the superlative compares *three or more* things.

This summer has been much hotter than last summer. (*hot*)

Grandpa says that this winter will be the snowiest winter that he has ever seen. (*snowy*)

Redwood trees are the tallest trees in the world. (*tall*)

The Redwood National Forest was even grander than I had imagined! (*grand*)

The Great Barrier Reef is the ___largest___ coral reef system in the world. (*large*)

The stout infantfish lives in the Great Barrier Reef and is the ___tiniest___ fish in the sea. (*tiny*)

Golden retriever dogs are much ___bigger___ and ___gentler___ than Chihuahuas. (*big, gentle*)

Golden retrievers may be the ___friendliest___ dogs in the world. (*friendly*)

Exercise 65C: Diagramming Comparative and Superlative Adjectives

On your own paper, diagram the following sentences. The first three sentences are from J. J. Scarisbrick's *Henry VIII.*

Note to Instructor: In the second and fourth sentences, *seemed* is acting as a linking verb.

Cromwell had been the most faithful servant.

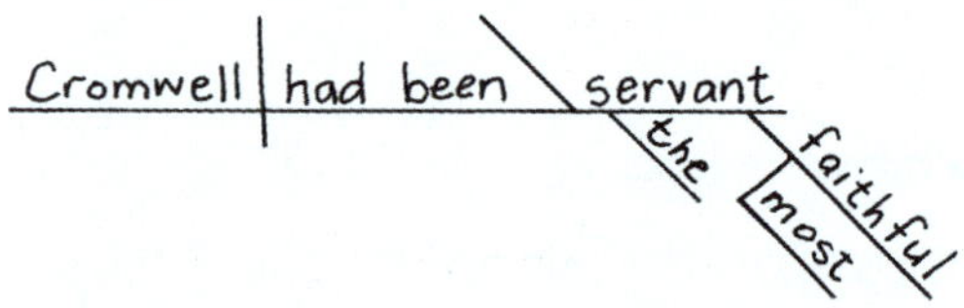

He seemed most assured and trustful.

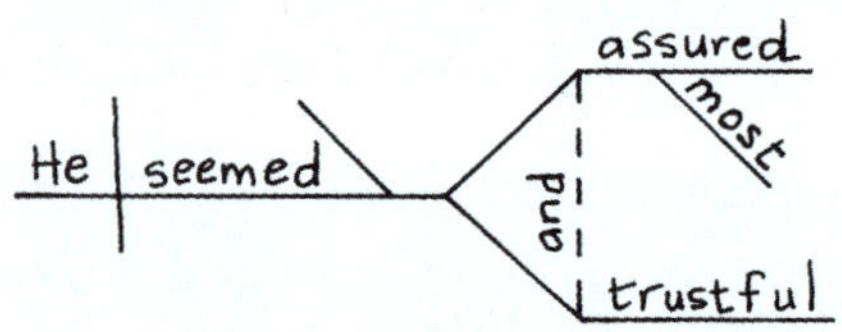

The smallest gesture could have opened the doors to forgiveness and reconciliation.

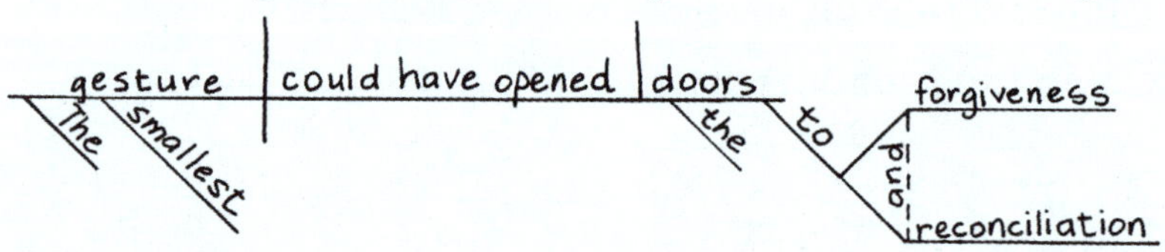

On this lovely autumn day, studying seemed most inappropriate.

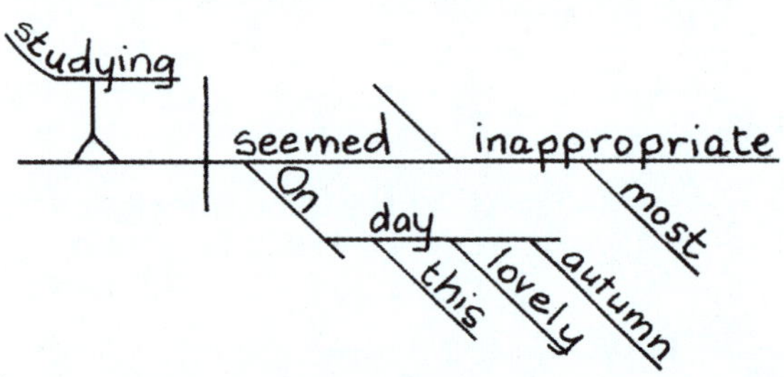

A more shocking discovery was around the corner.

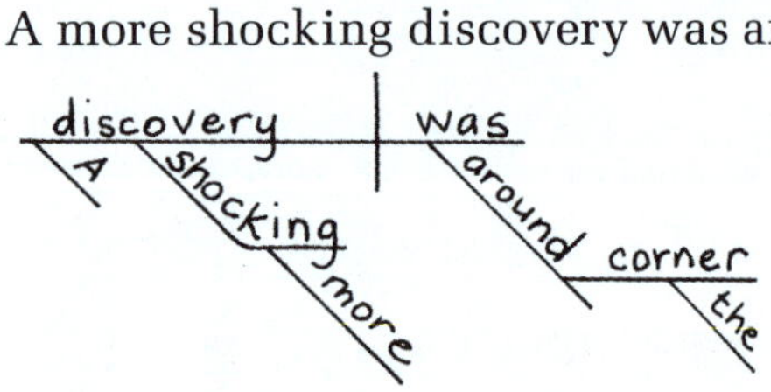

— LESSON 66 —

Adverbs
Comparative and Superlative Adverbs
Coordinating Conjunctions
Subordinating Conjunctions

Exercise 66A: Diagramming Comparatives

Diagram the first two sentences on the frames provided. Diagram the remaining sentences on your own paper.

The hare runs faster than the dog.

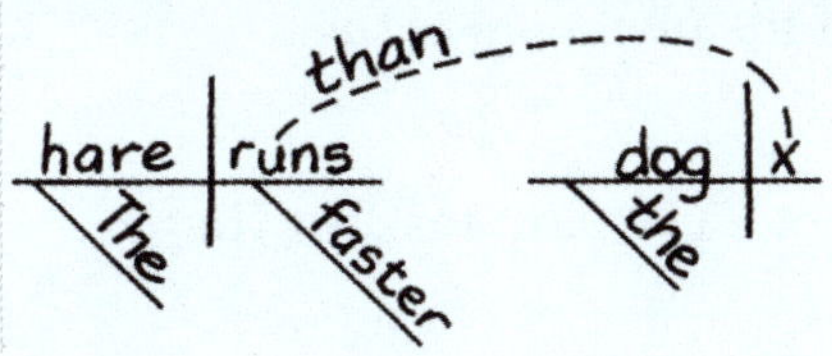

My right hand is working better than my left hand.

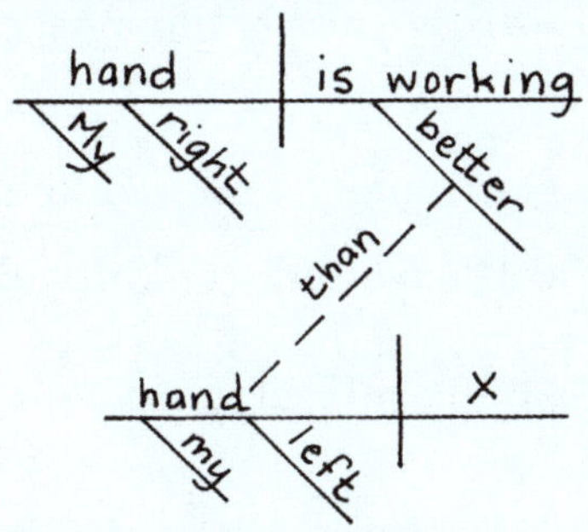

Today's movie is even sillier than yesterday's movie.

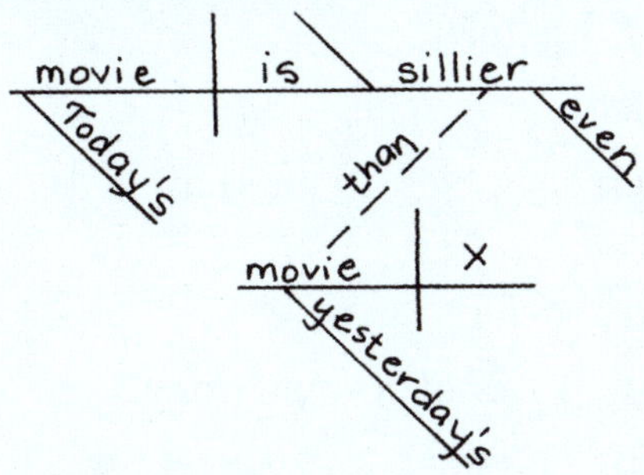

My brain thinks more slowly than yours does.

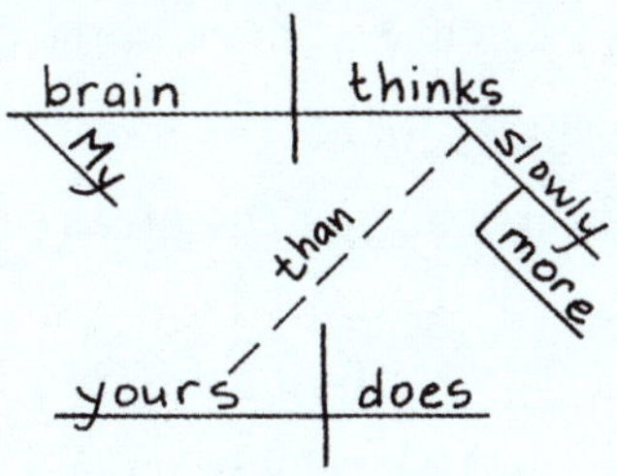

This cupcake is yummier than that one.

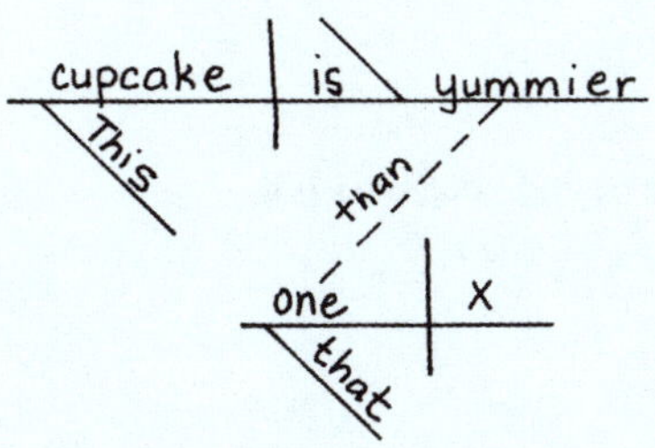

Exercise 66B: Identifying Positive, Comparative, and Superlative Adverbs

Identify the underlined adverb forms as *P* for positive, *C* for comparative, or *S* for superlative.

The first sentence is from Alan Schom's *Napoleon Bonaparte*; the last two sentences are from Alison Weir's *The Six Wives of Henry VIII.*

He rarely (P) moved, apart from his long bony hands.

If he walked any more slowly (C), he would have been standing still.

The child scooted closer (C) and clutched her hand more tightly (C).

His was the most grotesquely (S) twisted nose she had ever seen.

She played the most awkwardly (S) and yet the most skillfully (S) of any of the members of the tennis team.

Worse still, it oozed pus continually (P), and had to be dressed daily, not a pleasant task for the person assigned to do it as the wound stank dreadfully (P).

He would become increasingly (P) subject to savage and unreasonable rages.

Exercise 66C: Forming Comparative and Superlative Adverbs

Fill in the blank with the correct form of the adverb in parentheses.

Of all of the mountains in Africa, Mt. Kilimanjaro stands the tallest. (*tall*)

The cheetah runs the fastest of all the earth's land animals. (*fast*)

Courtney moved into the house across the street and now lives much closer to me than before. (*close*)

Freddy came to the party later than I did and left earlier. (*late, early*)

Tess can ride the roller coaster first; she has been waiting the longest of everyone. (*long*)

The birthday package arrived sooner than I had expected. (*soon*)

— LESSON 67 —

Irregular Comparative and Superlative Adjectives and Adverbs

Exercise 67A: Best and Worst Jobs

Put the following jobs in the column according to your opinion. (There are no *correct* answers—it all depends on you.)

There are no right/wrong answers!

Exercise 67B: Using Comparatives and Superlatives Correctly

Choose the correct form in parentheses. Cross out the incorrect form.

Maury eats (more wisely/~~wiser~~) than Frida.

Frida works (~~more hard~~/harder) than Maury does, so she fixes her meals (more quickly/~~quicker~~).

Buttons, their pet rabbit, probably eats the (most healthily/~~healthiest~~) of all.

When Frida eats lots of vegetables, she feels much (~~most cherrily~~/cheerier) and (~~more calmly~~ /calmer).

Frida sings "Happy Birthday" (more cheerily/~~cheerier~~) than Maury does.

> **Note to Instructor:** *Cheerily/most cheerily/most cheerily* is the adverb form (describing the verb *sings*). *Cheery/cheerier/cheeriest* is the adjective form (describing the pronoun *she*).

Frida goes jogging (more often/~~oftener~~) than Maury does.

Sometimes Maury goes jogging with Frida, but he jogs (more slowly/~~slower~~) than she does.

> **Note to Instructor:** *Slow/slower/slowest* is an adjective, not an adverb: *She is the slower runner of the two*, but *She runs more slowly*.

Frida doesn't mind. She is (~~more happy~~/happier) when she has company on her jogs.

Exercise 67C: Using Correct Comparative Forms of Modifiers

Choose the correct form in parentheses. Cross out the incorrect form. The last two sentences are from Albert Frederick Pollard's *Henry VIII.*

In a basketball game, the team that plays (~~best~~/better) wins.

Coach says that even if we play the (best/~~better~~) team in the league, we still have a chance.

If we play (harder/~~more harder~~) than they do and want to win (more/~~the most~~), then maybe we will beat them.

Sometimes even a very good team will play (worse/~~worst~~) than our team.

Today we will play against the Eagles. Compared to us, the Eagles have the (~~best~~/better) record.

They have (the most/~~more~~) wins in the entire league.

However, our record is not too much (~~more worse~~/worse) than theirs.

Let's play our (best/~~most best~~) game ever!

Vocal and instrumental pieces of his own composition, preserved among the manuscripts at the British Museum, rank among the (~~better~~/best) productions of the time.

His temper was getting (worse/~~worst~~).

Exercise 67D: Using Correct Adverbs and Adjectives

Choose the correct word in parentheses. Cross out the incorrect word.

The last sentence is from Isaac Newton Arnold's *The History of Abraham Lincoln, and the Overthrow of Slavery.*

I don't feel (~~good~~/well) today. I have a headache and a sore throat.

Ursula played so (~~good~~/well)! We would not have won the tournament without her.

The opponents did not play (~~bad~~/badly), but Ursula is extremely (good/~~well~~) at tennis.

Harriet smells (bad/~~badly~~). She should have showered!

Harriet smells (~~bad~~/badly). She can't tell if milk is sour by sniffing it.

Rattlesnakes taste (~~good~~/well). They have an organ called a Jacobson's organ that increases their sense of taste and smell.

Rattlesnakes taste (good/~~well~~). If you fry them, they taste just like chicken.

He analyzed (~~good~~/well); he saw and presented what lawyers call the very *gist* of every question.

— LESSON 68 —

Coordinating and Subordinating Conjunctions
Correlative Conjunctions

Exercise 68A: Coordinating and Subordinating Correlative Conjunctions

In each of the following sentences, circle the correlative conjunctions. Underline the words or groups of words that the conjunctions connect. In the blank, write *C* for coordinating or *S* for subordinating.

These sentences are adapted from Stanley A. Wolpert's *India*.

Note to Instructor: It is fine to accept underlined groups of words, even if the key underlines single words or smaller groups of words, as long as the underlined groups of words are connected by the conjunctions.

Devout Hindus (not only) wash themselves in the bubbling green of Varanasi water (but also) drink it. C

(If) we succumb, (then) we are done for. C

The immediate aftermath of that horrible war brought (neither) prosperity (nor) contentment. C

(Though) anathema to Muslims, (yet) pork is eaten by some Hindus (but not by others). S

Note to Instructor: *Anathema to Muslims* is a phrase while *pork is eaten . . .* is a sentence with subject and verb.

(Not only) time, (but) (both) river floods (and) monsoon rains have obscured ancient India's early millennia. C

Note to Instructor: This is a trick question—there are actually two sets of correlative conjunctions, *not only . . . but* and *both . . . and.* Both are coordinating because they all connect nouns (equal elements).

Most of the world had either begun to destroy nuclear-armed missiles or agreed to sign the test ban treaties. C

Although kept as traditional as possible, still British regiments were forced to adapt to some Bengali customs. S

> **Note to Instructor:** *Kept as traditional as possible* is a phrase while *British regiments were forced to adapt* . . . is a sentence with subject and verb.

All animals, both quadrupeds and birds, are larger than in other countries. C

Diwali generally falls either in our solar October or November. C

If the rains came late, then crows and other scavengers reaped the only harvest. C

Ingenious ancient Indian philosophers also reasoned that it was possible to feel both cold and hot upon entering the same room. C

Exercise 68B: Subject-Verb Agreement

Cross out the incorrect verb in each set of parentheses.

Not only the cat but also all of the dogs (~~is~~/ are) waiting by the rat's den.
Either the prince or his servants (~~is~~/ are) bringing the eighty pounds of mustard seed.
Both the tigers and the jackal (~~was~~/ were) lurking in the bushes.
Not only the little fishes but also the crab (was / ~~were~~) hiding beneath the lotus leaves.
Either the Raja's seven daughters or the Raja's wife (is / ~~are~~) preparing rice with care.
Neither the Fakir nor the dogs (~~was~~/ were) ever found.
Both the snake-king and the tiger-king (~~was~~/ were) sympathetic to the Brahman.
Neither the oats nor the ear of corn (was / ~~were~~) satisfying to the hungry horse.

Exercise 68C: Diagramming

On your own paper, diagram every word of the following sentences.

The King of Persia planned to destroy both him and his tribe.

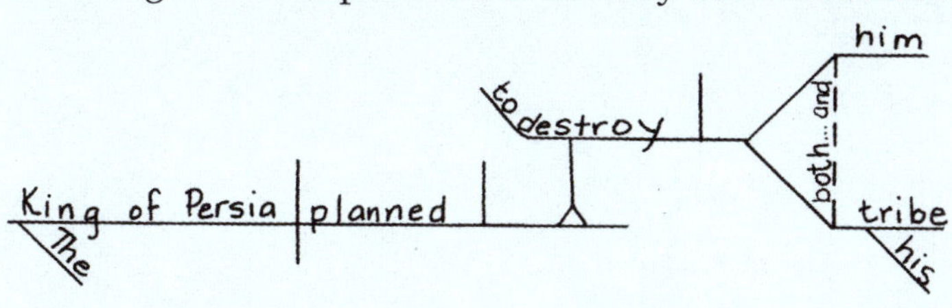

Neither wealth nor power does your slave desire!

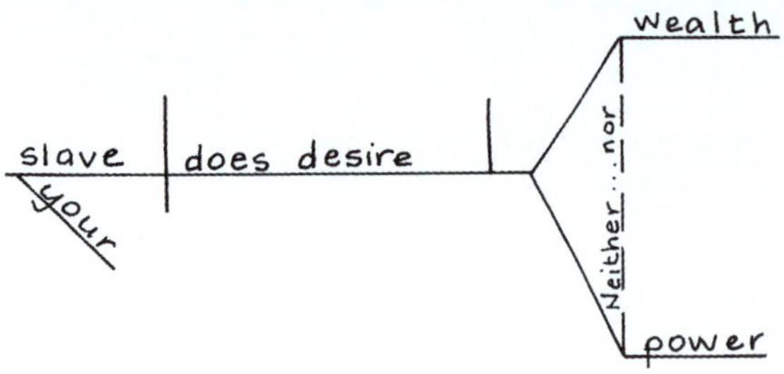

Either the new bride or the hospitable master of the house will welcome not only the expected guests but also the uninvited intruders.

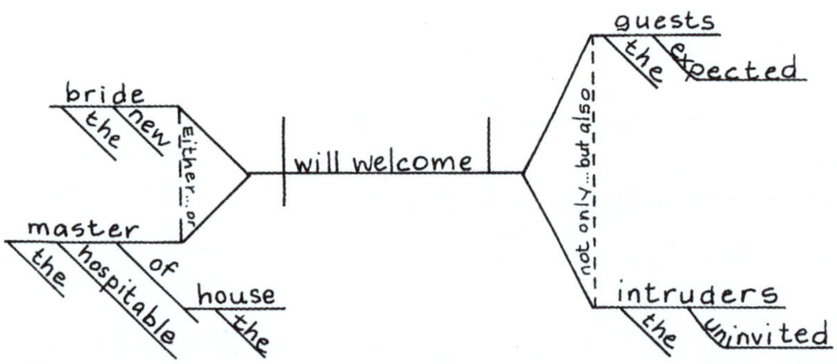

Both his wife and his brothers were delighted to see the coming of the dawn.

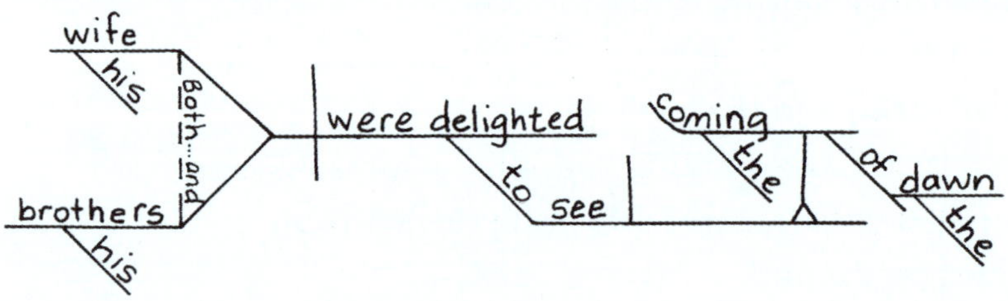

WEEK 18

Clauses

— LESSON 69 —

Phrases
Sentences
Introduction to Clauses

In the phrases and clauses below, the subjects are underlined once and the verbs twice for your reference

Behind the dusty wardrobe.	***phrase***	*no subject or verb*
Lucy opened the door.	***clause***	*subject and verb*
Leaping and bounding.	***phrase***	*two verbs, no subject*
They did not believe her.	***clause***	*subject and verb*
He tasted the delicious candy.	***clause***	*subject and verb*
Because he wanted more.	***clause***	*subject and verb*

(Although) Jamie didn't mean to eat the entire cake.	D
(Whether) they won or lost.	D
He picked up the pieces.	I
That milk is from Uncle Louie's cow.	I
(Since) she was already covered in mud.	D

Note to Instructor: Although the final clause does not have a stated subject, it is an imperative with an understood subject [you] that can stand on its own.

Exercise 69A: Distinguishing Between Phrases and Clauses

Identify the following groups of words as *phrases* or *clauses*. The clauses may be independent or dependent, but you only need to identify them as *clauses*. In each clause, underline the subject once and the verb twice.

Twisting and winding	phrase
The rooster fought the hen	clause
Because of the earthquake	phrase
Because the earthquake toppled a major building	clause
Macy was shocked	clause

Dribbling the basketball	phrase
Although eels and jellyfish are not	clause
It wasn't Brady's fault	clause
Through the bathrooms of the big bungalow	phrase
He was a mongoose	clause
Tickling under my chin	phrase

Exercise 69B: Distinguishing Between Independent and Dependent Clauses

Identify the following clauses as independent (*IND*) or dependent (*DEP*).

Unless he could clean his room in the next hour	DEP
He laid the bricks one by one	IND
As she munched chips on the train	DEP
Since the new baby was born	DEP
The balloon sailed high into the clouds	IND
If he hadn't heard the kitten mewing	DEP
It would have been awful	IND
Rikki-tikki-tavi tingled all over	IND
When morning came	DEP
Though Rikki-tikki-tavi had never met a live cobra before	DEP

Exercise 69C: Turning Dependent Clauses into Complete Sentences

Choose three of the dependent clauses in Exercise 69B and add independent clauses to them to form complete, complex thoughts. Write your three new sentences on your own paper. (The dependent clause can go before or after the independent clause.)

Answers will vary. Sample answers might include the following:

Unless he could clean his room in the next hour, he wouldn't be able to watch TV.

As she munched chips on the train, she watched the trees go by.

They have been very tired since the new baby was born.

If he hadn't heard the kitten mewing, he would have locked the door.

He got up when morning came.

Though Rikki-tikki-tavi had never met a live cobra before, he knew what to do.

— LESSON 70 —

Adjective Clauses
Relative Pronouns

Intro 70: Introduction to Adjective Clauses

Match the dependent clause on the right with the correct independent clause on the left. The first one has been done for you.

Beethoven, __A__, was deaf.	~~A.~~ who composed "Ode to Joy"
Many ships have sunk in the Bermuda Triangle, __E__.	B. that supposedly lives in the lakes of Scotland
Da Vinci, __D__, was a vegetarian.	C. whom many have called the greatest scientist of all time
Einstein, __C__, had speech problems as a child.	D. whose most famous painting is the *Mona Lisa*
Many people have reportedly seen the Loch Ness monster __B__.	E. which is a mysterious area in the Caribbean

Exercise 70A: Identifying Adjective Clauses and Relative Pronouns

Underline the adjective clauses in the following sentences, and circle the relative pronouns. Draw an arrow from each relative pronoun to its antecedent.

Many ships that sail between Europe and North America pass through the Bermuda Triangle.

Stories that tell of mysterious disturbances in the Triangle have frightened captains for years.

One captain, whose ship eventually sank in the Triangle, reported strange green waters.

Pilots who were flying over the Bermuda Triangle have also experienced trouble.

One possible explanation is unusual magnetic activity, which may cause compasses to malfunction.

The Gulf Stream, which is a strong ocean current, could also affect waters in the Triangle.

Other explanations that people have offered are less scientific.

Many superstitious sailors blame Atlantis, which is a mythical underwater city.

Exercise 70B: Choosing the Correct Relative Pronoun

In each sentence, cross out the incorrect relative pronoun. Above the correct pronoun, write *S* for subject, *OP* for object of the preposition, or *DO* for direct object to show how the relative pronoun is used within the dependent clause.

These sentences are adapted from classic Welsh fairy tales.

One day the queen's daughter, (who [S] / ~~whom~~) was now fifteen, decided to go and see the world.

She often visited the house of an old miser (who [S] / ~~whom~~) lived nearby.

She dressed the children (~~who~~ / whom [DO]) she did not like in rags.

One of them, (who [S] / ~~whom~~) seemed to be older than the rest, came up to him.

His favorite dog was a hound (who [S] / ~~whom~~) never missed his prey.

You have very bad neighbors, (~~who~~ / whom [DO]) I do not trust.

They returned to the king, (who [S] / ~~whom~~) at once sent forth his army.

He searched for the infant, about (~~who~~ / whom [OP]) he had had a vivid dream.

There was a lovely young woman (~~who~~ / whom [DO]) the fairies often visited.

Exercise 70C: Diagramming Adjective Clauses

On your own paper, diagram every word of the following sentences.

I am meeting Shirin, whose textbook I borrowed.

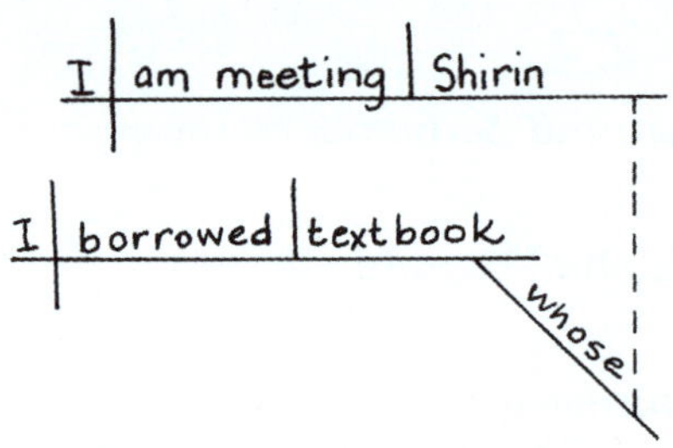

Thomas Jefferson, who was the third President of the United States, built the University of Virginia.

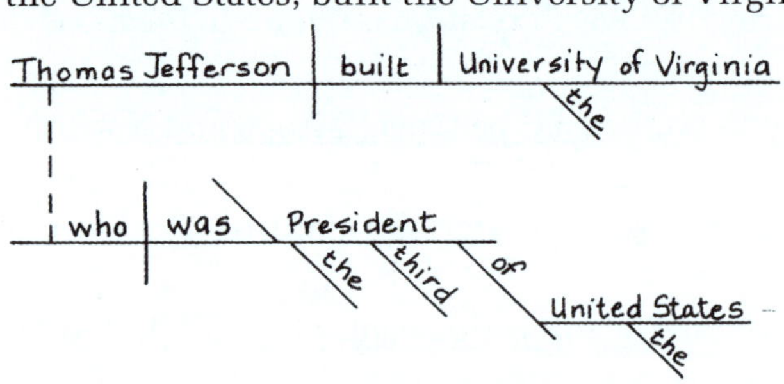

The first person that arrives will receive a free baseball.

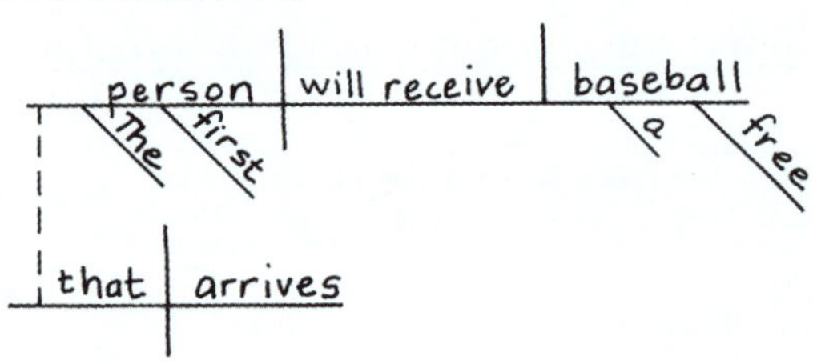

Horace ate the brownies that Mom had made for the picnic.

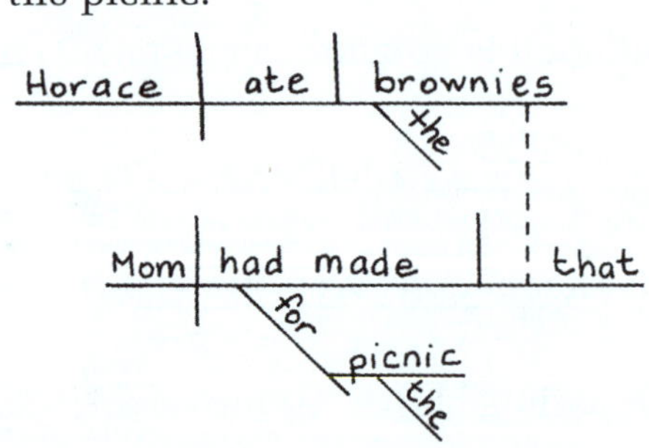

Ravi, whom I had given my number, called me this morning.

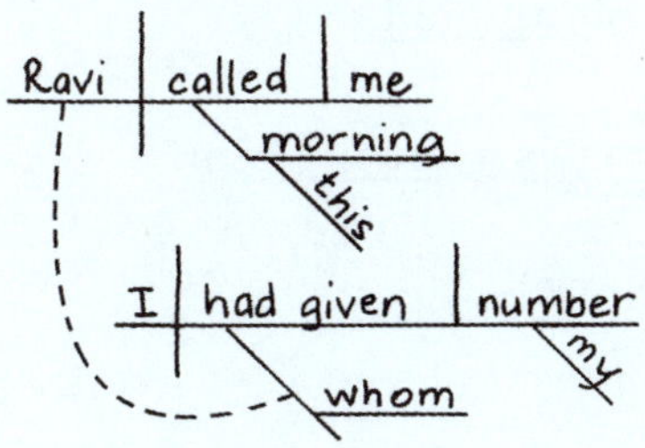

— LESSON 71 —

Adjective Clauses
Relative Adverbs
Adjective Clauses with Understood Relatives

Exercise 71A: Relative Adverbs and Pronouns

In the following sentences, underline each adjective clause. Circle each relative word and label it as *RP* for relative pronoun or *RA* for relative adverb. Draw an arrow from each relative word back to its antecedent in the independent clause.

These sentences are taken from Herman Melville's classic novel *Moby Dick*. Some have been slightly adapted or condensed.

He's the bird what (RP) catches the worm.

The sea is a green pasture where (RA) our children's grand-children will go for bread.

In the distance lay a ship whose (RP) furled sails conveyed a warning.

Nantucket was her great original, the Tyre of this Carthage, the place where (RA) the first dead American whale was stranded.

You look out a glass window where (RA) the frost is all on the outside.

Some few hands are called ship-keepers, whose (RP) province it is to work the vessel.

Father Mapple was in the hardy winter of an old age which (RP) was merging into a second flowering youth.

The ostensible reason why (RA) Ahab did not go on board was the coming storm.

The Guernsey-man, who (RP) had just got into the chains, had slung his nose in a sort of bag.

We should be furnished with the reason (why) his sense of smell seems obliterated. (RA)

He scarce heeds the moment (when) he drops seething into the yawning jaws awaiting him. (RA)

This was written at a time (when) the whalebone was largely used in ladies' bodices. (RA)

I was he (whom) the Fates ordained to take the place of Ahab's bowsman. (RP)

Exercise 71B: Missing Relative Words

Draw a caret in front of each adjective clause and insert the missing relative pronoun. (For the purposes of this exercise, *which* and *that* may be used interchangeably.)

> **Note to Instructor:** Increasingly, *which* and *that* are accepted as interchangeable. The distinction and the proper uses of each will be covered in a future lesson. Accept either.

Reykjavik is one of the finest cities ^ [which/that] I have visited.

The elderly woman ^ [whom] you met is not my grandmother.

The giraffe ^ [that/which] we saw was extremely tall and ravenously hungry.

The painting ^ [that/which] you admired was painted by me.

Of all the songs ^ [that] I have ever heard, this was the saddest.

The sloppy language ^ [which/that] the writer used is disgraceful.

The heritage seeds ^ [which/that] we planted have sprouted.

Exercise 71C: Diagramming

On your own paper, diagram the following sentences from your first two exercises.

The sea is a green pasture where our children's grand-children will go for bread.

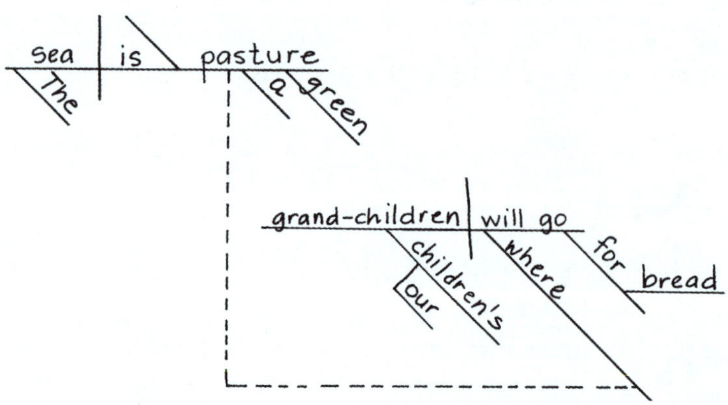

Nantucket was her great original, the Tyre of this Carthage, the place where the first dead American whale was stranded.

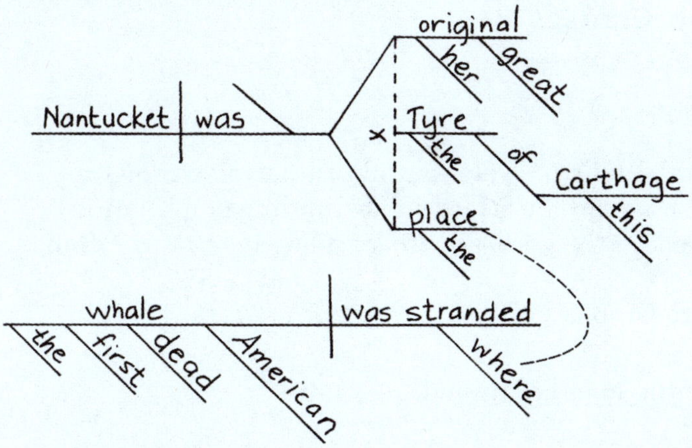

He scarce heeds the moment when he drops seething into the yawning jaws awaiting him.

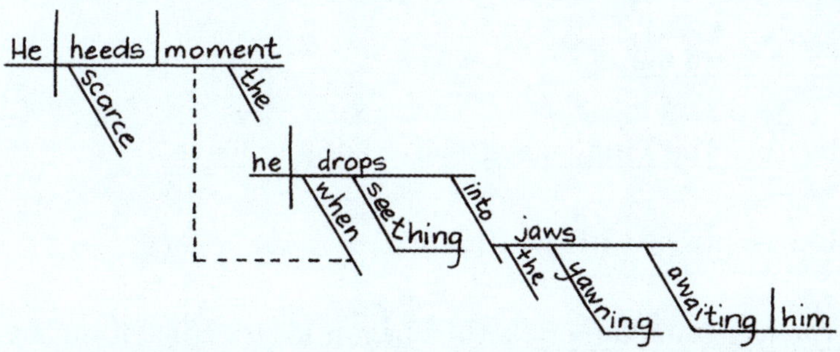

I was he whom the Fates ordained to take the place of Ahab's bowsman.

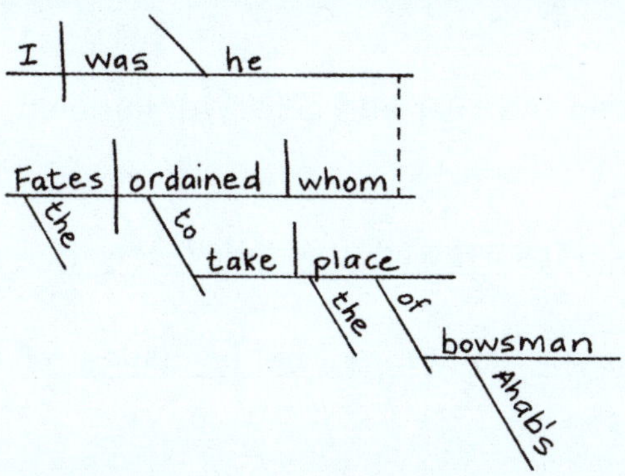

The giraffe we saw was extremely tall and ravenously hungry.

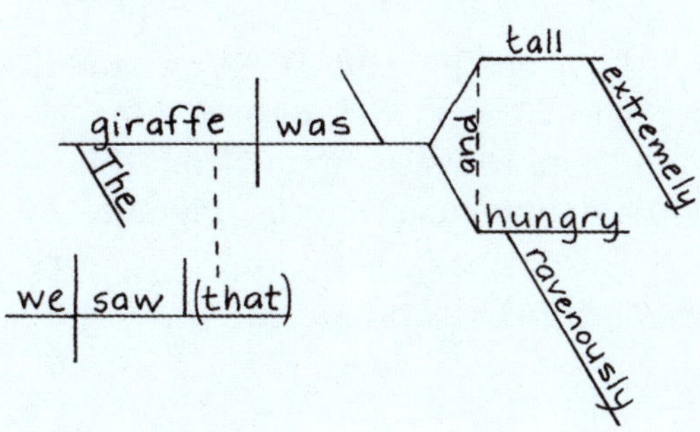

— LESSON 72 —

Adverb Clauses

Exercise 72A: Adverb Clauses

In the following sentences, underline each adverb clause. Circle the subordinating word(s) at the beginning of each clause and label it *ADV* for adverb or *SC* for subordinating conjunction. Draw an arrow from the subordinating word back to the verb, adverb, or adjective that the clause modifies.

These sentences are adapted from Alexandre Dumas's *The Man in the Iron Mask*.

The countenance of Aramis darkened as the young man continued.

When you have related it, leave us.

It was dangerous because his attempts to escape were many.

He drew the message from his pocket swiftly since the king was already rising to leave.

Since the king has given secret orders, I no longer possess his confidence.

While these affairs were separating forever the four musketeers, Athos began to pay his tribute.

Louis XIV continued as if he had seen nothing.

The moon, too, as if she had placed herself at his orders, silvered the trees and lake with her own bright and quasi-phosphorescent light.

This luminous square decreases from one till three, slowly, as if it sorrowed to bid me farewell.

The king would burn the whole building and its contents, in order that it might not be made use of by anyone else.

Exercise 72B: Descriptive Clauses

In the following sentences, underline each dependent clause. Above each, write *ADVC* for adverb clause or *ADJC* for adjective clause. Circle each subordinating word(s) and label it as *ADV* for adverb, *RP* for relative pronoun, or *SC* for subordinating conjunction. Draw an arrow from the subordinating word back (or forward) to the word in the independent clause that the dependent clause modifies.

These sentences are adapted from Alexandre Dumas's *The Man in the Iron Mask*.

For as my conscience does not accuse me, I aver my innocence.

He fell back to the cavern where the three rowers awaited him.

As soon as he was assured by the sound of their descending footsteps, he put the lantern on the table.

Speak to me of the religious order whose chief you are.

It is not you who will have to thank me, but rather the nation whom you will render happy, the posterity whose name you will make glorious.

D'Artagnan recoiled, as though the syllables had knocked the breath out of his body.

You remember the story of the Roman general who always kept seven wild boars roasting.

You see before you, my dear monsieur, a man who considers himself disgraced.

Will you meet me at Paris, in order that I may know your determination?

But already Percerin, goaded by the idea that the king was to be told, had offered Lebrun a chair.

He drank in delicious draughts of that mysterious air which interpenetrates at night the loftiest forests.

Exercise 72C: Diagramming

On your own paper, diagram every word of the following sentences.

These sentences are adapted from Alexandre Dumas's *The Man in the Iron Mask.*

Although the courier made a great noise, Baisemeaux heard nothing.

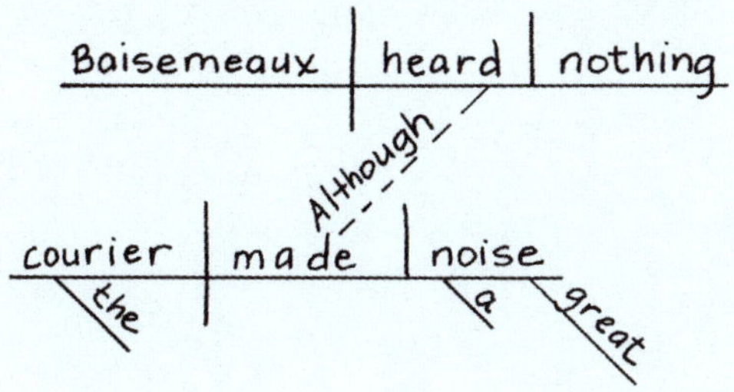

The latter, whose hands trembled in a manner to excite pity, turned a dull and meaningless gaze upon the letter.

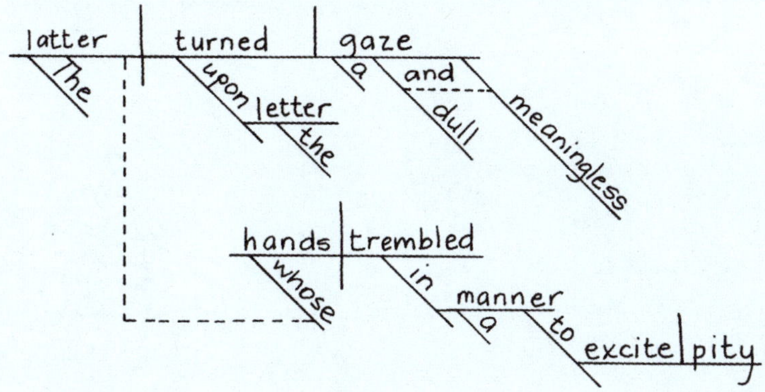

It was Aramis who brought me the invitation.

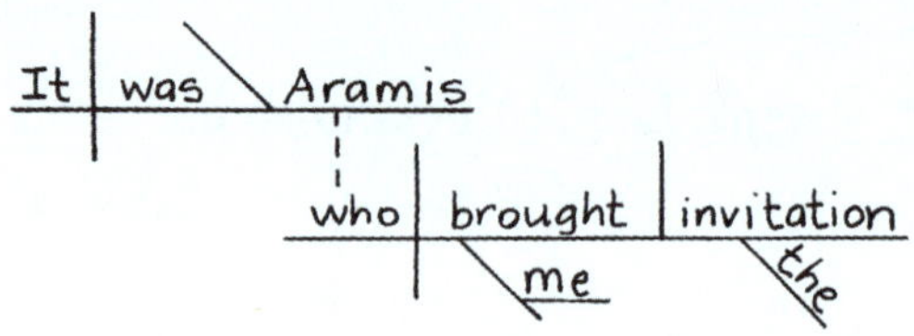

> **Note to Instructor:** It is also acceptable for the student to connect *who* to *It* with the dotted line.

D'Artagnan, pushing on Porthos, who scattered the groups of people right and left, succeeded in gaining the counter.

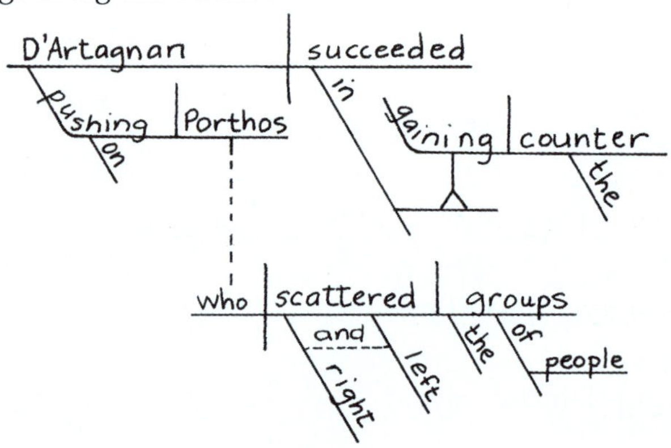

Moliere fixed upon Porthos one of those looks which penetrate the minds and hearts of men.

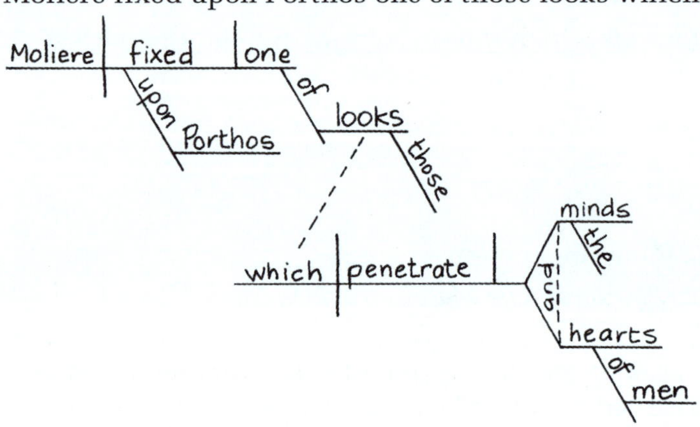

— REVIEW 6 —

Weeks 16-18

Topics

Personal Pronouns: Subject, Object, Possessive, Reflexive
Verb Voice (Active and Passive)
Verb Tense
Adjectives
Gerunds and Participles
Phrases
Clauses (Independent and Dependent)

Review 6A: Pronouns

In the following sentences, taken from the classic 1913 novel *The Custom of the Country*, by Edith Wharton, circle each pronoun. Label each as *S* (subject form of the personal pronoun), *O* (object form of the personal pronoun), *P* (possessive form of the personal pronoun), *R* (reflexive), *INT* (intensive), *I* (indefinite), *D* (demonstrative), or *RP* (relative pronoun).

"Yes—I suppose so. He said he'd like to paint me. Mabel Lipscomb introduced him. I don't care if I never see him again," the girl said, bathed in angry pink.

She meant to watch and listen without letting herself go, and she sat very straight and pink, answering promptly but briefly, with the nervous laugh that punctuated all her phrases—saying "I don't care if I do" when her host asked her to try some grapes, and "I wouldn't wonder" when she thought anyone was trying to astonish her.

Mrs. Marvell met this gravely. "It would depend, I should say, on the kind of people she wished to see."

Some she knew without being able to name them—fixed figure-heads of the social prow—others she recognized from their portraits in the papers; but of the few from whom she could herself claim recognition not one was visible, and as she pursued her investigations the whole scene grew blank and featureless.

He paused before answering, and she sat watching his shadowy profile against the passing lamps. "My mother's ideas are old-fashioned; and I don't know that it's anybody's business but yours and mine."

She kept her eyes fixed on her book while he entered the room and moved about behind her, laying aside his hat and overcoat; then his steps came close and a small parcel dropped on the pages of her book.

The old Marquis and his wife, who were content, when they came up from Burgundy in the spring, with a modest set of rooms looking out on the court of their ancestral residence, expected their son and his wife to fit themselves into the still smaller apartment which had served as Raymond's bachelor lodging.

Whenever Undine saw him after an absence she had a curious sense of his coming back from unknown distances and not belonging to her or to any state of things she understood. Then habit reasserted itself, and she began to think of him again with a querulous familiarity.

Review 6B: Using Comparative and Superlative Adjectives Correctly

Choose the correct form in parentheses. Cross out the incorrect form.

Rainforests are the earth's (~~diversest~~/most diverse) natural places.

Rainforests are (sunnier/~~more sunny~~) and (damper/~~most damp~~) than other forests.

The floor of the rainforest is the (darkest/~~most dark~~) and (~~humidest~~/most humid) place in the rainforest.

The canopy, or leafy part of the forest, is (richer/~~richest~~) in wildlife than the forest floor.

Rainforests are the earth's (~~more valuable~~/most valuable) natural wonder, hosting over half of the world's plant and animal species.

Every year rainforests are destroyed, and today they are (scarcer/~~most scarce~~) than they have ever been.

We must be (~~carefuller~~/more careful) than our ancestors, in order to protect this precious resource.

Review 6C: Verbs

Underline the main verb in each sentence. In the space above it, write the tense (*SIMP PAST, PRES, FUT; PROG PAST, PRES, FUT; PERF PAST, PRES, FUT*) and voice (*ACT* for active or *PASS* for passive) of the verb. If the verb is active, also note whether it is transitive (*TR*) or intransitive (*INTR*). The first is done for you.

These sentences are taken from *A History of China*, by Wolfram Eberhard.

PERF PRES, ACT, INTR
Chinese scholars have succeeded in deciphering some of the documents discovered.

SIMP PRES, PASS
The still existing fragments of writing of this period are found almost exclusively on tortoise-shells or on other bony surfaces.

SIMP PAST, PASS
No preference was shown to the son of the oldest brother.

PERF PAST, ACT, TR
At the time of the Han Dynasty, all citizens (slaves excluded) had accepted family names.

PERF PRES, ACT, INTR
Many of the old works have only come down to us in an imperfect state and with doubtful accuracy.

SIMP FUT, PASS
It will be remembered that Buddhism came to China overland and by sea in the Han epoch.

PROG PAST, ACT, INTR
Nomads were still living in the middle of China.

SIMP PAST, PASS
The younger sons were given independent pieces of land.

SIMP PRES, ACT, TR
Every feudal system harbours some seeds of a bureaucratic system of administration.

Review 6D: Identifying Dependent Clauses

Underline each dependent clause in the following sentences. Circle the subordinating word. Label each clause as either adjective (*ADJ*) or adverb clause (*ADV*), and draw a line from each subordinating word to the word it modifies.

These sentences are taken from "Rikki-Tikki-Tavi," by Rudyard Kipling.

ADJ
This is the story of the great war that Rikki-tikki-tavi fought single-handed.

ADV [answers the question "when"]
His war-cry, as he scuttled through the long grass, was: "Rikk-tikk-tikki-tikki-tchk!"

ADJ
He looked at Rikki-tikki with the wicked snake's eyes that never change their expression.

ADV
He jumped up in the air as high as he could go, and just under him whizzed by the head of Nagaina, Nag's wicked wife.

ADV
She had crept up behind him as he was talking, to make an end of him; and he heard her savage

ADV
hiss as the stroke missed.

The Coppersmith is a bird who makes a noise exactly like the beating of a little hammer on a copper pot.

From the thick grass at the foot of the bush there came a low hiss—a horrid cold sound that made Rikki-tikki jump back two clear feet.

Darzee was a feather-brained little fellow who could never hold more than one idea at a time in his head.

So he sang a very mournful song that he made up on the spur of the minute.

He was dizzy, aching, and felt shaken to pieces when something went off like a thunderclap just behind him.

Review 6E: Present and Past Participles

Underline each present participle and past participle in the following sentences. Indicate what part of the sentence each serves as with the labels *ADJ* for adjective, *ADV* for adverb, *S* for subject, *DO* and *IO* for direct and indirect object, and *OP* for object of the preposition. For adverbs and adjectives, draw an arrow back to the word modified.

Aloo tikki are made with mashed potatoes and cilantro, *garam* masala, and cumin.

Saute cumin seeds and onion in bubbling oil before adding other ingredients.

Divide the finished mixture into equal portions and shape into balls.

Flatten the balls on a greased tabletop.

Heat more oil in a frying pan and fry until the potato is golden.

You can make green pea *tikki* by mashing peas together with spinach and green chilis.

Aloo tikki is always hot and satisfying.

Eating *aloo tikki* is my favorite morning break activity.

The street vendor was very busy frying the morning's *aloo tikki.*

Note to Instructor: The student may choose *vendor,* but *frying* describes *in what manner* he was busy, so modifies the adjective and acts as an adverb.

You can also buy *aloo tikki* at *chaat* shops found in New Delhi.

You will find *aloo tikki chaat* heaped with yogurt and pomegranate in Pitampura.

Review 6F: Diagramming

On your own paper, diagram every word of the following sentences (taken from H. E. Macomber's biography of Samuel Finley Morse in *Stories of Great Inventors*).

There are many, many things, common and useful to us now, which were unknown to the world in 1800.

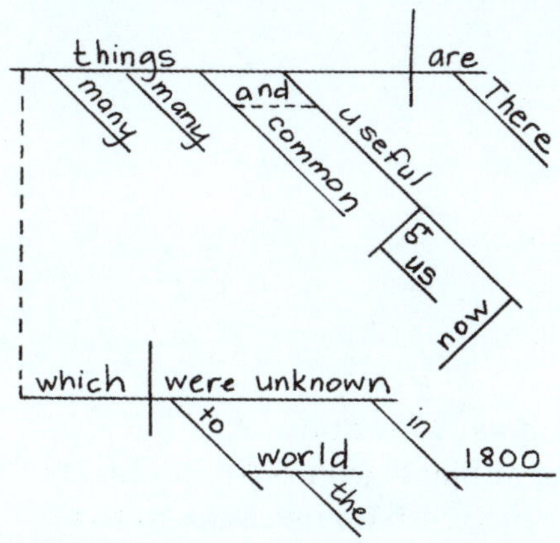

Note to Instructor: Sentences beginning with *there are* were covered in Lessons 28 and 34.

Lighting by means of gas was yet unknown.

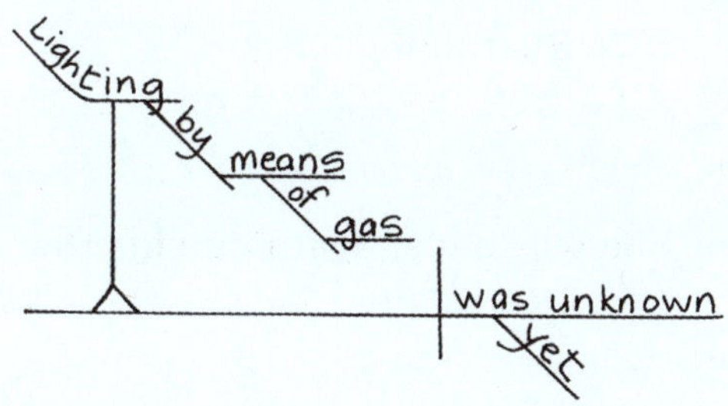

Even kerosene, which makes so poor a light, was then unused.

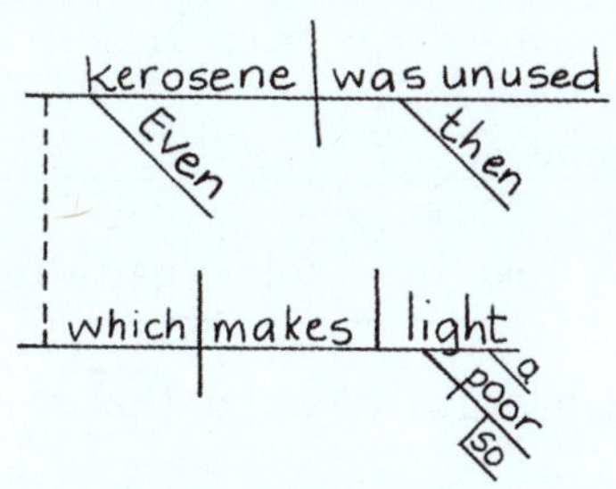

Though he did not snatch the thunder from the heavens, he gave the electric current thought, and bound the earth in light.

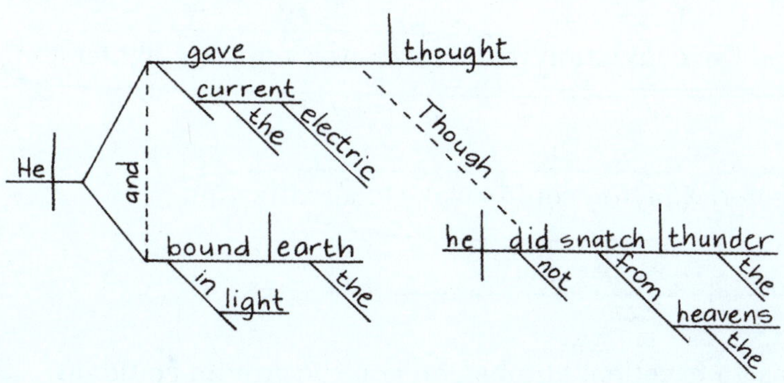

Note to Instructor: Although the adverb clause could modify either verb, it is more common to attach it to the first. *In light* is an adverb phrase because it answers the question *how. Electric current* could also be diagrammed as a single compound noun.

WEEK 19

More Clauses

— LESSON 73 —

Adjective and Adverb Clauses
Introduction to Noun Clauses

Exercise 73A: Identifying Clauses

In the following sentences, circle each dependent clause. Label each as *N* for noun, *ADJ* for adjective, or *ADV* for adverb. Indicate whether the noun clauses are subjects (*S*) or direct objects (*DO*). Draw a line from the subordinating word of each adjective and adverb clause back to the word it modifies.

Some of these clauses may have another clause within them! Do your best to find both, and ask your instructor for help if needed.

These sentences are taken from *Tarzan of the Apes*, by Edgar Rice Burroughs.

ADV ADV
Though Lady Greystoke lived for a year after her baby was born, she was never again outside the cabin, nor did she ever fully realize that she was not in England.
N DO

N S
That he had been able to turn his hands at all to such unaccustomed labor was a source of mild wonder to him.

ADJ
But deep in the minds of the apes was rooted the conviction that Tarzan was a mighty fighter and a strange creature.

ADV ADJ
So peaceful was her end that it was hours before Clayton could awake to a realization that his wife was dead.

ADJ
By the time Tarzan was ten years old he was an excellent climber, and on the ground could do many wonderful things which were beyond the powers of his little brothers and sisters.
ADJ

Note to Instructor: The adjective clause *Tarzan was ten years old* has an understood introductory *that* relating it back to *time.*

ADJ

Whatever his decision the apes accept it as final, and return to their occupations satisfied.

N DO

Tarzan wondered why the men had gone into the jungle.

ADJ

Occasionally they would enter a spot where the foliage above was less dense.

ADJ

It was the surprise at the blinding flash and the deafening roar that had caused her hasty but temporary retreat.

N S

ADJ

Still more wonderful was how it contained the likeness of one who might be a brother.

Note to Instructor: The sentence is in reverse order; the noun clause is the subject, *was* is a linking verb, and *wonderful* is the predicate adjective.

Exercise 73B: Creating Noun Clauses

For each of the following sentences, write a noun clause that fits into the blank.

If you have trouble coming up with a dependent clause, try starting out with one of the following subordinating words: *that, how, why, what/whatever, who/whoever* (these are always subjects within the dependent clause), *whom/whomever* (these are always objects within the dependent clause), *where, whether.* (This is not an exhaustive list of the possibilities—just a jumping-off place for you.)

Note to Instructor: Answers will vary; the sentences below are examples of possible clauses.

No one should know [where the Christmas presents are hidden].

No one should know [how we escaped].

[How they were supposed to cross the ravine] was not very clear.

[What the assignment required] was not very clear.

Tell your father [what you did for your science project].

Tell your father [who is going to the party with you].

[That the car ran out of gas on the highway] was extremely unfortunate.

[How he decided to solve the problem] was extremely unfortunate.

The starving colonists ate [whatever they could find in the woods].

The starving colonists ate [whoever didn't run fast enough to get away].

Exercise 73C: Diagramming

On your own paper, diagram every word of the following sentences (taken from *Tarzan of the Apes*).

There was no simian in all the mighty forest through which he roved that dared to challenge his right to rule.

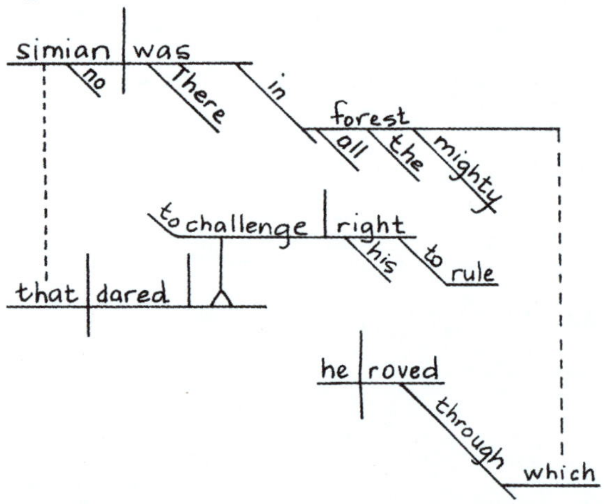

None of them could understand how a child could be so slow and backward in learning to care for itself.

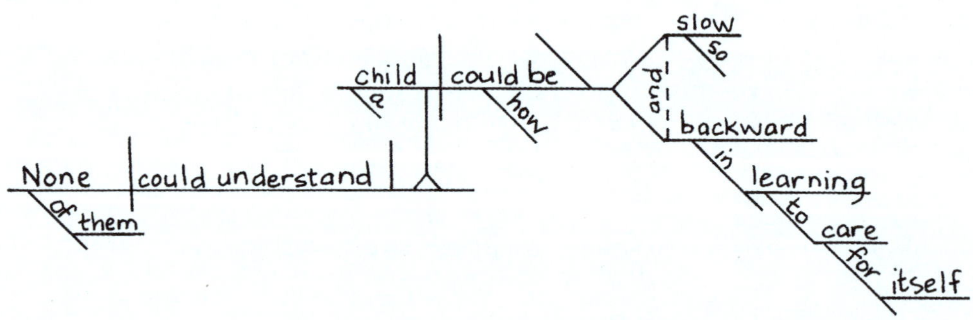

His thoughts were interrupted by the station agent who entered asking if there was a gentleman by the name of Tarzan in the party.

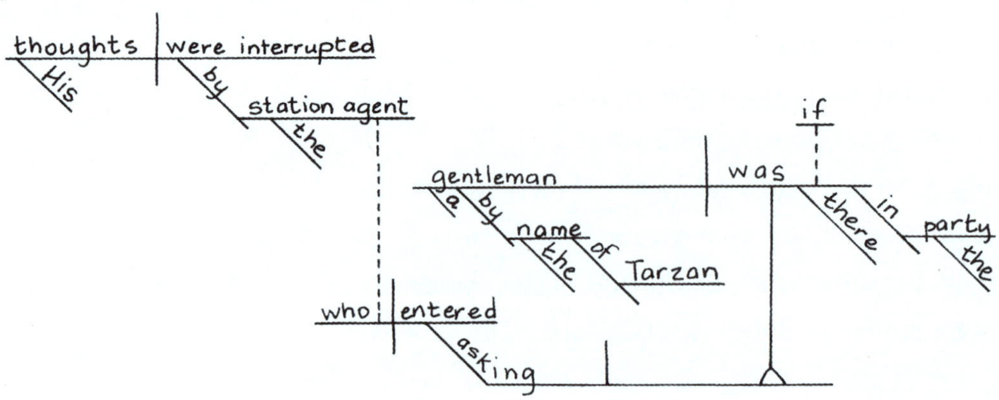

— LESSON 74 —

Clauses Beginning With Prepositions

Exercise 74A: Adjective Clauses Beginning with Prepositions

In the following sentences, circle each adjective clause. Draw a line from the subordinating word back to the word the clause modifies. If the clause begins with a preposition, underline that preposition and label its object with *OP*.

These sentences are adapted from *Native America: A History*, by Michael L. Oberg.

Drought killed the crops upon which the Chumash relied for food.

French weapons flowed from the Caddos to the Comanches, with whom they allied.

The Caddos entered into a treaty in which they ceded their lands.

He was a Cherokee hunter who lived for a time with bears.

Anthropologists searched for Algonquian remnants with which they could understand the past.

She felt sympathy for the Dakotas, with whom she identified in many ways.

Uncas found himself walking a treacherous path between the English and the natives over whom he exerted his influence.

We wish to return to the state in which we lived before these strangers came.

Aupaumut hoped to employ strong relations with the United States as a barrier against the Iroquois among whom his people lived.

They were a power with whom their rivals had to reckon.

The people who came to be known as the Cherokees told a different story.

The scarcity of game prevented the Senecas from the same hunts to which their fathers were accustomed.

Exercise 74B: Correct Use of *Who* and *Whom*

Choose the correct pronoun within the parentheses; cross out the incorrect pronoun.

(~~Who~~/Whom) does this belong to?
I think you should buy flowers for the girl (~~who~~/whom) you are interested in.
She is an official against (~~who~~/whom) no charge can be brought.
The mansion was inhabited by an old woman (who/~~whom~~) spent her days knitting.
He is the only one of them all (~~who~~/whom) I could make my friend.
(Who/~~Whom~~) is coming along with us all?
(~~Who~~/Whom) should you talk to?
This is the lady to (~~who~~/whom) I am indebted.
I was looking for my aunt and the two friends (~~who~~/whom) she was travelling with.
For those of us (who/~~whom~~) arrived on time, the evening went well.
There are only a few to (~~who~~/whom) this privilege is granted.
That is the family (~~who~~/whom) we were talking about.
I'm glad someone is here of (~~who~~/whom) I can ask advice.
This request should go to my partner, (who/~~whom~~) is already aware of the problem.

Exercise 74C: Formal and Informal Diction

On your own paper, rewrite the following informal sentences in formal English, placing the preposition before its object. In four sentences, you will also need to insert a relative pronoun! The first has been done for you.

Read both versions of each sentence out loud, and place a star by any sentence that sounds better in informal English.

> **Note to Instructor:** None of the informal sentences are "incorrect," and "sounds better" is a judgment call. Accept any answers from the student; the exercise is intended to begin to teach the student to read sentences out loud and listen to them.

Whom should I turn to?
  To whom should I turn?
The forest which the animals lived in was deep and dark.
  The forest in which the animals lived was deep and dark.
Sarya finally learned whom the presents were intended for.
  Sarya finally learned for whom the presents were intended.
He is the one I owe my thanks to.
  He is the one to whom I owe my thanks.
The men whom charges were brought against went on trial.
  The men against whom charges were brought went on trial.
The girl he's talking to is the daughter of the president.
  The girl to whom he's talking is the daughter of the president.
There are many other galaxies besides the ones we've given names to.
  There are many other galaxies besides the ones to which we've given names.
I'm very fond of the family I live with.
  I'm very fond of the family with whom I live.

Exercise 74D: Diagramming

On your own paper, diagram every word of the following two sentences from Exercise 74A.

French weapons flowed from the Caddos to the Comanches, with whom they allied.

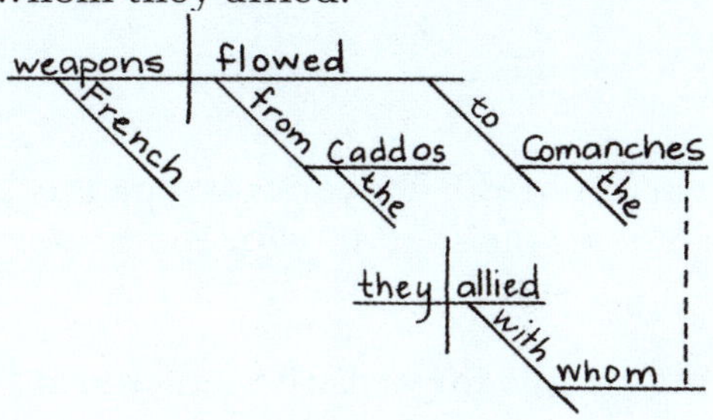

Uncas found himself walking a treacherous path between the English and the natives over whom he exerted his influence.

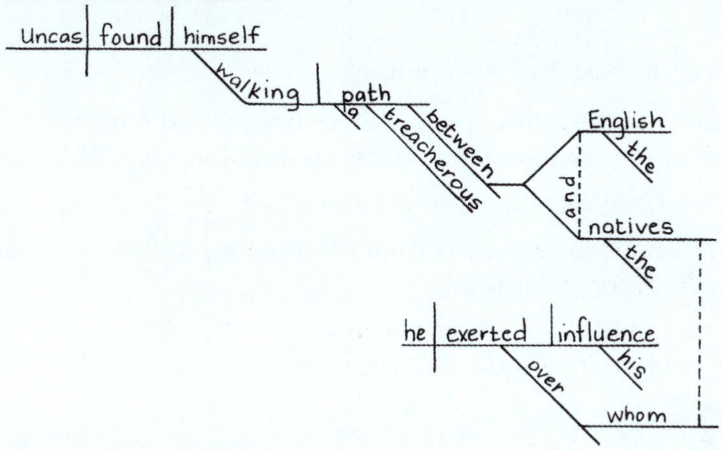

— LESSON 75 —

Clauses and Phrases
Misplaced Adjective Phrases
Misplaced Adjective Clauses

Exercise 75A: Correcting Misplaced Modifiers

Circle the misplaced adjective clauses and phrases in the following sentences. Draw an arrow to the place where each modifier should be.

The trees shaded the little girl with lush green branches.

The dog knocked over the vase that was running around the house.

The three girls walked down the street chewing gum.

I borrowed a sandwich for lunch with mayonnaise.

He gave a dog to his daughter named Rufus.

The lamp crashed onto the floor that Hillary had kicked.

With big fuzzy ears I gave a stuffed elephant to my sister Angie.

Tourists crowd the streets of Venice carrying cameras.

Kevin made Aunt Jean a strawberry pie, who is his mother's older sister

She tossed the fish in the bucket that was thrashing around

We served pizza to the children on paper plates that were too floppy

Exercise 75B: Diagramming

Each of the following sentences has at least one misplaced clause or phrase. On your own paper, diagram each sentence correctly, and then read the corrected sentence out loud to your instructor.

These sentences are adapted from Willa Cather's novel *O, Pioneers!*

The boys looked away from the shabby old barn with the flaming steeple towards the red church who were watching.

CORRECT: *The boys who were watching looked away from the shabby old barn towards the red church with the flaming steeple.*

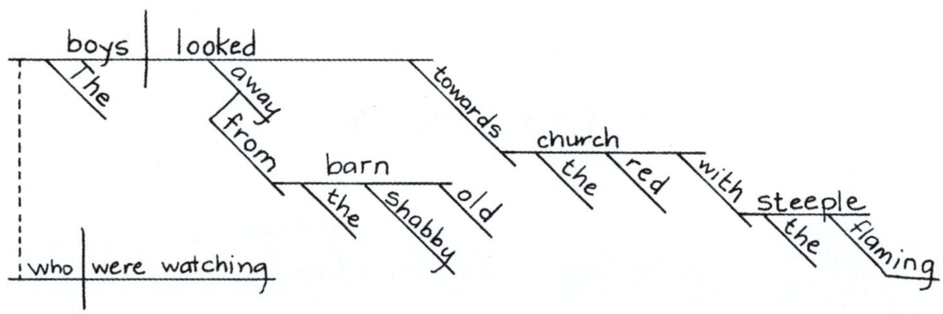

Huddled on the grey prairies, a mist of fine snowflakes was curling and eddying about the cluster of low drab buildings.

CORRECT: *A mist of fine snowflakes was curling and eddying about the cluster of low drab buildings huddled on the grey prairies.*

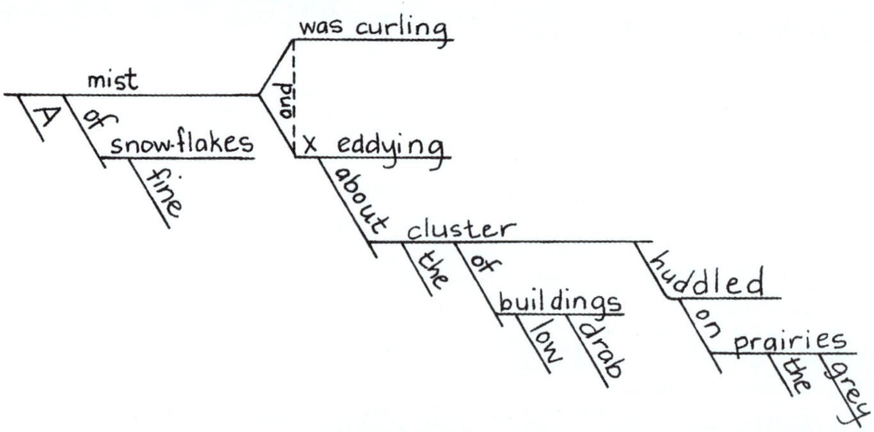

Note to Instructor: We have added an *x* to indicate that the helping verb *was* helps out both *curling* and *eddying*. It is fine for the student to simply put *eddying* on the diagram, but show her the diagram above and explain that the *x* indicates the understood helping verb *was*.

Her cousins sat in the pews dressed in black and weeping profusely.

CORRECT: *Dressed in black and weeping profusely, her cousins sat in the pews.*

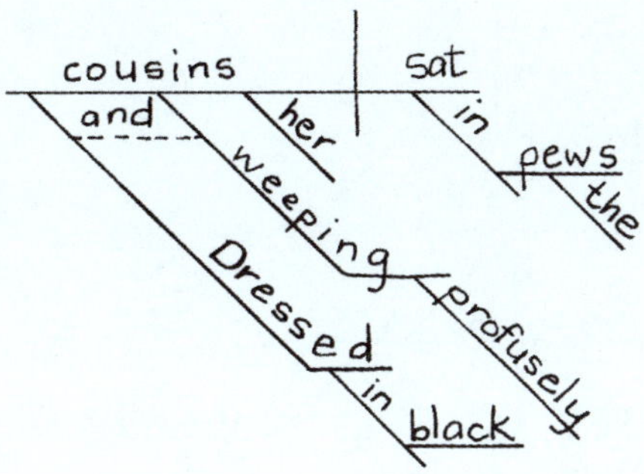

— LESSON 76 —

Noun, Adjective, and Adverb Clauses

Restrictive and Non-Restrictive Modifying Clauses

Exercise 76A: Clause Review

For each of the three sentences below, complete these steps:

1) Find and circle the dependent clauses. Label each one as *adjective*, *adverb*, or *noun*.
2) Identify and underline the subordinating word.
3) For the adverb and adjective clauses, draw a line from the subordinating word back to the word modified. For the noun clauses, identify the part of the sentence that each clause is serving as.
4) Diagram each sentence on your own paper.

These sentences are taken from *The Magic of Oz*, by L. Frank Baum.

ADVERB

The Glass Cat, (although it had some disagreeable ways and manners) nevertheless realized

NOUN–DIRECT OBJECT

(that Trot and Cap'n Bill were its friends)

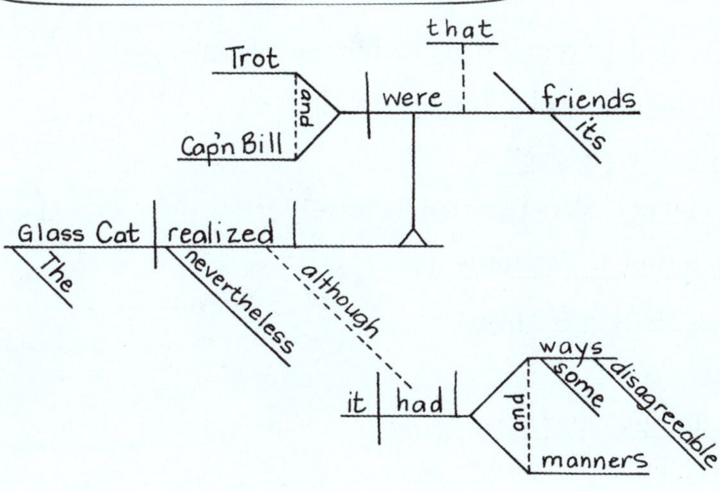

ADJECTIVE

There is the gold flower-pot containing the Magic Flower, which is very curious and beautiful.

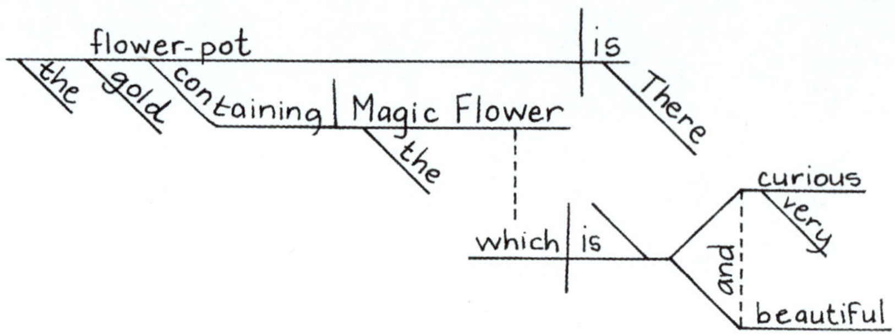

NOUN–DIRECT OBJECT

The Wizard did not know whether it would be better for him to hide himself until they

ADVERB

moved on again.

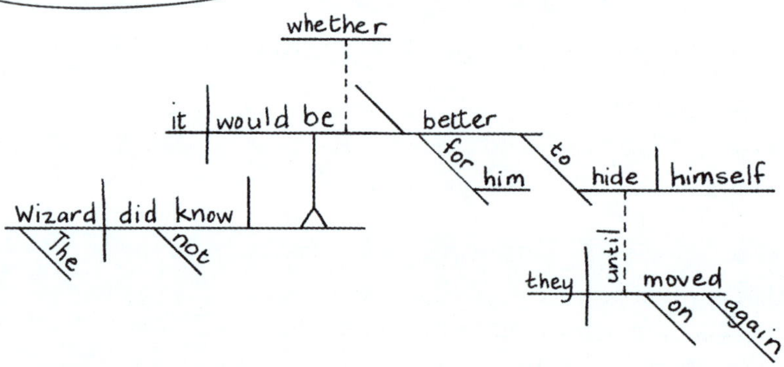

Exercise 76B: Non-Restrictive Clauses and Missing Commas

In the following sentences, taken from James Stephens' classic collection *Irish Fairy Tales*, underline each dependent clause. Place commas around each non-restrictive clause. Use proofreader's marks: ^,. Leave sentences with restrictive clauses as they are.

Although she was horrified by the battle, her interests lay in another direction.

The idea that a stranger may expire on your doorstep from hunger cannot be tolerated.

There came a sickness that bloated the stomach and purpled the skin.

The feast of Tara was held, at which all were gathered together.

Among the three hundred dogs which Fionn owned were two that he loved.

They stared dumbly at the stranger, as though they were utterly dazed.

There is a dense wood where every thorn is as sharp as a spear.

He did not loosen his knees when he walked.

She was singing lullabies to a cat that was yelping on her shoulder.

I am kinder than you, which no one can deny.

Exercise 76C: Restrictive Clauses and Unnecessary Commas

In the following sentences, taken from James Stephens' classic collection *Irish Fairy Tales,* underline each dependent clause. Delete the incorrect commas that have been placed around restrictive clauses. Use proofreader's marks: ℓ. Leave sentences with non-restrictive clauses as they are.

I was so alone that my own shadow frightened me.

They met him at the place where games are played.

For although Fionn loved Goll, he did not like him.

When the men saw his condition, they were distressed at his illness.

Each breeze that came from the right hand or the left brought me a tale.

For a while it did not matter to Fionn which way the hare jumped.

He remembered only an endless conversation, from which his mind slipped constantly away.

There is an eerie feeling abroad which I do not like.

I was that which I had dreamed.

WEEK 20

Constructing Sentences

— LESSON 77 —

Constructing Sentences

Exercise 77A: Making Sentences Out of Clauses and Phrases

The independent clauses below are listed in order and make up a story—but they're missing all their supporting pieces.

On your own paper, rewrite the story by attaching the dependent clauses and phrases in lists 2 and 3 to the independent clauses in List 1 to make complete sentences. You may insert dependent clauses that act as adjectives or adverbs into the beginning, middle, or end of independent clauses (usually by putting them right before or after the word they modify), and you may change any capitalization or punctuation necessary. But do not add or delete words.

The first sentence has been constructed for you.

Crossing out each clause or phrase as you use it will help you not to repeat yourself!

List 1. Independent Clauses

~~A terrible monster allowed no one to pass.~~
The Sphinx had the head of a woman.
The people were very much frightened.
They had lost their lives.
No one could harm the Sphinx.
The king had ridden off.
A messenger came.
He said.
Oedipus came.
The streets were filled.
The young prince soon learned the cause.
Oedipus immediately set out.
Oedipus walked.
What creature walks?
Oedipus answered.
Man creeps.
Man walks upright.
He supports his tottering steps.
The Sphinx, knowing, tried to get away.
Oedipus forced the Sphinx.

List 2. Dependent Clauses
that the creature of the riddle was man
if he wished to live
where it was dashed to pieces
since it ate up anyone
~~who could not answer a riddle~~
that the king and all of his servants had been killed
because he was sure
who could not guess its riddle
hoping to learn the answer to the riddle
listening to what they said
until he was stopped
that he could guess the riddle
which told him to answer a riddle
that its power was now at an end
although the bravest men had gone out to kill it
~~which it asked~~
unless he guessed the mysterious riddle

List 3. Phrases
and upon three at night
along the road
all talking at once
~~called the Sphinx~~
the body of a lion
drawing his sword
upon two at noon
with a staff
by the Sphinx
with excited people
after a few moments
over a cliff
in the morning of life
in the attempt
in the morning
and the wings of an eagle
onto the sharp stones below
of deep thought,
in old age
to find the monster
running into town
in manhood
in his chariot
to the city
upon four feet
soon afterwards
of their excitement
of Thebes
on hands and knees

Note to Instructor: The original sentences, adapted slightly from H. A. Guerber's *The Story of the Greeks,* are provided below (in chronological order). However, any sentences that the student assembles are acceptable as long as they make sense.

A terrible monster called the Sphinx allowed no one to pass who could not answer a riddle which it asked.

The Sphinx had the head of a woman, the body of a lion, and the wings of an eagle.

Since it ate up anyone who could not guess its riddle, the people were very much frightened.

Although the bravest men had gone out to kill it, they had lost their lives in the attempt.

No one could harm the Sphinx unless he guessed the mysterious riddle.

The king, hoping to learn the answer to the riddle, had ridden off in his chariot.

A messenger came running into town.

He said that the king and all of his servants had been killed.

Soon afterwards, Oedipus came to the city of Thebes.

The streets were filled with excited people, all talking at once.

The young prince, listening to what they said, soon learned the cause of their excitement.

Because he was sure that he could guess the riddle, Oedipus immediately set out to find the monster.

Oedipus walked along the road until he was stopped by the Sphinx, which told him to answer a riddle if he wished to live.

What creature walks upon four feet in the morning, upon two at noon, and upon three at night?

After a few moments of deep thought, Oedipus answered that the creature of the riddle was man.

In the morning of life man creeps on hands and knees.

In manhood, man walks upright.

In old age, he supports his tottering steps with a staff.

The Sphinx, knowing that its power was now at an end, tried to get away.

Drawing his sword, Oedipus forced the Sphinx over a cliff, onto the sharp stones below, where it was dashed to pieces.

— LESSON 78 —

Simple Sentences
Complex Sentences

Exercise 78A: Identifying Simple and Complex Sentences

In the sentences below, underline each subject once and each predicate twice. (Find the subjects and predicates in both independent and dependent clauses.) In the blank at the end of each sentence, write *S* for simple or *C* for complex.

These sentences are taken from *Knights of Art: Stories of the Italian Painters*, by Amy Steedman.

Many of the new artists shook off the old rules and ideas, and began to paint in quite a new way. S

There was one man especially, called Michelangelo, who arose like a giant, and with his new way and greater knowledge swept everything before him. C

As the boy grew up he clearly showed in what direction his interest lay. C

At school he was something of a dunce at his lessons. S

Every spare moment he spent making sketches on the walls of his father's house. S

Without needing a lesson he began to copy the statues in terra-cotta. S

Like all the other artists, he would often go to study Masaccio's frescoes in the little chapel of the Carmine. S

Michelangelo never forgot all that he owed to Lorenzo. C

Through the outer walls of stone he seemed to see the figure imprisoned in the marble. S

Michelangelo was obliged to lie flat upon a scaffolding and paint the ceiling above him. S

So, incomplete as they were, Michelangelo was obliged to uncover the frescoes that all Rome might see them. C

Exercise 78B: Forming Complex Sentences

On your own paper, rewrite each pair of simple sentences as a single complex sentence. The first is done for you. You will need to add a subordinating word to one of the sentences to turn it into a dependent clause.

There may be more than one way to rewrite each sentence, as you can see in the example.

Note to Instructor: Accept any answers that are grammatical and include one independent and one dependent clause (with subordinating word).

Young Titian had great talent in painting. His uncle sent him to study with Giovanni Bellini.

Because young Titian had great talent in painting, his uncle sent him to study with Giovanni Bellini.

OR

Young Titian, whose uncle sent him to study with Giovanni Bellini, had great talent in painting.

Titian began to paint with a marvelous richness of color. His color made his name famous.

Titian began to paint with a marvelous richness of color that made his name famous.

The Emperor Charles V was so delighted with Titian's work. He made Titian a knight.

The Emperor Charles V was so delighted with Titian's work that he made Titian a knight.

OR

The Emperor Charles V, who made Titian a knight, was so delighted with Titian's work.

Titian met Michelangelo. The great master looked at his paintings with much interest.

When Titian met Michelangelo, the great master looked at his paintings with much interest.

OR

Titian met the great master Michelango, who looked at his paintings with much interest.

In his famous picture, the Virgin is all alone. She has left her companions behind.

In his famous picture, the Virgin is all alone, for she has left her companions behind.

OR

The Virgin is all alone in his famous picture, because she has left her companions behind.

The crowd stands watching her from below. The high priest waits for her above.

The crowd stands watching her from below, while the high priest waits for her above.

OR

As the crowd stands watching her from below, the high priest waits for her above.

Exercise 78C: Diagramming

On your own paper, diagram the following four sentences. Beside each diagram, write the number of vertical lines dividing subjects from predicates, along with the label *S* for simple or *C* for complex.

This is the house Jack built.

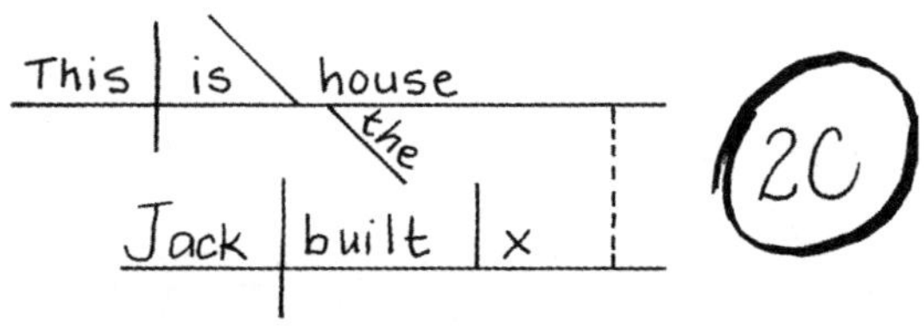

The horse and the hound and the horn belonged to the farmer sowing his corn.

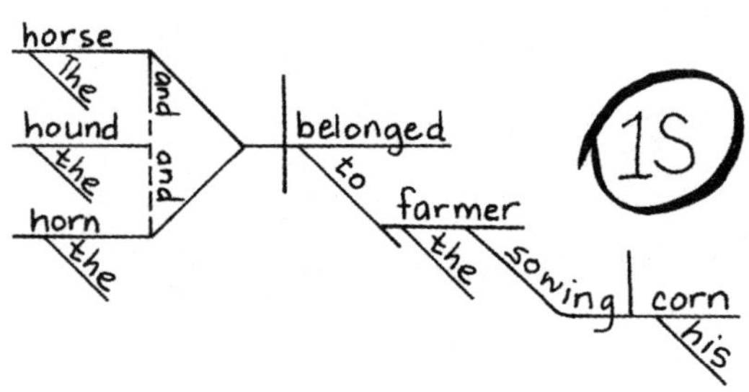

There was an old woman who lived in a shoe, who had so many children she didn't know what to do.

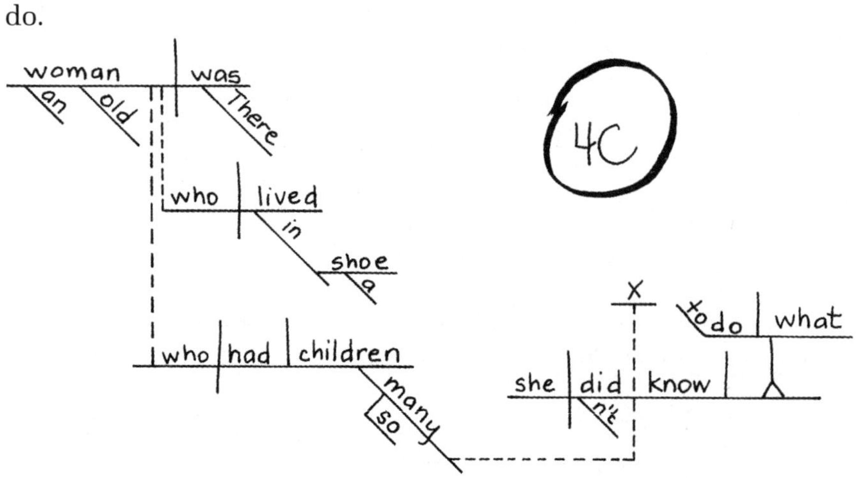

She gave them some broth without any bread and whipped them all soundly and put them to bed.

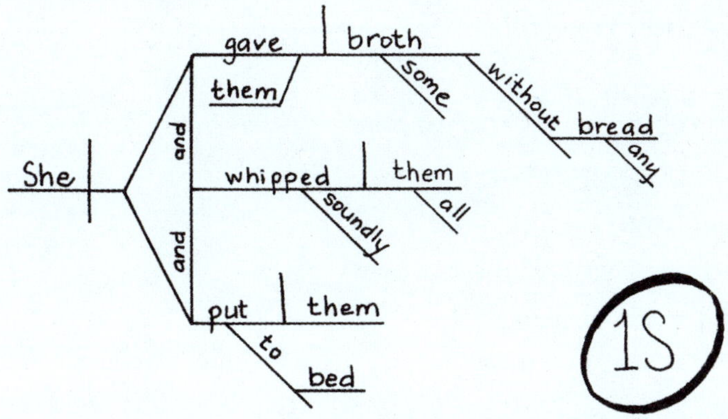

— LESSON 79 —

Compound Sentences
Run-on Sentences
Comma Splice

Exercise 79A: Forming Compound Sentences

Choose at least one independent clause from Column 1 and at least one independent clause from Column 2. Using correct punctuation and adding coordinating conjunctions as needed, combine the clauses into a compound sentence. (You may use more than two clauses, as long as your sentence makes sense!) Write your new compound sentences on your own paper. Use every clause at least once.

Column 1	Column 2
Master your temper.	The sun blazed down.
There was a strange look in his eyes.	The rains fell.
I might get up early.	It ought to be avoided
The fishermen could not launch their boats.	Treasures sink to the bottom.
It was August.	Your temper will master you.
The winds blew.	He was oddly cheerful.
The floods came.	I might sleep in.
Trash floats on the surface of the water.	The storm was raging fiercely.
The comma splice is a common mistake.	The corn grew green and thick.

Note to Instructor: The student may form other sentences than those below, as long as they make sense. However, she should *only* use the coordinating conjunctions. Watch out for subordinating conjunctions such as *before*, *while*, *because*, *after*, etc. Use of subordinating conjunctions transforms a clause from independent to dependent, and makes the sentence complex rather than compound.

No clauses should be joined with a comma splice (a comma without a coordinating conjunction), but all sentences can make use of either a semicolon (with or without coordinating conjunction) or a comma with a coordinating conjunction.

Master your temper, or your temper will master you.

There was a strange look in his eyes, yet he was oddly cheerful.

I might get up early, but I might sleep in.

The fishermen could not launch their boats, for the storm was raging fiercely.

It was August; the sun blazed down, and the corn grew green and thick.

The winds blew, and the rains fell, and the floods came.

Trash floats on the surface of the water, but treasures sink to the bottom.

The comma splice is a common mistake; it ought to be avoided.

Exercise 79B: Correcting Run-on Sentences (Comma Splices)

Using proofreader's marks (^ to insert a coordinating conjunction, ^, to insert a comma, ^; to insert a semicolon), correct each of the run-on sentences below.

> **Note to Instructor:** Answers may vary; each set of independent clauses should be connected by a semicolon (with or without a coordinating conjunction) or a comma and a coordinating conjunction.

The British Empire had to give up its colonies, ^so the colony of Singapore needed to become an independent nation.

At the beginning of the 20th century, 72 percent of Singapore's population was Chinese^; the rest of its residents were primarily Indian, Arab, European, and British.

In 1909 Singapore belonged to the Straits Settlements colony, ^and Penang and Malacca were in this colony as well.

During World War II, the Imperial Japanese occupied Singapore, ^but after the Surrender of Japan the British claimed Singapore again.

In 1948, the Communist Party of Malaya tried to take over Singapore by force^; this caused a state of emergency lasting for twelve years.

In 1965 Singapore became independent as the Republic of Singapore^, ^and it ruled itself from that point on.

British armed forces remained in Singapore until 1971, ^but the Republic had to build up its own defenses after that.

Exercise 79C: Diagramming

On your own paper, diagram every word of the following sentences from *Mr. Popper's Penguins*, by Richard and Florence Atwater.

He was spattered here and there with paint and calcimine, and there were bits of wallpaper clinging to his hair and whiskers, for he was rather an untidy man.

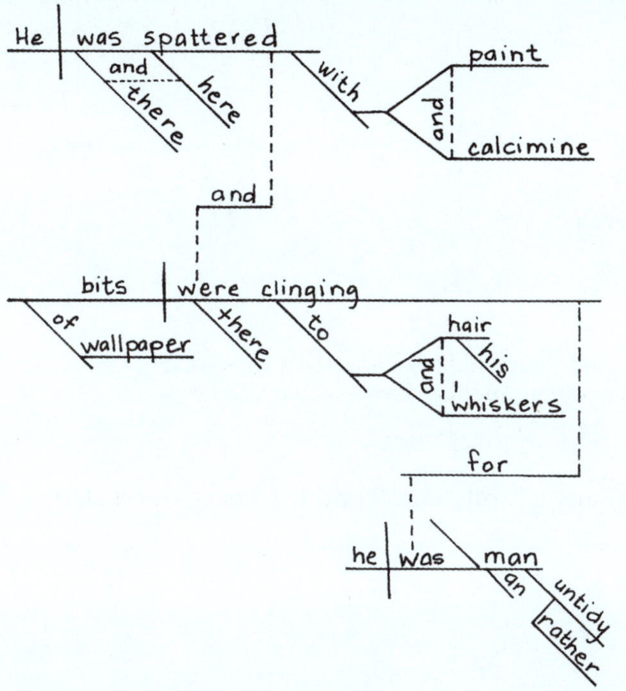

I have painted all of the kitchens in Stillwater; I have papered all of the rooms in the new apartment building on Elm Street.

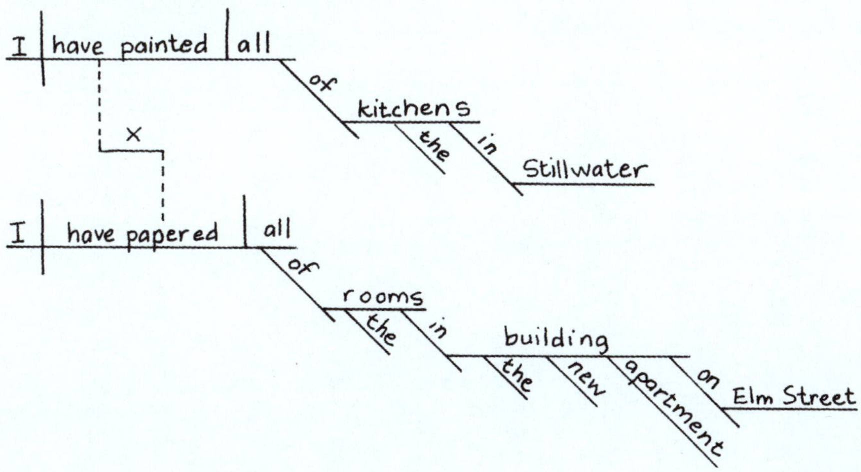

It will be nice to have you at home, but it is a little difficult to sweep with a man sitting around reading.

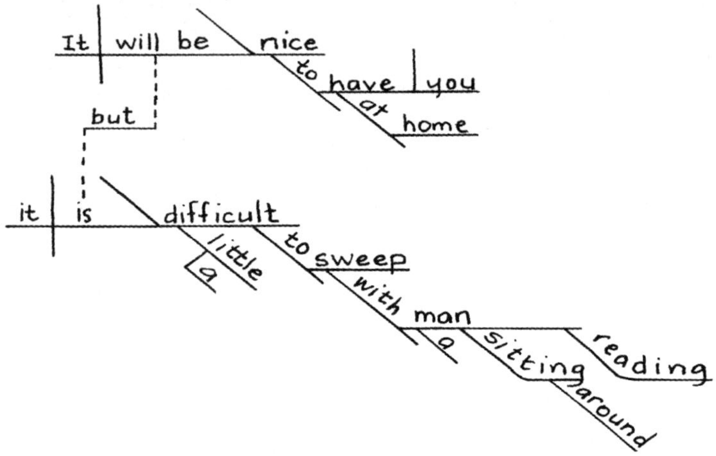

> **Note to Instructor:** This is an idiomatic use of the article *a* to modify an adverb—a somewhat unusual use of the article with a word other than a noun or pronoun. *Reading* could also be diagrammed as modifying *sitting*.

From the depths of the packing case, he suddenly heard a faint "Ork," and his heart stood still.

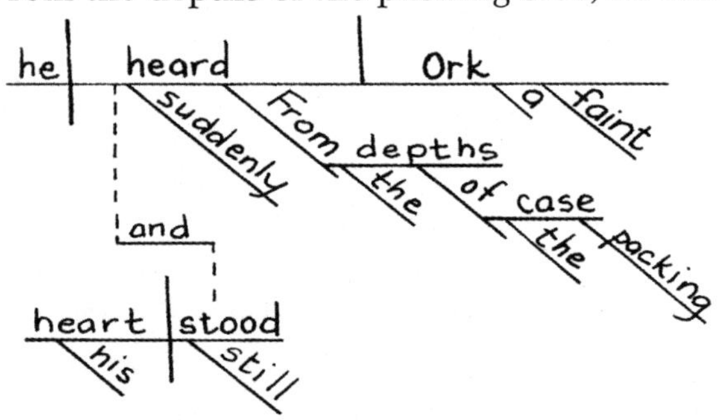

— LESSON 80 —

Compound Sentences
Compound-Complex Sentences
Clauses with Understood Elements

Exercise 80A: Analyzing Complex-Compound Sentences

The sentences below are all complex-compound sentences. For each sentence, carry out the following steps:

a) Cross out each prepositional phrase.
b) Circle any dependent clauses. Label them as *ADJ, ADV,* or *NOUN.* Draw a line from adjective and adverb clauses to the word modified. Label noun clauses with the part of the sentence that they function as.
c) Underline the subject of each independent clause once and the predicate twice.
d) Draw a vertical line between each simple or complex sentence.
e) Insert missing words (if any).

The first sentence has been done for you.

These sentences are taken from Isabel F. Hapgood's English translation of the complete five-volume novel *Les Miserables*, by Victor Hugo.

ADJ

Jean Valjean's mother had died of a milk fever, which had not been properly attended to; | his father, a tree-pruner, like himself, had been killed by a fall from a tree.

ADV

Maubert Isabeau, the baker on the Church Square at Faverolles, was preparing to go to bed, when he heard a violent blow on the grated front of his shop; | he arrived in time to see an arm passed through a hole made by a blow from a fist, through the grating and the glass.

ADV

While the bolt of his iron collar was being riveted behind his head with heavy blows from the hammer, he wept; | his tears stifled him; | they impeded his speech.

ADV

Then still sobbing, he raised his right hand and lowered it gradually seven times, as though he were touching in succession seven heads of unequal heights, and from this gesture they divined that the thing which he had done, whatever it was, was done for the sake of clothing and nourishing seven little children.

ADJ ADJ NOUN–DO

Note to Instructor: Within the final noun clause, *thing* is the subject of the entire noun clause and *was done* is the predicate.

NOUN–DO

He admitted (that he had committed an extreme and blameworthy act) | the loaf ~~of bread~~ would probably not have been refused ~~to him~~ if (had he asked ~~for it~~) ADV | ~~in any case~~, it would have been better ~~to wait~~ (until he could get it ~~through compassion~~ or ~~through work~~) ADV

> **Note to Instructor:** You may need to point out to the student that the dependent clause *if he had asked for it* is not only contracted, but the subject and verb are inverted as a result of the contraction.
>
> The student may have marked *until he could get it* as a prepositional phrase. If so, point out that since the "phrase" has a subject (*he*) and predicate (*could get*), it is a clause and not a phrase; *until* is acting as a subordinating word, not a preposition. Encourage the student to look at the preposition list and the subordinating conjunction list; *until* appears on both and can be used in either way.
>
> A later lesson will provide more practice in distinguishing the two.

~~From suffering~~ ~~to suffering~~, he had gradually arrived ~~at the conviction~~ (that life is a war) ADJ and that (~~in this war~~, he was the conquered.) ADJ

Exercise 80B: Constructing Complex-Compound Sentences

From each set of independent clauses, construct a single complex-compound sentence. You may turn any of the clauses into dependent clauses by adding subordinating words, insert any other words necessary, omit unnecessary words, and make any other needed changes, but try to keep the original meaning of each clause. You must use every clause in the set!

You may turn a clause into a prepositional phrase or another form, as long as your resulting sentence has at least two independent clauses and one dependent clause and contains all of the information in the listed clauses.

Write your new sentences on your own paper.

The first has been done for you.

We usually go to bed.
It is ten o'clock at night.
It is dark and cold outside.
We usually eat pie in the evening.

We usually go to bed when it is ten o'clock and dark and cold at night, but first we eat pie.

OR

When it is ten-o'clock at night and dark and cold outside, we usually eat pie and then go to bed.

> **Note to Instructor:** Other complex-compound sentences are also possible. If you're not sure whether the sentence qualifies, ask the student to locate and mark the subjects and predicates in the two independent clauses, and to circle the dependent clause.

The two boys sat on the beach.
The beach was at Sapzurro.
They could see through the clear green water to the white sand below.
The October afternoon was hot.
They sat in the shade of a clump of wax palms.

> It was a hot October afternoon, and the two boys who were sitting on the beach in Sapzurro beneath a clump of wax palms could see through the clear green water to the white sand below.

OR

> The two boys were sitting beneath the shade of a clump of wax palms, on the beach in Sapzurro; the October afternoon was hot, and they could see through the clear green water to the white sand below.

Benjamin Franklin discovered electricity.
He invented the lightning rod.
He wrote down thirteen virtues.
Order, silence, justice, and temperance were four of the virtues.
He wanted these virtues to become his habits.
He kept a little book to record his daily habits.

> Benjamin Franklin, who discovered electricity and invented the lightning rod, wrote down thirteen virtues such as order, silence, justice, and temperance; because he wanted these virtues to become his habits, he kept a little book to record his daily habits.

OR

> Benjamin Franklin discovered electricity and invented the lightning rod, but he also wanted thirteen virtues (such as order, silence, justice, and temperance) to become habits, so he kept a little book to record his daily habits.

Frozen raindrops collide with each other and create an electrical charge.
The electrical charge travels to the ground.
We call this charge "lightning."
Lightning creates a sound wave behind it.
We call this sound wave "thunder."
Light waves travel faster than sound waves.
We see the lightning before we hear the thunder.

> When frozen raindrops collide with each other and create an electrical charge, that charge can travel to the ground, creating a sound wave behind it; we call the charge "lightning" and the sound wave "thunder," and since light waves travel faster than sound waves, we see the lightning before we hear the thunder.

OR

> The electrical charge that we call "lightning" is created when frozen raindrops collide with each other and create an electrical charge that travels to the ground and creates a sound wave called "thunder" behind it; we see the lightning before we hear the thunder, because light travels faster than sound.

Tacos de papas are tacos filled with mashed potatoes.
The potatoes can be russet potatoes with butter and cumin.
They could be sweet potatoes with jalapeno peppers and red onions.
The tacos can be vegetarian.
They can also contain chorizo.
Spanish chorizo is sausage made from minced pork, smoked paprika, salt, and sometimes garlic.
Mexican chorizo is made from ground meat.
That ground meat can be pork, or beef, turkey, or venison.

Tacos de papas are tacos filled with mashed potatoes, which can be either russet potatoes with butter and cumin or sweet potatoes with jalapeno peppers and red onions; although the tacos can be vegetarian, they can also contain Spanish chorizo made from minced pork, smoked paprika, salt, and sometimes garlic, or Mexican chorizo made from ground pork, beef, turkey, or venison.

OR

Tacos de papas that are vegetarian are filled with mashed russet potatoes with butter and cumin, or sweet potatoes with jalapeno peppers and red onions; they can also contain Spanish chorizo with minced pork, smoked paprika, salt, and sometimes garlic, or Mexican chorizo that is made from ground pork, beef, turkey, or venison.

Exercise 80C: Diagramming

On your own paper, diagram the following epigrams. (Epigram: a short clever saying)

I have found you an argument; I am not obliged to find you an understanding.
—Samuel Johnson

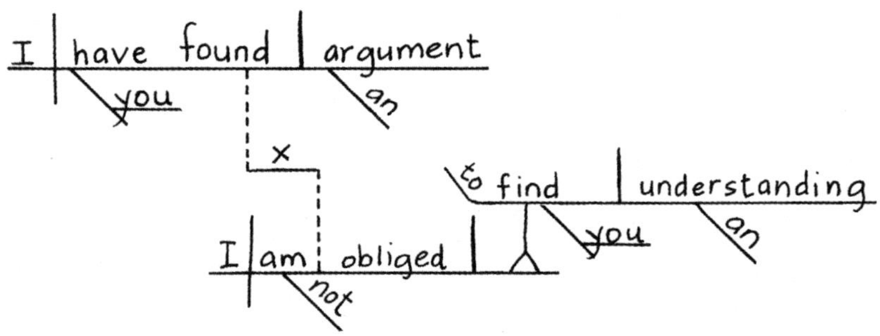

Note to Instructor: *To find you an understanding* could also be diagrammed as an adverb clause beneath *am obliged*.

A tart temper never mellows with age; and a sharp tongue is the only edged tool that grows keener with constant use.
—Washington Irving

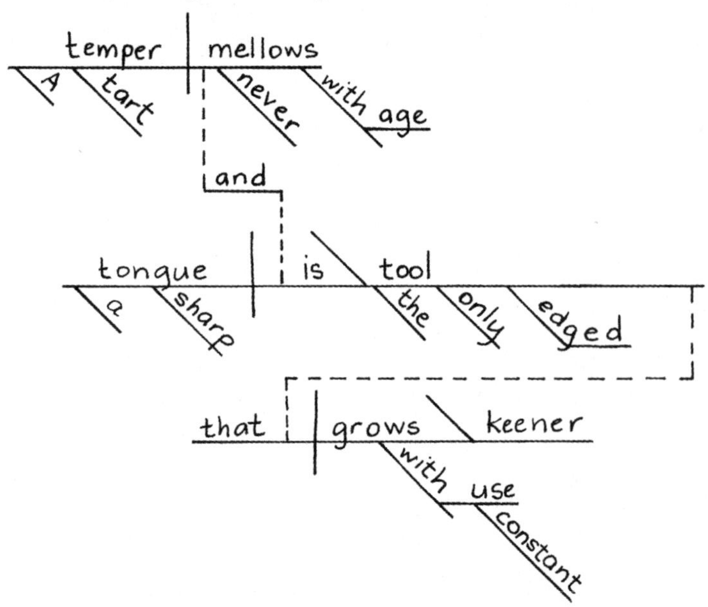

All actual heroes are essential men; and all men, possible heroes.
—Elizabeth Barrett Browning

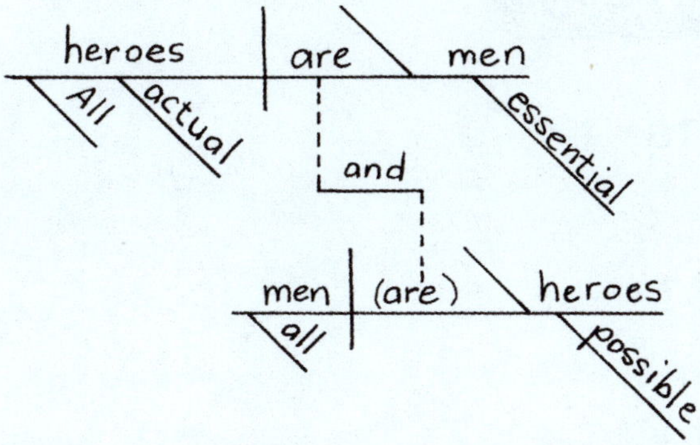

Improve yourself by other men's writings, thus attaining easily what they acquired through great difficulty.
—Socrates (translated by Michael R. Burch)

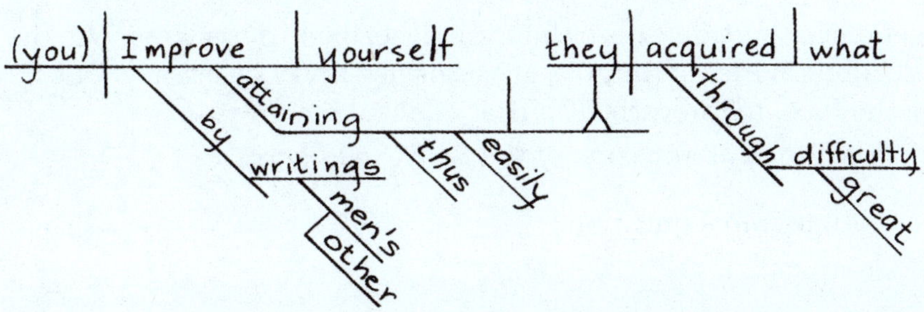

WEEK 21

Conditions

— LESSON 81 —

Helping Verbs
Tense and Voice
Modal Verbs

Exercise 81A: Using *Do, Does,* and *Did*

On your own paper, rewrite each sentence, putting it into the form described in brackets. Use the appropriate form of the helping verb along with any interrogatives or negatives necessary. Don't forget that you may have to change the form of the verb! The first one is done for you.

These sentences are taken from Jack Finney's *Invasion of the Body Snatchers.*

You heard of the Mattoon Maniac. [Change into a question.]
Did you hear of the Mattoon Maniac?

It happens. [Provide emphasis.]
It does happen.

I knew how to answer him. [Turn into a negative statement.]
I didn't know how to answer him.

A psychology instructor told me about an odd personality change. [Provide emphasis.]
A psychology instructor did tell me about an odd personality change.

I know how much noise I made. [Turn into a negative statement.]
I do not know how much noise I made.

We prefer the weird and thrilling to the dull and commonplace. [Provide emphasis.]
We do prefer the weird and thrilling to the dull and commonplace.

They drifted through space. [Provide emphasis.]
They did drift through space.

This street looks dead. [Change into a question.]
Does this street look dead?

This incredible alien life form "thinks" this or "knows" it. [Change into a question.]
Did this incredible alien life form "think" this or "know" it?

You know he isn't really Ira anymore. [Change into a question.]
How do you know he isn't really Ira anymore?

Exercise 81B: Modal Verbs

Fill in the blanks below with an appropriate helping verb (*should, would, may, might, must, can, could*) to form a modal verb. There may be more than one correct answer for each sentence. Use each helping verb at least once.

These sentences are taken from John Wyndham's wonderful novel *The Day of the Triffids*. After you finish the exercise, be sure to read the original sentence in the *Answer Key*.

Note to Instructor: The bolded words are John Wyndham's originals. Other acceptable answers are in brackets. If a substitution makes sense to you, accept it even if it isn't included in the bracketed options.

Fires and weather **would** [could, may, might, must] have worked on it; it **would** [could, may, might, must] be visibly dead and abandoned. But now, at a distance, it **could** [can] still masquerade as a living city.

It was evident that most of the foraging parties **must** [could, would, should] have returned by this hour.

Should [Must] we spend our time in prolonging misery when we believe that there is no chance of saving people in the end?

We **could** [should, might, can] do as he says. We **could** [should, might, can] show some, though only some, of these people where there is food. We **could** [might, can] do that for a few days, maybe for a few weeks, but after that— what?

I can't help feeling that there **must** [should, might, may, could] be something wrong about anything that starts with shooting.

Triffid stems do not snap—but they **can** [could] be mangled.

Some of us **may** [might, could] be feeling that it is the end of everything. It is not. But to all of you I will say at once that it **can** [could, would, might] be the end of everything—if we let it.

Any suspicion of illness **should** [must] be reported at once, since the effects of a contagious disease among us **would** [could, might] be serious.

Granted that they do have intelligence, then that **would** [could] leave us with only one important superiority—sight.

I couldn't get away from the feeling that they **might** [could, can, must] indeed be rattling out secret messages to one another.

Exercise 81C: Verb Tense and Voice

For each sentence below, underline each verb phrase (in both dependent and independent clauses) and identify the tense and voice of the verb. For state-of-being verbs which are neither active nor passive in voice, identify the tense and write *state-of-being*. Mark modal verbs as *perfect present* or *simple present*. The first sentence is done for you.

These sentences are taken from H. G. Wells's classic science fiction novel *The War of the Worlds*. Some have been slightly condensed.

simple past active — progressive present active
"Death!" I shouted. "Death is coming! Death!"

progressive past active — progressive past active
All night long the Martians were hammering and stirring, sleepless, indefatigable, at work upon
progressive past active
the machines they were making ready, and ever and again a puff of greenish-white smoke
simple past active
whirled up to the starlit sky.

simple past active
I wrenched the horse's head hard round to the right, and in another moment the dog-cart
perfect past active — simple past active — simple past passive — simple past active
had heeled over upon the horse; the shafts smashed noisily and I was flung sideways and fell heavily into a shallow pool of water.

simple future passive — simple present state-of-being
Lots will be worried by a sort of feeling that something is terribly wrong.

simple past state-of-being — simple past active — perfect past active — progressive past active
When his eyes were clear again, he saw the monster had passed and was rushing landward.

perfect present passive — simple past active
Beyond that, the tower of Shepperton Church—it has been replaced by a spire—rose above the trees.

perfect past active — perfect past active — perfect present modal
If I had fully realized the meaning of all the things I had seen, I should have immediately worked my way back to rejoin my wife.

perfect present active — perfect future active
The thread of life that has begun here will have streamed out to our sister planet.

perfect present active
Across the immensity of space, the Martians have watched the fate of these pioneers of theirs,
perfect present active
and perhaps on the planet Venus they have found a securer settlement.

simple present active — progressive present passive
I do not think that nearly enough attention is being given to the possibility of another attack from the Martians.

progressive future active
Presently the Martians will be coming this way again.

— LESSON 82 —

Conditional Sentences
The Condition Clause
The Consequence Clause

Exercise 82A: Identifying Conditional Sentences

Some of the sentences in this exercise are conditional sentences—and others are not! Identify each conditional sentence by writing a *C* in the margin. For each conditional sentence, label the clauses as *condition* or *consequence.*

Note to Instructor: If the student has trouble telling the difference, remind her that conditional sentences express situations that have not actually happened.

Although he was small and helpless, the mouse was a wise little creature.

condition / consequence
If he did not find a place to hide, he would serve as dinner to the great owl. C

condition / consequence
And if he went within reach of the cat's claws, he would suffer for it. C

As he thought and thought, his eyes grew brighter.

condition / consequence
"As long as I am near the cat, the owl will not dare to come after me." C

"While we have never been friends, dear cat, I have always considered you a noble enemy."

condition / consequence
"If you will promise never to do me any harm, I will nibble through the string around your neck and set you free." C

Although the mouse pretended to nibble the string, he took care not to bite it through.

consequence / condition
He knew that she would eat him up unless he took great care. C

Exercise 82B: Tense in Conditional Sentences

Fill in each blank below with the correct tense and form of the verb in brackets. Some sentences may have more than one possible correct answer.

First Conditional Sentences

If my sister sees [*see*] me eating her candy, I am [state-of-being verb] in big trouble. [or *will be*]

If he is [state-of-being verb] late, go [*go*] without him.

If that small child eats [*eat*] too much, she will be [state-of-being verb] sick.

If I find [*find*] the book, I will send [*send*] it to you.

Unless the patient stops [*stop*] smoking, he will become [*become*] very ill.

If she follows [*follow*] my advice about those investments, she will be [state-of-being verb] a very rich woman.

Second Conditional Sentences

> **Note to Instructor:** The helping verbs *might, could, would,* and *should* can all be used. If the student uses the same helping verb repeatedly, ask her to try one of the other verb options.

If I knew [*know*] what to do, I would do [*do*] it.

If I broke [*break*] my leg, I could not run [*run*] the marathon.

If I had [*have*] the book, I might send [*send*] it to you.

If the patient stopped [*stop*] smoking, he would feel [*feel*] much better.

Third conditional sentences

If I had known [*know*] what would happen, I would never have eaten [*eat*] the apple.

If the policemen had warned [*warn*] her about the consequences, she should have behaved [*behave*] differently.

If I had tried [*try*] to run a better campaign, I would be [state-of-being verb] President now.

If I had had [*have*] the book, I would have sent [*send*] it to you.

If the patient had stopped [*stop*] smoking, he would not cough [*cough*] so much now.

Had she followed [*follow*] my advice about those investments, she would be [state-of-being verb] a rich woman today.

Exercise 82C: Diagramming

On your own paper, diagram these sentences, taken from J. R. R. Tolkien's *The Hobbit.* A conditional clause should be diagrammed like any other dependent clause.

Goblins do not usually venture very far from their mountains, unless they are driven out and are looking for new homes, or are marching to war.

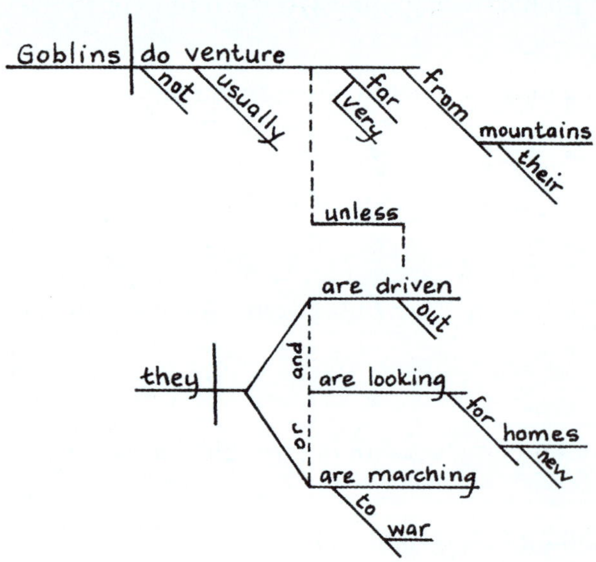

You would have dropped him, if a goblin had suddenly grabbed your legs from behind in the dark, tripped up your feet, and kicked you in the back!

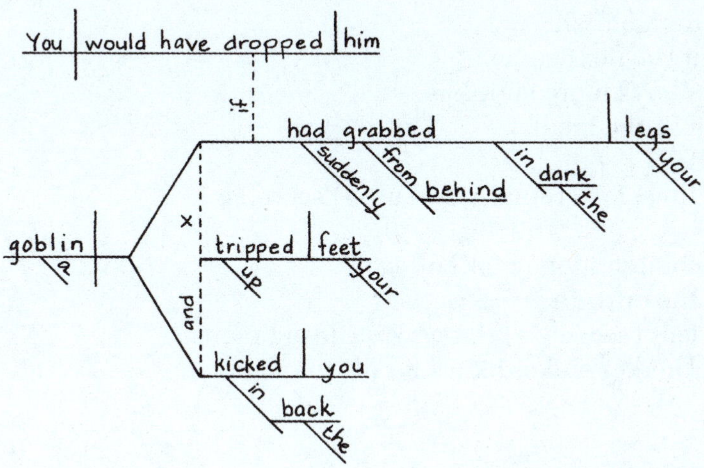

That only makes eleven and not four teen, unless wizards count differently than other people.

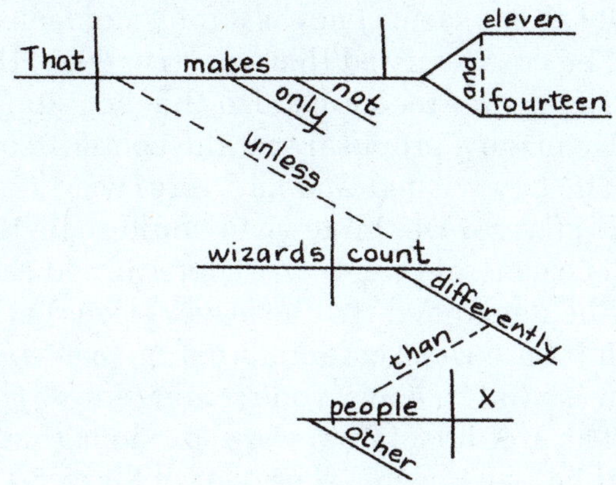

— LESSON 83 —

Conditional Sentences

The Subjunctive

Exercise 83A: Subjunctive Forms In Song Lyrics

Fill in each blank with the correct state-of-being verb.

If I were a rich man, all day long I'd biddy biddy bum.

If I were a wealthy man, I wouldn't have to work hard.

If I were rich, I'd have the time that I lack to sit in the synagogue and pray.

—From the musical *Fiddler on the Roof*

If I were a swan, I'd be gone.

If I were a train, I'd be late again.

And if I were a good man, I'd talk with you more often than I do.

—From the Pink Floyd song "If"

If I were a carpenter, and you were a lady, would you marry me anyway?

If a miller were my trade, at a mill wheel grinding, would you miss your colour box?

—From the Tim Hardin song "If I Were a Carpenter"

If she were only mine, I would build a house so fine.

She is as pretty as a queen.

—From the bluegrass song "Lulu Walls"

Exercise 83B: Subjunctive Forms in Complex Sentences

In each pair of verb forms, cross out the incorrect form.

It (~~seem~~/seems) now as if my stomach (were/~~was~~) as empty as a rich man's brain.
The cook insisted that she (try/~~tries~~) the cuttlefish dish.
The doctor recommended that he (~~sits~~/sit) out the next game.
He made a proposal that the committee (~~buys~~/buy) more supplies.
The boy wished that he (were/~~was~~) there to join the meal.
If I (were/~~was~~) like you I could scale the wall.
The general (~~were~~/was) determined that the invasion (remain/~~remains~~) secret.
She demanded that he leave/~~leaves~~) at once.
It (was/~~were~~) essential that he (~~saves~~/save) enough money for college.
It is vital that everyone (enter/~~enters~~) before the curtain rises.
The architect (was/~~were~~) anxious that his client (see/~~sees~~) the new building plans.
If he (~~was~~/were) president of Mars, he could (make/~~makes~~) laws for all the Martians.

— LESSON 84 —

Conditional Sentences
The Subjunctive
Moods of Verbs
Subjunctive Forms Using *Be*

Exercise 84A: Parsing Verbs

Underline each predicate, in both main clauses and dependent clauses. Above each, write the tense, voice, and mood of the verb.

Tenses: Simple past, present, future; progressive past, present, future; perfect past, present, future

Voice: Active, passive (or state-of-being)

Mood: Indicative, subjunctive, imperative, modal, subjunctive/modal

These sentences are taken from Lloyd Alexander's novel *The High King*, the final book in the *Chronicles of Prydain* series.

Note to Instructor: For the subjunctive and modal forms, the description within parentheses is optional, since we have not yet studied the progressive or perfect forms of these verbs.

perfect past, passive, indicative / simple past, passive, indicative

The socket from which the dragon's crest <u>had been torn</u> <u>was lined</u> with flat stones, and in it, as in

simple past, active, indicative

a narrow grave, <u>lay</u> Dyrnwyn, the black sword.

perfect present, active, indicative / present, active, imperative

You <u>have learned</u> much, but <u>learn</u> this last and hardest of lessons.

(simple) past, state-of-being, subjunctive — (simple) present, active, modal

Oh, if I were a giant again, you'd not find me lingering!

(simple) present, passive, subjunctive — (simple) present, state-of-being, modal/subjunctive

If any life be staked against Arawn Death-Lord, it must be mine.

> **Note to Instructor:** The form *it be* has to be subjunctive; the modal verb turns it into a combined modal/subjunctive verb.

simple future, active, indicative

They'll have no stomach for a fight now.

simple past, active, indicative — (perfect) past, state-of-being, subjunctive

Huge blocks of ice thundered down the slope, bounding and rolling as if they had been no more than pebbles.

simple present, active, imperative — (simple) present, active, modal/subjunctive — simple present, state-of-being, imperative

Mount up behind the King of Mona, if he can stand your company, and be quick about it.

simple present, state-of-being, indicative — perfect present, active, indicative

This is the most terrible thing that has ever happened.

perfect past, active, indicative — progressive past, active, indicative

Taran had already dismounted and was racing down the slope, waving at the bard to follow him.

Exercise 84B: Forming Subjunctives

Fill in the blanks in the following sentences with the correct verb form indicated in brackets.

> **Note to Instructor:** Any modal helping verbs (*should*, *might*, etc.) can be used in place of *would* as long as the finished sentence makes sense.

I wish [simple present indicative of *wish*] that my brother were [simple past subjunctive of *am*] here.

The judge's decision was [simple past indicative of *am*] that the driver be fined [simple present passive subjunctive of *fine*] five hundred dollars.

If he should be convicted [simple present passive subjunctive/modal of *convict*] of reckless driving, he will lose [simple future indicative of *lose*] his license.

If the earth were [simple past subjunctive of *am*] flat, adventurers would have been [perfect present modal of *am*] unable to sail all the way around it.

Far be [simple present subjunctive of *am*] it from me to question your motives!

If my boss were [simple past subjunctive of *am*] unhappy with my performance, he would have said [perfect present modal of *say*] so.

If only he had been determined [perfect past subjunctive of *determine*] to overcome his difficulties!

Were [simple past subjunctive of *am*] he to ask me to marry him, I would refuse [simple present modal].

It would have been [perfect present subjunctive of *am*] better to avoid the conversation altogether.

Exercise 84C: Diagramming

On your own paper, diagram the following sentences.

These are the first three sentences from the chapter "Shadows" in Lloyd Alexander's *The Castle of Llyr.*

The feast that evening was surely the merriest the castle had ever seen.

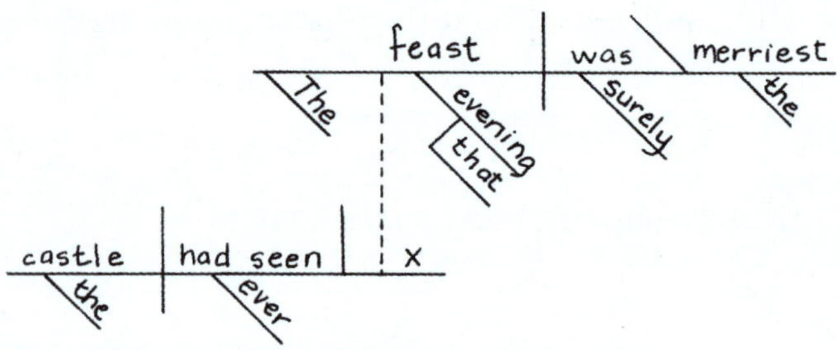

Note to Instructor: The phrase *that evening* can be diagrammed as an adjective phrase modifying *feast*, or as a participle phrase with an understood *[held] that evening* (or perhaps *[happening] that evening*), in which case it becomes an adverb phrase answering the question *when*. *Evening* can be an adjective, but not, on its own, an adverb.

Kaw, perched on the back of Taran's chair, bobbed up and down and looked as if the banquet had been the arranged entirely in his honour.

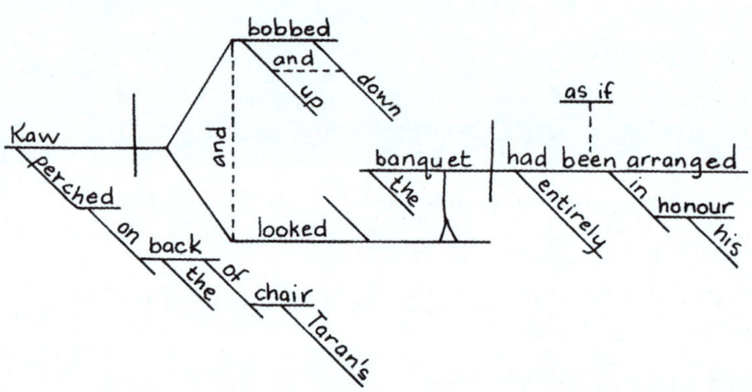

King Rhuddlum beamed with good spirits; the talk and laughter of the guests rang throughout the Great Hall.

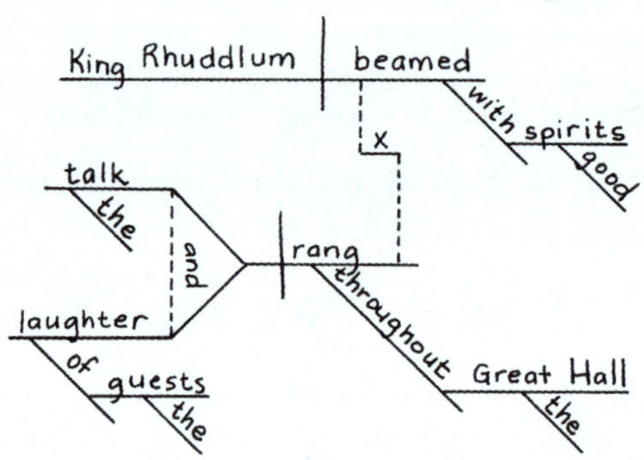

— REVIEW 7 —

Weeks 19-21

Topics
Phrases and Clauses
Adjective, Adverb, and Noun Clauses
Pronouns
Mood: Modal, Subjective, Imperative, Indicative
Conditional Sentences

Review 7A: Improving Sentences with Phrases

In the blanks below, supply phrases that meet the descriptions in brackets. You may supply more than one phrase in any blank, as long as at least one phrase fulfills the requirements (often, additional prepositional phrases may be needed). The first is done for you, with explanations provided.

The original sentences are taken from John Knowles's classic 1959 novel *A Separate Peace.* This is a challenging assignment—prepare to spend some time on it!

When you are finished, compare your sentences with the originals in the *Answer Key.*

> **Note to Instructor:** This is a difficult exercise, but it will begin to move the student towards using grammatical knowledge to construct more interesting sentences, while also giving a model from an excellent writer. If the student gets stuck, provide him with the first word or two of the original phrase.
>
> When the student is finished, ask him to read his sentence out loud first, follow by Knowles's original sentence. Encourage him to listen carefully to both sentences.

[adverbial prepositional phrase answering the question *where*] [adjectival present participle phrase modifying *anyone*]

I had rarely seen anyone go __________, or anyone ____________ or even an open window.

[adverbial prepositional phrase answering the question *where*] [adjectival present participle phrase modifying *anyone*]

I had rarely seen anyone go into one of them*, or anyone* playing on a lawn *or even an open window.*

EXPLANATION: The phrase modifies the verb *go* and tells us where *anyone* is going. Although Knowles could have written *into the houses* (a single prepositional phrase), he chose to put two phrases together (*into one* + *of them*).

EXPLANATION: The present participle *playing* describes what *anyone* is doing. Knowles has written a present participle phrase that includes a prepositional phrase (*on a lawn*). He could have written *playing happily* or another phrase containing *only* the participle and modifiers.

[adjectival prepositional phrase describing the houses; preposition should have a compound object]

Today with their failing ivy and stripped, moaning trees the houses looked both more elegant and more lifeless than ever.

[adverbial prepositional phrase answering the question *where*] [adverbial prepositional phrase answering the question *where*]

In through swinging doors I reached a marble foyer and stopped at the foot of a long white marble flight of stairs.

[adjectival prepositional phrase describing the wind] [adverbial subordinate cl phrase answering the question *when*]

With nothing to block it the wind flung wet gusts at me; at any other time I would have felt

[adjectival present participle phrase describing *fool*] [adjectival infinitive phrase describing *fool*]

like a fool slogging through mud and rain, only to look at a tree.

[adverbial prepositional phrase answering the question *where*] [adverbial subordinate clause answering the question *when*]

A little fog hung over the river so that as I neared it I felt myself becoming isolated from

[adjectival prepositional phrase describing *everything*]

everything except the river and the few trees beside it.

[adjectival present participle phrase describing *trees*]

There were several trees bleakly reaching into the fog.

[adjectival infinitive phrase describing *head*] [adjectival prepositional phrase describing *sounds*]

My head began to feel unnaturally light, and the vague rustling sounds from the nearby woods

[adverbial prepositional phrase answering the question *how* (manner)]

came to me as though muffled and filtered.

[present participle phrase acting as a noun and serving as the direct object of *risk*]

I would have to spring far out or risk falling into the shallow water next to the bank.

[adjectival past participle phrase describing *radio*]

Our illegal radio, turned too low to be intelligible, was broadcasting the news.

Review 7B: Improving Sentences with Clauses

Rewrite each sentence on your own paper, adding a dependent clause that meets the description in brackets. The first is done for you, with explanations provided.

The original sentences are taken from *A Christmas Carol*, by Charles Dickens. When you are finished, compare your sentences with the originals in the *Answer Key*.

[noun clause serving as the predicate nominative, renaming *doubt*]

There is no doubt ______________________________.

[noun clause serving as the predicate nominative, renaming *doubt*]

There is no doubt that Marley was dead.

[The subject of the sentence is *doubt*; the linking verb *is* connects the subject to the clause explaining what the *doubt* is. *There* and *no* are adverbs modifying *is*.]

This must be distinctly understood, or nothing wonderful can come of the story

[adjective clause describing *story*]

I am going to relate.

Scrooge had a very small fire, but the clerk's fire was so very much smaller
[adverb clause describing *how* much smaller]
that it looked like one coal.

[adjective clause describing *shops*]
The brightness of the shops where holly sprigs and berries crackled in the lamp heat of
[adverb clause telling *when*]
the windows made pale faces ruddy as they passed.

[adjective clause describing *chambers*]
He lived in chambers which had once belonged to his deceased partner.

[adjective phrase describing *noise*]
They were succeeded by a clanking noise, deep down below, as if some person were dragging a heavy chain over the casks in the wine-merchant's cellar.

[noun clause serving as the object of the infinitive *to have heard*]
Scrooge then remembered to have heard that ghosts in haunted houses were described as dragging chains.

Review 7C: Conditional Clauses

Label the following sentences as first, second, or third conditional by writing *1*, *2*, or *3* in the blank next to each one. Underline each conditional clause. Circle each consequence clause.

These sentences are taken from *The Hobbit*, by J. R. R. Tolkien.

I'll cook beautifully for you, a perfectly beautiful breakfast for you if only you won't have me for supper. 1

If we don't get blown off, or drowned, or struck by lightning, we shall be picked up by some giant and kicked sky-high for a football. 1

If their plan had been carried out there would have been none left there next day; all would have been killed except the few the goblins kept from the wolves and carried back as prisoners to their caves. 3

Bilbo began to feel there really was something of a bold adventurer about himself after all, though he would have felt a lot bolder still if there had been anything to eat. 3

Now scuttle off, and come back quick if all is well. 1

If precious asks, and it doesn't answer, we eats it, my precious 1

Note to Instructor: Technically there are two condition clauses, the second with an understood *if*: *If previous asks, and [if] it doesn't answer, we eats it.* Both conditions have to be fulfilled for the consequence clause to kick in.

They all thought their own shares in the treasure (which they quite regarded as theirs, in spite of their plight and the still unconquered dragon) would suffer seriously if the Wood-elves claimed part of it, and they all trusted Bilbo. 2

Note to Instructor: The entire consequence clause (subject: *treasure*; predicate: *would suffer*) contains an adjective clause (*which they . . . dragon*) within it.

Yet if they had known more about it and considered the meaning of the hunt and the white deer that had appeared upon their path, they would have known that they were at last drawing towards the eastern edge, and would soon have come, if they could have kept up their courage and their hope, to thinner trees and places where the sunlight came again. 3

Note to Instructor: There are two condition clauses (*Yet if they . . . path and if they . . . hope*) but only one consequence clause (subject: *they*; compound predicate: *were drawing, would have come*). The second condition clause interrupts the consequence clause.

Review 7D: Pronoun Review

The following paragraphs are taken from Russian fairy tales. Circle every pronoun. Label each as personal (*PER*), possessive (*POSS*), reflexive (*REF*), demonstrative (*DEM*), or indefinite (*IND*). Beside this label, add the abbreviation for the part of the sentence (or clause) that the pronoun serves as: adjective (*ADJ*), subject (*SUBJ*), direct object (*DO*), indirect object (*IO*), or object of the preposition (*OP*).

The first has been done for you.

On her [POSS/ADJ] deathbed the merchant's wife called her [POSS/ADJ] little daughter to her [PER/OP], took out from under the bed-clothes a doll, gave it [PER/DO] to her [PER/OP], and said, "Listen, Vasilissa, dear; remember and obey these last words of mine [POSS/OP]. I [PER/SUBJ] am going to die. And now, together with my [POSS/ADJ] parental blessing, I [PER/SUBJ] bequeath to you [PER/OP] this doll. Never show it [PER/DO] to anybody [IND/OP]; and whenever any misfortune comes upon you [PER/OP], give the doll food, and ask its [POSS/ADJ] advice. If you [PER/SUBJ] do this [DEM/DO], it [PER/SUBJ] will tell you [PER/IO] a cure for your [POSS/ADJ] troubles." Then the mother kissed her [POSS/ADJ] child and died.

This time there was no help for it [PER/OP]; Prince Ivan had to confess everything [IND/DO], and then he [PER/SUBJ] took to entreating the Sun's Sister to let him [PER/DO] go, that he [PER/SUBJ] might satisfy himself [REF/DO] about his [POSS/ADJ] old home. So at last he [PER/SUBJ] persuaded her [PER/DO], and she [PER/SUBJ] let him [PER/DO] go away to find out about his [POSS/ADJ] home. But first she [PER/SUBJ] provided him [PER/DO] for the journey with a brush, a comb, and two youth-giving apples. However old anyone [IND/SUBJ] might be, if he [PER/SUBJ] should eat one of these [DEM/ADJ] apples, he [PER/SUBJ] would grow young again in an instant.

Review 7E: Parsing

In the sentences below, underline every verb or verb phrase that acts as the predicate of a clause (dependent or independent). Label each verb with the correct tense, voice, and mood.

Tenses: Simple past, present, future; progressive past, present, future; perfect past, present, future

Voice: Active, passive, state-of-being

Mood: Indicative, subjunctive, imperative, modal, subjunctive/modal

The first is done for you.

These sentences are taken from Tom Holland's history *Persian Fire.*

simple present, active, modal — simple past, state-of-being, indicative — simple past, state-of-being, indicative

While Darius would soon prove himself as bold as he was ruthless, he was never one to flaunt his crimes.

perfect past, active, indicative

His calculations had been precise.

progressive past, active, indicative

A rare opportunity was indeed now opening.

simple present, active, modal

If the assassination squad could ambush him on open ground, somewhere on the road between

simple present, passive, modal/subjunctive

Ecbatana and the heartland of royal power in Persia, then he might be dispatched with relative ease.

simple past, active, indicative — simple past, passive, indicative

Horses, white horses, covered the plain—as many as 160,000 of them, it was said.

simple present, passive, modal/subjunctive — simple past, active, indicative

What happened next would be retold by all those who traced their lineage from the seven leaders of the assassination squad.

simple present, active, indicative — simple future, active indicative

The wretch who weaves deceit will bring death into his country.

perfect past, active, indicative

From that moment on, the King of Lydia had become the oracle's most generous patron.

simple past, active, subjunctive

If he were one of the greatest men of the kingdom—one of Darius's six co-conspirators, say—

simple present, active, modal

then he and his retinue might receive up to a hundred quarts of wine.

simple past, state-of-being, subjunctive — simple past, passive, subjunctive

If rivals proved obdurate, they were best murdered on the quiet.

Review 7F: Diagramming

On your own paper, diagram every word of the following sentence from J. R. R. Tolkien's *The Fellowship of the Ring.*

And if he often uses the Ring to make himself invisible, he *fades*; he becomes in the end invisible permanently, and walks in the twilight under the eye of the Dark Power that rules the Rings.

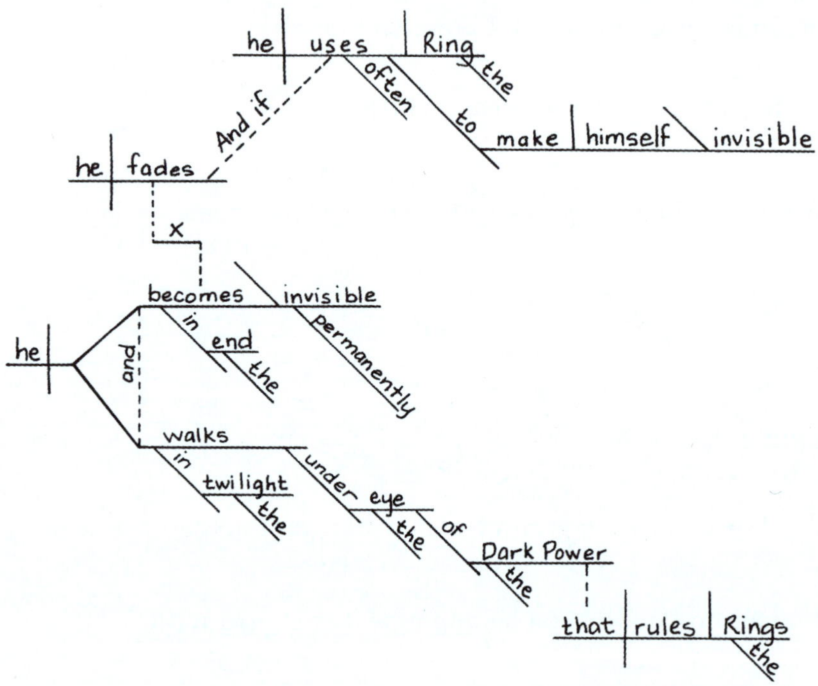

WEEK 22

Parenthetical Elements

— LESSON 85 —

Verb Review

Complete the following chart with the third-person singular form of the verb indicated in the left-hand column. If you need help, ask your instructor.

Note to Instructor: Ask the student to make his best guess at any forms that confuse him. Then, show him the answers and have him erase (or scratch out) his incorrect answers and write in the correct ones.

INDICATIVE TENSES

		Active	Passive
SIMPLE			
attack	Past	[he, she, it] attacked	[he, she, it] was attacked
paint	Present	[he, she, it] paints	[he, she, it] is painted
buy	Future	[he, she, it] will buy	[he, she, it] will be bought
PROGRESSIVE			
drink	Past	[he, she, it] was drinking	[he, she, it] was being drunk
forget	Present	[he, she, it] is forgetting	[he, she, it] is being forgotten
guide	Future	[he, she, it] will be guiding	[he, she, it] will be being guided
PERFECT			
embarrass	Past	[he, she, it] had embarrassed	[he, she, it] had been embarrassed
interrupt	Present	[he, she, it] has interrupted	[he, she, it] has been interrupted
scold	Future	[he, she, it] will have scolded	[he, she, it] will have been scolded

MODAL TENSES
(would *or* should, may, might, must, can, could)

		Active	Passive
SIMPLE			
dance	Present	[he, she, it] would dance	
PERFECT			
sleep	Past	[he, she, it] would have slept	

SUBJUNCTIVE TENSES

		Active	Passive
SIMPLE			
fall	Past	[he, she, it] fell	
fall	Present	[he, she, it] fall	

On your own paper, write sentences that use each of the forms above as the predicate of an independent or dependent clause. If you need help (or ideas), ask your instructor.

Note to Instructor: Model sentences using the forms in the chart are listed below. If the student needs assistance using a particular form, show him the sentence containing that form and then ask him to write a variation of it (different subject, different modifiers, etc.). Students should always be allowed to copy a model when they are confused.

She **was drinking** at the well when the ostrich **attacked** her.

The captain **would have slept** all night, but when his ship **was attacked** by pirates, his night's sleep was ruined.

Note to Instructor: Another modal helping verb can be substituted for *would*.

When an artist **paints** a landscape, she hopes that it **will be bought** by someone who loves it.

Lemonade **was being drunk**, hot dogs were being grilled, and the picnic was going full swing.

No one **will buy** this farm unless the barn **is painted** red.

The lecturer **is forgetting** a very important fact.

The old way **is** slowly **being forgotten.**

He will be on the ski slopes by then, and he **will be guiding** the ascent of Mount Everest in the cold and snow.

Part of the adventure **will be being guided** through the Himalayan foothills by experts.

He **had embarrassed** his family, which **had** already **been embarrassed** by losing all their money.

So far, nothing **has interrupted** my work.

When the little girl was happy, she **would dance** and spin in circles.

Note to Instructor: Another modal helping verb can be substituted for *would*.

If the rain **fell** any harder, it would wash the house itself away.

Should the captain **fall**, the lieutenant will take command.

— LESSON 86 —

Restrictive and Non-Restrictive Modifying Clauses
Parenthetical Expressions

Exercise 86A: Restrictive and Non-Restrictive Modifying Clauses

In the following sentences, mark each bolded clause as either *ADV* for adverb or *ADJ* for adjective, and draw an arrow from the clause back to the word modified. Some sentences contain more than one modifying clause.

Then, identify each bolded modifying clause as either restrictive (*R*) or non-restrictive (*N*).

Finally, set off all of the non-restrictive clauses with commas. Use the proofreader's mark: ^, for comma insertion. When you are finished, compare your punctuation with the original.

These sentences are slightly condensed from Lewis Carroll's *Alice's Adventures in Wonderland.* The original commas around the non-restrictive clauses have been removed.

R ADJ

How funny it'll seem to come out among the people **that walk with their heads downward**!

N ADJ

She found herself in a long, low hall **which was lit up by a row of lamps hanging from the roof.**

R ADJ

Soon her eye fell on a little glass box **that was lying under the table**: she opened it, and

N ADJ

found in it a very small cake **on which the words "EAT ME" were beautifully marked in currants**.

R ADJ

Now I'm opening out like the largest telescope **that ever was.**

R ADJ

However, she soon made out that she was in the pool of tears **which she had wept when**

R ADV

she was nine feet high.

R ADJ

They were indeed a queer-looking party **that assembled on the bank**—the birds with draggled feathers, the animals with their fur clinging close to them, and all dripping wet, cross, and uncomfortable.

N ADJ

At last the Mouse **who seemed to be a person of authority among them** called out, "Sit down, all of you, and listen to me! I'll soon make you dry enough!"

N ADJ

William the Conqueror **whose cause was favored by the pope** was soon submitted to by

N ADV

the English **who wanted leaders**.

N ADJ

"I have tasted eggs, certainly," said Alice **who was a very truthful child**.

N ADV R ADJ

While she was looking at the place where it had been it suddenly appeared again.

It was very provoking to find that the hedgehog had unrolled itself, and was in the act of crawling away: besides all this, there was generally a ridge or furrow in the way **wherever**

R ADJ

she wanted to send the hedgehog to.

R ADJ N ADJ

Those **whom she sentenced** were taken into custody by the soldiers **who of course had to leave off being arches to do this** so that by the end of half an hour or so there were no arches left, and all the players, except the King, the Queen, and Alice, were in custody and under sentence of execution.

R ADV

So she stood still **where she was** and waited.

Exercise 86B: Identifying Parenthetical Expressions

Identify each parenthetical expression as a phrase, dependent clause, or sentence.

CHALLENGE EXERCISE

Provide a fuller description of each expression. What kind of phrase, clause, or sentence? What does it do or modify?

When you are finished, ask your instructor for the fuller explanations. Compare your descriptions to these explanations.

Note to Instructor: As long as the student is able to identify the expression as phrase, clause, or sentence, you may consider the answer correct. The challenge exercise is optional. If the student has not provided the additional information included, go through each answer with her.

dependent clause acting as an adverb (answering the question "how did she give herself advice?" and so modifying the verb *gave*)

She generally gave herself very good advice (though she very seldom followed it), and sometimes she scolded herself so severely as to bring tears into her eyes.

dependent clause acting as an adverb (modifying the understood verb in the clause *on it [were] a fan and two or three pairs of tiny white kid gloves*)

By this time she had found her way into a tidy little room with a table in the window, and on it (as she had hoped) a fan and two or three pairs of tiny white kid gloves.

complete sentence, with *Alice* as the subject, containing a dependent clause acting as an adverb and describing *how* surprised Alice was

"Curiouser and curiouser!" cried Alice (she was so much surprised, that for the moment she quite forgot how to speak good English).

complete sentence, giving further details about the Caterpillar

"It is a very good height indeed!" said the Caterpillar angrily, rearing itself upright as it spoke (it was exactly three inches high).

phrase, acting as an adverb and describing *said*

"When I'm a Duchess," she said to herself (not in a very hopeful tone though), "I won't have any pepper in my kitchen at all."

dependent clause, acting as an adjective and describing *way*

As soon as she had made out the proper way of nursing it (which was to twist it up into a sort of knot, and then keep tight hold of its right ear and left foot, so as to prevent its undoing itself), she carried it out into the open air.

complete sentence, independent of the previous sentence

They very soon came upon a Gryphon, lying fast asleep in the sun. (If you don't know what a Gryphon is, look at the picture.)

complete sentence, a command to the reader

The judge, by the way, was the King; and as he wore his crown over the wig (look at the frontispiece if you want to see how he did it), he did not look at all comfortable, and it was certainly not becoming.

Exercise 86C: Punctuating Sentences with Parenthetical Expressions

Correct each of the following sentences, using the proofreader's marks listed below.

Insert quotation marks: ❞
insert comma: ^,
insert period: ⊙
insert question mark: ^?
insert exclamation point: ↑!
delete: ℓ
move punctuation mark: ↗

If the sentence is correct, write *C* in the margin next to it.

If young writers could learn grammar without a textbook, this workbook wouldn't be necessary⊙ (But, to be honest, a few intuitive types do figure it out on their own).

After seven weeks of instruction, the grammar class was frustrated with the teacher's knowledge, (or, to be frank, the lack thereof.)

I looked up the publication information for our grammar book (Harcourt Brace, 2002), but I still don't think that it reflects modern grammar usage. C

We checked our grammar book's explanation of parenthetical elements (we all thought it was adequate, if not great) against the explanation in the nineteenth-century grammar book (so hard to read!)⊙

I really do love grammar (and writing.)

Could you bring me a new grammar book quickly? (and cheaply)

That will help me to punctuate parentheses properly (and easily). C

It's a simple enough job, if you know exactly what you're saying (and where to put the punctuation)⊙

I've been researching grammar books (crazy hobby, isn't it)? for over a year now.

— LESSON 87 —

Parenthetical Expressions

Dashes

Exercise 87A: Types of Parenthetical Expressions

Identify each parenthetical expression as aphrase, dependent clause, or sentence.

CHALLENGE EXERCISE

- Provide a fuller description of each expression. What kind of phrase, clause, or sentence? What does it do or modify?
- When you are finished, ask your instructor for the fuller explanations. Compare your descriptions to these explanations.

These sentences are taken from *Through the Looking-Glass*, by Lewis Carroll.

Note to Instructor: This is an optional challenge; if the student chooses not to do it, go through the explanations provided below with her after she has finished identifying the parenthetical elements.

prepositional phrase, acting as an adverb describing how and why Alice *said*

"Here are the Red King and the Red Queen," Alice said (in a whisper, for fear of frightening them), "and there are the White King and the White Queen sitting on the edge of the shovel."

dependent clause introduced by a relative pronoun, which is the object of the preposition *in*, which is acting as an adjective, describing *book*

"What manner of things?" said the Queen, looking over the book (in which Alice had put "The White Knight is sliding down the poker. He balances very badly"). "That's not a memorandum of your feelings!"

"I should see the garden far better," said Alice to herself, "if I could get to the top of that hill: and

phrase preceding a complete sentence, no grammatical relationship to the rest of the sentence

here's a path that leads straight to it—at least, no, it doesn't do that—" (after going a few yards

participal phrase acting as an adverb and describing *said* (answers the question *when*)
(it could also be argued that the phrase has no clear grammatical relationship to the rest of the sentence)

along the path, and turning several sharp corners), "but I suppose it will at last."

For a few minutes all went on well, and she was just saying, "I really shall do it this time—"

dependent clause acting as an adverb, modifying *shook*

when the path gave a sudden twist and shook itself (as she described it afterwards), and the next moment she found herself actually walking in at the door.

complete sentence; describes the gentleman, but no grammatical relationship to the rest of the sentence

"So young a child," said the gentleman sitting opposite to her (he was dressed in white paper), "ought to know which way she's going, even if she doesn't know her own name!"

"Indeed I shan't!" Alice said rather impatiently. "I don't belong to this railway journey at all—I

complete sentence—no grammatical relationship

was in a wood just now—and I wish I could get back there."

complete sentence—no grammatical relationship

"Crawling at your feet," said the Gnat (Alice drew her feet back in some alarm), "you may observe a Bread-and-Butterfly. Its wings are thin slices of bread-and-butter, its body is a crust, and its head is a lump of sugar."

phrase, no grammatical relationship

"I mean to get under the—under the—under this, you know!" putting her hand on the trunk of the tree.

participle phrase acting as an adjective, describing *Alice*

"If I wasn't real," Alice said—half-laughing through her tears, it all seemed so ridiculous—"I shouldn't be able to cry."

complete sentence, no grammatical relationship

Exercise 87B: Punctuating Parenthetical Expressions

On either side of each bolded parenthetical expression, place parentheses, dashes, or commas. There are not necessarily *correct* answers for these, but compare them to the originals when you have finished.

These sentences are taken from *The Strange Case of Dr. Jekyll and Mr. Hyde*, by Robert Louis Stevenson.

Note to Instructor: The original versions of Stevenson's sentences are below and reflect the author's intentions; any grammatical answers are acceptable, but where the student has chosen different punctuation, ask him to read first his version, and then Stevenson's, out loud.

I met with one accident which, as it brought on no consequence, I shall no more than mention.

Poole admitted the visitor, as he spoke, into a large, low-roofed, comfortable hall, paved with flags, warmed (after the fashion of a country house) by a bright, open fire, and furnished with costly cabinets of oak.

He felt (what was rare with him) a nausea and distaste of life.

A good picture hung upon the walls, a gift (as Utterson supposed) from Henry Jekyll, who was much of a connoisseur.

I was struck besides with the shocking expression of his face, with his remarkable combination of great muscular activity and great apparent debility of constitution, and—last but not least—with the odd, subjective disturbance caused by his neighbourhood.

I believe his murderer (for what purpose, God alone can tell) is still lurking in his victim's room.

Evil, I fear, would come—evil was sure to come—of that connection.

He began to go wrong, wrong in mind, though of course I continue to take an interest in him for old sake's sake, as they say.

The fellow had a key, and, what's more, he has it still.

The smile withered from his face—happily for him—yet more happily for myself, for in another instant I had certainly dragged him from his perch.

This, then, is the last time, short of a miracle, that Henry Jekyll can think his own thoughts or see his own face (now how sadly altered!) in the glass.

He was small and very plainly dressed, and the look of him, even at that distance, went somehow strongly against the watcher's inclination.

And then all of a sudden he broke out in a great flame of anger, stamping with his foot, brandishing the cane, and carrying on (as the maid described it) like a madman.

Exercise 87C: Using Dashes for Emphasis

On your own paper, rewrite the next four sentences, substituting dashes for the underlined punctuation marks and making any other capitalization or punctuation changes needed.

These sentences are taken from *White Fang*, by Jack London.

They did not go far (a couple of days' journey).

Running at the forefront of the pack was a large grey wolf, one of its several leaders.

He had bred true to the straight wolf-stock. In fact, he had bred true to old One Eye himself, with but a single exception, and that was he had two eyes to his father's one.

So to him the entrance of the cave was a wall, a wall of light.

Original sentences:

They did not go far—a couple of days' journey.

Running at the forefront of the pack was a large grey wolf—one of its several leaders.

He had bred true to the straight wolf-stock—in fact, he had bred true to old One Eye himself, physically, with but a single exception, and that was he had two eyes to his father's one.

So to him the entrance of the cave was a wall—a wall of light.

— LESSON 88 —

Parenthetical Expressions
Dashes
Diagramming Parenthetical Expressions

Exercise 88A: Diagramming Parenthetical Expressions

On your own paper, diagram each of the following sentences.

The following sentences are slightly condensed from O. Henry's classic short story "The Gift of the Magi."

Quietness and value—Jim and the chain had quietness and value.

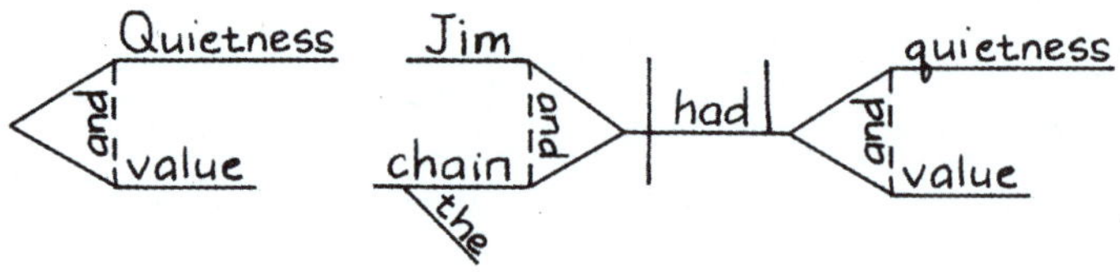

Note to Instructor: The phrase *quietness and value* is repeated and should be diagrammed in the same way both times, but the introductory parenthetical expression doesn't have a grammatical connection to the main clause.

He was only twenty-two—with a family of his own!

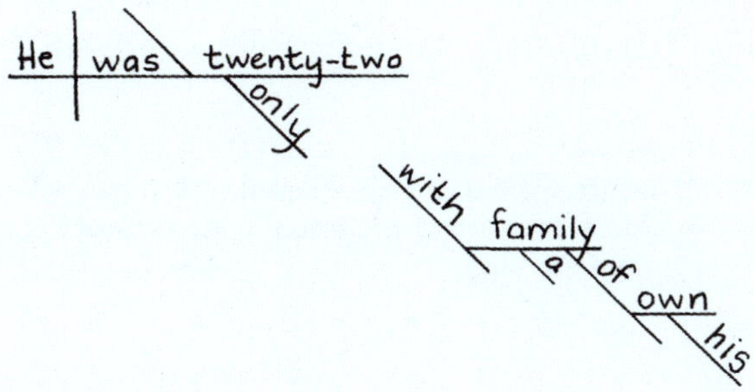

Note to Instructor: The parenthetical expression is a prepositional phrase but is unconnected to any particular word in the main clause.

There lay the Combs—the combs that Della had seen in a shop window and loved for a long time.

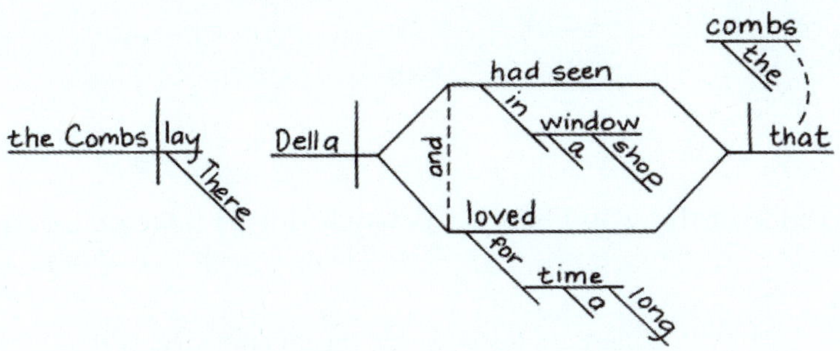

Note to Instructor: The parenthetical expression following the dash is unconnected to the main clause, but *the combs* is modified by the adjectival dependent clause beginning with *that*.

The magi, as you know, were wise men—wonderfully wise men— who brought gifts to the newborn Christ-child.

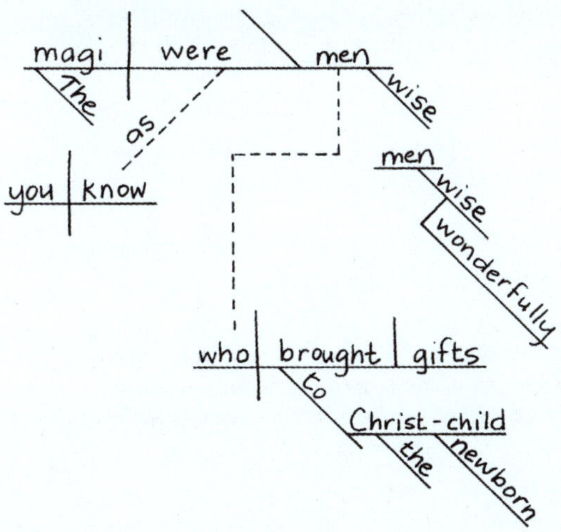

Note to Instructor: *Wonderfully wise men* is unconnected, but *as you know* is an adverbial dependent clause modifying the verb.

The following sentences are slightly condensed from *A Christmas Carol*, by Charles Dickens.

Marley's chain was made (for Scrooge observed it closely) of cash-boxes, keys, padlocks, ledgers, deeds, and heavy purses wrought in steel.

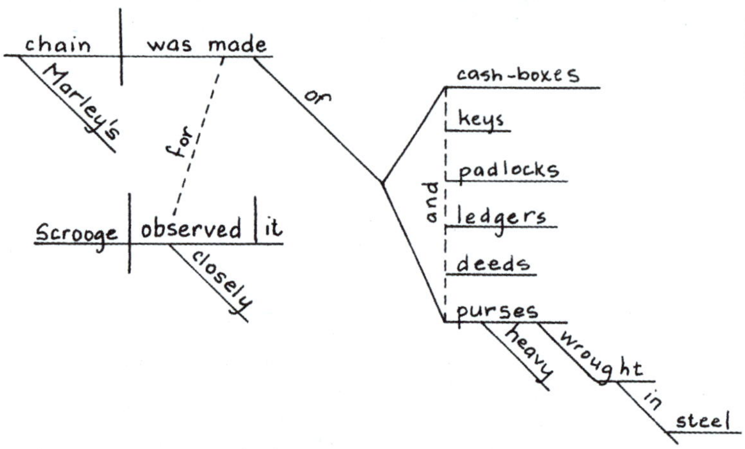

Note to Instructor: The parenthetical expression is an adverbial dependent clause.

The clerk, with the long ends of his white comforter dangling below his waist (for he boasted no greatcoat), went down a slide on Cornhill.

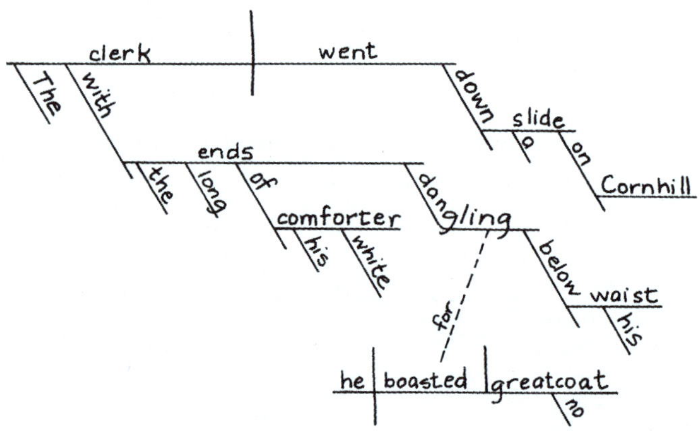

Note to Instructor: If the parenthetical expression were simply *he boasted no greatcoat*, it would have no grammatical relationship to the rest of the sentence, but the subordinating conjunction *for* creates a causal relationship between the dangling of the ends and the lack of a greatcoat: they dangled *because* he had no coat.

Mrs. Cratchit made the gravy (ready beforehand in a little saucepan) hissing hot.

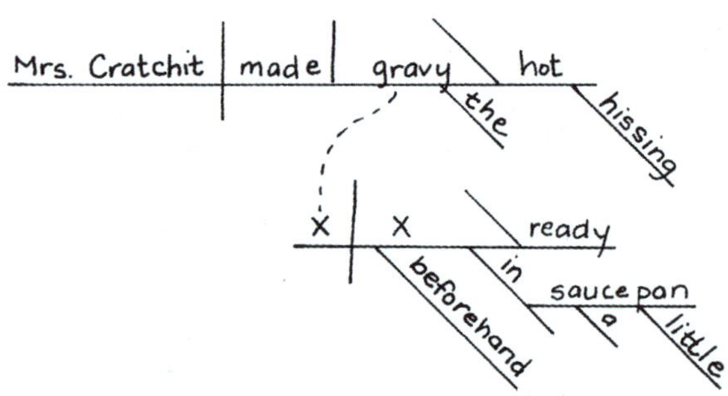

Note to Instructor: This may trip the student up—the parenthetical expression is actually a relative clause ([*which was*] *ready beforehand in a little saucepan*)—with an understood subject and predicate.

There was a little saucepan of gruel (Scrooge had a cold in his head) upon the hob.

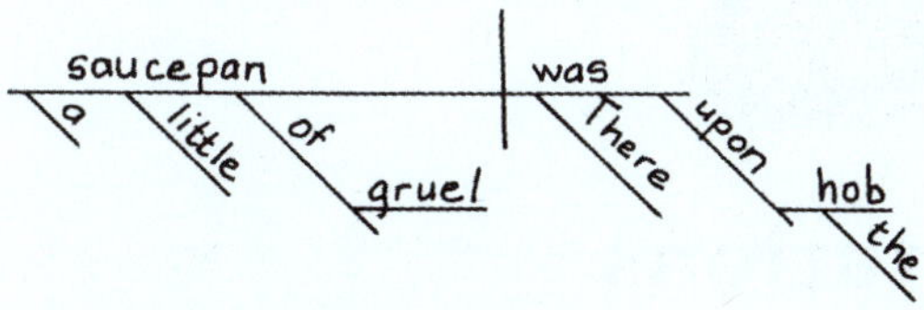

> **Note to Instructor:** The parenthetical expression is a completely separate sentence.

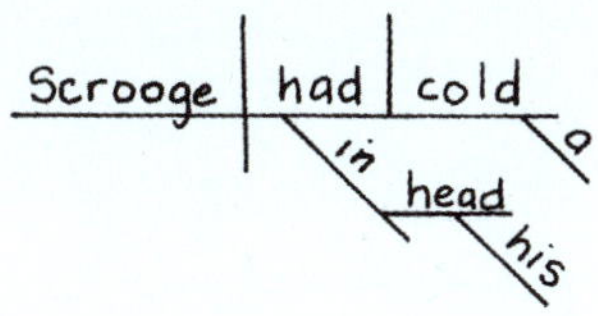

WEEK 23

Dialogue and Quotations

— LESSON 89 —

Dialogue

Exercise 89A: Punctuating Dialogue

The excerpt below is from H. G. Wells's classic science fiction novel *The Time Machine.* All of the dialogue is missing quotation marks, and some of it is missing ending punctuation as well. Do your best to supply the missing punctuation marks.

When you are finished, compare your version with the original.

Note to Instructor: The original version is below. You may assign the student the task of comparing the original punctuation with her edited version. Ask her to circle any differences with a colored pencil; this will help her pay close attention to the correct punctuation.

I took my eyes off the Time Traveller's face, and looked round at his audience. The Medical Man seemed absorbed in the contemplation of our host. The Editor was looking hard at the end of his cigar—the sixth. The Journalist fumbled for his watch. The others, as far as I remember, were motionless.

The Editor stood up with a sigh. "What a pity it is you're not a writer of stories!" he said, putting his hand on the Time Traveller's shoulder.

"You don't believe it?"

"Well—"

"I thought not." The Time Traveller turned to us. "Where are the matches?" he said.

He lit one and spoke over his pipe, puffing. "To tell you the truth . . . I hardly believe it myself. . . And yet—"

His eye fell with a mute inquiry upon the withered white flowers upon the little table. Then he turned over the hand holding his pipe, and I saw he was looking at some half-healed scars on his knuckles.

The Medical Man rose, came to the lamp, and examined the flowers. "The blooms are very odd," he said. The Psychologist leant forward to see, holding out his hand for a specimen.

"I'm hanged if it isn't a quarter to one," said the Journalist.

"How shall we get home?"

"Plenty of cabs at the station," said the Psychologist.

"It's a curious thing," said the Medical Man, "but I certainly don't know the natural order of these flowers. May I have them?"

The Time Traveller hesitated. Then suddenly he said, "Certainly not."

"Where did you really get them?" said the Medical Man.

The Time Traveller put his hand to his head. He spoke like one who was trying to keep hold of an idea that eluded him. "They were put into my pocket when I travelled into Time." He stared round the room. "I can feel that it is all going. This room and you and the atmosphere of every day is too much for my memory. Did I ever make a Time Machine, or a model of a Time Machine? Or is it all only a dream? They say life is a dream, a precious poor dream at times—but I can't stand another that won't fit. It's madness. And where did the dream come from? . . . I must look at that machine. If there is one!"

He caught up the lamp swiftly, and carried it, flaring red, through the door into the corridor. We followed him. There in the flickering light of the lamp was the machine sure enough, squat, ugly, and askew; a thing of brass, ebony, ivory, and translucent glimmering quartz. Solid to the touch—for I put out my hand and felt the rail of it—and with brown spots and smears upon the ivory, and bits of grass and moss upon the lower parts, and one rail bent awry.

The Time Traveller put the lamp down on the bench, and ran his hand along the damaged rail. "It's all right now," he said. "The story I told you was true. I'm sorry to have brought you out here in the cold."

He took up the lamp, and, in an absolute silence, we returned to the smoking-room.

Exercise 89B: Writing Dialogue Correctly

On your own paper, rewrite the following sentences as dialogue, using the past tense for the dialogue tags. Use the notations in parentheses to help you.

You may choose to place dialogue tags before, in the middle, or after dialogue, or to leave the tags out completely. But you must have at least one sentence with a dialogue tag that comes before, at least one sentence with a dialogue tag that comes after, at least one speech with the dialogue tag in the middle, and at least one speech with no dialogue tag at all.

When you are finished, compare your answers with the original. The first is done for you.

Sentences are taken from *Anne of Green Gables*, by Lucy Maud Montgomery.

(Anne asks) What am I to call you? Shall I always say Miss Cuthbert? Can I call you Aunt Marilla?

(Marilla answers) No; you'll call me just plain Marilla. I'm not used to being called Miss Cuthbert and it would make me nervous.

(Ann protests) It sounds awfully disrespectful to just say Marilla.

(Marilla says) I guess there'll be nothing disrespectful in it if you're careful to speak respectfully. Everybody, young and old, in Avonlea calls me Marilla except the minister.

(Anne says, wistfully) I'd love to call you Aunt Marilla. I've never had an aunt or any relation at all—not even a grandmother. It would make me feel as if I really belonged to you. Can't I call you Aunt Marilla?

(Marilla says) No. I'm not your aunt and I don't believe in calling people names that don't belong to them.

(Anne says) But we could imagine you were my aunt.

(Marilla says, grimly) I couldn't.

(Anne says, wide-eyed) Do you never imagine things different from what they really are?

(Marilla says) No.

(Anne says, drawing a long breath) Oh! Oh, Miss—Marilla, how much you miss!

(Marilla retorts) I don't believe in imagining things different from what they really are.

First answer:

"What am I to call you?" asked Anne. "Shall I always say Miss Cuthbert? Can I call you Aunt Marilla?"

Note to Instructor: Allow the student to compare her answers with the original text below, but accept any grammatical rewriting.

"What am I to call you?" asked Anne. "Shall I always say Miss Cuthbert? Can I call you Aunt Marilla?"

"No; you'll call me just plain Marilla. I'm not used to being called Miss Cuthbert and it would make me nervous."

Anne protested, "It sounds awfully disrespectful to just say Marilla."

"I guess there'll be nothing disrespectful in it if you're careful to speak respectfully. Everybody, young and old, in Avonlea calls me Marilla except the minister."

"I'd love to call you Aunt Marilla," said Anne wistfully. "I've never had an aunt or any relation at all—not even a grandmother. It would make me feel as if I really belonged to you. Can't I call you Aunt Marilla?"

"No. I'm not your aunt and I don't believe in calling people names that don't belong to them."

"But we could imagine you were my aunt."

"I couldn't," said Marilla grimly.

"Do you never imagine things different from what they really are?" asked Anne, wide-eyed.

"No."

"Oh!" Anne drew a long breath. "Oh, Miss—Marilla, how much you miss!"

"I don't believe in imagining things different from what they really are," retorted Marilla.

Exercise 89C: Proofreading

Using the following proofreader's marks, correct these incorrect sentences. They are from the O. Henry short story "The Ransom of Red Chief."

insert quotation marks: ⋎ insert comma: ⋏
insert period: ⊙ insert question mark: ⋏?
insert exclamation point: ↑! delete: —ℓ
move punctuation mark: ⤻

"Hey, little boy!" says Bill, "Would you like to have a bag of candy and a nice ride"?

The boy catches Bill neatly in the eye with a piece of brick.

"That will cost the old man an extra five hundred dollars", says Bill, climbing over the wheel.

"What you getting up so soon for, Sam" asked Bill.

"Me?" says I, "Oh, I got a kind of a pain in my shoulder. I thought sitting up would rest it."

"You're a liar" says Bill! "You're afraid. You was to be burned at sunrise, and you was afraid he'd do it. And he would, too, if he could find a match. Ain't it awful, Sam? Do you think anybody will pay out money to get a little imp like that back home?"

"Sure." said I "A rowdy kid like that is just the kind that parents dote on. Now, you and the Chief get up and cook breakfast, while I go up on the top of this mountain and reconnoiter."

— LESSON 90 —

Dialogue

Direct Quotations

Exercise 90A: Punctuating Dialogue

The six sentences below, from E. B. White's *The Trumpet of the Swan*, are missing punctuation. Write in all of the missing punctuation marks (insert them directly rather than using proofreader's marks). When you are finished, compare your answers to the original.

One evening a few weeks later, when the cygnets were asleep, the swan said to the cob Have you noticed anything different about one of our children, the one we call Louis

Different replied the cob In what way is Louis different from his brothers and sisters? Louis looks all right to me. He is growing well; he swims and dives beautifully. He eats well. He will soon have his flight feathers

Oh, he looks all right said the swan. And heaven knows he eats enough. He's healthy and bright and a great swimmer. But have you ever heard Louis make any sound, as the others do? Have you ever heard him use his voice or say anything? Have you ever heard him utter a single beep or a single burble

Come to think of it, I never have replied the cob, who was beginning to look worried.

Have you ever heard Louis say good night to us, as the others do? Have you ever heard him say good morning, as the others do in their charming little way, burbling and beeping

Now that you mention it, I never have said the cob Goodness! What are you getting at?

Note to Instructor: The original text is found below.

One evening a few weeks later, when the cygnets were asleep, the swan said to the cob, "Have you noticed anything different about one of our children, the one we call Louis?"

"Different?" replied the cob. "In what way is Louis different from his brothers and sisters? Louis looks all right to me. He is growing well; he swims and dives beautifully. He eats well. He will soon have his flight feathers."

"Oh, he looks all right," said the swan. "And heaven knows he eats enough. He's healthy and bright and a great swimmer. But have you ever heard Louis make any sound, as the others do? Have you ever heard him use his voice or say anything? Have you ever heard him utter a single beep or a single burble?"

"Come to think of it, I never have," replied the cob, who was beginning to look worried.

"Have you ever heard Louis say good night to us, as the others do? Have you ever heard him say good morning, as the others do in their charming little way, burbling and beeping?"

"Now that you mention it, I never have," said the cob. "Goodness! What are you getting at?"

Exercise 90B: Punctuating Direct Quotations

Write in all of the missing punctuation marks (insert them directly rather than using proofreader's marks). When you are finished, compare your answers to the original sentences.

Pinney concludes with the observation There is little reason to make the swan an unclean animal.

As a young woman, Goodall liked to go along her English river where she saw water birds, moor hens, kingfishers, and swans The swans were a bit scary she says especially when they had a nest or babies, because then they are sometimes aggressive. I knew one man who once had his leg broken when an angry swan, thinking he was after one of her babies, attacked him.

While on a hunting expedition on rivers of Missouri and Kentucky, Audubon writes of the Trumpeter To form a perfect conception of the beauty and elegance of these Swans, you must observe them when they are not aware of your proximity.

Waterfowl migration according to Simpson and Day is very apparent in the Northern Hemisphere where vast numbers leave northern breeding areas, moving south to warmer regions along fairly defined flyways.

—Alice L. Price, *Swans of the World: In Nature, History, Myth and Art*

A garden dung-heap recommends Mr. Baily overgrown with artichokes, mallows, and other weeds, is an excellent cover for chickens, especially in hot weather.

There is no sort of insect notes Mr. Dickson which fowls will not eat. They are exceedingly fond of flies, beetles, grasshoppers, and crickets, but more particularly of every sort of grub, caterpillar, and maggot.

Mr. Baily adds Do not give fowls meat, but always have the bones thrown out to them after dinner; they enjoy picking them, and perform the operation perfectly.

We never ourselves now attempt to assist a chick from the shell explains Mr. Wright.

—Hugh Piper, *Poultry: A Practical Guide*

Note to Instructor: The original sentences are found below.

Pinney concludes with the observation, "There is little reason to make the swan an unclean animal."

As a young woman, Goodall liked to go along her English river where she saw water birds, moor hens, kingfishers, and swans. "The swans were a bit scary," she says, "especially when they had a nest or babies, because then they are sometimes aggressive. I knew one man who once had his leg broken when an angry swan, thinking he was after one of her babies, attacked him."

While on a hunting expedition on rivers of Missouri and Kentucky, Audubon writes of the Trumpeter, "To form a perfect conception of the beauty and elegance of these Swans, you must observe them when they are not aware of your proximity."

"Waterfall migration," according to Simpson and Day, "is very apparent in the Northern Hemisphere where vast numbers leave northern breeding areas, moving south to warmer regions along fairly defined flyways."

—Alice L. Price, *Swans of the World: In Nature, History, Myth and Art*

"A garden dung-heap," recommends Mr. Baily, "overgrown with artichokes, mallows, and other weeds, is an excellent cover for chickens, especially in hot weather."

"There is no sort of insect," notes Mr. Dickson, "which fowls will not eat. They are exceedingly fond of flies, beetles, grasshoppers, and crickets, but more particularly of every sort of grub, caterpillar, and maggot."

Mr. Baily adds, "Do not give fowls meat, but always have the bones thrown out to them after dinner; they enjoy picking them, and perform the operation perfectly."

"We never ourselves now attempt to assist a chick from the shell," explains Mr. Wright.

—Hugh Piper, *Poultry: A Practical Guide*

Exercise 90C: Attribution Tags

In the following paragraphs, adapted from the classic 19th-century animal guide *Beeton's Book of Poultry and Domestic Animals*, find and underline the direct quotes that are missing their attribution tags. When you are finished, ask your instructor to check your work.

Then, compare the paragraphs with the originals found in the *Answer Key*. Circle each attribution tag in the *Answer Key*.

Note to Instructor: The original paragraphs follow the exercise. A key below identifies the attribution tag that should be underlined in each paragraph. Do not allow the student to read the key before he identifies each tag.

It is essential that the keepers of Dorkings must provide a good long run for the chickens. If this is carefully done, the Dorkings will thrive and grow well. There are two species: the white and the colored. White Dorkings are the favorite of many poultry raisers. "They lay well, and are excellent sitters and mothers." However, the colored Dorking is also a handsome bird.

The fantail pigeon is the most elegant of all the pigeons. It is pure white with a long, delicately curved neck, so long that at times the bird's head will nestle among the tail feathers. The fantail pigeon is also known by other names. One of the most successful pigeon breeders calls it a *broad-tailed shaker.* "They are called shakers," he writes, "because they constantly shake their heads up and down; broad-tailed, from the great number of feathers they have in their tails."

The limbs of the Manx cat are gaunt, its fur close-set, its eyes staring and restless, and it possesses no tail. As one cat-fancier says, "A black Manx cat, with its staring eyes and its stump of a tail, is an almost unearthly looking beast." The Angol cat, on the other hand, is one of the most beautiful of cats, with long and silky fur, and a remarkably full and brush-like tail.

George Henry Lewes has furnished us with some curious facts about the tail of the tadpole. If it is cut off, the tail will continue to live for several days, and not only live but grow. "I have kept tails alive for up to eleven days, and they not only grow, but twist about with a rapid swimming movement when irritated." However, when the tails reach the point when they require circulation of blood for their further development, they die.

The Dhole, or Kholsun, is a wild dog living in the depths of the Indian jungles. Like other wild dogs, it forms packs and hunts down game. The dhole is a brave dog, and has no fear even of the terrible tiger. "From the observations which have been made, hardly any animal, with the exception of the elephant and the rhinoceros, can cope with the dhole." Only the leopard is safe, because the dogs cannot follow their spotted quarry into the tree branches.

The Rocky Mountain squirrel lurks, bat-like, in the gloom of the pine forests during the day, and becomes active at night. The Australian physician and naturalist George Bennet says, "Their flying membrane is a folding of the skin along either side, clothed by a dense fur, enabling the squirrel to take leaps of almost incredible extent." Flying squirrels are also found in Sri Lanka and in India.

Note to Instructor: Here are the original paragraphs for the student's reference. She should circle each attribution tag.

It is essential that the keepers of Dorkings must provide a good long run for the chickens. If this is carefully done, the Dorkings will thrive and grow well. There are two species: the white and the colored. White Dorkings are the favorite of many poultry raisers; as the *Poultry Chronicle* remarks, "They lay well, and are excellent sitters and mothers." However, the colored Dorking is also a handsome bird.

The fantail pigeon is the most elegant of all the pigeons. It is pure white with a long, delicately curved neck, so long that at times the bird's head will nestle among the tail feathers. The fantail pigeon is also known by other names. One of the most successful pigeon breeders calls it a *broadtailed shaker*. "They are called shakers," he writes, "because they constantly shake their heads up and down; broad-tailed, from the great number of feathers they have in their tails."

The limbs of the Manx cat are gaunt, its fur close-set, its eyes staring and restless, and it possesses no tail. As one cat-fancier says, "A black Manx cat, with its staring eyes and its stump of a tail, is an almost unearthly looking beast." The Angol cat, on the other hand, is one of the most beautiful of cats, with long and silky fur, and a remarkably full and brush-like tail.

George Henry Lewes has furnished us with some curious facts about the tail of the tadpole. If it is cut off, the tail will continue to live for several days, and not only live but grow. "I have kept tails alive for up to eleven days," Lewes claims, "and they not only grow, but twist about with a rapid swimming movement when irritated." However, when the tails reach the point when they require circulation of blood for their further development, they die.

The Dhole, or Kholsun, is a wild dog living in the depths of the Indian jungles. Like other wild dogs, it forms packs and hunts down game. The dhole is a brave dog, and has no fear even of the terrible tiger. "From the observations which have been made," writes a naturalist, "hardly any animal, with the exception of the elephant and the rhinoceros, can cope with the dhole." Only the leopard is safe, because the dogs cannot follow their spotted quarry into the tree branches.

The Rocky Mountain squirrel lurks, bat-like, in the gloom of the pine forests during the day, and becomes active at night. The Australian physician and naturalist George Bennet says, "Their flying membrane is a folding of the skin along either side, clothed by a dense fur, enabling the squirrel to take leaps of almost incredible extent." Flying squirrels are also found in Sri Lanka and in India.

Key: **The following attribution quotes should be circled.**
Student: **Do not read this key until you have completed the exercise!**

Paragraph #1: as the *Poultry Chronicle* remarks
Paragraph #2: he writes
Paragraph #3: As one cat-fancier says
Paragraph #4: Lewes claims
Paragraph #5: writes a naturalist
Paragraph #6: The Australian physician and naturalist George Bennet says

— LESSON 91 —

Direct Quotations
Ellipses
Partial Quotations

Exercise 91A: Using Ellipses

The following three paragraphs are taken from Charles Morris's *The 1906 San Francisco Earthquake and Fire: As Told by Eyewitnesses.*

This excerpt is 368 words long. On your own paper, rewrite it so that it has no more than 200 words.

Use ellipses wherever you omit words. Do not cut the opening or closing words of any paragraph. Make sure that you don't end up with run-on sentences or fragments!

When you are finished, compare your version with the condensed version found in the *Answer Key.*

The work of fighting the fire was the first and greatest duty to be performed, but from the start it proved a very difficult, almost a hopeless, task. With fierce fires burning at once in a dozen or more separate places, the fire department of the city would have been inadequate to cope with the demon of flame even under the best of circumstances. As it was, they found themselves handicapped at the start by a nearly total lack of water. The earthquake had disarranged and broken the water mains and there was scarcely a drop of water to be had, so that the engines proved next to useless. Water might be drawn from the bay, but the center of the conflagration was a mile or more away, and this great body of water was rendered useless.

The only hope that remained to the authorities was to endeavor to check the progress of the flames by the use of dynamite, blowing up buildings in the line of progress of the conflagration. This was put in practice without loss of time, and soon the thunder-like roar of the explosions began, blasts being heard every few minutes, each signifying that some building had been blown to atoms. But over the gaps thus made the flames leaped, and though the brave fellows worked with a desperation and energy of the most heroic type, it seemed as if all their labors were to be without avail, the terrible fire marching on as steadily as if a colony of ants had sought to stay its devastating progress.

It was with grief and horror that the mass of the people gazed on this steady march of the army of ruin. They were seemingly half dazed by the magnitude of the disaster, strangely passive in the face of the ruin that surrounded them, as if stunned by despair and not yet awakened to a realization of the horrors of the situation. Among these was the possibility of famine. No city at any time carries more than a few days' supply of provisions, and with the wholesale districts and warehouse regions invaded by the flames the shortage of food made itself apparent from the start. Water was even more difficult to obtain, the supply being nearly all cut off.

Note to Instructor: A sample condensation is shown below. The student may choose to omit different parts of the passage. When she is finished, check her paragraphs for sense and readability. Ask her to read her paragraphs out loud, listening for meaning. Then, allow her to read the sample answer below.

Each omission must be marked by ellipses.

The work of fighting the fire . . . proved a very difficult . . . task. With fierce fires burning . . . in a dozen or more . . . places, the fire department . . . found themselves handicapped . . . by a nearly total lack of water. The earthquake had . . . broken the water mains . . . Water might be drawn from the bay, but the centre of the conflagration was a mile or more away, and this great body of water was rendered useless.

The only hope . . . was . . . the use of dynamite, blowing up buildings in the line of progress of the conflagration . . . and soon the thunder-like roar of the explosions began . . . But over the gaps . . . the flames leaped, and . . . all their labors were . . . without avail, the terrible fire marching on steadily.

It was with grief and horror that the mass of the people gazed on this . . . ruin. They were . . . stunned by despair and not yet awakened to . . . the horrors of the situation.

Among these was the possibility of famine. No city at any time carries more than a few days' supply of provisions, and . . . the shortage of food made itself apparent from the start. Water was . . . nearly all cut off.

Exercise 91B: Partial Quotations

On your own paper, rewrite the five statements below so that each one contains a partial quotation. Draw the partial quotation from the bolded sentences that follow each statement. The authors of the bolded sentences are provided for you—be sure to include an attribution tag for each direct quote!

You may change and adapt the statements freely.

One of your sentences should contain a very short one- to three-word quote; one should contain a prepositional phrase, gerund phrase, participle phrase, or infinitive phrase; and one should quote a dependent clause.

If you need help, ask your instructor to show you sample answers.

Note to Instructor: If the student needs a jump-start, show her *one* of the three sample sentences that follow each statement.

Jane Seymour was the third wife of Henry VIII.

"But the predominant impression given by her portrait . . . is of a woman of calm good sense. And contemporaries all commented on Jane Seymour's intelligence . . . She was also naturally sweet-natured (no angry words or tantrums here) and virtuous—her virtue was another topic on which there was general agreement."

—Antonia Fraser, historian

One- to three-word quote

The historian Antonia Fraser writes that Jane Seymour, the third wife of Henry VIII, was "naturally sweet-natured."

Prepositional phrase

Jane Seymour, Henry VIII's third wife, was intelligent, virtuous, and "a woman of calm good sense," as Antonia Fraser puts it.

Dependent clause

Antonia Fraser writes that the virtue of Jane Seymour, Henry VIII's third wife, was a "topic on which there was general agreement."

In the nineteenth century, candy-makers could add anything they wanted to candy.

"Unscrupulous manufacturers would resort to any number of devious and even dangerous practices to sell their goods. Some, for example, varnished their candies with shellac to make them shinier and more attractive. Brick dust was added to some candies to make them redder, while other candies contained lead, insect parts and other contaminants."

—Joël Glenn Brenner, financial journalist

One- to three-word quote

In the nineteenth century, candy might contain lead, pieces of insects, or even "brick dust," according to financial journalist Joël Glenn Brenner.

Infinitive phrase

As journalist Joël Glenn Brenner writes, candy manufacturers in the nineteenth century sometimes shellacked their candies "to make them shinier and more attractive."

Dependent clause

In the nineteenth century, candy-makers could add anything they wanted to candy; Joël Glenn Brenner writes that some were reddened with brick dust, "while other candies contained lead, insect parts and other contaminants."

Vampire bats drink the blood of other animals.

"Vampire bats are unique among mammals for their habit of subsisting on the blood of other warm-blooded vertebrates . . . The bats do preferentially bite the capillary-rich tips of fingers, toes and noses; and through a small circular aperture made in the victim's skin, they indeed can lap large quantites of blood for their size—thanks to an anticoagulant in their saliva that also can lead to excessive bleeding in their victims after they drink their fill and flap away."

—Bill Wasik and Monica Murphy, science writers.

One- to three-word quote

Vampire bats drink the blood of "warm-blooded vertebrates," as Bill Wasik and Monica Murphy write.

Participle phrase

Vampire bats drink the blood of other animals; according to Bill Wasik and Monica Murphy, they prefer "subsisting on the blood of . . . warm-blooded vertebrates."

Dependent clause

Science writers Bill Wasik and Monica Murphy tell us that when vampire bats drink the blood of other animals, their saliva can cause "excessive bleeding" which continues even "after they drink their fill and flap away."

Brain development happens very quickly in babies.

"When babies are born, their brains have about the same number of connections as adults have. That doesn't last long. By the time children are 3 years old, the connections in specific regions of their brains have doubled or even tripled."

—John Medina, molecular biologist

One- to three-word quote

Brain development happens quickly in babies; molecular biologist John Medina tells us that by the time they reach the age of three, the connections in some parts of their brains have "doubled" or "tripled."

Prepositional phrase

In babies, brain development "in specific regions" happens very quickly before age 3, according to John Medina.

Dependent clause

John Medina writes that brain development happens so quickly in babies that "by the time children are 3 years old," brain connections have "doubled or even tripled."

Medieval town clocks could be very elaborate.

"The clock made about 1350 for the cathedral of Strasbourg . . . included a moving calendar and an astrolabe whose pointers indicated the movements of the sun, moon and planets. The upper compartment was adorned with a statue of the Virgin before whom at noon the Three Magi bowed while a carillon played a tune. On top of the whole thing stood an enormous cock which, at the end of the procession of the Magi, opened its beak, thrust forth its tongue, crowed and flapped its wings."

—Carlo M. Cipolla, economic historian

One- to three-word quote

Medieval town clocks could be very elaborate, like the Strasbourg clock which, according to Carlo Cipolla, had a "moving calendar" and astrolabe as well as a giant rooster on top of it.

Prepositional phrase

Medieval town clocks could be very elaborate; Carlo Cipolla writes that some included calendars, astrolabes that tracked the paths "of the sun, moon, and planets," and moving statues.

Dependent clause

Carlo Cipolla tells us that elaborate medieval town clocks might include calendars, astrolabes, and statues of Mary "before whom . . . the Three Magi bowed."

Exercise 91C: Diagramming

On your own paper, diagram every word of the following sentences.

These are slightly adapted from *Rabid: A Cultural History of the World's Most Diabolical Virus*, by Bill Wasik and Monica Murphy.

These are difficult! Do your best, and then compare your answers with the *Answer Key.*

Skunks do not attack (or even approach) humans except when in the demented throes of rabies.

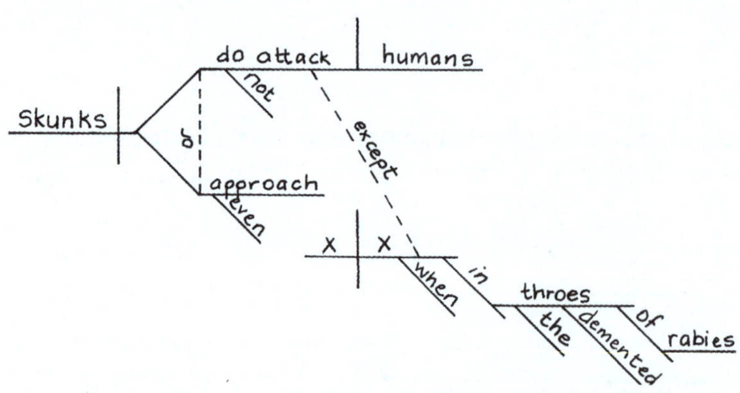

Note to Instructor: *Or even approach,* although set off by parentheses, has a clear grammatical relationship as part of the compound predicate, so should be diagrammed as part of the sentence. *Except when in the demented throes of rabies* is an adverb clause with an understood subject and predicate, introduced by a subordinating conjunction. It is diagrammed as if it were *Except when [they are] in the demented throes of rabies. Except* is a connector, so is diagrammed on the dotted line, and *when* is an adverb modifying *are.*

It was a yellow bat—a species that only eats insects—but today it seemed determined to make a meal of the boy.

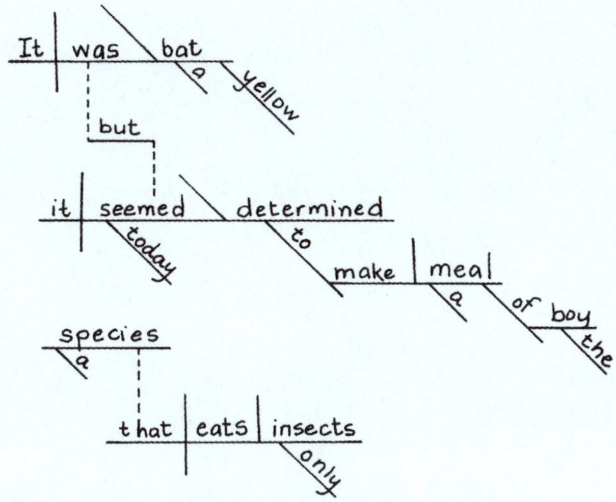

After hearing reports of a rabid wolf marauding through the region of Arbois, furiously biting man and beast, Pasteur and his friends witnessed one victim being brought to the blacksmith's shop for treatment.

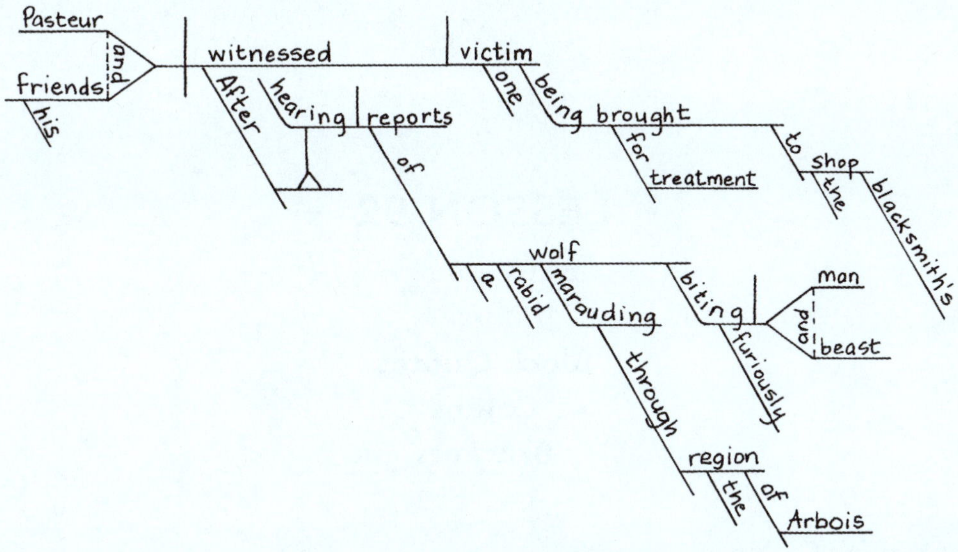

He devised a simple experimental protocol; twenty-five sheep would be vaccinated against anthrax, fifty including these would be infected, and an additional ten would be untreated controls.

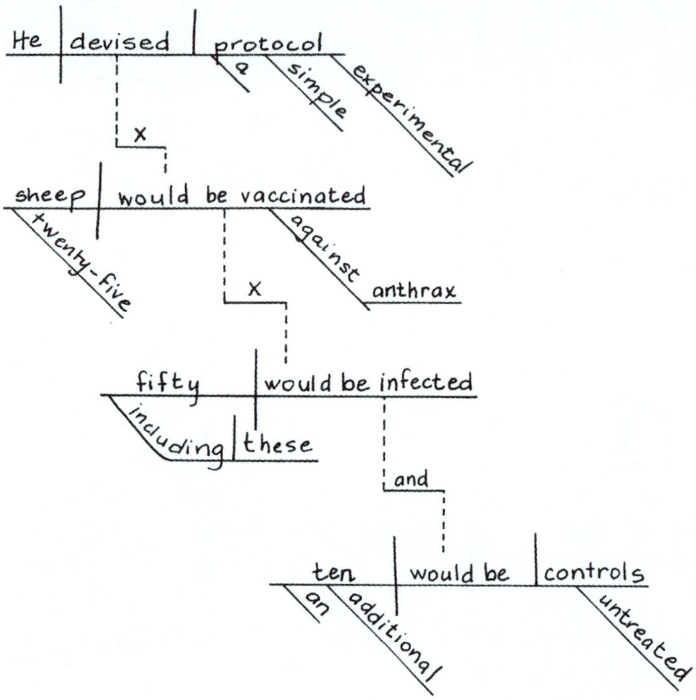

— LESSON 92 —

Partial Quotations
Ellipses
Block Quotes
Colons
Brackets

Exercise 92A: Writing Dialogue Correctly

The following speeches, from *Little Women*, by Louisa May Alcott, are listed in the correct order, but are missing the dialogue tags. On your own paper, rewrite the speeches as dialogue, making use of the dialogue tags below. You must place at least one dialogue tag before a speech, one in the middle of a speech, and one following a speech.

A list of the rules governing dialogue follows, for your reference.

When you are finished, compare your dialogue to the original passage in the *Answer Key*.

List 1. Dialogue (in Correct Order)

Meg, I wish you'd go and see the Hummels. You know Mother told us not to forget them.
I'm too tired to go this afternoon.
Can't you, Jo?

Too stormy for me with my cold.
I thought it was almost well.
It's well enough for me to go out with Laurie, but not well enough to go to the Hummels.
Why don't you go yourself?
I have been every day, but the baby is sick, and I don't know what to do for it. I think you or Hannah ought to go.
Ask Hannah for some nice little mess, and take it round, Beth, the air will do you good. I'd go but I want to finish my writing.
My head aches and I'm tired, so I thought maybe some of you would go.
Amy will be in presently, and she will run down for us.

List 2. Dialogue Tags (Not in Correct Order)
asked Beth
said Beth, ten days after Mrs. March's departure
Beth said earnestly
Beth said
Meg asked
suggested Meg
replied Meg, rocking comfortably as she sewed
said Jo, laughing, but looking a little ashamed of her inconsistency
said Jo, adding apologetically

List 3. For Reference: Rules for Writing Dialogue
A dialogue tag identifies the person making the speech.
When a dialogue tag comes after a speech, place a comma, exclamation point, or question mark inside the closing quotation marks.
When a dialogue tag comes before a speech, place a comma after the tag. Put the dialogue's final punctuation mark inside the closing quotation marks.
Speeches do not need to be attached to a dialogue tag as long as the text clearly indicates the speaker.
Usually, a new paragraph begins with each new speaker.
When a dialogue tag comes in the middle of a speech, follow it with a comma if the following dialogue is an incomplete sentence. Follow it with a period if the following dialogue is a complete sentence.

> **Note to Instructor:** As long as the above rules are followed, the student's rewritten dialogue does not need to match the original (below) exactly. Ask the student to point out the differences between her dialogue and the passage below.

Original Dialogue:

"Meg, I wish you'd go and see the Hummels. You know Mother told us not to forget them," said Beth, ten days after Mrs. March's departure.

"I'm too tired to go this afternoon," replied Meg, rocking comfortably as she sewed.

"Can't you, Jo?" asked Beth.

"Too stormy for me with my cold."

"I thought it was almost well."

"It's well enough for me to go out with Laurie, but not well enough to go to the Hummels," said Jo, laughing, but looking a little ashamed of her inconsistency.

Meg asked, "Why don't you go yourself?"

"I have been every day," Beth said earnestly, "but the baby is sick, and I don't know what to do for it. I think you or Hannah ought to go."

"Ask Hannah for some nice little mess, and take it round, Beth, the air will do you good," said Jo, adding apologetically, "I'd go but I want to finish my writing."

Beth said, "My head aches and I'm tired, so I thought maybe some of you would go."

"Amy will be in presently, and she will run down for us," suggested Meg.

Exercise 92B: Using Direct Quotations Correctly

On your own paper, rewrite the following three paragraphs, inserting at least one quote from each of the following three sources into the paragraph. Use the following guidelines:

a) At least one quote must be a block quote.
b) At least one quote must be a complete sentence.
c) At least one quote must be a partial sentence incorporated into your own sentence.
d) Each quote must have an attribution tag.
e) At least one quote must be condensed, using ellipses.
f) You must make at least one change or addition that needs to be put in brackets.

A list of the rules governing direct quotations follows, for your reference.

You may make whatever changes are needed to the paragraphs. When you are finished, compare your paragraphs to the sample answer in the Answer Key.

These paragraphs are adapted from Chapter Ten of *The History of the Renaissance World*, by Susan Wise Bauer.

List 1. Paragraphs

After Babur the Tiger died in 1530, he left his oldest son Humayan in charge of his empire. But not long after Humayan came to the throne, he was driven out of India by invaders. He spent the next fifteen years trying to get the throne of India back! Finally, Humayan was able to return to his palace in Delhi. But he had lost much of his father's empire.

Just one year after Humayan returned to India, he slipped on the steps of his library, hit his head, and died. In 1556, his thirteen-year-old son Akbar was crowned emperor in his place. Akbar was young, but he was determined to restore the glory of his grandfather's empire. He launched a furious campaign to reconquer the lands that Humayan had lost. And after he got those lands back under his control, he added even more cities to his empire. By the time he died, after a reign of forty-nine years, Akbar ruled an empire that covered half of India.

Like his grandfather Babur, Akbar was a fair and just ruler. Although he himself was a Muslim, Akbar believed that he would need to be popular with his Hindu subjects if he wanted to stay on the throne. So he married a Hindu princess and allowed Hindu worship to continue in his country.

List 2. Sources

"Humayan walked out upon the terrace of the library, and sat down there for some time to enjoy the fresh air. When the Emperor began to descend the steps of the stair from the terrace, the crier, according to custom, proclaimed the time of prayer. The King stood still upon this occasion and repeated his creed, then sat down upon the second stair till the proclamation was ended. When he was going to rise, he supported himself on a staff, which unfortunately slipped upon the marble, and the King fell headlong from the top to the bottom of the stair; he was taken up insensible and laid upon his bed; he soon recovered his speech, and the physicians administered all their art but in vain; for upon the 11th of the month, about sunset, his soul took flight to Paradise."

—Alexander Dow, translator and historian

"Akbar further underscored toleration as a major concern of state by declaring his policy of *sulh-i kul,* universal toleration. That extended the canopy of justice to all, regardless of religious affiliation."

—Catherine Asher, historian

"During his reign of nearly half a century Akbar had his fill of fighting. Noted as an administrator and a broadminded statesman, he was forced to distinguish himself first as a soldier. At the outset of his reign he possessed only the Punjab and Delhi, and he had to struggle even to maintain himself on the throne of Delhi. Twenty years of severe fighting was needed to bring the country into subjection and numerous campaigns ensued during the twenty years to round off the boundaries of the kingdom.

—*The Cyclopedia of India: Biographical, Historical, Administrative, Commercial*

List 3. For Reference: Rules for Using Direct Quotations

When an attribution tag comes after a direct quote, place a comma, exclamation point, or question mark inside the closing quotation marks.

When an attribution tag comes before a direct quote, place a comma after the tag. Put the dialogue's final punctuation mark inside the closing quotation marks.

When an attribution tag comes in the middle of a direct quotation, follow it with a comma if the remaining quote is an incomplete sentence. Follow it with a period if the remaining quote is a complete sentence.

Direct quotes can be words, phrases, clauses, or sentences, as long as they are set off by quotation marks and form part of a grammatically correct original sentence.

An ellipsis shows where something has been cut out of a sentence.

Every direct quote must have an attribution tag.

If a direct quotation is longer than three lines, indent the entire quote one inch from the margin in a separate block of text and omit quotation marks.

If you change or make additions to a direct quotation, use brackets.

Note to Instructor: You will need to check the student's paragraphs against the rules above. The sample answer below is just one way to insert the direct quotations.

If the student needs prompting, allow her to read the sample answer below and then require her to use different parts of the sources in her own rewritten paragraphs.

Notice that the student has not been asked to provide footnotes or in-text citations; the focus of this lesson is on incorporating quotes properly into a piece of written work.

After Babur the Tiger died in 1530, he left his oldest son Humayan in charge of his empire. But not long after Humayan came to the throne, he was driven out of India by invaders. He spent the next fifteen years trying to get the throne of India back! Finally, Humayan was able to return to his palace in Delhi. But he had lost much of his father's empire.

Just one year after Humayan returned to India, he slipped on the steps of his library, hit his head, and died. The translator and historian Alexander Dow describes the accident:

> When the Emperor began to descend the steps of the stair from the terrace, the crier, according to custom, proclaimed the time of prayer. The King . . . sat down upon the second stair till the proclamation was ended. When he was going to rise, he supported himself on a staff, which unfortunately slipped upon the marble, and the King fell headlong from the top to the bottom of the stair; he was taken up insensible and laid upon his bed . . . [and] upon the 11th of the month, about sunset, his soul took flight to Paradise.

In 1556, his thirteen-year-old son Akbar was crowned emperor in his place. Akbar was young, but he was determined to restore the glory of his grandfather's empire. He launched a furious campaign to reconquer the lands that Humayan had lost. And after he got those lands back under his control, he added even more cities to his empire. As The Encyclopedia of India tells us, "Twenty years of severe fighting was needed to bring the country into subjection and numerous campaigns ensued during the twenty years to round off the boundaries of the kingdom." By the time he died, after a reign of forty-nine years, Akbar ruled an empire that covered half of India.

Like his grandfather Babur, Akbar was a fair and just ruler. Although he himself was a Muslim, Akbar believed that he would need to be popular with his Hindu subjects if he wanted to stay on the throne. So he married a Hindu princess and allowed Hindu worship to continue in his country. He also put into place a policy called sulh-i kul; as the historian Catherine Asher writes, this "extended . . . justice to all, regardless of religious affiliation."

WEEK 24

Floating Elements

— LESSON 93 —

Interjections
Nouns of Direct Address
Parenthetical Expressions

Exercise 93A: Using Floating Elements Correctly

On your own paper, rewrite the following sentences in List 1, inserting interjections, nouns of direct address, and parenthetical expressions from List 2. You must use every item in List 2 at least once. Every sentence in List 1 must have at least one insertion. Interjections may either come before or after sentences on their own, or may be incorporated directly into the sentence.

List 1. Sentences

Pluto is no longer considered to be a planet.
This milk has spoiled.
I think I'd better kill that rattlesnake.
Go take a nap.
You finally understand quadratic equations!
Is that dog really a St. Bernard-Chihuahua mix?
That is the exact book I was looking for.

List 2. Interjections, Nouns of Direct Address, Parenthetical Expressions

come what may
children
congratulations
sweetheart
Mother
eureka
oh, well
Mr. President
no doubt
in fact
of course

Note to Instructor: The answers below are samples. Any grammatical, properly punctuated versions of these sentences are acceptable.

Oh, well, Pluto is no longer considered to be a planet.
Children, this milk has spoiled, of course.
Sweetheart, I think I'd better kill that rattlesnake, come what may.

Go take a nap, Mother.
Congratulations! You finally understand quadratic equations!
Is that dog really, in fact, a St. Bernard-Chihuahua mix?
Eureka! That, no doubt, is the exact book I was looking for.

Exercise 93B: Parenthetical Expressions

In the following pairs of sentences, underline each subject once and each predicate twice. In each pair, cross out the parenthetical expression that is not essential to the sentences. If the expression is used as an essential part of the sentence, circle it and label it with the correct part of the sentence (e.g., *prep phrase acting as adj*, etc.). If it acts as a modifier, draw an arrow back to the word it modifies.

The meeting was, ~~after all~~, a failure.

prep phrase acting as adv
(After all) that preparation, the meeting was a failure.

You must appeal, ~~in a word~~, to the reader's imagination.

prep phrase acting as adv
There is great power (in a word) that is carefully chosen.

~~As it happens,~~ I will be too late to see the presentation.

prep phrase acting as adv
Thanks to the live broadcast, we will be able to see the presentation (as it happens).

inf phrase acting as noun/subject
To be sure of yourself is a good quality, but can also become a weakness.

The laws governing self-defense are, ~~to be sure~~, complicated and confusing.

~~In fact~~, autobiographies are notoriously unreliable.

prep phrase acting as adv
Autobiographies are often unreliable (in fact).

Exercise 93C: Diagramming

On your own paper, diagram every word of the following sentences.

These are slightly adapted from Sir Walter Scott's historical novel *Waverley*.

Oh, Squire, we should have followed you through flood and fire, to be sure!

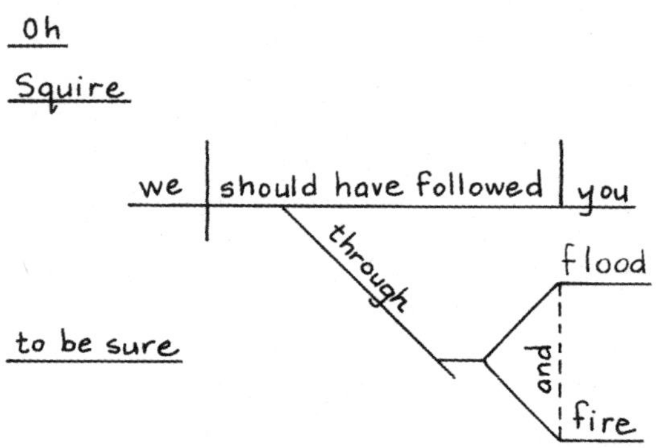

Alas, Mr. Waverley, I have no better advice.

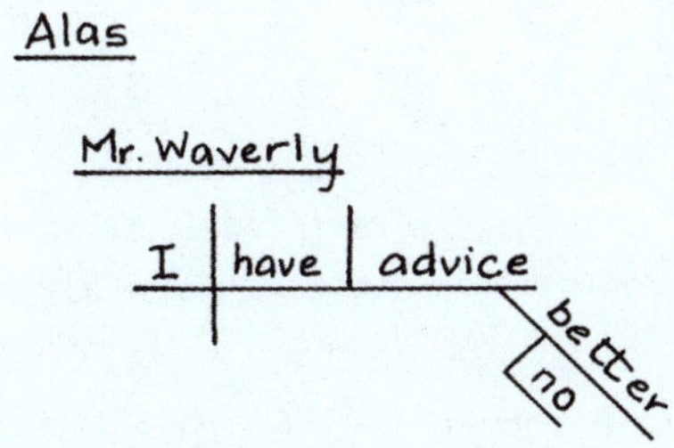

Distance, in truth, produces the same effect.

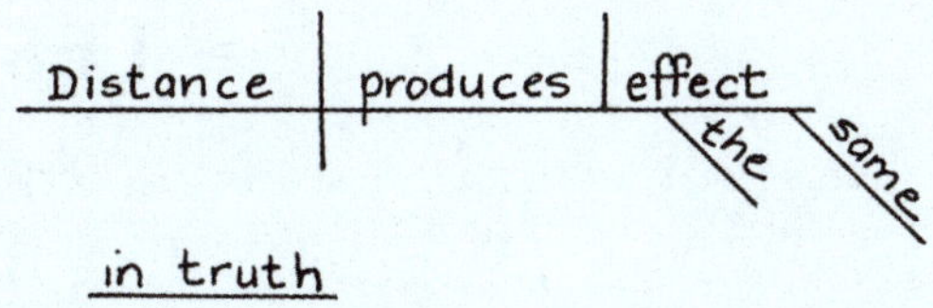

The starlight was lost as the stars faded before approaching day, and the head of the marching column, continuing its descent, plunged as it were into the heavy ocean of fog, which rolled its white waves over the whole plain, and over the sea by which it was bounded.

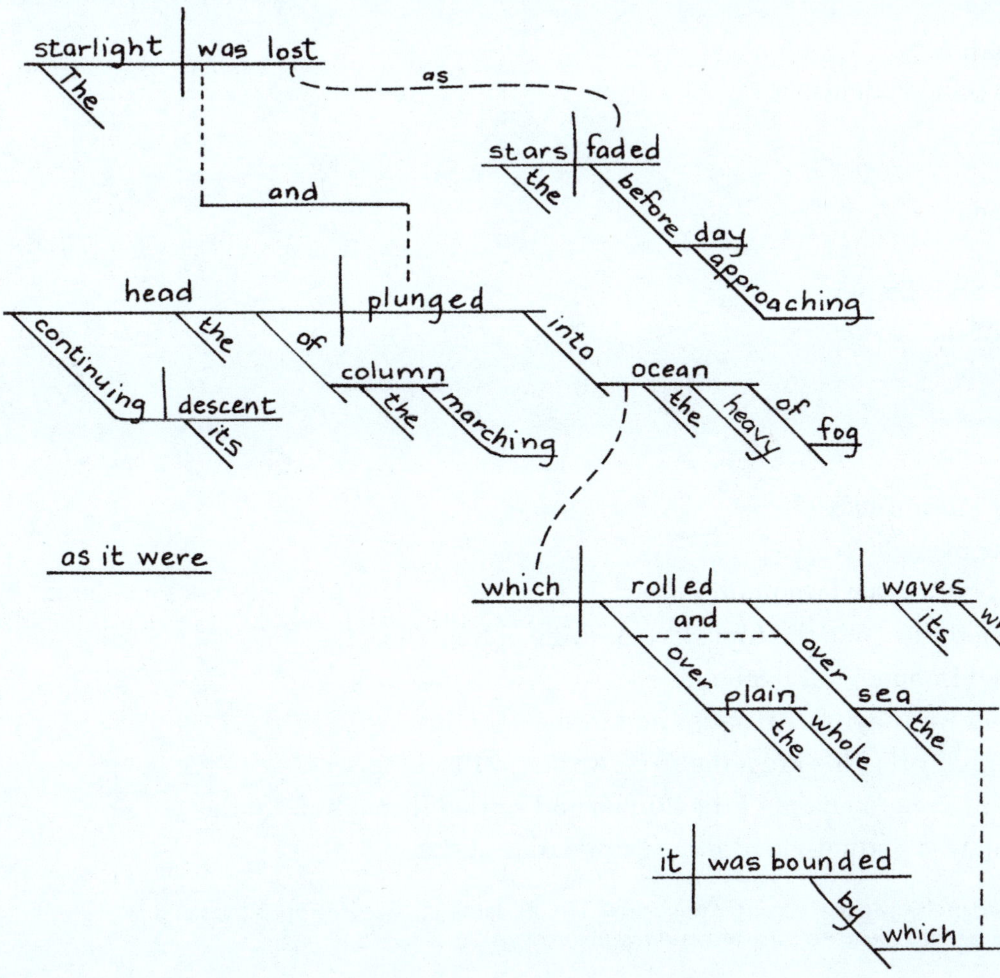

— LESSON 94 —

Appositives

Exercise 94A: Using Appositives

Rewrite the following sentences on your own paper, inserting at least one appositive or appositive phrase from List 1 into each of the sentences in List 2, and using correct punctuation. You may insert more than one appositive into each sentence, but you must use each appositive or phrase in List 1 at least once.

List 1. Appositives

Henry
the Duke of Normandy
the year of Indian independence
George III
Lahore
their ancestral home
the Virgin Queen
the founder of the Sikh Empire
the author of *Robinson Crusoe*
Haryana and Punjab
the blind poet

List 2. Sentences

John Milton wrote *Paradise Lost*.
Daniel Defoe wrote over 250 works.
Jane Austen's brother became her literary agent.
William the Conqueror became the first Norman king of England.
Virginia was named in honor of Elizabeth.
The king of England was paying little attention to the colonies.
Maharaja Ranjit Singh ruled his kingdom from Aurangzeb's old fortress.
After 1947, the Sikhs emigrated out of the Punjab and settled throughout India.
In 1966, the Punjab was again divided into two separate states.

Note to Instructor: The original sentences are below. The student may mix the appositives and phrases up as long as the sentences are punctuated properly.

Original Sentences:

John Milton, the blind poet, wrote *Paradise Lost*.

Daniel Defoe, the author of *Robinson Crusoe*, wrote over 250 works.

Jane Austen's brother, Henry, became her literary agent.

William the Conqueror, the Duke of Normandy, became the first Norman king of England.

Virginia was named in honor of Elizabeth, the Virgin Queen.

The king of England, George III, was paying little attention to the colonies.

Maharaja Ranjit Singh, the founder of the Sikh Empire, ruled his kingdom from Aurangzeb's old fortress, Lahore.

After 1947, the year of Indian independence, the Sikhs emigrated out of the Punjab, their ancestral home, and settled throughout India.

In 1966, the Punjab was again divided into two separate states, Haryana and Punjab.

Exercise 94B: Identifying Appositives

In each of the following sentences, underline the subject of each independent clause once, and the predicate twice. Circle each appositive or appositive phrase.

These sentences are taken from Constance Garnett's translation of *Crime and Punishment*, by Fyodor Dostoyevsky.

I am Raskolnikov, a student; I came here a month ago.

He was a man over fifty, bald and grizzled, of medium height, and stoutly built.

The persons still in the tavern were a man who appeared to be an artisan, drunk, but not extremely so, sitting before a pot of beer, and his companion, a huge, stout man with a grey beard.

This man, this most reputable and exemplary citizen, will on no consideration give you money.

Her stockings, her stockings I have sold for drink!

Note to Instructor: The first *stockings* is the appositive because it is set off with commas.

She married her first husband, an infantry officer, for love, and ran away with him from her father's house.

You can judge the extremity of her calamities, that she, a woman of education and culture and distinguished family, should have consented to be my wife.

Boots, cotton shirt-fronts—most magnificent, a uniform—they got up all in splendid style, for eleven roubles and a half.

The first morning I came back from the office I found Katerina Ivanovna had cooked two courses for dinner—soup and salt meat with horseradish—which we had never dreamed of till then.

And here I, her own father, took thirty copecks of that money for a drink.

There is the house of Kozel, the cabinet-maker, a German, well-to-do.

In the far distance, a copse lay, a dark blur on the very edge of the horizon.

A few paces beyond the last market garden stood a tavern, a big tavern.

Exercise 94C: Diagramming (Challenge!)

On your own paper, diagram every word of the following five sentences from Exercise 94B.

NOTE: The last three sentences each contain a diagramming challenge! Try to come up with solutions on your own—how can you make the sentence structure clear? If you get frustrated, ask your instructor for help. And when you're finished, compare your diagrams to those in the *Answer Key*.

Note to Instructor: Diagramming is not an exact science! As long as the student understands, grammatically, the sentences below, and as long as her diagram solution makes the grammatical relationships clear, she does not necessarily have to diagram the difficult elements in exactly the way you see below.

Encourage the student to have fun with this assignment, and try to avoid unnecessary frustration.

Her stockings, her stockings I have sold for drink!

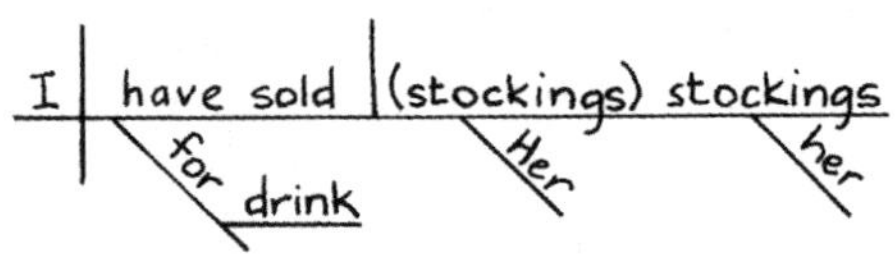

I am Raskolnikov, a student; I came here a month ago.

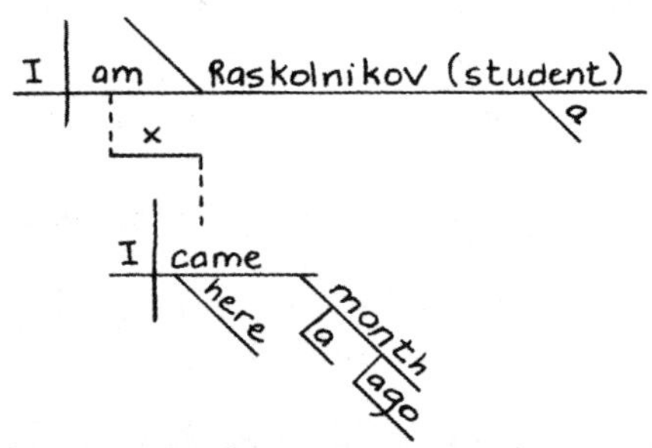

Note to Instructor: In this idiomatic use of *month*, the noun is actually functioning as an adverb answering the question *when*, so it is diagrammed on an adverb line beneath the verb.

The persons still in the tavern were a man who appeared to be an artisan, drunk, but not extremely so, sitting before a pot of beer, and his companion, a huge, stout man with a grey beard.

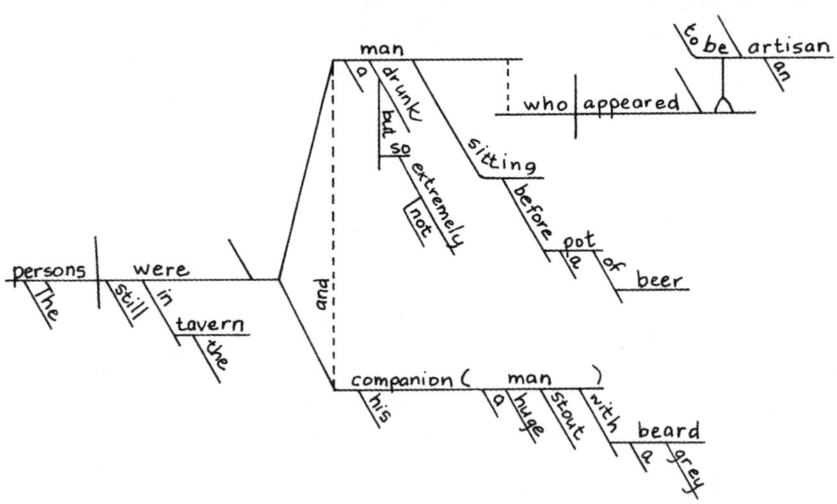

Note to Instructor: If the student cannot classify *but not extremely so*, ask her to look up *but* and *so* in a dictionary. In this usage, *so* is functioning as a pronoun (referring back to the state of drunkenness: *[He was] drunk, but not extremely [drunk]*). *But* can also work as a preposition: the pronoun *so* is its object. *Extremely* describes *so*. Normally *extremely* is an adverb, but since *so* is actually replacing the adjective *drunk*, *extremely* can modify it. (*He was not extremely drunk.*)

To be an artisan is an infinitive phrase functioning as a predicate adjective and following the linking verb *appeared*. Within the infinitive phrase, *artisan* functions as a predicate nominative, not a direct object.

Boots, cotton shirt-fronts—most magnificent, a uniform—they got up all in splendid style, for eleven roubles and a half.

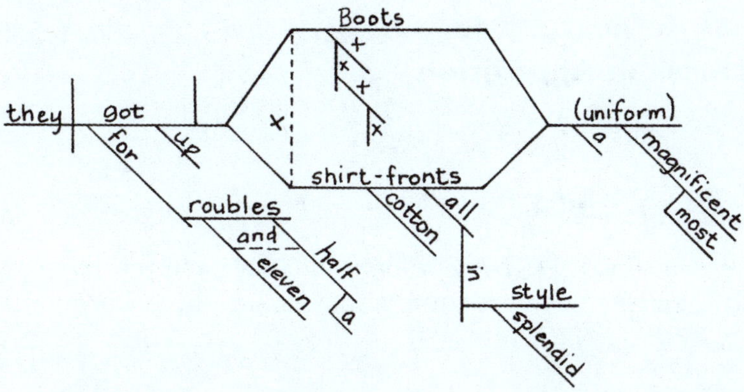

Note to Instructor: The appositive, *a uniform*, refers to *both* of the compound direct objects (*boots* and *shirt-fronts*), so the two lines should be brought back together before the appositive is inserted. *All in splendid style* is an adjective phrase (*all* here functions as an adjective with *in splendid style* modifying it) that modifies both direct objects, so it is diagrammed beneath the nearest direct object, and the phrase is repeated beneath the first direct object with *X* taking the place of the actual words, to show that the phrase only occurs once but modifies both nouns.

Additional Note: Some grammarians might choose to identify *all* as a pronoun here, functioning as a predicate nominative in the understood relative clause *that were all in splendid style*:

> "For eleven and a half roubles, they got up boots [and] cotton shirt-fronts (a most magnificent uniform) [that were] all in splendid style."

Since this sentence is taken from a line of dialogue, its structure is less regular.

The first morning I came back from the office I found Katerina Ivanovna had cooked two courses for dinner—soup and salt meat with horseradish—which we had never dreamed of till then.

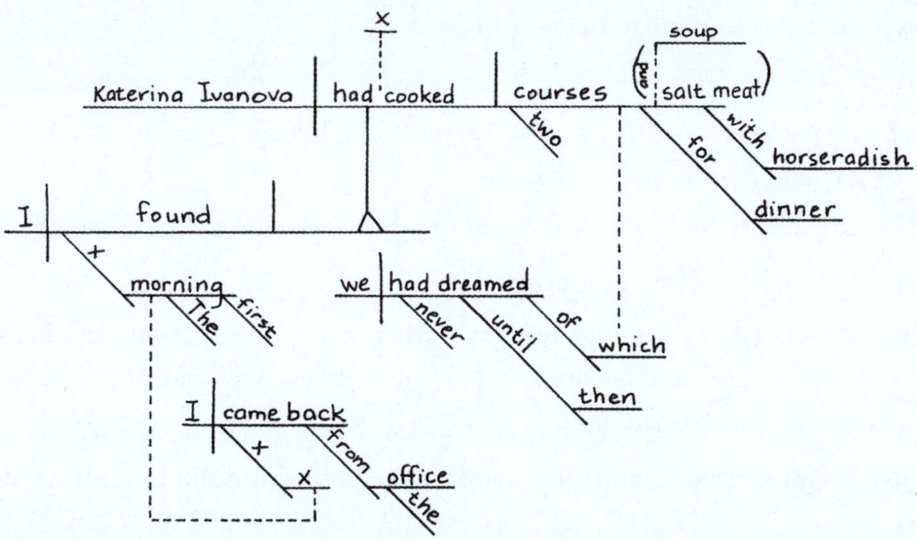

Note to Instructor: There are three relative clauses in this sentence, but the relative pronouns in two of them are understood. There is also an understood prepositional phrase. Spelled out (but without the appositive), this sentence would be:

> "[On] The first morning [on which] I came back from the office, I found [that] Katerina Ivanovna had cooked two courses (of which we had never dreamed until then) for dinner."

Soup and salt meat with horseradish is a compound appositive. Here it is diagrammed as though it were a compound subject, but if the student can indicate this clearly in another way, that's acceptable.

— LESSON 95 —

Appositives
Intensive and Reflexive Pronouns
Noun Clauses in Apposition
Object Complements

Exercise 95A: Reflexive and Intensive Pronoun Review

In the following sentences from Fyodor Dostoyevsky's novel *The Idiot*, underline each reflexive or intensive pronoun. Put parentheses around each intensive pronoun. Label each reflexive pronoun with the correct part of the sentence (*S, DO, IO, PA, PN, OP*, etc.).

"No, he didn't, for I saw it all (myself)," said Colia.

Might he suggest, for instance, such a thing as a marriage between himself (OP) and one of the general's daughters?

Everyone gasped; some even crossed themselves (DO).

"Prince, be so kind as to come to me for a moment in the drawing-room," said Nina Alexandrovna (herself), appearing at the door.

It hid itself (DO) under the cupboard and under the chest of drawers, and crawled into the corners.

Why, it was yourself (PN) who advised me to bring him over.

Judge for yourselves (OP).

But I'll tell you why I have been awaiting you so impatiently, because I believe that Providence (itself) sent you to be a friend and a brother to me.

You see, prince, I'll tell you privately, Evgenie and ourselves (S) have not said a word yet.

Not that Varia was afraid of standing up for herself (OP).

Yet we feel that we ought to limit ourselves (DO (of inf.)) to the simple record of facts, without much attempt at explanation, for a very patent reason: because we (ourselves) have the greatest possible difficulty in accounting for the facts to be recorded.

They had (themselves) decided that it would be better if the prince did not talk all the evening.

Exercise 95B: Distinguishing Noun Clauses in Apposition from Adjective Clauses

In the following sentences, identify each noun, noun phrase, or noun clause acting as an appositive by underlining it and writing the abbreviation *APP* above it. Draw an arrow from each appositive back to the noun it renames or explains.

Circle each adjective clause and draw an arrow from each circle back to the noun that the adjective clause modifies.

He sincerely believed the impossible, that aliens were living among us (APP).

APP
The court's conclusion, that the convicted man deserved a retrial, was immediately challenged in the press.

I smashed the spider (that was dangling from the corner of my bed.)

APP
The mystery, how the treasure had disappeared without a trace, was still unsolved.

APP
The truth, that I was bored and wanted to leave, would have hurt my host's feelings.

The sailors hoped to capture the ship (which was anchored close by.)

APP
The skater's conviction, that he would win an Olympic medal, sustained him through long hours of practice.

APP
The shepherd, a gnarled mountain man (who carried an ancient weathered crook,) whistled to

APP
his dog, a whippet-thin border collie.

APP
He hefted the weapon, a sword (that had been forged by his grandfather,) and turned towards the enemy.

APP
My mother's advice, that I should leave early to avoid traffic, turned out to be very good advice indeed.

The musical instrument (that I love the most) is the violin.

APP
Her hope, that he would return from the war unharmed, began to fade away.

APP
His greatest fault, that he works so slowly, is a difficult one to overcome.

APP
The book never really answers the question, which ambition is better to pursue.

Vegetables (that are grown organically) are much more expensive.

APP
My car, the blue one (that is parked by the fire hydrant,) won't start.

Exercise 95C: Diagramming

On your own paper, diagram every word of these two sentences from Frederick Marryat's classic adventure novel *The Pirate.* Do your best to place each word on the diagram, but ask your instructor if you need help.

Our little party was now threatened with a new danger, that we might be run over by the frigate, which was now within a cable's length of us, driving the seas before her in one widely extended foam, as she pursued her rapid and impetuous course.

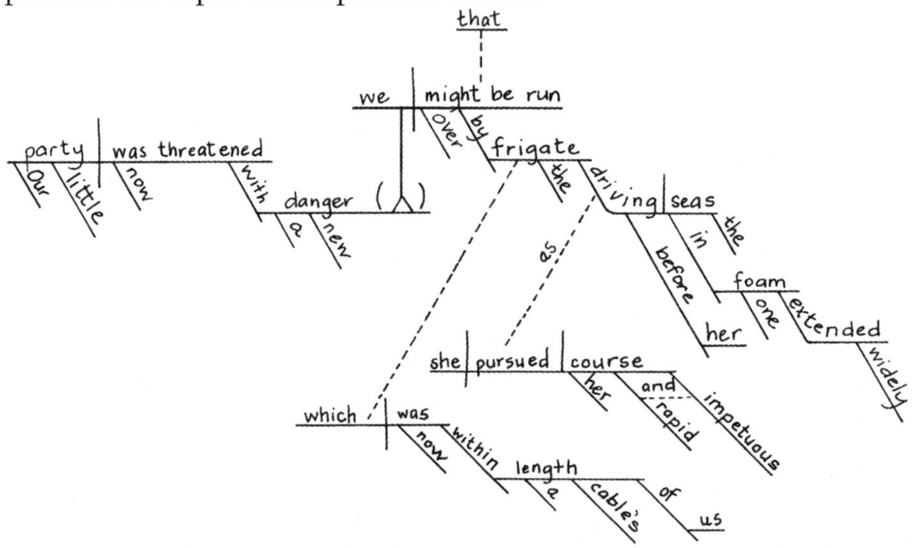

Note to Instructor: *In one widely extended foam* is ambiguous. It describes the seas, so I have diagrammed it as an adjective. It could also be taken as adverbial, describing *how* the frigate is driving, so if the student diagrams it beneath *driving,* accept this answer.

The indignation and rage which were expressed by the captain as he rapidly walked the deck in company with his first mate—his violent gesticulation—proved to the crew that there was mischief brewing.

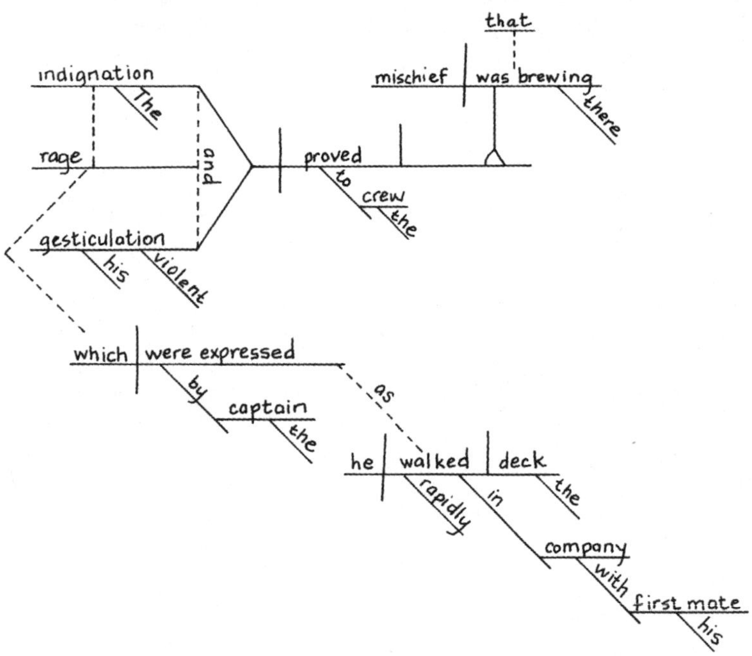

Note to Instructor: The adjective clause *which were expressed by the captain* modifies *indignation and rage*, but not the third subject, *gesticulation*, which is punctuated like a parenthetical element but actually has a grammatical function within the sentence. The student should attempt to link *indignation* and *rage* to the relative pronoun *which* without linking *gesticulation*. This *Answer Key* offers one possible solution; you could accept another arrangement as long as the relationship of *which* to the first two subjects is clear.

As he rapidly walked the deck in company with his first mate is an adverb clause modifying *were expressed* and answering the question *when*.

— LESSON 96 —

Appositives

Noun Clauses in Apposition

Absolute Constructions

Exercise 96A: Identifying Absolute Constructions

The excerpts below are taken from classic works of poetry and prose. Circle the absolute construction in each one. Label each absolute construction as *CL* for clause or *PHR* for phrase. For clauses, underline the subject of each clause once and the predicate twice.

PHR
A fellow presently passing by, Adams asked him if he could direct him to an ale-house.

—Henry Fielding

Note to Instructor: *Passing*, like *being locked* and *being* below, is an adjective, not a predicate.

PHR
As to the door being locked, it is a very ordinary lock.

—Agatha Christie

Thinkest thou this heart could feel a moment's joy,
PHR
Thou being absent?

—Henry Wadsworth Longfellow

CL
We sitting, as I said, the cock crew loud.

—Alfred, Lord Tennyson

PHR
He went down, rider and steed, before his lance.

—Edward Bulwer-Lytton

CL
He was buried in Westminster Abbey, the stone that bears his inscription resting at the feet of Addison.

—Thomas Macaulay

Note to Instructor: The dependent clause *that bears his inscription* acts as an adjective modifying *stone*. The entire clause beginning with *the stone* and ending with *of Addison* serves as the absolute construction.

PHR
He speaks three or four languages, word for word.

—William Shakespeare

PHR
As to my cargo, it was, a great part of it, lost.

—Daniel Defoe

Note to Instructor: *A great part of it* is an appositive renaming the subject *it*.

PHR

Here lies, his head upon the lap of earth
A youth to fortune and to fame unknown.
—Thomas Gray

Exercise 96B: Appositives, Modifiers, and Absolute Constructions

The sentences below, taken from *The Mysterious Affair at Styles*, by Agatha Christie, each contain phrases or clauses set off by dashes. Some are appositives, some are modifiers, and some are absolute constructions. Identify them by writing *APP*, *MOD*, or *AC* above each one. For appositives and modifiers, draw an arrow back to the word being renamed or modified.

AC

Very well—but it's all extremely mysterious.

AC

We will look at the chest—but no matter—we will examine it all the same.

APP

It was the expression on his face that was extraordinary—a curious mingling of terror and agitation.

AC

She had bolted the door leading into his room—a most unusual proceeding on her part.

Note to Instructor: This cannot be a modifier because the noun *proceeding* cannot act as an adverb describing the verb *had bolted*.

AC

She was not extravagantly loved—no.

AC

Call for me in passing—the last house in the village.

APP

A very dark shadow is resting on this house—the shadow of murder.

AC

Miss Howard had been on afternoon duty on Tuesday, and—a convoy coming in unexpectedly—she had kindly offered to remain on night duty.

MOD

Mary Cavendish was there, shaking the girl—who must have been an unusually sound sleeper—and trying to wake her.

APP

My idea was—a very ridiculous one—that she had intended to poison him.

AC

But I decided that if I made any interesting and important discoveries—as no doubt I should—I would keep them to myself.

AC

I think—I am sure—he cared for me at first.

APP

They had already arranged their infamous plot—that he should marry this rich, but rather foolish old lady, induce her to make a will leaving her money to him, and then gain their ends by a very cleverly conceived crime.

MOD

Did you—while you happened to be alone for a few seconds—unlock the poison cupboard, and examine some of the bottles?

Exercise 96C: Diagramming

On your own paper, diagram every word of the following sentences, taken from Agatha Christie's mystery novel *Murder on the Orient Express.*

Round her neck was a collar of very large pearls which, improbable though it seemed, were real.

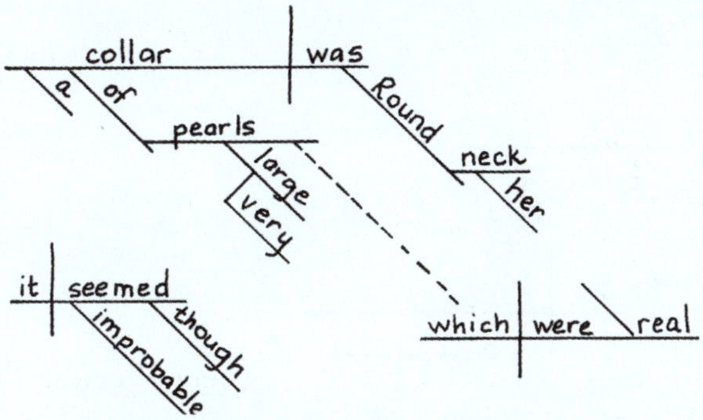

Note to Instructor: The absolute construction is diagrammed below and to the left of the dependent clause, since it refers to the realness of the pearls rather than to the collar itself, but the placement is not vitally important. *Though* acts as an adverb within the construction. It could possibly be argued that *though* is the subordinating word connecting the adverbial clause *improbable though it seemed* to the verb *were*. Accept either answer.

Poirot passed along the corridor, a somewhat slow progress, as most of the people travelling were standing outside their carriages.

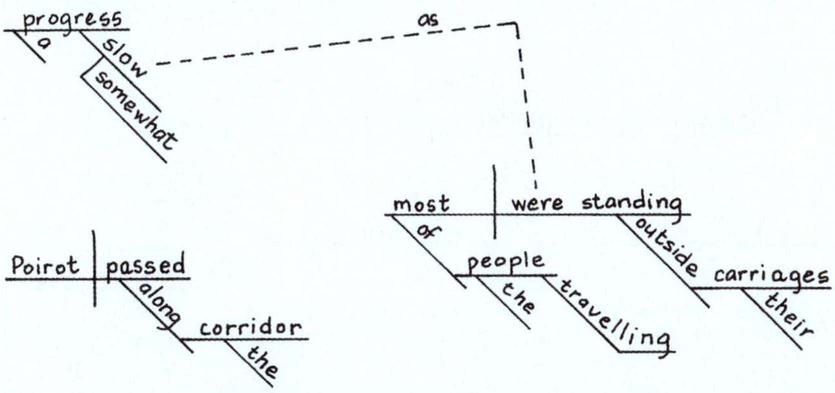

Note to Instructor: *A somewhat slow progress* is the first part of the absolute construction; *as most of the people travelling were standing outside their carriages* is a dependent clause acting as a modifier to explain the slowness of the progress; since it modifies the adjective *slow*, it is adverbial.

There was a kind of cool efficiency in the way she was eating her breakfast and in the way she called to the attendant to bring her more coffee, which bespoke a knowledge of the world and of travelling.

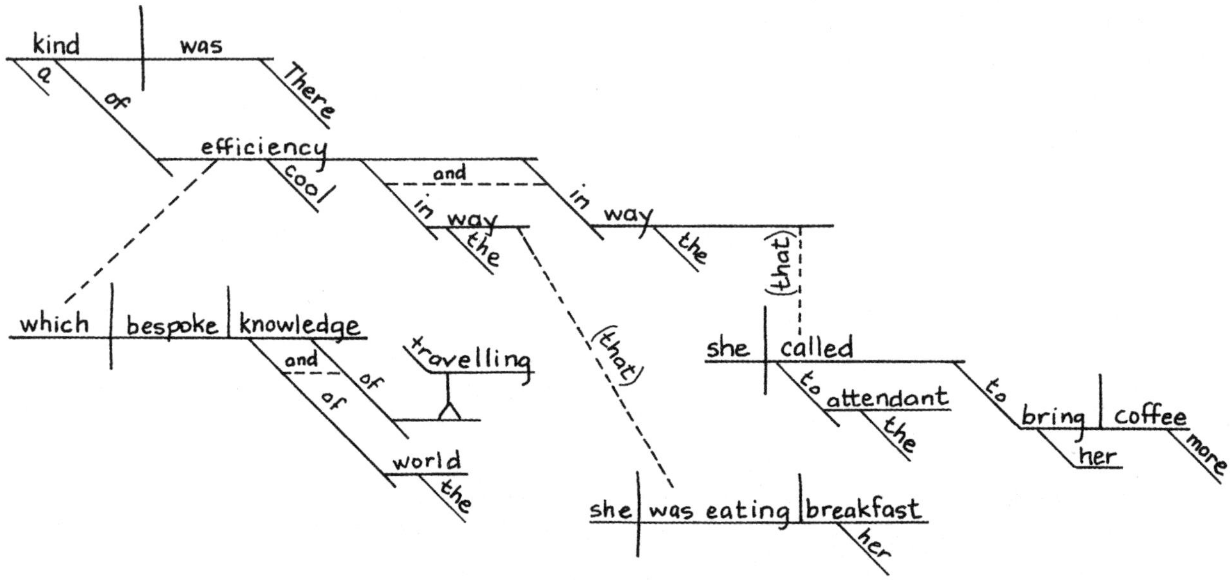

To look up the antecedents of all these people, to discover their *bona fides*—that takes time and endless inconvenience.

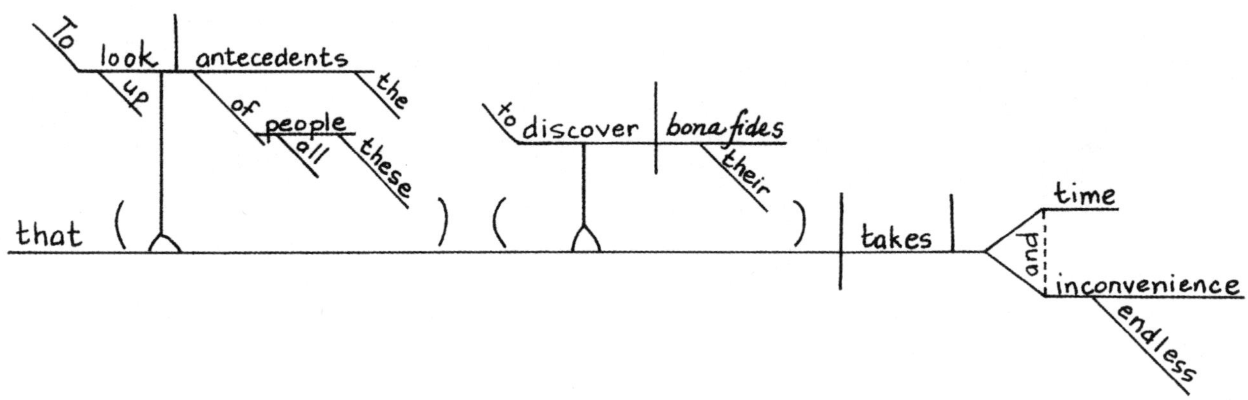

— REVIEW 8 —
Weeks 22-24

Topics
Parenthetical Expressions
Dashes, Colons, and Brackets
Dialogue and Dialogue Tags
Direct Quotations and Attribution Tags
Ellipses and Partial Quotations
Block Quotes
Interjections
Nouns of Direct Address
Appositives
Noun Clauses in Apposition
Absolute Constructions

Review 8A: Definition Fill-in-the-Blank

You learned many definitions in the past three weeks! Fill in the blanks in the definitions below with one of the terms from the list. Many of the terms will be used more than once.

Note to Instructor: Allow the student to look back through the workbook and find definitions as necessary; the value of the exercise comes in the student's completing each definition, whether from memory or not.

commas	comma	parentheses
line space	dashes	coordinating conjunction
semicolon	colon	paragraph
appositive	appositives	absolute construction
period	attribution tag	exclamation point
parenthetical expression	interjections	dialogue tag
question mark	brackets	ellipses
restrictive modifying clause	nouns of direct address	quotation marks
non-restrictive modifying clause	closing quotation marks	short parenthetical expressions

A restrictive modifying clause **defines the word that it modifies. Removing the clause changes the essential meaning of the sentence.**

A non-restrictive modifying clause **describes the word that it modifies. Removing the clause doesn't change the essential meaning of the sentence.**

Only a non-restrictive modifying clause **should be set off by commas.**

Parentheses **can enclose words that are not essential to the sentence.**

A parenthetical expression **often interrupts or is irrelevant to the rest of the sentence.**

Punctuation goes inside the parentheses **if it applies to the** parenthetical expression**; all other punctuation goes outside the** parentheses**.**

A parenthetical expression **only begins with a capital letter if it is a complete sentence with ending punctuation.**

A parenthetical expression **can also be set off by commas.**

Short parenthetical expressions **such as the following are usually set off by commas: *in short, in fact, in reality, as it were, as it happens, no doubt, in a word, to be sure, to be brief, after all, you know, of course.***

Dashes **can enclose words that are not essential to the sentence.**

Dashes **can also be used singly to separate parts of a sentence.**

Commas **make a parenthetical element a part of the sentence.**

Dashes **emphasize a parenthetical element.**

Parentheses **minimize a parenthetical element.**

The independent clauses of a compound sentence must be joined by a comma **and a** coordinating conjunction**, a** semicolon**, or a** semicolon **and a** coordinating conjunction**. They cannot be joined by a** comma **alone.**

When a dialogue tag **comes before a speech, place a** comma **after the tag. Put the dialogue's final punctuation mark inside the** closing quotation marks**.**

Speeches do not need to be attached to a dialogue tag **as long as the text clearly indicates the speaker.**

Usually, a new paragraph **begins with each new speaker.**

When an attribution tag **comes in the middle of a speech, follow it with a** comma **if the following dialogue is an incomplete sentence. Follow it with a** period **if the following dialogue is a complete sentence.**

When an attribution tag **comes after a direct quote, place a** comma**,** exclamation point**, or** question mark **inside the closing quotation marks.**

When an attribution tag **comes before a direct quote, place a** comma **after the tag. Put the dialogue's final punctuation mark inside the** closing quotation marks**.**

When an attribution tag **comes in the middle of a direct quotation, follow it with a** comma **if the remaining quote is an incomplete sentence. Follow it with a** period **if the remaining quote is a complete sentence.**

Every direct quote must have an attribution tag**.**

Ellipses **show where something has been cut out of a sentence.**

A second or third quote from the same source does not need another attribution tag**, as long as context makes the source of the quote clear.**

Direct quotes can be words, phrases, clauses, or sentences, as long as they are set off by quotation marks **and form part of a grammatically correct original sentence.**

If a direct quotation is longer than three lines, indent the entire quote one inch from the margin in a separate block of text and omit quotation marks**.**

If you change or make additions to a direct quotation, use brackets**.**

When using word processing software, leave an additional line space **before and after a block quote.**

Block quotes should be introduced by a colon **(if preceded by a complete sentence) or a** comma **(if preceded by a partial sentence).**

Interjections **express sudden feeling or emotion. They are set off with** commas **or stand alone with a closing punctuation mark.**

Nouns of direct address **name a person or thing who is being spoken to. They are set off with** commas**. They are capitalized only if they are proper names or titles.**

An appositive **is a noun, pronoun, or noun phrase that usually follows another noun and renames or explains it.** Appositives **are set off by** commas**.**

A dependent clause can act as an appositive **if it renames the noun that it follows.**

An absolute construction **has a strong semantic relationship but no grammatical connection to the rest of the sentence.**

Review 8B: Punctuating Restrictive and Non-Restrictive Clauses, Compound Sentences, Interjections, and Nouns of Direct Address

The sentences below contain restrictive clauses, non-restrictive clauses, interjections, and nouns of direct address. Some are compound sentences. But all of them have lost their punctuation! Insert all necessary punctuation directly into the sentences (use the actual punctuation marks rather than proofreader's marks).

These sentences are taken from Harriet Jacobs's 1861 memoir, *Incidents in the Life of a Slave Girl, Written by Herself.*

Note to Instructor: The original sentences are below; explanations have been inserted in brackets where necessary.

"Ah, Ellen, is that you?" he said, in his most gracious manner. [The comma after *said* is optional.]

Five of them were my grandmother's children, and had shared the same milk that nourished her mother's children. [The comma after *children* is optional.]

Alas, the thought was familiar to me, and had sent many a sharp pang through my heart, [The comma after *me* is optional.]

She may be an ignorant creature, degraded by the system that has brutalized her from childhood, but she has a mother's instincts, and is capable of feeling a mother's agonies. [The comma after *instincts* is optional, but the others are required; the first sets off the non-restrictive descriptive clause *degraded by . . . childhood*, and the second comma and coordinating conjunction *but* connect the two independent clauses together into a compound-complex sentence.]

Forgive me for what, mother? For not letting him treat me like a dog?

We that loved him waited to bid him a long and last farewell. [*That loved him* is a restrictive clause necessary to the meaning of the sentence.]

I asked her to prepare a poultice of warm ashes and vinegar, and I applied it to my leg, which was already much swollen. [Both commas are necessary; the first, along with the coordinating conjunction *and,* connects the two independent clauses, and the second comes before the non-restrictive descriptive clause *which was already much swollen.*]

My uncle Phillip, who was a carpenter, had very skillfully made a concealed trap door, which communicated with the storeroom. [Both descriptive relative clauses are non-restrictive.]

I had slunk down behind a barrel, which entirely screened me, but I imagined that Jenny was looking directly at the spot, and my heart beat violently. [The first two commas are necessary; the first relative clause is non-restrictive, and the comma and coordinating conjunction *but* connects the two independent sentences. The last comma is optional.]

My grandmother loved this old lady, whom we all called Miss Fanny. [The descriptive clause is non-restrictive.]

This wounded my grandmother's feelings, for she could not retain ill will against the woman whom she had nourished with her milk when a babe. [The comma and coordinating conjunction *for* connect the two independent sentences.]

There the prisoners rest together; they hear not the voice of the oppressor; the servant is free from his master. [The three independent clauses (sentences) have no coordinating conjunctions so must be connected with semicolons instead of commas.]

Well, Martha, I've brought you a letter from Linda.

Review 8C: Dialogue

In the following passage of dialogue, taken from Harriet Beecher Stowe's classic anti-slavery novel *Uncle Tom's Cabin,* all of the punctuation around, before, and after the lines of dialogue is missing. Insert all necessary punctuation directly into the sentences (use the actual punctuation marks rather than proofreader's marks).

Note to Instructor: The original excerpt, with original punctuation, is found below.

Marie was busy, turning over the contents of a drawer, as she answered, "Well, of course, by and by, Eva, you will have other things to think of besides reading the Bible round to servants. Not but that is very proper; I've done it myself, when I had health. But when you come to be dressing and going into company, you won't have time. See here!" she added, "these jewels I'm going to give you when you come out. I wore them to my first ball. I can tell you, Eva, I made a sensation."

Eva took the jewel-case, and lifted from it a diamond necklace. Her large, thoughtful eyes rested on them, but it was plain her thoughts were elsewhere.

"How sober you look, child!" said Marie.

"Are these worth a great deal of money, mamma?"

"To be sure, they are. Father sent to France for them. They are worth a small fortune."

"I wish I had them," said Eva, "to do what I pleased with!"

"What would you do with them?"

"I'd sell them, and buy a place in the free states, and take all our people there, and hire teachers, to teach them to read and write."

Eva was cut short by her mother's laughing.

"Set up a boarding-school! Wouldn't you teach them to play on the piano, and paint on velvet?"

"I'd teach them to read their own Bible, and write their own letters, and read letters that are written to them," said Eva, steadily. "I know, mamma, it does come very hard on them that they can't do these things. Tom feels it—Mammy does,—a great many of them do. I think it's wrong."

"Come, come, Eva; you are only a child! You don't know anything about these things," said Marie. "Besides, your talking makes my head ache."

Marie always had a headache on hand for any conversation that did not exactly suit her.

Review 8D: Parenthetical Expressions, Appositives, Absolute Constructions

Each one of the sentences below (from Frederick Douglass's 1845 memoir *Narrative of the Life of Frederick Douglass, an American Slave, Written by Himself*) contains an element not closely connected to the rest of the sentence: parenthetical, appositive, or absolute.

In each sentence, find and circle the unconnected element (word, phrase, or clause).

Above it, write *PAR* for parenthetical, *APP* for appositive, or *AB* for absolute.

In the blank at the end of the sentence, note whether the element is set apart with commas (*C*), parentheses (*P*), or dashes (*D*).

She was nevertheless left a slave—a slave for life—a slave in the hands of strangers. ___D___

I started off to Covey's in the morning (Saturday morning) wearied in body and broken in spirit. ___P___

We went, as usual, to our several fields of labor. ___C___

As to my own treatment while I lived on Colonel Lloyd's plantation, it was very similar to that of the other slave children. ___C___

There being little else than field work to do, I had a great deal of leisure time. ___C___

In the afternoon of that day, we reached Annapolis, the capital of the state. ___C___

His reply was, as well as I can remember, that Demby had become unmanageable. ___C___

I shall never forget the ecstasy with which I received the intelligence that my old master (Anthony) had determined to let me go to Baltimore, to live with Mr. Hugh Auld, brother to my old master's son-in-law, Captain Thomas Auld. ___P C___

The slave was made to say some very smart as well as impressive things in reply to his master—things which had the desired though unexpected effect; for the conversation resulted in the voluntary emancipation of the slave on the part of the master. ___D___

AB

In hottest summer and coldest winter, I was kept almost naked—no shoes, no stockings, no jacket, no trousers, nothing on but a coarse tow linen shirt, reaching only to my knees. D

Review 8E: Direct Quotations

The following paragraph about Abraham Lincoln, from *The Emancipation Proclamation: Ending Slavery in America*, by Adam Woog, contains two different direct quotations from Lincoln himself. Those quotations are bolded, but they are not properly punctuated. Rewrite the paragraph on your own paper, spacing and punctuating both quotations correctly.

When you are finished, circle any places where words have been left out of the direct quotations. Underline any places where words have been added to the direct quotations.

Abraham Lincoln became a celebrity through his eloquent appearances in debates with his opponent, Stephen Douglas. In one of these now-famous debates, Lincoln stated that slavery was **the issue that will continue in this country when these poor tongues of Judge Douglas and myself shall be silent.** He went on **It is the eternal struggle between these two principles—right and wrong—throughout the world . . . The one is the common right of humanity, and the other the divine right of kings . . . No matter what shape it comes [in] . . . it is the same tyrannical principle.** As the public learned during these debates, Lincoln was not a polished politician.

Note to Instructor: The original passage is shown below.

The student could place a comma rather than a colon after the tag *He went on*; either is correct.

The final sentence returns to the margin because this is a single paragraph—it should not be indented.

Abraham Lincoln became a celebrity through his eloquent appearances in debates with his opponent, Stephen Douglas. In one of these now-famous debates, Lincoln stated that slavery was "the issue that will continue in this country when these poor tongues of Judge Douglas and myself shall be silent." He went on:

> It is the eternal struggle between these two principles—right and wrong—throughout the world . . . The one is the common right of humanity, and the other the divine right of kings . . . No matter what shape it comes [in] . . . it is the same tyrannical principle.

As the public learned during these debates, Lincoln was not a polished politician.

Review 8F: Diagramming

On your own paper, diagram every word of the following sentences—twice! Each sentence can legitimately be diagrammed in two different ways. (Remember, the English language doesn't operate by strictly scientific laws. Sometimes grammar is a matter of interpretation.) Try to diagram both options for each. One option will contain a floating element (a parenthetical expression or an absolute), while the second will place all words on a single diagram.

These sentences are taken from *The Underground Railroad*, by Raymond Bial.

If you need help, or a hint, ask your instructor.

Note to Instructor: Explanations follow each version of the diagrams below. Give the student all necessary help.

The Underground Railroad was, in fact, an informal yet intricate network of routes leading north, eventually to Canada.

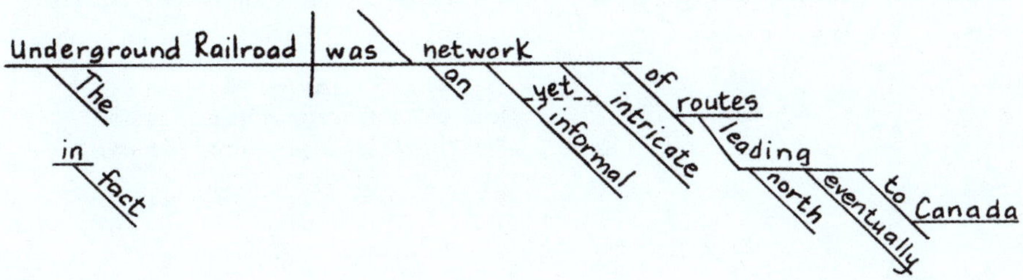

Note to Instructor: *In fact* is diagrammed as a parenthetical expression.

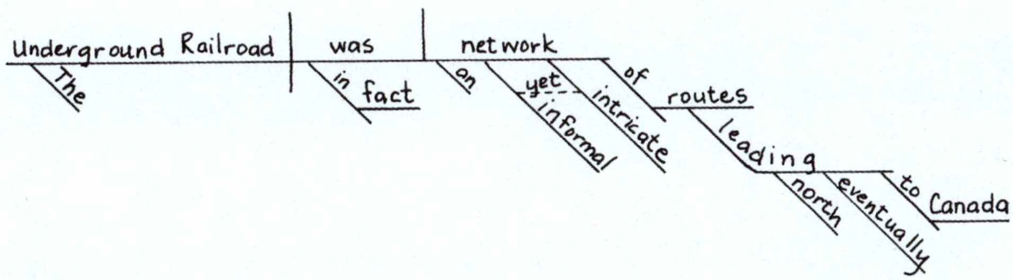

Note to Instructor: *In fact* is diagrammed as a parenthetical expression.

Yet I believed I could accurately capture the spirit of drama in these otherwise quiet places—both the courage of flight and the nobility of the aid extended to fugitive slaves.

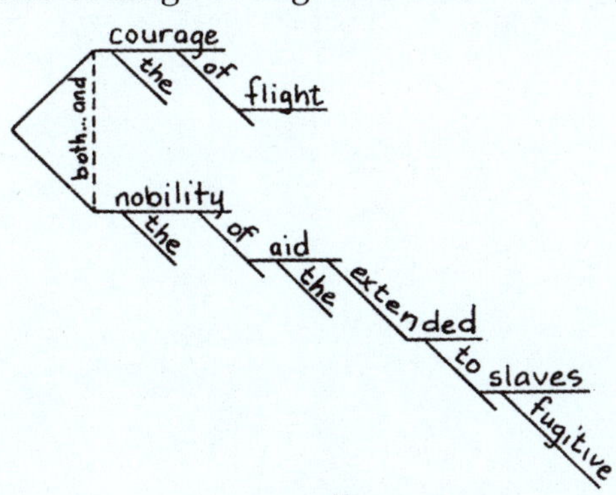

Note to Instructor: The expression after the dash is diagrammed as an absolute construction.

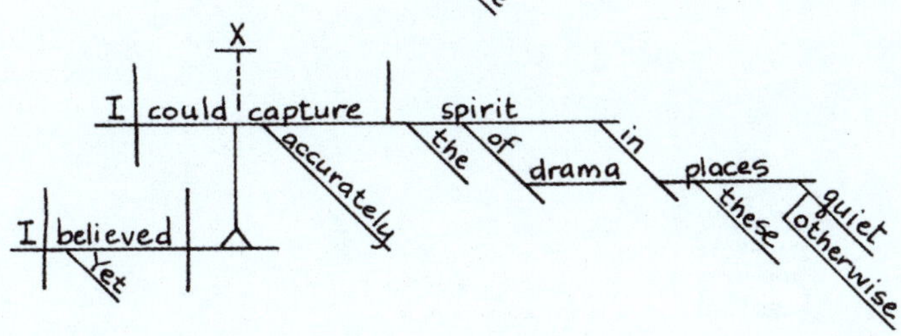

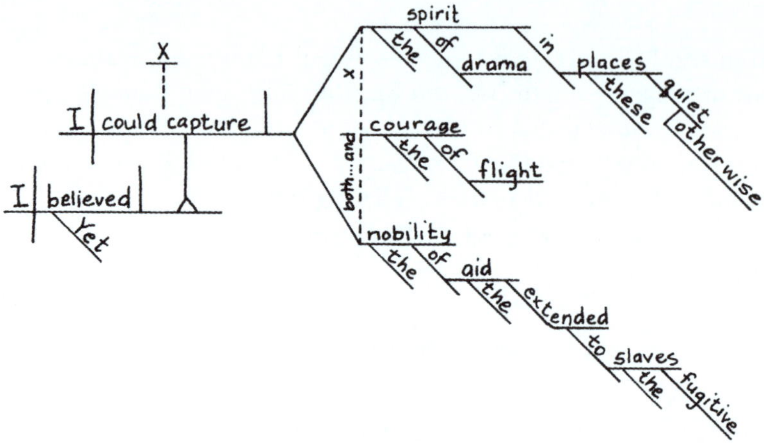

Note to Instructor: The expression after the dash is diagrammed as additional direct objects of the verb *could capture.*

I was left with a feeling of reverence for those brave people—both runaways and workers on the Railroad—who had gone before us.

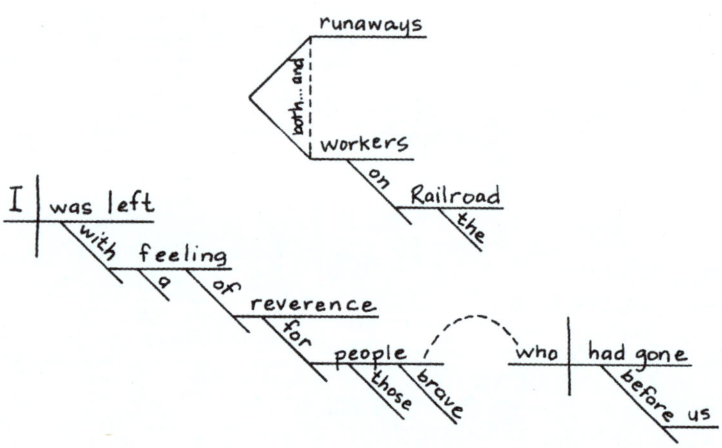

Note to Instructor: The expression after the dash is diagrammed as an absolute construction.

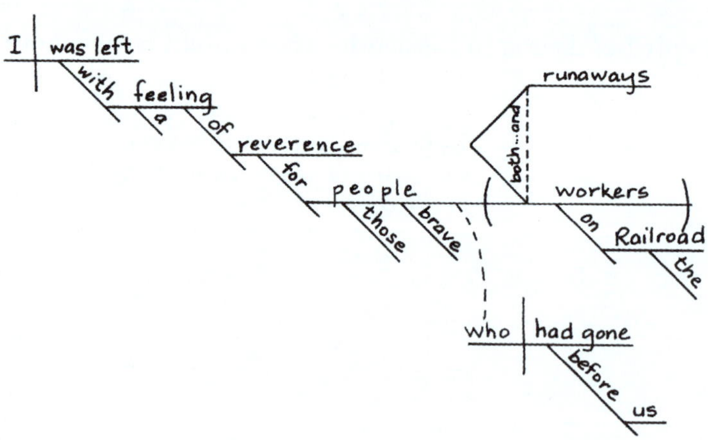

Note to Instructor: The expression after the dash is diagrammed as an appositive.

WEEK 25

Complex Verb Tenses

— LESSON 97 —

Verb Tense, Voice, and Mood
Tense Review (Indicative)
Progressive Perfect Tenses (Indicative)

Exercise 97A: Review of Indicative Tenses

The following partially completed chart shows the active and passive tenses of the regular verb *refuse* (in the third-person singular), the irregular verb *tell* (in the third-person plural), and the irregular verb *bring* (in the first-person singular). Review your indicative tenses by completing the chart now.

		Active	Passive
SIMPLE TENSES			
refuse *tell* *bring*	Past	he refused they told I brought	he was refused they were told I was brought
refuse *tell* *bring*	Present	he refuses they tell I bring	he is refused they are told I am brought
refuse *tell* *bring*	Future	he will refuse they will tell I will bring	he will be refused they will be told I will be brought
PROGRESSIVE TENSES			
refuse *tell* *bring*	Past	he was refusing they were telling I was bringing	he was being refused they were being told I was being brought
refuse *tell* *bring*	Present	he is refusing they are telling I am bringing	he is being refused they are being told I am being brought
refuse *tell* *bring*	Future	he will be refusing they will be telling I will be bringing	he will be being refused they will be being told I will be being brought

		Active	Passive
PERFECT TENSES			
refuse *tell* *bring*	Past	he had refused they had told I had brought	he had been refused they had been told I had been brought
refuse *tell* *bring*	Present	he has refused they have told I have brought	he has been refused they have been told I have been brought
refuse *tell* *bring*	Future	he will have refused they will have told I will have brought	he will have been refused they will have been told I will have been brought

Exercise 97B: Parsing Verbs

In the following sentences, underline the main verb of every clause (both independent and dependent). Above each verb, write the tense and voice. For state-of-being verbs, write the tense and add *state-of-being*.

You may abbreviate: *PROG, PERF, SIMP, PAST, PRES, FUT, ACT, PASS*, or *SB* for state-of-being.

SIMP PRES, ACT — PROG PERF FUT, ACT
When he reaches the summit of Everest, he will have been climbing for over eleven hours.

PROG PERF PAST, ACT — PERF PAST, ACT — SIMP PAST, ACT
He had been wondering for the past few years what had happened to the seer who made the prophecy.

SIMP PAST, ACT — PROG PERF PAST, PASS
They removed the feeder because too many birds had been being killed by stray cats.

PROG PERF FUT, PASS
By this point, the new cook will have been being introduced to her duties for several days.

PERF PAST, PASS — PROG PAST, ACT
He had been tempted for years by the dreams of freedom; they were calling him to move West into the wide open spaces.

SIMP PAST, ACT — SIMP PRES, SB — PROG PERF FUT, ACT
An hour that is spent walking is an hour well spent, because you will have been thinking for all that time.

PROG PERF PAST, ACT — SIMP PAST, ACT
The exhaustion that I had been experiencing, off and on, ever since my arrival swept over me again.

PROG PERF PRES, ACT — SIMP PRES, SB — SIMP PAST, ACT
He has been implying that I am behind on my rent, even though I paid up on the first of the month as usual.

SIMP PAST, ACT — PROG PERF PAST, ACT
Ever since the Russians beat them into space, the Americans had been desperately striving to seize the initiative.

PROG PERF FUT, ACT — SIMP PAST, ACT — SIMP PAST, ACT
The director will have been wondering how a performance which began so well suddenly fell apart.

Exercise 97C: Completing Sentences

Complete the following sentences by providing an appropriate verb in the tense and voice indicated beneath each blank. For state-of-being verbs, simply provide an appropriate state-of-being verb in the tense indicated.

Note to Instructor: As long as the verbs are in the correct tense, any verbs that make sense are acceptable.

The historian has been illuminating (progressive perfect present, active) his readers for over twenty years.

By this time next week, I will have been working (progressive perfect future, active) at this company for eight years.

I have been sweating (progressive perfect present, active) in that sauna all morning.

The nuts have been soaking (progressive perfect present, active) in the brandy and cinnamon mixture all morning.

By dinner, he will have been cleaning (progressive perfect future, active) his room for five solid hours.

He will be disappointed (simple future, passive), because he will have been expecting (progressive perfect future, active) a complete meal.

That stupid dog has been swimming (progressive perfect present, active) in the slimy pond again.

The operatic soprano has been singing (progressive perfect present, active) ever since she was (simple past, state-of-being) able to talk.

My mother is weeping (progressive present, active), but not with grief; she has been chopping (progressive perfect, present, active) onions for the spaghetti sauce.

The pilot has been flying (progressive perfect present, active) ever since he earned (simple past, active) his license in 2009.

— LESSON 98 —

Simple Present and Perfect Present Modal Verbs

Progressive Present and Progressive Perfect Present Modal Verbs

Exercise 98A: Parsing Verbs

Write the tense, mood, and voice of each verb above it. The first is done for you. These sentences have been slightly adapted from *King Arthur's Knights*, by Henry Gilbert.

The king refused (simple past, indicative, active) to give the signal to sit to meat until he should have experienced (perfect present, modal, active) some strange adventure.

simple present, modal, passive

The cook and his scullions came to and fro with anxious faces, for they feared that the meat could be overdone.

simple present, modal, passive

Each great baron, strong in men, plotted to win the overlordship when the king should be gone.

perfect present, modal, passive

If Lancelot had dared his enemies to prove his treason, they would have been instantly discountenanced.

progressive present, modal, active

Others believed that what rumour said might be coming true.

simple present, modal, active

I fear war must come of it all.

simple past, indicative, passive — perfect present, modal, active

Men were all amazed, and would have gone instantly to see this marvel, but the archbishop bade them stay.

simple present, modal, passive

No man or child could be seen anywhere.

simple present, modal, active

The kings and lords for angry spite would have slain Arthur, but the archbishop threatened them with the most dreadful ban of Holy Church.

progressive present, modal, active

His wound could be bleeding afresh.

perfect present, modal, passive

Many of the dead may have been slain by their own kindred.

simple future, indicative, active — simple present, modal, passive

The dead shall lie uncoffined, for no prayers may be said over them.

Exercise 98B: Forming Modal Verbs

Fill in the blanks with the missing modal verbs. Using the helping verbs indicated, put each action verb provided into the correct modal tense.

You __can go__ back to the beginning of the book only after you have read the end.
helping verb: *can*
simple present active of *go*

The rice beds __must have been flooded__ to just the right depth, and the first rice seeds sown, before the farmers can rest.
helping verb: *must*
perfect present passive of *flood*

After counting the rings of the giant live oak, the researcher believed that it __could have been growing__ during Tecumseh's lifetime.
helping verb: *could*
progressive perfect present active of *grow*

An article in *Palaeodiversity* suggests that dinosaurs __might have eaten__ hallucinogenic fungi.
helping verb: *might*
perfect present active of *eat*

Cosmologists may be changing their ideas about infinity.
helping verb: *may*
progressive present active of *change*

Instead of learning to use weapons, the young men should have been being taught to be compassionate.
helping verb: *should*
progressive perfect present passive of *teach*

Everybody has to die, but I always believed that an exception would be made in my case (William Saroyan).
helping verb: *would*
simple present passive of *make*

The additional food bank is helpful, but there are so many other important needs that could be being met instead!
helping verb: *could*
progressive present passive of *meet*

— LESSON 99 —

Modal Verb Tenses
The Imperative Mood
The Subjunctive Mood
More Subjunctive Tenses

Exercise 99A: Complete the Chart

Fill in the missing forms on the following chart. Use the verbs indicated above each chart, in order. The first form on each chart is done for you.

INDICATIVE
(confuse, trick, read, add, allow, paint, pass, save, school, lead, kiss, mark)

Indicative Tense	Active Formation	Examples	Passive Formation	Examples
Simple present	Add *-s* in third-person singular	I confuse he, she, it confuses	*am/is/are* + past participle	I am confused you are confused he, she, it is confused
Simple past	Add *-d* or *-ed*, or change form	I tricked	*was/were* + past participle	I was tricked you were tricked

Indicative Tense	Active Formation	Examples	Passive Formation	Examples
Simple future	+ *will* OR *shall*	they will read	*will be* + past participle	it will be read
Progressive present	*am/is/are* + present participle	I am adding you are adding he, she, it is adding	*am/is/are being* + past participle	I am being added you are being added he, she, it is being added
Progressive past	*was/were* + present participle	I was allowing you were allowing he, she, it was allowing	*was/were being* + past participle	I was being allowed you were being allowed he, she, it was being allowed
Progressive future	*will be* + present participle	I will be painting	*will be being* + past participle	it will be being painted
Perfect present	*has/have* + past participle	I have passed you have passed he, she, it has passed	*has/have been* + past participle	I have been passed you have been passed he, she, it has been passed
Perfect past	*had* + past participle	they had saved	*had been* + past participle	you had been saved
Perfect future	*will have* + past participle	we will have schooled	*will have been* + past participle	they will have been schooled
Progressive perfect present	*have/has been* + present participle	I have been leading he, she, it has been leading	*have/has been being* + past participle	I have been being led he, she, it has been being led

Indicative Tense	Active Formation	Examples	Passive Formation	Examples
Progressive perfect past	*had been* + present participle	you had been kissing	*had been being* + past participle	you had been being kissed
Progressive perfect future	*will have been* + present participle	you will have been marking	*will have been being* + past participle	they will have been being marked

MODAL

(match, quarry, nibble, obey)

Note to Instructor: Student's choice of modal helping verb may vary. *Should, would, may, might, must, can,* and *could* are all acceptable.

Modal Tense	Active Formation	Examples	Passive Formation	Examples
Simple present	modal helping verb + simple present main verb	I could match you could match he, she, it could match	modal helping verb + *be* + past participle	I could be matched they could be matched
Progressive present	modal helping verb + *be* + present participle	I might be quarrying	modal helping verb + *be* + *being* + past participle	it might be being quarried
Perfect present	modal helping verb + *have* + past participle	you could have nibbled	modal helping verb + *have* + *been* + past participle	it could have been nibbled
Progressive perfect present	modal helping verb + *have been* + present participle	I should have been obeying	modal helping verb + *have been being* + past participle	we should have been being obeyed

IMPERATIVE
(number, feed)

Imperative Tense	Active Formation	Examples	Passive Formation	Examples
Present	simple present form without subject	Number ! Feed !	*be* + past participle	Be numbered ! Be fed !

SUBJUNCTIVE
(fear, feel, rattle, wave, wear, call, carry, dash)

Subjunctive Tense	Active Formation	Examples	Passive Formation	Examples
Simple present	no change in any person	I fear you fear he, she, it fear we fear you fear they fear	*be* + past participle	I be feared they be feared
Simple past	**same as indicative:** Add *-d* or *-ed*, or change form	I felt you felt he, she, it felt	*were* + past participle	he were felt you were felt
Progressive present	**same as indicative:** *am*/*is*/*are* + present participle	I am rattling you are rattling he, she, it is rattling	**same as indicative:** *am*/*is*/*are being* + past participle	I am being rattled you are being rattled he, she, it is being rattled
Progressive past	*were* + present participle	I were waving you were waving he, she, it were waving	*were being* + past participle	I were being waved you were being waved he, she, it were being waved
Perfect present	**Same as indicative:** *has*/*have* + past participle	I have worn he, she, it has worn they have worn	**same as indicative:** *has*/*have been* + past participle	I have been worn he, she, it has been worn they have been worn

Subjunctive Tense	Active Formation	Examples	Passive Formation	Examples
Perfect past	**same as indicative:** *had* + past participle	we had called	**same as indicative:** *had been* + past participle	we had been called
Progressive perfect present	**same as indicative:** *have/has been* + present participle	I have been carrying you have been carrying he, she, it has been carrying	**same as indicative:** *have/has been being* + past participle	I have been being carried you have been being carried he, she, it has been being carried
Progressive perfect past	**same as indicative:** *had been* + present participle	you had been dashing	**same as indicative:** *had been being* + past participle	you had been being dashed

Exercise 99B: Parsing

Write the mood, tense, and voice of each underlined verb above it. These sentences are taken from Mary Shelley's classic novel *Frankenstein.* The first is done for you.

indicative simple present active

The sun is yet high in the heavens; before it descends to hide itself behind your snowy precipices

indicative perfect future active — modal simple present active

and illuminate another world, you will have heard my story and can decide.

indicative simple future passive

She is to be tried today, and I hope, I sincerely hope, that she will be acquitted.

indicative perfect past active — indicative progressive past active

The moon had reached her summit in the heavens and was beginning to descend

indicative perfect present passive

Instead of being spent in study, as you promised yourself, the year has been consumed in my sick room.

subjunctive perfect past passive

Perhaps, if my first introduction to humanity had been made by a young soldier, burning for

modal perfect present passive

glory and slaughter, I should have been imbued with different sensations.

indicative simple future active — modal simple present active — imperative present active

Shall I create another like yourself, whose joint wickedness might desolate the world. Begone! I

indicative perfect present active — modal simple present active

have answered you; you may torture me, but I will never consent.

subjunctive past passive — modal simple present active OR state-of-being

If he were vanquished, I should be a free man.

subjunctive perfect past active — modal simple present active OR state-of-being

If for one instant I had thought what might be the hellish intention of my fiendish adversary, I

modal perfect present active

would rather have banished myself forever from my native country and wandered a friendless

indicative perfect present active

outcast over the earth than have consented to this miserable marriage.

— LESSON 100 —

Review of Moods and Tenses
Conditional Sentences

Exercise 100A: Conditional Sentences

Identify the following sentences (taken from *Japanese Fairy Tales*, by Yei Theodora Ozaki) as first, second, or third conditional by writing a *1*, *2*, or *3* in the margin next to each.

If it goes on much longer like this, not only shall I lose all my children, but I myself must fall a victim to the monster. 1

The warrior saw that he had now only one arrow left in his quiver, and if this one failed he could not kill the centipede. 2

If I had made a mistake, I would have begged you to forgive me! 3

I shall soon take my leave if you will give me the big box—that is all I want! 1

Very well, Ojisan, we will give you the tortoise if you give us the money! 1

It must be very far away, if it exists at all! 1

If you would like to see the Sea King's land, I will be your guide. 1

If you open it, something dreadful will happen to you! 1

If the Princess Hase were to write a poem and offer it in prayer, might it not stop the noise of the rushing river and remove the cause of the Imperial illness? 1

If only you had spoken in time I should have remembered it, and should have brought it along with me! 3

Exercise 100B: Parsing

Write the correct mood, tense, and voice above each underlined verb. These sentences are taken from *Japanese Fairy Tales*, by Yei Theodora Ozaki.

indicative progressive past active — indicative simple past active

While he was speaking, a train of fishes appeared, all dressed in ceremonial, trailing garments.

indicative simple past passive — modal simple present active

Then the happy fisherman, following his bride, the Sea King's daughter, was shown all the wonders of that enchanted land where youth and joy go hand in hand and neither time nor age can touch them.

indicative progressive perfect present active — indicative simple present passive — indicative simple present active — indicative perfect present active

Surely someone has been telling you lies, and you are dazed, and you know not what you say—or some evil spirit has taken possession of your heart.

indicative perfect past active — indicative perfect past active — indicative perfect past passive

The old man tried to pacify her by showing her the box of presents he had brought back with him, and then he told her of all that had happened to him, and how wonderfully he had been entertained at the sparrow's house.

modal progressive present active

Seized with curiosity as to who could be studying so diligently in such a lonely spot, he dismounted, and leaving his horse to his groom, he walked up the hillside and approached the cottage.

imperative present active — imperative present active

Never neglect to keep the anniversaries of your ancestors, and make it your duty to provide for your children's future.

indicative simple past passive — indicative simple past passive

It seemed as if she were made of light, for the house was filled with a soft shining, so that even in the dark of night it was like daytime.

indicative perfect past active — indicative simple past passive

They said that they had worked for over a thousand days making the branch of gold, with its silver twigs and its jeweled fruit, that was now presented to her by the Knight, but as yet they had received nothing in payment.

modal simple present active — imperative present active

You must sit where you are and not move, and whatever happens don't go near or look into the inner room.

subjunctive perfect past active — modal perfect present active — indicative perfect past passive

The Happy Hunter said he blamed himself; if he had understood how to fish properly he would never have lost his hook, and therefore all this trouble had been caused in the first place by his trying to do something which he did not know how to do.

indicative simple past active
A great darkness now overspread the heavens, the thunder rolled and the lightning flashed, and
subjunctive progressive past active
the wind roared in fury, and it seemed as if the world were coming to an end.

indicative perfect present active / indicative progressive perfect present active
I have made the badger soup and have been waiting for you for a long time.

indicative simple past passive
When the branch was finished, he took his journey home and tried to make himself look as if he
subjunctive simple past passive
were wearied and worn out with travel.

Exercise 100C: Diagramming

On your own paper, diagram every word of the following sentences from *Japanese Fairy Tales*, by Yei Theodora Ozaki.

I cannot forgive you unless you bring me back my own hook.

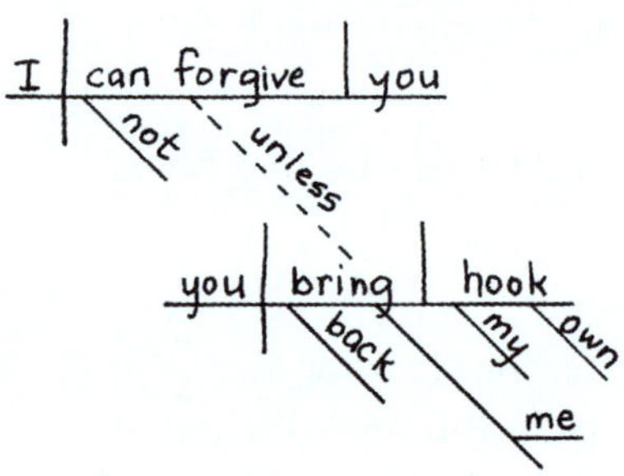

The warrior saw that he had now only one arrow left in his quiver, and if this one failed he could not kill the centipede.

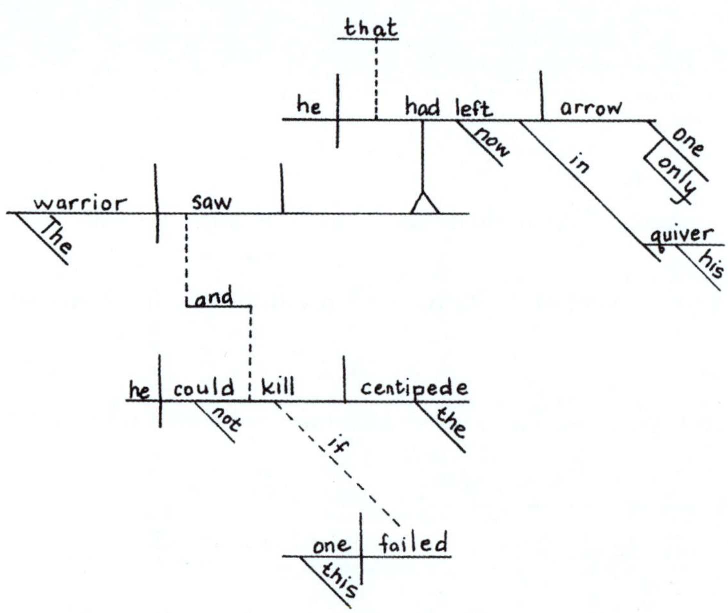

But the Sun and the Moon still hesitated, saying that they had heard that one of the pillars of heaven had been broken as well, and they feared that, even if the roads had been remade, it would still be dangerous for them to sally forth on their usual journeys.

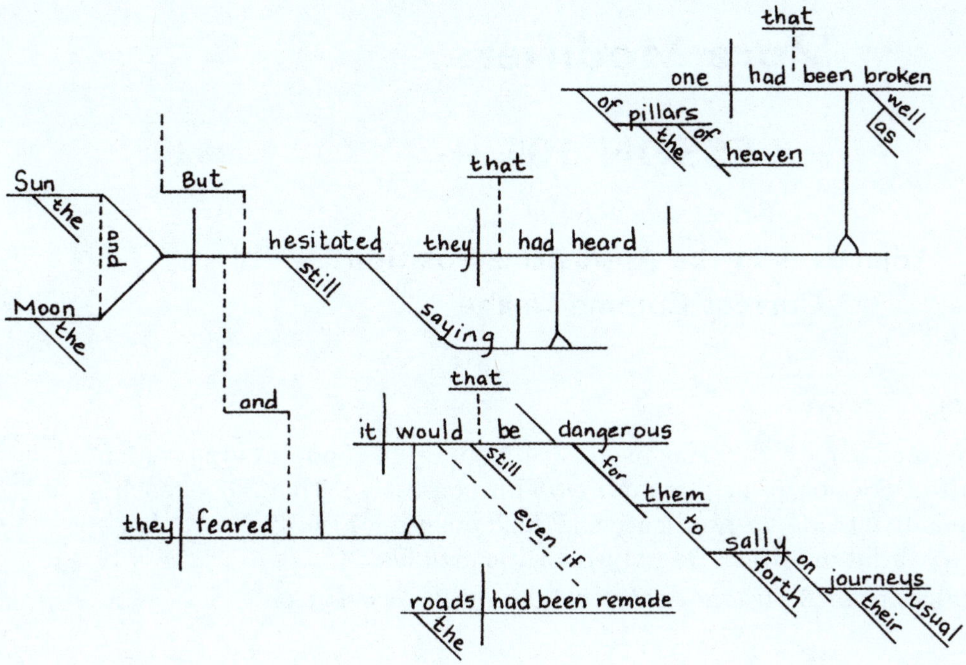

WEEK 26

More Modifiers

— LESSON 101 —

Adjective Review
Adjectives in the Appositive Position
Correct Comma Usage

Exercise 101A: Identifying Adjectives

Underline every adjective (including verb forms used as adjectives) in the following sentences. Above each adjective, write *DESC* for descriptive or *POSS* for possessive. Then, label each as in the attributive (*ATT*), appositive (*APP*), or predicative (*PRED*) position. Finally, draw an arrow from each adjective to the word it modifies. Do not underline articles.

These sentences are taken from *A Strange Story*, by Edward Bulwer-Lytton.

And the tall guttering candle by the bedside, and the flicker from the fire, threw their reflection on the ceiling just over my head in a reek of quivering blackness.

An ascent, short, but steep and tortuous, conducted at once to the old Abbey Church, nobly situated in a vast quadrangle, round which were genteel and gloomy dwellings.

She seemed listless and dejected, and was very pale; but she denied that she felt unwell.

As to his antecedents, he had so frankly owned himself a natural son, a nobody, a traveller, an idler; his expenses were so unostentatious; he was so wholly the reverse of the character assigned to criminals, that it seemed as absurd to bring a charge of homicide against a butterfly or a goldfinch as against a seemingly innocent and delightful favourite of humanity and nature.

My bride was on the floor prostrate, insensible: my first dreadful thought was that life had gone.

The entrance of the arcade was covered with parasite creepers, in prodigal luxuriance, of variegated gorgeous tints,—scarlet, golden, purple; and the form, an idealized picture of man's youth fresh from the hand of Nature, stood literally in a frame of blooms.

I applied the flame of the candle to the circle, and immediately it became lambent with a low steady splendour that rose about an inch from the floor; and gradually from the light there emanated a soft, gray, transparent mist and a faint but exquisite odour.

Exercise 101B: Punctuation Practice

The sentences below are missing all of their punctuation marks! Using everything you have learned about punctuation, insert correct punctuation. You may simply write the punctuation marks in, rather than using proofreader's marks.

These sentences are slightly adapted from Horace Walpole's 1764 novel, *The Castle of Otranto,* generally thought to be the first gothic novel.

Note to Instructor: The sentences with original punctuation are listed below.

They heard a confused noise of shrieks, horror, and surprise.
He examined the bleeding, mangled remains of the young prince.
The portrait of his grandfather, which hung over the pitted oak bench where they had been sitting, uttered a deep sigh.

Note to Instructor: This is a non-restrictive adjective clause because there are not multiple portraits that need to be defined by descriptive clauses.

He printed a thousand kisses on her clay-cold hands, and uttered every expression that love, sincere, deep, and despairing, could dictate.

Note to Instructor: The comma between *hands* and *is* optional.

The lower part of the castle was hollowed into several intricate cloisters; it was not easy to find the door that opened into the dark, awful cavern.
His steady, composed manner and the gallantry of his last reply, which were the first words she heard distinctly, interested her.

Note to Instructor: The adjective clause is non-restrictive.

His person was noble, handsome, and commanding, but his countenance soon engrossed her whole attention.
Surprise, doubt, tenderness, respect succeeded each other in the youth's face.
Pride, ambition, and his reliance on ancient prophecies, which had pointed out a possibility of preserving his family, combated that thought.

Note to Instructor: The adjective clause is non-restrictive.

His hot-headed, impious passion subsided.
Savage, inhuman monster! What have you done?

Exercise 101C: Diagramming

On your own paper, diagram the following sentences from *The Mysteries of London*, an 1844 gothic novel by George W. M. Reynolds.

The sun had set behind huge piles of dingy purple clouds, which, after losing the golden hue with which they were for awhile tinged, became somber and menacing.

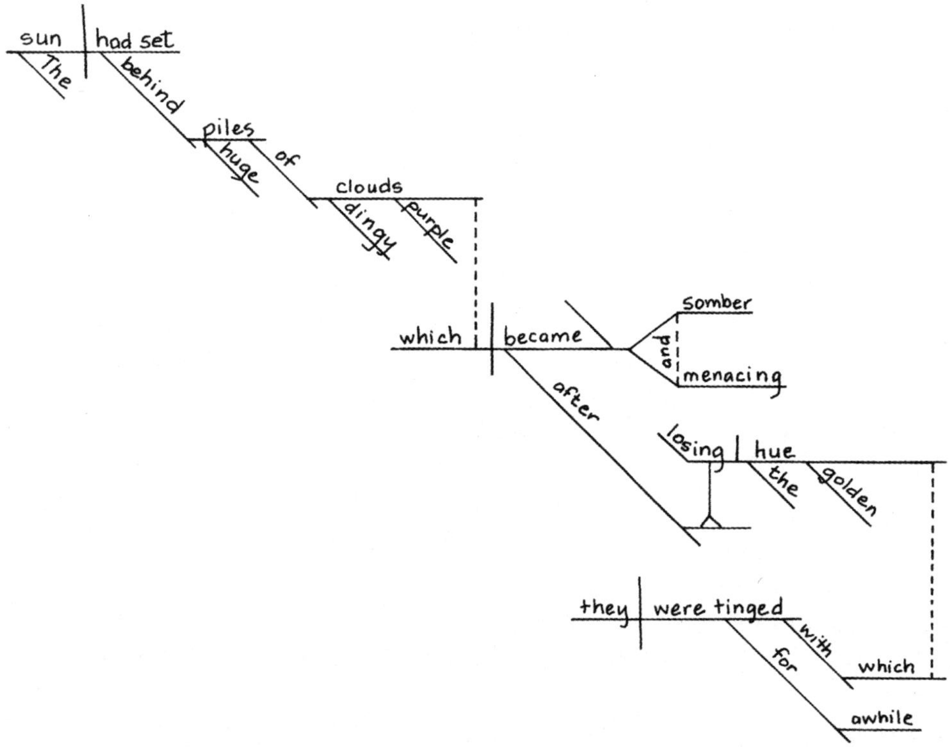

He was a man about fifty years of age, with a jolly red face, a somewhat bulbous nose, small laughing eyes, short grey hair standing upright in front, whiskers terminating above his white cravat.

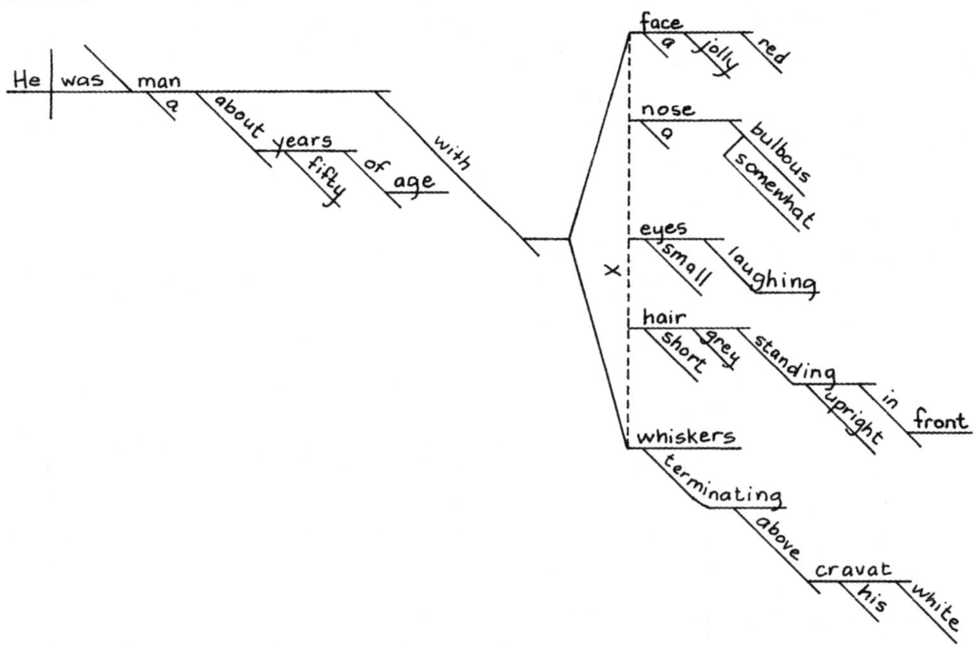

Note to Instructor: *Fifty years* can also be diagrammed as a compound noun on the line where *years* is diagrammed.

When the two ruffians stooped down to take him up again, fear surmounted all other sentiments, all feelings, all inclinations; and his deep—his profound—his heartfelt agony was expressed in one long shriek, loud and piercing.

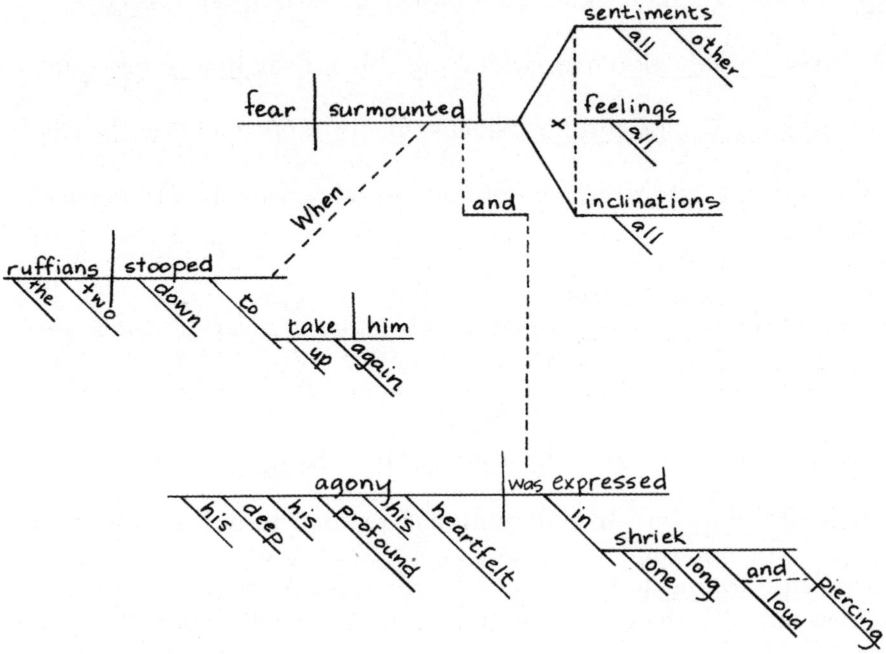

— LESSON 102 —

Adjective Review
Pronoun Review
Limiting Adjectives

Exercise 102A: Identifying Adjectives

The following paragraph has been condensed slightly from the opening of "The Fall of the House of Usher," by Edgar Allan Poe. Underline every word that acts as an adjective.

Do not include phrases or clauses acting as adjectives. Also, do not include articles. (There are just too many!)

Label each one using the following abbreviations:

Descriptive Adjectives		**Limiting Adjectives**	
Regular	*DA-R*	Possessives	*LA-P*
Present participles	*DA-PresP*	~~Articles~~	~~*LA-A*~~
Past participles	*DA-PastP*	Demonstratives	*LA-D*
		Indefinites	*LA-IND*
		Interrogatives	*LA-INT*
		Numbers	*LA-N*

During the whole of a <u>dull</u> (DA-R), <u>dark</u> (DA-R), and <u>soundless</u> (DA-R) day in the autumn of the year, when the clouds hung oppressively low in the heavens, I had been passing alone, on horseback, through a singularly dreary [DA-R] tract of country, and at length found myself, as the shades of the evening drew on, within view of the melancholy [DA-R] House of Usher. I know not how it was—but, with the first [LA-N] glimpse of the building, a sense of insufferable [DA-R] gloom pervaded my [LA-P] spirit. I say insufferable [DA-R]; for the feeling was unrelieved [DA-PastP] by any of that [LA-D] half-pleasurable [DA-R], because poetic [DA-R], sentiment, with which the mind usually receives even the sternest [DA-R] natural [DA-R] images of the desolate or terrible. I looked upon the scene before me—upon the mere [DA-R] house, and the simple [DA-R] landscape [DA-R] features of the domain—upon the bleak [DA-R] walls—upon the vacant [DA-R] eye-like [DA-R] windows—upon a few [LA-IND] rank [DA-R] sedges—and upon a few [LA-IND] white [DA-R] trunks of decayed [DA-PastP] trees—with an utter [DA-R] depression of soul which I can compare to no earthly [DA-R] sensation more properly than to the after-dream of the reveller upon opium—the bitter [DA-R] lapse into every-day [DA-R] life—the hideous [DA-R] dropping off of the veil. There was an iciness, a sinking, a sickening of the heart—an unredeemed [DA-PastP] dreariness of thought. What was it—I paused to think—what was it that so unnerved me in the contemplation of the House of Usher? It was a mystery insoluble [DA-R]; nor could I grapple with the shadowy [DA-R] fancies that crowded upon me as I pondered. I was forced to fall back upon the unsatisfactory [DA-R] conclusion, that while, beyond doubt, there are combinations of very simple [DA-R] natural [DA-R] objects which have the power of thus affecting us, still the analysis of this [LA-D] power lies among considerations beyond our [LA-P] depth. It was possible [DA-R], I reflected, that a different [DA-R] arrangement of the particulars of the scene, of the details of the picture, would be sufficient [DA-R] to modify, or perhaps to annihilate its capacity for sorrowful [DA-R] impression; and, acting upon this [LA-D] idea, I reined my [LA-P] horse to the precipitous [DA-R] brink of a black [DA-R] and lurid [DA-R] tarn that lay in unruffled [DA-PastP] lustre by the dwelling, and gazed down—but with a shudder even more thrilling [DA-PresP] than before—upon the remodelled [DA-PastP] and inverted [DA-PastP] images of the gray [DA-R] sedge, and the ghastly [DA-R] tree-stems, and the vacant [DA-R] and eye-like [DA-R] windows.

Exercise 102B: Analysis

The passage above shows you how a good writer uses adjectives: a mix of colorful descriptive adjectives and sparer, simpler limiting adjectives.

The total word count of the excerpt is 394 words. Now count each type of adjective and fill out the following chart:

> **Note to Instructor:** This exercise is intended to engage statistically-inclined thinkers in a way that grammar usually doesn't. You may certainly skip it if the student finds this sort of calculation frustrating or unhelpful.

Descriptive Adjectives		**Limiting Adjectives**	
Regular	39	Possessives	2
Present participles	1	~~Articles~~	
Past participles	6	Demonstratives	3
		Indefinites	2
		Interrogatives	0
		Numbers	1
Total Descriptive Adjectives	46	Total Limiting Adjectives	8

Total Adjectives Used 54

Good prose can't be reduced to *just* formulas—but formulas can give you some extra help in writing well. The total word count of the excerpt is 394 words. You can figure out what fraction of the total word count is taken up by adjectives by dividing the total word count by the total number of adjectives used. Work that sum now, and ask your instructor for help if necessary.

```
      7 r.16
54 ) 394
     378
      16
```

> **Note to Instructor:** This isn't math class; show answers as necessary!

The sum above tells you that 1 out of every 7 r 16 [insert answer to division problem!] words in this passage is an adjective. In other words, adjectives do not make up more than about 1/7 [or 1/7–1/8] of this descriptive writing.

Now let's look at the relationship between limiting and descriptive adjectives. Complete the following division problem:

[number of limiting adjectives] 8 | 54 [number of descriptive adjectives] =

The sum above tells you that 1 out of every 8 r 5 [insert answer to second division problem!] adjectives used is a limiting adjective. In other words, limiting adjectives do not make up more than about 1/8 [or 1/8–1/9] of this descriptive writing.

Ask your instructor to share the last part of this exercise with you.

> **Note to Instructor:** Share the following conclusion with the student.

So, 1/7 to 1/8 of Poe's words are adjectives (1 out of every 7 or 8 words). Of those adjectives, 1/8 to 1/9 are limiting (1 out of every 8 or 8 adjectives). The rest are descriptive.

Exercise 102C: Using Adjectives

On your own paper, rewrite the passage below. It is taken from Edgar Allen Poe's sea adventure *Narrative of A. Gordon Pym*—but all of the adjectives (except for articles) have been removed.

Where adjectives could be removed without making the sentence ungrammatical, they have simply been deleted without a trace. Where removing an adjective made the sentence unreasonable, a blank has been inserted instead. So you *know* that adjectives go in the blanks—but you'll have to find a lot of other places to put them as well!

You can also insert adverbs, additional articles, and conjunctions as necessary to make your insertions work.

Use the same proportions as the passage in Exercise 102B. This excerpt originally had 325 words, so use 45-48 total adjectives, not including articles.

Use no more than seven to nine limiting adjectives. Use at least three different kinds of limiting adjectives (your choice!).

The remainder should be descriptive adjectives. Use at least three participles (present or past) as adjectives.

When you are finished, compare your work with the original passage in the *Answer Key*.

The brig came on slowly, and now more steadily than before, and—I cannot speak calmly of ____________ event— ____________ hearts leaped up wildly within us, and we poured out ____________ souls in shouts and thanksgiving to God for the deliverance that was so palpably at hand. Of a sudden, and all at once, there came wafted over the ocean from the vessel (which was now close upon us) a smell, a stench, such as the world has no name for—no conception of. I gasped for breath, and turning to ____________ companions, perceived that they were ____________ than marble. But we had now no time left for question or surmise—the brig was within feet of us, and it seemed to be ____________ intention to run under ____________ counter, that we might board her without putting out a boat. We rushed aft, when, suddenly, a yaw threw her off full ____________ points from the course she had been running, and, as she passed under our stern at the distance of about ____________ feet, we had a view of ____________ decks. Shall I ever forget the horror of ____________ spectacle? Bodies, among whom were females, lay scattered about between the counter and the galley in the state of putrefaction. We plainly saw that not a soul lived in ____________ vessel! Yet we could not help shouting to the dead for help! Yes, long and loudly did we beg, in the agony of the moment, that those images would stay for us, would not abandon us to become like them, would receive us among their company! We were raving with horror and despair—thoroughly ____________ through the anguish of our disappointment.

Notes to Instructor: The original passage, found below and on the next page, actually had 39 adjectives, of which 17 were limiting adjectives. When the student has finished, show her the original and point out that proportions can change depending on the purpose of the passage.

This exercise is intended to make students more aware of, and sensitive to, the presence and proportion of adjectives in good descriptive writing—not to establish some sort of firm rule.

You may need to remind her that she can add more than one descriptive adjective to any given noun or pronoun.

If she gets frustrated, show her one or more lines of the original and encourage her to use a thesaurus.

The brig came on slowly, and now more steadily than before, and—I cannot speak calmly of **this** event—**our** hearts leaped up wildly within us, and we poured out **our whole** souls in shouts and thanksgiving to God for the **complete, unexpected**, and **glorious** deliverance that was so palpably at hand. Of a sudden, and all at once, there came wafted over the ocean from the **strange** vessel (which was now close upon us) a smell, a stench, such as the **whole** world has no name for—no conception of—**hellish**—utterly **suffocating**—**insufferable, inconceivable**. I gasped for breath, and turning to **my** companions, perceived that they were **paler** than marble. But we had now no time left for question or surmise—the brig was within **fifty** feet of us, and it seemed to be **her** intention to run under **our** counter, that we might board her without putting out a boat. We rushed aft, when, suddenly, a **wide** yaw threw her off full **five** or **six** points from the course she had been running, and, as she passed under our stern at the distance of about **twenty** feet, we had a **full** view of **her** decks. Shall I ever forget the **triple** horror of **that** spectacle? **Twenty-five** or **thirty human** bodies, among whom were **several** females, lay scattered about between the counter and the galley in the **last** and most **loathsome** state of putrefaction. We plainly saw that not a soul lived in **that fated** vessel! Yet we could not help shouting to the dead for help! Yes, long and loudly did we beg, in the agony of the moment, that those **silent** and **disgusting** images would stay for us, would not abandon us to become like them, would receive us among **their goodly** company! We were raving with horror and despair—thoroughly **mad** through the anguish of our **grievous** disappointment.

— LESSON 103 —

Misplaced Modifiers
Squinting Modifiers
Dangling Modifiers

Exercise 103A: Correcting Misplaced Modifiers

Circle each misplaced modifier and draw an arrow to the place in the sentence that it should occupy.

I can't even consider leaving you without pain.

He was a man with one ear named William White.

My brother would like to play a piece on the piano of his own composing.

The housekeeper could see that the floor had been mopped with half an eye.

The fishermen were up before daybreak at 3 a.m.

Here are some ideas for protecting your property from the sheriff's department.

After robbing the bank, the getaway car took the robbers to the airport.

The dress that she wore to the wedding, splattered with cake frosting, has been cleaned.

Carefully baked by my mother, my brother brought cookies to the party.

Lost: A cow belonging to an old woman (with brass knobs on her horns)

Rewritten Sentences

I can't even consider, without pain, leaving you.

BETTER: The thought of leaving you always gives me pain.

He was a man named William White, with one ear.

BETTER: The man named William White had only one ear.

My brother would like to play a piece of his own composing on the piano.

The housekeeper could see with half an eye that the floor had been mopped.

The fishermen were up at 3 a.m., before daybreak.

Here are some ideas from the sheriff's department for protecting your property.

The getaway car took the robbers, after robbing the bank, to the airport.

BETTER: After they robbed the bank, the robbers took a getaway car to the airport.

The dress splattered with frosting that she wore to the wedding has been cleaned.

BETTER: Her dress that got splattered with frosting at the wedding has been cleaned.

My brother brought cookies, carefully baked by my mother, to the party.

Lost: A cow with brass knobs on her horns, belonging to an old woman.

Exercise 103B: Clarifying Squinting Modifiers

Circle each squinting modifier. On your own paper, rewrite each sentence twice, eliminating the ambiguity by moving the squinting modifier to produce sentences with two different meanings. Insert commas and change capitalization/punctuation as needed.

The first is done for you. (Warning: the last one has a catch!)

Note to Instructor: Explanatory notes in italics follow each set of sentences. Use these to help the student understand as needed.

Writing out the points on 3x5 cards (clearly) gave the second debater an edge.

Clearly, writing out the points on 3x5 cards gave the second debater an edge.

Writing out the points clearly on 3x5 cards gave the second debater an edge.

Aspiring pianists who practice (often) become proficient in a short time.

Often, aspiring pianists who practice become proficient in a short time.

Aspiring pianists who often practice become proficient in a short time.

The difference is between pianists who just practice, and those who practice often.

Children who watch TV (rarely) turn out to be readers.

Children who rarely watch TV turn out to be readers.

Rarely, children who watch TV turn out to be readers.

OR Children who watch TV turn out, rarely, to be readers.

OR Children who watch TV turn out to be readers rarely.

The difference is between children who watch TV (without qualification) and children who rarely watch TV.

The ancient Greeks understood human dignity (at least) as well as we do.

The ancient Greeks understood at least human dignity as well as we do.

At least the ancient Greeks understood human dignity as well as we do.

OR The ancient Greeks understood human dignity as well as we do, at least.

> The distinction drawn is between the ancient Greeks understanding *just* human dignity (not other human qualities) as well as we do, and the ancient Greeks having, at a minimum, the same grasp on human dignity that we do.

The vet explained (eventually) the dog would need to go back to the SPCA.

Eventually, the vet explained the dog would need to go back to the SPCA.

The vet explained the dog would eventually need to go back to the SPCA.

OR The vet explained the dog would need to go back to the SPCA eventually.

> The difference is between the vet explaining eventually, and the dog going back eventually.

The pollen I breathed in (intensely) made me cough.

The pollen I breathed intensely in made me cough.

The pollen I breathed in made me cough intensely.

> The difference is between breathing intensely and coughing intensely.

The king promised (after his coronation) to declare war on the kingdom's enemies.

After his coronation, the king promised to declare war on the kingdom's enemies.

The king promised to declare war on the kingdom's enemies after his coronation.

> The distinction is between the king promising, before his coronation, to declare war; and the king promising, at some unspecified time, to be coronated and then declare war.

Tell the caller (if he is in the living room) I will not see him.

If he is in the living room, tell the caller I will not see him.

Tell the caller I will not see him if he is in the living room.

> In the first sentence, the caller will not be seen—but the speaker doesn't know where he is. In the second sentence, whether or not he's in the living room determines whether or not he'll be seen.

Although the patient at first improved (gradually) he became sicker.

Although the patient at first gradually improved, he became sicker.

Although the patient at first improved, he gradually became sicker.

OR Although the patient at first improved, he became sicker gradually.

> The distinction is between the parent gradually improving and then becoming sicker, or improving and then becoming sicker gradually.

I (only) spoke to him.

I only spoke to him.

I spoke only to him.

> *Only* is a much misused adverb. Technically, the first sentence means that the narrator just spoke—didn't sing, dance, complain, or do anything other than speak. The second sentence means that the narrator spoke to *him* and to no one else. In colloquial English, however, the first version of the sentence is often used for both meanings, with context determining the final meaning.

Exercise 103C: Rewriting Dangling Modifiers

On your own paper, rewrite each of these sentences twice, using each of the strategies described in the lesson.

> **Note to Instructor:** Answers may vary; as long as they follow the rules in "How to Fix a Dangling Modifier," you may accept different versions.

Hiking down the trail, the birds sang beautifully and the sweet scent of flowers drifted past.

Hiking down the trail, the pilgrim heard the birds singing beautifully, and smelled the sweet scent of flowers drifting past.

As the pilgrim hiked down the trail, the birds sang beautifully and the sweet scent of flower drifted past.

The ferry departed, having eaten our lunch.

We departed on the ferry, having eaten our lunch.

The ferry departed, after we had eaten our lunch.

Looking at the mountain from the east, it has a plume of snow and ice blowing from its peak.

Looking at the mountain from the east, we could see a plume of snow and ice blowing from its peak.

As we look at the mountain from the east, it has a plume of snow and ice blowing from its peak.

Tearing open the envelope, a thick wad of bills fell out.

Tearing open the envelope, the blackmailer found a thick wad of bills.

As the blackmailer tore open the envelope, a thick wad of bills fell out.

After pointing out my errors, I was sent out of the room.

After pointing out my errors, the teacher sent me out of the room.

After the teacher pointed out my errors, I was sent out of the room.

— LESSON 104 —

Degrees of Adjectives

Comparisons Using *More*, *Fewer*, and *Less*

Exercise 104A: Positive, Comparative, and Superlative Adjectives

Using the following chart to review spelling rules for forming degrees of adjectives. Fill in the missing forms. Then, fill in the blank in each sentence with each adjective indicated in brackets (properly spelled!).

These sentences are all drawn from Emily Bronte's classic novel *Wuthering Heights.*

Spelling Rules:

If the adjective ends in -*e* already, add only -*r* or -*st*.

noble	nobler	noblest
pure	purer	purest
cute	cuter	cutest

If the adjective ends in a short vowel sound and a consonant, double the consonant and add *-er* or *-est*.

red	redder	reddest
thin	thinner	thinnest
flat	flatter	flattest

If the adjective ends in *-y*, change the *y* to *i* and add *-er* or *-est*.

hazy	hazier	haziest
muddy	muddier	muddiest

A wild, wicked slip she was—but she had the bonniest eye, the sweetest smile, and the lightest foot in the parish. [in order, the superlatives of *bonny, sweet,* and *light*]

Our young lady returned to us saucier and more passionate, and haughtier than ever. [in order, the comparatives of *saucy, passionate,* and *haughty*]

"It is not so buried in trees," I replied, "and it is not quite so large, but you can see the country beautifully all round; and the air is healthier for you—fresher and drier." [in order, the comparatives of *healthy, fresh,* and *dry*]

Catherine, his happiest days were over when your days began. [superlative of *happy*]

"But you have been worse," persisted his cousin; "worse than when I saw you last; you are thinner." [in order, the comparatives of *bad, bad* again, and *thin*]

I went, at the earliest opportunity, and besought him to depart. [superlative of *early*]

He had grown sparer, and lost his colour. [comparative of *spare*]

Many a time I've cried to myself to watch them growing more reckless daily. [comparative of *reckless*]

I discerned a soft-featured face, exceedingly resembling the young lady at the Heights, but more pensive and amiable in expression. [in order, the comparative of pensive and the positive of *amiable*]

Your presence is a moral poison that would contaminate the most virtuous: for that cause, and to prevent worse consequences, I shall deny you hereafter admission into this house. [in order, the superlative of *virtuous* and the comparative of *bad*]

That is the most diabolical deed that ever you did. [superlative of *diabolical*]

Linton was very reluctant to be roused from his bed at five o'clock, and astonished to be informed that he must prepare for further travelling [comparative of *far*]

Let them say the least word to her, and she'll curl back without respect of any one. [superlative of *less*]

Exercise 104B: Forming Comparisons

Rewrite each set of independent clauses so that they form a comparative sentence making use of *more*, *less*, *fewer*, and/or comparative forms of the adjectives indicated. The first is done for you.

When you are finished, ask your instructor to show you the original sentences, which are taken from Charlotte Bronte's novels *Villete* and *Shirley*.

> **Note to Instructor:** This may be a challenging assignment for some students; give all help needed. If necessary, read the first part of the sentence out loud and encourage the student to try to finish it. When the student is finished, show her the original sentences. Her sentences do not need to be identical as long as they incorporate a comparison.

The humor is inflexibly stubborn.
The tone is sadder and softer.
The more inflexibly stubborn the humor, the sadder, the softer the tone.

My mien was impassible and prosaic.
She laughed more merrily.
The more impassible and prosaic my mien, the more merrily she laughed.

I did more.
I worked harder.
He seemed less content.
The more I did, the harder I worked, the less he seemed content.

They say.
They have more to say.
The more they say, the more they have to say.

I look further into this matter.
I see plainly.
The further I look into this matter, the more plainly I see.

We live longer.
Our experience widens.
We are less prone to judge our neighbour's conduct.
The longer we live, the more our experience widens, the less prone are we to judge our neighbour's conduct.

Exercise 104C: Using *Fewer* and *Less*

Complete the sentences by filling in each blank with either *fewer* or *less*.

The original sentences are taken from Charlotte Bronte's novels *Villete* and *Shirley*.

Her attainments were fewer than were usually possessed by girls of her age and station.

With little ceremony, and less courtesy, he pointed out what he termed her errors.

I am cheated in fewer things than you imagine.

Once or twice she addressed him with suddenness and sharpness, saying that he hurt her, and must contrive to give her less pain.

Such men may have less originality, less force of character than you, but they are better friends to mankind.

Exercise 104D: Diagramming

On your own paper, diagram every word of the following sentences from *Wuthering Heights.*

The more the worms writhe, the more I yearn to crush out their entrails!

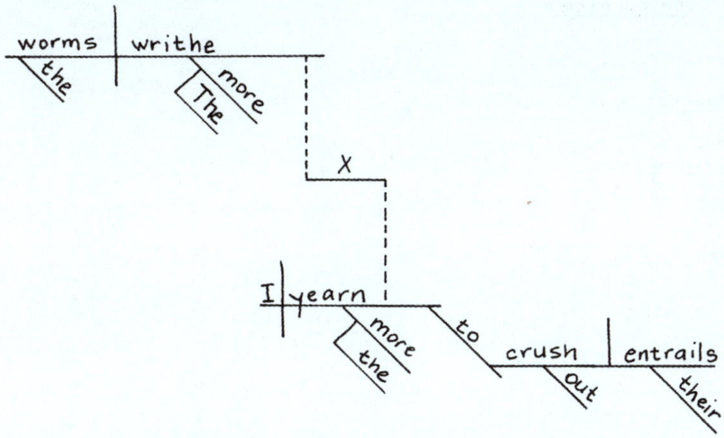

Note to Instructor: *Yearn* is intransitive, so *to crush* is adverbial, not a direct object.

The nearer I got to the house the more agitated I grew; and on catching sight of it I trembled in every limb.

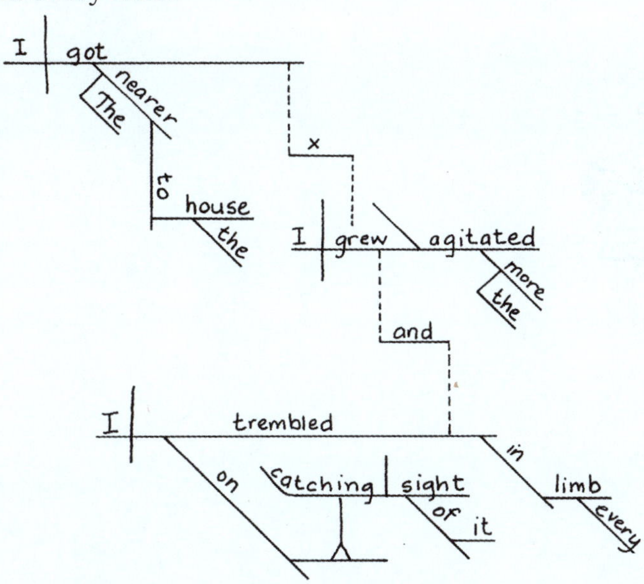

By his knack of sermonising and pious discoursing, he contrived to make a great impression on Mr. Earnshaw; and the more feeble the master became, the more influence he gained.

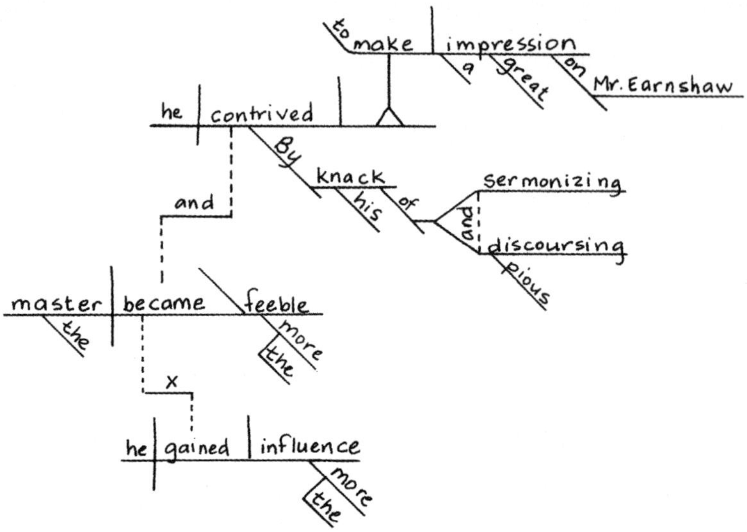

Note to Instructor: *Contrived* is a transitive verb, so *to make* serves as the object (the thing contrived). *Yearned* (above) is an intransitive verb, so *to crush* serves as an adverb describing *how*.

WEEK 27

Double Identities

— LESSON 105 —

Clauses with Understood Elements
Than as Conjunction, Preposition, and Adverb
Quasi-Coordinators

Exercise 105A: Comparisons Using *Than*

Each of the following sentences, taken from Charles Darwin's account of his travels in *The Voyage of the Beagle*, contains a comparison clause introduced by *than* and missing some of its words. Using carets, do your best to insert the missing words.

Note to Instructor: The student's phrasing may differ. Words in brackets can be inserted by the student, but do not mark the answer as wrong if they are left out. When the student is finished, ask him to compare his work to the answers below.

Considering that there is no natural boundary between the two places, and that the character of the country is nearly similar, the difference was much greater than I should have expected^it to be.

At Bahia Blanca, a recent establishment in Northern Patagonia, I was surprised to find how little the deer cared for the noise of a gun; one day I fired ten times from within eighty yards at one animal; and it was much more startled at the ball cutting up the ground than^it was at the report of the rifle.

I allude only to the butterflies; for the moths, contrary to what might have been expected from the rankness of the vegetation, certainly appeared in much fewer numbers than^they do *or* they appear in our own temperate regions.

Nothing can be more striking than the effect of these huge rounded masses of naked rock rising out of the most luxuriant vegetation^is [striking].

It is as flat and elastic as an ivory paper-cutter, and the lower mandible, differing from every other bird, is an inch and a half longer than the upper^[mandible] is.

Exercise 105B: Identifying Parts of the Sentence

In the following sentences, drawn from *The Life and Letters of Charles Darwin,* Vol. I, identify each bolded word or phrase as *SC* for subordinating conjunction, *QC* for quasi-coordinator, *PREP* for preposition, or *ADV* for adverb.

In the old days the practice of bleeding largely was universal, but my father maintained that far more evil was thus caused SC **than** good done; and he advised me if ever I were myself ill not to allow any doctor to take ADV **more than** an extremely small quantity of blood.

He gave one the idea that he had been active QC **rather than** strong; his shoulders were not broad for his height, though certainly not narrow.

I think I shall go for a few days to town to hear an opera and see Mr. Hope, QC **not to mention** my brother also, whom I should have no objection to see.

I am nothing ADV **more than** a lions' provider: I do not feel at all sure that they will not growl and finally destroy me.

The author begins by stating that varieties differ from each other less SC **than** species.

The origin of a new species by PREP **other than** ordinary agencies would be a vastly greater "catastrophe" than any of those which Lyell successfully eliminated from sober geological speculation.

We felt that we saw more of him in a week's holiday SC **than** in a month at home.

He had more dread SC **than** have most people of repeating his stories, and continually said, "You must have heard me tell," or "I dare say I've told you."

Your engraving is exactly true, but underrates QC **rather than** exaggerates the luxuriance.

How much ADV **more than** delightful to go to some good concert or fine opera.

Exercise 105C: Diagramming

On your own paper, diagram every word of the following sentences, slightly condensed from *The Voyage of the Beagle.*

In five little packets which I sent him, he has ascertained no less than sixty-seven different organic forms!

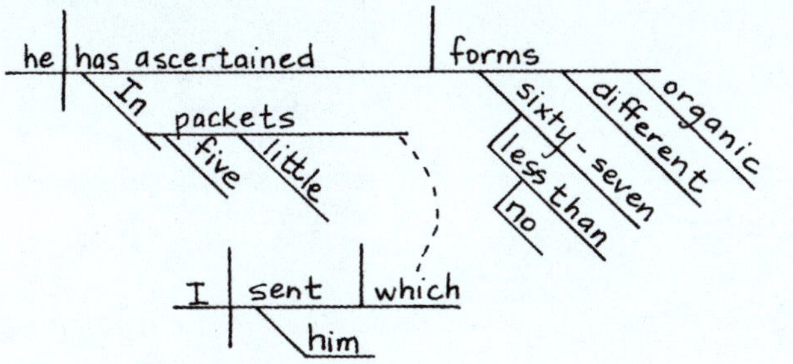

has [a tail]

One is a small kingfisher (*Ceryle Americana*); it has a longer tail than the European species^, and hence does not sit in so stiff and upright a position.

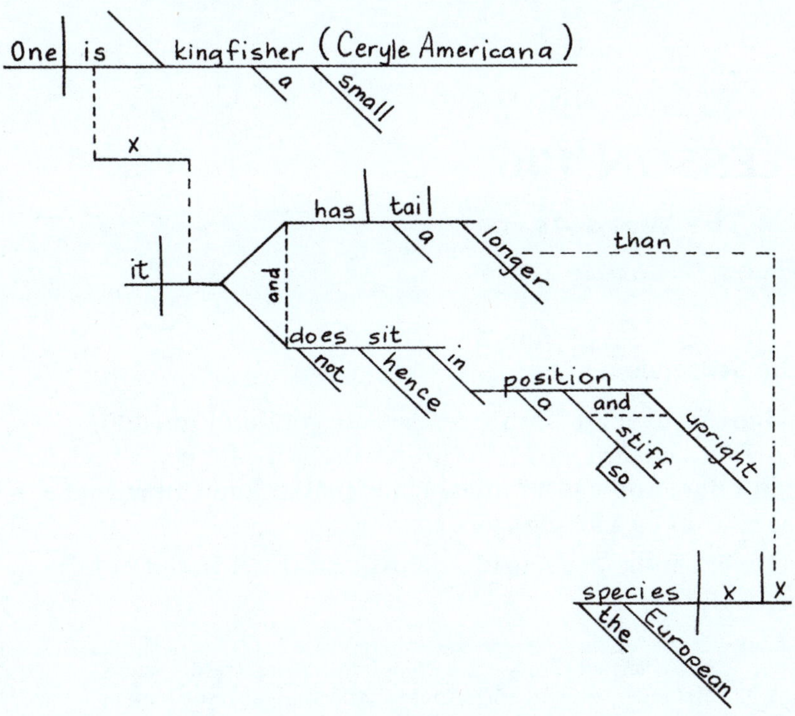

Note to Instructor: The understood words are inserted above so that you can explain the diagram to the student; the dotted line showing the comparison goes from the descriptive word *longer* to the understood word *tail.*

Much of the snow at these great heights is evaporated rather than thawed.

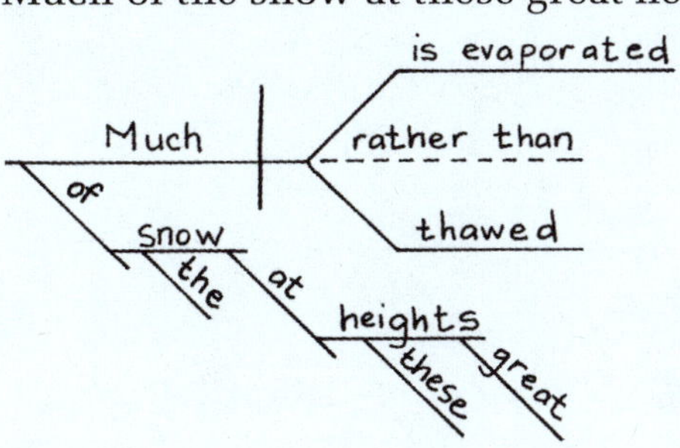

If Vesuvius, Etna, and Hecla in Iceland (all three relatively nearer than the corresponding points
are [nearer]
in South America^), suddenly burst forth in eruption on the same night, the coincidence would be remarkable.

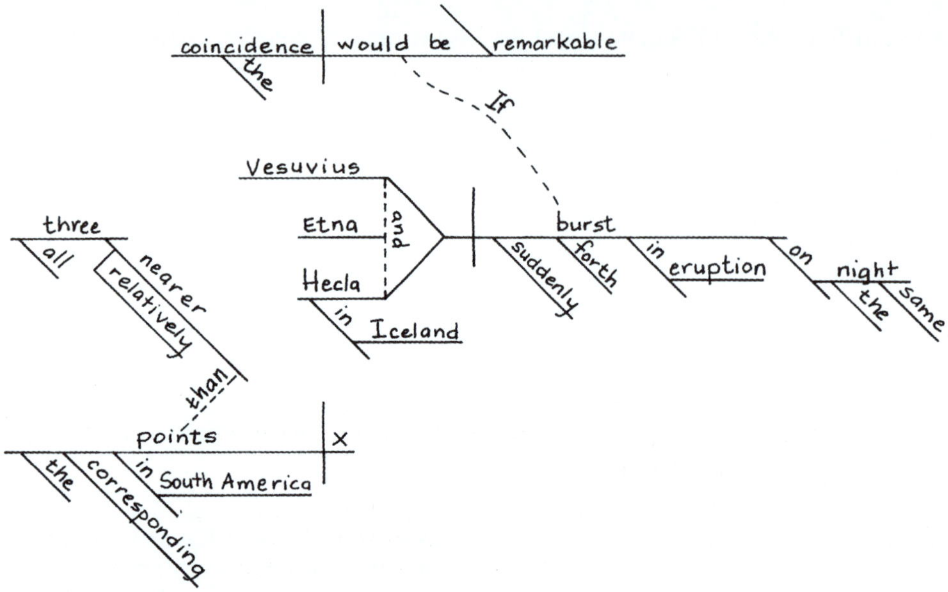

> **Note to Instructor:** The parenthetical element is diagrammed separately, as described in Week 22. The comparison introduced by *than* is completed for your reference in the sentence above.

— LESSON 106 —

The Word *As*

Quasi-Coordinators

Exercise 106A: Identifying Parts of the Sentence

In the following sentences, find and underline every adverb, preposition, conjunction, and quasi-coordinator. Then label each as *ADV* for adverb, *PREP* for preposition, *CC* for coordinating conjunction, *SC* for subordinating conjunction, and *QC* for quasi-coordinator. Remember that a quasi-coordinator can be a short phrase as well as a single word.

These sentences are adapted from Oliver Goldsmith's 1816 scientific study, *A History of the Earth and Animated Nature.*

> **Note to Instructor:** Where subordinating conjunctions introduce incomplete clauses, the missing words have been inserted below for your reference. You may show them to the student if she has trouble identifying the clauses.

PREP SC serve PREP
Pectoral fins serve the same purpose to fish as wings do^ to birds.

ADV SC
Fishes are as deaf as they are mute.

ADV ADV
The frogs began to be agitated, more than before.

PREP PREP ADV
The tail of the whale serves as a great oar to push its mass along.

ADV SC
The sword-fish is as active as the whale is strong.

PREP PREP PREP PREP
He describes his countrymen as living for part of the year upon salted gulls.

QC ADV
Sharks, as well as rays, bring forth their young alive.

PREP ADV PREP
The animal, in less than two days, grows a hard skin over its body.

ADV ADV PREP SC is [nimble]
The land tortoise is much more nimble upon land than the sea turtle ^.

CC PREP SC
The Pike-headed Whale and the Round-lipped Whale differ from each other, as their names
ADV
obviously imply.

PREP QC PREP
Larger fish will swallow a living small fish upon a hook, sooner than any bait that can be put on it.

ADV PREP PREP SC CC are [furnished]
The fish seems as well furnished with the means of happiness as quadrupeds or birds ^.

QC
Those tiny bones are dangerous as well as troublesome to be eaten.

Exercise 106B: Diagramming

On your own paper, diagram every word of the following sentences, slightly adapted from Oliver Goldsmith's 1816 scientific study, *A History of the Earth and Animated Nature.*

These are difficult! Do your best to think through the sentences, but ask for help if you need it.

Note to Instructor: Provide all necessary help.

A roach appears more bony than a carp, because it is leaner and smaller; and it is actually more bony than an eel, because it has a greater number of fins.

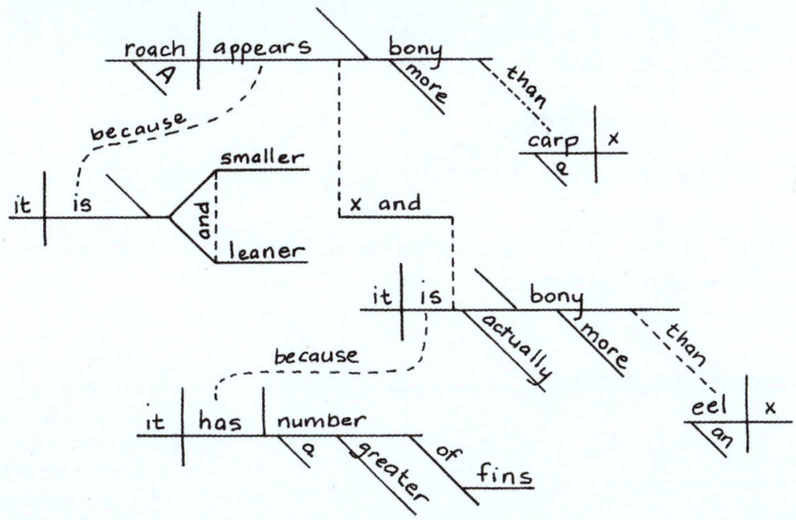

Note to Instructor: In the comparison, the incomplete clause *than a carp* has been diagrammed as though it were *than a carp does* (with the *X* standing in for the predicate *does*), but the student could also add a direct object space with another *X*, on the assumption that the incomplete clause should be finished out *than a carp appears bony*. In the same way, the incomplete clause *than an eel* has been diagrammed as *than an eel is*, but could also include a predicate adjective space (*than an eel is bony*).

In a single season, a cod can produce as many potential offspring as there are people in England; the cod spawns in one season more than ten million eggs.

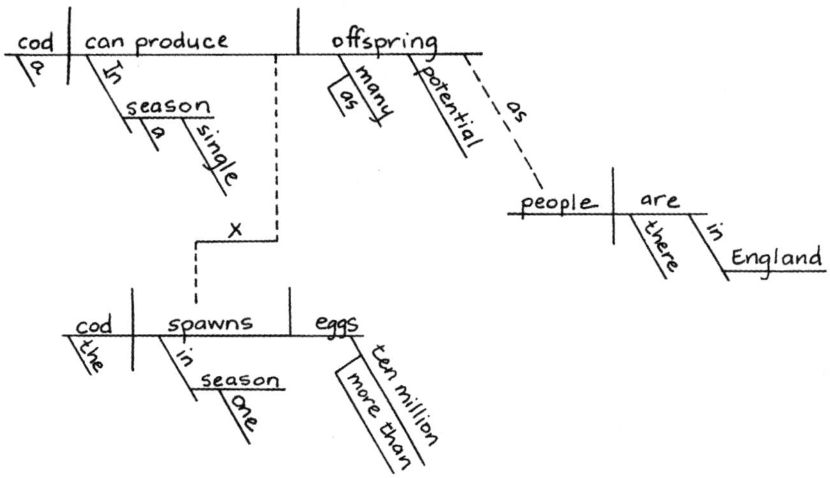

The scorpion's head seems, as it were, joined to the breast, in the middle of which are seen two eyes.

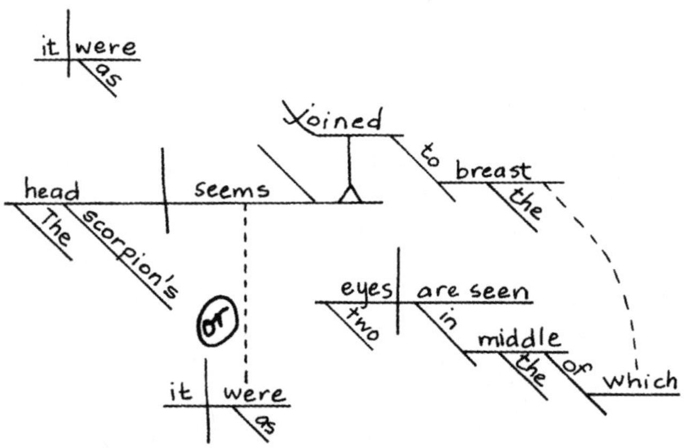

Note to Instructor: In the sentence above, the clause *as it were* can be interpreted either as a parenthetical expression (with *as* as an adverb) or as a relative clause introduced by the subordinating conjunction *as*. Both can be accepted as correct (and both are illustrated on the diagram).

It is a good thing that scorpions are so destructive to each other, or they would multiply so greatly as to make some countries uninhabitable.

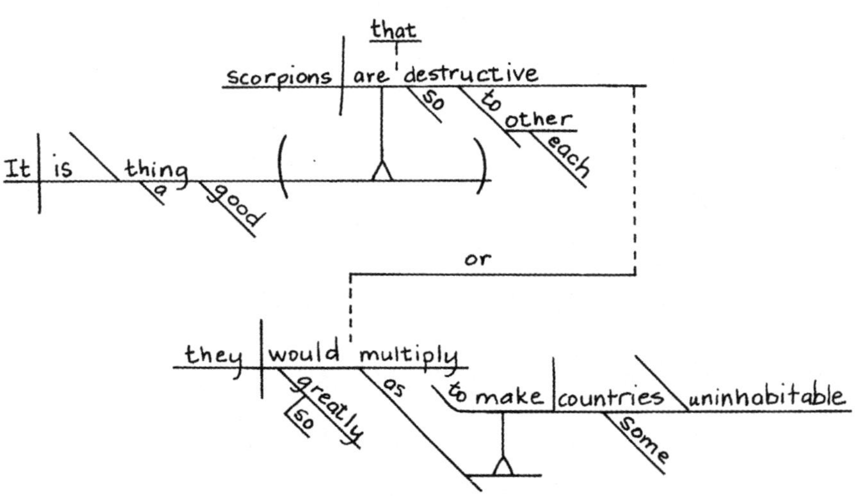

Note to Instructor: In the sentence above, *uninhabitable* is an object complement describing the object *countries* and *as* serves as a preposition. The clause *that scorpions are so destructive to each other* is an appositive renaming *thing*. Give the student all necessary help!

— LESSON 107 —

Words That Can Be Multiple Parts of Speech

Exercise 107A: Identifying Parts of Speech

Identify the part of speech of each underlined word (adapted from *Bleak House, by Charles Dickens*) by writing the correct abbreviation above it: *N* (noun), *PRO* (pronoun), *V* (verb), *ADJ* (adjective), *ADV* (adverb), *PREP* (preposition), *CC* (coordinating conjunction), or *SC* (subordinating conjunction).

PREP
I came off laughing, and red, and anything but tidy.

SC
After we got home, he haunted a post opposite our house.

ADJ
We stood aside, watching for any countenance we knew.

PREP
They meet again at dinner—again, next day—again, for many days in succession.

ADV
Mr. Snagsby is doubtful of his being awake and out—doubtful of the reality of the streets through which he goes—doubtful of the reality of the moon that shines above.

ADV
We were charmed by his fine hilarious manner and his engaging candour and his genial way of lightly tossing his own weaknesses about.

PRO PREP
Business has prevented me from mixing much with general society in any but a professional character.

SC ADV ADV ADV PREP
As the bell was yet ringing and the great people were not yet come, I had leisure to glance over the church, which smelt as earthy as a grave.

ADV
Her fingers were white and wrinkled with washing, and the soap-suds were yet smoking which she wiped off her arms.

CC
Well, my dear, it's a pretty anecdote, nothing more; still I think it charming.

SC
I said I would be ready at half-past six, and after she was gone, stood looking at the basket, quite lost in the magnitude of my trust.

CC
I cannot describe the tenderness with which he spoke to her, half playfully yet all the more compassionately and mournfully.

> **Note to Instructor:** linking *playfully* and *compassionately*, just as *and* links *compassionately* and *mournfully*—all three adverbs modifying *spoke*.

ADJ
I don't think there's any harm in that.

CC
The men's consent I bought, but her help was freely given.

PREP PRO ADV
In no way wearied by his sallies on the road, he was in the drawing-room before any of us; and I heard him at the piano while I was yet looking after my housekeeping.

PREP
The sky had partly cleared, but was very gloomy—even above us, where a few stars were shining.

PREP
And have the children looked after themselves at all, sir?

PREP
I have no purpose but to die.

ADJ
On this blooming summer morning, they sat beneath the cloudless sky above.

CC
It appeared to be something droll, for occasionally there was a laugh and a cry of "Silence!"

ADV
Keep the whole thing quiet ever after.

ADV
Don't you worry any more.

ADV
He will get into some trouble or difficulty otherwise.

ADJ
"I hear a voice," says Chadband; "Is it a still small voice, my friends?"

PREP
It was so delicious to see the clouds about his bright face clearing, and to see him so heartily pleased.

Exercise 107B: Diagramming

On your own paper, diagram every word of the following sentences from *Bleak House.*

Weariness of soul lies before her, as it lies behind.

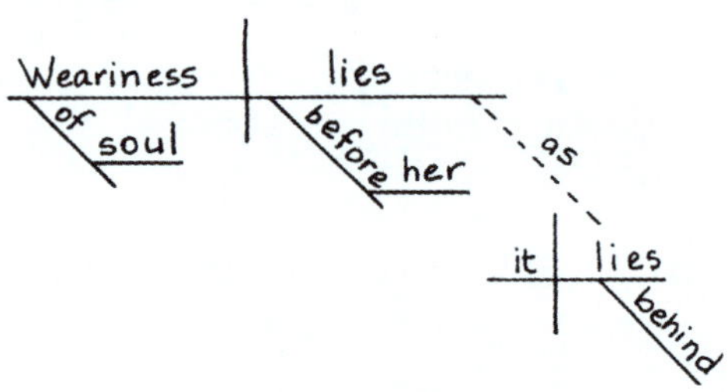

Everything the dear child wore was either too large for him or too small.

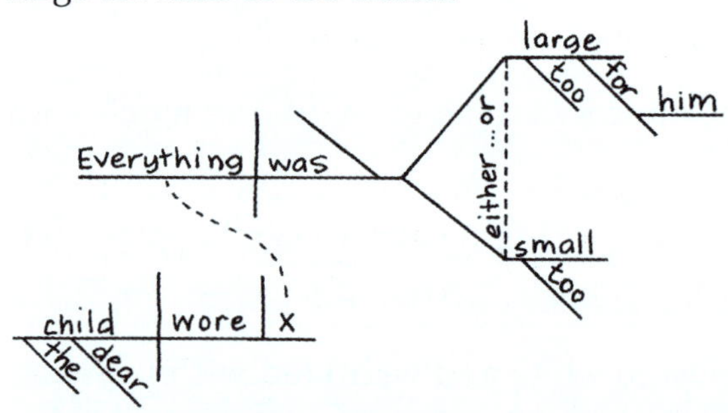

Note to Instructor: Diagramming correlative conjunctions such as *either . . . nor* was covered in Lesson 68.

They straggle about in wrong places, look at the wrong things, don't care for the right things, gape when more rooms are opened, and exhibit profound depression of spirits.

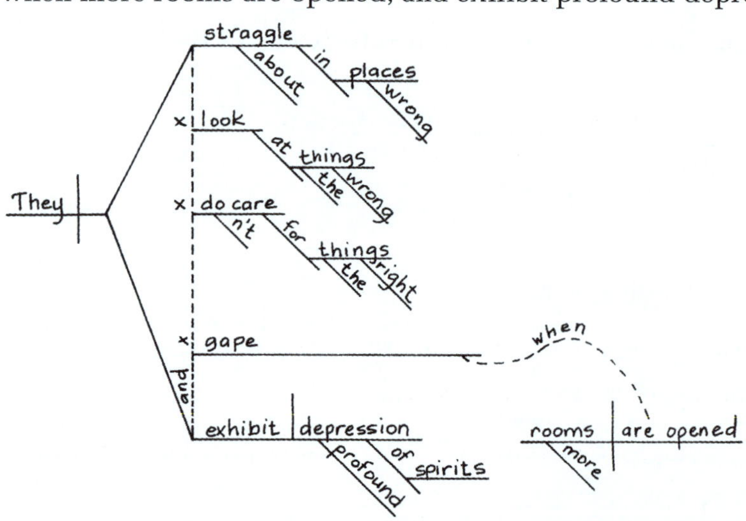

Note to Instructor: Inserting the *X* marks to indicate commas is optional.

The next two sentences are **CHALLENGE EXERCISES**—ask for help when necessary!

She should be an upper servant by her attire, yet in her air and step, though both are hurried and assumed—as far as she can assume in the muddy streets, which she treads with an unaccustomed foot—she is a lady.

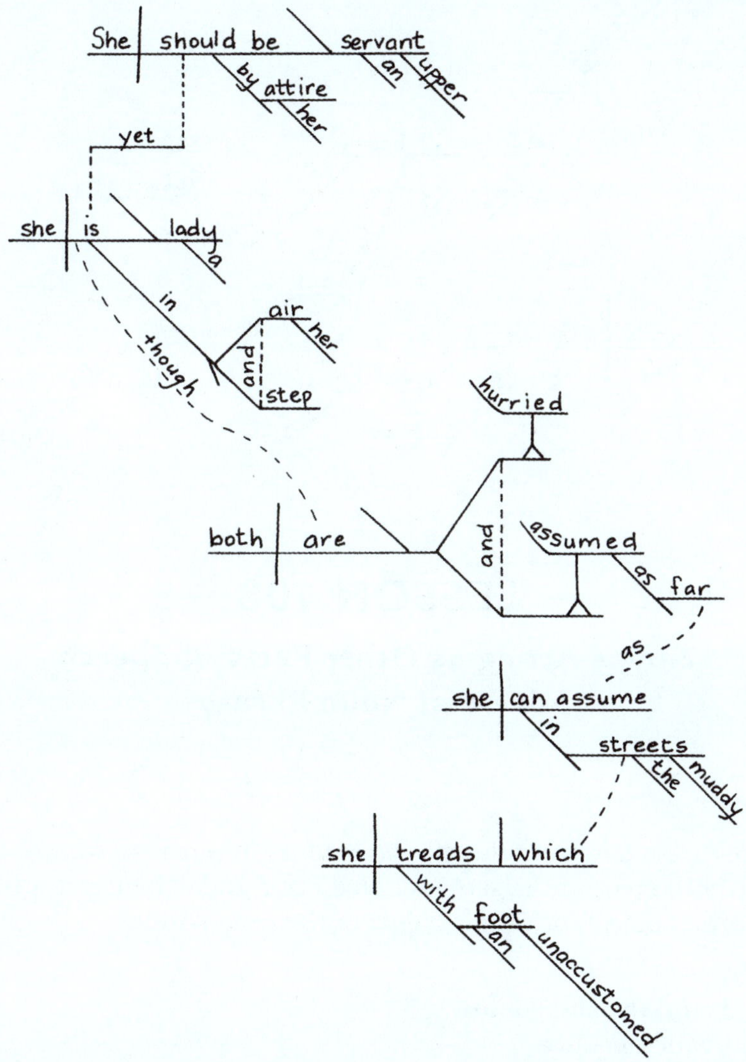

Notes to Instructor: *By her attire* is diagrammed as an adverb phrase because it answers the question *how.* (She is not *a servant by her attire*—rather, *by her attire,* she *should be.*)

The same is true of *in her air and step.* It does not modify *lady* because it does not answer the questions *which one? what kind? how many? whose?* about the noun lady.

Although *both* is a pronoun referring back to *air* and *step,* the relative clause *though both are hurried and assumed* is attached to the verb, not to *air* and *step,* because grammatically it is not an adjective clause—the subject is not a relative pronoun.

Can assume is connected to *far* because the clause explains *far*—the extent to which she can assume.

Beyond it was a burial ground—a dreadful spot in which the night was very slowly stirring, where I could dimly see heaps of dishonored graves and stones, hemmed in by filthy houses with a few dull lights in their windows, on whose walls a thick humidity broke out like a disease.

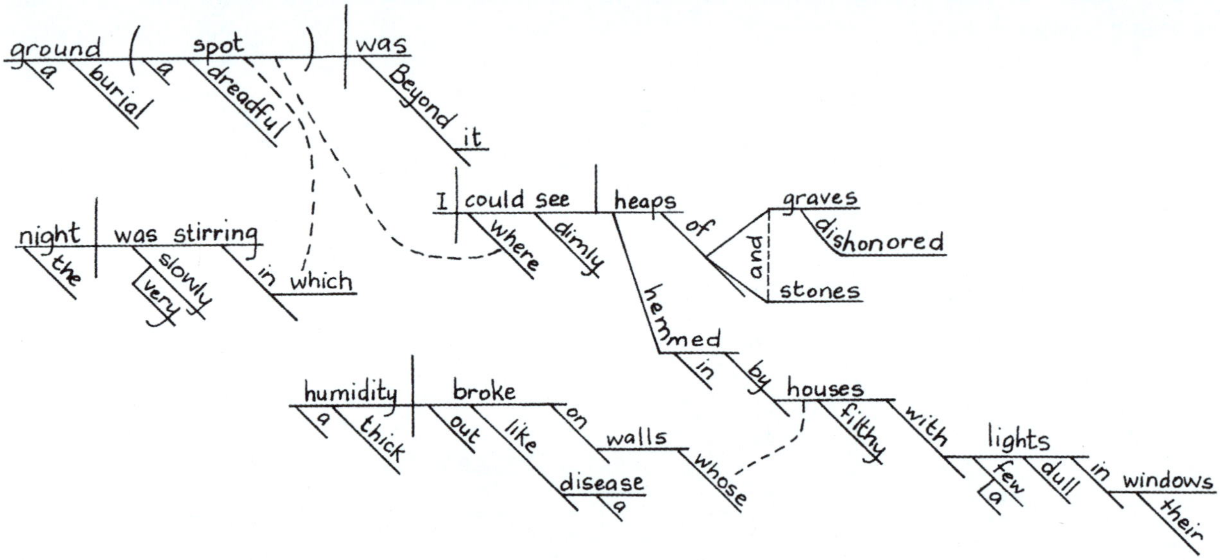

— LESSON 108 —

Nouns Acting as Other Parts of Speech
Adverbial Noun Phrases

Exercise 108A: Nouns

The next five sentences are taken from the classic reader *Animal and Nature Stories*, edited by William Patten. Identify the part of the sentence that each underlined noun plays by labeling it as *S* for subject, *DO* for direct object, or *OP* for object of the preposition.

S
The afternoon wore on, and the sun got low.
—Anna Sewell, *Black Beauty*

DO
Afterward, he made the round of the camps.
—Rush Hawkins, "Jeff the Inquisitive"

S
The well, when we reached it, was dried up, and few of the pilgrims survived.
—Lillian Gask, "Ships of the Desert"

DO
She staked her all on the answers to those eager questions.
—John Brown, "Rab and His Friends"

OP
After a while, they carried them all away.
—John Lubbock, "The intelligence of Ants"

Exercise 108B: Nouns as Other Parts of Speech

Each of the following sets of sentences is missing one of the nouns from the exercise above. Your task: figure out which of those nouns can fill every blank in one set of sentences, according to the parts of speech given in parentheses. Each set must use the *same* word in each blank!

These sentences are slightly adapted from *Animal and Nature Stories*, edited by William Patten.

The good Doctor did nothing to stop the round of gayeties. (noun)
—Harriet Beecher Stowe, "The Katy-Did's Party"

The wind shook the boughs and scattered the fruit round far and wide. (adv)
—Carl Ewald, "The Beech and the Oak"

The anemones burst into flower and bashfully bowed their round heads to the earth. (adj)
—Carl Ewald, "The Anemones"

He helped round up the cows, casting furtive glances ahead. (verb)
—M. Cornell, "Anna and the Rattler"

I found, in that afternoon walk, some curiously shaped splinters of jasper. (adj)
—Charles C. Abbott, "How the Stone-Age Children Played"

They went one afternoon to drink tea with Lady Margaret. (noun)
—Octave Thanet, "Marcus Aurelius"

I'll take good care of you while you are mine. (subordinating conjunction)
—Octave Thanet, "Marcus Aurelius"

I will while away the time by geologizing. (verb)
—Charles C. Abbott, "How the Stone-Age Children Played"

All the while, he continued to be an incorrigible rogue and thief. (noun)
—W. H. G. Kingston, "Some True Stories of Tigers, Wolves, Foxes and Bears"

All camels are by nature patient, and strong to endure. (adj)
—Lillian Gask, "Ships of the Desert"

The papa fox took a survey all round. (adv)
—W. H. G. Kingston, "Some True Stories of Tigers, Wolves, Foxes and Bears"

All of these arrow-points are very neatly made. (pronoun)
—David Starr Jordan, "The Story of a Stone"

He seemed so glad to give his all that I was ashamed of myself. (noun)
—Louisa May Alcott, *Little Women*

The frosts came early, but we are all well. (adj)
—Lillian Gask, "Two Enemies of the Beavers"

We know very well that if we once catch a bad cold we are done for. (adv)
—Carl Ewald, "The Anemones"

Well, you must wait until Father Beaver comes home. (int)
—Lillian Gask, "At Home with the Beavers"

They drank from the well at Blackfriars Wynd. (noun)
—John Brown, "Rab and His Friends"

Tears well in her eyes as she reads the letter. (verb)
—Octave Thanet, "Marcus Aurelius"

Exercise 108C: Identifying Parts of Speech

Identify the part of speech of each underlined word by writing the correct abbreviation above it: *N* (noun), *ADV-N* (adverbial noun), *PRO* (pronoun), *V* (verb), *ADJ* (adjective), *ADV* (adverb), *PREP* (preposition), *CC* (coordinating conjunction), *SC* (subordinating conjunction), or *QC* (quasi-coordinator).

These sentences are taken from *Great Astronomers*, by Robert S. Ball.

> **Note to Instructor:** Explanations are provided in brackets; provide all necessary help to the student.

The effect of this instrument is to show an object at a distance of fifty miles as [SC] if it were but [PREP] five miles. [*as* introduces the subordinate clause *if it were but five miles*; the prepositional phrase *but five miles* acts as an adverb modifying the verb]

Kepler had himself assigned no reason why the orbit of a planet should be an ellipse rather than [QC] any [ADJ] other of the infinite number of closed curves which might be traced around the sun. [*rather than* connects the double predicate nominatives *ellipse* and *other*, renaming *orbit* and following the linking verb *should be*; *any* modifies *other*]

It was, no doubt, not so large as [SC] Saturn, it was certainly very much less than [SC] Jupiter; on the other hand, the new body was very much larger than [SC] Mercury, than [SC] Venus, or than [SC] Mars, and the earth itself seemed quite an insignificant object in comparison with this newly added member of the Solar System. [in each case, *than* introduces a subordinate clause with an understood verb: *not so large as Saturn [was], much less than Jupiter [was], much larger than Mercury [was], than Venus [was], or than Mars [was]*]

There was no argument in favour of this notion, other than [PREP] the merely imaginary reflection that circular movement, and circular movement alone, was "perfect," whatever "perfect" may have meant. [compound preposition with *reflection* as the object]

No doubt others, before [PREP] Copernicus, had from time to time in some vague fashion surmised, with more or less plausibility, that the sun, and not the earth, was the centre about [PREP] which the system really revolved. [prepositional phrases *before Copernicus* and *about which* modify *others* and *centre*, respectively]

Tycho, however, speedily made it plain to his teachers that though he was an ardent student, yet [CC] the things which interested him were the movements of the heavenly bodies and not the subtleties of metaphysics. [coordinating conjunction links the clauses *he was an ardent student* and *the things which interested him were . . .*, both of which are equal because they are both subordinated in the same way by the subordinating conjunction *that*]

This new Pope, while [PREP] a cardinal, had been an intimate friend of Galileo's, and had indeed written Latin verses in praise of the great astronomer and his discoveries. [adverbial prepositional phrase modifies *had been* and answers the question *when?*]

It must be remembered that it was the almost universal belief in those days, that all (ADJ) the celestial spheres revolved in some mysterious fashion around the earth, which appeared by far the most important body in the universe. [modifies *spheres*]

The absurdity of this doctrine is obvious enough, especially when we observe that, as (SC) it is now well (ADV) known, there are two large planets, and a host of small planets, over and above (PREP) the magical number of the regular solids. [*as* introduces the subordinate clause *it is now well known*; *well* modifies the passive verb *is known*; *above* is part of the compound preposition *over and above*]

Kepler rightly judged that the number of days which a planet required to perform its voyage round (PREP) the sun must be connected in some manner with the distance from the planet to the sun; that is to say, with the radius of the planet's orbit, inasmuch as (SC) we may for our present object regard the planet's orbit as (SC) circular. [*round the sun* is a prepositional phrase describing voyage and answering the question *which?*; *as* introduces the subordinate clause *we may for our present object regard . . .* ; the second *as* introduces the subordinate clause with missing words *as [if it were] circular* (*as* cannot be a preposition because it has no object; *circular* is an adjective, not a noun)]

It would have been almost impossible to refuse to draw the inference that the stars thus brought into view were still (ADV) more remote objects which the telescope was able to reveal, just in the same way as (SC) it showed certain ships to the astonished Venetians, when at the time these ships were beyond the reach of unaided vision. [*still* modifies the adverb *more*; *as* introduces the subordinate clause *it showed certain ships . . .*]

Exercise 108D: Adverbial Noun Phrases

Circle each adverbial noun or noun phrase, and draw an arrow from the circle to the word modified.

These sentences are taken from *Great Astronomers*, by Robert S. Ball.

It was not unusual for him to work **twelve hours** at a stretch.

On the 11th of November in that year, he was returning **home** to supper after a day's work in his laboratory, when he happened to lift his face to the sky, and there he beheld a brilliant new star.

Rouge was then introduced as the polishing powder, and the operation was continued **nine hours**, by which time the great mirror had acquired the appearance of highly polished silver.

After an uneventful voyage lasting **three months**, the astronomer landed on St. Helena with a telescope **24 feet** long, and forthwith plunged with ardor into his investigation of the southern skies.

The King took so great a fancy to the astronomer that he first, as I have already mentioned, duly pardoned his desertion from the army, **some twenty-five years** previously.

It appears that sitting **one day** in the Cathedral of Pisa, Galileo's attention became concentrated on the swinging of a chandelier which hung from the ceiling.

So long as a bird was perched on a tree, he might very well be carried onward by the moving earth, but the moment he took wing, the ground would slip from under him at a frightful pace, so that when he dropped down again he would find himself at a distance perhaps ten times as great as that which a carrier-pigeon or a swallow could have traversed in the same time.

Exercise 108E: Diagramming

On your own paper, diagram every word of the following sentences from *Great Astronomers*, by Robert S. Ball.

In those days the doctrines of Aristotle were regarded as the embodiment of all human wisdom in natural science, as well as everything else.

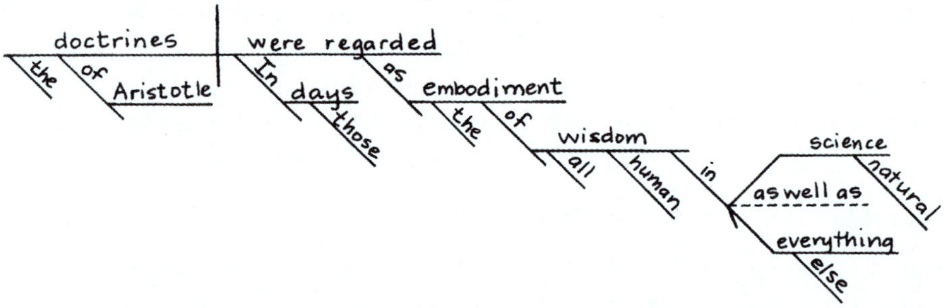

Brinkley was eighteen years waiting for his telescope,
and he had eighteen years more in which he could use it.

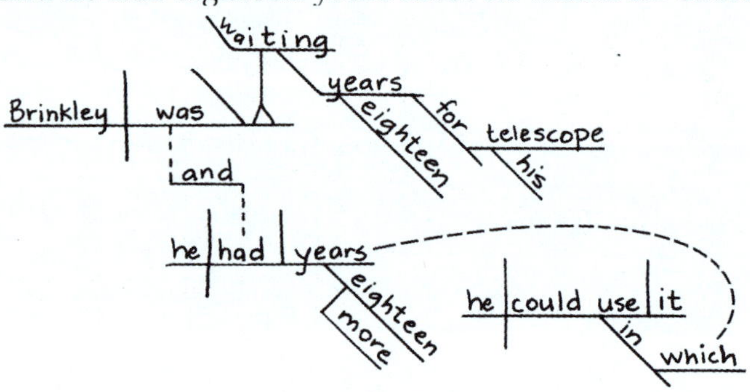

On the other hand, constellations new to the inhabitants of northern climes were seen to rise above the southern horizon.

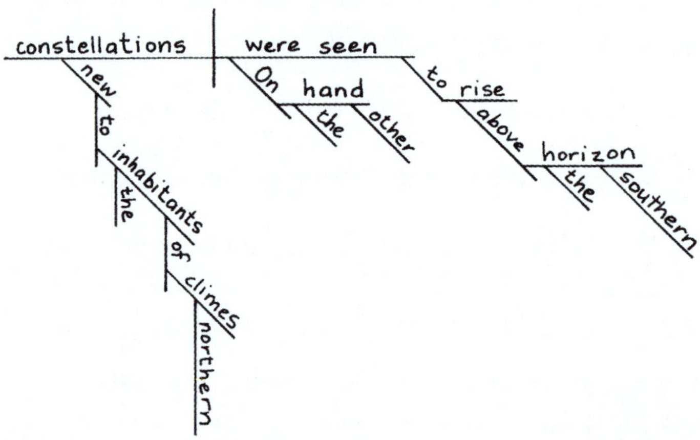

Note to Instructor: It is also acceptable to diagram *on the other hand* as a parenthetical expression.

By this reasoning he arrives at the fundamental conclusion that the earth is a globular body freely lying in space, and surrounded above, below, and on all sides by the glittering stars of heaven.

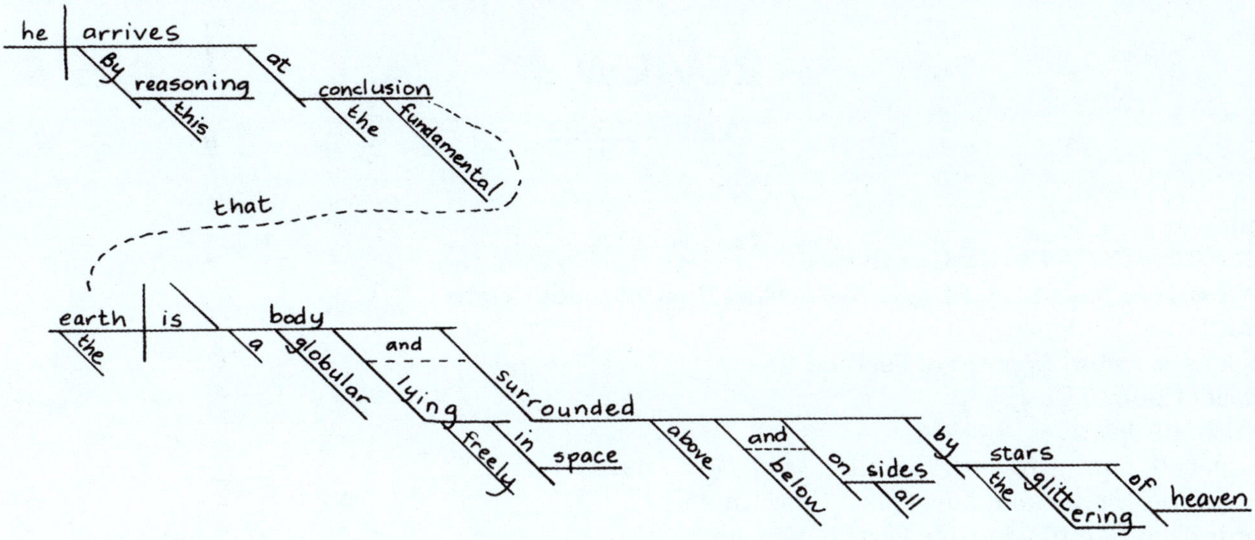

As the earth turns round, the stars over your head will change, and unless it should happen that you have taken up your position at either of the poles, new stars will pass into your view, and others will disappear, for at no time can you have more than half of the whole sphere visible.

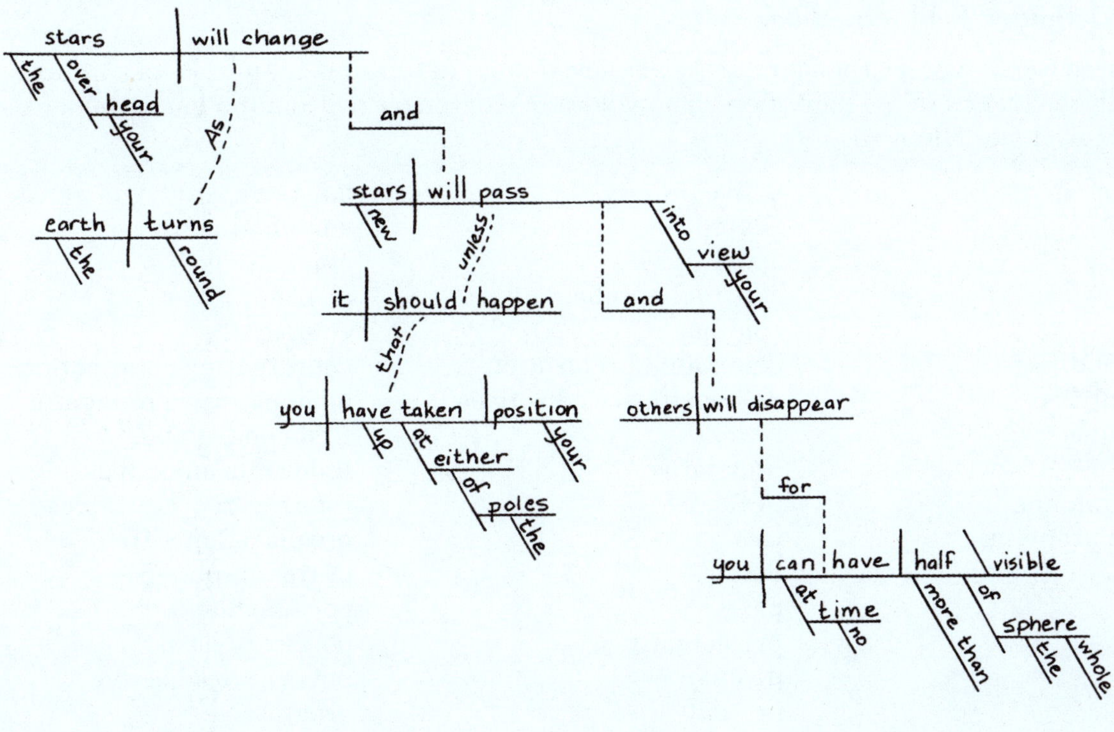

WEEK 28

— REVIEW 9 —

Weeks 25-27

Topics
Progressive Perfect Indicative Tenses
Progressive Present and Progressive Perfect Present Modal Verbs
Conditional Sentences
Adjectives in the Appositive Position
Correct Comma Usage
Limiting Adjectives
Misplaced, Squinting, and Dangling Modifier Comparisons
Using *More*, *Fewer*, and *Less* Quasi-Coordinators
Words That Can Be Multiple Parts of Speech
Nouns Acting as Other Parts of Speech
Adverbial Nouns

Review 9A: Definition Fill-in-the-Blank

In the last three weeks, you learned (and reviewed) even *more* definitions than in Weeks 22, 23, and 24! Fill in the blanks in the definitions below with one of the terms from the list. Many of the terms will be used more than once.

abstract noun	active	adjective
adjectives	adverb	adverbial noun
adverbs	apostrophe	appositive
attributive	cardinal numbers	clause
comma	commas	comparative
compound modifiers	compound preposition	coordinating conjunction
dangling modifier	demonstrative adjectives	demonstrative pronouns
descriptive adjective	fewer	first conditional
future	imperative	indefinite adjectives
indefinite pronouns	indicative	interrogative adjectives
interrogative pronouns	less	misplaced modifier
modal	noun	ordinal numbers
passive	past	past participle
perfect	perfect past	perfect present
plural	positive	possessive adjective
predicative	present	progressive
progressive perfect	progressive present	quasi-coordinators
second conditional	simple	simple present
singular	squinting modifier	state-of-being
subjunctive	subordinating conjunction	superlative
third conditional		

> **Note to Instructor:** Allow the student to look back through the workbook and find definitions as necessary; the value of the exercise comes in the student's completing each definition, whether from memory or not.

Indicative verbs express real actions.

Subjunctive verbs express situations that are unreal, wished for, or uncertain.

Imperative verbs express intended actions.

Modal verbs express possible actions and situations that have not actually happened.

In a sentence with an active verb, the subject performs the action.

In a sentence with a passive verb, the subject receives the action.

A simple verb simply tells whether an action takes place in the past, present, or future.

A progressive verb describes an ongoing or continuous action.

A perfect verb describes an action which has been completed before another action takes place.

A progressive perfect verb describes an ongoing or continuous action that has a definite end.

The present passive imperative is formed by adding the helping verb *be* to the past participle of the verb.

The present passive subjunctive is formed by pairing *be* with the past participle of a verb.

Use the simple past subjunctive state-of-being verb, plus an infinitive, to express a future unreal action.

First conditional sentences express circumstances that might actually happen. The predicate of the condition clause is in a present tense. The predicate of the consequence clause is an imperative or is in a present or future tense.

Second conditional sentences express circumstances that are contrary to reality. The predicate of the condition clause is in a past tense. The predicate of the consequence clause is in the simple or progressive present modal tense.

Third conditional sentences express past circumstances that never happened. The predicate of the condition clause is in the perfect past tense. The predicate of the consequence clause is in the perfect present modal or simple present modal tense.

A descriptive adjective tells what kind.

A descriptive adjective becomes an abstract noun when you add *-ness* to it.

A possessive adjective tells whose.

A noun becomes an adjective when it is made possessive.

Form the possessive of a singular noun by adding an apostrophe and the letter *s.*

Form the possessive of a plural noun ending in *-s* by adding an apostrophe only.

Form the possessive of a plural noun that does not end in *-s* as if it were a singular noun.

An adjective that comes right before the noun it modifies is in the attributive position.

An adjective that follows the noun it modifies is in the predicative position.

Appositive adjectives directly follow the word they modify.

When three or more nouns, adjectives, verbs, or adverbs appear in a series, they should be separated by commas.

When three or more items are in a list, a coordinating conjunction before the last term is usual but not necessary.

When three or more items are in a list and a coordinating conjunction is used, a comma should still follow the next to last item in the list.

When two or more adjectives are in the attributive position, they are only separated by commas if they are equally important in meaning.

Demonstrative pronouns demonstrate or point out something. They take the place of a single word or a group of words.

Demonstrative adjectives modify nouns and answer the question *which one*.

Indefinite pronouns are pronouns without antecedents.

Indefinite adjectives modify nouns and answer the questions *which one* and *how many*.

Interrogative pronouns take the place of nouns in questions.

Interrogative adjectives modify nouns.

Cardinal numbers represent quantities (one, two, three, four . . .).

Ordinal numbers represent order (first, second, third, fourth . . .).

A misplaced modifier is an adjective, adjective phrase, adverb, or adverb phrase in the wrong place.

A squinting modifier can belong either to the sentence element preceding or the element following.

A dangling modifier has no noun or verb to modify.

The positive degree of an adjective describes only one thing.

The comparative degree of an adjective compares two things.

The superlative degree of an adjective compares three or more things.

Most regular adjectives form the comparative by adding *-r* or *-er*.

Most regular adjectives form the superlative by adding *-st* or *-est*.

Many adjectives form their comparative and superlative forms by adding the word *more* or *most* before the adjective instead of using *–er* or *–est*. In comparative and superlative adjective forms, the words *more* and *most* are used as adverbs.

Use *fewer* for concrete items and *less* for abstractions.

In comparisons using *more . . . fewer* and *more . . . less*, *more* and *less* can act as either adverbs or adjectives and *the* can act as an adverb.

In comparisons using two comparative forms, the forms may act as either adverbs or adjectives, and *the* can act as an adverb.

A coordinating conjunction joins equal words or groups of words together.

A <u>subordinating conjunction</u> joins unequal words or groups of words together.

When *than* is used in a comparison and introduces a <u>clause</u> with understood elements, it is acting as a <u>subordinating conjunction</u>.

Other than is a <u>compound preposition</u> that means "besides" or "except."

More than and *less than* are <u>compound modifiers</u>.

<u>Quasi-coordinators</u> link compound parts of a sentence that are unequal. <u>Quasi- coordinators</u> include *rather than, sooner than, let alone, as well as,* and *not to mention.*

An <u>adverbial noun</u> tells the time or place of an action, or explains how long, how far, how deep, how thick, or how much. It can modify a verb, <u>adjective</u>, or <u>adverb</u>.

An <u>adverbial noun</u> plus its modifiers is an <u>adverbial noun</u> phrase.

Review 9B: Parsing

Above each underlined verb, write the complete tense, the voice or the state-of-being, and the mood. The first sentence is done for you.

These sentences are from *Otto of the Silver Hand* by Howard Pyle.

I <u>was walking</u> [progressive past, active, indicative] there, and my wits <u>were running</u> [progressive past, active, indicative] around in the grass like a mouse.

A moment more, and he <u>might have promised</u> [perfect present, active, modal] what she besought; a moment more, and he <u>might have been saved</u> [perfect present passive, modal] all the bitter trouble that was to follow.

A stranger was in the refectory, standing beside the good old Abbot, while food and wine <u>were being brought</u> [progressive past, passive, indicative] and set upon the table for his refreshment; a great, tall, broad-shouldered man, beside whom the Abbot <u>looked</u> [simple past, active, indicative] thinner and slighter than ever.

A few inches more and he <u>would have been discovered</u> [perfect present, passive, modal];—what <u>would have happened</u> [perfect present, active, modal] then <u>would have been</u> [perfect present, state-of-being, modal] no hard matter to foretell.

First, it <u>shone</u> [simple past, active, indicative] white and thin like the moon in the daylight; but it <u>grew</u> [simple past active, indicative] brighter and brighter, until it hurt one's eyes to look at it, as though it <u>had been</u> [perfect past, state-of-being, indicative] the blessed sun itself.

And then, in her own fashion she related to him the story of how his father <u>had set</u> [perfect past, active, indicative] forth upon that expedition in spite of all that Otto's mother had said, beseeching him to abide at home;

perfect past, passive, indicative

how he had been foully wounded, and how the poor lady had died from her fright and grief.

simple present, passive, subjunctive — simple present, active, modal

If you be slain, what then would become of me?

progressive perfect past, active, indicative — progressive perfect past, active, indicative

One by one those barons who had been carrying on their private wars, or had been despoiling the

perfect past, passive, indicative

burgher folk in their traffic from town to town, and against whom complaint had been lodged,

simple past, passive, indicative — simple past, passive, indicative

were summoned to the Imperial Court, where they were compelled to promise peace and to swear allegiance to the new order of things.

simple past, active, indicative

Otto lay watching the rope as it crawled up to the window and out into the night like a great

simple present, passive, modal

snake, while one-eyed Hans held the other end lest it should be drawn too far.

There was no room now to swing the long blade, but holding the hilt in both hands, Baron

simple past, active, indicative — simple past, state-of-being, subjunctive

Conrad thrust with it as though it were a lance, stabbing at horse or man, it mattered not.

perfect past, active, indicative — perfect past, active, indicative

Many folk said that the one-eyed Hans had drunk beer with the Hill-man, who had given him the

simple present, active, modal — simple present, active, modal

strength of ten, for he could bend an iron spit like a hazel twig, and could lift a barrel of wine from the floor to his head as easily as though it were a basket of eggs.

simple past, state-of-being, subjunctive

I wish that I were back in the monastery again; I am afraid out here in the great wide world;

simple present, active, modal — simple present, state-of-being, indicative — simple present, active, modal

perhaps somebody may kill me, for I am only a weak little boy and could not save my own life

simple past, active, indicative

if they chose to take it from me.

simple past, active, indicative — simple past, active, indicative

So at last they reached the chasm that yawned beneath the roadway, and there they stopped, for

perfect past, active, indicative — progressive perfect past, active, indicative

they had reached the spot toward which they had been journeying.

simple future, state-of-being, indicative — simple present, active, modal — simple present, passive, indicative

Night will be upon you before you can reach home again, and the forests are beset with wolves.

Review 9C: Provide the Verb

Complete each song lyric by providing an appropriate verb in the tense indicated. You may want to use the chart in Lesson 99 for reference. In some cases, the missing verb is also part of the title of the song!

If there are two blanks for a single verb, the helping verb is divided from the main verb by another part of the sentence.

If you can't think of a verb, ask your instructor for help.

When you are finished, compare your answers to the original lyrics.

> **Note to Instructor:** If the student has trouble coming up with a verb, simply tell him the verb used and then allow him to put it into the proper tense.

progressive perfect present, active, modal

And I'll finally show you how I should have been being with you every day.

—"Train," Lincoln Avenue

> **Note to Instructor:** Prompt is *Use the state-of-being verb.*

progressive future, active, indicative

So if you've a date in Constantinople/ She 'll be waiting in Istanbul.

—"Istanbul," They Might Be Giants [*lyrics by Jimmy Kennedy*]

simple present, active, modal

I could say that I'll always be here for you.

—"I Could Say," Lily Allen

progressive perfect present, active, indicative

Time . . . I 've been passing time watching trains go by.

—"It Might Be You," Steven Bishop

progressive present, active, modal

We should be sleeping now,/ We're wide awake, but we're dead on our feet.

—"We Should Be Sleeping," Eddie Money

simple future, active, indicative / *progressive future, active, indicative*

I 'll set you free, and then just like me you 'll be being / In love with me.

—"My Best Friend," Jefferson Airplane

> **Note to Instructor:** Prompt for the second verb is *Use the state-of-being verb.*

perfect future, active, indicative

Oh, if only love comes 'round again,/ It will have been worth the ride.

—"It's Only Love," Sheryl Crow

> **Note to Instructor:** Prompt is *Use the state-of-being verb.*

progressive perfect past, active, indicative

You were the answer that I had been looking for.

—"The Best I Had," Taken

perfect present, passive, indicative

They may be false; they may be true, but nothing has been proved.

—"Nothing Has Been Proved," Dusty Springfield

both *perfect present, active, indicative*

Since I have found you, my life has just begun.

—"Love, Thy Will Be Done," Martika

progressive present, active, modal

Could I be coming home, with the waves rolling back?

—"Could I Be," Sylvan Esso

simple present, active, modal *simple present, active, indicative*

I must leave this place before they break my heart.

—"Shall I Tell You What I Think of You?" Oscar Hammerstein, from *The King and I*

Review 9D: Identifying Adjectives and Punctuating Items in a Series

In the following stanzas (from the poem "Hakon's Lay," by the American poet James Russell Lowell), carry out the following three steps:

a) Underline once and label all adjectives (except for articles), using the following abbreviations:

Descriptive Adjectives		Limiting Adjectives	
Regular	*DA-R*	Possessives	*LA-P*
Present participles	*DA-PresP*	~~Articles~~	~~*LA-A*~~
Past participles	*DA-PastP*	Demonstratives	*LA-D*
Infinitives	*DA-Inf*	Indefinites	*LA-IND*
		Interrogatives	*LA-INT*
		Numbers	*LA-N*

b) Circle all adjectives that are in the predicate or in the predicative position, and draw an arrow from each back to the noun it modifies.

c) The passage contains one indefinite pronoun, two demonstrative pronouns, and two interrogative pronouns. Find each, underline them twice, and identify them as part of the sentence (*SUBJ* for subject, *DO* for direct object, *IO* for indirect object, *OP* for object of the preposition).

Then the old (DA-R) man arose; white-haired (DA-R) he stood,
White-bearded (DA-R) with eyes that looked afar
From their (LA-P) still (DA-R) region of perpetual (DA-R) snow,
Over the little (DA-R) smokes and stirs of men:
His (LA-P) head was bowed with gathered (DA-PastP) flakes of years,
As winter bends the sea-foreboding (DA-PresP) pine,

SUBJ LA-P
But something triumphed in his brow and eye,
SUBJ
Which whoso saw it, could not see and crouch: [*whoso* is a variant form of the interrogative pronoun *who*]
DA-PastP
Loud rang the emptied beakers as he mused,
LA-P DA-PastP
Brooding his eyried thoughts; then, as an eagle [*brooding* is an adverb modifying *mused*]
Past-P DA-PastP
Circles smooth-winged above the wind-vexed woods,
LA-P
So wheeled his soul into the air of song
DA-R
High o'er the stormy hall; and thus he sang:
LA-P
"The fletcher for his arrow-shaft picks out
Past-P Past-P DA-R
Wood closest-grained, long-seasoned, straight as light;
DA-R
And, from a quiver full of such as these,
Past-P LA-P
The wary bow-man, matched against his peers,
PresP
Long doubting, singles yet once more the best. [*best* is here acting as a noun]
SUBJ LA-D
Who is it that can make these shafts as Fate?
LA-INT LA-P DA-R
What archer of his arrows is so choice,
Or hits the white so surely? They are men, [*white* is here acting as a noun]
LA-P
The chosen of her quiver; nor for her [*chosen* is here acting as a noun in apposition to *men*]
DA-PastP DA-PastP
Will weakened reed suffice, or cross-grained stick
LA-P DA-R DA-PastP
At random from life's vulgar stick-heap plucked:
DA-R
Such answer household ends; but she will have [*such* is a pronoun referring back to *stick*]
DA-R DA-R DA-R DA-R
Souls straight and clear, of toughest fibre, sound
OP
Down to the heart of heart; from these she strips
LA-IND DA-R LA-IND DO
All needless stuff, all sapwood; hardens them;
DA-R
From circumstance untoward feathers plucks
OP DA-R DA-R
Crumpled and cheap; and barbs with iron will:
LA-P
The hour that passes is her quiver-boy;
When she draws bow, 'tis not across the wind,
LA-P DA-PastP
Nor 'gainst the sun, her haste-snatched arrow sings,
For sun and wind have plighted faith to her
Ere men have heard the sinew twang, behold,
LA-P LA-P DA-PresP
In target's heart her trembling messenger!"

Review 9E: Correcting Modifiers

The following sentences all have modifier problems! Correct each sentence, using proofreader's marks, and be ready to explain the problems to your instructor. The first is done for you.

Note to Instructor: Use the explanations below to prompt the student if necessary. These sentences may also be rewritten/corrected in other ways as long as the central error is corrected.

As I was w
Wandering through the zoo, my attention was caught by the new baby panda.

Explanation: The adjectival participle phrase at the beginning is a misplaced modifier—*my attention* was not *wandering through the zoo*, I was!

more
The goal of this book is the development of correcter grammar.

Explanation: The comparative form of the adjective *correct* is formed with the adverb *more*.

The patient was whisked to the hospital before more symptoms were suffered by the first responders.

Explanation: The adverb phrase *by the first responders* is misplaced; they did not suffer the symptoms.

scarier
Ghost stories are more scary when it is completely dark.

Explanation: *Scary* is a regular adjective and forms a regular comparative.

I was
Once finished with college, my favorite professor was able to find me a great internship.

Explanation: The adjectival participle phrase *once finished with college* shouldn't modify *professor.*

The dog under the table that tried to snatch food off my plate is badly trained.

Explanation: The subordinate clause *that tried to snatch food off my plate* follows *table* and so acts to modify *table*. Instead, it should modify *dog*. As long as the subordinate clause no longer modifies *table*, accept any reasonable answers. If *badly trained* goes in front of *dog*, it should be hyphenated because it becomes attributive.

he was
While eating the steak, Dr. Mulrooney's pager went off and called him to surgery.

Explanation: Without the addition of the subject *he*, the initial phrase describes pager, not Dr. Mulrooney.

fastest
The marathoner ran the most fast of all the competitors.

Explanation: The correct superlative form of *fast* is *fastest*.

When the party guest ed her
Realizing that she was two hours late, it seemed simplest for the party guest to give up and go back home.

Explanation: The opening phrase is dangling—it is not grammatically related to any word in the main clause. In meaning, it modifies *party guest*, so the altered sentence moves *party guest* to become the subject of an opening subordinate clause.

Rabbits kept in a hutch require ^less ~~fewer~~ food than rabbits that run around outside.

Explanation: *Food* cannot be easily quantified or counted, so *less* is more appropriate. *Fewer feedings* or *fewer scoops of rabbit food* could be quantified or counted.

Her favorite sweater was the one she bought at the little thrift store (with the asymmetrical hem).

Explanation: *With the asymmetrical hem* does not modify the thrift store! It also goes more naturally after the predicate nominative *one* rather than after *sweater*, since *the one with the asymmetrical hem* defines *favorite sweater. Her favorite sweater with the asymmetrical hem* implies that she has many sweaters with asymmetrical hems.

She married a man with a vast country estate (in a small church in the Cotswolds.)

Explanation: The circled prepositional phrase acts as an adverb, answering the question *where*. It goes most naturally at the beginning of the sentence rather than after the verb *married* (which it modifies).

To do well in school, ^students must hand in work ~~must be handed in~~ on time.

Explanation: The infinitive phrase that begins the sentence is dangling in both grammar and meaning—it has no relationship to the rest of the sentence. The sentence could also be changed to *Work must be handed in on time for students to do well in school.*

January is usually ^colder ~~more cold~~ than March.

Explanation: The correct comparative form is *colder.*

The young woman in the very high heels, ^ (I introduced myself to) ^who turned out to be my cousin.

Explanation: You introduced yourself to the young woman, not her heels! So that *I introduced myself to* (a subordinate clause with an understood *whom*) modifies *young woman*, the sentence can either be corrected to read *I introduced myself to the young woman in the very high heels, who turned out to be my cousin* or perhaps *The young woman I introduced myself to, the one wearing very high heels, turned out to be my cousin.*

After winning the competition, ~~a first-class flight took~~ the singer ^took a first-class flight to Disneyland.

Explanation: *After winning the competition* modifies *singer*, not *flight*, so it should come immediately before *singer*. Another possible correction might be *A first-class flight took the singer to Disneyland after she won the competition.*

Katsuji gave away his books to his brother (that he was finished with.)

Explanation: The circled clause modifies the *books*, not the *brother.*

Nothing is ^more beautiful ~~beautifuller~~ than a flower meadow filled with colorful butterflies in the country.

Explanation: The correct comparative form of *beautiful* is *more beautiful.*

Review 9F: Identifying Adverbs

In the following sentences, taken from J. M. Barrie's novel *Peter Pan,* carry out the following steps:

a) Underline each word, phrase, or clause that is acting as an adverb.
b) Draw a line from the word/phrase/clause to the verb, adjective, or adverb modified.
c) Above the word or phrase, note whether it is a regular adverb (*ADV*), an adverbial noun (*AN*), a prepositional phrase (*PrepP*), an infinitive phrase (*INF*), a present participle phrase (*PresP*), a past participle phrase (*PastP*), or an adverbial clause (*C*).

Remember: within a phrase or clause acting as an adverb, there might also be an adverb modifying an adjective or verb form within the phrase or clause. Underline these adverbs a second time.

ADV ADV
"How clever I am!" he crowed rapturously, "oh, the cleverness of me!"

ADV ADV ADV PrepP ADV AN
"You see, children know such a lot now, they soon don't believe in fairies, and every time a child
ADV PrepP ADV ADV ADV ADV
says 'I don't believe in fairies,' there is a fairy somewhere that falls down dead."

Note to Instructor: *Dead* can function as an adverb, as it does in this sentence.

ADV ADV C ADV ADV PrepP
When at last the heavens were steady again, John and Michael found themselves alone in the darkness.

Note to Instructor: *At last* is a compound adverb with a single meaning.

ADV AN ADV
It was the tail of a kite, which Michael had made some days before.

ADV C PrepP
While that smile was on his face no one dared address him; all they could do was to stand
ADV INF
ready to obey.

Note to Instructor: *On his face* is adverbial because it answers the question *where*. If the student is puzzled by *address*, it is an understood infinitive acting as the direct object of the verb *dared*:

S	V	DO
one	dared	(to) address

PresP
ADV AN ADV PrepP
All night they sat above, keeping watch over the home under the ground and awaiting the
PresP ADV ADV ADV ADV
big attack by the pirates which obviously could not be much longer delayed.

Note to Instructor: *Under the ground* is an adjectival prepositional phrase modifying *home*. *By the pirates* is an adjectival prepositional phrase modifying *attack*. *Obviously*, *not*, and *longer* all modify the verb *could be delayed*, so the arrows point to the main action verb (but could also point to the helping verbs).

No watch was kept on the ship, it being Hook's boast that the wind of his name guarded the ship for a mile around.

> **Note to Instructor:** In the phrase *for a mile around, mile* is acting as a noun (object of the preposition), not an adverbial noun; *around* is thus acting as an adjective, not an adverb, because it modifies the noun *mile.*

Left so fearfully alone, any other man would have lain with his eyes shut where he fell: but the gigantic brain of Hook was still working, and under its guidance he crawled on his knees along the deck as far from the sound as he could go.

> **Note to Instructor:** *With his eyes shut* is a phrase, not a clause, because *shut* is a past participle acting as an adjective, not a verb like *fell* in the following clause. *Far* modifies *crawled* because it answers the question *to what extent*; *from the sound* and *as he could go* both tell *how* far.

None too soon, Peter, every inch of him on tiptoe, vanished into the cabin; for more than one pirate was screwing up his courage to look round.

> **Note to Instructor:** *More than* is a single compound adverb.

When Wendy returned diffidently she found Peter sitting on the bed-post crowing gloriously, while Jane in her nighty was flying round the room in solemn ecstasy.

> **Note to Instructor:** The clause *while Jane in her nighty was flying round the room in solemn ecstasy* describes *when* Peter was crowing and sitting, so the arrow can go to either or both of those verb forms.

Review 9G: Comma Use

The following sentences have lost all of their commas. Insert commas directly into the text (no need to use proofreader's marks) wherever needed.

The first four sentences are from *The Structure of Atoms*, by Suzanne Slade.

> **Note to Instructor:** The Oxford comma is used in every text below. Additional explanatory notes, when needed, are found in brackets after each sentence.

Atoms make up every animal, plant, and rock.

Matter is any solid, liquid, or gas that takes up space.

Matter that is made of only one kind of atom is called an element.

This book, the peanut-butter sandwich you ate for lunch, and the helium gas inside a balloon are all matter made from atoms.

> **Note to Instructor:** The three items (*book, sandwich, gas*) are found in phrases, not as single words. The Oxford comma rule still applies.

(The following sentences are from *Discovering Atoms*, by Margaret Christine Campbell and Natalie Goldstein.)

Rather, Empedocles believed that water, air, fire, and earth were the four fundamental "elements," or building blocks, of matter.

> **Note to Instructor:** The introductory word *Rather* should be set off by commas so that it does not appear to be an adjective. Commas surround *or building blocks* because it is an appositive. The comma should go inside the closing quotation marks of *elements*, because it separates the appositive from *elements*, which it renames.

In medieval Europe, alchemists began to gain a bad reputation, often being viewed as counterfeiters, thieves, and cheats.

> **Note to Instructor:** Commas normally set off opening prepositional phrases such as *In medieval Europe* and adjectival past participial phrases such as *often being viewed.*

In 1803, Dalton came up with his own law, the law of multiple proportions, which stated that the same elements can combine in different ways to form different compounds.

> **Note to Instructor:** The adjectival clause beginning with *which stated* . . . is non-restrictive; the rest of the sentence would still make sense without it.

He thought of atoms as solid, indestructible spheres that had no internal structure.

> **Note to Instructor:** *Solid* and *indestructible* can be reversed without changing the sentence, so they need a comma between them. *That had no internal structure* is a restrictive clause, so no comma precedes it.

Thomson had discovered a particle that was smaller than the atom, which was supposedly the smallest indivisible particle that existed.

> **Note to Instructor:** The *which* clause is non-restrictive.

Rutherford called these rays "beta rays," and they had properties remarkably like electrons, which is what they were.

> **Note to Instructor:** The two parts of the sentence joined by *and* are both independent clauses, so a comma should precede the coordinating conjunction. The *which* clause is non-restrictive.

Bohr had created a model of the Rutherford atom that was stable.

> **Note to Instructor:** *That was stable* is a restrictive clause, so no comma precedes it.

Radium emits alpha particles that pierce a sheet of gold foil.

> **Note to Instructor:** *That pierce a sheet of gold foil* is a restrictive clause, so no comma precedes it.

(The following sentences are from *A Tale of Seven Elements*, by Eric Scerri.)

Mendeleev had sketched out a periodic table, which included sixty-three known elements.

> **Note to Instructor:** The *which* clause is non-restrictive.

Mendeleev wrongly placed mercury with copper and silver, misplaced lead with calcium, strontium, and barium, and also misplaced thallium along the alkali metals.

> **Note to Instructor:** The three items in a series are the phrases that accompany each of the verbs: *placed mercury . . .* , *misplaced lead . . .* , and *misplaced thallium*. The first two are thus followed by commas. In addition, commas separate the series of nouns *calcium, strontium, and barium*.

Another discovery by Rutherford consisted of the nuclear model of the atom, a concept that is taken more or less for granted these days.

> **Note to Instructor:** The portion of the sentence beginning *a concept* is an appositive, so it is separated from *the atom* (which it renames) by a comma. Within the appositive, the *that* clause is restrictive, so it isn't preceded by a comma.

In 1913, it was known that there were three main radioactive decay series that began with radium, thorium, and actinium.

Another unusual aspect of the element argon was its complete chemical inertness, which meant that its compounds could not be studied because none existed.

> **Note to Instructor:** The *which* clause is non-restrictive.

In the minerals which contain these elements, a certain amount of weak acid forms.

> **Note to Instructor:** The *which* clause is restrictive.

The next column contains the elements magnesium, calcium, iron, strontium, uranium, and barium.

Seaborg succeeded in synthesizing and identifying the two new elements, which were subsequently named americium and curium.

> **Note to Instructor:** The *which* clause is non-restrictive.

Review 9H: Conjunctions

In the following sentences from Rudyard Kipling's *The Jungle Book*, find and circle every conjunction. Label each as coordinating (*C*), subordinating (*SUB*), coordinating correlative (*CC*), subordinating correlative (*SC*), or quasi-coordinator (*QC*).

The monkeys never fight (unless [SUB]) they are a hundred to one, (and [C]) few in the jungle care for those odds.

Mowgli had never seen an Indian city before, (and [C]) (although [SC]) this was almost a heap of ruins, still it seemed very wonderful and splendid.

(And [C]) (yet [CC]) they never knew what the buildings were made for (nor [CC]) how to use them.

Shere Khan heard the thunder of their hoofs, picked himself up, (and [C]) lumbered down the ravine, looking from side to side for some way of escape, (but [C]) the walls of the ravine were straight, (and [C]) he had to keep on, heavy with his dinner (and [C]) his drink, willing to do anything (rather than [QC]) fight.

Both beasts dropped down with a snort of disgust, for (C) neither (CC) horse nor (CC) mule can bear to listen to an elephant's voice.

The boy could climb almost as well as (QC) he could swim, and (C) swim almost as well as (QC) he could run; so (SUB) Baloo, the Teacher of the Law, taught him the Wood and Water laws: how to tell a rotten branch from a sound one; how to speak politely to the wild bees when he came upon a hive of them fifty feet aboveground; what to say to Mang, the Bat, when he disturbed him in the branches at midday; and (C) how to warn the water-snakes in the pools before he splashed down among them.

Review 9I: Identifying Independent Elements

The following sentences, taken from J. M. Barrie's novel *Peter Pan*, all contain independent elements: absolutes (*ABS*), parenthetical expressions (*PE*), interjections (*INT*), nouns of direct address (*NDA*), appositives (*APP*), and noun clauses in apposition (*NCA*). Locate, underline, and label each one.

Some elements may legitimately be labeled in more than one way. The difference between an absolute and a parenthetical expression is particularly tricky; generally, a parenthetical element can be removed without changing the meaning of the sentence, while an absolute construction cannot. Be ready to explain your answers.

Note to Instructor: This is a challenging exercise, since the student must locate as well as label the elements. If the student struggles, read the underlined elements out loud and then ask him to identify them.

If the student marks an absolute as a parenthetical expression (or vice versa), ask him to read the sentence out loud without the marked phrase or clause to see whether the meaning changes. Accept any reasonable answer.

For reply Peter rose and kicked John out of bed, blankets and all (ABS); one kick (ABS).

That, Peter had told Wendy (PE), was the way to the Neverland; but even birds, carrying maps and consulting them at windy corners, could not have sighted it with these instructions.

Indeed (PE), sometimes when he returned he did not remember them, at least not well.

Note to Instructor: The concluding phrase *at least not well* could possibly be understood as a parenthetical expression. However, since it modifies *remember* and is set off with commas rather than other punctuation, I have interpreted it as adverbial.

One green light squinting over Kidd's Creek, which is near the mouth of the pirate river, marked where the brig, the *Jolly Roger* (APP), lay, low in the water; a rakish-looking craft foul to the hull (NCA), every beam in her detestable, like ground strewn with mangled feathers (ABS).

> **Note to Instructor:** It is also acceptable for the student to identify the entire text following the semicolon as NCA; if she does so, point out that the text *every beam . . . mangled feathers* has no clear grammatical relationship to *craft*. It is also acceptable for the student to simply identify *every beam in her detestable* as ABS; if she chooses this option, point out that *like ground strewn with mangled feathers* is a adverbial prepositional phrase modifying *detestable* and answering the question *how* (and also containing a second adverbial prepositional phrase, *with mangled feathers*, modifying the adjectival past participle *strewn*).

Strange to say (ABS), they all recognized it at once, and until fear fell upon them they hailed it, not as something long dreamt of and seen at last, but as a familiar friend to whom they were returning home for the holidays.

> **Note to Instructor:** *Not as something long dreamt of and seen at last* is an adjectival clause modifying *it*, not an absolute.

Poor kind Tootles (NDA), there is danger in the air for you to-night.

With the exception of Nibs, who has darted away to reconnoiter, they are already in their home under the ground, a very delightful residence of which we shall see a good deal presently (NCA).

They had indeed (PE) discovered the chimney of the home under the ground.

He knocked politely, and now the wood was as still as the children, not a sound to be heard (ABS), except from Tinkerbell, who was watching from a branch and openly sneering.

> **Note to Instructor:** The underlined text could possibly be identified as a noun clause modifying *still* and acting as an adverb, but it is more easily classified as an absolute.

Hurrah (INT), I am in a story, Nibs (NDA).

Adventures, of course (PE), as we shall see (PE), were of daily occurrence; but about this time Peter invented, with Wendy's help, a new game that fascinated him enormously, until he suddenly had no more interest in it, which, as you have been told (PE), was what always happened with his games.

No watch was kept on the ship, it being Hook's boast that the wind of his name guarded the ship for a mile around (ABS).

And then at last they all got into bed for Wendy's story, the story they loved best (NCA), the story Peter hated (NCA).

Review 9J: Words with Multiple Identities

In the following sentences, taken from *The History of Korea* (2nd ed.) by Djun Kil Kim, identify each underlined word as an adverb (*ADV*), adjective (*ADJ*), pronoun (*PRO*), preposition (*PREP*), subordinating conjunction (*SC*), coordinating conjunction (*CC*), or quasi-coordinator (*QC*).

The nascent Tang dynasty was not yet (ADV) prepared to make any (ADJ) conquering moves of expansion.

During his reign (391-413), King Gwanggaeto's conquered territory was the largest yet [ADV] in northeast Asian history.

> **Note to Instructor:** The adverb modifies the predicate adjective *largest.*

Yet [CC] many Americans know very little about [PREP] the histories of nations with which the United States relates.

Korea, smaller than [SC] China, was a perfect size to become thoroughly orthodox and thoroughly committed to Confucian ideals.

> **Note to Instructor:** The conjunction introduces a comparison clause with an understood verb: *than China was*.

Given the two different ways of life that divided Korea for more than [ADV] six decades, some language difference, vocabulary in particular, as well as [QC] some unique regional dialects have been found between the north and south.

True Bone status consisted of the Kim clan whose maternal lines were other than [ADJ] Bak.

Finally, Yeongjo saw no other alternative but [CC] to eliminate his son.

> **Note to Instructor:** *Alternative* and *to eliminate* are the compound direct objects of the verb *saw.*

Silla, though grievously insulted, complied, for [CC] it was waiting for [PREP] the right opportunity to circumvent the Tang's imperial ambition for [PREP] rule of the peninsula.

On April 19, about [ADV] 20,000 students, mostly from universities and high schools, took to the street in Seoul, shouting, "Down with dictatorship!"

Both the "explode" and "implode" predictions of North Korean scenarios remain possible to bring about [ADV] the regime change.

> **Note to Instructor:** *About* modifies the infinitive phrase *to bring*, and *change* is the direct object of the infinitive.

In any [PRO] of the three scenarios, North Korea would change toward the democratic, market-oriented South Korea.

Tang China was distracted by the emerging Tibetan power in the west and therefore could not devote any [ADV] more resources to Silla.

> **Note to Instructor:** The adverb modifies the adjective *more.*

The sons of Yeon Gaesomun, unable to resolve their bickering, fell easily before (PREP) the enemy.

After these unexpected victories, Japan strengthened its diplomacy with the United States and Britain before (SC) it started peace negotiations with Russia.

Among (PREP) the high-tech goods mentioned above (ADV), the mobile phone and semiconductor productions rank top in the world.

In 589, the Sui dynasty finally unified the Chinese continent after (PREP) more than (ADV) three and a half centuries of disunity.

The daughters' descendants were usually not recorded at all, but an exception was made if one of their sons achieved a prominent position in the government; otherwise (CC), the daughters' line ended.

South Korea is globally acknowledged as an advanced country, although some Koreans believe otherwise (ADV).

Others were recruited as (PREP) part of the police or constabulary, and still (ADJ) others became members of political youth groups like the Korean Democratic and Patriotic Youth Union.

The kingdom of Goryeo, however, was still (ADV) plagued by Chinese rebels from the north and Japanese marauders from the south.

Review 9K: Verb Forms Functioning in Other Ways

The following excerpt, from *Disasters and Accidents in Manned Spaceflight*, by David Shayler, describes the explosion of the space shuttle *Challenger* on January 28, 1986.

In the following sentences, present participles, past participles, and infinitives are used as nouns and modifiers. Circle each of these verb forms and label each one as noun (*N*), adjective (*ADJ*), or adverb (*ADV*).

For adjectives and adverbs, draw a line back to the word modified. For nouns, add a label describing the part of the sentence it fulfills: subject (*S*), direct object (*DO*), indirect object (*IO*), predicate nominative (*PN*), or object of the preposition (*OP*).

By now a rapid sequence of events that had begun the moment that Challenger lifted off the ground was unfolding, unseen (ADJ) by the crew and most of the onlookers on the ground.

Long Range Camera 207—one of several located (ADV) around the launch complex—recorded a bright glow on the right-hand side of the external tank, which increased in size and brightness until the whole cloud engulfed *Challenger* and her crew.

Unlike earlier programs such as Mercury and Apollo—which employed escape towers to pull the crew module clear of an exploding launch vehicle—the shuttle did not have such an escape system.

What had started as relaxed expectations for the 25th mission, carrying the first schoolteacher into space, ended with the American space program in disarray and its most appalling disaster played out in full view of the world's media.

TV monitors recorded debris splashing into the sea, preventing search aircraft from entering the area for more than an hour, despite being airborne two minutes after the accident.

The plan was to recover all surface debris before starting the much more difficult underwater search.

Whilst the ocean search was running above and below the surface, the investigation panel set up by the President continued to piece together the events leading up to the tragic accident, as well as putting forward recommendations to begin the long road back to space.

> **Note to Instructor:** *To piece* and *putting* are both adverbs modifying *continued*, but because one is an infinitive and the other is a present participle, they are unequal and linked by a quasi-coordinator (*as well as*).

Review 9L: Diagramming

On your own paper, diagram every word of the following sentences.

> **NOTE:** The next two sentences contain understood elements that have been left out. If you cannot locate them, ask your instructor for help.

Had it been so with Peter at that moment I would admit it.

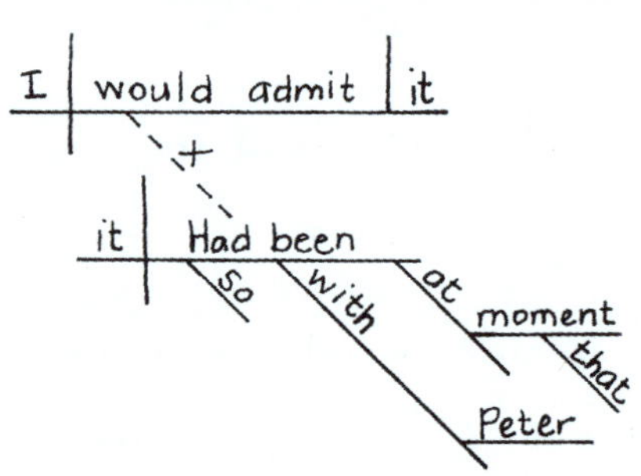

> **Note to Instructor:** This is a conditional sentence with an understood *if* before *had*, so that *Had it been so with Peter at that moment* is actually a subordinate clause. Provide the student with this information if necessary.

A few moments afterwards the other boys saw Hook in the water striking wildly for the ship; no elation on the pestilent face now, only white fear, for the crocodile was in dogged pursuit of him.

—From *Peter Pan*, by J. M. Barrie

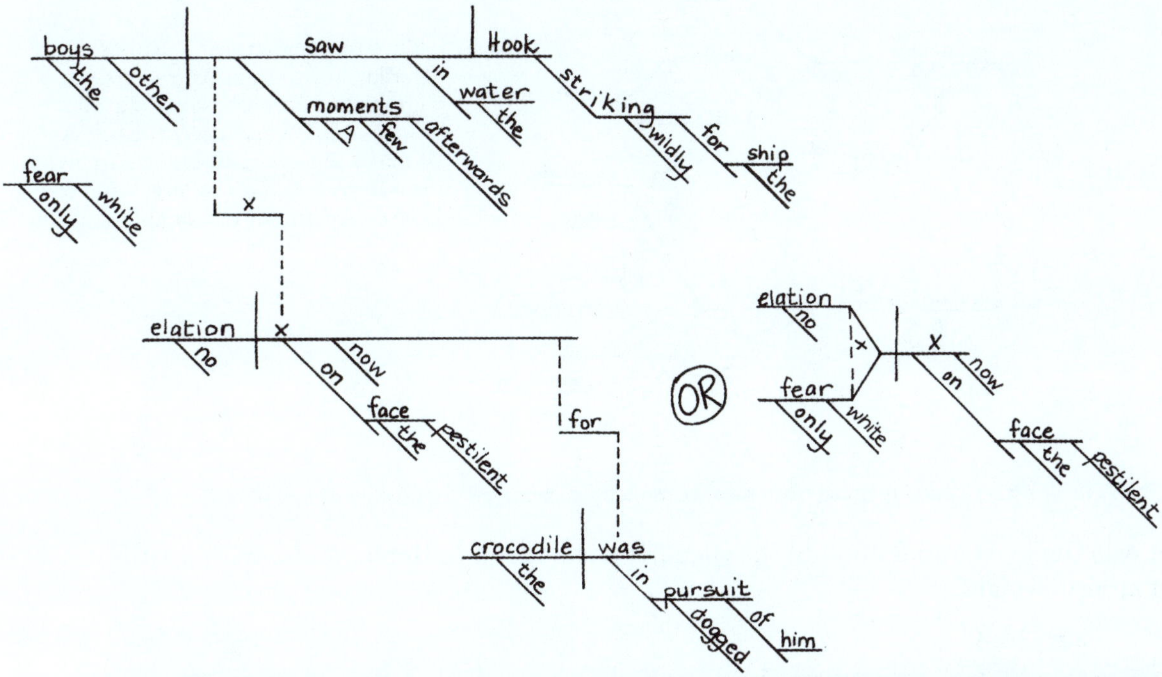

Note to Instructor: *A few moments afterwards* is an adverbial noun phrase. *No elation on the pestilent face now* contains an understood verb and is an implied independent clause. *Only white fear* can be diagrammed as an absolute element (not parenthetical because it is essential to the sentence) *or* as part of a compound subject with an understood coordinating conjunction. Both are illustrated on the diagram above. *In the water* answers the question *where did the boys see Hook?*, but could also be classified as an adjective phrase modifying Hook.

NOTE: The next two sentences contain multiple compound elements.

Painters began to create native pastoral scenes in Korea rather than the commonly copied landscapes of south China, which they had never seen.

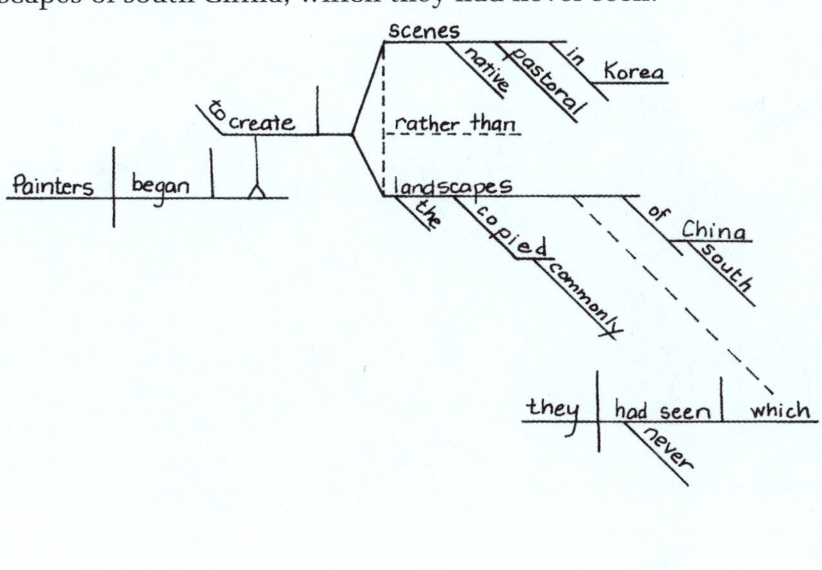

As tax payments, the government now collected rice, bolts of cloth, or currency, and no longer demanded necessary goods—weapons, paper, nails, ceramics, silks, brassware, and coins.

—From *The History of Korea*, 2nd ed., by Djun Kil Kim

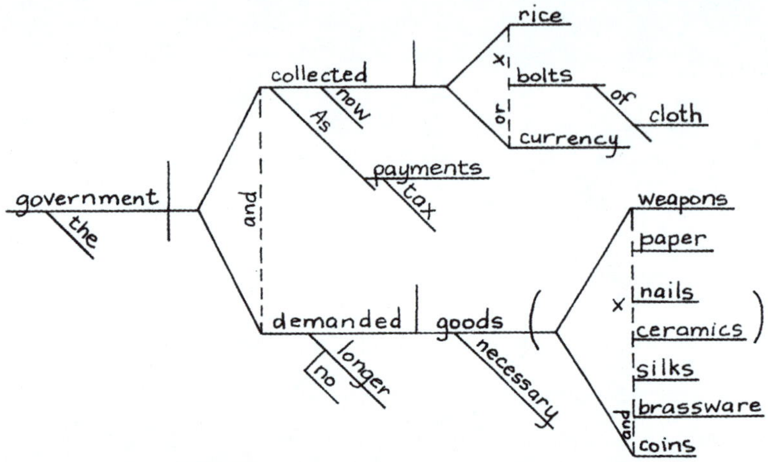

Note to Instructor: The student could choose to put a tree in the appositive parentheses and attach the multiple appositives to that. As long as all seven appositives are in parentheses after the direct object *goods*, accept any reasonable solution.

NOTE: The next two sentences both have complicated elements that follow the verbs.

Actinium was the least understood of the recently discovered radioelements, with a still unknown atomic weight.

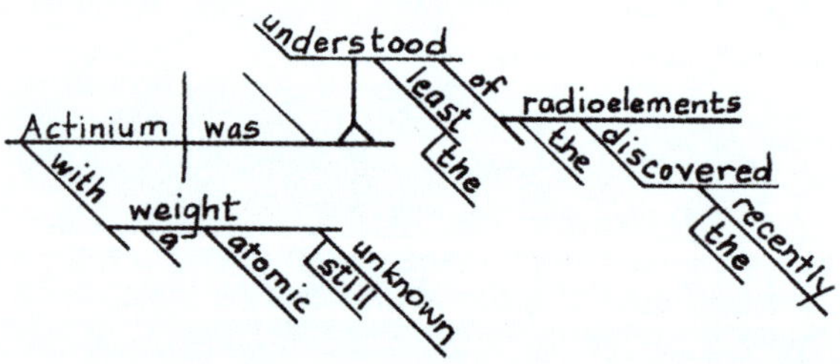

Lavoisier then rediscovered oxygen but went much further than his contemporaries in making this element the centerpiece for a new theory of combustion that overthrew the notion that burning resulted in the evolution of a substance called phlogiston.

—From *A Tale of Seven Elements*, by Eric Scerri

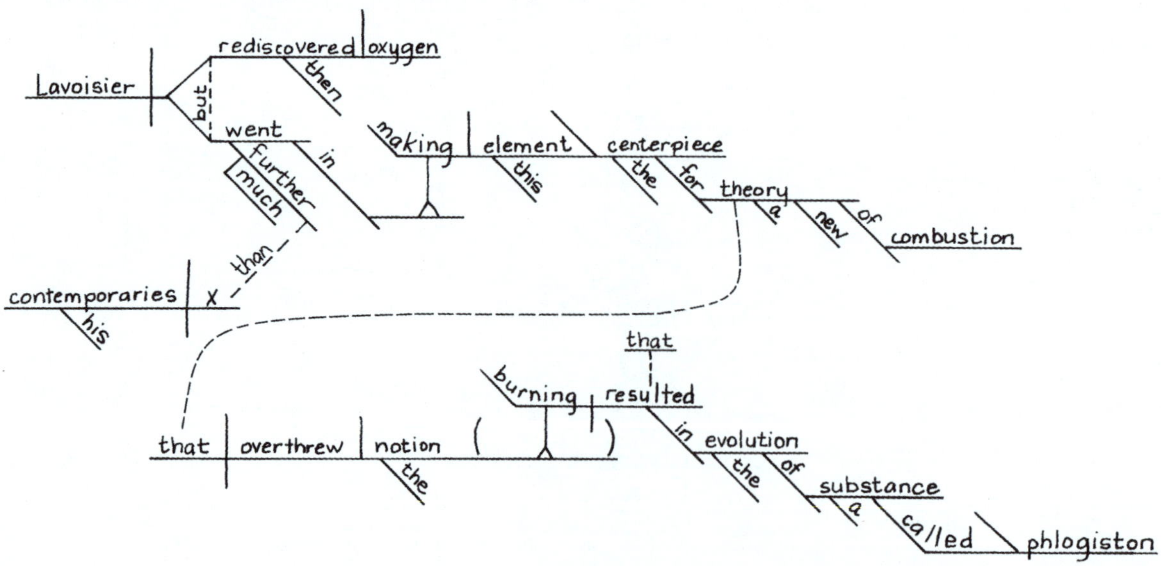

> **NOTE:** The next three sentences all have at least one part of speech that you may have trouble identifying.

We told your friend here that there was nothing to be afraid of, but he knew so much that he thought otherwise.

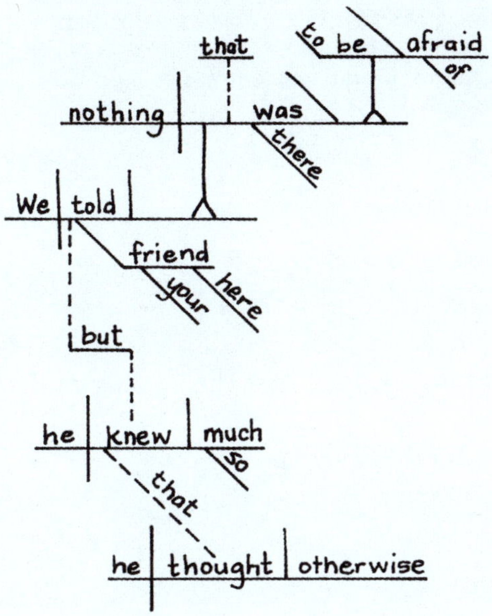

> **Note to Instructor:** *Afraid* is always an adjective so must be diagrammed as an additional predicate adjective—it can't modify *to be*. *Here* is usually an adverb, but when it is used to describe a noun, it functions as an adjective.

This time, if I have any eye-sight, they have pecked down trouble for themselves, for Baloo is no fledgling and Bagheera can, as I know, kill more than goats.

—From *The Jungle Book*, by Rudyard Kipling

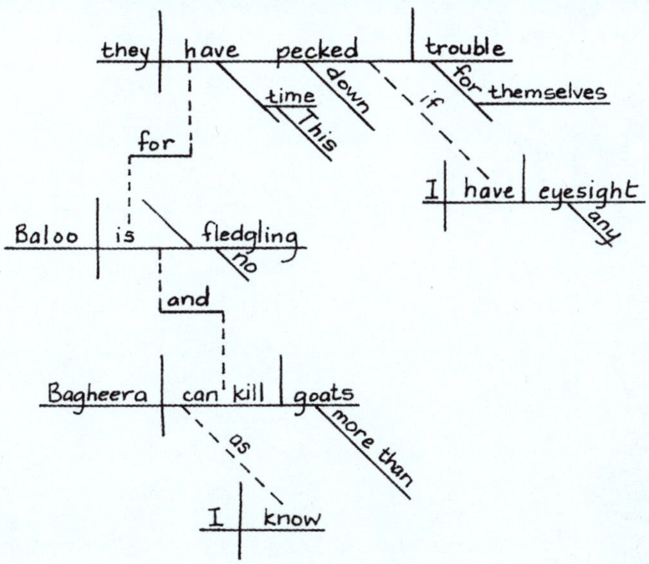

> **Note to Instructor:** *Time* is an adverbial noun. *More than* is a compound adjective. Both subordinate clauses are acting as adverbs.

Partly as a result of the *Challenger* accident, many astronauts decided to leave the agency to pursue new careers.

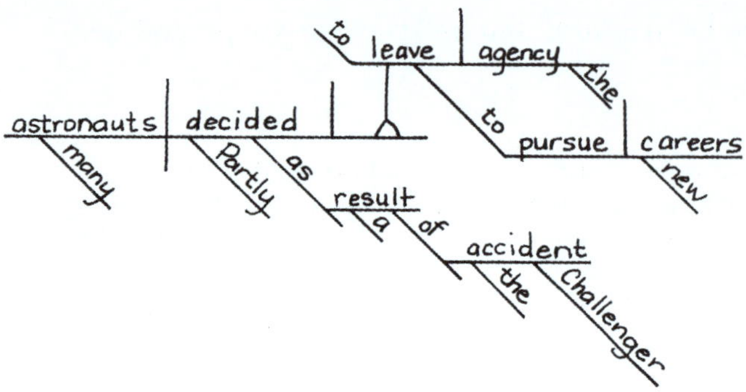

Note to Instructor: In this sentence, *as* is acting as a preposition (the prepositional phrase is adverbial, modifying the verb), and a preposition cannot be modified by another word. *Partly* is an adverb, so cannot modify *result*. It has to modify the verb *decided*.

NOTE: You can figure this last sentence out without a hint!

Some were critical of the agency and the accident, but many just recognised that the agency and the program they had joined would never be the same again.

—From *Disasters and Accidents in Manned Spaceflight*, by David Shayler

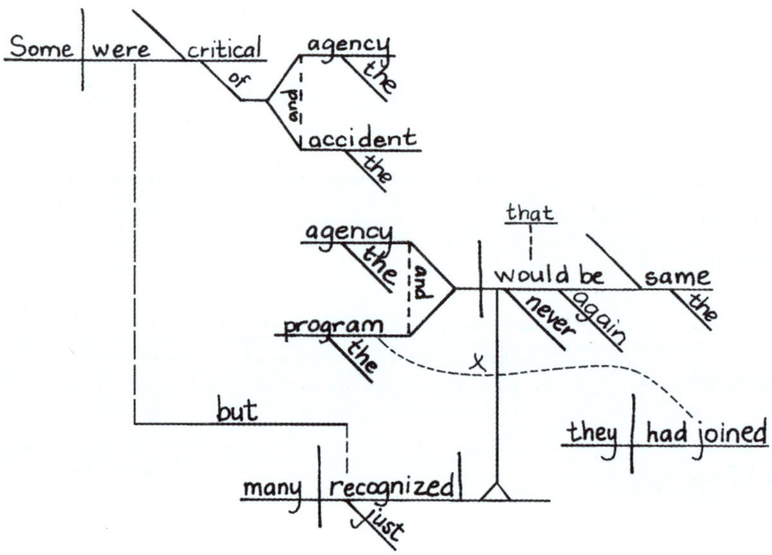

WEEK 29

Still More Verbs

— LESSON 109 —

Hortative Verbs

Subjunctive Verbs

Exercise 109A: Identifying Hortative Verbs

Sacred and religious texts are often exhorting their readers—so they tend to use many hortative verbs! In the following sentences, underline twice every element of each hortative verb (*let* or *may*, any other helping verbs, and the main verb). Above the verb, identify it as state-of-being, active, or passive. If the person or thing being exhorted is present in the sentence, circle the noun or pronoun that identifies him/her/it, and identify it as *S* for subject or *O* for object.

The first is done for you.

Note to Instructor: Modal verbs using *may* and *let* are mixed into the sentences below; the verbs that have not been underlined are not hortative.

state-of-being
O

Let my servants be few and secret: they shall rule the many and the known.

—*The Book of the Law*

state-of-being
S

May it be thy will, O Lord my God and God of my fathers, to suffer me to lie down in peace and to

active O — active O

let me rise up again in peace. Let not my thoughts trouble me.

—The Authorized Daily Prayer Book

active O — O active

Let us fill ourselves with costly wine and ointments: and let no flower of the spring pass by us.

—*Wisdom,* Chapter 2 (The Apocrypha)

active O — active O

Let us live happily then, not hating those who hate us! Among men who hate us let us dwell free from hatred!

—The *Dhammapada*

active O

If a man find no prudent companion who walks with him, is wise, and lives soberly, let him walk alone, like a king who has left his conquered country behind.

—The *Dhammapada*

May the radiance of the three wisdoms increase.
—*Aspirations for Mahamudra*

May ignorance and confusion be completely resolved.
—*Aspirations for Mahamudra*

So may this his pyramid endure, and this his temple likewise, for ever and ever.
—The Pyramid Texts

Without going out of doors one may know the whole world; without looking out of the window, one may see the Way of Heaven.
—The Sayings of Lao-Tzu

O cobbler! mend me this shoe, that I may walk.
—*Liber*

And God said: "Let there be a firmament in the midst of the waters, and let it divide the waters from the waters."
—Genesis 1 (The Bible, King James Version)

So let it come to pass, that the damsel to whom I shall say: Let down thy pitcher, I pray thee, that I may drink; and she shall say: Drink, and I will give thy camels drink also; let the same be she that Thou hast appointed for Thy servant, even for Isaac; and thereby shall I know that Thou hast shown kindness unto my master.
—Genesis 24 (The Bible, King James Version)

And afterward Moses and Aaron went in, and told Pharaoh, Thus saith the Lord God of Israel, Let my people go, that they may hold a feast unto me in the wilderness.
—Exodus 5 (The Bible, King James Version)

Let us therefore, with all haste, put an end to this; and let us fall down before the Lord, and beseech Him with tears, that He would mercifully be reconciled to us, and restore us to our former seemly and holy practice of brotherly love.
—Clement of Rome

In hunger I have come to thee; let me not go unfed. I have come in poverty to the Rich, in misery to the Compassionate; let me not return empty and despised.
—St. Anselm

It casts aside cares, and excludes all thoughts save that of God, that it may seek Him.
—St. Anselm

Exercise 109B: Rewriting Indicative Verbs as Hortative Verbs

Hortative verbs are also common in speeches. In the excerpts from famous speeches below, the statements and commands in bold type originally contained hortative verbs. On your own paper, rewrite each bolded clause so that the main verbs are hortative. Then, compare your answers with the original.

If you need help, ask your instructor.

Note to Instructor: Each excerpt with bolded clauses is followed by the original, hortative version. Accept any reasonable answers, but ask the student to read both her rewritten sentences and the originals out loud, listening carefully to both.

If the student needs help, give her the first three or four words of the original sentence and ask her to continue rewriting from there.

The enterprise itself, then, the opportunity, your property, your dangers, and the glorious spoils of war should animate you far more than my words.

Let the enterprise itself, then, let the opportunity, let your property, your dangers, and the glorious spoils of war, animate you far more than my words.

—Catiline, "To the Conspirators" (c. 70 BC)

Would we be free? If we no longer desire it, **we should perish,** for we have all sworn it. If we wish it, **we will all march to defend our independence.**

Would we be free? If we no longer desire it, let us perish, for we have all sworn it. If we wish it, let all march to defend our independence.

—Georges Jacques Danton, "Let France Be Free" (1793)

Be generous toward the good, compassionate with the unfortunate, inexorable with the evil, just toward every one.

Let us be generous toward the good, compassionate with the unfortunate, inexorable with the evil, just toward every one.

—Robespierre, "The Festival of the Supreme Being" (1794)

We will perish before we break a pledge which has saved the country and the life of her children.

May we perish before we break a pledge which has saved the country and the life of her children.

—Simon Bolivar, "Address at Angostura" (1819)

No matter what happens in the coming days, the French are going to suffer. **They will be worthy of the past of their nation. They will become brothers.**

No matter what happens in the coming days, the French are going to suffer. May they be worthy of the past of their nation. May they become brothers.

—Paul Reynaud, "France Will Live Again" (June 13, 1940)

Exercise 109C: Diagramming

On your own paper, diagram every word of each sentence.

These, my friends, are some of the evils visited upon us by a hateful and contentious spirit, from which may the good Lord deliver us.

—Oliver Wendell Holmes

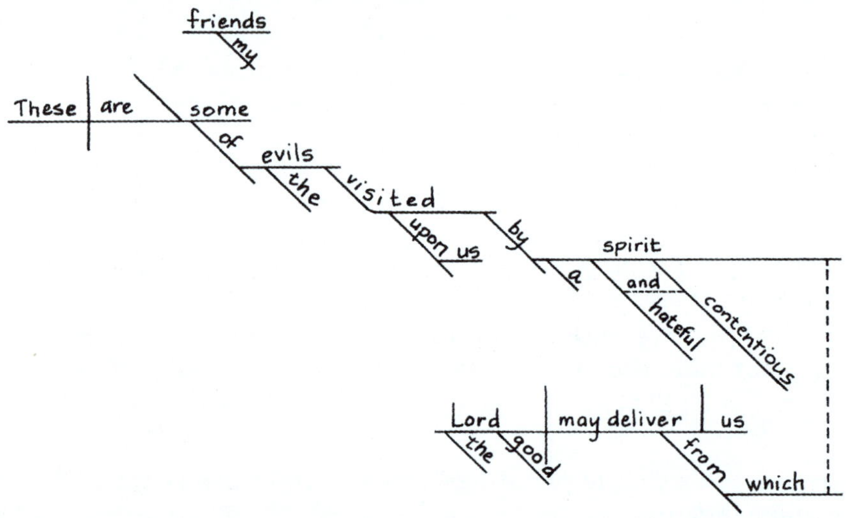

So let us begin anew—remembering on both sides that civility is not a sign of weakness, and sincerity is always subject to proof. Let us never negotiate out of fear, but let us never fear to negotiate.

—John F. Kennedy, Inaugural Address

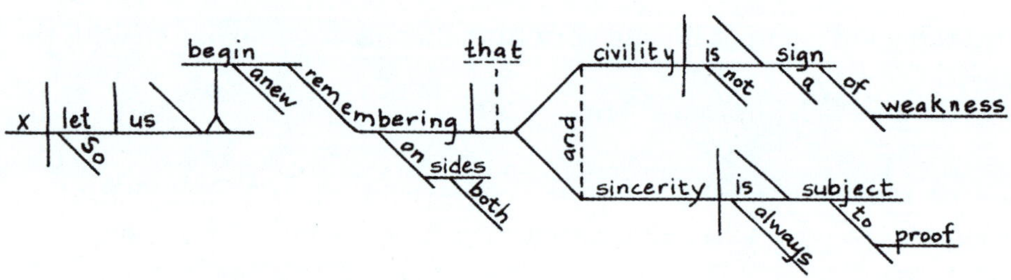

Note to Instructor: *That* introduces both noun clauses acting as a compound direct object.

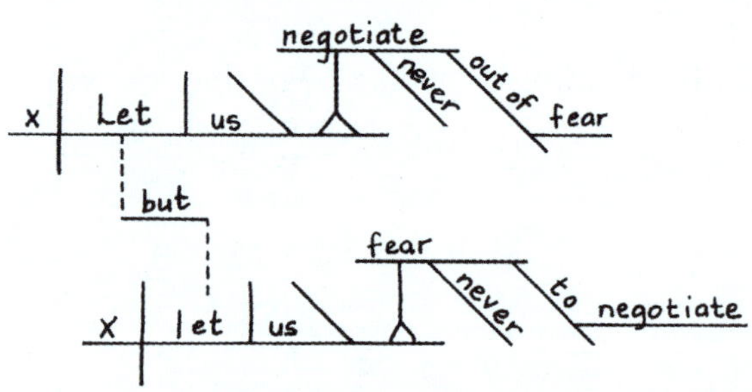

Note to Instructor: *Out of* functions here as a single compound preposition.

— LESSON 110 —

Transitive Verbs
Intransitive Verbs
Sit/Set, Lie/Lay, Rise/Raise
Ambitransitive Verbs

Exercise 110A: Ambitransitive Verbs

Each one of the sentences below (adapted from traditional Eskimo folk tales) contains at least one ambitransitive verb. For each sentence, carry out the following steps:

a) Underline the verbs that are acting as predicates, and label each one as *TR* for transitive or *INTR* for intransitive.

b) Label each transitive verb as *A* for active or *P* for passive.

c) Label the direct object of each active transitive verb as *DO* (*TR*) and the subject of each passive transitive verb as *S* (*TR*).

d) Choose two sentences with active transitive verbs. On your own paper, rewrite them so that the verb becomes passive.

INTR
A lamp burned at one end of the house.

TR A DO (TR)
The man burned the tops of the grass blades down.

TR A DO (TR)
The grass plant changed itself quickly into a small tuber plant.

S (TR) TR P
The mouse was changed at once into a beautiful white owl.

INTR
The white owl changed immediately into a fine young man.

INTR S (TR) TR P
In those days people grew very fast, so that the earth would be peopled.

TR A DO (TR)
The new earth grew grass thickly across her surface.

TR A DO (TR)
I will not eat the meat of a whale!

INTR INTR
You must eat, or you will die.

S (TR) TR P
And then the man was eaten by the young thunderbirds.

TR A DO (TR)
I will cook you a very good supper.

INTR
The grandmother cooked for the guests.

INTR TR A DO (TR)
The bear entered, and frightened her very much.

TR A DO (TR) TR A DO (TR)
I will enter the house; do not shoot me!

TR A DO (TR)
We have followed him a long way.

INTR INTR
Run quickly, and I will follow.

Note to Instructor: The student's two rewritten sentences should resemble two of the following.

The tops of the grass blades were burned down by the man.

The grass plant was changed quickly into a small tuber plant.

Grass was grown thickly by the new earth across her surface.

The meat of a whale will not be eaten by me!

A very good supper will be cooked by me for you.

The bear entered, and she was frightened by the bear very much.

The house will be entered by me; let me not be shot by you!

He has been followed by us a long way.

Exercise 110B: The Prefix *Ambi-*

Using a dictionary or thesaurus, find two more words using the prefix *ambi*, where the prefix carries the meaning of *both*. On your own paper, write the words and their definitions, and then use each correctly in a sentence. If the word is too technical for you to write an original sentence, you may locate a sentence using an Internet search and write it down.

Note to Instructor: These are sample answers; the student's answers may vary. Make sure that the words the student chooses carry the meaning of *both* rather than *around*, another possible meaning of the prefix *ambi-* (so: *ambivalent*, but not *ambiance* or *ambition*).

ambivalent: having mixed feelings or more than one feeling, having trouble choosing between two different options

The six-year-old felt ambivalent about the family's enormous new dog.

ambilateral: affecting both sides

The patient's muscle weakness was ambilateral.

ambipolar: having both positive and negative charge carriers

"Ambipolar diffusion is important in redistributing magnetic flux." (From *Issues in Astronomy and Astrophysics*)

ambisinister: equally clumsy with both hands

The ambisinister cook dropped the tureen of soup, cut both hands with his paring knife, and burned his left elbow while trying to turn on the burner with his right hand.

ambivert: someone who is both introverted and extroverted

Ambiverts make good salespeople because they enjoy talking to customers but don't overwhelm them with too much attention.

Exercise 110C: Diagramming

On your own paper, diagram every word of the following quotations.

When you are finished, label each action verb occupying a predicate space with *T* for transitive or *INT* for intransitive.

Progress is impossible without change, and those who cannot change their minds cannot change anything.

—George Bernard Shaw

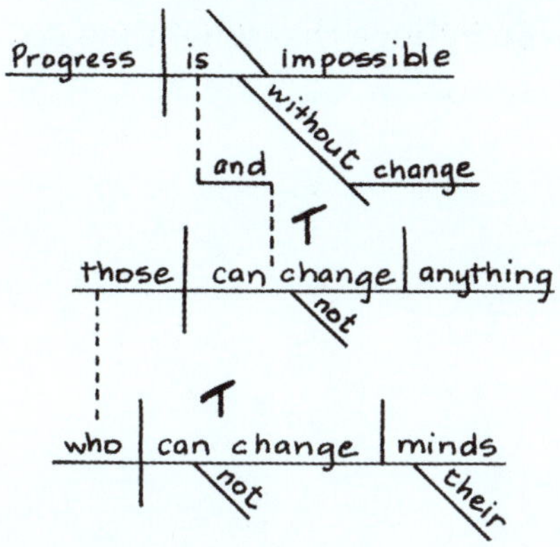

Note to Instructor: *Without change* is an adverb phrase because it answers the adverb question *how*.

Just when I think I have learned the way to live, life changes.

—Hugh Prather

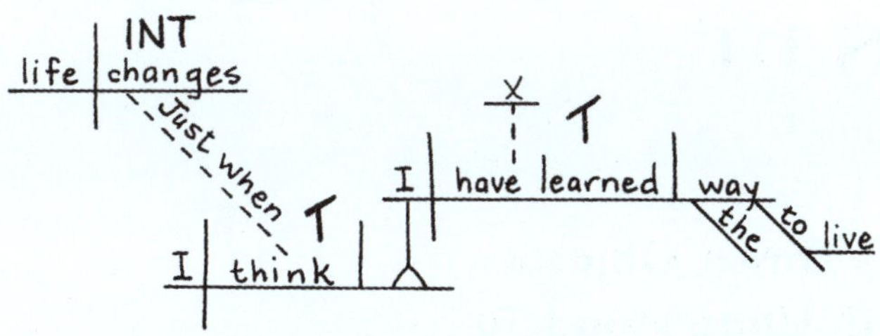

Note to Instructor: *Just when* is functioning as a single relative adverb, linking the introductory subordinate clause to the main clause *life changes*.

Space can bend and twist and stretch, and probably the best way to think about space is to imagine a big piece of rubber that you can twist.

—Alan Guth

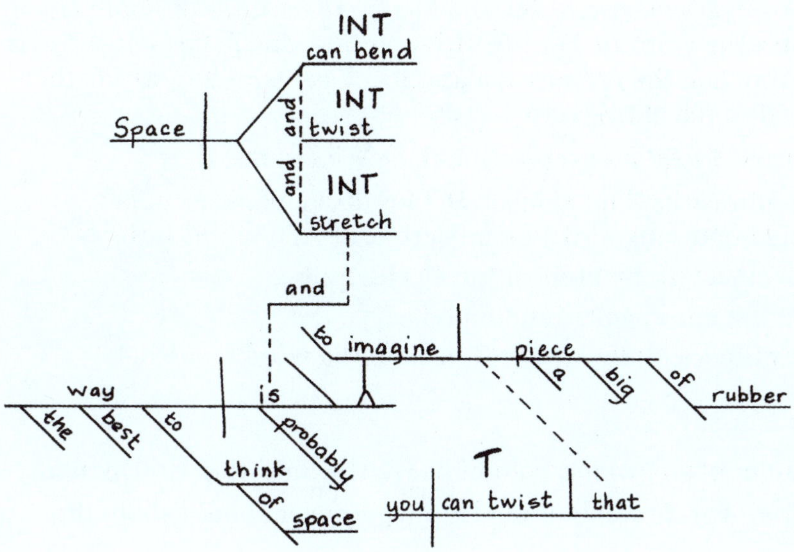

If a man can't manage his own life, he can't manage a business.
— S. Truett Cathy

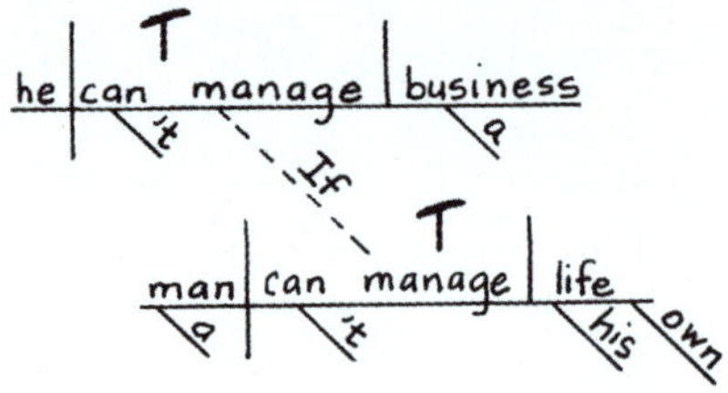

When evil acts in the world it always manages to find instruments who believe that what they do is not evil but honorable.
—Max Lerner

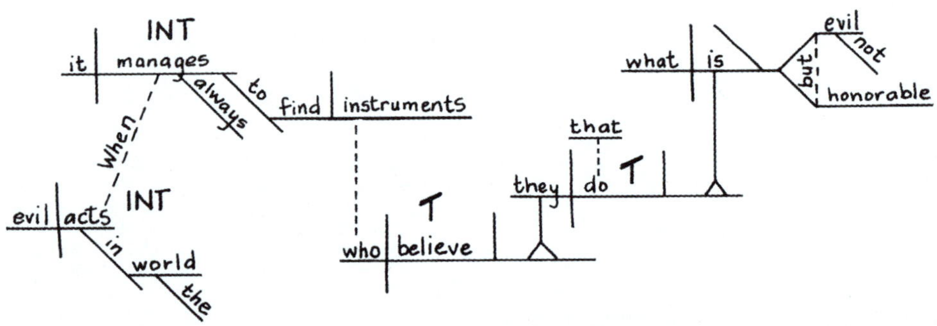

— LESSON 111 —

Ambitransitive Verbs
Gerunds and Infinitives
Infinitive Phrases as Direct Objects
Infinitive Phrases with Understood *To*

Exercise 111A: Infinitives and Other Uses of *To*

In the following sentences from Howard Pyle's classic novel *The Merry Adventures of Robin Hood*, underline every phrase that incorporates the word *to*. For infinitives, underline just the infinitive itself; for prepositional phrases, underline just the preposition and its object (and any words that come between); for verb phrases, underline the entire verb.

- Label each phrase as INF for infinitive, PREP for prepositional, or V for verb.
- For infinitives, further identify the phrase as S for subject, DO for direct object, PA for predicate adjective, PN for predicate nominative, ADJ for adjective, or ADV for adverb.
- For prepositional phrases, label the object of the preposition as OP.
- For verb phrases, parse the verb, giving tense, voice, and mood.
- For infinitive adjective and adverb phrases, draw an arrow back to the word modified.

The first is done for you.

When Robin was a youth of eighteen, stout of sinew and bold of heart, the Sheriff of Nottingham proclaimed a shooting match and offered a prize of a butt of ale to (PREP) whosoever (OP) should shoot the best shaft in Nottinghamshire.

But his heart was bitterly angry, for his blood was hot and youthful and prone to boil [INF ADV].

And so he came to dwell in the greenwood that was to be his home for many a year to come [INF ADJ], never again to see [INF ADJ] the happy days with the lads and lasses of sweet Locksley Town; for he was outlawed, not only because he had killed a man, but also because he had poached upon the King's deer, and two hundred pounds were set upon his head, as a reward for whoever would bring him to [PREP] the court [OP] of the King.

Besides this, they swore never to harm [INF DO] a child nor to wrong [INF DO] a woman, be she maid, wife, or widow; so that, after a while, when the people began to find that no harm was meant to them [PREP OP], but that money or food came in time of want to many a poor family [PREP OP], they came to praise [INF ADV] Robin and his merry men, and to tell [INF ADV] many tales of him and of his doings in Sherwood Forest.

Then when the feast was ready they all sat down, but Robin placed Little John at his right hand, for he was henceforth to be [INF PN] the second in the band.

And now I will tell how the Sheriff of Nottingham three times sought to take [INF DO] Robin Hood, and how he failed each time.

Then he told how none could be found in all Nottingham Town to serve [INF ADV] this warrant, for fear of cracked pates and broken bones, and how that he, the messenger, was now upon his way to [PREP] Lincoln Town [OP] to find [INF ADV] of what mettle the Lincoln men might be.

As the Sheriff looked around ere he ordered his men to string [INF DO] the three youths up to [PREP] the oak tree [OP], his eyes fell upon this strange old man.

Then of a sudden it came to him [PREP OP] like a flash that were he to proclaim [INF ADV] a great shooting match and offer some grand prize, Robin Hood might be over-persuaded by his spirit to come [INF ADV] to the butts [PREP OP]; and it was this thought which caused him to cry [INF DO] "Aha!" and smite his palm upon his thigh.

"I take thy meaning, Robin Hood," said the Queen, "and that thou dost convey reproach to me [PREP OP], as well thou mayst, for I know that I have not done by thee as I ought to have done [V present perfect, active, modal]."

Note to Instructor: If necessary, translate the sentence from archaic English into modern English for the student: "I take your meaning, Robin Hood," said the Queen, "and that you do convey reproach to me, as well you may, for I know that I have not done by you as I ought to have done."

Exercise 111B: Diagramming

On your own paper, diagram every word of the following sentences from *The Merry Adventures of Robin Hood.*

Truly, no one likes to go on this service, for fear of cracked crowns and broken bones.

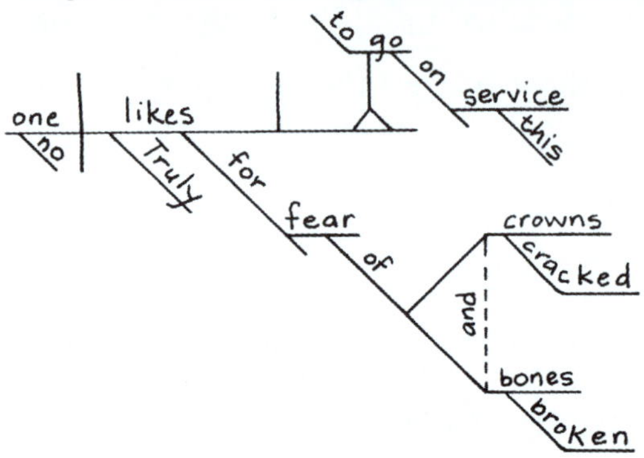

So saying, he went within and whispered to the host to add a measure of Flemish strong waters to the good English ale, which the latter did and brought it to them.

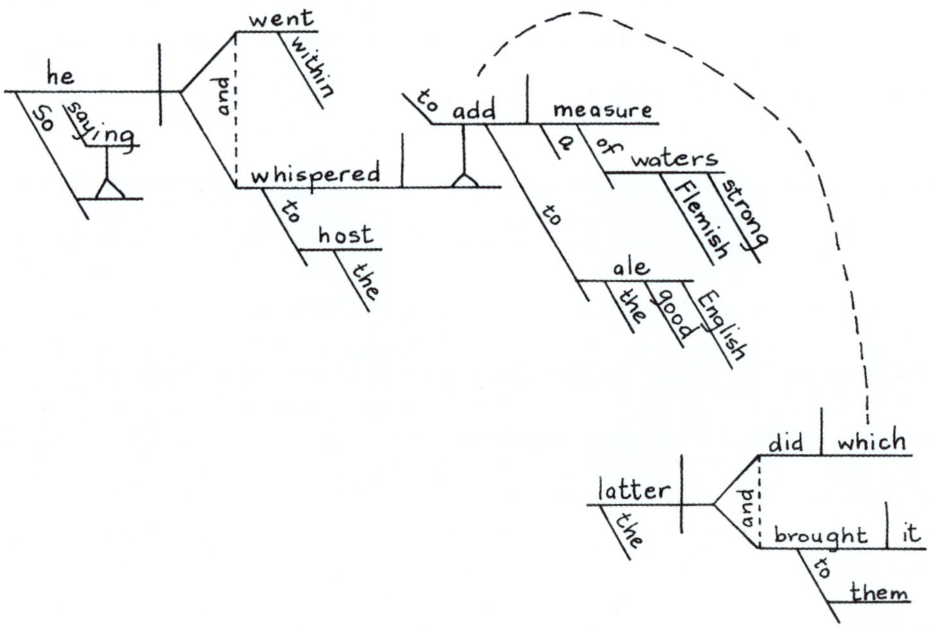

Note to Instructor: In this sentence, *so* is acting as a preposition. The prepositional phrase *So saying*, which describes *he* and answers the question *which one?*, could also be interpreted to be an adverb phrase describing *went* and answering the question *how.*

Then he bade all his servants and retainers to make ready to go to London Town, to see and speak with the King.

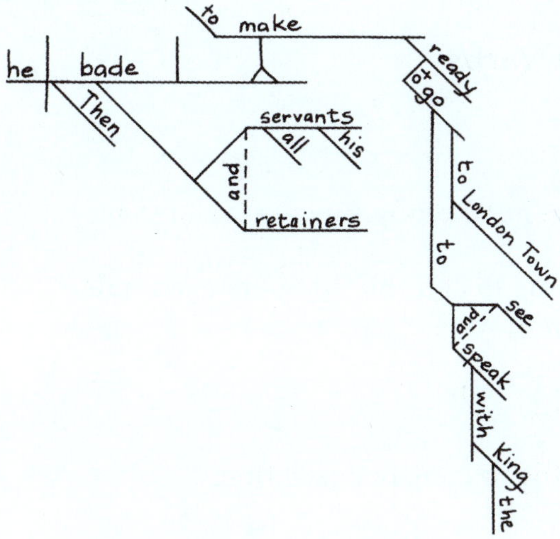

Note to Instructor: This is a tricky sentence—give all necessary help! *To make* is the direct object of the verb *bade* (it is the thing that he ordered them to do), while *servants and retainers* is a compound indirect object. *To go* is an adverbial infinitive phrase modifying the adverb *ready*, while *to see and speak* is a compound infinitive modifying *go* and answering the question *why*.

At last Robin gave the stranger a blow upon the ribs that made his jacket smoke like a damp straw thatch in the sun.

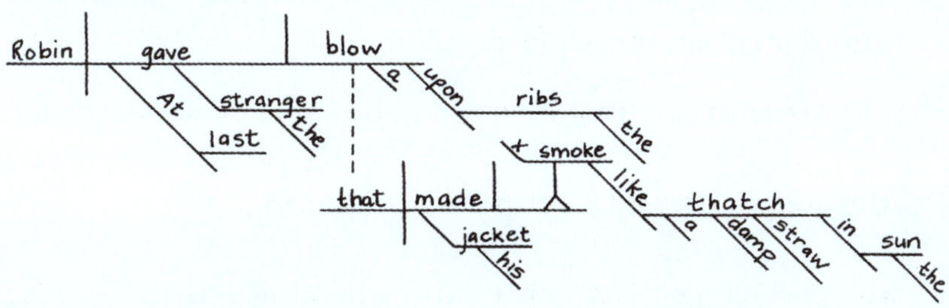

Note to Instructor: In this sentence, *like* functions as a preposition. *Like* can also be an adjective meaning *of the same* ("I remember a like instance"), an adverb meaning *approximately* ("He's more like seventy than sixty"), a conjunction meaning *as if* ("He acted like he was king of the world"), a noun ("I have never seen the like"), and, infamously, an interjection ("She was, like, so cool"). At your discretion, you may share these different meanings with the student or have her look them up.

Then, of a sudden, with a twist and a wrench, the stranger loosed himself, and he of the scar found himself locked in a pair of arms that fairly made his ribs crack.

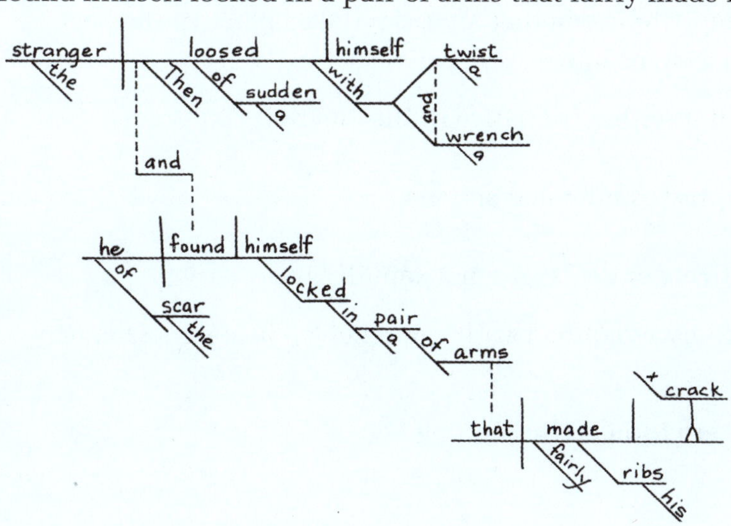

Note to Instructor: It is also acceptable to link *that fairly made his ribs crack* to *pair* rather than *"arms,"* since the antecedent of *that* is unclear.

— LESSON 112 —

Principal Parts

Yet More Troublesome Verbs

Exercise 112A: Verb Definitions

Match the terms on the left with the definitions on the right by drawing lines between them.

hortative	formed by combining *to* and the first-person singular present form of a verb
first principal part	expresses possible actions
transitive verb	describes an ongoing or continuous action
indicative	present participle acting as a noun
gerund	describes an action which has been completed before another action takes place
infinitive	expresses action that is received by some person or thing
present participle	the simple present (first-person singular)
ambitransitive verb	the perfect past verb form, minus helping verbs
simple verb	the same as the simple past verb form
modal	encourages or recommends an action
perfect verb	expresses situations that are unreal, wished for, or uncertain
second principal part	simply tells whether an action takes place in the past, present, or future
progressive verb	can be either transitive or intransitive
intransitive verb	expresses intended actions
subjunctive	affirms or declares what actually is
imperative	expresses action that is not received by any person or thing
third principal part	a verb form ending in *-ing*

Exercise 112B: Using Troublesome Verbs Correctly

In the following sentences from Indian myths, fill in the blanks.

The first blank (above the sentence) should be filled in with the first principal part of the correct verb: *lie* or *lay* in the first set of sentences, *sit* or *set* in the second set, and *rise* or *raise* in the third set of sentences.

You will be able to tell from the context of the sentence whether you should use the transitive verbs *lay, set,* and *raise* (if the verb is passive, or has a direct object), or the intransitive verbs *lie, sit,* and *rise* (if the action of the verb is not passed on to any other word in the sentence).

The second blank (in the sentence itself) should be filled in with the correct form of that verb.

The first sentence in each section is done for you.

The first eight sentences are from *Hindu Tales from the Sanskrit*, by N. D'Anvers and Siddha Mohana Mitra.

simple past active indicative of lie

Then, thinking she had been dreaming, Patala lay down again.

perfect past active indicative of lie

The princess too was tired, because she had lain awake so many nights.

simple past active indicative of lay

Buddhi-Mati led her husband to the garden where she had found the beetle and laid it tenderly on the ground.

simple present active indicative of lie

"Whoever wins the fight will get them all. There they lie on the ground."

infinitive of lay

If he wishes my death, I am ready to lay down my life.

simple past passive indicative of lay

Very happily Buddhi-Mati obeyed, and soon the cotton thread and twine were laid aside.

The piles of seed were gone, and flocks of birds were gathering in the hope of securing
simple past active indicative of lie
some of the seed as it lay in the furrows.

infinitive of lie

The lizard loved to lie and bask in the sunshine, catching the flies on which he lived,
gerund of lie
lying so still that they did not notice him.

The following sentences are from Volume 1 of *The Mahabharata of Krishna-Dwaipayana Vyasa*, trans. by Kisari Mohan Ganguli.

simple past active indicative of rise

And saying this, she quickly rose, with tearful eyes, to go to her father.

perfect present active indicative of rise

The low have risen, and the high have fallen.

simple future active indicative of rise

And the lowest orders of men will rise to the position of the intermediate ones.

simple past active indicative of raise

He raised a great quantity of dust that overspread the firmament.

simple present active indicative of rise

And this will slake their thirst after they rise refreshed from sleep.

simple past active indicative of rise

That wicked youth who had nectar in his tongue and a razor in his heart, rose at length, and in a friendly way.

simple past passive indicative of raise

His tail, covered with long hair and a little bent at the end, was raised like a banner.

perfect past passive indicative of raise

In that lake, a pillar had been raised.

gerund of rise

Both Arjuna and Vasudeva, hastily rising from their seats, stood waiting.

gerund of raise

And the monarch, promptly raising her from the pit, sweetly and courteously returned to his capital.

perfect past active indicative of rise

Kunti, frightened by a tiger, had risen up suddenly, unconscious of the child that lay asleep on her lap.

simple past active indicative of sit

What also did all the kings who sat in that assembly say?

perfect past active indicative of sit

And when all had sat down, Salya spoke.

simple present active modal of set

After carefully deliberating on all things, a person should set before the king those topics that are both profitable and pleasant.

Note to Instructor: The student could choose to use any of the helping verbs associated with modal tenses (*should, would, may, might, must, can, could*).

Those princes, the sons of Draupadi, rivalling their fathers in valour, strength, grace, and prowess,

simple past active indicative of sit

sat upon excellent seats inlaid with gold. And when those mighty heroes

perfect past active indicative of set

wearing shining ornaments and robes had set themselves down, that gorgeous assembly of kings looked beautiful, like the firmament spangled with resplendent stars.

simple past passive indicative of set

Upon that chariot was set a tall standard bearing a lion of golden maces.

simple past active indicative of sit
None of his friends or kinsmen could venture to look at or speak to Arjuna, as he sat there exceedingly afflicted with grief on account of his son, and with face bathed in tears.

progressive present active indicative of sit
Let these rulers of earth that are sitting here say what the answer should be!

simple present active modal of sit — simple present active modal of sit
A learned man should sit either on the king's right or the left; he should not sit

infinitive of sit
behind him for that is the place appointed for armed guards, and to sit before him is always forbidden.

Note to Instructor: The student could choose to use any of the helping verbs associated with modal tenses (*should, would, may, might, must, can, could*).

Exercise 112C: More Irregular Principal Parts

Fill in the chart below with the missing principal parts of each verb. (You may use a dictionary if necessary.) Then, in the sentences below (from *Watership Down*, by Richard Adams), fill in the blanks with the correct verb, in the tense, mood, and voice indicated in brackets at the end of each sentence. Each verb is used one time.

	First Principal Part **Present**	Second Principal Part **Past**	Third Principal Part **Past Participle**
I	fight	fought	fought
	shake	shook	shaken
	weave	wove	woven
	split	split	split
	fly	flew	flown
	draw	drew	drawn
	show	showed	shown
	freeze	froze	frozen
	tear	tore	torn

Then the Black Rabbit told such a tale of fear and darkness as froze the hearts of Rabscuttle and El-Ahrairah where they crouched on the rock, for they knew that every word was true. [simple past, active, indicative]

Dandelion took up his cue with the same plucky readiness that he had shown in the wood. [perfect past, active, indicative]

They noticed for the first time that the grass in front of it was torn and scored with lines. [simple past, passive, indicative]

The does, disturbed from their thoughts, looked at him resentfully and drew back. [simple past, active, indicative]

More than once he had fought alone and imposed his will on crowds of other rabbits. [perfect past, active, indicative]

Fiver looked as though he were about to speak, but then shook his ears and turned to nibbling at a dandelion. [simple past, active, indicative]

But down in the grass itself, between the bushes, in that thick forest trodden by the beetle, the spider, and the hunting shrew, the moving light was like a wind that danced among them to set them scurrying and weaving . [gerund (present participle)]

The bird split the stick three ways in as many seconds and snapped up the few insects inside. [simple past, active, indicative]

"What does that prove?" said Blackberry, his teeth chattering. "He may have flown off the surface or put his great webbed feet down. It's not he that's soaked through and shivering and twice as heavy with wet fur." [perfect present, active, modal]

> **Note to Instructor:** The original sentence uses *may*, but the student may make use of any of the modal helping verbs.

WEEK 30

Still More About Clauses

— LESSON 113 —

Clauses and Phrases

Exercise 113A: Phrases and Clauses

Identify each bolded set of words as *PH* for phrase or *CL* for clause.

Then, identify the part of the sentence (*S, DO, IO, OP, PN, PA, ADV, ADJ*) that each set of words functions as.

- For adjective and adverb phrases and clauses, draw an arrow to the word modified.
- For phrases, further identify the phrase as *PREP, INF* (infinitive), *GER* (gerund), or *PP* (past participle).
- For clauses, underline the subject of the clause once and the predicate twice.

The first is done for you. All of these sentences are taken from *Martin the Warrior*, by Brian Jacques.

PH ADV PREP

The mole gazed at it **for a while** before giving his verdict.

Their foraging had proved extremely fruitful: apples, early wild plums and some green acorns,

CL ADJ

parsley, dandelion, wild oats and a piece of honeycomb, **which Pallum had found floating in a small rivulet of ice-cold mountain water.**

PH ADJ GER

Rising above the mists into the summer day, it towered in solitary splendor, the lower slopes

PH ADV PREP CL ADJ

clad **in verdant pine**, rising to shrub and wild lupin, **which gave way to naked dun-hued rock all the way to its majestic peak**.

CL ADV

Brome sighed and voiced aloud the thought that tormented him constantly, **whenever he looked out over the deep waters of the main**.

PH ADJ PREP CL ADV

A small cloud **of dust** arose **where the otter toiled away**, digging the sandy clayish ground

PH ADV PREP

with both paws.

PH ADV PREP
She had been following his paw tracks **since early noon**; they stood out clearly in the smooth wet sand, marked with a straight furrow **where the sword point trailed at Martin's side.**
CL ADJ

PH DO PREP
She had thought **of giving her eagle call**, but if Martin or Dinjer were in the nest they would be crushed under the gannet, **which would naturally sit on its nest to defend the chicks against anything.**
CL ADJ

> **Note to Instructor:** Although the object of the preposition, *giving*, is a gerund, the phrase itself is a prepositional phrase acting as a direct object.

PH ADV PREP
The lizards stood motionless, tongues in, eyes filmed over **as if completely cowed** by the mad intensity **of the heron's stare.**
PH ADJ PREP

PH ADJ PREP
The marks **of the deep scratches on his cheeks** were still there, and his face was thinner though the resolute jaw was firm and the eyes **that stared back at him** shone with the light of determination.
CL ADJ

CL ADJ
There was a considerable interval **when nobeast was on the walltop**, and she took advantage of this **to sneak up to the fortress.**
PH INF ADV

> **Note to Instructor:** The clause is an adjective clause describing a time and introduced by a relative adverb.

CL ADV
You were coming this way **because a band of ruffians were chasing you.**

PH ADV PREP
Unable to see **because of the bright light burning in their eyes**, the walltop troops were hit hard.

> **Note to Instructor:** *Because* acts here as a compound preposition along with *of* rather than as a subordinating conjunction.

CL ADV
While the wounded were treated by Rose and Brome, food was divided up among the groups of creatures **seated around the low hillock.**
PH ADJ PP

PH ADV INF PH ADJ PREP
They continued **to play the game**, this time **with Clogg's paw straying close to his cutlass**, while Badrang toyed with the bone handle of a long skinning dagger.

> **Note to Instructor:** In the second phrase, *with* is acting as a preposition. *Straying* is a gerund modifying *paw*, not a predicate, so this is not a clause. It modifies *to play*.

Exercise 113B: Diagramming

On your own paper, diagram every word of the following sentences, taken from *Rakkety Tam*, by Brian Jacques.

The volethief munched on his rations whilst he analyzed what he had just witnessed.

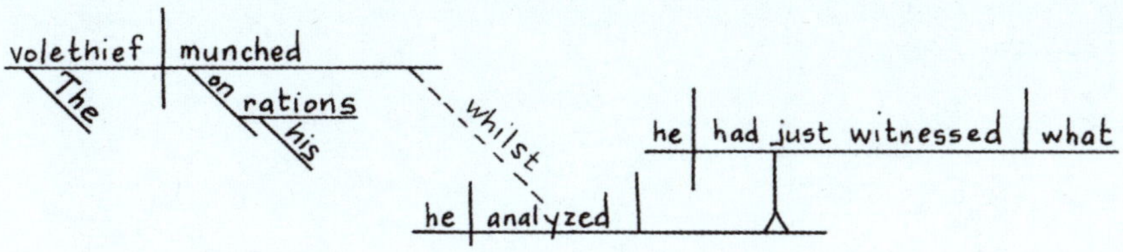

Snow, that silent invader, fell deep and soft upon Redwall Abbey in Mossflower Country.

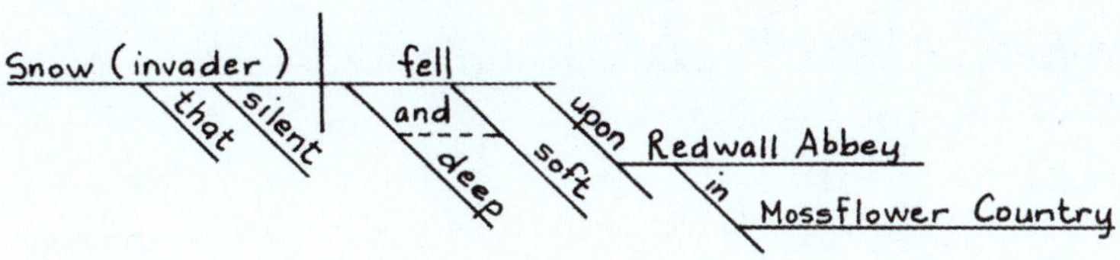

Turning his attention to the trembling king, Tam tried to make sense of all that was going on.

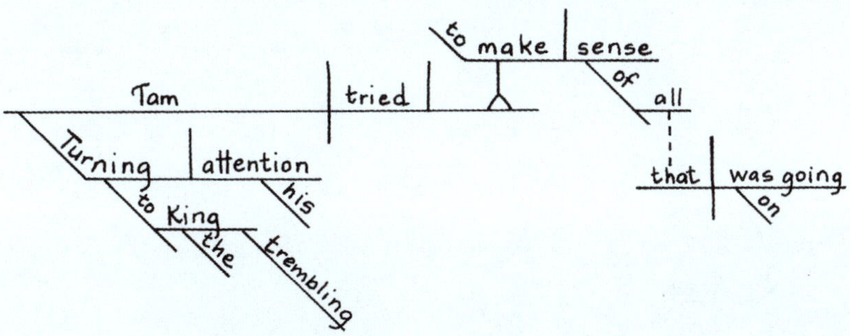

Note to Instructor: The adjectival gerund phrase *Turning his attention to the trembling king* describes *Tam*, but could also be interpreted as an adverbial phrase describing *tried.*

It was some twelve seasons since they had arrived and had enforced their authority over the tree groves.

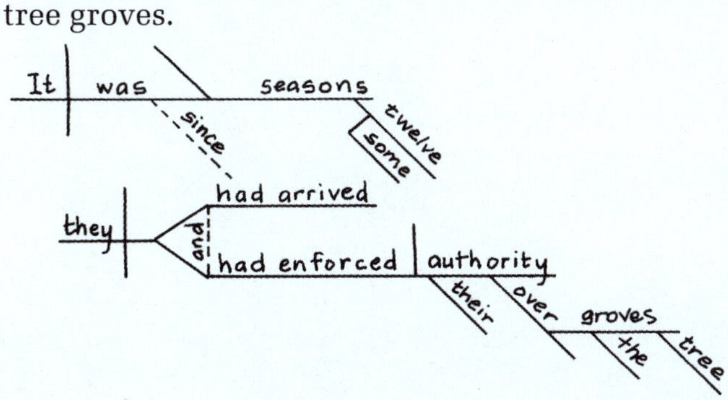

Those two beasts were the only creatures who moved through this territory since the rats have been here.

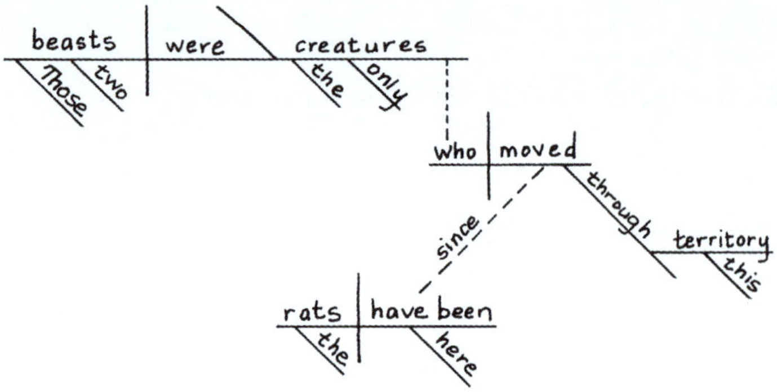

It had been a long time since the traveller's last visit, and the Abbey creatures were anxious to hear the news from places beyond Redwall.

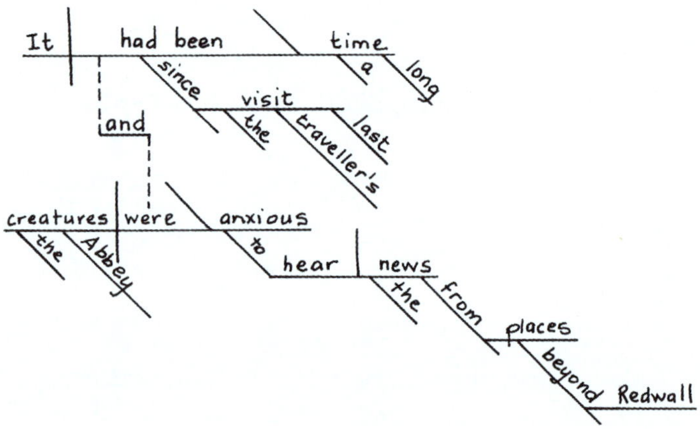

Where the sun falls from the sky, and dances at a pebble's drop, where little leaves slay big leaves, where wood meets earth I stop.

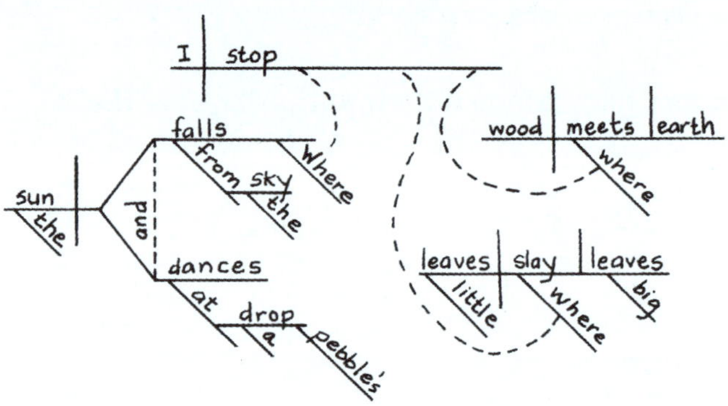

— LESSON 114 —

Restrictive and Non-Restrictive Modifying Clauses
Punctuating Modifying Clauses
Which and *That*

Exercise 114A: Restrictive and Non-Restrictive Adjective Clauses

Find every adjective clause in the following sentences, taken from *A History of Mathematics*, by Florian Cajori, and then follow these steps:

a) Underline each adjective clause.
b) Circle the relative pronoun that introduces each clause.
c) Draw an arrow from the pronoun back to the word modified.
d) Label each clause as *R* for restrictive or *NR* for non-restrictive.
e) Draw an asterisk or star next to each sentence that does *not* follow the *which/that* rule.

In it are also found the theorems that the sum of the three sides of a spherical triangle is less than a great circle, and that the sum of the three angles exceeds two right angles. R R

*The principal defect of Egyptian arithmetic was the lack of a simple, comprehensive symbolism—a defect which not even the Greeks were able to remove. R

During middle life he engaged in commercial pursuits, which took him to Egypt. NR

Later another regular solid was discovered, namely the dodecahedron, which, in absence of a fifth element, was made to represent the universe itself. NR

The fact that trigonometry was cultivated not for its own sake, but to aid astronomical inquiry, explains the rather startling fact that spherical trigonometry came to exist in a developed state earlier than plane trigonometry. R R

The geometry of the circle, which had been entirely neglected by the Pythagoreans, was taken up by the Sophists. NR

*The equations which constitute the foundation of the theory of fluid motion were fully laid down at the time of Lagrange. R

It contains the proposition that the number of primes is greater than any given number. R

*Two questions which have occupied geometers of all periods may be regarded as having originated with them. R

R

Poisson drew from Fresnel's formulæ the seemingly paradoxical deduction that a small circular disc, illuminated by a luminous point, must cast a shadow with a bright spot in the centre.

Exercise 114B: Dependent Clauses Within Dependent Clauses

The following sentences all contain dependent clauses that have other dependent clauses within them.

Underline the entire dependent clause, including additional dependent clauses that act as nouns or modifiers within it. Draw a box around the subject of the main dependent clause, and underline its predicate twice. In the right-hand margin, write the abbreviation for the part of the sentence that the main dependent clause is fulfilling: *N-SUB* for a noun clause acting as subject, *N-PN* for predicate nominative, *N-DO* for direct object, *N-OP* for object of the preposition, and then *ADJ* for adjective and *ADV* for adverb.

Then, circle any additional clauses that fall within the main dependent clause. Label each clause, above the circle, in the same way: N-SUB for a noun clause acting as subject, *N-PN* for predicate nominative, *N- DO* for direct object, *N-OP* for object of the preposition, and then *ADJ* for adjective and *ADV* for adverb. For adjective and adverb clauses, draw a line from the circle back to the word in the main dependent clause modified.

The first sentence is done for you.

The following sentences are from *Philosophy & Fun of Algebra*, by Mary Everest Boole.

It often happens that two or three problems are so entangled up together that it seems impossible to solve any one of them until the others have been solved. ADV

ADV ADV

Note to Instructor: The entire underlined clause describes *happens* (which is an intransitive verb).

That is what will happen to you if you learn your algebra properly when you are no longer tied down to a, b, c, and $\sqrt{-1}$, as the values of x. N-PN

ADV ADV

The next sentences are from *Zero: The Biography of a Dangerous Idea*, by Charles Seife.

Hippasus had revealed a secret that threatened to undermine the entire philosophy that the brotherhood had struggled to build. ADJ

ADJ

The bad news was that the river destroyed many of the boundary markers, erasing all of the landmarks that told farmers which land was theirs to cultivate. N-PN

ADJ N DO

Note to Instructor: The noun clause *which land was theirs to cultivate* is the direct object of the predicate *told* in the clause before. *Farmers* is the indirect object of the verb *told*.

The only real difference was that instead of basing their numbers on 60 as the Babylonians did, the Mayans had a vigesimal, base-20 system that had the remnants of an earlier base-10 system in it.

Pythagoras noticed that plucking the string segments creates two notes that form a perfect fifth, which is said to be the most powerful and evocative musical relationship.

(The following sentences are from *Things to Make and Do in the Fourth Dimension: A Mathematician's Journey Through Narcissistic Numbers, Optimal Dating Algorithms, at Least Two Kinds of Infinity, and More*, by Matt Parker.)

To do that, we'll prove that no sum of consecutive numbers can give a total which is a power of two.

Note to Instructor: Use the notes following each of the following three sentences to prompt the student if necessary.

NOTE: Be careful—the next sentence has a missing word, *and* a clause within a clause within a clause! Ask your instructor if you need help.

You'll notice we're not using the original number as one of its own factors, which means we're adding the so-called "proper factors", i.e., all the factors including 1 but excluding the number itself.

Note to Instructor: The dependent clause *we're not using . . . the number itself* has an understood *that* introducing it. Within the main dependent clause beginning *which means . . .*, the dependent clause beginning *we're adding the so-called . . .* is also missing its introductory *that*. The noun clause beginning *we're adding . . .* is a direct object, not a predicate nominative or adjective, because *means* is a transitive verb, not a linking verb.

NOTE: Don't relax yet—the next sentence has even more clauses within clauses, plus unusual word order. Ask your instructor if you need help.

The factors of 220 are 1, 2, 4, 5, 10, 11, 20, 22, 44, 55, and 110, which may not seem very special—until you realize that, if you add them all together, the total is 284.

NOTE: See if you can figure out what makes this last sentence difficult! You've already met these complications in your other sentences—just not in this particular combination.

Note to Instructor: The entire dependent clause set actually modifies the whole predicate nominative—the 11 numbers following the linking verb are, collectively, the predicate nominative. (That's why the student isn't asked to diagram this sentence!) The entire dependent clause *until you realize . . . total is 284* modifies the verb *may seem* and answers the question *when. That . . . the total is 284* is the direct object of the verb *realize*, and *if you add them all together*, inserted between the subordinating word *that* and the rest of its dependent clause, is an adverbial clause answering the question *how* and modifying *realize*.

Mills' constant is a great reminder that if we want a number with a certain property, we can simply construct it ourselves—which is not to say it isn't a real number.

ADV N-DO ADJ N-DO

Note to Instructor: The entire dependent clause set modifies *reminder* (and answers the question *What kind of reminder?*). This adjectival clause is interrupted by the adverb clause *if we want . . . certain property*, which modifies the verb of the main dependent clause, *can construct*. (*Why? If we want. . . .*)

The adjective clause *which is not . . . real number* describes *it*. Within that adjective clause, there is a third clause with an understood *that*: *[that] it isn't a real number*. This clause serves as the direct object of the infinitive *to say*, which is itself an infinitive acting as a predicate nominative renaming *which*.

Exercise 114C: Diagramming

On your own paper, diagram every word of the following sentences. If you need help, ask your instructor.

Note to Instructor: Use the notes below to provide all necessary help.

In fact, this idea underlies what in mathematics we call the law of the excluded middle—which says that there is no middle ground between true and not true.

—From Amir D. Aczel, *Finding Zero: A Mathematician's Odyssey to Uncover the Origins of Numbers*

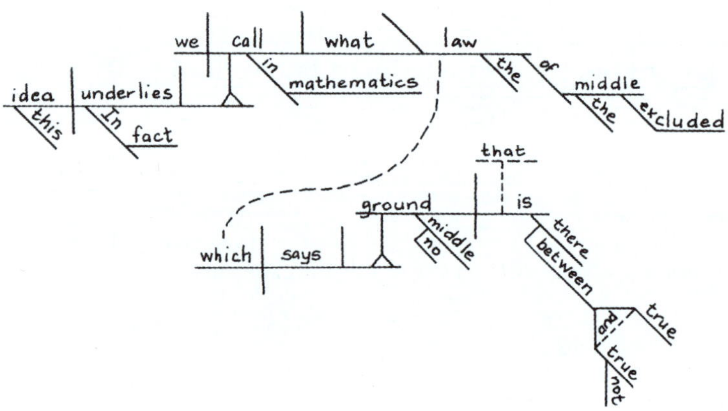

Note to Instructor: *Law* is an object complement; if you need to remind the student about object complements, see Lesson 40). If the student diagrams *between true and not true* as an adverbial prepositional phrase directly between the verb *is*, do not correct her. We have diagrammed it as an adverbial prepositional phrase modifying the adverb *there* because *between true and not true* seems to modify the adverb *there* and answer the question *where* but the ground is also *between true and not true*. This one is a judgment call.

But nowadays everybody knows that zero can't really sit anywhere on the number line, because it has a definite numerical value of its own.

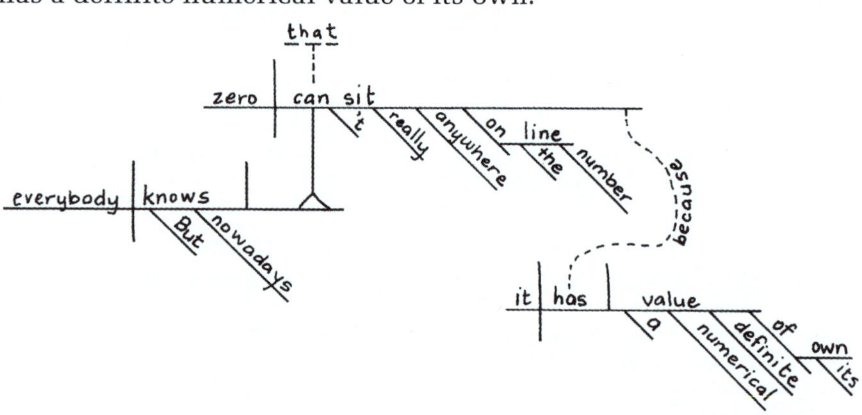

Note to Instructor: The noun clause *that zero . . . of its own*, serving as the direct object of *knows*, contains the adverb clause *because it . . . of its own*.

This violates a basic principle of numbers called the axiom of Archimedes, which says that if you add something to itself enough times, it will exceed any other number in magnitude.

—From Charles Seife, *Zero: The Biography of a Dangerous Idea*

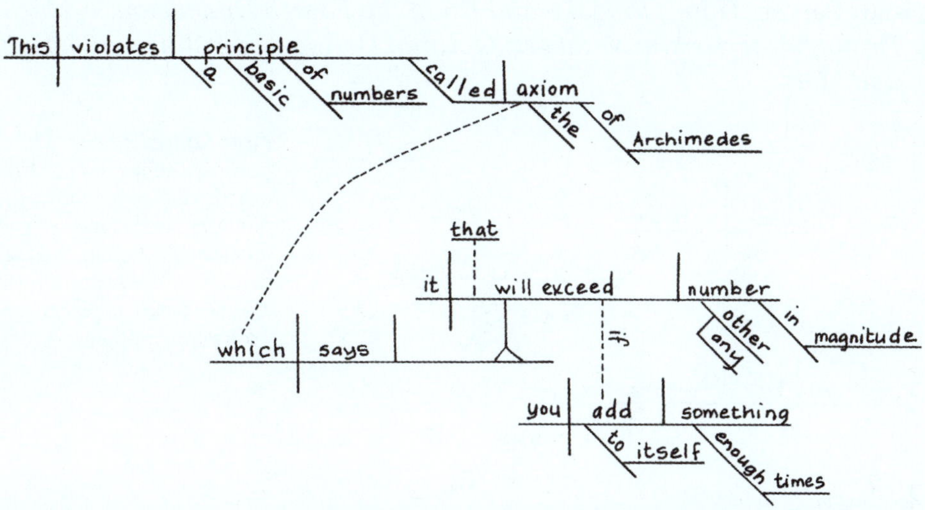

Note to Instructor: I have attached the entire adjective clause *which says that, if . . . in magnitude* to the noun *axiom*, which is the direct object of the past participle *called*. It is perfectly acceptable for the student to attach that clause to *principle*, since it is not completely clear which one of those nouns (which are synonyms) the clause describes. If the student is confused about the phrase *if that*, suggest that she read the sentence out loud but put the dependent clause *if you add something to itself enough times* at the end. This should make clear that the noun clause *that it will exceed any other number in magnitude* is the direct object of the verb *says*, while the clause *if you . . . enough times* is an adverb clause that interrupts the noun clause.

We've already used whole numbers as well as fractions, which are what I call the "well-behaved" numbers.

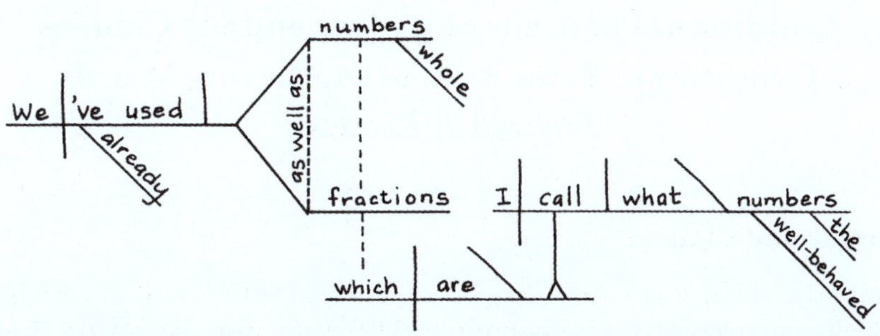

Note to Instructor: *Numbers* and *fractions* are compound direct objects joined by the quasi-coordinator *as well as* (see Lesson 106). The student may attach the adjective clause *which are . . . numbers* to either *numbers* or *fractions*. Since it technically modifies both, a dotted line connects both nouns with the relative pronoun *which*. Show the student this option in the *Answer Key*. The noun clause *what I call the "well-behaved" numbers* is a predicate nominative renaming *which*. The phrase *the "well-behaved numbers"* is an object complement; for review, see Lesson 40.

If you list all the factors of any composite number, they form pairs which multiply to give you back the original number, but square numbers have an extra lonely factor which has to pair with itself.

—From Matt Parker, *Things to Make and Do in the Fourth Dimension: A Mathematician's Journey Through Narcissistic Numbers, Optimal Dating Algorithms, at Least Two Kinds of Infinity, and More*

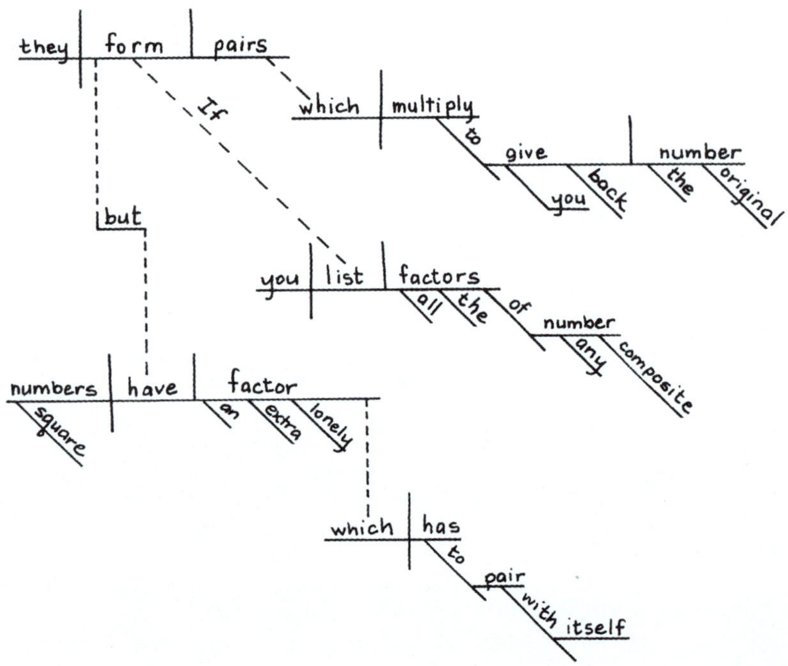

Note to Instructor: This compound-complex sentence contains both adjective (*which multiply . . . original number*) and adverb (*If you list . . . number*) clauses in the first part of the sentence; the second independent clause (*square numbers . . . with itself*) contains an adjective clause.

— LESSON 115 —

Conditional Sentences

Conditional Sentences as Dependent Clauses
Conditional Sentences with Missing Words
Formal *If* Clauses

Exercise 115A: Conditional Clauses

In the following sentences from *Pride and Prejudice and Zombies*, by Jane Austen and Seth Grahame-Smith, circle every conditional sentence. This may mean circling the entire sentence, or circling simply the part of it that makes up the conditional-consequence clause set, or circling the conditional and consequence clauses separately if they are divided by other words.

After you have circled the conditional sentences, underline twice and then parse the predicate in each conditional and consequence clause.

Finally, write a *1, 2,* or *3* in the blank to indicate *first, second, or third* conditional.

The first is done for you.

simple future, state-of-being, indicative — simple present, active, subjunctive

Will you be very angry with me, my dear Lizzy, if I take this opportunity of saying how much I like him? 1

perfect past, active, subjunctive

All Elizabeth's anger against him had been long done away, but had she still felt any, it could hardly have stood its ground against the unaffected cordiality with which he expressed himself on seeing her again. 3

perfect present, active, modal

simple present, state-of-being, subjunctive — simple present, active, indicative

If this be the case, he deserves you. 1

simple present, active, indicative — simple present, state-of-being, subjunctive

I now give it to you, if you are resolved on having him. 1

simple past, active, subjunctive — perfect present, active, modal (both verbs)

Had she her dagger, Elizabeth would have dropped to her knees and administered the seven cuts of dishonor without a moment's hesitation. 2

simple present, active, subjunctive — simple future, active, indicative (both verbs)

"If he does not come to me, then," said she, "I shall give him up for ever, and shall never again divert my eyes from the end of my blade." 2

Note to Instructor: *Does come* is an emphatic form (see Lesson 81), but it is still simple present.

simple present, active, modal — simple present, active, imperative

And, if I may mention so delicate a subject, endeavour to check Miss Bennet's unladylike affinity for guns, and swords, and exercise, and all those silly things best left to men or ladies of low breeding. 1

simple present, active, modal — perfect past, state-of-being, subjunctive

Elizabeth highly approved his forbearance, which was greater than her own, for she confessed that a duel would have almost certainly ensued, had she been in his place. 3

simple present, active, imperative — simple present, active, subjunctive

Prattle on if you must, but leave me to the defense of my estate! 1

simple present, active, subjunctive — simple future, active, indicative

But if I go on, I shall displease you by saying what I think of persons you esteem. 1

simple present, passive, subjunctive — simple present, state-of-being, indicative

If Mr. Darcy is neither by honour nor inclination confined to his cousin, why is not he to make another choice? 1

simple present, active, subjunctive — simple present, active, modal

I should prefer you have speed at your disposal; besides, if it rains, you must stay all night. 1

simple past, active, subjunctive — simple present, active, modal — simple past, state-of-being, subjunctive — simple present, active, modal

If they believed him attached to me, they would not try to part us; if he were so, they would not succeed. 2

simple past, state-of-being, subjunctive — simple present, state-of-being, modal — simple past, state-of-being, subjunctive — simple present, state-of-being, modal

He really believed, that were it not for the inferiority of her connections, he should be in some danger of falling in love, and were it not for his considerable skill in the deadly arts, that he should be in danger of being bested by hers—for never had he seen a lady more gifted in the ways of vanquishing the undead. 2

perfect past, active, subjunctive — perfect past, state-of-being, modal

Had he done his duty in that respect, Lydia need not have been indebted to her uncle for whatever of honour or credit could now be purchased for her. 3

Exercise 115B: Diagramming

On your own paper, diagram every word of the following two sentences from Exercise 115A.

All Elizabeth's anger against him had been long done away, but had she still felt any, it could hardly have stood its ground against the unaffected cordiality with which he expressed himself on seeing her again.

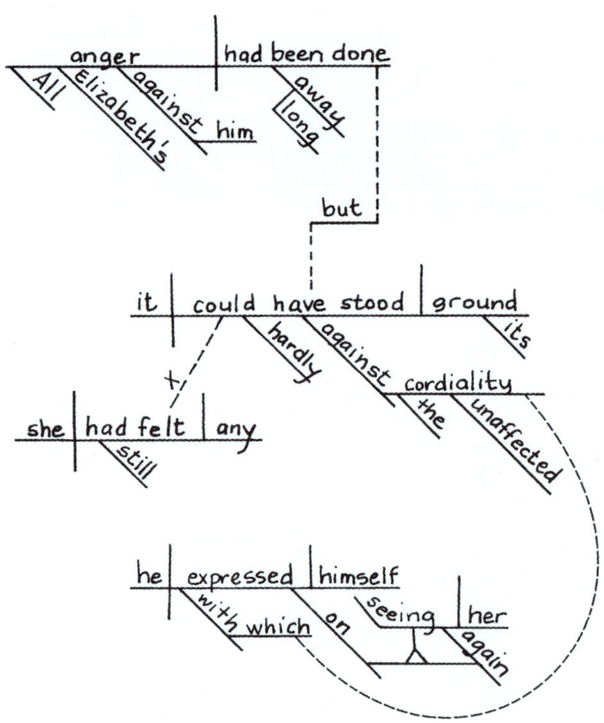

Note to Instructor: The conditional sentence is *[If] she had felt any, it could hardly have stood its ground.* The *X* on the diagram represents the missing *if*.

NOTE: This is a hard one! Use scratch paper, and ask for help if you need it.

He really believed, that were it not for the inferiority of her connections, he should be in some danger of falling in love, and were it not for his considerable skill in the deadly arts, that he should be in danger of being bested by hers—for never had he seen a lady more gifted in ways of vanquishing the undead.

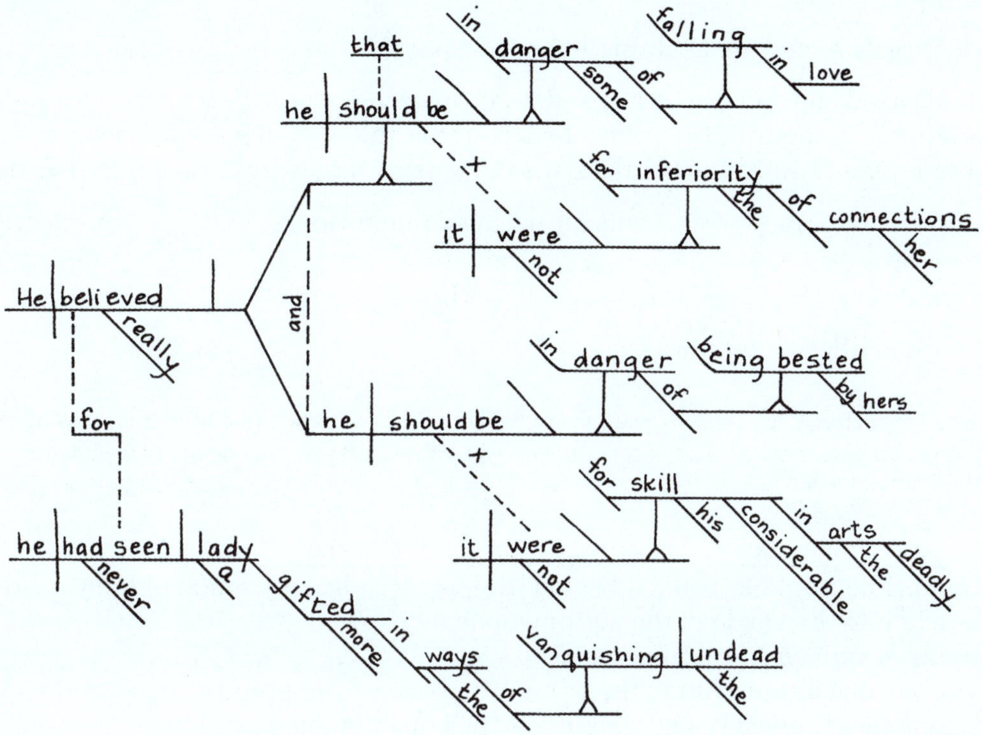

Note to Instructor: Provide all necessary help! This sentence is made up of two independent sentences joined by the coordinating conjunction *for*. The first sentence has *He believed* as subject and predicate. *Believed* has a compound direct object made up of two conditional sentences, each subordinated by *that*. This turns each conditional sentence into a noun clause, acting as direct object, with an understood *if* in the formal conditional clause, and as prepositional phrases following the state-of-being verbs and acting as predicate adjectives and predicate nominatives. The consequence clauses are linked to the condition clauses by the understood *if* and also have prepositional phrases following the state-of-being verbs and acting as predicate adjectives and predicate nominatives.

—LESSON 116—

Words That Can Be Multiple Parts of Speech
Interrogatives
Demonstratives
Relative Adverbs and Subordinating Conjunctions

Exercise 116A: Words Acting as Multiple Parts of Speech

Use these sentences, taken from Zane Grey's classic western novel *Riders of the Purple Sage* (some very slightly adapted), to identify the parts of speech that the bolded words can serve as. The first blank is filled in for you. Fill in the blanks with the correct labels from the following list:

coordinating conjunction	subordinating conjunction	interjection
preposition	adverb	adjective
noun	verb	

The first blank is filled in for you.

Note to Instructor: The parts of speech in the blanks are listed in the same order that they occur in each group of sentences. Explanatory notes are listed in brackets; provide the student with any assistance needed.

But coordinating conjunction preposition adverb

The rider did not bridle him, but walked beside him, leading him by touch of hand, and together they passed slowly into the shade of the cottonwoods.
[connects compound verbs *bridle* and *walked*]
There never was any one but her in my life till now. [object of the preposition is *her*]
I never had but one idea. I never rested. [modifies the adjective *one*]

For preposition coordinating conjunction

A thousand excuses he invented for himself, yet not one made any difference in his act or his self-reproach. [object of the preposition is *himself*]
But death, while it hovered over him, did not descend, for the rider waited for the twitching fingers, the downward flash of hand that did not come. [connects two complex sentences to form a compound-complex sentence]

Yet adverb coordinating conjunction adjective

"The world seems very far away," he muttered, "but it's there—and I'm not yet done with it." [modifies the adjective *done*]
He smiled a flinty smile that was more than inhuman, yet seemed to give out of its dark aloofness a gleam of righteousness. [connects the compound predicate adjective phrases *more than inhuman* and *seemed to give out . . .*]
But that's a good many miles yet. [modifies the noun "miles"]

Before preposition adverb subordinating conjunction

Her clear sight intensified the purple sage-slope as it rolled before her.
[object of the preposition is *her*]
Once, long before, on the night Venters had carried Bess through the canyon and up into Surprise Valley, he had experienced the strangeness of faculties singularly, tinglingly acute.
I lost all before I knew it. [subordinates the adverb clause *before I knew it*]

Out adverb adjective interjection

A sharp clip-crop of iron-shod hoofs deadened and died away, and clouds of yellow dust drifted from under the cottonwoods out over the sage. [modifies the verb *drifted*]

I reckon, Jane, that marriage between us is out of all human reason. [modifies the noun *marriage*]

Out! Out! Leave Utah and leave me in peace!

Around preposition noun adverb

But I feel something dark and terrible closing in around me. [object of the preposition is *me*]

When the two men entered the immense barnyard, from all around the din increased. [noun serving as the object of the preposition "from," modified by the adjective *all*]

I've seen them drunk with joy and dance and fling themselves around. [modifies the verb *fling*]

Below adjective preposition noun adverb

Venters had a moment's notice of the rock, which was of the same smoothness and hardness as the slope below, before his gaze went irresistibly upward to the precipitous walls of this wide ladder of granite. [modifies the noun *slope*]

Next on the slope, just below the third and largest lake, were corrals and a wide stone barn and open sheds and coops and pens. [object of the preposition is *lake*]

He knew that behind the corner of stone would be a cave or a crack which could never be suspected from below. [serves as the object of the preposition "from"]

The dog growled below and rushed into the forest. [modifies the verb *growled*]

Except preposition subordinating conjunction

I've no more to lose—except my life. [object of the preposition is *life*]

Swiftly, resolutely he put out of mind all of her life except what had been spent with him. [subordinates the adverb clause *what had been spent with him*]

Up adjective verb adverb preposition

On the morrow he was up bright and early, glad that he had a surprise for Bess. [predicate adjective modifying the pronoun *he*]

Once again he upped his bet. [action verb for raising a bet in poker]

Low swells of prairie-like ground sloped up to the west. [modifies the verb *sloped*]

A group of riders cantered up the lane, dismounted, and threw their bridles. [object of the preposition is *lane*]

Since adverb preposition subordinating conjunction

It was he of whom Judkins had long since spoken. [modifes the verb *had spoken*]

Bess, I haven't seen that since last summer. [object of the preposition is *summer*]

How many years had passed since the cliff-dwellers gazed out across the beautiful valley as he was gazing now? [subordinates the adverb clause *the cliff-dwellers gazed out across the beautiful valley*]

Exercise 116B: Words Introducing Clauses

In the following sentences, taken from Zane Grey's classic Western novel *The Lone Star Ranger* (some slightly condensed), underline every subordinate clause. Then, carry out the following steps:

a) Circle the introductory word of the clause.
(**NOTE**: When the introductory word is the object of a preposition, circle the word itself, not the preposition that precedes it. See the sample sentence.)

b) Label the clause as *N* (for noun), *ADJ* (for adjective), or *ADV* (for adverb).

c) For noun clauses, further identify them *S* (as subject) or *OBJ* (as object).

d) For adjective or adverb clauses, draw an arrow back to the word modified.

e) Finally, label the introductory word as one of the following: *RP* for relative pronoun, *RAdj* for relative adjective (a relative pronoun functioning as an adjective and introducing an adjective clause), *RAdv* for relative adverb, *SC* for subordinating conjunction, or *A-SC* for adverb functioning as a subordinating conjunction.

Note to Instructor: Explanatory notes follow each sentence, when necessary. Use them to prompt the student as needed.

And these images naturally are of the men with whom I have dealt.

When he had looked after the needs of his horse he returned to the group before the inn.

Note to Instructor: Because *when* simply answers the question *when*, rather than referring to a noun or pronoun in the main clause following, it is an adverb acting as a subordinating conjunction rather than a relative adverb.

These riders, whoever they were, had approached too closely.

Note to Instructor: *Whoever* is a compound form of the relative pronoun *who*.

The reward was offered by the woman's husband, whose name appeared at the bottom of the placard.

Note to Instructor: *Whose* refers back to *husband* but modifies *name*, so it introduces the adjective clause but does not stand alone as a pronoun.

Without the horse he made better time and climbed through deep clefts, wide canyons, over ridges, up shelving slopes, along precipices—a long, hard climb—till he reached a divide.

Note to Instructor: *Till* is a shortened form of *until*, which always appears with a subject and predicate following it, never alone as an adverb.

Who heads the gang, anyway?

Note to Instructor: This is a trick sentence—*who* is the subject of the sentence and there are no dependent clauses.

About three in the afternoon he came to a little river which marked the boundary line of his hunting territory.

The bottom-lands through which the river wound to the southwest were more inviting.

He looked among his effects for a hobble, and, finding that his uncle had failed to put one in, he suddenly remembered that he seldom used a hobble, and never on this horse.

Note to Instructor: Since *that* serves no grammatical function in either clause, it is a subordinating conjunction, not a pronoun.

He's the only person in this awful place who's been good to me.

Hardly once since Jennie had entered into his thought had those ghosts returned to torment him.

Note to Instructor: The student may be unsure whether the adverb clause modifies *once* or *had returned*. Since the clause seems to tell more about the timing of the thoughts returning, rather than their actual return, *once* makes more sense. However, if the student makes an argument for the clause modifying the verb, accept it.

There were four other men whom Duane knew by sight, several whose faces were familiar, and half a dozen strangers, all dusty horsemen.

Darkness had about set in when he reached his destination.

Note to Instructor: This adverb clause answers the question *when* and modifies the verb.

Those who were his real friends on the border would have been the last to make inquiries.

Note to Instructor: *Those* is sometimes a relative pronoun/adjective, but in this sentence, it is a pronoun acting as the subject of the main clause (subject: *those*; predicate, *would have been*) and is modified by an adjective clause.

There were more coming round the cut where the road curved.

Note to Instructor: The clause is adjectival because it modifies a place (*cut*).

He had gathered from the words of one of his pursuers that the brake was a kind of trap.

The way out of it was along the bank where he had entered, and where obviously all night long his pursuers had kept fires burning.

Note to Instructor: The clauses are adjectival because it modifies a place (*bank*).

After supper the guests assembled in a big sitting-room where an open fire place with blazing mesquite sticks gave out warmth and cheery glow.

> **Note to Instructor:** The clause is adjectival because it modifies a place (*sitting-room*).

He followed it until a late hour, when he picketed his horse and lay down to rest.

> **Note to Instructor:** The clause is adjectival because it modifies a time (*hour*).

It can't be done unless you want to sacrifice everything.

Wellston was a small town, but important in that unsettled part of the great state because it was the trading-center of several hundred miles of territory.

> **Note to Instructor:** The clause could also modify the adjective *important*.

Exercise 116C: Diagramming

(You didn't think you'd escape diagramming, did you?)

On your own paper, diagram every word of the following sentences from Zane Grey's classic Western novel *The Rainbow Trail.*

If you need help, ask your instructor.

> **Note to Instructor:** Use the notes following to give all possible help to the student.

By and by they had a little girl whom they named Jane.

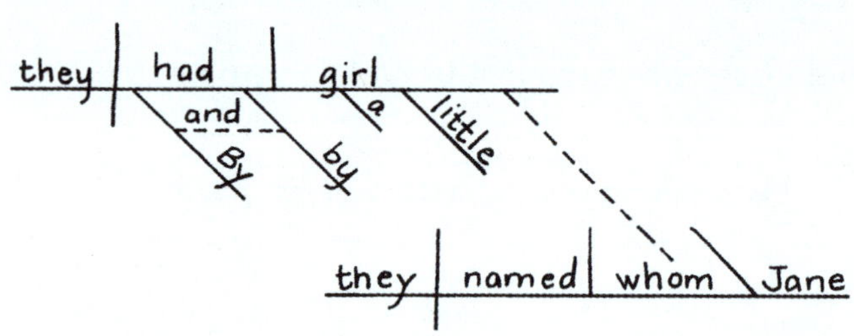

> **Note to Instructor:** *Jane* is an object complement; see Lesson 49. *By and by* is a compound adverb connected by the coordinating conjunction *and*. The adjective clause *whom they named Jane* is connected to the noun *girl* by the relative pronoun *whom*, which serves as the direct object within the subordinate clause.

We raised corn and fruit, and stored what we didn't use.

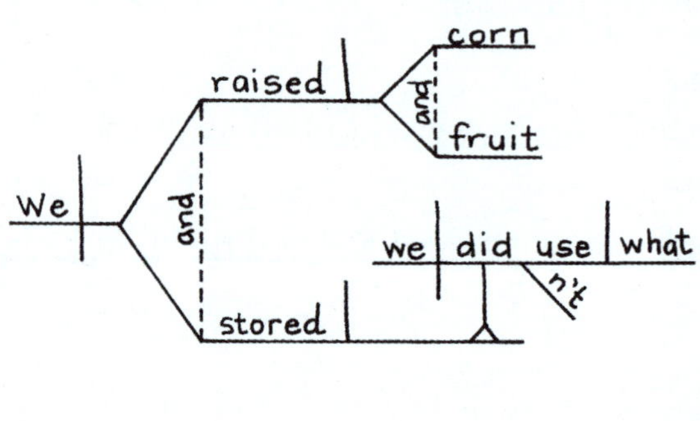

> **Note to Instructor:** The noun clause *what we didn't use* is the direct object of the verb *stored*, and the relative pronoun *what* has an unexpressed antecedent.

When he assured her he was unhurt she said he had agreed to go where she went.

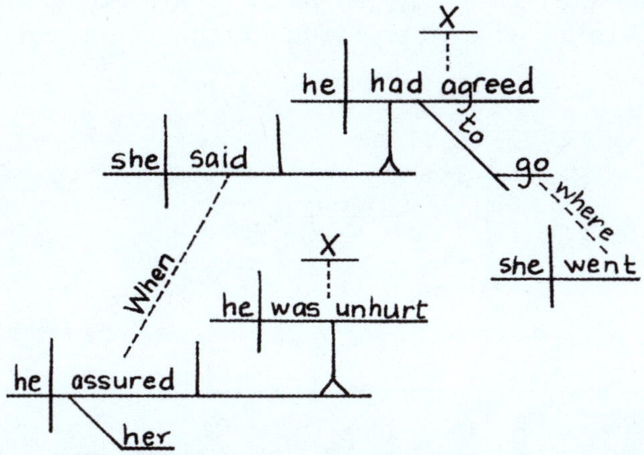

Note to Instructor: The main clause of the sentence is *she said*, followed by the direct object noun clause (with understood subordinating conjunction *that*) *[that] he had agreed to go where she went.* Within that noun clause, *to go* is an adverbial infinitive modifying *had agreed.* (To what extent had he agreed?) *Where she went* is an adverb clause modifying the infinitive. *Where* is an adverb acting as a subordinating conjunction.

When he assured her he was unhurt is an adverb clause answering the question *when*, modifying *said*, and connected to the verb by the adverb *when* (acting as a subordinating conjunction). The clause *[that] he was unhurt*, with the understood subordinating word *that*, is the direct object: it is the thing that *he* assured, with *her* serving as the indirect object.

In the gray of dawn, when the hush of the desert night still lay deep over the land, the Navajo stirred in his blanket and began to chant to the morning light.

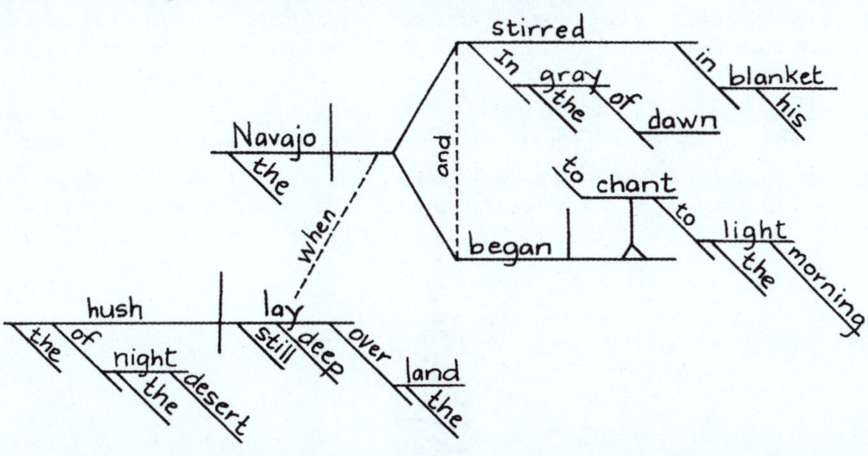

Note to Instructor: *When* is an adverb acting as a subordinating conjunction for the adverb clause *when the hush . . . the land.* Since the Navajo both stirs and begins *when the hush lay*, the dotted line connecting the adverb clause is drawn from the line *after* the subject-predicate divider but before the predicate branches into the compound verb. If the student inserts the dotted line from one verb or the other, this is not incorrect, but show him the diagram above and point out that the line placement allows the adverb clause to modify both verbs, not just one.

He had not often walked with her beyond the dark shade of the pinyons round the cottage, but this night, when he knew he must tell her, he led her away down the path, through the cedar grove to the west end of the valley where it was wild and lonely and sad and silent.

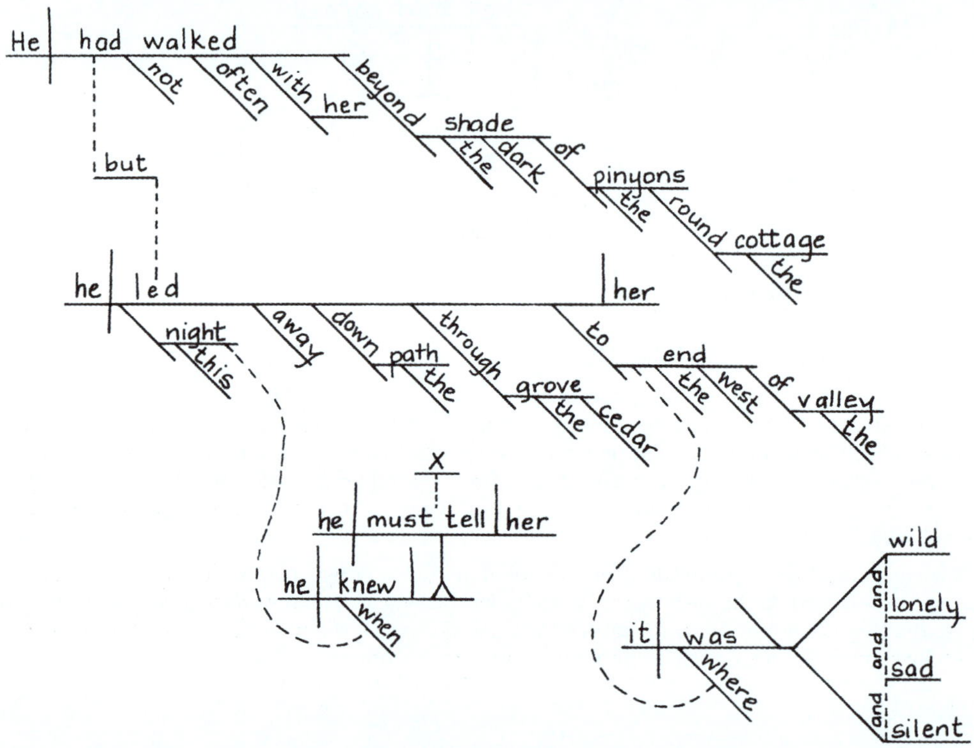

Note to Instructor: The first main clause is *He had not often walked with her beyond the dark shade of the pinyons round the cottage*. This is connected to the second main clause *he led her away down the path, through the cedar grove to the west end of the valley* (forming a compound sentence) with the coordinating conjunction *but*.

The adverb clause *when he knew he must tell her* is connected to *night* by the relative adverb *when*. (What night? The night when . . .) The relative adverb clause refers back to a time (*night*).

The adverb clause *where it was wild and lonely and sad and silent* is connected to *end* by the relative adverb *where*. This is an adverb clause because it describes a place (*the end of the valley*).

WEEK 31

Filling Up the Corners

— LESSON 117 —

Interrogative Adverbs
Noun Clauses
Forming Questions
Affirmations and Negations
Double Negatives

Exercise 117A: Identifying Adverbs, Interrogative and Demonstrative Pronouns and Adjectives, and Relatives

In the following sentences from *Charlie and the Chocolate Factory* by Roald Dahl, follow these steps:

a) Label each bolded word as one of the following:
  ADV for adverb
    Draw an arrow from the adverb to the word modified.
    If the adverb also introduces a clause, underline the clause.
  PRO for pronoun
    If the pronoun has an antecedent, label the antecedent as *ANT.*
    If the pronoun introduces a clause, underline the clause.
    Label each pronoun as *S* for subject, *PN* for predicate nominative, *DO* for direct object, *IO* for indirect object, *OP* for object of the preposition, or *ADJ* (see below).
  ADJ for adjective
    Draw an arrow from the adjective to the word modified. If the adjective introduces a clause, underline the clause.
  SC for subordinating conjunction
    Underline the dependent clause introduced by the conjunction.

b) Label each underlined clause as *ADV-C* for adverb clause, *ADJ-C* for adjective clause, or *N-C* for noun clause.

c) Draw an arrow from each *ADV-C* and *ADJ-C* clause back to the word modified. Label each *N-C* noun clause as *S* for subject, *DO* for direct object, *IO* for indirect object, or *OP* for object of the preposition.

The first is done for you. Notice that *whose* has two labels because it is both an adjective and a relative pronoun.

ANT ADJ/PRO ADJ-C
Mr. and Mrs. Bucket have a small boy **whose** name is Charlie Bucket.

N-C DO ADV ADJ

I shall now tell you **how this** amazing television set of mine works.

ADV PRO OP N DO

And oh, **how** he wished he could go inside the factory and see **what** it was like!

> **Note to Instructor:** The main clause of the sentence is *how he wished*, with *how* as an adverb modifying the verb. The entire noun clause *he could go inside the factory and see what it was like* has an understood *that* before it and serves as the direct object of *wished*. The noun clause *what it was like* is the direct object of the second verb within the noun clause; *like what* is a prepositional phrase modifying *was* (*it was like what*).

ADV-C ADV

They suck up the chocolate and carry it away to all the other rooms in the factory **where** it is needed!

> **Note to Instructor:** You may need to explain to the student that while the relative adverb *where* does point back to *rooms*, within the clause itself, it is an adverb modifying the verb *is needed*.

ADV ADJ

Why do we have to go rushing on past all **these** lovely rooms?

> **Note to Instructor:** There is no subordinate clause in this sentence. The predicate is *do have*. *To go* is an adverbial infinitive modifying *do have*, and *rushing* is the object of the infinitive.

ADJ ADV ADV-C

The wallpaper has pictures of all **these** fruits printed on it, and **when** you lick the picture of a banana, it tastes of banana.

PRO S ADV ADV-C

So **who** is going to run the factory **when** I get too old to do it myself?

ADJ ADV ADV

If **these** people can break up a photograph into millions of pieces and send the pieces whizzing through the air and **then** put them together again at the other end, **why** can't I do the same thing with a bar of chocolate?

> **Note to Instructor:** The main clause is the question *Why can't I do the same thing with a bar of chocolate?* All other words in front of the comma belong to the subordinate adverb clause introduced by the subordinating conjunction *if*.

ADV ANT PRO DO PRO PN ADV ADV-C ADV

But **there** was one other thing **that** the grownups also knew, and it was **this: however** small the chance might be of striking lucky, the chance was **there**.

> **Note to Instructor:** *That* is a relative pronoun, referring back to *thing* and serving as the direct object, within its own clause of the verb *knew*. *This* has no antecedent, although the entire following clause defines it.

ADJ PRO PN

What sort of nonsense is **this**?

ADV-C ADV ADV-C ADV

He worked in a toothpaste factory, **where** he sat all day long at a bench and screwed the little caps onto the tops of the tubes of toothpaste **after** the tubes had been filled.

> **Note to Instructor:** The entire adverb clause modifying *factory* begins with *where he sat* and ends with *had been filled*. The adverb clause *after the tubes had been filled* comes within the larger adverb clause and modifies *screwed*. You may need to explain to the student that while the relative adverb *where* does point back to *factory*, within the clause itself, it is an adverb modifying the verb *sat*.

Exercise 117B: Forming Questions

On your own paper, rewrite the following statements as questions.

Use each of the three methods for forming questions (adding an interrogative pronoun, reversing the subject and helping verb, or adding the helping verb *do, does,* or *did* in front of the subject and adjusting the tense of the main verb) at least once. You may change tenses, add or subtract words, or alter the statements in any other necessary ways, as long as the meaning remains the same.

These statements are all adapted from famous questions in books and movies. When you have transformed your statements into questions, compare them with the originals.

Note to Instructor: The student's questions do not need to be identical to the originals, but each question should be grammatically correct, and each method should be used at least once.

STATEMENT	QUESTION
The rum is gone.	But why is the rum gone? —*Pirates of the Caribbean: The Curse of the Black Pearl*
I feel lucky	Do I feel lucky? —*Dirty Harry*
The air speed velocity of an unladen swallow is unknown.	What is the air speed velocity of an unladen swallow? —*Monty Python and the Holy Grail*
You're a little short for a storm trooper.	Aren't you a little short for a storm trooper? —*Star Wars: A New Hope*
We shall play a game.	Shall we play a game? —*WarGames*
Mirror, mirror on the wall, the fairest one of all is unknown.	Mirror, mirror on the wall, who is the fairest one of all? —*Snow White*
You are Sarah Connor.	Are you Sarah Connor? —*The Terminator*
It always has to be snakes.	Why does it always have to be snakes? —*Raiders of the Lost Ark*
It has something in its pocketses.	What has it got in its pocketses? —*The Hobbit*
A white dove must sail many seas before she sleeps in the sand.	How many seas must a white dove sail before she sleeps in the sand? —"Blowin' in the Wind," Bob Dylan
While you're at it, give me a nice nice paper cut and pour lemon juice on it.	While you're at it, why don't you give me a paper cut and pour lemon juice on it? —*The Princess Bride*

Exercise 117C: Affirmations and Negations

On your own paper, rewrite each of the following affirmative statements as a negation, using one adverb or adjective of negation. You may add or subtract words or change tenses as necessary.

- Rewrite each negative statement as an affirmative, using at least one adverb of affirmation.
- Rewrite each double negation as an affirmative, also using at least one adverb of affirmation.

When you are finished, compare your answers with the original sentences, slightly adapted from Lamar Underwood's *1001 Fishing Tips: The Ultimate Guide to Finding and Catching More and Bigger Fish.*

Note to Instructor: The student's answers do not need to be identical to the original sentences, as long as the guidelines above are followed. Check to see that the student has included adverbs of affirmation and negation in each sentence; these are bolded in the original sentences below.

ASSIGNED SENTENCES	ORIGINAL VERSIONS
Fishing in the big wind is not tough.	Fishing in the big wind can be **very** tough.
The mealworm isn't a deadly bait.	The mealworm is an **absolutely** deadly bait.
The fish sucked the worm into its mouth.	The fish **never** sucked the worm into its mouth.
The film *Bigmouth 35* will not help you catch more bass.	The film *Bigmouth 35* will **definitely** help you catch more bass.
You can't count on the seven lures featured here.	You can **absolutely** count on the seven lures featured here.
Chum salmon get respect.	Chum salmon get **no** respect.
A hair-trigger reaction to a strike is the way to go.	A hair-trigger reaction to a strike is **not** the way to go.
People who tell you that bass don't school don't know nothing about what they're talking about.	People who tell you that bass do**n't** school do**n't** know what they're talking about.
Worm fishing doesn't make anglers yawn.	**Yes**, worm fishing makes some anglers yawn.

— LESSON 118 —

Diagramming Affirmations and Negations
Yet More Words That Can Be Multiple Parts of Speech
Comparisons Using *Than*
Comparisons Using *As*

Exercise 118A: Identifying Parts of Speech

Label each of the bolded words in these sentences (from Roald Dahl's novel *The BFG*, about a big friendly giant) with one of the following abbreviations: *ADV* for adverb, *ADV-N* for adverb of negation, *ADV-A* for adverb of affirmation, *ADV-R* for relative adverb, *SC* for subordinating conjunction, *PREP* for preposition, *RP* for relative pronoun, or *N* for noun.

Where a subordinating conjunction introduces a comparison clause with missing words, draw a caret and insert the missing words.

Note to Instructor: Explanatory notes are provided below, where necessary; give the student all needed help.

ADV SC is clear
It was **as** clear **as** crystal^.

ADV-A ADV SC
Yes, **now that** you come to mention it, I did.

ADV
They had never seen the likes of it **before.**

ADV ADV ADV SC
The Giant reached **out** and rolled the stone to one side **as easily as** if it had been a football, and
ADV ADV-R ADV
now, **where** the stone had been, **there** appeared a vast black hole.

Note to Instructor: *As if* is actually a compound subordinating conjunction, but since that has not yet been covered, only *as* is bolded. The relative adverb *where* refers to *hole* (the student may be confused because the relative adverb clause comes *before* the place that it describes).

ADV ADV SC PREP
Suddenly, **there** was a crunch **as** the Bloodbottler bit a huge hunk **off** the end.

PREP N ADV-N ADV-A ADV-A ADV ADV
By now Sophie was beginning to feel **not** only **extremely** hungry, but **very** thirsty **as well**.

Note to Instructor: Although *now* is generally an adverb, in this sentence it serves as a noun (equivalent to *the time*) and is the object of the preposition *by*.

PREP ADV-A SC ADV ADV PREP
The wind rushing **against** Sophie's face became **so** strong **that** she had to duck **down again into**
PREP ADV
the blanket to prevent her head **from** being blown **away**.

Note to Instructor: If the student simply labels *so* as *ADV*, point out that it is equivalent to *really* or *very*. The list of adverbs of affirmation in the lesson was not exhaustive. *Being blown* serves as the object of the preposition *from*.

ADV SC is big
It was **as** big **as** a house^.

The ninth, **who** (RP) happened to be the Fleshlumpeater, was causing trouble for the soldiers **because** (SC) he was lying with his right arm tucked **underneath** (PREP) his enormous body.

Fleshlumpeater says he is **never** (ADV-N) eating a queen and he thinks **perhaps** (ADV) she has an **especially** (ADV-A) scrumdiddlyumptious flavour.

> **Note to Instructor:** The student may think that *perhaps* introduces the clause *she has an especially scrumdiddlyumptious flavour,* but that clause actually has an understood *that* introducing it, so *perhaps* actually is an adverb modifying *has.*

It is the same with trees **as** (SC) it is with flowers.

> **Note to Instructor:** This comparison clause is actually complete. Dahl could have written *It is the same with trees as with flowers* but chose to finish out the final subordinate clause.

No noise came **out** (ADV), but it was obvious to Sophie **that** (SC) **whatever** (RP) had been in the jar had **now** (ADV) been blown through the trumpet into the Goochey children's bedroom.

Exercise 118B: Diagramming

On your own paper, diagram every word of the following sentences. Ask your instructor for help if you need it.

> **Note to Instructor:** Use the notes below to give all necessary help.

Do you know what they are really thinking?

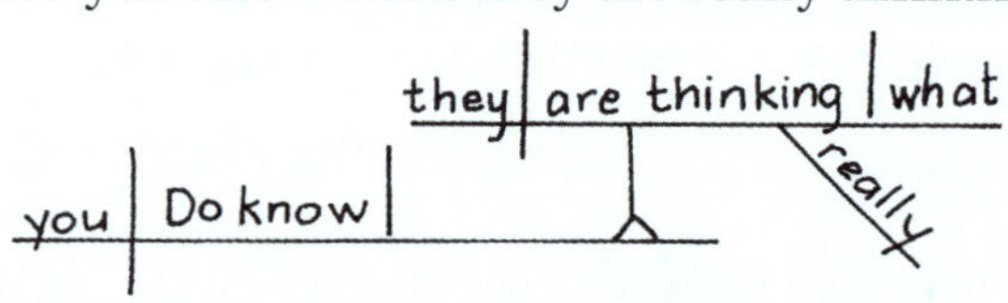

His memories of the understory of the great forest burst into lyrical phrases, as resinous as the sap of a pinecone, as crisp as the shell of a beetle.

—From *The Dreamer,* by Pam Muñoz Ryan

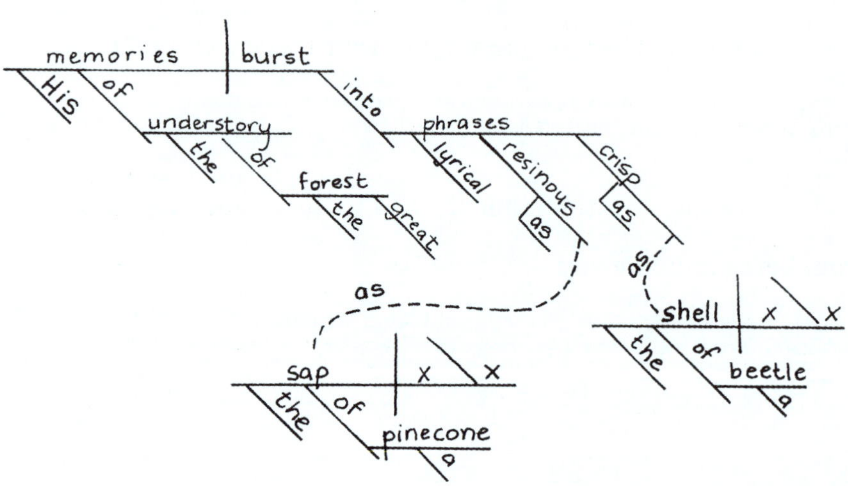

> **Note to Instructor:** The comparison clauses, completed, are *as resinous as the sap of a pinecone [is resinous], as crisp as the shell of a beetle [is crisp].*

Yes, really and truly, I want you to keep it.

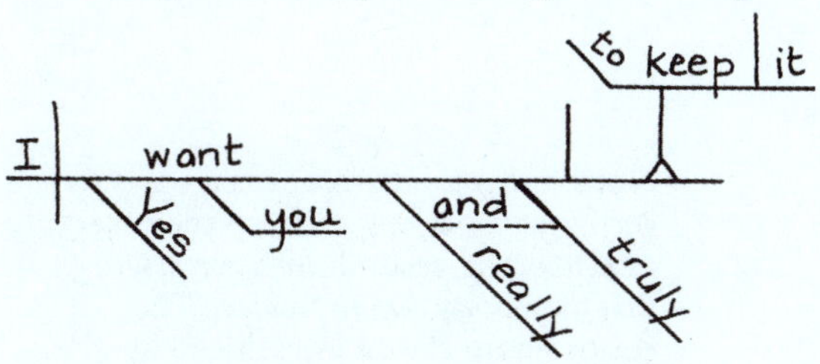

Well, Diary, I was about to say, No!

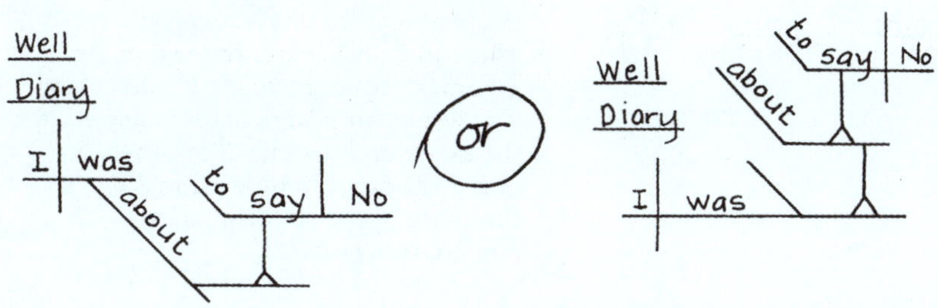

> **Note to Instructor:** In this sentence, *well* is an interjection, not an adverb of any kind. *No* serves as a noun, the object of the infinitive *to say*. It is a judgment call whether the prepositional phrase *about to say, No* serves as a predicate adjective (describing *I*) or an adverb phrase answering the question *how I was*. An argument can be made for either interpretation.

After that call, we were all very nervous as we always are when we hear news of someone being nabbed by *la migra*.

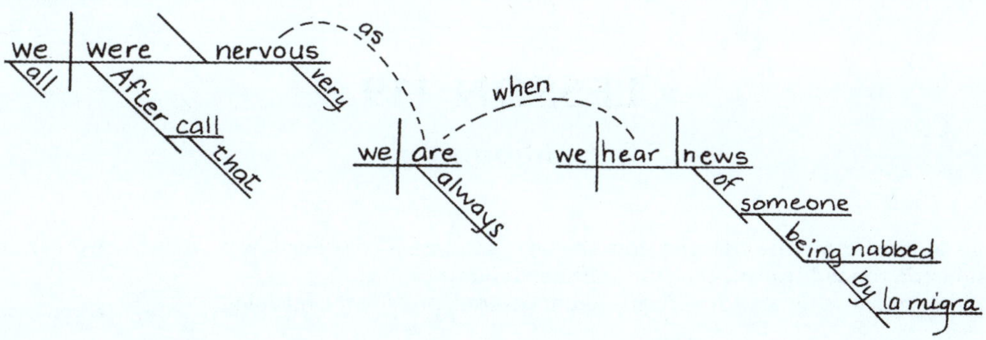

> **Note to Instructor:** Foreign phrases are usually treated as names and diagrammed on one line, but it is not incorrect for the student to diagram the article *la* beneath *migra*. *As we always are* is an adverb clause modifying the predicate adjective *nervous* and answering the questions *how* and *when*. *When we hear news . . .* is an adverb clause answering the question *when*.

We have missed you terribly the eight months and a day (yes, Mama, I am keeping count!) that you have been gone.

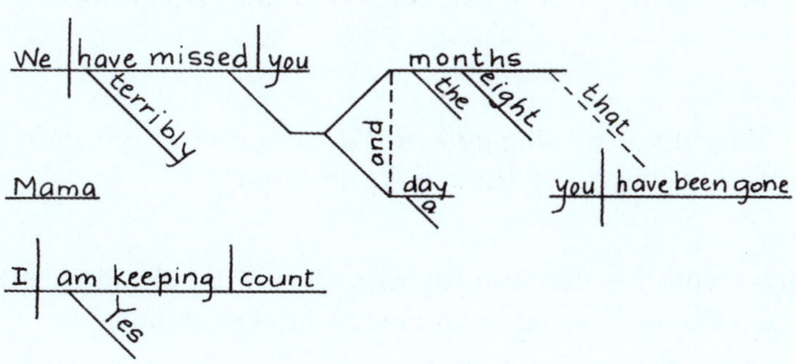

> **Note to Instructor:** *Months* and *day* are adverbial nouns. The subordinate clause *that you have been gone* can be connected to either of these adverbial nouns. The parenthetical element is diagrammed separately (see Lesson 88). *Yes* is an adverb of affirmation and *Mama* is a term of direct address.

Papa kept reassuring us that the journey home was no problem, as you would be entering your birth land on an airplane, not on foot through a desert.

—From *Return to Sender*, by Julia Alvarez

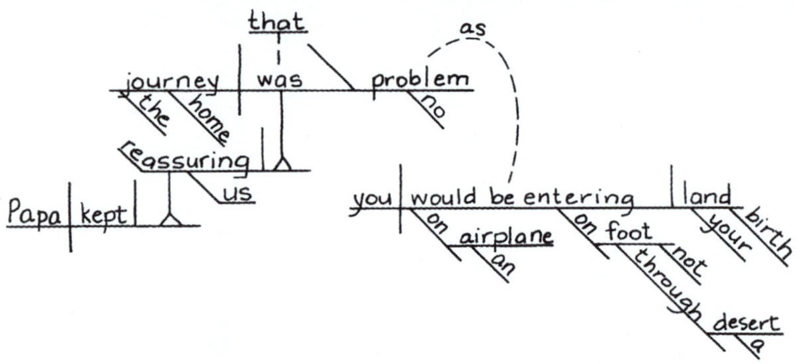

Note to Instructor: *Keep* is a transitive verb, not a helping verb, so the object of *kept* is the gerund phrase *reassuring that the journey was no problem*. The subordinate clause introduced by *that* is the object of the gerund itself. The remaining subordinate clause, introduced by *as*, explains more about the problem, so I have attached it as an adjective clause to *problem*. An argument could be made for attaching it to *was* as an adverb clause answering the question *how*—this is another judgment case. *As* here expresses the sense of the subordinating conjunction *because*.

— LESSON 119 —

Idioms

Note to Instructor: The dialogue from the *Core Handbook* is continued here, in the *Answer Key*, so that instructor and student can study different idioms each year.

If the student is unfamiliar with any idiom covered, provide the meaning.

Instructor: We can divide idioms into two types. In the first type, all of the words in the idiom are serving a clear, familiar grammatical function—but the idiom itself means something completely different from its literal meaning. The next sentences in your *Workbook* are this type of idiom. Read me the first sentence.

Student: One day it's sunny and warm and the next it's raining cats and dogs.

Instructor: The verb *rain* can be transitive—you can say, for example, "It rained confetti" or "The king rained gifts and favors upon the lucky knight." But unless you're watching cartoons, you'll never see cats and dogs falling out of the sky. What does this idiom mean?

Student: It's raining hard.

Instructor: Put your right index finger on the diagram of *raining cats and dogs* and your left index finger on the diagram of *rained gifts and favors*. Do they look the same?

Student: Yes.

Instructor: Except for the fact that cats and dogs would never actually rain down, the idiom works just like any transitive verb with two direct objects. Read me the next sentence.

Student: The pilot was getting into the groove of the airplane, was flying it every day.

Instructor: The pilot was, literally, flying the airplane every day. But was he actually sitting down into a groove in the airplane?

Student: No.

Instructor: What does *getting into the groove* mean?

Student: Getting comfortable with, getting used to.

Instructor: Put the sentence onto the frame in your workbook.

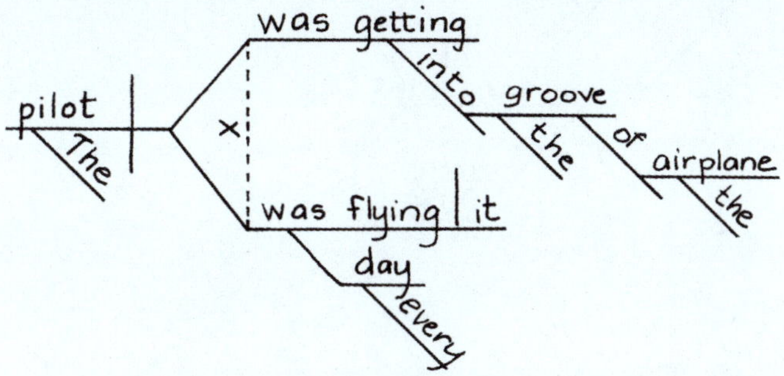

Instructor: If you can diagram an idiom without any trouble, you know that it has regular grammar—even if it has an unusual meaning.

The second type of idiom uses combinations of words that you might not be able to fit into patterns you've already learned. Read me the next sentence.

Student: No doubt the gypsy had stolen my earring as I lay unconscious.

Instructor: Underline the subject once and the predicate twice.

No doubt the gypsy had stolen my earring as I lay unconscious.

Instructor: *No* modifies *doubt*, and *no doubt* modifies the verb *had stolen*. But *doubt* isn't an adverb. What two parts of speech can *doubt* serve as?

> **Note to Instructor:** If the student needs help, give him the example sentences, *I doubt that* and *It is normal to feel doubt*.

Student: Verb and noun.

Instructor: There's no way to make a verb, or a noun, modify *had stolen*! So you have to treat *no doubt* like a single adverb that means "certainly." When you can sum up the meaning of an idiom with one word, it should always go on a single line in your diagram. Diagram this sentence onto the frame in your workbook.

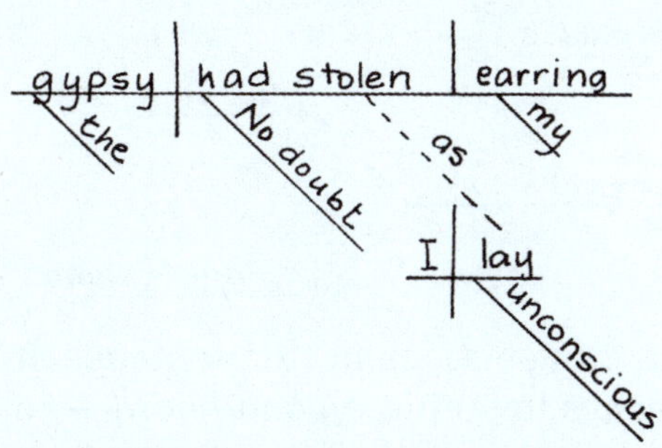

Instructor: Sometimes, an idiom expresses a single meaning even though you can't easily boil it down to one word. In the next sentence, why does she wash the butter with ice water?

Student: To separate the curd from the whey.

Instructor: You could rephrase this as "She would wash the butter with ice water *for the purpose of separating* the curd from the whey." Or you could just say simply "She would wash the butter with ice water *to* separate the curd from the whey." Either way, the phrase *in order to* works as a single unit to introduce the adverb phrase. Treat *in order to* as a single idiom and place the sentence on the diagram frame.

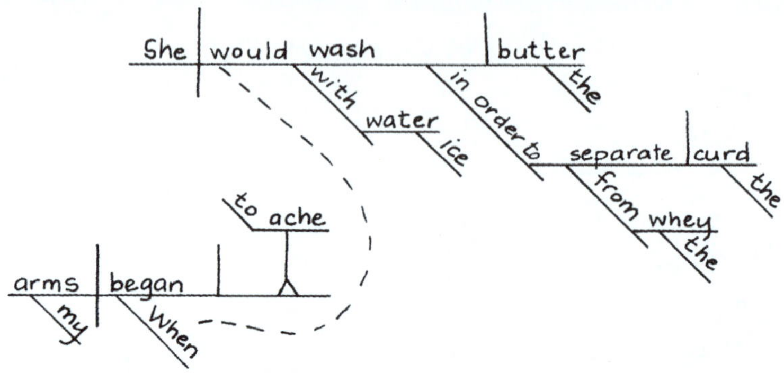

Note to Instructor: *When my arms began to ache* is a relative adverb clause because it refers back to a time in the main clause.

Instructor: In the next sentence, the idiom introduces the phrase *As for the ghosts*. Can you think of another way to say *as for*?

Note to Instructor: If the student cannot think of an alternative, say, "Read the sentence out loud and substitute as *for* with *concerning*. Then read it out loud and substitute as for with *regarding*."

Instructor: Idioms using *as* can be confusing, because *as* has so many different uses. But generally, when *as* is combined with other prepositions, it is acting as a single unit. *As for* often introduces phrases that are absolute constructions. What is an absolute construction?

Student: An absolute construction has a strong semantic relationship but no grammatical connection to the rest of the sentence.

Instructor: You learned about absolute constructions in Lesson 96. This phrase doesn't act as an adverb, or an adjective, so although it adds to the meaning of the sentence, it is diagrammed separately—*above* the sentence, to show it's more important than a parenthetic expression (which is usually diagrammed *below*). Place the absolute construction on the empty part of your diagram frame now.

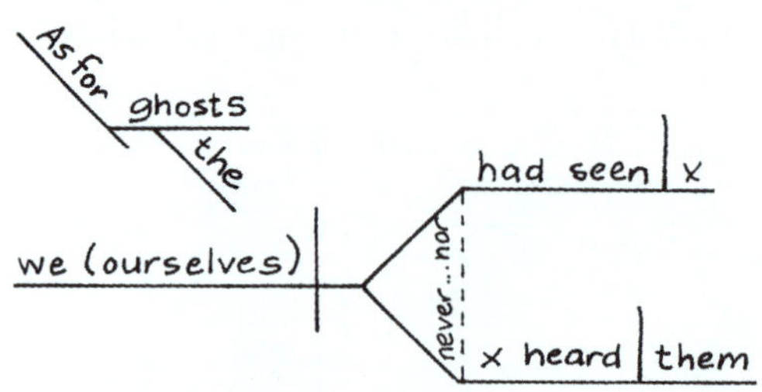

Instructor: I want you to notice something else about this sentence. It has some missing words. The helping verb *had* belongs to both *seen* and *heard*— and the direct object *them* belongs to both *seen* and *heard* as well. The sentence is actually, *We ourselves had never seen them nor had heard them.* English sentences often drop out repetitions of compound helping verbs and direct objects. It's usually best to mark these missing words with an *X* on your diagram. Write the missing words above each *X* on the diagram.

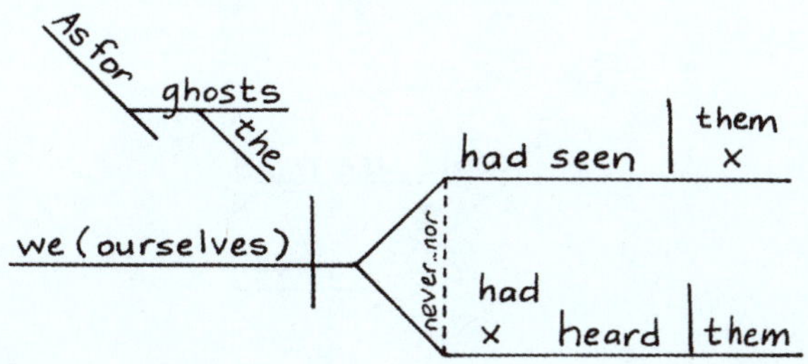

Instructor: Instead of diagramming the next two sentences, we'll circle the idioms. See if you can find them yourself.

Well, Thomas Keller and Jean-Georges wouldn't be caught dead using the same salt in their kitchens as you use in yours, so they had to up the ante, turning to such exotics as African clay salt and black lava salt from Hawaii.

It felt kind of weird.

—From *52 Loaves: A Half-Baked Adventure*, by William Alexander

Note to Instructor: If the student has trouble, simple tell her which words to circle.

Instructor: In the first sentence, *wouldn't be caught dead* just means *wouldn't do it.* The whole thing, all together, carries a single meaning. There's no way to pull it apart—because being *caught dead* doesn't make literal sense. If you were diagramming this, you'd put *wouldn't be caught dead* all on the predicate line. You wouldn't even put the adverb *not* below it—because *would be caught dead* would be a completely different verb. *To up the ante* means "to raise the stakes" and is taken from poker. It could be diagrammed exactly as written—as an infinitive with an object.

In the second sentence, can you substitute a single word that means *kind of*?

Student: [Somewhat, moderately, partially, slightly, rather].

Note to Instructor: If the student can't think of a word, supply several of the options above, and have her repeat the sentences two or more times, substituting several of the words for *kind of.*

Instructor: *Kind of* would be diagrammed below *weird* as a single adverb.

Let's look at one last odd little idiom—only one word long. Does the last sentence mean that he *can* use a job, or *can't* use a job?

Student: He should take a job.

Instructor: You've learned that when *no* is part of a sentence, it is an adverb of negation. But in this idiom, it has turned into an adverb of affirmation! Read the sentence out loud and change *no* to *yes*.

Student: And he could use a job after school, yes?

Instructor: If you put the idiom *no* on the diagram as a modifier, it will reverse the meaning of the sentence. So it's best to diagram it as an interjection, even though it's part of the sentence. Notice one more thing about this sentence: It begins with a conjunction, even though it's not joined to anything. When this happens, you diagram the conjunction above the verb—you just don't connect it to another verb. Put the sentence on the frame in your workbook.

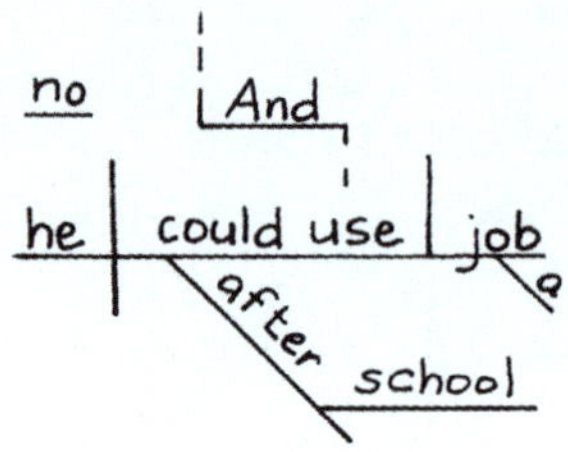

Instructor: Complete your exercises now.

Exercise 119A: Identifying Idioms

In the following sentences, circle each complete idiom. Write its meaning above it in your own words. (You can use more than one word!)

The first is done for you.

> **Note to Instructor:** If the student cannot find the idiom, point it out and ask the student to describe (or act out) its literal meaning. Encourage the student to include helping verbs when idioms contain a verb. If the student cannot explain the meaning of the idiom, allow her to look it up in a print or online reference tool; idioms are often listed in dictionaries under the first or primary word in the idiom.
>
> The definitions below are suggestions; any explanation that carries a similar meaning is acceptable.

somewhat like, similar to

The tea was beautiful, served in a tall glass filled with mint leaves, kind of like the mojito I'd have greatly preferred, but without ice.

would notice, would think it strange

If I were baking a different kind of bread each week, no one would blink an eyelash, but somehow this pursuit of trying to do one thing very well made me eccentric.

in order, intending

I took a step back so as to not destroy an entire production cycle with my clumsiness.

> **Note to Instructor:** It's acceptable for the student to include *to* in the circle, but the actual idiom, expressing a result, is *so as*.

A third row of tables, reserved for guests, ran plumb down the center, just so everyone

watch over

could keep an eye on us.

something so big it can't be controlled

This was apparently her cue to invite a most unwelcome eight-hundred-pound gorilla into the garden.

to happen a certain way / the most important part

Chlorine, it turned out, wasn't even the half of it.

—From *52 Loaves: A Half-Baked Adventure*, by William Alexander

admit wrong, stop being so proud

You'd think he'd come off his high horse after the fool he made of himself at the mine, but he's worse than ever.

pretend not to see her

She rather expected that Mrs. Mablett would cut her dead, but she had reckoned without that lady's firm grasp on mine politics.

forced to leave — very quickly

You'll be right out on your ear in nothing flat.
—From *Foxfire*, by Anya Seton

extreme desperation

Because nothing in the world is so disheartening as being in dire straits after once enjoying prosperity, the formerly rich man suffered terribly from the plight he found himself in.

being destroyed

Persuading her husband that it was a good idea for him to visit some of his estates, because she had heard that things were going to rack and ruin there, she got him out of the house for an indeterminate number of days.

in front of them — believe them

Many ignorant people, when lauded to their face by flatterers, tend to take them at their word, but this king, who was truly meritorious, wanted people to think the opposite.

dependable

The seventh and last unit was led by the emperor himself, with four thousand Germans, all tried and true, who looked as if they had been born in armor.
—From *Medieval Tales and Stories*, ed. Stanley Appelbaum

Exercise 119B: Diagramming

On your own paper, diagram every word of the following sentences.

Note to Instructor: Give the student all necessary help. Remember that diagramming is a tool, not an end in itself; if the student can give a good reason for diagramming a word or phrase differently, accept it.

After all, he had often used this excuse in order to avoid going back to school on Monday.

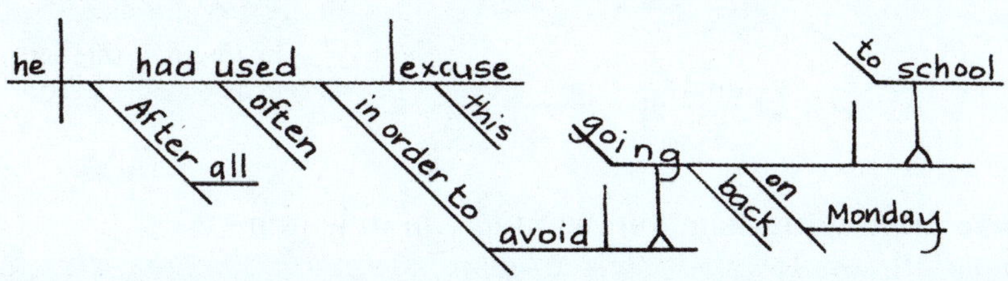

Note to Instructor: *After all* is not diagrammed as an idiom because the literal meaning (*after everything else*) and the idiom's meaning are so close together. However, do not mark it as incorrect if the student diagrams this phrase on a single line (but it should be diagrammed as an adverb beneath the verb). *In order to* is a single idiomatic phrase replacing the simple *to* of the infinitive.

He pushed an old ice-cream cart throughout the city, visiting a new neighborhood each day, as if to give everyone a chance to taste the delicious flavors of his ice cream: pineapple, coconut, cherimoya, and more.

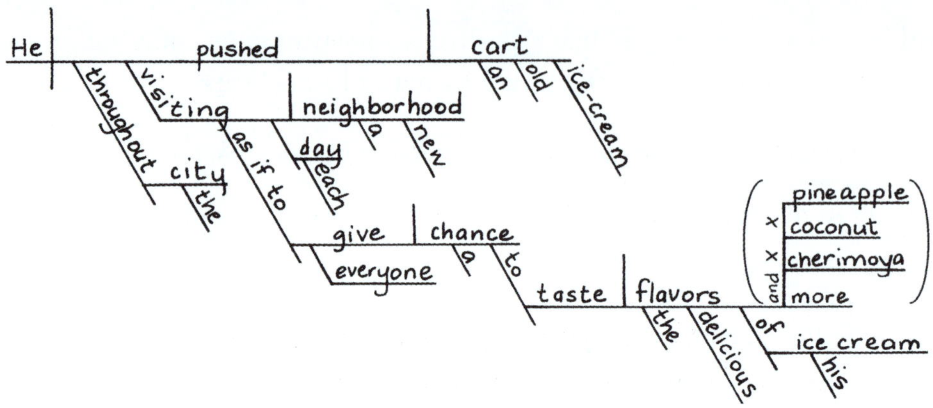

Note to Instructor: The idiom in this sentence is *as if to*, which stands in for *to* in the infinitive phrase *to give everyone a chance . . .*" The noun *flavors* has four appositives (*pineapple, coconut, cherimoya, more*). As long as the student places them in parentheses after *flavors*, you should give some latitude in how they are diagrammed.

Ever since their mother had died when my father was fifteen and my uncle only ten, my father had taken care of Mario.

—From *Where the Flame Trees Bloom*, by Alma Flor Ada

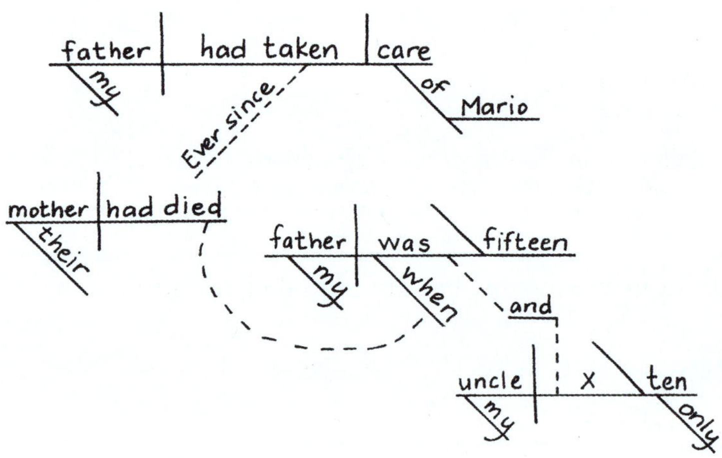

Note to Instructor: The student will probably first attempt to diagram *father* and *uncle* as a compound subject with the single shared linking verb *was*; this will not work, since *father* and *uncle* have two different predicate adjectives (*fifteen* and *ten*), so cannot share the same linking verb. The second *was* is understood.

When is a relative adverb because it refers back to a time (the time when mother died) in the previous clause.

The idiom in this sentence is *Ever since*, acting as a single subordinating conjunction.

I was fighting tooth and nail with them and wanted you to help me.

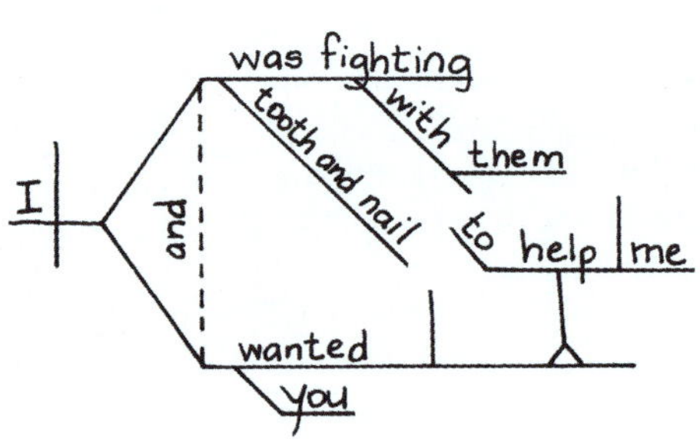

Note to Instructor: The phrase *tooth and nail* is a single idiom expressing *fiercely*.

Katerina Ivanovna had just begun, as she always did at every free moment, walking to and fro in her little room from window to stove and back again, with her arms folded across her chest, talking to herself and coughing.

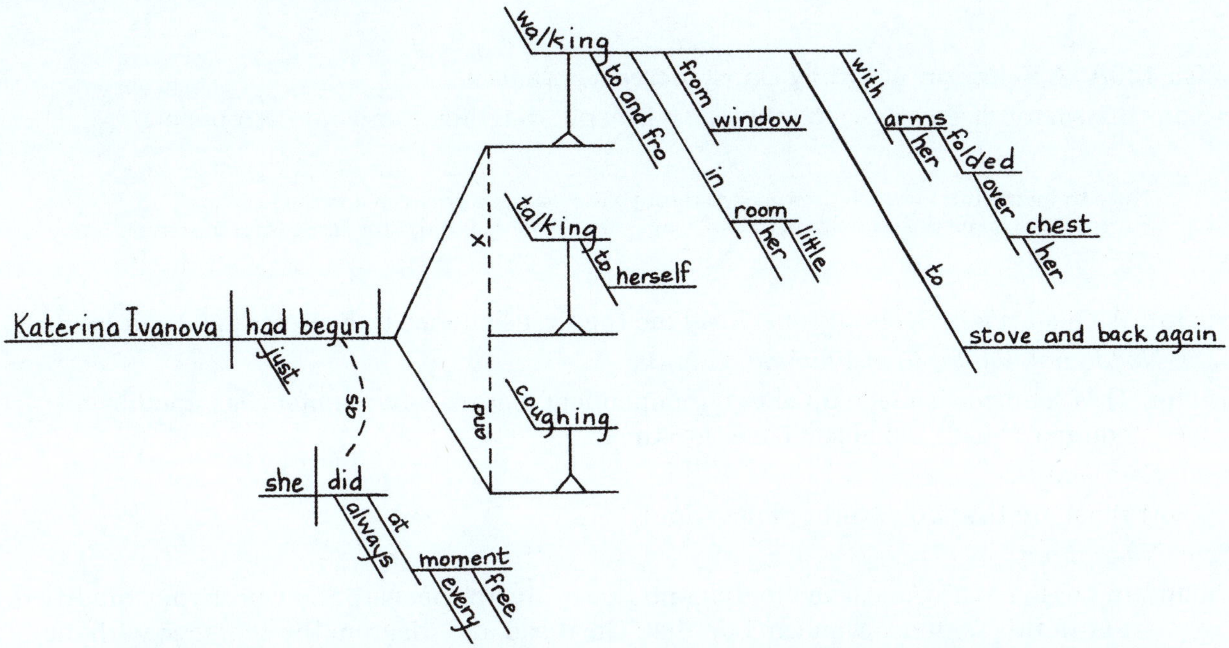

Note to Instructor: This sentence contains two idioms: *to and fro* and *to . . . and back again*. *To and fro* should be diagrammed as a single adverb answering the question *where*.

From window to stove and back again could also be diagrammed as follows:

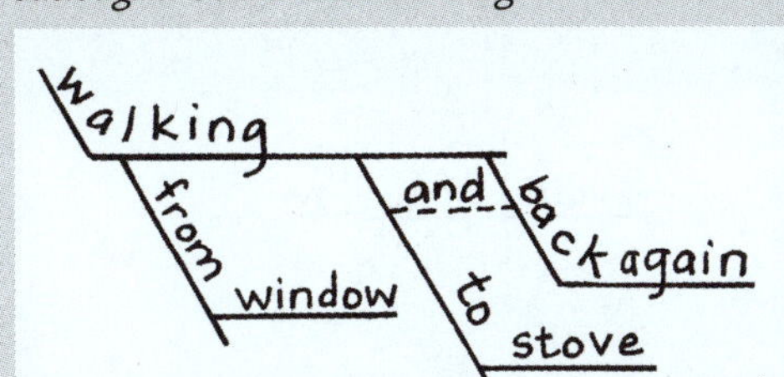

But this requires classifying *again* as a noun (the time known as again), which most dictionaries don't recognize.

On the other hand: if the student is now good enough at grammar to recognize this problem, he's already good enough to pass any standardized exam (and already knows more than 99% of all his potential bosses).

— LESSON 120 —

Troublesome Sentences

Exercise 120A: A Selection of Oddly Constructed Sentences

After your instructor discusses each sentence with you, diagram it on your own paper.

> **Note to Instructor:** For each sentence, go through the dialogue provided and then ask the student to diagram the sentence before moving on to the next. Prompt the student for answers as necessary.

Instructor: We'll start with a simple one. Read me the first sentence in Exercise 120A out loud.

Student: No, do not hand it to me, fan me with it!

Instructor: This sentence is made up of two independent clauses—two sentences joined by a comma. What kind of sentences are they?

Student: Commands.

Instructor: What are the two adverbs of negation?

Student: No and not.

Instructor: In Lesson 117, you learned to diagram these adverbs beneath the words they modified. But in this sentence, you can't do that. Go ahead and diagram the sentence without diagramming the *no* at the beginning.

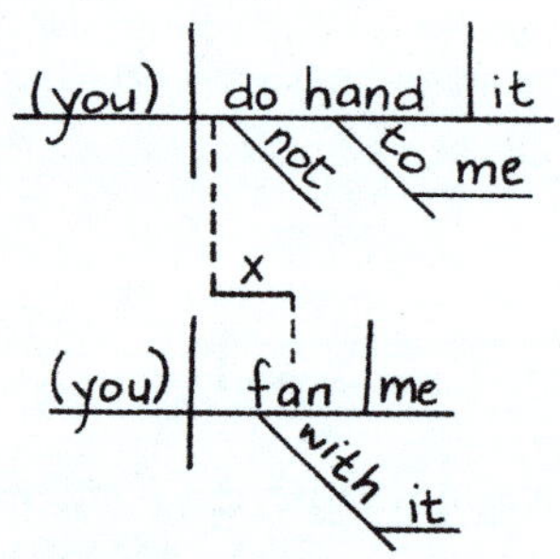

Instructor: If you diagram *no* with the first command, what grammatical error does this introduce?

Student: A double negative.

Instructor: If you diagram it with the second command, what happens?

Student: The meaning changes.

Instructor: Even though *no* is an adverb of negation, you have to treat it as an interjection. Go ahead and diagram that now.

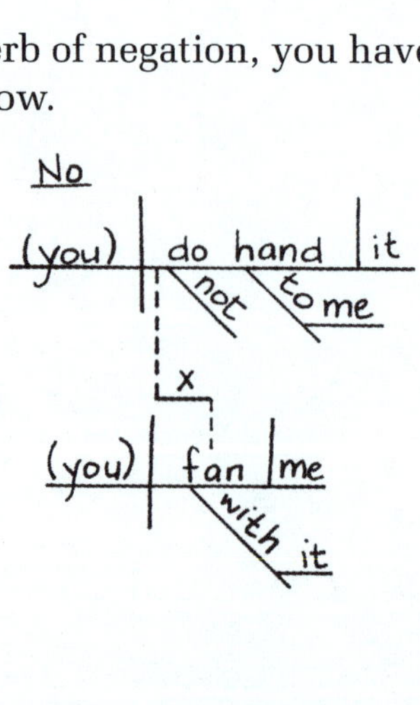

Instructor: Read me the second sentence.

Student: Now I had never been called Señor Pareja in my life.

Instructor: Diagram *only* the subject and the predicate.

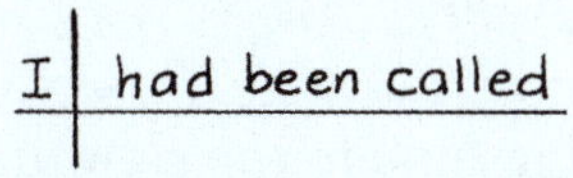

Instructor: Now we have to figure out what to do with the name *Señor Pareja.* It follows the verb, but it can't be a direct object. Why?

Student: The verb is passive.

Instructor: The subject is already receiving the action of the passive verb, so a passive verb cannot also have a direct object. It cannot be a predicate nominative either. Why not?

Student: Call isn't a linking verb.

Instructor: Predicate nominatives have to follow linking verbs, not action verbs. Can you think of anything else that *Señor Pareja* could be in this sentence?

> **Note to Instructor:** Give the student a chance to come up with the answer; continue with the dialogue below as necessary.
>
> Grammatically, there are two possibilities: either Señor Pareja is an appositive placed in an unusual position, or else it is one of two compound subjects along with I. However, since Señor Pareja and I are the same person, not two different people, the appositive solution works better to preserve the meaning.

Instructor: *Señor Pareja* receives the action of the verb, just like *I* does. So *I* and *Señor Pareja* could be compound subjects. But that makes them sound like two different people. Since *I* and *Señor Pareja* both refer to the same person, *Señor Pareja* renames *I.* It is actually an appositive in a very unusual position—following the verb. Re-diagram the sentence now, treating *Señor Pareja* as an appositive.

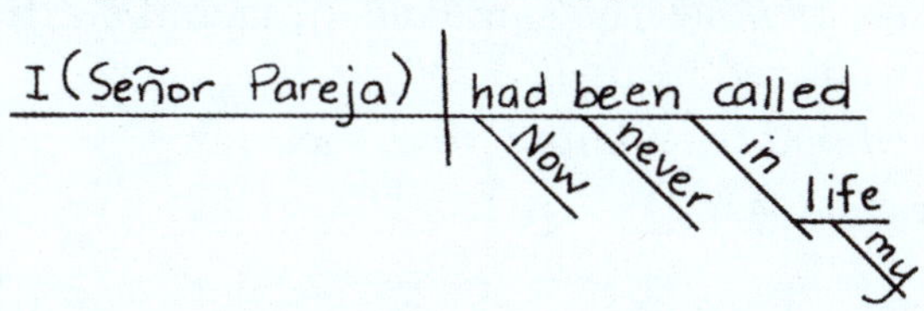

Instructor: The next two sentences, from *The Dreamer,* don't exactly *break* rules—but they're a little more complicated than they might look at first glance. Read me the first.

Student: Neftali felt the river breathing beneath him, as if keeping time to the slow and sorrowful tune.

Instructor: Underline the subject once and the predicate twice.

> Neftali felt the river breathing beneath him, as if keeping time to the slow and sorrowful tune.

Instructor: What part of the sentence is *river*?

Student: The direct object.

Instructor: *River* receives the action of the action verb *felt.* What does the participle phrase *breathing beneath him* describe?

Student: The river.

Instructor: What does the phrase *as if keeping time to the slow and sorrowful tune* tell you more about?

Student: The breathing.

Instructor: What part of speech is *breathing* acting as?

Student: An adjective.

Instructor: Since the phrase *as if keeping time to the slow and sorrowful tune* describes an adjective, what is it working as?

Student: An adverb.

Instructor: So you have two participles acting as two different parts of speech. What part of speech does the introductory pair of words *as if* act as?

Student: A preposition.

> **Note to Instructor:** If the student says subordinating word, point out that the phrase does not contain a subject and a predicate, so it is not a clause. Subordinating words only introduce clauses.

Instructor: *As if* is a compound preposition that means *like* or *in the same way*. Diagram the sentence now.

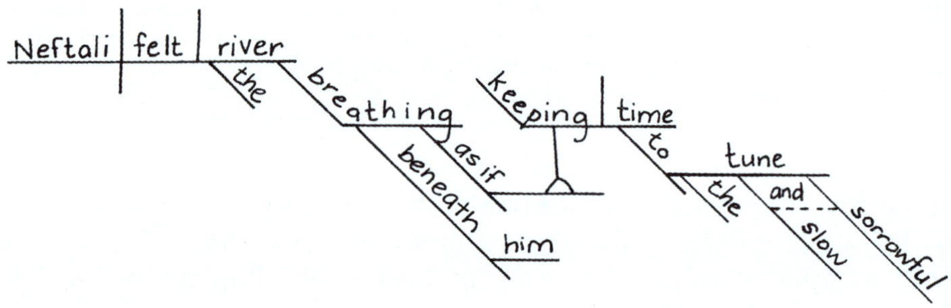

Instructor: In the next sentence, *as if* has the same meaning, but a different function. Read the group of words introduced by *as if*.

Student: As if a piece of himself had been left behind, too.

Instructor: Is this a phrase or a clause?

Student: A clause.

> **Note to Instructor:** If the student says "phrase," ask him to underline the subject and predicate of the clause: *as if a piece of himself had been left behind, too.*

Instructor: So what part of speech does *as if* act as in this sentence?

Student: A subordinating conjunction.

Instructor: The entire clause follows the verb *felt*. What part of speech does the clause serve as?

Student: Predicate adjective.

> **Note to Instructor:** If the student says "Direct object," say, "Did he actually feel that with his hands or see it with his eyes or sense it with his physical body?"

Instructor: *Feel* is one of the linking verbs that can also be an action verb. In the first sentence, it's an action verb. In the second, it links the subject to a clause that *describes* the subject, so it has become a linking verb. Diagram the sentence now.

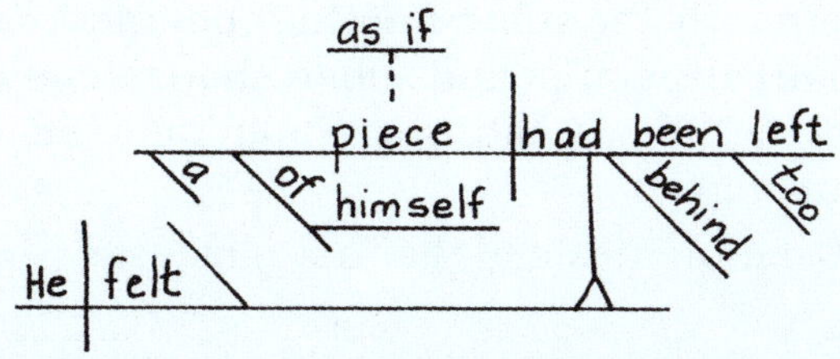

Note to Instructor: *Left behind* is not an idiom because the addition of the adverb *behind* does not change the meaning of *left*.

Instructor: In your next sentence, from *Crime and Punishment,* Dostoyevsky wins the prize for subordinate clauses! To start, go through the sentence and circle every separate clause. Then, underline the subject of the main clause once, and the predicate twice.

And if at that moment he had been capable of seeing and reasoning more correctly, if he had been able to realize all the difficulties of his position, the hopelessness, the hideousness and the absurdity of it, if he could have understood how many obstacles and, perhaps, crimes he had still to overcome or to commit, to get out of that place and to make his way home, it is very possible that he would have flung up everything, and would have gone to give himself up, and not from fear, but from simple horror and loathing of what he had done.

Note to Instructor: Give all necessary help. Asking the student to underline all predicates twice might help him to find the clauses. For the clause *he had still to overcome or commit*, you might suggest that the student insert a caret and the word *that* in front of *he* in order to make the presence of the clause clearer. You may also tell the student that the main clause is the shortest one in the whole sentence.

Instructor: Let's talk about this sentence. You can either outline each clause as we go, or you can wait until we've discussed the entire sentence and then outline it.

Start with the main clause. What is *possible*?

Student: Predicate adjective.

Instructor: That's a very simple main clause!

Now read me the first three *if* clauses. Stop at the word *crimes*.

Student: And if at that moment he had been capable of seeing and reasoning more correctly, if he had been able to realize all the difficulties of his position, the hopelessness, the hideousness and the absurdity of it, if he could have understood how many obstacles and, perhaps, crimes . . .

Instructor: All three of these clauses express possible causes. There's an understood *then* in front of the main clause: *If he had been capable, if had been able, if he could have understood . . . then* it is possible. So the clauses tell us *how, under what conditions,* and *to what extent* the possibility *is.* All three are adverb clauses that should be connected to the verb *is* by the subordinating conjunctions *if.* Notice that the very first conjunction is actually the compound subordinating conjunction *and if.* In this case, *and* acts like part of the subordinating conjunction, instead of acting like a plain old coordinating conjunction.

What is the subject and predicate of the first *if* clause?

Student: He had been capable.

Instructor: The preposition *of* has two direct objects. What are they?

Student: Seeing and reasoning.

Instructor: What is the subject and predicate of the second *if* clause?

Student: He had been.

Instructor: What is *able*?

Student: Predicate adjective.

Instructor: The infinitive *to realize* tells you more about the adjective *able.* It has four objects. What are they?

Student: Difficulties, hopelessness, hideousness, absurdity.

Instructor: What is the subject and predicate of the third *if* clause?

Student: He could have understood.

Instructor: What are the two direct objects of the verb?

Student: Obstacles and crimes.

Instructor: An adjective clause introduced by an understood *that* describes both *obstacles* and *crimes.* What is that adjective clause?

Student: [That] he had still to overcome or commit.

Instructor: Since the clause modifies both direct objects, draw a dotted line that connects the predicate of the adjective clause to both direct object lines in the diagram. What is the subject and predicate of the adjective clause?

Student: He had.

Instructor: The verb *have* is ambitransitive—it can be either transitive or intransitive. In this clause, it's intransitive. The infinitives following the verb answer the question *how,* so you would diagram them as adverbs. What coordinating conjunction connects the infinitives?

Student: Or.

Instructor: Just as those two infinitives connected by *or* describe the verb, two more infinitives connected by *and* describe the infinitive *commit.* What are they?

Student: To make way and to get.

> **Note to Instructor:** It is not always completely clear whether an infinitive is acting as an adverb or a direct object. In this case, the dictionary defines the verb *commit* as intransitive when followed by an infinitive, so the infinitives are diagrammed as adverbs. If the student asks, tell her that she can always consult a dictionary if she's not sure.

Instructor: In this sentence, *out of* is an idiom, an emphatic form of *out*—if you just said *get of,* it wouldn't make sense, so diagram *out of* as a single preposition. What is the direct object of the infinitive *to make*?

Student: Way.

Instructor: Make way where?

Student: Home.

Instructor: *Home* almost looks like an adverbial noun—but it can't be an adverb. Why not?

Student: It's modifying a noun.

Instructor: In this case, there's an understood preposition, *to*, forming the adjectival prepositional phrase *to home*. You would diagram this phrase with an *X* on the preposition line.

Time for the final clause! Read me the rest of the sentence that follows *possible*.

Student: That he would have flung up everything, and would have gone to give himself up, and not from fear, but from simple horror and loathing of what he had done.

Instructor: This is an adverb clause, because it tells you more about the predicate adjective *possible*. The subject of the clause is *he*. What is the compound predicate?

Student: Would have flung [up] and would have gone.

Instructor: *Fling up* is an idiom meaning "relinquish, give away, get rid of," so you would diagram *would have flung up* all on one line. One of these predicates is followed by a direct object, and one is followed by an adverb phrase. What is the direct object?

Student: Everything.

Instructor: The adverb phrase begins with the infinitive *to give*. What is the direct object of that infinitive?

Student: Himself.

Instructor: *Give up* is an idiom meaning "surrender," so you would diagram *give up* on a single line. Two parallel prepositional phrases describe *give up*. What preposition introduces each phrase?

Student: From.

Instructor: The two phrases are joined by correlative conjunctions. These work in pairs to join words or groups of words. What are the two correlative conjunctions?

Student: And, but.

Instructor: These are diagrammed on a single dotted line connecting the two prepositions, with ellipses coming between them. The object of the first *from* is *fear*. What is the compound object of the second *from*?

Student: Horror and loathing.

Instructor: One more clause describes *loathing*. The clause is the object of the preposition *of*. What is the subject and predicate of this adjective clause?

Student: He had done.

Instructor: What is the direct object of *had done?*

Student: What.

Instructor: Diagram the sentence now [or finish diagramming the sentence now]. When you are finished, compare your diagram with the one in this *Answer Key.*

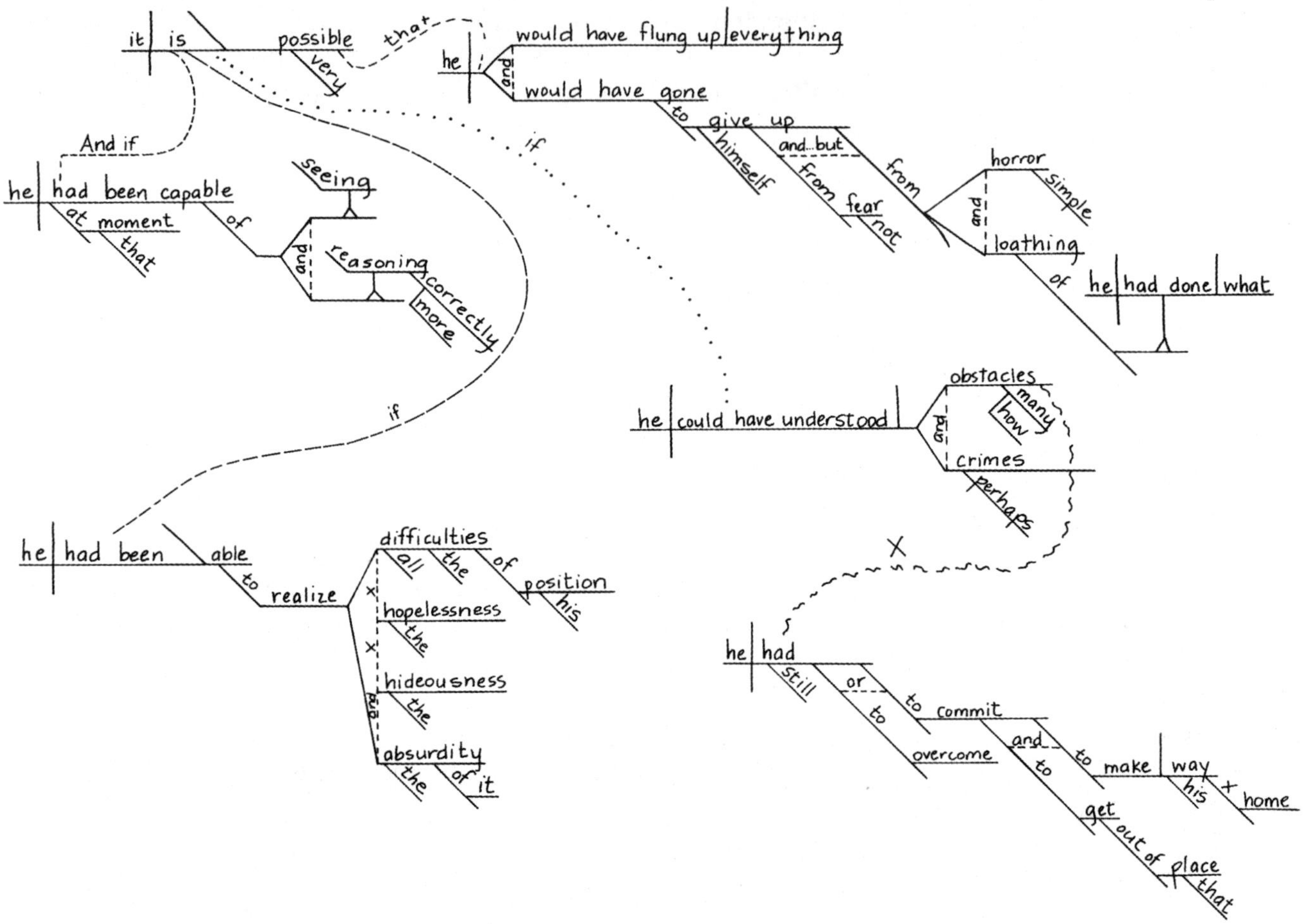

WEEK 32

—REVIEW 10—

Weeks 29-31

Topics
Hortative Verbs
Ambitransitive Verbs
Infinitive Phrases as Objects
Infinitive Phrases with Understood "To"
Principal Parts of Irregular Verbs
Noun Clauses as Appositives
Which/That in Restrictive and Non-Restrictive Clauses
Formal Conditionals
Words Acting as Multiple Parts of Speech
Affirmations and Negations
Idioms

Review 10A: The Missing Words Game

Fill in each blank below with the exact *form* described—but choose your own words!

Show your answers to your instructor, who will insert them into the matching blanks in the short essay in the *Answer Key*.

Your instructor will then show you the original essay—and your version.

Note to Instructor: Write the student's answers into the blanks below. The fill-in-the-blank version of the essay is followed by the original. You may decide which version to show the student first.

ORNAMENTS FOR HOMES (student version)

It is not the most ____________ (regular adverb) ____________ (past participle acting as adjective) houses that are the most ____________ (adjective). Comparatively few persons have the means ____________ (active infinitive of transitive verb) their love of pretty little ____________ (plural concrete noun) with which to beautify their homes. It is ____________ (adverb of affirmation) ____________ (adjective) to visit some houses; there ____________ (adjective) walls and ____________ (adjective) rooms meet you, ____________ (coordinating conjunction) there are many such, and ____________ (plural noun) in them too. ____________ (interrogative adverb) ____________ (regular adverb) ____________ (**Note**: modal helping verb here) these homes ____________ (**Note**: *be* + past participle here) (simple present modal passive verb, third-person plural) by careful ____________ (abstract singular noun) in ____________ (present participle of transitive verb) some little ornaments that are ____________ (adverb of affirmation) of no expense, save the ____________ (singular noun)?

Comb-cases, ______________ (plural concrete compound noun), letter-holders, ______________ (plural concrete compound noun), paper-racks, ______________ (plural concrete noun), and many other pretty and ______________ (adjective) things can ______________ (regular adverb) be made of ________ (adjective) ______________ (adjective) pasteboard boxes (and the boxes are ______________ (passive infinitive) in a variety of ______________ (plural noun)). For any of ______________ (plural demonstrative pronoun), cut out the parts and ______________ (adverb) sew them together, and the seams and ______________ (adjective) edges ______________________________ (simple present modal passive verb, third-person plural) with narrow strips of ______________________ (compound adjective) paper or tape. ______________________ (present active imperative, singular, of transitive verb) them with transfer or scrap pictures.

I ______________________ (perfect present active indicative transitive verb, first-person singular) ____________________ (adverb of affirmation) pretty vases for ______________________ (present participle of transitive verb) dried flowers and grasses, made of plain dark brown pasteboard, and the seams neatly covered with narrow strips of ______________ (singular concrete noun). __________ (adjective) ottomans can be made by ______________ (present participle of transitive verb) any suitable box with a bit of carpeting, and ________________ (present participle of transitive verb) the top with straw or cotton. Or, __________ (subordinating conjunction introducing an adverb clause) the carpeting is ________ (adverb of negation) ______________ (adjective) ______________ (present active imperative, singular, of transitive verb) a covering of wool.

______________ (active infinitive of transitive verb) the children during the long winter months, ______________ (present active imperative, singular, of transitive verb) a scrap-book of pictures. Collect __________ (indefinite pronoun that can be either singular or plural) the old illustrated books, papers, and ______________ (plural concrete noun), and cut out the pictures and with __________ (singular concrete noun) nicely paste __________ (plural object pronoun) in a ______________ (singular concrete noun), first ______________ (present participle of transitive verb) alternate leaves ______________ (subordinating conjunction) it will ______________ (adverb of negation) be too bulky.

Perhaps ____________ (singular demonstrative pronoun) last remark is ____________ (regular adverb) wandering from my subject, but I love the little ______________ (plural concrete noun) and want them happy. Cares and trouble ______________ (simple future active indicative verb, first-person plural) to them soon enough. For the wee ______________ (adjective) girl make a nice rag ______________ (singular concrete noun); it ______________ (simple future active indicative of transitive verb, third-person singular) her quite as well as a bought one, and __________ (adverb of affirmation) last much ____________ (regular adverb).

Ornaments for Homes (original)

It is not the most expensively furnished houses that are the most homelike. Comparatively few persons have the means to gratify their love of pretty little ornaments with which to beautify their homes. It is really painful to visit some houses; there naked walls and cheerless rooms meet you, yet there are many such, and children in them too.

How much might these homes be brightened by careful forethought in making some little ornaments that are really of no expense, save the time?

Comb-cases, card-receivers, letter-holders, match-safes, paper-racks, cornucopias, and many other pretty and useful things can easily be made of nice clean pasteboard boxes (and the boxes are to be found in a variety of colors). For any of these, cut out the parts and nicely sew them together, and the seams and raw edges can be covered with narrow strips of bright-hued paper or tape. Ornament them with transfer or scrap pictures.

I have seen very pretty vases for holding dried flowers and grasses, made of plain dark brown pasteboard, and the seams neatly covered with narrow strips of paper. Pretty ottomans can be made by covering any suitable box with a bit of carpeting, and stuffing the top with straw or cotton. Or, if the carpeting is not convenient, knit a covering of wool.

To amuse the children during the long winter months, make a scrap-book of pictures. Collect all the old illustrated books, papers, and magazines, and cut out the pictures and with glue nicely paste them in a book, first removing alternate leaves so it will not be too bulky. Perhaps this last remark is slightly wandering from my subject, but I love the little folks and want them happy. Cares and trouble will come to them soon enough. For the wee little girl make a nice rag doll; it will please her quite as well as a bought one, and certainly last much longer.

Review 10B: Identifying Infinitive Phrases, Noun Clauses, and Modifying Clauses

In the following essay, follow these four steps:

a) Identify every set of underlined words as *INF* for infinitive phrase, *PREP* for prepositional phrase, or *CL* for clause.

b) Label each phrase or clause as *ADV* for adverb, *ADJ* for adjective, or *N* for noun.

c) For adjective and adverb phrases and clauses, draw an arrow from the label to the word modified.

d) For noun phrases and clauses, add the appropriate part of the sentence label: *S* for subject, *DO* for direct object, *IO* for indirect object, *PN* for predicate nominative, *OP* for object of the preposition, *APP* for appositive.

The first is done for you.

RAISING ONIONS

CL ADJ — CL N PN

There are two causes of failure that make this crop uncertain. One is because the soil is not

CL N PN

kept clear of weeds, and the other is that it is not properly enriched.

INF N S — PREP ADV

To raise a good crop of onions requires a light, loamy soil, worked to as fine a condition as

INF ADV

possible, to render cultivation easy. The greater part of the preparation should be done in the

CL ADJ

fall, especially the application of the manure. Well-rotted manure is the best, and that which

is free from grass, oats, or weed seeds should always be selected. Of course, if the manure is

CL ADV

properly rotted the vitality of the larger portion of the seed in it will be killed, but unless this

CL ADV

is done it will render the cultivation much more difficult. Stiff, clayey, or hard, poor land can

INF N DO

be made a great deal better for the onion crop by a heavy application of ashes. I prefer to apply

PREP ADV

ashes to the soil as a top dressing in the spring, working it in the surface, as I find by experience

[CL N DO] that they are not only valuable as a fertilizer, but are also of great benefit in keeping down the weeds.

A plot of ground [CL ADJ] that is seeded with crab-grass should not be selected, as the pulling up of the grass injures the growth of the onions. Of course it is too late now [INF ADV] to talk about fall preparation. [CL ADV] If we want a crop of onions from seed this spring, [CLN S] whatever preparation there is must be done between now and seeding.

Another important point in raising a good crop of onions is [INF N PN] to have good seed and sow it early. The first favorable time in the spring must be taken advantage of, [CL ADV] if you would have the best success with your crop. I always take advantage of the first chance in March [INF ADV] to sow my onion seed. We usually have a few warm days sometime about the middle of the month when this work can be done. Of course I do not say that this is the case every year. [CL N S] That the first favorable opportunity should be taken advantage of is [CL N PN] what I want to impress upon those [CL ADJ] who expect to make a crop; let this time come [CL ADV] when it will, any time early in the spring.

[CL ADV] If you have well-rotted poultry manure, now is the best time [INF ADV] to apply it. This strategy, [CL N APP] that you begin your spring cultivation by working fertilizer into the top of the soil with a rake, will guarantee a healthy sprouting of the seeds.

As soon [CL ADV] as the shoots make their appearance above the ground a good raking with a fine steel rake can be given. This will give them a good start and destroy the young weeds [CL ADJ] that will make their appearance at the same time. [CL ADV] After the onions start growing, cultivation is the making of the crop.

Review 10C: Parsing

Parse every bolded verb in the following essay.

Provide the following information:

Person:	First, second, or third
Number:	Sing. or pl.
Tense:	Simple past, present, or future; perfect past, present, or future; progressive past, present, or future; or progressive perfect present
Voice:	Active, passive, or state-of-being
Mood:	Indicative, subjunctive, imperative, hortatory, or modal If the verb is also emphatic, add this label to the mood.

The first bolded verb is done for you.

CHICKEN CHAT

One of my correspondents **writes** [3rd sing., simple present, active, indicative]: "My hens don't eat well—they just **pick** [3rd pl., simple present, active, indicative] over the food as if

3rd sing., simple past, state-of-being, subjunctive
it **were** not good enough for them—and they don't lay well; in fact they don't do much of anything
except to mope about—not as if sick, but as if lazy."

2nd sing., perfect present, active, indicative
Probably you **have fed** the same thing every day for the last six months, and the hens
3rd pl., progressive present, active, indicative — 3rd pl., simple present, state-of-being, indicative
are getting tired of it. Hens **are** like other people—they like a change of provender once in a while,
3rd sing., simple future, active, indicative
especially when confined indoors. Sometimes over-feeding **will cause** indigestion, and then the
2nd sing., simple present, active, hortative
biddies will exhibit the symptoms you describe. In either case, **let** the fowls **fast** for a whole day,
2nd sing., simple present, active, imperative — 3rd pl., progressive present, perfect, active, indicative
and then for a few days **feed** lightly with food that is different from what they **have been living** on.

Another correspondent wants to know why I always advise giving cooked food to fowls and
3rd sing., simple present, state-of-being, indicative — 3rd sing., perfect present, active, indicative
chicks when uncooked food **is** the natural diet. I advise cooked food because experience **has taught**
me that it is much better for poultry than the raw articles would be. Because raw bugs and worms
3rd sing., simple present, active, indicative, emphatic
constitute the "natural diet" of fowls in their wild state, it **does** not **follow** that raw meal and pota-
3rd pl., simple present, state-of-being, modal
toes **would be** the best and most economical food for our domestic fowls. Other things being equal,
3rd pl., simple present, passive, indicative
chicks that **are fed** on cooked food grow fatter, are less liable to disease, and thrive better gener-
ally than those who worry along on uncooked rations.

2nd sing., simple present, active, imperative
If you are short of sitting hens and don't own an incubator, **make** the hens do double duty. Set
two or more at the same time, and when the chicks come out, give two families to one hen, and
3rd sing., simple present, passive, modal
set the other over again. To do this successfully, the chicks **must be taken** from the nest as soon as
dry and given to the hen that is to raise them; for if a hen once leaves the nest with her chicks, no
3rd sing., simple future, active, indicative
amount of moral persuasion **will induce** her to go back. Before giving the hen fresh eggs, the nest
3rd sing., simple present, passive, modal
should be renovated and the hen dusted with sulphur or something to prevent lice.

Review 10D: *Which* and *That* Clauses

In the following sentences, underline each clause introduced by *which or that*. If *that* is understood, use a caret to insert it. If a *which* or *that* clause falls within another clause, underline the entire larger clause once, and the clause-within-a-clause a second time.

- Label each clause as *ADJ* for adjective, *ADV* for adverb, or *N* for noun.
- For adjective and adverb clauses, draw an arrow back to the word modified.
- For noun clauses, label the part of the sentence that the clause fulfills (*S, PN, DO, IO, APP*).
- Finally, label each adjective clause as R for restrictive or *NON-R* for non-restrictive.

The first sentence is done for you.

ADJ R

We have been looking for a grass that would supply good grazing to our cattle and sheep after the native grasses have become dry and tasteless.

ADJ R

Two twisted No. 11 wires were used for this fence, and the posts are the best that could be procured.

Note to Instructor: Although *best* is usually an adjective, in this sentence it serves as a noun.

ADV

I came away satisfied that it was reliable; it ought to be in the home of every farmer in this great

ADV that ADJ R

country of ours, so that their children can learn and know what a grand heritage ^ they have got.

ADV

The weather was so nice the first part of this month that the farmers did a large amount of plowing.

Those who planted seed of their own raising and got a stand have fair corn, while much of

ADJ R N OP

that which was raised from Kansas and Nebraska seed was caught by the frost.

Note to Instructor: The entire clause is the object of the preposition *of*, and the entire prepositional phrase modifies *much*. Notice that the *that* clause actually comes within yet another clause—the adverb clause *while much . . . by the frost*. This is an example of a restrictive clause introduced by *which* (in order to prevent the double occurrence of *that*).

ADJ R

For some reason a barrel that has once held beef will never do for a pork barrel.

ADJ R

The potato which has sold for the highest price in Boston all season is the Early Rose; this has been one of the most remarkable potatoes known.

N DO

I remarked that this was pretty rough farming.

ADJ R

The red ears of maize have a constancy of color which is truly remarkable.

Note to Instructor: The student could make a case for this being a non-restrictive clause, since removing *which is truly remarkable* does not change the statement about *constancy*. I have labeled it as *restrictive* because it is not set off by a comma (a comma would definitely make the clause inessential), and the point of the sentence seems to be the remarkable nature of the *constancy*, rather than merely the *constancy itself*. However, you may accept the label *NON-R* if the student can explain her choice.

Every Northern farmer knows the common coarse grass called door-yard grass, which has long, broad leaves, a tough, bunchy root, and a three-fingered spreading head, which contains large, round seeds.

ADJ NON-R; ADJ NON-R

Great numbers of these caterpillars were killed by a contagious disease, which swept them off just as they were ready to transform to the chrysalis.

ADJ NON-R

We often see in the papers the amount, in dollars and cents, that strong drink costs the people of this country.

ADJ R

That year he grew about 1,000 bushels of oats, some 250 bushels of wheat, and raised 100 hogs.

> **Note to Instructor:** This is a trick sentence; *that* is a demonstrative adjective and does not introduce a clause.

We must have a grass that the hogs will relish, and on which they will both grow and fatten.

ADJ R; ADJ NON-R

In three or four days after the cheeses are placed in the drying-room they become speckled; in another week they are covered with a thick crop of white mold, which by degrees deepens to a dark yellow, the outside of the cheese becoming less and less sticky.

ADJ NON-R

In about two hours, when it is dark, go out again with a lantern and a pail containing salt and water, and pick up each piece on which the slugs are found feeding, and throw slugs and bran into the brine, where they instantly die.

ADJ R

He thought that Iowa was one of the best places in the world in which to raise sheep.

N DO; ADJ R

Review 10E: Words Acting as Multiple Parts of Speech

In each set of sentences below, underline the repeated word. Label each occurrence as *N* for noun, *V* for verb, *PRO* for pronoun, *ADV* for adverb, *ADJ* for adjective, *PREP* for preposition, *CC* for coordinating conjunction, or *SC* for subordinating conjunction.

At day-break we rode home. (ADV)

> **Note to Instructor:** This could also be labeled as an adverbial noun.

For a hardy, early, red raspberry that is sweet and delicious for home (ADJ) use, plant the Turner.

The new home (N) will be established on the fertile prairie next summer.

Shaffer's Colossal raspberry is excellent for canning, or for table use, if you like a fruit full of raspberry flavor though (CC) a little tart.

> **Note to Instructor:** *Though* acts as a coordinating conjunction connecting the compound adjectives *full* and *tart*, both of which describe *fruit*. It cannot be a preposition because it has no noun or pronoun to serve as its object.

The honest breeder, though[PREP] a man of ideas, acknowledges he does not know all.

Though[SC] blue grass is the best for pasture, timothy is the best for hay.

Our race[ADJ] horses of to-day would make a sorry comparison to those in the days of the pony express.

There are some people in every business who, in the race[N] for success, far outrun their competitors.

Huge cakes of ice of every shape and size race[V] past us.

Prudent farmers spare neither time nor expense in providing themselves with a full set[N] of improved furnishings for their dairies, all the way down to good, substantial three-legged milking stools.

It set[V] him to thinking, and before next morning he was of the same opinion.

A set[ADJ] smile was fixed upon his round face.

Should the ground prove weedy, cut the weeds down[ADV] with the mowing machine in June, and leave them upon the surface.

It is quite appalling how much the average lawyer in Congress expects, in money down[ADJ], in the way of a retainer.

A large cake of ice had come floating down[PREP] the river.

She sells duck eggs, breeding ducks, and feathers and down[N] at the local market.

Mr. I. L. Ellwood was experimenting to accomplish a like[ADJ] result with a thin band of metal, the barbs cut and curved outward from the strip.

The blueberry, like[PREP] the cranberry, appears to be a potash plant.

Some members did not like[V] to have hogs running in their orchards.

Musty stained drawers, dusty baskets, old barrels, and the like[N] do not help to sell fruit.

Does the basket willow have to be cultivated like[SC] a field crop?

> **Note to Instructor:** The subordinating conjunction functions in the same way that *as* would function and introduces a clause with understood elements: *like a field crop [is cultivated].*

I have found the very opposite[N] to be true, and I believe I have carefully and faithfully tested the matter.

Mr. Glidden had had in his mind the idea of a barb of wire twisted about the main wire of the fence, leaving two projecting points on opposite[ADJ] sides.

PREP
The statue stands opposite the far corner, next to the path.

Review 10F: Idioms

Circle each idiom in the following sentences. Above each one, write its meaning within the sentence. The first is done for you.

suitable for, will do well in
Strawberries are (at home) in a young orchard.

taken care of my own affairs, organized myself
To begin the work, I have (set my own house in order).

nothing to gain, nothing to be lost
I think the Kieffer pear is better than the Bartlett, but I have (no axe on the grindstone) in this matter.

refresh, improve
I must (brush up) my memory by asking you a question or two.

prevent bad things from happening, take precautions
I have always tried (to keep a lock on the stable door before the horse is stolen).

considering, knowing about
Who can be indifferent (in the face of) our great perils?

think it is a good idea
If you (think best), you can blow the candle out and allow the wick to cool.

have a high opinion
I used to (think a great deal) of Mrs. Goode, who was always so kind to me.

fulfill the purpose, meet the need
An orchard owner who could import European pear varieties that will (fill the bill) required by the necessities of our soil and climate would have a fortune at his command.

Review 10G: Ambitransitive Verbs

Underline each predicate in the following sentences. Mark each verb as *T* for transitive or *IT* for intransitive. For transitive verbs, circle the word that receives the action of the verb.

The first is done for you.

This mill will stand (T) a heavier (wind), run (IT) steadier, and last (IT) longer than any other mill.

Two men run (T) the old-fashioned cross-cut (saw), which makes (T) two (backs) sore every day that they use (T) (it).

The (trees) should (T) then be set against the sloping side of the trench.

The cells of the frosted corn ruptured (IT) when hard weather set (IT) in.

She set (T) several (hens) and the (incubator) at the same time.

The corn-plant louse, an early and destructive enemy of the crop, throttled (T) the young (shoots).

before they had broken ground

The lark broke into song.

The snow will melt away when warm air rises from the unfrozen earth.

The engineers melted copper for the strong but thin wire.

Young horses frighten easily at every fresh or strange object that they see.

The raging torrent frightened him.

He strung two wires between two trees and twisted them together with a stick.

The vines will twist around the arbor if you tie them up with twine.

Gates open from each field into a private central road belonging to the farm.

Linnæus opened the way in botany, and the world profited by his blunders.

Review 10H: Hunt and Find

In the following essay, find, underline, and label each of the following:

Infinitive phrase acting as a noun
Infinitive phrase acting as an adjective
Infinitive phrase acting as an adverb
To as a preposition
Hortative verb
That acting as a demonstrative pronoun
Restrictive clause introduced by *which*
Non-restrictive clause introduced by *which*
Noun clause in apposition
Indirect object
Clause with an understood *that*
Comparison
Participle phrase acting as a noun
Compound subordinating conjunction
Adverbial noun

THE HORSE AND HIS TREATMENT

The horse is naturally a wild animal and therefore, though domesticated, he demands such food as nature would provide for him. But man forgets this. Nature's food would be largely grass. It is true that when domesticated and put to hard work he needs some food of a more concentrated and highly nutritious nature than grass; but while labor may necessitate grain, the health of his system yet demands a liberal allowance of grass.

I have found that when the horses were allowed the range of a blue grass pasture at night, they endured work the best because they digested their grain and hay better, and good digestion made good appetites. In fact, I consider pasture the best food and the best medicine a horse can be given. If his coat is rough, if he is stiff and lifeless, if he is losing flesh and strength, turn him on pasture and he will soon grow better.

For winter, hay is provided. I am convinced that the great majority of farmers do not feed their horses enough forage. I know of farmers who do not feed hay at all when their horses are at work, which is more than half the year [non-restrictive clause introduced by *which*]. Grain is fed exclusively. Yet they wonder why their horses lose flesh and have rough coats. Feeding a horse all grain [participle phrase acting as a noun (subject)] is like feeding a man all meat [participle phrase acting as a noun (object of preposition *like*)] [comparison]. The food is so oily and difficult of digestion that it soon deranges the digestive organs. The horse should have all the hay he wishes, at all seasons of the year.

The horse should have at least ninety minutes for each meal. A large number of farmers do not give him [indirect object] this much time. Their reason for neglecting [participle phrase acting as noun (OP *for*)] to do so [infinitive phrase acting as noun (DO of *neglecting*)], that it would be a loss of time [noun clause in apposition (renames *reason*)], is untrue. Time is gained. The horse has the opportunity to eat slowly [infinitive phrase acting as adjective (modifies *opportunity*)], can eat all he wishes [clause with an understood *that* (adjective clause modifies *all*)], and can rest after eating, giving the organs of digestion a chance to work. Let him have [hortative verb] an hour and a half to eat his noon-day meal [infinitive phrase acting as adverb (modifies *have*)], at least, and at the end of the season you will find that you have gained time. He may not have walked before the plow and harrow so many hours [adverbial noun (modifies *walked*)], but he has stepped faster and pulled more energetically.

Another error is the feeding of too much grain [participle phrase acting as noun (predicate nominative)]. Some farmers have grain in the feeding troughs all the time during the spring and summer. This may do for a hog, whose only business is to lie around, grunt, and put on fat; but for a horse it will not do.

One more error which I notice [participle phrase acting as noun (predicate nominative)] is the giving of too much dry food. The horse does best upon moist food, or that [*that* acting as demonstrative pronoun] which has a large percentage of water in its composition [restrictive clause introduced by *which*]. Carrots, turnips, beets, pumpkins, etc., may be given in small quantities with decided advantage, especially in the winter. In summer the hay should be sprinkled with water, and the oats soaked. This will make the food more palatable and easily digested.

One of the other evils of stable management often allowed is the accumulation of manure. The accumulation of the manure in the stable hurts the horse. Its fermentation gives off obnoxious gases which pollute and poison the air [non-restrictive clause introduced by *which*] the horse is compelled [clause with an understood *that*] to breathe [infinitive phrase used as adverb (modifies *is compelled*)].

The manure should be cleaned out morning [adverbial noun (modifies *cleaned*)], noon [adverbial noun (modifies *cleaned*)], and again at night. Use sawdust or straw liberally for bedding. It will absorb the urine, and as soon as [compound subordinating conjunction (introduces clause with understood elements: *as soon as [it is] foul*)] foul, should be removed to [*to* as a preposition] the compost heap with the dung, where it will soon be converted into fine, excellent manure.

Review 10I: Conditionals and Formal Conditionals

In each of the following conditional sentences, parse the underlined verbs, giving tense, voice (*active*, *passive*, or *state-of-being*), and mood. Then, classify the sentences as first, second, or third conditional by placing a *1*, *2*, or *3* in the blank at the end.

If the sentence is a formal conditional, write *FC* next to the blank.

The first is done for you.

simple future, active, indicative — simple present, passive, indicative
Oak planks will last many years if they are turned over occasionally. 1

simple present, state-of-being, indicative — simple present, state-of-being, modal
If pork is to be kept all summer, twice boiling the brine may be necessary. 1

perfect present, passive, modal — perfect present, passive, modal
Much loss from frost would have been avoided had the seed been carefully selected from the best corn grown in the immediate neighborhood. 3 FC

Note to Instructor: Although the indicative and subjunctive are often identical in form, verbs that express unreal situations (as in the condition clause of a second or third conditional sentence) are in the subjunctive mood. You may need to remind the student of this.

simple present, passive, indicative — simple present, passive, hortative
If arbors or rests are needed, let them be placed at the points where they are obviously required, and be made of graceful patterns. 1

simple present, state-of-being, subjunctive — simple present, state-of-being, indicative
The coat is rough and staring if the horse is in lean condition. 1

simple past, state-of-being, subjunctive — simple present, state-of-being, modal
Were they successful, it would be a sad commentary upon our system of government. 2 FC

perfect present, state-of-being, modal — perfect past, active, subjunctive
She labored early and late to make both ends meet, something she would not have been able to accomplish had she not possessed skill as a dressmaker. 3 FC

perfect past, active, subjunctive — perfect present, active, modal
If every scientist had attempted to master the majority of scientific truths before concentrating his time on some special branch of science, science would have progressed little or none at all. 3

simple past, state-of-being, subjunctive — simple present, active, modal
Were I the owner of a whole herd of Jerseys, I should endeavor to engage this genius to write them up for me. 2 FC

simple present, active, indicative — simple present, passive, modal
If you want a crop of onions from seed this spring, whatever preparation there is must be done between now and seeding. 1

simple present, active, indicative — simple present, active, modal
If farmers expect a good crop of corn they should not get seed from a southern latitude. 1

Review 10J: Affirmations and Negations

The following sentences all contain adverbs of affirmation and negation. Circle each one, and label them as *AFF* or *NEG*.

Then, choose three sentences and rewrite them on your own paper, turning affirmatives into negatives and vice versa. Show your sentences to your instructor.

The first is done for you.

Note to Instructor: The rewritten sentences below are just examples; the student may choose to use other affirmative or negative adverbs.

There is (no) [NEG] new thing under the sun.

There is certainly a new thing under the sun.

(Never) [NEG] since I was a boy can I remember experiencing so perfect a repose.

I surely experienced the most perfect repose I have had since I was a boy.

(Indeed) [AFF] the whole tribe of willows love cool, moist situations.

The whole tribe of willows does not love cool, moist situations.

If at the end of forty-eight hours the water turns milky, there can be (no) [NEG] doubt of its impurity.

If at the end of forty-eight hours the water turns milky, you can be certain of its impurity.

(No) [NEG] crop is free from immaturity or imperfection.

The crop is certainly free from immaturity or imperfection.

The eucalyptus proved to be (no) [NEG] more hardy than the orange.

The eucalyptus proved very much more hardy than the orange.

I have (never) [NEG] seen a large variety of corn that suited me so well.

I have certainly seen a large variety of corn that suited me well.

The cattle there were (certainly) [AFF] fine animals.

The cattle there were not fine animals.

(Surely) [AFF] every farmer can afford to build a wind break, at least a pile of brush and old hay, around the stock yards.

Not every farmer can afford to build a wind break, not even a pile of brush and old hay, around the stock yards.

This is (indeed) [AFF] a fearful showing.

This is not a fearful showing.

In fields of maize, the cornroot worm was again (very) [AFF] destructive.

In fields of maize, the cornroot worm was never destructive.

AFF NEG
It (surely) will (not) be lasting.

It will never be lasting.
Certainly, it will be lasting.
Indeed, it will never be lasting.

Review 10K: Diagramming
On your own paper, diagram every word of the following sentences.

The railway folks feared it would injure stock, the damages for which they would be forced to pay.

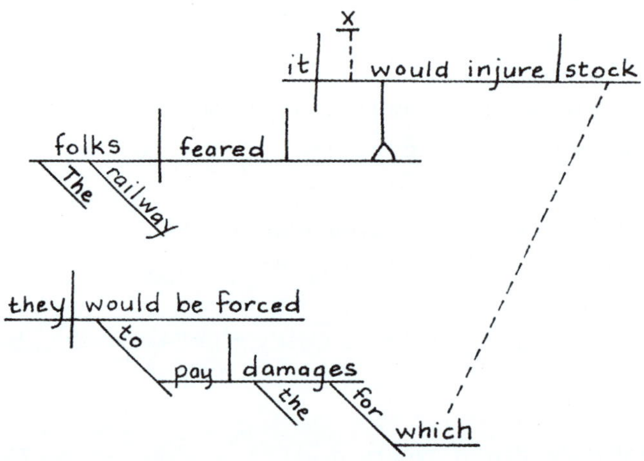

Now why could we not make some use of this grass, and of others, such as quack-grass, which defy so persistently all our efforts to destroy them?

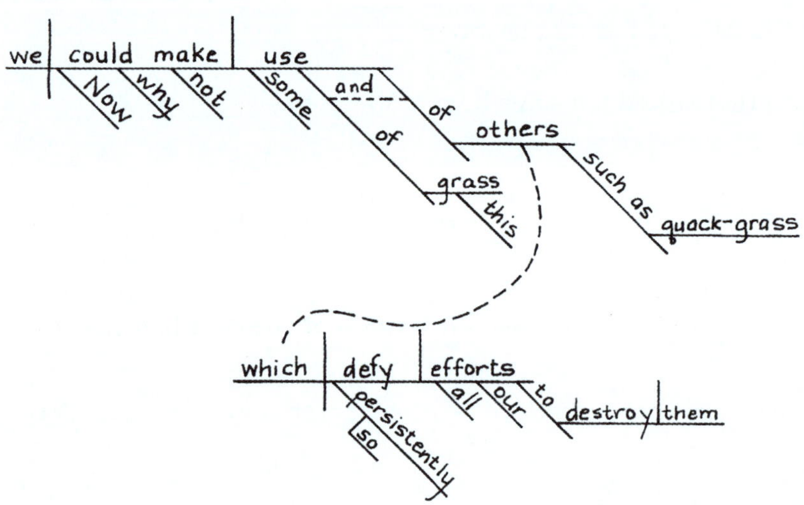

Note to Instructor: *Such as* is an idiom meaning *for example* and functioning in this sentence as a preposition.

With the first of June the field was green indeed, and from then until frost we pastured sixty large hogs, which, with one ear of corn for each, morning and evening, became thoroughly fat.

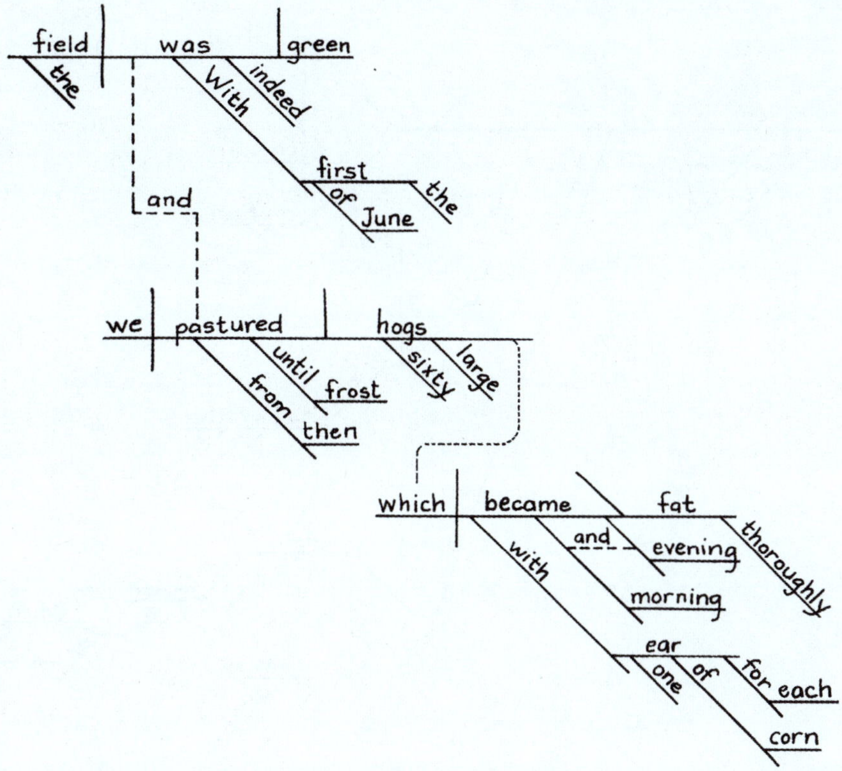

A good farmer must be quick in his judgment of what should be done at the present time, and he should have a good perception to show him the best thing to do for the future.

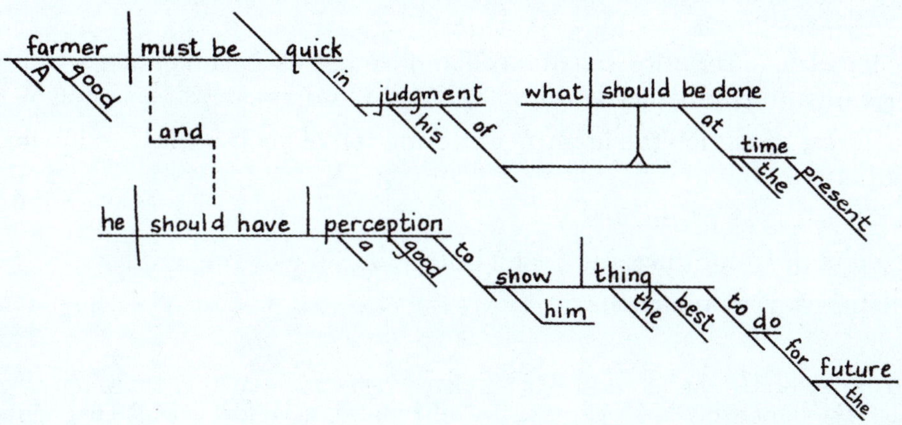

With a liberal supply of corn fodder for winter feeding and a good pasture, with hay and corn during the coldest weather, this branch of farming is not only easy, but certain and profitable.

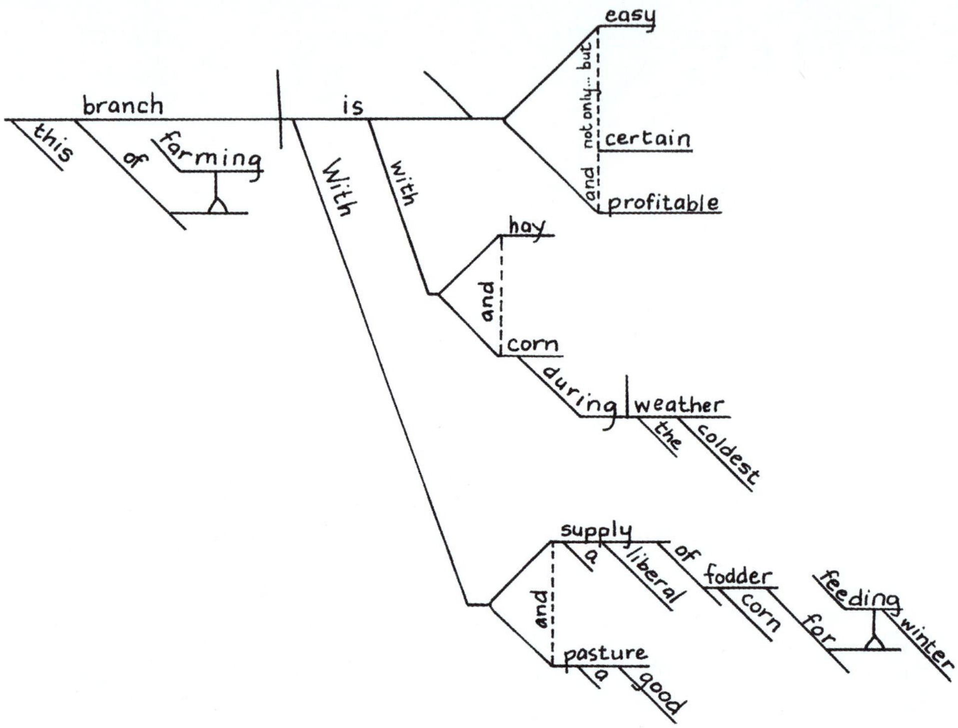

Review 10L: Explaining Sentences

Tell your instructor every possible piece of grammatical information about the following sentences. Follow these steps:

a) Underline each clause. Describe the identity and function of each clause and give any other useful information (introductory word, relationship to the rest of the sentence, etc.)

b) Circle each phrase. Describe the identity and function of each phrase and give any other useful information.

c) Parse all verbs acting as predicates.

d) Describe the identity and function of each individual remaining word.

If you need help, ask your instructor.

Note to Instructor: Use the information in the Notes, below, to prompt the student as necessary. The purpose of this exercise is to build the student's confidence in defining and explaining sentences out loud. Give all necessary help and encourage the student to answer loudly and in complete sentences.

Have you no butter, eggs, fowls, honey, or bees-wax to sell from this good farm?

a) Have you no butter, eggs, fowls, honey, or bees-wax to sell from this good farm?

Note to Instructor: This sentence is made up of one independent clause with a single subject and predicate. It is an interrogative sentence; the question is formed by placing the predicate in front of the subject.

b) Have you no butter, eggs, fowls, honey, or bees-wax to sell from this good farm?

> **Note to Instructor:** The infinitive phrase *to sell from this good farm* modifies all of the compound direct objects and acts as an adjective, answering the question *what kind*.
> *From this good farm* is a prepositional phrase acting as an adverb and modifying the infinitive *to sell*.
> *From* is the preposition; *farm* is the object of the preposition; the demonstrative adjective *this* and the adjective *good* both modify the noun *farm*.

c) The predicate *have* is simple present, active, indicative.

d) The pronoun *you* is the subject.
The nouns *butter, eggs, fowls, honey* and *bees-wax* are all direct objects of the predicate *have*.
Or is a coordinating conjunction connecting the direct objects.

How has science advanced—is it not by the invaluable aid of men who have given their whole lives to the solution of some special problem?

a) How has science advanced—is it not by the invaluable aid of men who have given their whole lives to the solution of some special problem?

> **Note to Instructor:** This sentence is made up of two independent clauses (*How . . . advanced* and *is it not . . . special problem*) with a subordinate clause (*who have given their whole lives*) within the second clause.
> Both independent clauses are interrogatives. They are connected by a dash.
> The first is formed with the interrogative adverb *How* and the second is formed simply by placing the predicate in front of the subject.
> The subordinate clause functions as an adjective. It is introduced by the relative pronoun *who* and modifies *men*, which is also the antecedent of the relative pronoun.

b) How has science advanced—is it not by the invaluable aid of men who have given their whole lives to the solution of some special problem?

> **Note to Instructor:** The entire prepositional phrase *by the invaluable aid of men who have given their whole lives to the solution of some special problem* is an adverb phrase modifying *is* and answering the question *how*. (It is not a predicate nominative or adjective because *is it* refers to *how has science advanced*, not *what science is*.)
> *Of men who have given their whole lives* is an adjectival prepositional phrase modifying *aid*.
> *To the solution* is an adverbial prepositional phrase modifying *have given*.
> *Of some special problem* is an adjectival prepositional phrase modifying *solution*.

c) The predicate *has advanced*, in the first independent clause, is perfect present, active, indicative.
The predicate *is*, in the second independent clause, is simple present, state-of-being, indicative.
The predicate *have given*, in the subordinate clause, is perfect present, active, indicative.

d) The noun *science* is the subject of the first independent clause.
The pronoun *it* is the subject of the second independent clause.
The noun *aid* is the object of the preposition *by*, and the article *the* and the adjective *invaluable* modify *aid*.
The noun *men* is the object of the preposition *of*.

The noun *lives* is the direct object of the verb *have given*. The possessive adjective *their* and the adjective *whole* modify *lives*.
The noun *solution* is the object of the preposition *to*. The article *the* modifies *solution*.
The noun *problem* is the object of the preposition *of*. The indefinite adjective *some* and the adjective *special* modify *problem*.

This is a mistaken idea that many possess who think there is no brain work needed on a farm.

a) This is a mistaken idea that many possess who think there is no brain work needed on a farm.

> **Note to Instructor:** This sentence begins with the independent clause *This is a mistaken idea.* (Technically, the entire sentence could be underlined, since the independent clause contains the three remaining subordinate clauses within it, but for simplicity it is underlined separately.)
>
> The adjective clause *that many possess who think there is no brain work needed on a farm* modifies *idea* and is introduced by the relative pronoun *that*, which is the direct object of the verb *possess; idea* is the antecedent of *that*.
>
> The adjective clause *who think there is no brain work needed on a farm* modifies the pronoun *many* and is introduced by the relative pronoun *who*, which is the subject of the clause and also refers back to its antecedent *many*.
>
> Finally, the noun clause *there is no brain work needed on a farm* is introduced by an understood *that*. It serves as the direct object of the verb *think*.
>
> All three subordinate clauses are contained within the main clause; the first subordinate clause contains the other two; the second subordinate clause contains the last.

b) This is a mistaken idea that many possess who think there is no brain work needed (on a farm)

> **Note to Instructor:** The prepositional phrase *on a farm* acts as an adverb and modifies the past participle *needed*.

c) The predicate *is* is simple present, state-of-being, indicative.
The predicate *possess* is simple present, active, indicative.

d) The second *is* is also simple present, state-of-being, indicative.
The demonstrative pronoun *this* is the subject of the first independent clause.
The noun *idea* is a predicate nominative renaming *this*.
The article *a* and the adjective *mistaken* modify *idea*.
The pronoun *many* is the subject of the first subordinate clause.
In the third subordinate clause, *there* is an adverb modifying *is*.
The compound noun *brain work* is the subject of the third subordinate clause.
No is functioning as an adjective of negation, modifying *brain work*.
Needed is a past participle acting as an adjective and modifying *needed*.
Farm is the object of the preposition *on*.
The article *a* modifies *farm*.

WEEK 33

Mechanics

— LESSON 121 —

Capitalization Review
Additional Capitalization Rules
Formal and Informal Letter Format
Ending Punctuation

Exercise 121A: Proofreading

Use proofreader's marks to insert the missing capital letters and punctuation marks into the following sentences.

capitalize letter: ≡	make letter lowercase: /
insert period: ⊙	insert exclamation point: ^!
insert comma: ^,	insert question mark: ^?

If a word or phrase should be italicized, indicate this by underlining.

Note to Instructor: The original sentences are below. Accept all reasonable corrections.

Oh, dear, the subject is difficult.

I was a moviegoer, a magazine-reader, a CNN-watcher.

And so, after my sophomore year, I had moved out of the dorms with friends and into an apartment on 112th Street between Broadway and Amsterdam, and I had escaped whenever possible into the city—to Carnegie Hall or folk clubs in the Village or to the movie revival houses on the Upper West Side.

In 1897, the distinguished architectural firm of McKim, Mead & White had given the campus an integral design, but I had never encountered anyone who was passionate about the neo-Renaissance, red-brick buildings with limestone trim and pale green copper roofs that surrounded the large open space between Low Library to the north and the blockish, Herbert Hooverish Butler Library to the south.

I now understood better than ever that my dismay when Odysseus kills the suitors at the end of the *Odyssey* was an emotion Homer couldn't possibly have intended his listeners to feel.

—David Denby, *Great Books: My Adventures with Homer, Rousseau, Woolf, and Other Indestructible Writers of the Western World*

Note to Instructor: If the student does not capitalize *Toad*, *Mole*, and *Rat* in the sentences below, do not correct him, but point out that the author treated these words as proper names.

Oh, I am a smart Toad, and no mistake!

For a few weeks it was all well enough, but afterwards, O the weary length of the nights!

Alas! what am I saying?

Well, well, we won't linger over that now.

But the Mole was bent on enjoying everything, and although just when he had got the basket packed and strapped up tightly he saw a plate staring up at him from the grass, and when the job had been done again the Rat pointed out a fork which anybody ought to have seen, and last of all, behold! the mustard pot, which he had been sitting on without knowing it—still, somehow, the thing got finished at last, without much loss of temper.

—Kenneth Grahame, *The Wind in the Willows*

Nicholas was standing with his back to the curtain, now contemplating the first scene, which was a Gothic archway, about two feet shorter than Mr. Crummles, through which that gentleman was to make his first entrance.

Mr. Crummles lived in Thomas's Street, at the house of one Bulph, a pilot, who sported a boat-green door, with window-frames of the same colour, and had the little finger of a drowned man on his parlour mantelshelf, with other maritime and natural curiosities.

Smike, the boys, and the phenomenon went home by a shorter cut, and Mrs. Grudden remained behind to take some cold Irish stew and a pint of porter in the box-office.

At Mr. Wackford Squeers's Academy, Dotheboys Hall, at the delightful village of Dotheboys, near Greta Bridge in Yorkshire, youth are boarded, clothed, booked, furnished with pocket-money, provided with all necessaries, instructed in all languages living and dead, mathematics, orthography, geometry, astronomy, trigonometry, the use of the globes, algebra, single stick (if required), writing, arithmetic, fortification, and every other branch of classical literature. Terms, twenty guineas per annum. No extras, no vacations, and diet unparalleled. Mr. Squeers is in town, and attends daily, from one till four, at the Saracen's Head, Snow Hill.

—Charles Dickens, *The Life and Adventures of Nicholas Nickleby*

Exercise 121B: Correct Letter Mechanics

The following text is the actual rejection letter written to Edgar Rice Burroughs, the author of *Tarzan of the Apes*, when he sent his story to the Chicago publisher Rand McNally & Company in 1913.

On your own paper (or with your own word processing program), rewrite or retype the text so that it is properly formatted, punctuated, and capitalized. You may choose either letter format from this lesson.

Notice that there are no ZIP codes, because ZIP codes were only created by the U.S. Post Office in 1963.

Each sentence in the letter is a separate paragraph. The last sentence/paragraph ends with the comma after *we are*, and the closing is *Yours very truly.* This is an old-fashioned but correct way to end a letter.

When you are finished, compare your letter with the two versions in the *Answer Key.*

rand mcNally & company 168 adams street chicago illinois august 20, 1913 mr edgar rice burroughs 2008 park avenue chicago illinois dear sir we are returning under separate cover *the all-story* magazine (oct. 1912) containing your story, "tarzan of the apes." we have given the work careful consideration and, while interesting, we find it does not fit in with our plans for the present year. thanking you for submitting the story to us, we are, yours very truly, rand mcNally & company

Note to Instructor: Two correct versions of the letter are given below.

Rand McNally & Company
168 Adams Street
Chicago, Illinois

August 20, 1913

Mr. Edgar Rice Burroughs
2008 Park Avenue
Chicago, Illinois

Dear Sir:

We are returning under separate cover *The All-Story* magazine (Oct. 1912) containing your story, "Tarzan of the Apes."

We have given the work careful consideration and, while interesting, we find it does not fit in with our plans for the present year.

Thanking you for submitting the story to us, we are,

Yours very truly,

Rand McNally & Company

Rand McNally & Company
168 Adams Street
Chicago, Illinois

August 20, 1913

Mr. Edgar Rice Burroughs
2008 Park Avenue
Chicago, Illinois

Dear Sir:

We are returning under separate cover *The All-Story* magazine (Oct. 1912) containing your story, "Tarzan of the Apes."

We have given the work careful consideration and, while interesting, we find it does not fit in with our plans for the present year.

Thanking you for submitting the story to us, we are,

Yours very truly,

Rand McNally & Company

— LESSON 122 —

Commas
Semicolons
Additional Semicolon Rules
Colons
Additional Colon Rules

Exercise 122A: Comma Use

In the blank at the end of each sentence, write the number from the list above that describes the comma use. If more than one number seems to fit equally well, write all suitable numbers.

These sentences are taken from *Fifty Famous People*, by James Baldwin.

This happened six hundred years ago, in the city of Florence in Italy. 11

And you, grandfather, were as bad as the rest. 5, 8

There was one such king who had four sons, Ethelbald, Ethelbert, Ethelred, and Alfred. 2, 4

"Shoe him quickly, for the king wishes to ride him to battle," said the groom who had brought him. 17, 1

Two children, brother and sister, were on their way to school. 8

Daniel, you must be up early in the morning. 5

King Solomon lived 3,000 years ago. 15

His grandfather, whose name was Astyages, was king of Media, and very rich and powerful. 6, 19

The caliph, Al Mansur, lived nearly twelve hundred years ago. 8

He looked at the bright, yellow pieces and said, "What shall I do with these coppers, mother?" 3, 5, 16

He saw that Cyrus had a will of his own, and this pleased him very much. 1

He was always reading, learning, inquiring. 2

He sang of war, and of bold rough deeds, and of love and sorrow. 2

They looked, or so they thought, in every place where the lambs might have taken shelter. 7

He shouted, "A horse! A horse! My kingdom for a horse." 16

Oh, yes, I know she is anxious, and I will go. 9, 10, 1

"Let us call the neighbors together and have a grand wolf hunt tomorrow," said Putnam. 17

No, no, I am going to be a sailor; I am going to see the world. 10

Exercise 122B: Commas, Capitals, Closing Punctuation, Colons, and Semicolons

Insert all missing punctuation and correct all capitalization in the text that follows. Use these proofreader's marks:

capitalize letter: ≡	make letter lowercase: /
insert period: ⊙	insert exclamation point: ^!
insert comma: ^,	insert question mark: ^?
insert colon: ^:	insert semicolon: ^;

Note to Instructor: The original sentences are found below. Where there is a legitimate judgment call over which punctuation mark to admit, a note has been inserted. Make sure that the student looks at the original sentences once the exercise is finished, so that she can be familiar with the different ways in which these punctuation marks may be used.

Be sure to check the student's proofing of the citations as well as the sentences themselves.

122B.1: Sentences

We have divided time into segments of every conceivable size: nanoseconds, milliseconds, seconds, minutes, hours, days, weeks, months, years, decades, centuries, millennia, eons, eras, and on and on.

Note to Instructor: *On and on* is a single idiom, so the final item before the conjunction (the one that takes the Oxford comma) is *eras*.

The watches on our wrists today are the culmination of a long, slow, arduous process of invention and discovery which ultimately began about four millennia ago when someone stuck a stick in the ground and watched its shadow change throughout the day.

Note to Instructor: A comma before *which* is also acceptable, since it is not entirely clear whether that clause is restrictive or non-restrictive.

Our ancestors, of course, had no idea of any of the things discussed in the previous chapter.

Early efforts at time-counting still did not quite deal with the whole day/night unit; instead, they usually tallied repetitions of an easily recognized event within the unit, namely, sunrise or sunset.

In addition to the flat dial with which we are most familiar, sundials were also invented in the form of sunken hemispheres and cones, cubes, columns, open rings, and opened tablets, to name only a few.

—Jo Ellen Barnett, *Time's Pendulum: From Sundials to Atomic Clocks, the Fascinating History of Timekeeping and How Our Discoveries Changed the World*

Jewelers also regulated, maintained, and repaired timepieces.

The jewelers who crowded beneath the Chicago clock when it debuted might have recalled the years when they belonged to the ranks of time specialists: those artisans, tinkerers, and scientists who reckoned the time and made clocks for its conveyance.

Note to Instructor: *Those* could also be preceded by a comma, but the colon is neater since the items that followed are separated by commas.

The clock itself was an elaborate period piece: illuminated with electric lights, decorated in the oriental motifs favored in twenties' design, and topped with a figure of Father Time holding a scythe and an hourglass.

> **Note to Instructor:** The colon could also be eliminated completely.

The parameters within which the earliest clocks functioned were broad; a hand moved either direction (rather than only "clockwise"), and dials indicated three, four, sixteen, or twenty-four hours, in addition to the now conventional twelve hours.

> **Note to Instructor:** The comma before *in addition to* is the Oxford comma and should be included.

They decorated their homes with clocks; included clocks and watches in their poetry, sermons, stories, and songs; and enlivened their visual culture with representations of timekeepers.

And even on land, calculating longitude was no small feat; just an estimation of it required a well-regulated clock, astronomical instruments, and observatory charts.

Steam engines, gas-light, telegraphs, telephones, electricity, phonography, photography, combustion engines, and wireless communications fundamentally changed our experiences of time and space.

—Alexis McCrossen, *Marking Modern Times: A History of Clocks, Watches, and Other Timekeepers in American Life*

122B.2: Letter Format

The following letters are adapted from the book *Mark Twain's Letters*, Vol. 1 (1917).

September 28, 1860

Orion Clemens
Keokuk, Iowa

Dear Brother,

Yesterday I spent ten dollars on dinner at a French restaurant, where we ate sheep-head, fish with mushrooms, shrimps and oysters, birds, and coffee with brandy burnt in it.

Please find $20 enclosed.

In haste,

Sam

January 27, 1868

American Publishing Company
Hartford, Connecticut

Dear Sir:

I agree to your propositions and will furnish you with manuscript sufficient for a volume of 500 to 600 pages for a book to be sold by the American Publishing Company by subscription.

For this manuscript, the APC will pay me a copyright of 5 percent upon the subscription price of the book for all copies sold.

Very truly yours,

Samuel L. Clemens

122B.3: Quotes

In his book *About Time,* Bruce Koscielniak writes, "The Greeks used three ten-day weeks per month." He adds, "The Romans used an eight-day week with the eighth day reserved for market festivities."

We think of time as something natural, normal, and inevitable. But in *About Time,* Bruce Koscielniak points out that our ideas of time are invented:

> Time is what is measured by a regular or standard interval—a second, a minute, an hour, for example—that is chimed, ticked, beeped, or in some way displayed by a time-measuring device called a clock.

— LESSON 123 —

Colons
Dashes
Hyphens
Parentheses
Brackets

Exercise 123A: Hyphens

Some (but not all) of the following sentences (from *Around the World in Eighty Days*, by Jules Verne) contain words that should be hyphenated. Insert a hyphen into each word that needs one.

Phileas Fogg passed ten hours out of the twenty-four in Saville Row.

He was never seen in the counting-rooms of the City.

Note to Instructor: *Counting rooms* is also correct.

He was served by the gravest waiters, in dress coats, and shoes with swan–skin soles.

The club decanters contained his sherry, his port, and his cinnamon–spiced claret.

I've been an itinerant singer and a circus–rider.

> **Note to Instructor:** *circus rider* is also correct.

From this moment, twenty–nine minutes after eleven, you are in my service.

Seen in the various phases of his daily life, he gave the idea of being perfectly well balanced.

He appeared to be about forty years of age, with handsome features, and a well–shaped figure.

A moderate–sized safe stood in his bedroom.

A package of banknotes, to the value of fifty–five thousand pounds, had been taken.

On the day of the robbery, a well–dressed gentleman of polished manners, and with a well–to–do air, had been observed going to and fro in the paying room where the crime was committed.

> **Note to Instructor:** *Paying-room* is also correct.

The other was a small, slight-built personage, with a nervous, intelligent face.

According to habit, he scrutinized the passers–by with a keen, rapid glance.

This is a family watch, monsieur, which has come down from my great–grandfather!

Three–quarters of an hour afterwards we were off.

The celebrated East India Company was all powerful from 1756.

He lost no time in knocking down two of his long–gowned adversaries with his fists.

In the semi–obscurity they saw the victim, quite senseless.

The whole multitude prostrated themselves, terror stricken, on the ground.

Exercise 123B: Parenthetical Elements

The following sentences are all from *Robinson Crusoe*, by Daniel Defoe. Defoe liked to write very long sentences filled with parenthetical elements! Set off each bolded set of words with commas, dashes, or parentheses. Choose the punctuation marks that seem to fit best. Then, compare your answers with the original punctuation in the *Answer Key.*

> **NOTE:** Depending on what punctuation marks you choose, you may have to add an additional comma or semicolon following some the parenthetical elements. Be sure to look at the entire sentence to decide whether additional punctuation should be added. Keep in mind that, in contemporary English punctuation, a parenthesis can be followed by another punctuation mark, but a dash almost never is.

> **Note to Instructor:** The original sentences follow, but in almost all cases, all three types of punctuation (commas, dashes, or parentheses) will work. If the student chooses different punctuation than Defoe, ask her to compare the two versions side by side and decide which one she prefers. This exercise is simply intended to demonstrate the many different correct ways in which sentences with parenthetical elements can be punctuated.

Nature—**as if I had been fatigued and exhausted with the very thoughts of it**—threw me into a sound sleep.

About a year and a half after I entertained these notions **(and by long musing had, as it were, resolved them all into nothing, for want of an occasion to put them into execution),** I was surprised one morning by seeing no less than five canoes all on shore together on my side of the island, and the people who belonged to them all landed and out of my sight.

> **Note to Instructor:** The comma after the closing parenthesis divides the initial adverb clause, which contains the parenthetical element, from the main clause. It is unnecessary if commas or dashes set off the parenthetical material.

I loaded all my cannon, as I called them—**that is to say, my muskets, which were mounted upon my new fortification**—and all my pistols, and resolved to defend myself to the last gasp—**not forgetting seriously to commend myself to the Divine protection, and earnestly to pray to God to deliver me out of the hands of the barbarians.**

So, **after some days,** I took Friday to work again by way of discourse, and told him I would give him a boat to go back to his own nation; and, **accordingly,** I carried him to my frigate, **which lay on the other side of the island,** and having cleared it of water **(for I always kept it sunk in water),** I brought it out, showed it him, and we both went into it.

> **Note to Instructor:** The additional comma after the closing parenthesis divides the adverb clause *and having cleared it of water (for I always kept it sunk in water)* from the main clause *I brought it out*. It is optional.

While this was doing, I sent Friday with the captain's mate to the boat with orders to secure her, and bring away the oars and sails, **which they did;** and by-and-by three straggling men, that were **(happily for them)** parted from the rest, came back upon hearing the guns fired; and seeing the captain, **who was before their prisoner,** now their conqueror, they submitted to be bound also; and so our victory was complete.

> **Note to Instructor:** The parenthetical element *which they did* can be set off by two commas, rather than a comma and semicolon, since a coordinating conjunction introduces the next sentence. If the student chooses parentheses for this element, the closing parenthesis should be followed by a comma or semicolon. If the student chooses dashes, no additional punctuation is necessary.

Accordingly, we went on board, took the arms which were left on board out of her, and whatever else we found there—which was a bottle of brandy, and another of rum, a few biscuit-cakes, a horn of powder, and a great lump of sugar in a piece of canvas **(the sugar was five or six pounds):** all which was very welcome to me, especially the brandy and sugar, **of which I had had none left for many years.**

> **Note to Instructor:** If the student chooses parentheses for *the sugar was five or six pounds*, it may be followed by either a comma or a colon. The colon in the original follows the rule *A colon may introduce an item that follows a complete sentence, when that item is closely related to the sentence.* Note that the closing words *all which was very welcome to me, especially the brandy and sugar, of which I had had none left for many years* is not a complete sentence and should not be preceded by a semicolon.

As the bear is a heavy, clumsy creature, and does not gallop as the wolf does, **who is swift and light,** so he has two particular qualities, which generally are the rule of his actions; first, as to men, who are not his proper prey **(he does not usually attempt them, except they first attack him, unless he be excessively hungry, which it is probable might now be the case, the ground being**

covered with snow), if you do not meddle with him, he will not meddle with you; but then you must take care to be very civil to him, and give him the road, for he is a very nice gentleman; he will not go a step out of his way for a prince; nay, **if you are really afraid,** your best way is to look another way and keep going on; for sometimes if you stop, and stand still, and look steadfastly at him, he takes it for an affront; but if you throw or toss anything at him, **though it were but a bit of stick as big as your finger,** he thinks himself abused, and sets all other business aside to pursue his revenge, and will have satisfaction in point of honour—**that is his first quality**; the next is, if he be once affronted, he will never leave you, **night or day,** till he has his revenge, but follows at a good round rate till he overtakes you.

Note to Instructor: The first two parenthetical elements must be followed by a comma if they are set off with parentheses; the element *that is his first quality must* be followed by a semicolon, since the next clause is an independent sentence that does not begin with a coordinating conjunction.

— LESSON 124 —

Italics
Quotation Marks
Ellipses
Single Quotation Marks
Apostrophes

Exercise 124A: Proofreading Practice

The sentences below have lost most punctuation and capitalization. Insert all missing punctuation marks, and correct all capitalization errors. When you are finished, compare your sentences with the originals.

Use these proofreader's marks:

capitalize letter: ≡	make letter lowercase: /
insert period: ⊙	insert exclamation point: ^!
insert comma: ^,	insert question mark: ^?
insert colon: ^:	insert semicolon: ^;
insert dash: (—)	insert quotation marks: ∨"
insert hyphen: △	

Note to Instructor: The original versions of the sentences are found below.

All of the sentences in this exercise are from *Glinda of Oz* by L. Frank Baum. This book has twenty-four chapters, including "The Magic Stairway," "The Enchanted Fishes," and "Glinda's Triumph."

Note to Instructor: The comma after *Oz* is optional. The period after *Baum* can also be a semicolon followed by a lowercase letter.

When evening came, they saw the Diamond Swan, still keeping to the opposite shore of the lake, walk out of the water to the sands, shake her diamond-sprinkled feathers, and then disappear among the bushes to seek a resting place for the night.

> **Note to Instructor:** The comma after *came* is optional. Baum uses *Diamond Swan* as a proper name, but the student does not need to capitalize it.

The fairy Ruler of Oz only needed her silver wand—tipped at one end with a great sparkling emerald—to provide through its magic all that they might need.

> **Note to Instructor:** Capitalizing *Ruler* is optional. The phrase set off by dashes may also be set off by commas.

She placed her two hands before her mouth, forming a hollow with them, and uttered a clear, thrilling, bird-like cry.

I've lost all the poison I had to kill the fishes with, and I can't make any more because only my wife knew the secret of it, and she is now a foolish Pig and has forgotten all her magic.

> **Note to Instructor:** While both commas are technically optional, the student should insert both since each clause is independent. *Pig* does not need to be capitalized (Baum is using it as the name of a tribe or race, like European or Cherokee).

A different sort of person was Jack Pumpkinhead, one of Ozma's oldest friends and her companion on many adventures.

The one who had been a goldfish had beautiful golden hair and blue eyes and was exceedingly fair of skin; the one who had been a bronzefish had dark brown hair and clear gray eyes and her complexion matched these lovely features.

The others, too, seemed to think the Wizard's plan the best, and Glinda herself commended it, so on they marched toward the line of palm trees that hid the Skeezers' lake from view.

> **Note to Instructor:** *Too* does not have to be surrounded by commas, but it makes the sentence easier to read. *Wizard* does not need to be capitalized. *Skeezers* is a proper name.

By this time Ozma had made up her mind as to the character of this haughty and disdainful creature, whose self-pride evidently led her to believe herself superior to all others.

> **Note to Instructor:** A comma may follow *time*.

At ordinary times Ozma was just like any little girl one might chance to meet—simple, merry, lovable as could be—yet with a certain reserve that lent her dignity in her most joyous moods.

> **Note to Instructor:** A comma may follow *times*. The dashes may be parentheses. They may also be commas, although dashes or parentheses better suit the nature of the parenthetical expression.

"There is more magic in my fairyland than I dreamed of," remarked the beautiful Ozma, with a sigh of regret.

> **Note to Instructor:** The comma after *Ozma* is optional.

That is all that makes life worth our while—to do good deeds and to help those less fortunate than ourselves.

> **Note to Instructor:** The dash may also be a comma, although the dash suits the character of the set-off phrase, which is a definition, better.

Exercise 124B: Foreign Phrases That Are Now English Words

The following phrases and words are now part of English and are usually not italicized. Using a dictionary, look up each one. In the blank, write the original language that the word belongs to, the meaning in English, and the meaning in the original language. The first is done for you.

Note to Instructor: The most common meanings are listed below, but the student may choose others as long as they are in the dictionary.

cul-de-sac	French, a dead-end street, "bottom of the sack"
status quo	Latin, an existing state or condition, "state in which"
résumé	French, a written summary of your qualifications, "to sum up"

Note to Instructor: The accents are the clue that this is the noun of French origin rather than the English verb meaning *to start again.*

doppelganger	German, a ghostly double of a living person, "double-walker"
en masse	French, all together as a group, "in mass"
vice versa	Latin, the other way around from the original, "to alternate, to turn"
non sequitur	Latin, a conclusion that doesn't follow from the premises, "it does not follow"
addendum	Latin, a thing to be added, "to be added"
hors d'oeuvre	French, an appetizer, "outside the main course"
per diem (noun)	Latin, an allowance for each day of expenses, "by the day"

WEEK 34

Advanced Quotations & Dialogue

LESSONS 125 and 126

No exercises in these lessons.

— LESSON 127 —

Practicing Direct Quotations and Correct Documentation

Note to Instructor: The student's instructions and the resources given are provided below for your reference. You will need to check the paper for each of the five required elements and compare the student's formatting to the rules in the workbook.

A simple retelling of each story is all that's necessary. The essay may be any length, as long as it is over 200 words.

A sample essay is provided at the end of this lesson for your reference. If the student has trouble getting started, read her the first paragraph of the sample essay (don't let her look at it, since formatting the quotes properly is part of the challenge) and tell her she can use it as a model for the first paragraph of her own essay.

The student's Works Cited section should be identical to the Works Cited section of the sample essay.

The student may write an introduction and conclusion, but since the focus of this assignment is on documentation, four paragraphs that just retell important parts of the four stories are perfectly acceptable.

After the assignment is completed, ask the student to read the sample essay and the explanatory notes.

Your assignment: Write a short essay called "Four Famous Pirates." It should be at least 250 words, although it will probably need to be longer.

You must quote directly from all four of the sources listed below, footnote each direct quote, and put all four on your Works Cited page.

Your essay must include the following:

a) A brief quote that comes before its attribution tag.
b) A brief quote that comes after its attribution tag.
c) A brief quote divided by its attribution tag.
d) A block quote.
e) A quote that is incorporated into a complete sentence and serves a grammatical function within that sentence.
f) A quote that has been altered with either brackets or ellipses.
g) A second quote from the same source.

One quote can fulfill more than one of these requirements.

If you need help, ask your instructor.

Author: Daniel Defoe
Title of Book: *A General History of the Pyrates, From Their First Rise and Settlement in the Island of Providence, to the Present Time*
City of Publication: London
Publisher: T. Warner
Date: 1724

Page 44
In the Times of Marius and Sylla, Rome was in her greatest Strength, yet she was so torn in Pieces by the Factions of those two great Men, that every Thing which concerned the publick Good was altogether neglected, when certain Pyrates broke out from Cicilia, a Country of Asia Minor, situated on the Coast of the Mediterranean, betwixt Syria on the East, from whence it is divided by Mount Tauris, and Armenia Minor on the West. This Beginning was mean and inconsiderable, having but two or three Ships, and a few Men, with which they cruised about the Greek Islands, taking such Ships as were very ill arm'd or weakly defended; however, by the taking of many Prizes, they soon increased in Wealth and Power: The first Action of theirs which made a Noise, was the taking of Julius Cæsar, who was as yet a Youth, and who being obliged to fly from the Cruelties of Sylla, who sought his Life, went into Bithinia, and sojourned a while with

Page 45
Nicomedes, King of that Country; in his Return back by Sea, he was met with, and taken, by some of these Pyrates, near the Island of Pharmacusa: These Pyrates had a barbarous Custom of tying their Prisoners Back to Back and throwing them into the Sea; but, supposing Cæsar to be some Person of a high Rank, because of his purple Robes, and the Number of his Attendants, they thought it would be more for their Profit to preserve him, in hopes of receiving a great Sum for his Ransom; therefore they told him he should have his Liberty, provided he would pay them twenty Talents, which they judg'd to be a very high Demand, in our Money, about three thousand six hundred Pounds Sterling; he smiled, and of his own Accord promised them fifty Talents; they were both pleased, and surpriz'd at his Answer, and consented that several of his Attendants should go by his Direction and raise the Money; and he was left among these Ruffians with no more than three

Page 46
Attendants. He pass'd eight and thirty Days, and seemed so little concerned or afraid, that often when he went to sleep, he used to charge them not to make a Noise, threatening, if they disturbed him, to hang them all; he also play'd at Dice with them, and sometimes wrote Verses and Dialogues, which he used to repeat, and also cause them to repeat, and if they did not praise and admire them, he would call them Beasts and Barbarians, telling them he would crucify them. They took all these as the Sallies of a juvenile Humour, and were rather diverted, than displeased at them.

At length his Attendants return'd with his Ransom, which he paid, and was discharged; he sail'd for the Port of Miletum, where, as soon as he was arriv'd, he used all his Art and Industry in fitting out a Squadron of Ships, which he equipp'd and arm'd at his own Charges; and sailing in Quest of the Pyrates, he surpriz'd them as they lay at Anchor

Page 47
among the Islands, and took those who had taken him before, with some others; the Money he found upon them he made Prize of, to reimburse his Charges, and he carry'd the Men to Pergamus or Troy, and there secured them in Prison: In the mean Time, he apply'd himself to Junius, then Governor of Asia, to whom it belonged to judge and determine of the Punishment of these Men; but Junius finding there was no Money to be had, answered Cæsar, that he would think at his Leisure, what was to be done with those Prisoners; Cæsar took his Leave of him, returned back

to Pergamus, and commanded that the Prisoners should be brought out and executed, according to Law in that Case provided; which is taken Notice of, in a Chapter at the End of this Book, concerning the Laws in Cases of Pyracy: And thus he gave them that Punishment in Earnest, which he had often threatened them with in Jest.

Author/Editor/Sponsoring Organization: *Time* Magazine
Name of Web Article: "Peril on the High Seas: Francis Drake Raids Cadiz: 1584"
URL: http://content.time.com/time/specials/packages/article/0,28804,1860715_1860714_1860707,00.html
Date of access: Use the date on which you are writing your essay

The Englishman may be remembered for circumnavigating the world, but Sir Francis Drake also happened to be Queen Elizabeth I's favorite pirate. Indeed, part of his globetrotting mission was to take treasure from the Spaniards, which he brought back to his appreciative monarch (who got a half-share of the loot). The pirate-patriot's greatest act was also a blow against the King of Spain: a raid on the Spanish port of Cadiz that destroyed several ships being assembled for the great Armada that was to be launched against England.

Author: Ta Chen
Title of Book: *Chinese Migrations, With Special Reference to Labor Conditions*
City of Publication: Washington, DC
Publisher: Government Printing Office
Date: 1923

Page 41

EXPLOITS OF KOXINGA

At this time the Ming dynasty was declining and the Chinese coast fell into the hands of Cheng Ch'in-kung (Koxinga), a pirate patriot, who checked the invading Manchus. Koxinga's father, Tse-lung, was a tailor of Chuanchow, who, because of his defeat of the pirate Liu Hiang-lao in 1639, was promoted to a high rank by the court of Ming. In 1644, Brigadier General Ching Hung-tah proclaimed himself Emperor of Fukien and made Tse-lung a prince, and Ch'in-kung, his son, a marquis. When Tse-lung was executed in Nanking, Ch'm-kung (Koxinga) succeeded him in control of the coast of Fukien and Formosa. Using the Kulan Islands off Fukien as the base for food supplies, Koxinga made raids upon the coast villages of the Province. Ho Bien, who was known to the Dutch as Pinqua, had been with the Japanese pirates, but was dismissed by them because of crimes he had committed. He was now in the employ of the Dutch in Formosa as a treasurer and was heavily in debt. In order to meet his own debts, as well as for the political and commercial advantages to Koxinga, he persuaded Koxinga to invade Taiwan.

With about 25,000 men, in 400 junks, Koxinga attacked Fort Provintia, which was surrendered May 4, 1661. Castle Zeelandia fell soon after. A treaty of peace was signed by Koxinga and the Dutch on February 1, 1662, by which the fort was evacuated by the Dutch.

KOXINGA'S SUCCESSORS

Koxinga's advisor, Chen Yung-hua'tiien persuaded him to promulgate just laws, open lands for cultivation, appoint civil officers, make adequate military preparations, establish schools, and treat emigrants of the old Ming dynasty with magnanimity. He founded the prefecture of Chen Tien on the site of the old Tayouan, and also put two districts under its jurisdiction: Tien Shun and Wan Nien.

When Yin, his son, came to succeed him from Amoy, the Manchus persuaded him to submit himself to the Emperor, but his conditions of surrender were refused, and frequent fighting ensued.

Name of Article: "Morgan the Buccanee"r
Author: None listed
Magazine: *Harper's New Monthly Magazine*
Date: June 1859
Volume and issue number: Volume 11, No. 6
Page range of article: 20-37

Page 20

About the year 1666 there was an old pirate at Jamaica named Mansvelt. At the same time an adventurer by the name of Morgan, a Welsh man by birth, and the commander of a good vessel, had acquired the reputation of being a bold and successful cruiser. Mansvelt having resolved to make a descent on Costa Rica, fitted out an expedition consisting of fifteen vessels, manned with 900 men. Making Morgan his vice-admiral, he set sail for St. Catherine's Isle, near Costa Rica. The Spaniards in possession of it were unprepared for such a force, and after a mere

Page 21

show of resistance surrendered. Demolishing all the forts but one, Mansvelt laid a bridge over the channel to an adjacent isle, and soon became master of that also. Leaving a hundred men here he re-embarked, intending to plunder the coast of Costa Rica as far north as Nata. But finding that the Governor of Panama had been informed of his approach, he turned back with his fleet to St. Catherine's. The Sieur Simon, whom he had left as Governor, having during his absence put the main island in a good state of defense, and begun to cover the smaller one with fertile plantations, Mansvelt determined to keep possession of it. To carry out this plan he went to Jamaica with proposals to the Governor for its retention. Being met with a refusal, and knowing he could not hold it against the Spanish force in those seas, he retired to Tortuga, where he suddenly died.

Morgan succeeded to the command, and hoped, like his predecessor, to retain St. Catherine's; but the Spaniards, during his absence, made a sudden descent upon it and took it. He then resolved to collect a large force in some of the ports of Cuba; and in two months' time he succeeded in assembling twelve vessels and 700 men. It was first proposed to plunder Havana, but fearing that his force was insufficient, he resolved to attack Puerto del Principe.

Having arrived abreast of the place in the night, he waited for daylight to land and surprise it. But a Spanish prisoner aboard one of the vessels contrived to escape unobserved, and swimming ashore alarmed the town. The news spread consternation through the place; and the inhabitants, aroused from their slumbers by the cry, "The pirates have come!" swarmed through the streets in affright, bearing bags of gold and other valuables and fled—men and women and children—into the surrounding forest. Soon every house was empty; and nothing was heard save the steady tramp of 800 soldiers as they defiled through the streets toward the port, which lay some distance off. Halting where the road was narrow, they cut down trees and made barricades, behind which they were stationed by the Governor, and awaited the approach of the pirates. Morgan, finding the high-road to the town thus defended, landed his men some distance off, and taking a circuitous march through the woods, at length emerged on the open plain in front of the place. As the troops defiled from the forest and formed into line, they saw the Governor with a large body of horse drawn up in order of battle. Morgan had scarcely time to throw his men into the form of a half moon when the Spanish bugles sounded the charge, and the horse came gallantly on. The pirates, reserving their fire till the enemy were within close range, took deadly aim, and emptied nearly a hundred saddles at the first discharge. The Spaniards wheeled and charged again and again, but were unable to break the firm formation, while the deadly volleys mowed them down by scores. At length the few survivors turned and fled.

Morgan then marched on the town, but was met at the entrance by the foot-soldiers, who defended it for a long time with determined bravery. The pirates, made desperate by this protracted resistance, dashed with a loud yell so fiercely on the gate-way that they bore back all opposition, and poured through the street. The Spaniards then retired to their houses, from whence they continued to fire on their assailants until the latter threatened to fire the town, when they surrendered. After the surrender some were locked up in the houses and burned to death; others underwent the most dreadful tortures to make them confess where they had hidden away their riches; their cries and groans mingling in with the shouts and laughter of those who, in the meantime, grew merry over the deep potations of liquor which the inhabitants had left behind.

Having tried every other means in vain, Morgan told them if they did not pay a handsome ransom he would take them all to Jamaica and sell them as slaves. The Spaniards then deputized four of their number to get the required contribution. These brought back word that they could not find any of their own party, but that they would raise the money in fifteen days. This was granted, and the pirates gave themselves over to reveling and pleasure.

In a few days, however, a servant was caught with letters on his person from the Governor of Santiago to the chief officers of the town urging them to detain the pirates as long as they could, for he would soon be there with a large force to their assistance. Morgan immediately ordered all the booty he had collected to be sent aboard his vessel, and demanded that the ransom should be paid next day. This being declared impossible, he directed them to send him immediately five hundred sides of beef, with salt enough to cure them. This being done, he liberated the prisoners and set sail for an uninhabited island to divide the plunder.

> **Note to Instructor:** The numbers of the required elements are in marginal brackets below, followed by additional explanation where necessary at the end of the essay.

SAMPLE ESSAY

In ancient times, Julius Caesar was kidnapped by pirates when he was a young man. Instead of throwing him overboard, as was their custom, the pirates decided to hold him for ransom. Caesar spent thirty-eight days with the pirates and grew very comfortable with them; he played dice with them, and wrote poetry for them. Daniel Defoe writes, "He seemed so little concerned or afraid, that often when he went to sleep, he used to charge them not to make a Noise, threatening, if they disturbed him, to hang them all."[1] Finally the pirates received ransom for Caesar [b]
and set him free. Caesar then assembled a fleet, found the pirates, captured them, and had them put to death.

Centuries later, Sir Francis Drake, "Queen Elizabeth I's favorite pirate,"[2] raided [e]
Spanish ships for treasure and brought it back to Elizabeth I, who then took half of it. When Drake destroyed Spanish ships at Cadiz, he weakened the Armada that the King of Spain was getting ready to attack England with.

On the other side of the world, the Chinese pirate known as Koxinga invaded Taiwan. "[B]ecause of his defeat of the pirate Liu Hiang-lao," the historian Ta Chen writes, ". . . [Koxinga's father] was promoted to a high rank by the court of Ming."[3] Ironically, [c] [f]
his son became a pirate. Koxinga raided villages on the coast and, in 1661, he captured Fort Provintia and Castle Zeelandia from the Dutch.

The Welsh pirate Morgan, who started out as vice-admiral for an old Jamaican pirate named Mansvelt, attacked Puerto del Principe in Cuba. Word of the raid got to the town ahead of him, so the people of the town were able to seize their treasures and hide in the forest. When the Spanish army tried to keep the pirates away, Morgan's crew killed them by the score. Some of them surrendered instead. This did not turn out well. The article "Morgan the Buccaneer" says:

> After the surrender some were locked up in the houses and burned to death; others underwent the most dreadful tortures to make them confess where they had hidden away their riches; their cries and groans mingling in with the shouts and laughter of those who, in the meantime, grew merry over the deep potations of liquor which the inhabitants had left behind.[4] [d]

Morgan demanded a large ransom for the survivors, but instead accepted a large ransom of "five hundred sides of beef, with salt enough to cure them,"[5] as "Morgan the Buccaneer" tells us. Then he left for a deserted island with his men, the beef, and all of his plunder. [a] [g]

---

[1] Daniel Defoe, *A General History of the Pyrates, From Their First Rise and Settlement in the Island of Providence, to the Present Time* (T. Warner, 1724), p. 46.

[2] *Time*, "Peril on the High Seas: Francis Drake Raids Cadiz: 1584," http://content.time.com/time/specials/packages/article/0,28804,1860715_1860714_1860707,00.html (accessed Sept. 27, 2016).

[3] Ta Chen, *Chinese Migrations, With Special Reference to Labor Conditions* (Government Printing Office, 1923), p. 41.

[4] "Morgan the Buccaneer." *Harper's New Monthly Magazine*, June, 1859, p. 21.

[5] "Morgan the Buccaneer," p. 21.

WORKS CITED

Chen, Ta. *Chinese Migrations, With Special Reference to Labor Conditions.* Washington, D.C.: Government Printing Office, 1923.

Defoe, Daniel. *General History of the Pyrates, From Their First Rise and Settlement in the Island of Providence, to the Present Time.* London: T. Warner, 1724.

"Morgan the Buccaneer." *Harper's New Monthly Magazine* 11:6 (June 1859), pp. 20-37.

Time. "Peril on the High Seas: Francis Drake Raids Cadiz: 1584." http://content.time.com/time/specials/packages/article/0,28804,1860715_1860714_1860707,00.html (accessed Sept. 27, 2016).

Instructor Notes to Bracketed Numbers:

[b] The attribution tag, *Daniel Defoe writes*, comes before the quote.

[e] The direct quote *Queen Elizabeth's favorite pirate* is an appositive for *Sir Frances Drake*.

[c] The attribution tag *the historian Ta Chen writes* comes in the middle of the direct quote.

[f] Brackets turn the beginning of the quote into the start of the sentence and insert the missing subject. Ellipses show where words were left out of the quote.

[d] This block quote is introduced by an attribution tag followed by a colon.

[a] The attribution tag, *as "Morgan the Buccaneer" tells us*, comes after the direct quote.

[g] This is the second quote from "Morgan the Buccaneer". Since no author is listed, the name of the article stands in for the author's last name. Technically, when a footnote cites the same information as the footnote immediately before it, you merely write "Ibid." However, that's advanced documentation, and this assignment is intended to give the student a chance to practice the *second quote* format, so the student should use the *second quote* format even if the reference is identical.

WEEK 35

Introduction to Sentence Style

— LESSON 128 —

Sentence Style: Equal and Subordinating
Sentences with Equal Elements: Segregating, Freight-Train, and Balanced

Exercise 128A: Identifying Sentence Types

In the blank that follows each sentence, write *S* for segregating, *FT* for freight-train, or *B* for balanced.

Her good will could not be denied, and her capacity could not be disregarded.
—Lytton Strachey, *Eminent Victorians* B

I make them. But they are not mine. The artillery is not mine. I must put in for it.
—Ernest Hemingway, *For Whom the Bell Tolls* S

The rain is beating on the windows. It was not midnight. It was not raining.
—Samuel Beckett, *Molloy* (translated by Patrick Bowles) S

It had rained in the night, and the lane was awash with thin red mud, and puddles stood in the ruts and potholes.
—Berton Roueché, *What's Left* FT

The nurse sat down again. The nurse's shoes were white. Pelletier's and Espinoza's shoes were black. Morini's shoes were brown.
—Roberto Bolaño, *2666: A Novel* S

Then God said, "Let there be lights in the firmament of the heavens to divide the day from the night; and let them be for signs and seasons, and for days and years; and let them be for lights in the firmament of the heavens to give light on the earth"; and it was so.
—Genesis 1:14-15 FT

We are such stuff as dreams are made on, and our little life is rounded with a sleep.
—William Shakespeare, *The Tempest* B

The shadows are lengthening for me. The twilight is here. My days of old have vanished, tone and tint.
—Douglas MacArthur, "Duty, Honor, Country" S

What the white whale was to Ahab, has been hinted; what, at times, he was to me, as yet remains unsaid.
—Herman Melville, *Moby-Dick* B

Let freedom ring from the mighty mountains of New York. Let freedom ring from the heightening Alleghenies of Pennsylvania. Let freedom ring from the snow-capped Rockies of Colorado. Let freedom ring from the curvaceous slopes of California.
—Martin Luther King, "I Have a Dream" S

Cowards die many times before their deaths; the valiant never taste of death but once.
—William Shakespeare, *Julius Caesar* B

The grass was wet and the earth smelled of springtime.
—E. B. White, *Charlotte's Web* B

They are waiting on the street in the late afternoon. The air is thin as paper. The day is raw.
—James Salter, *A Sport and a Pastime* S

Mrs. Cratchit made the gravy (ready beforehand in a little saucepan) hissing hot; Master Peter mashed the potatoes with incredible vigour; Miss Belinda sweetened up the apple-sauce; Martha dusted the hot plates; Bob took Tiny Tim beside him in a tiny corner at the table; the two young Cratchits set chairs for everybody, not forgetting themselves, and mounting guard upon their posts, crammed spoons into their mouths, lest they should shriek for goose before their turn came to be helped.
—Charles Dickens, *A Christmas Carol* FT

— LESSON 129 —

Subordinating Sentences: Loose, Periodic, Cumulative, Convoluted, and Centered

Exercise 129A: Identifying Subordinating Sentences

In each sentence, underline the subject(s) of the main clause once and the predicate twice. Label each sentence in the blank that follows it as *L* for loose, *P* for periodic, *CUMUL* for cumulative, *CONV* for convoluted, or *CENT* for centered.

For the purpose of this exercise, any sentence with four or more phrases and dependent clauses before or after the main clause should be considered cumulative. If three or fewer phrases or dependent clauses come before or after the main clause, the sentence should be classified as loose or periodic.

If phrases or clauses come before *and* after the main clause, the sentence is centered, no matter how many phrases or clauses there are.

If any phrases or clauses come between the subject, predicate, and any essential parts of the main clause (objects, predicate nominatives or predicate adjectives), the sentence is convoluted.

A phrase serving as an object or predicate nominative should be considered a single part of speech, not a subordinate phrase.

All emotions, and that one particularly, were abhorrent to his cold, precise but admirably balanced mind. CONV
—Arthur Conan Doyle, "A Scandal in Bohemia"

She had heard Papa sing so many songs about the heart; the heart that was breaking—was aching—was dancing—was heavy laden—that leaped for joy—that was heavy in sorrow—that turned over—that stood still. CUMUL

—Betty Smith, *A Tree Grows in Brooklyn*

I am a convicted prisoner serving five years for leaving the country without a permit and for inciting people to go on strike at the end of May 1961. L

—Nelson Mandela, "I Am Prepared to Die"

The answer, Galileo came to see, was that four objects were in orbit around Jupiter. CONV

—Edward Dolnick, *The Clockwork Universe: Isaac Newton, the Royal Society, and the Birth of the Modern World*

As she read, at peace with the world and happy as only a little girl could be with a fine book and a little bowl of candy, and all alone in the house, the leaf shadows shifted and the afternoon passed. CUMUL

—Betty Smith, *A Tree Grows in Brooklyn*

Note to Instructor: I have counted this as four phrases/clauses preceding the main clause, since *as only a little girl could be* is a dependent clause that falls within the phrase *happy...candy*, but if the student marks this as a periodic sentence, accept that answer. Since *leaf* is a noun, I have treated *leaf shadows* as a compound noun rather than a noun (*shadows*) modified by an adjective (*leaf*).

Shall we acquire the means of effectual resistance, by lying supinely on our backs, and hugging the delusive phantom of hope, until our enemies shall have bound us hand and foot? L

—Patrick Henry, "Liberty or Death"

Seeing the self-confident and refined expression on the faces of those present he was always expecting to hear something very profound. P

—Leo Tolstoy, *War and Peace*

Note to Instructor: Because the infinitive phrase *to hear something very profound* is the direct object of the verb *was expecting*, it is an essential part of the main clause and does not turn the sentence into a centered sentence.

The other students—most of them white, some of them Asian, and from Russia, Japan, and Spain, as well as from cities and small towns throughout the States—had been dancing their entire lives. CONV

—Misty Copeland, *Life in Motion: An Unlikely Ballerina*

In this land, he may be what he will, if he has the good heart and the way of working honestly at the right things. CENT

—Betty Smith, *A Tree Grows in Brooklyn*

For my part, whatever anguish of spirit it may cost, I am willing to know the whole truth—to know the worst and to provide for it. CENT

—Patrick Henry, "Liberty or Death"

And when he speaks of Irene Adler, or when he refers to her photograph, it is always under the honourable title of "the woman." P

—A. Conan Doyle, "A Scandal in Bohemia"

Note to Instructor: Because the prepositional phrase *under the honourable title of 'the woman'* serves as a predicate adjective, it is an essential part of the main clause and does not turn the sentence into a centered sentence.

The San Bernardino Valley lies only an hour east of Los Angeles by the San Bernardino Freeway but is in certain ways an alien place: not the coastal California of the subtropical twilights and the soft westerlies off the Pacific but a harsher California, haunted by the Mojave just beyond the mountains, devastated by the hot dry Santa Ana wind that comes down through the passes at 100 miles an hour and whines through the eucalyptus windbreaks and works on the nerves. CUMUL

—Joan Didion, *Some Dreamers of the Golden Dream*

Note to Instructor: Because nothing comes between the subject and the first verb, we have classified this as cumulative rather than convoluted, particularly since the number of clauses and phrases after the main clause are clearly intended to produce the effect of a cumulative sentence.

While the spread of the plague could be charted from the Bills, its origins were uncertain. P

—Stephen Porter, *The Great Plague*

It is a big, airy room, the whole floor nearly, with windows that look all ways, and air and sunshine galore. L

—Charlotte Perkins Gilman, *The Yellow Wallpaper*

But you must believe me when I tell you that I have found it impossible to carry the heavy burden of responsibility and to discharge my duties as King as I would wish to do without the help and support of the woman I love. CUMUL

—Edward VIII, Abdication Speech

Often, after shows, the dancers would do outreach, speaking to young people who'd been in the audience. CENT

—Misty Copeland, *Life in Motion: An Unlikely Ballerina*

The last of the great naked-eye astronomers, Tycho was a meticulous observer with an unsurpassed knowledge of the sky. CENT

—Edward Dolnick, *The Clockwork Universe: Isaac Newton, the Royal Society, and the Birth of the Modern World*

No thinker of that age, no matter how brilliant, could imagine an alternative. CONV

—Edward Dolnick, *The Clockwork Universe: Isaac Newton, the Royal Society, and the Birth of the Modern World*

If his father was a carpenter, he may be a carpenter. P

—Betty Smith, *A Tree Grows in Brooklyn*

She had so much of tenderness in her, so much of wanting to give of herself to whoever needed what she had, whether it was her money, her time, the clothes off her back, her pity, her understanding, her friendship or her companionship and love. CUMUL

—Betty Smith, *A Tree Grows in Brooklyn*

Tonight, I will become the first black woman to star in Igor Stravinsky's iconic role for American Ballet Theatre, one of the most prestigious dance companies in the world. L

—Misty Copeland, *Life in Motion: An Unlikely Ballerina*

With the exception of the aunt, beside whom sat only one elderly lady, who with her thin careworn face was rather out of place in this brilliant society, the whole company had settled down. P

—Leo Tolstoy, *War and Peace*

In the loveliest town of all, where the houses were white and high and the elm trees were green and higher than the houses, where the front yards were wide and pleasant and the back yards were bushy and worth finding out about, where the streets sloped down to the stream and the stream flowed quietly under the bridge, where the lawns ended in orchards and the orchards ended in fields and the fields ended in pastures and the pastures climbed the hill and disappeared over the top toward the wonderful wide sky, in this loveliest of all towns Stuart stopped to get a drink of sarsaparilla. CUMUL

—E. B. White, *Stuart Little*

> **Note to Instructor:** We have classified this a cumulative because even though there is a brief adverb phrase after the verb, the sheer weight of all of the phrases in front of the main clause clearly reveal the author's intentiont that this sound like a cumulative sentence.

When he smiled, his grave, even rather gloomy, look was instantaneously replaced by another—a childlike, kindly, even rather silly look, which seemed to ask forgiveness. CENT

—Leo Tolstoy, *War and Peace*

If a physician of high standing, and one's own husband, assures friends and relatives that there is really nothing the matter with one but temporary nervous depression—a slight hysterical tendency—what is one to do? CUMUL

—Charlotte Perkins Gilman, *The Yellow Wallpaper*

> **Note to Instructor:** The phrase *what is one to do* borders on the idiomatic. I have marked *one* as the subject, *is* as the predicate, and am considering *what* to be a direct object modified by the adjectival infinitive *to do*. An argument could be made for *what* as the subject, and *one to do* as an idiom serving as a predicate nominative.

If you had somehow happened to guess the Pythagorean theorem, how would you prove it? P

—Edward Dolnick, *The Clockwork Universe: Isaac Newton, the Royal Society, and the Birth of the Modern World*

These mothers, instead of being able to work for their honest livelihood, are forced to employ all their time in strolling to beg sustenance for their helpless infants. CONV

—Jonathan Swift, *A Modest Proposal*

Wrapped in their torn blankets, they would sit or lie on the ground, staring vacantly into space, unaware of who or where they were, strangers to their surroundings. CENT

—Elie Wiesel, "The Perils of Indifference"

If they but knew it, almost all men in their degree, some time or other, cherish very nearly the same feelings towards the ocean with me. CONV

—Herman Melville, *Moby-Dick*

The stout gentleman half rose from his chair and gave a bob of greeting, with a quick little questioning glance from his small fat-encircled eyes. L

—Arthur Conan Doyle, "The Red-Headed League"

— LESSON 130 —

Practicing Sentence Style

Note to Instructor: The student may choose one of the assignments below. The first (rewriting) will suit students who do not easily come up with creative ideas; the second is intended for students who find creative writing natural.

A sample composition, along with the original Grimm tale, has been provided for the first, but there is no way to provide a sample or rubric for the second.

Choose one of the following assignments:

Exercise 130A: Rewriting

The following list of events, from the Brothers Grimm tale "The Mouse, the Bird, and the Sausage," needs to be rewritten as a story.

This story must have at least one of each of the following types of sentences:

Segregating (at least three sentences in a row)
Freight-Train
Balanced
Loose
Periodic
Cumulative (with four or more subordinate phrases/clauses; main clause can come either first or last)
Convoluted
Centered

You may add, change, and subtract, as long as the finished story is at least 400 words long and makes good sense.

mouse, bird, sausage lived together
it went well
they were comfortable
they were prosperous

they all had different duties
the bird fetched wood for the fire
the mouse fetched water
the sausage cooked
the sausage jumped in the broth
the sausage rolled in the vegetables
this seasoned them
the bird met another bird
he told the other bird about the duties
the other bird called him a simpleton
the other bird said that the bird did too much hard work
the other bird said the mouse could spend all day in her room
the other bird said the sausage did nothing until dinner
the first bird went home
the next morning he refused to fetch wood for the fire
the mouse and sausage begged
he refused to go
the sausage went for wood
the bird made the fire
the mouse got ready to cook
the sausage never came back
the bird flew out to find him
a dog had eaten him
the bird went home and told the mouse
they were unhappy
the bird set the table
the mouse got ready to cook
she jumped into the broth
she got cooked
the bird could not find the mouse
the bird hunted for the mouse
no one watched the fire
a coal fell out of the fire
the kitchen began to burn
the bird went to the well for water
he fell in the well and drowned

Note to Instructor: This sample composition shows one way in which the assignment could be completed. Each sentence fulfilling one of the required elements is underlined, with the label of the required element written in the margin next to the line where the sentence ends.

The original Grimm fairy tale, which does not meet the requirements for sentence styles, is also included. If the student has trouble rewriting, allow her to read the original tale.

SAMPLE COMPOSITION

Long, long ago, in a charming cottage that was set just at the edge of deep, dark woods, a mouse, a bird, and a sausage lived together. Their household was comfortable and prosperous. Each one of them had different duties. The bird fetched firewood. The mouse fetched water. And the sausage cooked. The sausage had an unusual way of cooking. Jumping into the broth, stewing in it to give it flavor, heating the vegetables and then rolling in them, climbing out of the skillet leaving the vegetables seasoned and flavorful—these were his methods. periodic segregating cumulative

One day, the bird met another bird while out fetching wood, and told the second bird all about his household. This bird, who was a quarrelsome troublemaker, called the first bird a simpleton. He said, "You do too much hard work. The mouse spends all day in her room, and the sausage does not work until your dinner." convoluted balanced

The quarrelsome bird flew away, and the first bird thought, and then he thought some more, and then he began to think that the quarrelsome bird was right, and then finally he went home. The next morning, he announced that he would not go and fetch wood for the fire. freight-train

The mouse and the sausage were surprised, and then alarmed, begging the bird to go instead, hoping that he would change his mind, worried about what this would mean for the future. Finally, they gave up. The sausage said that he would get the wood, if the bird went for firewood and if the mouse did the cooking. loose loose

So, the three friends decided to change jobs. The next morning, excited about his new job, the sausage went for wood, hopping happily through the woods, pleased to have a new adventure. The bird busily made the fire, and the mouse got ready to cook. centered

But the sausage never came back. Finally, the bird flew out to find him. Instead, he found a dog licking his chops. The dog had eaten the sausage.

The bird flew sadly home and told the mouse what had happened. Although they grieved over the loss of the sausage, they decided to carry on. The bird started to set the table, and the mouse began to cook. Copying the sausage, hoping to season the broth, trying to do a good job as cook, she leaped in. periodic periodic

But the broth was hot. She was not the sausage. It cooked her. She was dead. The bird came into the kitchen, finished with the table, ready for the meal, looking forward to spending time with his friend, hoping for a good dinner. He called for the mouse, but could not find her. While he was hunting for her, a coal fell out of the fire. It began to blaze up, and the kitchen began to burn. segregating cumulative periodic

The bird went to the well for water, but as he tried to dip it out, he fell into the well. He could not get out, and he drowned.

That was the end of the three friends.

THE MOUSE, THE BIRD, AND THE SAUSAGE
(Original Grimm Tale)

Once upon a time, a mouse, a bird, and a sausage, entered into partnership and set up house together. For a long time all went well; they lived in great comfort, and prospered so far as to be able to add considerably to their stores. The bird's duty was to fly daily into the wood and bring in fuel; the mouse fetched the water, and the sausage saw to the cooking.

When people are too well off they always begin to long for something new. And so it came to pass, that the bird, while out one day, met a fellow bird, to whom he boastfully expatiated on the excellence of his household arrangements. But the other bird sneered at him for being a poor simpleton, who did all the hard work, while the other two stayed at home and had a good time of it. For, when the mouse had made the fire and fetched in the water, she could retire into her little room and rest until it was time to set the table. The sausage had only to watch the pot to see that the food was properly cooked, and when it was near dinner-time, he just threw himself into the broth, or rolled in and out among the vegetables three or four times, and there they were, buttered, and salted, and ready to be served. Then, when the bird came home and had laid aside his burden, they sat down to table, and when they had finished their meal, they could sleep their fill till the following morning: and that was really a very delightful life.

Influenced by those remarks, the bird next morning refused to bring in the wood, telling the others that he had been their servant long enough, and had been a fool into the bargain, and that it was now time to make a change, and to try some other way of arranging the work. Beg and pray as the mouse and the sausage might, it was of no use; the bird remained master of the situation, and the venture had to be made. They therefore drew lots, and it fell to the sausage to bring in the wood, to the mouse to cook, and to the bird to fetch the water.

And now what happened? The sausage started in search of wood, the bird made the fire, and the mouse put on the pot, and then these two waited till the sausage returned with the fuel for the following day. But the sausage remained so long away, that they became uneasy, and the bird flew out to meet him. He had not flown far, however, when he came across a dog who, having met the sausage, had regarded him as his legitimate booty, and so seized and swallowed him.

The bird picked up the wood, and flew sadly home, and told the mouse all he had seen and heard. They were both very unhappy, but agreed to make the best of things and to remain with one another.

So now the bird set the table, and the mouse looked after the food and, wishing to prepare it in the same way as the sausage, by rolling in and out among the vegetables to salt and butter them, she jumped into the pot; but she stopped short long before she reached the bottom, having already parted not only with her skin and hair, but also with life.

Presently the bird came in and wanted to serve up the dinner, but he could nowhere see the cook. He called and searched, but no cook was to be found.

No one was tending the fire, and as the bird searched, a coal fell out onto the kitchen floor and began to blaze. The bird hastened to fetch some water, but his pail fell into the well, and he after it, and as he was unable to recover himself, he was drowned.

Exercise 130B: Original Composition

Write an original composition of at least 400 words, with at least one of each of the following types of sentences:

Segregating (at least three sentences in a row)
Freight-Train
Balanced
Loose
Periodic
Cumulative (with four or more subordinate phrases/clauses; main clause can come either first or last)
Convoluted
Centered

This composition may be one of the following:

a) A plot summary of one of your favorite books or movies,
b) A narrative of some event, happening, trip, or great memory from your past,
c) A scene from a story that you create yourself, or
d) Any other topic you choose.

WEEK 36

— REVIEW 11 —

Final Review

Note to Instructor: This is not a "test"—it is a review and a challenge to the student to use the knowledge acquired. Give all necessary assistance.

Review 11A: Explaining Sentences

Tell your instructor every possible piece of grammatical information about the following sentences. Follow these steps (notice that these are slightly different than the instructions in your previous "explaining" exercise):

1) Identify the sentence type and write it in the left-hand margin.
2) Underline each subordinate clause. Describe the identity and function of each clause and give any other useful information (introductory word, relationship to the rest of the sentence, etc.)
3) Label each preposition as *P* and each object of the preposition as *OP*. Describe the identity and function of each prepositional phrase.
4) Parse, out loud, all verbs acting as predicates.
5) Describe the identity and function of each individual remaining word. Don't worry about the articles, though.
6) Provide any other useful information that you might be able to think of.

Note to Instructor: Use the information below to prompt the student as necessary. (Numbered information sections correspond to instruction steps above.) Give all necessary help. Encourage the student to answer loudly and in complete sentences.

The Sound in front of me was like a sheet of blue silk, with just the distant murmur of moving water as a reminder that there were tides here.

—Hans Kruuk, *Wild Otters: Predation and Populations*

1) loose (or cumulative) **The Sound in front of me was like a sheet of blue silk, with just the distant murmur of moving water as a reminder that there were tides here.**

Note to Instructor: 1) The sentence can be interpreted either as loose (with *The Sound in front of me was* followed by three prepositional phrases and a subordinate clause) or as convoluted (if *in front of me* is interpreted as an interrupting element). This is an example of a sentence that rhetoricians would disagree over, since *in front of me* is somewhere between an actual interrupting element and a brief modifying phrase.

The Sound in front of me was like a sheet of blue silk, with just the distant murmur of moving water as a reminder that there were tides here.

Note to Instructor: 2) The single subordinate clause, introduced by the subordinating conjunction *that*, is an adjective clause modifying *reminder.*

P OP P OP P OP P OP

The Sound in front of me was like a sheet of blue silk, with just the distant

P OP P OP

murmur of moving water as a reminder that there were tides here.

Notes to Instructor: 3) While it is correct to label two prepositions and two *OPs* in the phrase *in front of me*, as done above, *in front of* is an idiom that acts as a single preposition. The student may begin to realize this if she tries to treat *in front* as one prepositional phrase and *of me* as a second (this would turn *front* into a noun, but then *of me* would have to be an adjective phrase—and it doesn't answer any of the adjective questions in relationship to *front*). *Me* is the object of this idiomatic preposition.

The entire prepositional phrase *like a sheet of blue silk* acts as a predicate adjective following *was* and describing *Sound.*

Of blue silk is an adjective phrase describing *sheet.*

Although the student might identify the prepositional phrase *with just the distant murmur* as describing either *sheet* or *Sound*, it is actually an adverb phrase answering the question *how the Sound was*, and so modifying the verb *was.*

As a reminder is an adjective phrase describing *murmur* (in this case, *as* is a preposition).

4) *Was* is simple past, state-of-being (linking), indicative.

Were is simple past, state-of-being, indicative.

5) *Sound* is a proper noun acting as the subject.

Blue is an adjective modifying *silk.*

Just is tricky—it is the equivalent of *only*, and, although it appears to be part of the prepositional phrase, it actually is an adverb modifying the verb *was.* (This is *just* how it *was.*) *Just* is only an adjective when it means *fair, true, correct.*

Distant is an adjective modifying *murmur.*

Moving is a present participle acting as an adjective and modifying *water.*

Within the subordinate clause, *tides*, is the subject, and *there* and *here* are both adverbs modifying the verb *were.*

6) Optional: The entire prepositional phrase *with just the distant murmur of moving water as a reminder that there were tides here* is adverbial and modifies the predicate of the main clause.

I had come to cooking late in life, and knew from firsthand experience how frustrating it could be to try to learn from badly written recipes.

1) loose **I had come to cooking late in life, and knew from firsthand experience how frustrating it could be to try to learn from badly written recipes.**

Note to Instructor: 1) The sentence is loose because the main clause *I had come* is first, followed by phrases and clauses. Since nothing comes between the subject and the first of the compound predicates (*had come* and *knew*), this is classified as a loose, not convoluted, sentence.

I had come to cooking late in life, and knew from firsthand experience how frustrating it could be to try to learn from badly written recipes.

Note to Instructor: 2) The subordinate clause *how frustrating it could be to try to learn from badly written recipes* serves as the direct object of the verb *knew.* The subject of the subordinate clause is *it*, the predicate is *could be*, *frustrating* is the predicate adjective describing *it*, and the adverb *how*, modifying the adjective *frustrating*, is serving double-duty as the subordinating word.

P OP P OP P OP

I had come to cooking late in life, and knew from firsthand experience how

P OP

frustrating it could be to try to learn from badly written recipes.

Notes to Instructor: 3) *To cooking* is a prepositional phrase acting as an adverb and modifying the verb *come* (*Come where?*). Note that in the line below, both occurrences of *to* are parts of infinitives, not prepositions.

In life is a prepositional phrase acting as an adverb and modifying the adverb *late*.

From firsthand experience is a prepositional phrase acting as an adverb and modifying the verb *knew*.

From badly written recipes is a prepositional phrase modifying the infinitive *to learn* and acting as an adverb.

4) *Had come* is perfect past, active, indicative.

Knew is simple past, active, indicative. It is the second verb of the compound verb.

Could be is simple present, state-of-being, modal.

5) The personal pronoun *I* is the subject.

To cooking is an infinitive acting as an adverb and modifying *had come* (answering the question *where*).

Late is an adverb modifying *had come* and answering the question *when*.

Firsthand is an adjective modifying *experience*.

To try is an infinitive acting as an adverb, modifying the adjective *frustrating* and answering the question *how*.

To learn is an infinitive acting as the object of the infinitive *to try*.

Written is a past participle acting as an adjective and modifying the noun *recipes*.

Badly is an adverb modifying the adjective *written*.

6) None.

Along the quay, dozens of wooden fishing boats were parked, stern in, and wizened old men and enormous fishwives sold the day's catch from little stalls or sometimes right from the back of their boats.

—Julia Child, *My Life in France*

1) centered **Along the quay, dozens of wooden fishing boats were parked, stern in, and wizened old men and enormous fishwives sold the day's catch from little stalls or sometimes right from the back of their boats.**

Notes to Instructor: 1) This is actually a compound centered sentence—the first main clause, *dozens were parked*, has phrases both before and after it (the single modifying phrase *of boats* does not transform it into a convoluted sentence), while the second main clause, *men and fishwives sold* has the entire first main clause (plus phrases) before it, and modifying phrases following it.

2) This sentence has no subordinate clauses; instead, it has two main clauses.

P OP P OP

Along the quay, dozens of wooden fishing boats were parked, stern in, and

P OP

wizened old men and enormous fishwives sold the day's catch from little stalls or

P OP P OP

sometimes right from the back of their boats.

Notes to Instructor: 3) *Along the quay* is an adverb phrase modifying *were parked*.

Of wooden fishing boats is an adjective phrase modifying *dozens*.

From little stalls and *from the back* are both adverb phrases modifying *sold*.

Of their boats is an adjective phrase modifying *back*.

4) *Were parked* is simple past, passive, indicative.

Sold is simple past, active, indicative.

5) *Dozens* is a noun acting as the subject.
Wooden and *fishing* are both adjectives. *Fishing* can also be classified as a present participle acting as an adjective.
Stern in is an idiomatic expression acting as a single adverb and modifying *were parked.*
Wizened and *old* are adjectives modifying *men.*
Enormous is an adjective modifying *fishwives.*
Day's is a possessive adjective modifying *catch.*
Catch is a noun acting as the direct object.
Little is an adjective modifying *stalls.*
Sometimes and *right* are both adverbs modifying *sold.*
Their is a possessive pronoun acting as an adjective and modifying *boats.*
6) None.

The wind was blowing a gale now, and there was little danger of oars being heard.

1) loose **The wind was blowing a gale now, and there was little danger of oars being heard.**

Notes to Instructor: 1) Like the sentence before, this has two main clauses strung loosely together; the only phrase there is (*of oars being heard*) follows the second main clause.
2) There are no subordinate clauses.

P OP
The wind was blowing a gale now, and there was little danger of oars being heard.

Notes to Instructor: 3) The prepositional phrase *of oars being heard* is adjectival and describes *danger.*
4) *Was blowing* is progressive past, active, indicative.
Was is simple past, state-of-being, indicative.
5) *Wind* is a noun acting as the subject of *was blowing.*
Gale is a noun acting as the direct object of *was blowing.*
Now is an adverb modifying *was blowing.*
And is the coordinating conjunction joining the two independent clauses.
There is an adverb modifying *was.*
Little is an adjective modifying *danger.*
Danger is a noun acting as the subject of *was.*
Being heard is a present passive participle, acting as an adjective and modifying *oars*. This is a rare form; you may need to direct the student to the final chart in Lesson 61 to review it.
6) None.

Frankly, had I been the King, the further they had gone the better should I have been pleased.
—Anthony Hope, *The Prisoner of Zenda*

1) periodic **Frankly, had I been the King, the further they had gone the better should I have been pleased.**
—Anthony Hope, *The Prisoner of Zenda*

Note to Instructor: 1) The main clause in the sentence is *I should have been the better pleased.* It is preceded by two subordinate clauses with understood subordinating words; since it comes at the end of the sentence, the sentence is periodic in structure.

Frankly, <u>had I been the King</u>, <u>the further they had gone</u> the better should I have been pleased.

Notes to Instructor: 2) The first subordinate clause is a formal version of a condition clause, which drops the *if* and reverses the order of the subject and helping verb (*If I had been the king . . .*). Although it may appear to be an independent clause, it depends on the consequence clause and is subordinate.

The second subordinate clause, *the further they had gone*, is introduced by an understood subordinating *that*: *The further that they had gone, the better should I have been pleased.*

3) This is a rare sentence—no prepositional phrases!

4) *Had been* is perfect past, state-of-being, subjunctive (it is in a condition clause and expresses a circumstance contrary to reality).

Had gone is perfect past, active, subjunctive. Although it is identical in form to the indicative, it also expresses a circumstance contrary to reality.

Should have been pleased is present perfect, passive, modal.

5) *Frankly* is an adverb that modifies the main verb in the sentence, *should have been pleased*. The *frankly* refers to the narrator's statement about his own emotion, not to the hypothetical statement *had I been the king* or to the imaginary circumstance *the further they had gone*.

I is a personal pronoun acting as the subject of *had been*.

King is a proper noun acting as the predicate nominative and renaming *I*.

Further is an adverb modifying the verb *had gone*.

They is a personal pronoun acting as the subject of the subordinate clause *the further [that] they had gone*.

Better is an adverb modifying *should have been pleased*.

6) This is a third conditional sentence, expressing past circumstances that never happened.

In the constructions *the further* and *the better*, *the* is acting in an extremely unusual way: it is *not* an article, but rather an adverb! The dictionary definition of *the* as an adverb notes that it *modifies an adjective or adverb in the comparative degree, in one instance with relative force and in the other with demonstrative force, and signifying "by how much . . . by so much" or "in what degree . . . in that degree."* (If the student does not bring this up, point it out!)

But whatever the incarnation of the "small difference," whether it be a missing horse shoe nail, a butterfly, a sea gull, or most recently, a mosquito "squished" by Homer Simpson, the idea that small differences can have huge effects is not new.

—Leonard Smith, *Chaos: A Very Short Introduction*

1) convoluted **But whatever the incarnation of the "small difference," whether it be a missing horseshoe nail, a butterfly, a sea gull, or most recently, a mosquito "squished" by Homer Simpson, the idea that small differences can have huge effects is not new.**

—Leonard Smith, *Chaos: A Very Short Introduction*

Notes to Instructor: Point out to the student that although she has learned the rule *Italicize words if they are the subject of discussion*, some style guides use quotation marks instead of italics for this purpose, as in this sentence.

1) The main clause is *the idea is not new*. It is divided by the subordinate clause *that small differences can have huge effects*, making the sentence convoluted.

But whatever the incarnation of the *small difference*, <u>whether it be a missing horseshoe nail, a butterfly, a sea gull, or most recently, a mosquito *squished* by Homer Simpson</u>, the idea <u>that small differences can have huge effects</u> is not new.

Note to Instructor: 2) The first subordinate clause is introduced by the subordinating conjunction *whether*. It acts as an adjective, modifying the compound noun (see below) *small difference*. Note that it is possible to make an argument for this subordinate clause as an appositive to *small difference*, since it does rename, but because there are four different *small* *differences* listed, only one of which can actually be the *small difference* at any given time, this is better identified as an adjective clause.

The second subordinate clause, introduced by the subordinating conjunction *that*, is unambiguously an appositive. It renames *the idea*.

Note that *whatever the incarnation of the "small difference"* is *not* a clause (see below) because it has no predicate.

But whatever the incarnation of (P) the "small difference," (OP) whether it be a missing horseshoe nail, a butterfly, a sea gull, or most recently, a mosquito "squished" by (P) Homer Simpson (OP), the idea that small differences can have huge effects is not new.

Notes to Instructor: 3) The prepositional phrase *of the "small difference"* describes *incarnation* and is adjectival.

The prepositional phrase *by Homer Simpson* is adverbial and modifies *squished*.

4) *Be*, in the first subordinate clause, is simple present, state-of-being, subjunctive.

Can have, in the second subordinate clause, is simple present, active, modal.

Is, in the independent clause, is simple present, state-of-being, indicative.

5) *But* is a coordinating conjunction, connecting the entire sentence to the separate sentence preceding it.

Whatever is an adjective describing *incarnation*.

Incarnation is a noun. Because *but whatever the incarnation of the "small difference"* is an absolute construction, it is difficult to identify the exact part that *incarnation* plays within the construction (see below).

It is the subject of the subordinate class.

Nail, *butterfly*, *seagull*, and *mosquito* are all four predicate nominatives, all of them following the state-of-being/linking verb *be* and renaming *it*.

Missing is a present participle acting as an adjective and modifying *nail*.

Horseshoe is a single compound adjective modifying *nail*.

Recently is an adverb modifying the verb *be* (expressing the circumstances under which the mosquito *is*). *Most* is an adverb modifying *recently*.

Squished is a past participle acting as an adjective and modifying *mosquito*.

Idea is a noun acting as the subject of the main clause.

Small is an adjective modifying *differences*.

Differences is a noun acting as the subject of the subordinate clause.

Huge is an adjective modifying *effects*.

Effects is a noun acting as the direct object of the verb *can have*.

Not is an adverb of negation.

New is a predicate adjective describing *idea*.

6) The sentence begins with the absolute construction *but whatever the incarnation of the "small difference"* which syntactically (in meaning) has a strong connection to the rest of the sentence—it repeats the *small differences* in the appositive clause that renames the subject, *idea*—but which has *no* clear grammatical connection to the rest of the sentence. (Note: The student could possibly make an argument for this being a subordinate clause with an understood predicate: *But whatever the incarnation of the "small difference" [is]*. In that case it would act as an adjective, modifying *small differences* later in the sentence. This is possible, but since a clause is generally defined by the presence of a predicate, I prefer to see this as an absolute construction.)

Small difference acts as a single compound noun because it is set off with quotation marks. Both this and *squished* are direct quotes from other contexts/sources. The first quote is actually a quote from the end of the writer's own sentence, while the second, *squished*, is a quote from the television show *The Simpsons* (as context makes clear).

Review 11B: Correcting Errors

Rewrite the following sets of sentences on your own paper (or with a word processing program), inserting all necessary punctuation and capitalization.

Include the citations in your corrections!

Note to Instructor: The original sentences are listed below. In some cases, there are multiple correct options for punctuation. As many acceptable alternatives as possible are listed below, but if the student chooses an option not listed and it appears to follow the rules, you may choose to accept it.

When the student is finished, show him the original sentences for comparison.

One night—it was on the twentieth of March, 1888—I was returning from a journey to a patient (for I had now returned to civil practice) when my way led me through Baker Street.

Note to Instructor: The dashes may be parentheses instead, but not commas (that would introduce a comma splice). The parentheses may also be dashes or commas.

"Let me see!" said Holmes. "Hum! Born in New Jersey in the year 1858. Contralto—hum! La Scala, hum! Prima donna Imperial Opera of Warsaw—yes! Retired from operatic stage—ha! Living in London—quite so! Your Majesty, as I understand, became entangled with this young person, wrote her some compromising letters, and is now desirous of getting those letters back."

—Arthur Conan Doyle, "A Scandal in Bohemia"

Note to Instructor: The first exclamation point could also be a comma. The first dialogue tag could be punctuated as

"Let me see," said Holmes. "Hum! Born . . ."

or

"Let me see," said Holmes, "hum. Born . . ."

The remaining exclamation points could all be periods (or possibly semicolons). The dashes could be commas:

"Contralto, hum. La Scala, hum. Prima donna Imperial Opera of Warsaw, yes. Retired . . ."

I have always understood that the word *mob* was derived from the Latin expression *mobile vulgus*, which is, I believe, in Virgil.

Note to Instructor: *Mob* should be italicized because it is the subject under discussion, and *mobile vulgus* should be italicized because it is a foreign word.

In some of the most beautiful pictures of "The Virgin and Child" of Raphael, and other old masters, the right foot of Jesus is placed upon the right foot of the Virgin. What is the symbolism of this position?

Note to Instructor: "The Virgin and Child" could also be *The Virgin and Child*, since whether it's a major or minor work is up for interpretation. The comma after Raphael is optional. *Virgin* is capitalized because it is a title. The period after *Virgin* could also be a semicolon or dash.

The letter is fully quoted by Mr. Tytler in his book *England under Edward VI and Mary.*

—*Notes and Queries: A Medium of Inter-communication for Literary Men, Artists, Antiquaries, Genealogists, Etc.* Number 243, June 24, 1854

Note to Instructor: *By Mr. Tytler* could also be set off by commas.

This lady was the Countess Amelia, whose picture my sister-in-law wished to remove from the drawing-room in Park Lane; and her husband was James, fifth Earl of Burlesdon and twenty-second Baron Rassendyll, a Knight of the Garter.

> **Note to Instructor:** The semicolon after *Park Lane* could also be a comma. *Knight of the Garter* is a formal title. *Drawing-room* can be either hyphenated or unhyphenated.

I could see only three yards ahead; I had then good hopes of not being seen, as I crept along close under the damp, moss-grown masonry.

> **Note to Instructor:** The semicolon after *ahead* could also be a period. The comma after *seen* is preferable, but optional. The comma after *damp* is necessary because the adjectives cannot easily be reversed (*moss-grown damp masonry*).

They came one by one and kissed my hand—De Gautet, a tall lean fellow, with hair standing straight up and waxed moustache; Bersonin, the Belgian, a portly man of middle height with a bald head (though he was not far past thirty); and last, the Englishman, Detchard, a narrow-faced fellow, with close-cut fair hair and a bronzed complexion.

—Anthony Hope, *The Prisoner of Zenda*

> **Note to Instructor:** The dash after *hand* could be a colon. The comma after *fellow* is optional. The clause *though he was not far past thirty* could be preceded by a comma rather than surrounded by parentheses. The comma after *Englishman* is optional. The comma after *fellow* is optional.

Review 11C: Fill-in-the-Blank

Each of the following sentences is missing one of the elements listed. Provide the correct required form of a word that seems appropriate to you. When you are finished, compare your sentences with the originals.

On all __sides__ (plural noun), except the wash by __which__ (relative pronoun) we __reached__ (simple past active indicative verb) the river, the place appeared __to be walled__ (passive infinitive) in by towering mountains whose bare sides __were sculptured__ (simple past passive indicative verb) into __fantastic__ (adjective) and __colossal__ (adjective) forms.

From a dark, __repulsive__ (adjective), __hurrying__ (present participle) mass, the river __was transformed__ (simple past passive indicative verb) into a __shimmering__ (present participle), __scintillating__ (present participle) stream which seemed __to murmur__ (infinitive) its gratitude at __escaping__ (present participle) from the gloom of the great canyon.

—Josiah F. Gibbs, *Kawich's Gold Mine: An Historical Narrative of Mining in the Grand Canyon of the Colorado*

In a posthumous vindication of Charles's belief in the Divine Right of Kings, __some__ (indefinite pronoun) rushed forward __to dip__ (active infinitive) their handkerchiefs in the royal blood, __believing__ (present active participle) it to have sacred properties.

—Charles Spencer, *Killers of the King*

I felt we __should strive__ (present active modal indicative verb) to show our readers __how__ (subordinating adverb) to make everything top notch, and explain, if possible, __why__ (subordinating adverb) things work one way __but__ (coordinating conjunction) not another.

The little restaurant could only hold about twenty patrons, but it had survived,
present active modal indicative verb — perfect past active indicative verb
quite nicely, largely on the strength of its *beurre blanc*—a thick, creamy sauce that is really
relative pronoun
nothing but warm butter held in suspension by an acidic flavor base of shallots, wine,
past participle acting as adjective
vinegar, salt, and pepper.

—Julia Child, *My Life in France*

This book would probably never have been written if it had not been for my first few
perfect present passive modal verb — adverb of negation — possessive pronoun
years in the wonderful study area in Shetland, at Lunna, and I will describe some of its details
adjective — simple future active indicative verb
to provide a background for many of the results mentioned here.
infinitive — indefinite pronoun — past participle acting as adjective

On the other hand, we could sit or lie in full view of the animals, as long as we remained
idiom introducing an alternative point of view — simple present active modal verb — adverb — subordinating conjunction — simple past active indicative verb
absolutely still, wearing rather dark clothing and sitting against a bank or a rock or whatever.
present participle — present participle — indefinite pronoun

—Hans Kruuk, *Wild Otters: Predation and Populations*

But whatever solution we choose (and most modern speculation has not been very convincing),
progressive perfect present active indicative verb
an even bigger puzzle is that fact that one of the founding twins really was redundant—
demonstrative pronoun — subordinating conjunction — adjective
since Remus was killed by Romulus, or in other versions by, one of his henchmen, on the very
simple past passive indicative verb
first day of the city.

—Mary Beard, *SPQR: A History of Ancient Rome*

If the blob were far out in space, appearing as an unresolved point of light in the sky, our
present state of being subjunctive — present participle — possessive pronoun
five senses would offer us no insight to its distance, velocity through space, or its rate of rotation.
adjective of negation — possessive pronoun

—Neil DeGrasse Tyson, *Death by Black Hole and Other Cosmic Quandaries*

Review 11D: Diagramming

On your own paper, diagram every word of the following sentences.

To ignore the Romans is not just to turn a blind eye to the distant past.

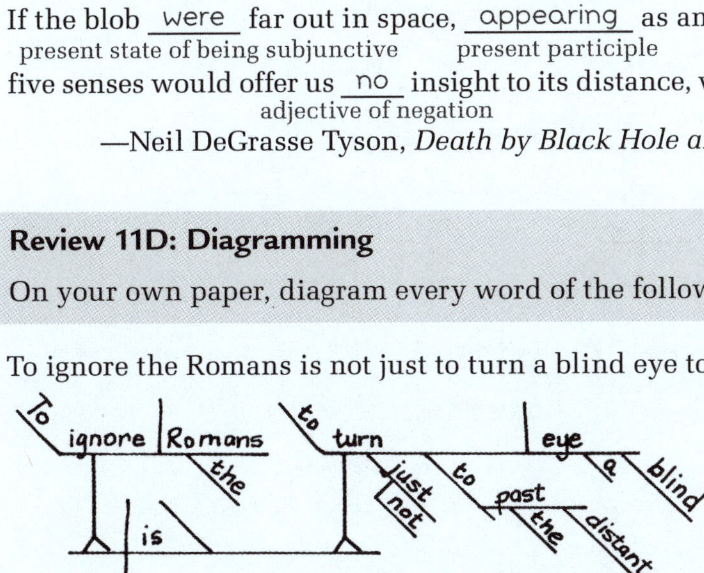

Romulus and the new citizens of his tiny community were fighting their neighbours, a people known as the Sabines, on the site that later became the Forum, the political centre of Cicero's Rome.

—Mary Beard, *SPQR: A History of Ancient Rome*

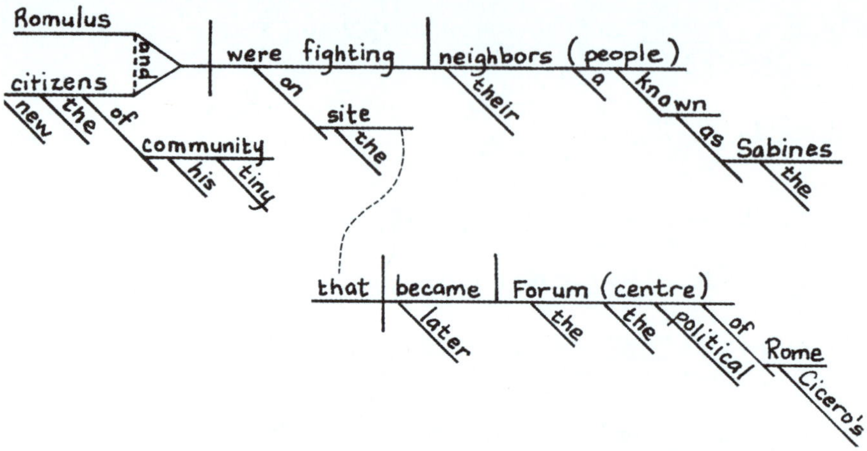

Either there's a missing part of Einstein's gravity that enables it to acept the tenets of quantum mechanics, or there's a missing part of quantum mechanics that enables it to accept Einstein's gravity.

—Neil deGrasse Tyson, *Death by Black Hole and Other Cosmic Quandaries*

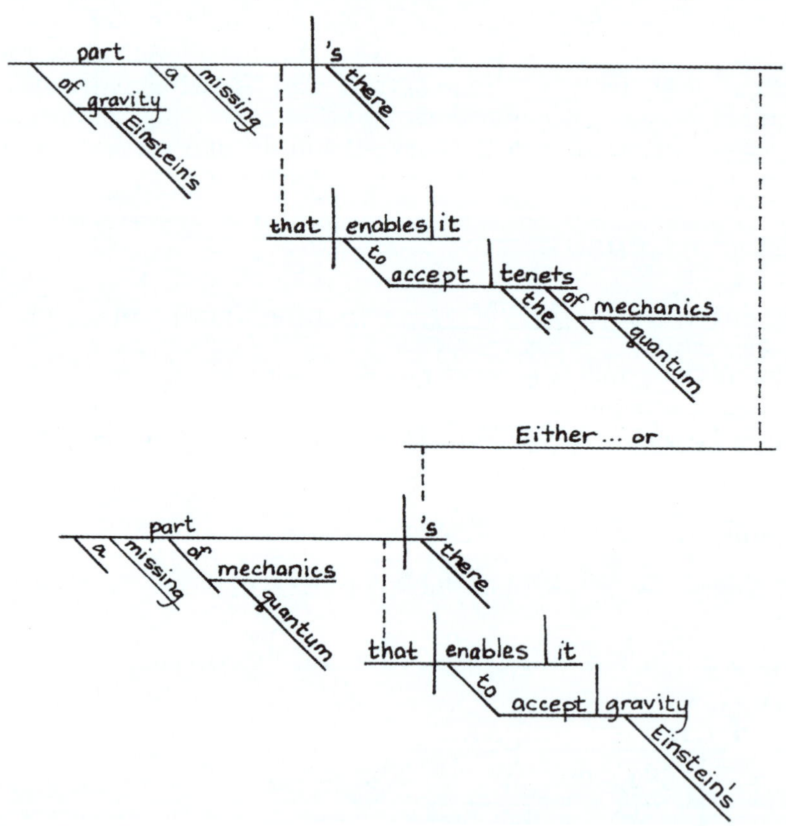

Note to Instructor: *Missing* can be diagrammed either as a plain adjective or as a present participle.

Yet, at about the same time that I was sitting there along the Yell Sound, the last otter disappeared from Holland, the land where I grew up with its sea, lakes, dykes, and rivers, a paradise for otters if ever there was one.

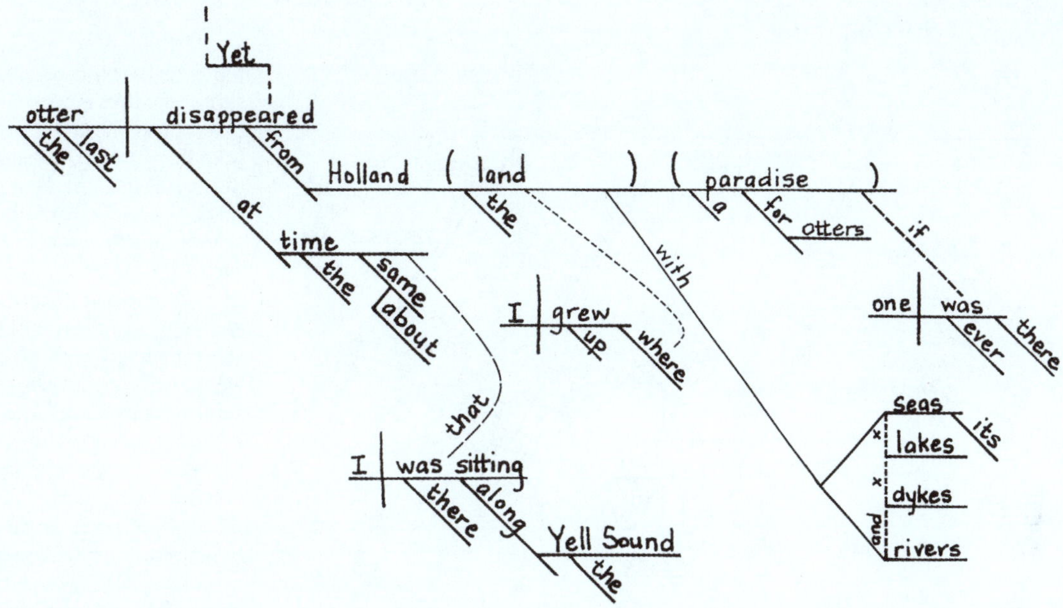

A tiny brook moved through the meadow, then noisily tumbled over the sharp descent toward the river, ten miles distant by the winding trail.

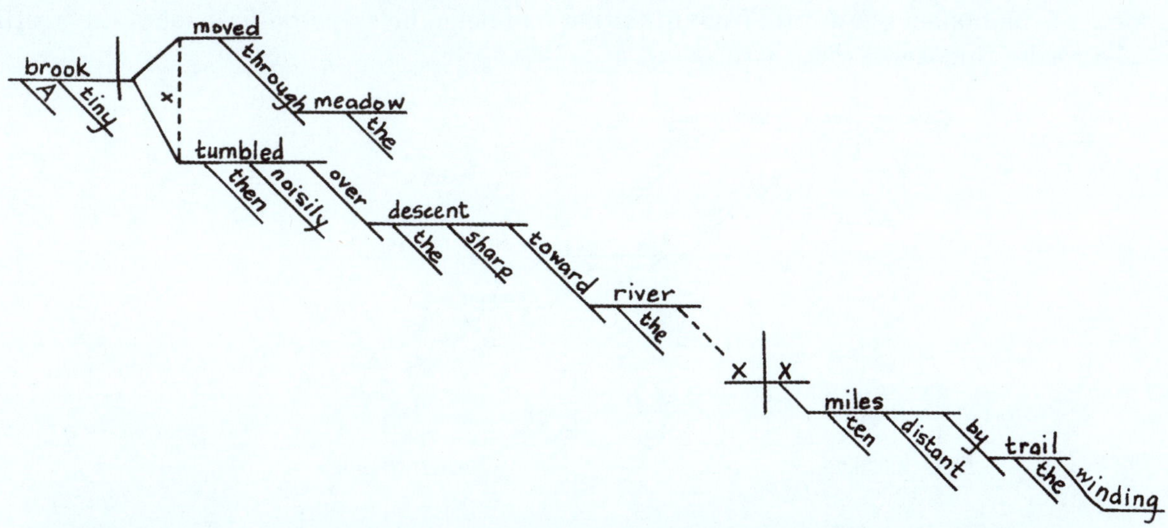

Note to Instructor: If the student chooses to diagram *miles* directly beneath *river* as an adverbial noun, accept the answer, but show him the alternative above.

On the southeast side of the river the walls rose terrace above terrace, like giant stairs, composed of granite, marble, lime and sandstone, and each so variegated with sculptured forms and tints as to baffle the most skillful artist.

—Josiah F. Gibbs, Kawich's Gold Mine: An Historical Narrative of Mining in the Grand Canyon of the Colorado

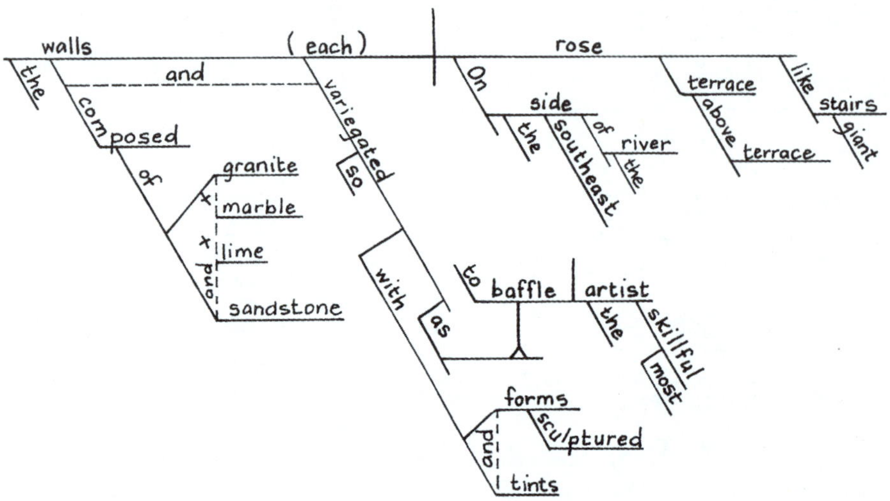

Note to Instructor: The sentence above presents several challenges. *Terrace above terrace* (like *like giant stairs*) actually describes *how* the walls rose, so this is an example of an adverbial noun modifying a verb.

Composed describes the walls. It would only describe *stairs* if the comma after *stairs* were missing, but the comma separates *stairs* off into a different adverbial expression. *The walls rose like giant stairs; the walls were composed of . . .*

Each is a pronoun functioning as an appositive, renaming *walls.* The expression *variegated* describes *each*, not *walls.*

Charles was determined to talk of his innocence, particularly on the greater charges against him; he insisted with disdain that he had not begun the war with Parliament, pointing instead to how his opponents had taken his militia from him; that had been, he said, the first act of the hostilities.

—Charles Spencer, *Killers of the King*

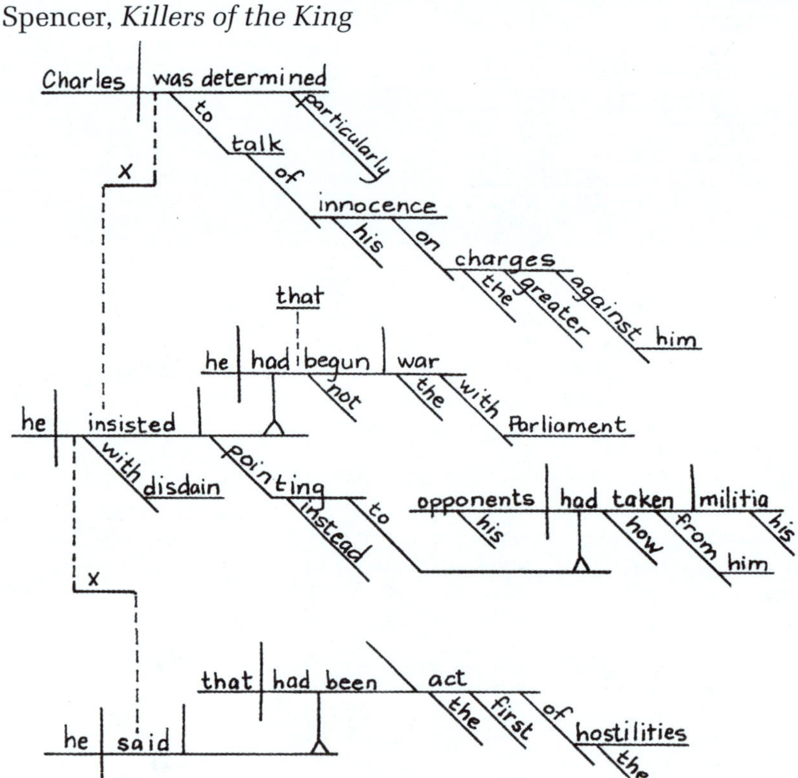

An intellect which at a certain moment would know all forces that set nature in motion, and all positions of all items of which nature is composed—if this intellect were also vast enough to submit these data to analysis, it would embrace in a single formula the movements of the greatest bodies of the universe and those of the tiniest atom; for such an intellect nothing would be uncertain and the future, just like the past, would be present before its eyes.

—Pierre Laplace, quoted in Leonard Smith, *Chaos: A Very Short Introduction*

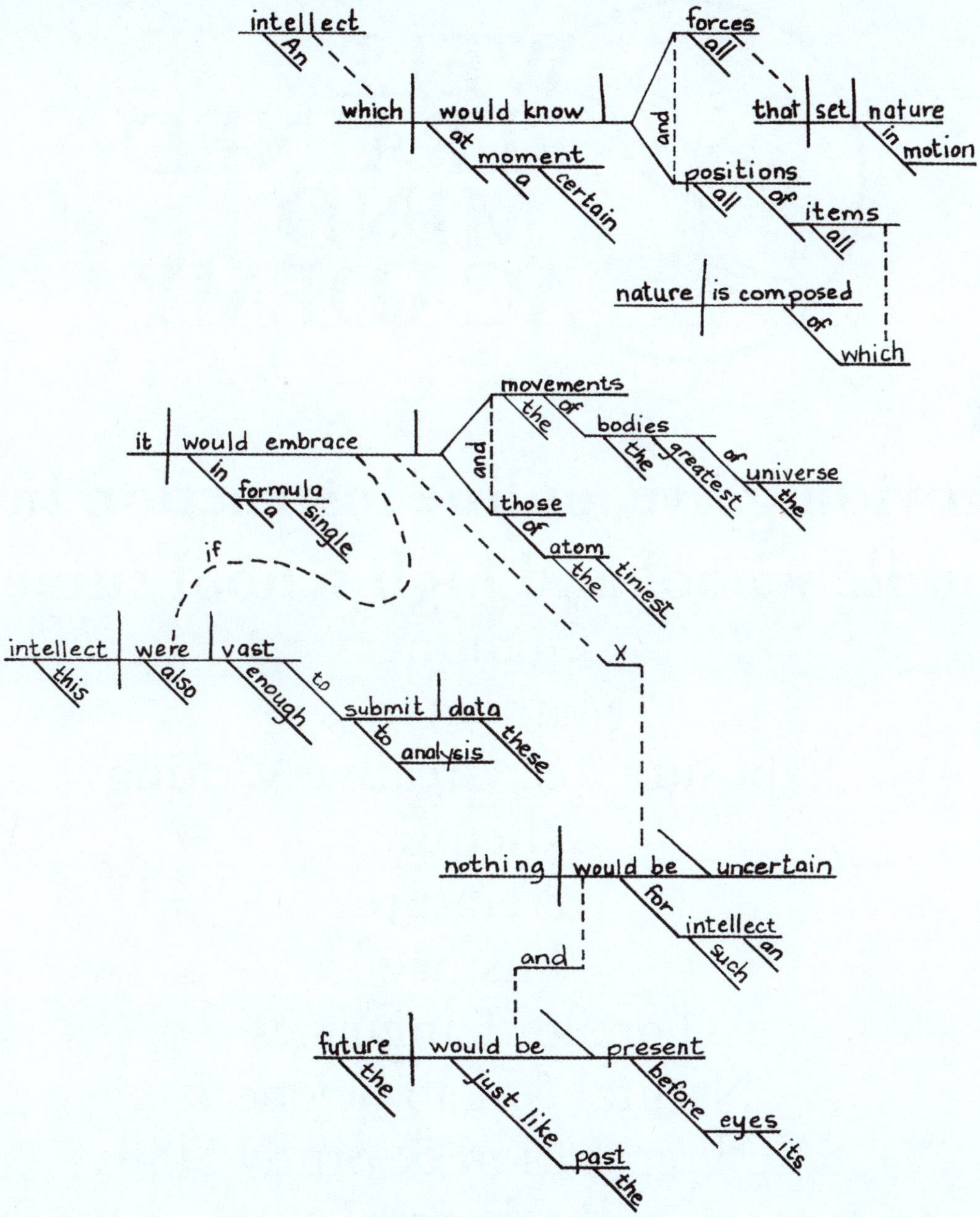